Teaching Pronunciation

A Reference for Teachers of English to Speakers of Other Languages

Marianne Celce-Murcia
Donna M. Brinton
Janet M. Goodwin

CAMBRIDGE
UNIVERSITY PRESS

CAMBRIDGE UNIVERSITY PRESS
Cambridge, New York, Melbourne, Madrid, Cape Town, Singapore, São Paulo, Delhi

Cambridge University Press
32 Avenue of the Americas, New York, NY 10013–2473, USA

www.cambridge.org
Information on this title: www.cambridge.org/9780521406949

First published 1996
16th printing 2007

Printed in the United States of America

A catalog record for this publication is available from the British Library

Library of Congress Cataloging in Publication Data
Celce-Murcia, Marianne.
Teaching pronunciation: a reference for teachers of English to
speakers of other languages Marianne Celce-Murcia, Donna M. Brinton,
Janet M. Goodwin.
p. cm.
Includes bibliographical references and index.
ISBN 978-0-521-40694-9 (pbk.).– ISBN 978-0-521-40504-1 (hbk.). –
ISBN 978-0-521-40695-6 (cassette)
1. English language–Pronunciation–Study and teaching.
2. English language–Study and teaching–Foreign speakers.
3. English language–Pronunciation by foreign speakers.
I. Brinton, Donna M. II. Goodwin, Janet M. III. Title.
PE1137.C415 1996
428.007–dc20   96-20132

ISBN 978-0-521-40504-1 hardback   ISBN 978-0-521-40695-6 cassette
ISBN 978-0-521-40694-9 paperback

Book design and text composition: Edward Smith Design, Inc.
Illustrations: Edgar Blakeney, Daisy De Puthod, Edward Smith Design, Inc.,
Suffolk Technical Illustrators
Photographs: p. 128 (left to right): Robert Burke/Gamma Liaison, Leo de Wys Inc.TPL/DeWys,
Bruce Laurence/Gamma Liaison; p. 294 (woman on beach): Paul Aresu/FPG; p. 301 (all): Anna Veltfort

Every effort has been made to trace the owners of copyrighted materials in this book. We would be grateful to
hear from anyone who recognizes their material and who is acknowledged. We will be pleased to make the
necessary corrections in future edition of this book.

IN FOND MEMORY OF
CLIFFORD H. PRATOR AND J. DONALD BOWEN,
OUR MENTORS IN THE TEACHING OF PRONUNCIATION

CONTENTS

FIGURES AND TABLES

Figures

Tables

PREFACE

We have written *Teaching Pronunciation: A Reference for Teachers of English to Speakers of Other Languages* to serve as the core of a comprehensive course in pronunciation pedagogy designed to provide ESL/EFL teachers with the following: (1) an overview of the issues involved in teaching pronunciation, such as how pronunciation has been viewed from various methodological perspectives and what we know about the acquisition of second language phonology; (2) a thorough grounding in the sound system of North American English (NAE), including both the segmental and suprasegmental aspects; (3) insight into the ways in which this sound system intersects with other skills and areas of language, such as listening, inflectional morphology, and orthography, (4) a framework for developing teaching techniques, ranging from structured exercises to more holistic and communicative classroom activities, including alternative teaching techniques; (5) a discussion of options in syllabus design as it relates to the teaching of pronunciation; and (6) a treatment of pronunciation diagnosis and assessment measures.

Based on our collective experience at UCLA (both in teaching pronunciation to ESL/EFL students and in training prospective teachers in practical phonetics), we address the current debate on teaching segmentals versus suprasegmentals, and suggest ways in which teachers can deal with both of these critical areas of the sound system within a communicative teaching framework that includes the accuracy–fluency continuum. Accompanying each chapter are discussion questions and exercises that encourage current and prospective teachers to bring their own personal language learning and teaching experience to bear on the topic at hand. The cassette that accompanies the text provides opportunities to develop transcription skills, to assess ESL/EFL learners' pronunciation, and to develop original exercises and activities.

The volume is organized as follows: In Part 1 we cover the history of and research on teaching pronunciation (Chapters 1 and 2). In Part 2 we present the sound system of North American English and some basic teaching techniques by focusing first on the consonants (Chapter 3), next the vowels (Chapter 4), then rhythm, stress, and adjustments in connected speech (Chapter 5), and finally prominence and intonation at the discourse level (Chapter 6). In Part 3 we address the intersection of the NAE sound system with other areas of the language, such as the listening skill (Chapter 7), morphological inflections (Chapter 8), and orthography (Chapter 9). Part 4 deals with issues of implementation; here we treat alternative teaching techniques (Chapter 10), the place of pronunciation in curriculum design (Chapter 11), and techniques and tools for the assessment of pronunciation (Chapter 12).

We have used the material in this text to train prospective ESL/EFL teachers who have already taken at least one introductory course in linguistics. Thus Chapters 1 and 2 presuppose some of the more basic information presented in detail in Chapters 3–6. For teacher trainers whose students have no prior linguistic or phonetic preparation, we suggest starting the course with Part 2 and then having students read Part 1 either after Part 2 or after Part 3.

It has been a long but enjoyable process for us to collaborate on this course text. We hope that you and your students will find it useful and that you will share your comments and suggestions with us.

Marianne Celce-Murcia
Donna M. Brinton
Janet M. Goodwin

ACKNOWLEDGMENTS

This text would not exist without the immense encouragement which we received along the way from our editors at Cambridge University Press. In particular, we owe a great debt to Ellen Shaw, who initiated the project; to Mary Vaughn, who was inordinately supportive and patient throughout the manuscript's extended "birthing process;" and Colin Hayes, who encouraged our efforts from the beginning. For the production phase we acknowledge the excellent assistance of Suzette André, Sandra Graham, and Olive Collen.

Our team writing effort was augmented by the enormous contributions of an anonymous reviewer and Wayne Dickerson, both of whom not only provided insightful critiques of the entire manuscript but also reconceptualized and reworded lengthy passages for us. We also received extremely helpful comments on the manuscript from Janet Anderson-Hsieh and Dick Suter, who caught many inconsistencies and provided much-needed encouragement along the way. Many of our colleagues graciously responded to portions of the manuscript, lending their expertise to correct inaccuracies, flesh out examples, and provide reference sources. In particular, we wish to highlight the contributions of the following individuals: Peter Ladefoged and Patricia Keating (Chapter 3, Appendix 1); John Esling, George Yule, and Julietta Shakhbagova (Appendix 1); John Schumann (Chapter 2); Patsy Duff (Chapter 4); Laura Hahn, and Greta Levis (Chapter 5); Linda Jensen (Appendix 13); Thor Nilsen (Appendix 1 and Chapters 3, 4, 7, and 9); Laurel Brinton (Chapter 5 and Appendix 8); and Francisco Gomes de Matos (general comments).

We are indebted to the work of several graduates of the Applied Linguistics Program at UCLA whose doctoral work we draw on – specifically, Bob Jacobs, Barbara Baptista and Yuichi Todaka. We also consulted with or were influenced by numerous colleagues in constructing and refining pronunciation activities. Although it is often difficult to identify the source of activities which we may have acquired during our many cumulative years of teaching, we specifically want to thank the following individuals (and apologize to those whom we may have unintentionally omitted here): Bill Acton, Judy Gilbert, Joan Morley, Rita Wong, Marsha Chan, Pat Grogan, Susan Stern, Jim Purpura, Karl Lisovsky, Georgiana Farnoaga, Roann Altman, Judith Weidman, Nitza Llado-Torres, Patrice Dally, Lorraine Megowan, Ann Aguirre, Lief Nielsen, and Kathy Jensen-Gabriel.

In field testing the manuscript, we received much helpful feedback from our TESL and ESL students. We particularly wish to acknowledge Andrea Kahn, Gabriela Solomon, Tetsuo Harada, Linda Choi, Denise Babel, Bob Agajeenian, and Cara Wallis.

For assistance in preparing the cassette, we are indebted to the UCLA Phonetics Laboratory and especially to Henry Tehrani and all of the ESL students who graciously consented to be taped for this project.

We would be remiss if we didn't mention other forms of support which we received. For their artwork assistance, we are grateful to Cathy Johnson, Sasha Mosely, and Motoko Ueyama. For access to reference sources, we thank Susan Ryan, formerly of Cambridge University Press. And above all we are indebted to Sandy Wallace for graciously inputting portions of the manuscript and assisting with permissions.

Needless to say, we have appreciated the patience and encouragement of friends and family throughout the writing of this book.

Although so many knowledgeable colleagues have generously given us detailed and extensive feedback, we know that there will be inevitable errors or shortcomings in an undertaking of this scope and size. Any such residual errors are solely our responsibility.

TRANSCRIPTION KEY

	Sound	Examples		Sound	Examples
I.	**The consonants of North American English**				
1.	/b/	boy, cab	13.	/ʒ/	leisure, beige
2.	/p/	pie, lip	14.	/ʃ/	shy, dish
3.	/d/	dog, bed	15.	/h/	his, ahead
4.	/t/	toe, cat	16.	/tʃ/	cheek, watch
5.	/g/	go, beg	17.	/dʒ/	joy, budge
6.	/k/	cat, back	18.	/m/	me, seem
7.	/v/	view, love	19.	/n/	no, sun
8.	/f/	fill, life	20.	/ŋ/	sing(er), bang
9.	/ð/	the, bathe	21.	/l/	long, full
10.	/θ/	thin, bath	22.	/r/	run, car
11.	/z/	zoo, goes	*23.	/w/	win, away
12.	/s/	see, bus	24.	/hw/	which, what
			*25.	/y/	you, soya

	II.	**The vowels of North American English**			

Stressed Vowels

	Sound	Examples		Sound	Examples
1.	/iy/	pea, feet	8.	/ow/	pole, toe
2.	/ɪ/	pin, fit	9.	/ʊ/	put, foot
3.	/ey/	pain, fate	10.	/uw/	pool, stew
4.	/ɛ/	pen, fed	11.	/ay/	pine, fight
5.	/æ/	pan, fad	12.	/aw/	pound, foul
6.	/ɑ/	pot, doll	13.	/ɔy/	poise, foil
7.	/ɔ/	bought, talk	14.	/ʌ/	pun, cut
			15.	/ɜʳ/	bird, third

Unstressed Vowels

	Sound	Examples		Sound	Examples
16.	/ə/	focus, allow	19.	/ɪ/	music, coping
17.	/əʳ/	father, bitter	20.	/o/	hotel, narrow
18	/i/	city, prefer	21.	/u/ yuw	into, igloo

	III.	**Other frequently used symbols and diacritical markings**	
22.	[ʔ]	glottal stop	_uh-_oh
23.	[Cʰ]	aspirated consonant	time, pick, kitchen
24.	[ɫ]	velarized or dark /l/	ball, told, coal
25.	[ɾ]	flap allophone	little, butter, put on
26.	[V:, C:]	lengthening	pa, bid, June night
27.	[C°]	unreleased consonant	but, cap, back
28.	[C̩]	syllabic consonant	kitten, riddle, battle

*Note that /y/ and /w/ function as consonants and also as vowel glides
in vowels 1, 3, 8, 10, 11, 12, and 13.

PART I

PRONUNCIATION INSTRUCTION IN PERSPECTIVE

In the first of these two introductory chapters, we provide a historical overview of how pronunciation has been treated in language teaching over the past hundred years: the types of teaching approaches and techniques that have been used as well as the degree of phonetic analysis or explanation that teachers have provided learners. The second chapter surveys the theories and findings from studies focusing on the acquisition of the sound system of a second language. We then show how this information can help teachers better understand the pronunciation acquisition process and thus be in a better position to set instructional priorities. Together, these two chapters prepare the reader for the specific descriptive and pedagogical information presented in Parts 2 and 3 of this volume as well as the problems of implementation that we discuss in Part 4.

CHAPTER 1

The History and Scope
of Pronunciation Teaching

In his very comprehensive history of language teaching, Kelly (1969) dubs pronunciation the "Cinderella" area of foreign language teaching. He shows that Western philologists and linguists have studied grammar and vocabulary much longer than pronunciation. For this reason, grammar and vocabulary have been much better understood by most language teachers than pronunciation, which began to be studied systematically shortly before the beginning of the twentieth century.

The field of modern language teaching has developed two general approaches to the teaching of pronunciation: (1) an intuitive-imitative approach and (2) an analytic-linguistic approach. Before the late nineteenth century only the first approach was used, occasionally supplemented by the teacher's or textbook writer's impressionistic (and often phonetically inaccurate) observations about sounds based on orthography (Kelly 1969).

An *intuitive-imitative approach* depends on the learner's ability to listen to and imitate the rhythms and sounds of the target language without the intervention of any explicit information; it also presupposes the availability of good models to listen to, a possibility that has been enhanced by the availability first of phonograph records, then of tape recorders and language labs in the mid-twentieth century, and more recently of audio- and videocassettes and compact discs.

An *analytic-linguistic approach,* on the other hand, utilizes information and tools such as a phonetic alphabet, articulatory descriptions, charts of the vocal apparatus, contrastive information, and other aids to supplement listening, imitation, and production. It explicitly informs the learner of and focuses attention on the sounds and rhythms of the target language. This approach was developed to complement rather than to replace the intuitive-imitative approach, which was typically retained as the practice phase used in tandem with the phonetic information.

When we look at the various language teaching methods that have had some currency throughout the twentieth century, we must acknowledge that there are methods, such as *Grammar Translation* and *reading-based approaches,* in which the teaching of pronunciation is largely irrelevant. In such methods grammar or text comprehension is taught through the medium of the learner's native language, and oral communication in the target language is not a primary instructional objective. In the following overview of methods we focus on those methods and approaches for which the teaching and learning of pronunciation is a genuine concern.

DIRECT METHOD AND MORE RECENT NATURALISTIC APPROACHES

In *Direct Method* foreign language instruction, which first gained popularity in the late 1800s and early 1900s, pronunciation is taught through intuition and imitation; students imitate a model – the teacher or a recording – and do their best to approximate the model through imitation and repetition. This instructional method was grounded on observations of children learning their first language and of children and adults learning foreign languages in noninstructional settings. Successors to this approach are the many so-called *naturalistic methods*, including comprehension methods that devote a period of learning solely to listening before any speaking is allowed. Examples include Asher's (1977) Total Physical Response and Krashen and Terrell's (1983) Natural Approach. Proponents maintain that the initial focus on listening without pressure to speak gives the learners the opportunity to internalize the target sound system. When learners do speak later on, their pronunciation is supposedly quite good despite their never having received explicit pronunciation instruction.

THE REFORM MOVEMENT

The first linguistic or analytic contribution to the teaching of pronunciation emerged in the 1890s as part of the *Reform Movement* in language teaching. This movement was influenced greatly by phoneticians such as Henry Sweet, Wilhelm Viëtor, and Paul Passy, who formed the International Phonetic Association in 1886 and developed the *International Phonetic Alphabet (IPA)*. This alphabet resulted from the establishment of phonetics as a science dedicated to describing and analyzing the sound systems of languages. A phonetic alphabet made it possible to accurately represent the sounds of any language because, for the first time, there was a consistent one-to-one relationship between a written symbol and the sound it represented.

The phoneticians involved in this international organization, many of whom had also had experience teaching foreign languages, did much to influence modern language teaching by specifically advocating the following notions and practices:

• The spoken form of a language is primary and should be taught first.

• The findings of phonetics should be applied to language teaching.

• Teachers must have solid training in phonetics.

• Learners should be given phonetic training to establish good speech habits.

THE 1940s AND 1950s

Many historians of language teaching (e.g., Howatt 1984) believe that the Reform Movement played a role in the development of *Audiolingualism* in the United States and of the Oral Approach in Britain during the 1940s and 1950s. In both the Audiolingual and Oral Approach classrooms, pronunciation is very important and is taught explicitly from the start. As in the Direct Method classroom, the teacher (or a recording) models a sound, a word, or an utterance and the students imitate or repeat. However, the teacher also typically makes use of information from phonetics, such as a visual transcription system (modified IPA or some other system) or charts that demonstrate the articulation of sounds.

Furthermore, the teacher often uses a technique derived from the notion of contrast in structural linguistics: the *minimal pair drill* – drills that use words that differ by a single sound in the same position. This technique, based on the concept of the phoneme as a minimally distinctive sound (Bloomfield 1933), is used for both listening practice and guided oral production:

SAMPLE MINIMAL PAIR TEACHING MATERIALS

Word Drills

A	B
/iy/	/i/
sheep	ship
green	grin
least	list
meet	mitt
deed	did

Sentence Drills

I. Syntagmatic drills (contrast within a sentence)

Don't <u>sit</u> in that <u>seat</u>.

Did you at <u>least</u> get the <u>list</u>?

II. Paradigmatic drills (contrast across two sentences)

Don't <u>slip</u> on the floor.

Don't <u>sleep</u> on the floor.

Is that a black <u>sheep</u>?

Is that a black <u>ship</u>?

Using such *minimal pairs* the teacher first has the students practice listening skills.[1] The teacher says two words (e.g., "sheep, sheep" or "sheep, ship") and asks the students to decide if they are the same or different. Alternatively, the teacher might read a word or words from either list A or list B and ask the student to identify which sound (A or B) is being produced.

Listening

1. Same or different? (*sheep, sheep; ship, sheep*)
2. A or B? (*ship; ship; sheep*)

Such listening discrimination practice is followed by guided oral production practice. Following a teacher model, students practice lists A and B first in isolation (i.e., reading list A and then list B), then in contrast (i.e., reading across columns A and B).

Guided Oral Production

1. Read down column A, then column B (*sheep, green,* etc.)
2. Read across the columns (*sheep, ship,* etc.)

Finally, the teacher asks individual students to read the lists without a model.

THE 1960s

In the 1960s the *Cognitive Approach*, influenced by transformational-generative grammar (Chomsky 1959, 1965) and cognitive psychology (Neisser 1967), viewed language as rule-

---

[1]This technique can be adapted to all minimal pair contrasts involving vowel or consonant discrimination.

governed behavior rather than habit formation. It deemphasized pronunciation in favor of grammar and vocabulary because, its advocates argued, (1) nativelike pronunciation was an unrealistic objective and could not be achieved (Scovel 1969); and (2) time would be better spent on teaching more learnable items, such as grammatical structures and words.

THE 1970s

As can be seen from the preceding discussion, the language teaching profession changed positions many times with respect to the teaching of pronunciation. Various methods and approaches placed this skill either at the forefront of instruction, as was the case with Reform Movement practices and the Audiolingual/Oral Method, or in the back wings, as with the Direct Method and naturalistic comprehension-based approaches, which operated under the assumption that errors in pronunciation (and other errors, for that matter) were part of the natural acquisition process and would disappear as students gained in communicative proficiency. Other methods and approaches either ignored pronunciation (e.g., Grammar Translation, reading-based approaches, and the Cognitive Approach) or taught pronunciation through imitation and repetition (Direct Method), or through imitation supported by analysis and linguistic information (Audiolingualism).

The methods that came to attention during the 1970s, such as the Silent Way and Community Language Learning, continued to exhibit interesting differences in the way they dealt with pronunciation. This aspect of both methods is described in the following two sections.[2]

THE SILENT WAY

Like Audiolingualism, the **Silent Way** (Gattegno 1972, 1976) can be characterized by the attention paid to accuracy of production of both the sounds and structures of the target language from the very initial stage of instruction. Not only are individual sounds stressed from the very first day of a Silent Way class, but learners' attention is focused on how words combine in phrases – on how blending, stress, and intonation all shape the production of an utterance. Proponents claim that this enables Silent Way learners to sharpen their own inner criteria for accurate production. The difference between Audiolingualism and the Silent Way, however, is that in the Silent Way learner attention is focused on the sound system without having to learn a phonetic alphabet or a body of explicit linguistic information.

How does the Silent Way work in terms of teaching pronunciation? The teacher, true to the method's name, speaks as little as possible, indicating through gestures what students should do. This includes an elaborate system in which teachers tap out rhythmic patterns with a pointer, hold up their fingers to indicate the number of syllables in a word or to indicate stressed elements, or model proper positioning of the articulators by pointing to their own lips, teeth, or jaw. The Silent Way teachers also use several indispensable tools of the trade such as a sound-color chart, the Fidel charts, word charts, and colored rods.[3]

The **sound-color chart** was created by Gattegno to bypass the ear (Gattegno 1985). This large rectangular wall chart contains all the vowel and consonants sounds of a target language in small colored rectangles. In the upper half of the chart are the vowels. The primary vowels are represented by one color each, the diphthongs by two colors. The consonants are located in the bottom half of the chart, and are divided from the vowels by a solid line. Colors for consonants are assigned randomly, although there is consistency in color from language to language when sounds overlap.

[2]See the excellent volumes by Blair (1982), Larsen-Freeman (1986), and Stevick (1980) for further details about all aspects of these methods, and not just their treatment of pronunciation.
[3]All tools are available from Educational Solutions in New York, the late Caleb Gattegno's company.

```
          a   rod  -s  -s  blue
        green    yellow   black
        brown  take  red  give
          as   to  it  and  not
        back  here  her  is  the
        them  two  him  an  me
    orange the are one he another these white
          put  end  too  his
```

Figure 1.1 Word Chart 1 for English as a Second Language (Reproduced with permission from C. Gattegno, *Teaching foreign languages in schools: The Silent Way,* New York: Educational Solutions, 1972)

The set of *Fidel wall charts* contains all the possible spelling patterns for each sound in the language. Each letter or combination of letters is color coded: Sounds that are pronounced alike are colored alike. Because of the complex nature of English spelling, eight charts in the set represent sound–spelling correspondence.

The large colored word charts (1 to 12; see Figure 1.1) are similar in size to the sound-color chart; they reflect and reinforce the system used in the sound-color chart.[4] The wall charts contain common words of the target language, along with some words utilitarian to the method (e.g., rod). These are grouped semantically in a way that allows the leader (teacher or proficient student) to "silently dictate" or tap out phrases, which are then practiced orally and/or written down as a dictation. For example, the class might take several steps to progress from "Take a blue rod" to "Take a blue rod and a red rod. Give the blue one to him and the red one to her."

The final tool is a set of small colored blocks of wood or plastic of varying lengths, with all red rods being the same size, all white the same size, and so on. The rods are used for many purposes, but when the focus is pronunciation, the rods can be used to build and visually demonstrate intonation patterns, and to indicate the differing pronunciations of morphological endings (past tense, plural marker, etc.).

In one Silent Way lesson that we observed, the students were foreign-born professionals, advanced in English but with heavy accents. As an accent reduction exercise, the instructor was helping students to introduce themselves in a way that would be intelligible and acceptable to native English speakers. They first practiced giving their names (e.g., "My name is Christos Eliopoulos") by placing the colored rods on the table in front of them in a configuration that approximated the stress, intonation, and blending of the phrase. This visual configuration was adjusted as students discovered ways in which they could produce a more intelligible form of the phrase. For example, contracting *name* and *is* to produce *name's* was achieved by moving the small white rod representing *is* directly next to the red rod representing *name*. The teacher remained very much in the background, and there was intense peer assistance both in monitoring the utterances and suggesting alternatives. Once a high level of intelligibility had been attained for the first phrase, students then practiced their professions (e.g., "I'm a commercial real estate broker") in the same manner. Finally, they combined the two phrases and introduced themselves to their peers.[5]

The Silent Way is better understood if experienced rather than read about, since any description fails to capture actual learner engagement. The method appears to have a spe-

---

[4]Since the Fidel wall chart is not reproduced in color, some of the important clues to pronunciation are lost here.

[5]We thank Judith Weidman for allowing us to observe and videotape her 818 class at the American Language Center of UCLA Extension.

cial focus on teaching pronunciation, and many language educators agree that the principle of sound–color correspondence, which the Silent Way invokes, provides learners with an "inner resource to be used" (Stevick 1980: 46), which helps to establish a true feel for the language, "its diction, rhythm, and melody" (Blair 1991: 32).[6]

COMMUNITY LANGUAGE LEARNING

Rooted in the humanistic client-centered learning exemplified by Carl Rogers (1951), *Community Language Learning* (CLL) is a method developed by Charles A. Curran (1976) for teaching second and foreign languages. A typical lesson in a CLL classroom proceeds as follows. Students sit around a table with a tape recorder – a key tool of the method. The counselor (i.e., the teacher) stands behind one of the students, with hands on the student's shoulders. After speaking reassuringly, the counselor asks the student to say something in the native language he or she wishes to be able to say in the target language. This utterance is then provided by the teacher in the target language, who takes care to phrase it idiomatically. The counselor provides the phrase (broken into chunks for ease of repetition), the student repeats, and once the student can produce the whole utterance fluently, it is recorded on tape.

In the next phase of the lesson, the utterances are played back and students match the new target language with the word-for-word translation provided by the counselor. Next, the teacher asks if the students wish to further practice the pronunciation of any of the new utterances they have learned. If they do, the counselor again stands behind the student who requests further practice and engages in a technique known as *human computer*. The counselor/computer can be turned on or off at will by the student, who can request the correct pronunciation of a given phrase or piece of a phrase from the computer. This provides the raw data for the student to mimic and repeat until he or she is satisfied with the pronunciation.

Several tools and techniques are critical to the treatment of pronunciation in CLL. First, the audiotape recorder not only captures what is said in the student-generated utterances but also provides a way for students to distance themselves from what was said so they can focus on how it was said and compare their pronunciation with that of the counselor. Second, the human computer technique, which gives no overt correction of pronunciation, allows the student to initiate pronunciation practice by selecting the item(s) to practice and deciding the amount of repetition needed. In this way, students are able to approximate the target pronunciation to the extent that they desire. Thus the teaching approach is intuitive and imitative as in the Direct Method, but its exact content and the extent to which practice takes place are controlled by the learner/client rather than the teacher or textbook.

PRONUNCIATION TEACHING TODAY

The *Communicative Approach*, which took hold in the 1980s and is currently dominant in language teaching, holds that since the primary purpose of language is communication, using language to communicate should be central in all classroom language instruction. This focus on language as communication brings renewed urgency to the teaching of pronunciation, since both empirical and anecdotal evidence indicates that there is a threshold level of pronunciation for nonnative speakers of English; if they fall below this threshold level, they will have oral communication problems no matter how excellent and extensive their control of English grammar and vocabulary might be. (For research supporting this claim, see Hinofotis and Bailey 1980).

---

[6]The same principle could, of course, be a limitation for those 10% of male learners who are color blind.

Morley (1987: 2) suggests that there are currently at least four groups of English language learners whose oral communication needs mandate a high level of intelligibility and therefore require special assistance with pronunciation:

1.   foreign teaching assistants – and sometimes foreign faculty – in colleges and universities in English-speaking countries

2.   foreign-born technical, business, and professional employees in business and industry in English-speaking countries

3.   international business people and diplomats who need to use English as their working lingua franca

4.   refugees (adult and adolescent) in resettlement and vocational training programs wishing to relocate in English-speaking countries

To Morley's four categories we should add at least two more groups:

5.   teachers of English as a foreign language who are not native speakers of English and who expect to serve as the major model and source of input in English for their students

6.   people in non–English-speaking countries working as tour guides, waiters, hotel personnel, customs agents, and the like, who use English for dealing with visitors who do not speak their language

The goal of teaching pronunciation to such learners is not to make them sound like native speakers of English. With the exception of a few highly gifted and motivated individuals, such a goal is unrealistic. A more modest and realistic goal is to enable learners to surpass the threshold level so that their pronunciation will not detract from their ability to communicate.

Having established that intelligible pronunciation is one of the necessary components of oral communication, the next issue is methodological: How can teachers improve the pronunciation of unintelligible speakers of English so that they become intelligible? This is a problem for Communicative Language Teaching, since proponents of this approach have not dealt adequately with the role of pronunciation in language teaching, nor have they developed an agreed-upon set of strategies for teaching pronunciation communicatively.[7]

We can begin to answer the question of how to teach pronunciation as part of the Communicative Approach by reviewing the kinds of techniques and practice materials that have traditionally been used – and are still being used – to teach pronunciation. The following is a fairly comprehensive list:

1.   *Listen and imitate:* A technique used in the Direct Method in which students listen to a teacher-provided model and repeat or imitate it.[8] This technique has been enhanced by the use of tape recorders, language labs, and video recorders.

2.   *Phonetic training:* Use of articulatory descriptions, articulatory diagrams, and a phonetic alphabet (a technique from the Reform Movement, which may involve doing phonetic transcription as well as reading phonetically transcribed text).

3.   *Minimal pair drills:* A technique introduced during the Audiolingual era to help students distinguish between similar and problematic sounds in the target language through listening discrimination and spoken practice. Minimal pair drills typically

---

[7]See Celce-Murcia (1983) and Pica (1984) for some of the earliest practical suggestions for teaching pronunciation communicatively.
[8]This includes, for example, having a Spanish speaker imitate the accent of an English speaker in Spanish in order to then transfer that "accent" to English.

begin with word-level drills and then move on to sentence-level drills (both paradigmatic and syntagmatic).

4. *Contextualized minimal pairs:* Bowen's (1972, 1975b) attempt to make minimal pair drills responsive to Cognitive Approach criticisms of meaninglessness and lack of context. In the technique, the teacher establishes the setting (e.g., a blacksmith shoeing a horse) and presents key vocabulary; students are then trained to respond to a sentence stem with the appropriate meaningful response (a or b):[9]

Sentence stem

The blacksmith (a. hits / b. heats) the horseshoe.

Cued student response

a. with the hammer / b. in the fire.

5. *Visual aids:* Enhancement of the teacher's description of how sounds are produced by audiovisual aids such as sound-color charts, Fidel wall charts, rods, pictures, mirrors, props, realia, etc. These devices are also used to cue production of the target sounds.

6. *Tongue twisters:* A technique from speech correction strategies for native speakers (e.g., "She sells seashells by the seashore.")

7. *Developmental approximation drills:* A technique suggested by first-language acquisition studies in which second language speakers are taught to retrace the steps that many English-speaking children follow as they acquire certain sounds in their first language. Thus just as children learning English often acquire /w/ before /r/ or /y/ before /l/, adults who have difficulty producing /l/ or /r/ can be encouraged to begin by pronouncing words with initial /w/ or /y/, and then shift to /r/ or /l/, respectively:

/w/ → /r/		/y/ → /l/	
wed	red	yet	let
wag	rag	yes	less
witch	rich	you	Lou
wipe	ripe	young	lung

8. *Practice of vowel shifts and stress shifts related by affixation:* A technique based on rules of generative phonology (Chomsky and Halle 1968) used with intermediate or advanced learners. The teacher points out the rule-based nature of vowel and stress shifts in etymologically related words to raise awareness; sentences and short texts that contain both members of a pair may be provided as oral practice material:[10]

Vowel shift: mime (long i) mimic (short i)

Sentence context: Street *mimes* often *mimic* the gestures of passersby.

Stress shift: PHOtograph   phoTOGraphy

Sentence context: I can tell from these *photographs* that you are very good at *photography*.

9. *Reading aloud/recitation:* Passages or scripts for learners to practice and then read aloud, focusing on stress, timing, and intonation. This technique may or may not involve memorization of the text, and it usually occurs with genres that are intended to be spoken, such as speeches, poems, plays, and dialogues.

---

[9]The Bowen technique is described more fully in Chapters 3 and 4.
[10]For a more comprehensive treatment of this topic see Chapter 9.

10. *Recordings of learners' production:* Audio- and videotapes of rehearsed and spontaneous speeches, free conversations, and role plays. Subsequent playback offers opportunities for feedback from teachers and peers as well as for teacher, peer, and self-evaluation.

With the exception of the last two techniques listed, we can see that the emphasis in pronunciation instruction has been largely on getting the sounds right at the word level – dealing with words in isolation or with words in very controlled and contrived sentence-level environments.[11] Although the last two techniques allow for practice at the discourse level, the practice material is often fully scripted and sometimes highly contrived. There is thus some doubt about whether such reading-aloud exercises can actually improve a learner's pronunciation in spontaneous conversation.[12]

When the Communicative Approach to language teaching began to take over in the mid- to late 1970s (see Brumfit and Johnson 1979; Widdowson 1978), most of the aforementioned techniques and materials for teaching pronunciation at the segmental level were flatly rejected on theoretical and practical grounds as being incompatible with teaching language as communication. Influenced by the discourse-based approaches and materials being used to teach language communicatively, materials developers and teachers began to search for more appropriate ways to teach pronunciation. They decided that directing most of their energy to teaching suprasegmental features of language (i.e., rhythm, stress, and intonation) in a discourse context was the optimal way to organize a short-term pronunciation course for nonnative speakers. McNerney and Mendelsohn (1992: 186) express this position very clearly:

> . . . a short term pronunciation course should focus first and foremost on suprasegmentals as they have the greatest impact on the comprehensibility of the learner's English. We have found that giving priority to the suprasegmental aspects of English not only improves learners' comprehensibility but is also less frustrating for students because greater change can be effected in a short time.[13]

Today we see signs that pronunciation instruction is moving away from the segmental/suprasegmental debate and toward a more balanced view. This view recognizes that both an inability to distinguish sounds that carry a high functional load (such as /ɪ/ in *list* and /iy/ in *least*) and an inability to distinguish suprasegmental features (such as intonation and stress differences in yes/no and alternative questions) can have a negative impact on the oral communication – and the listening comprehension abilities – of nonnative speakers of English. Today's pronunciation curriculum thus seeks to identify the most important aspects of both the segmentals and suprasegmentals, and integrate them appropriately in courses that meet the needs of any given group of learners.[14] In addition to segmental and suprasegmental features of English, there is also the issue of voice quality setting; that is, each language has certain stereotypical features such as pitch level, vowel space, neutral tongue position, and degree of muscular activity that contribute to the overall sound quality or "accent" associated with the language.[15]

This book represents our own best effort to compile a comprehensive volume on the teaching of North American English (NAE) pronunciation to nonnative speakers of

[11]A classic text of this "sounds-in-words" approach is Nilsen and Nilsen (1973).
[12]For a more detailed discussion of recitation and reading-aloud techniques as they relate to pronunciation training, see Chapter 10.
[13]One of the best-known textbooks that follows this line of thinking is Gilbert (1993).
[14]See the excellent volume by Morley (1994a) for an overview of recent pronunciation research and pedagogy.
[15]Chapter 2 reviews what is currently known about voice quality setting in English and some other languages.

English. As such, the text provides a detailed treatment of both the NAE sound system and a grounding in classroom methods and techniques for the teaching of pronunciation. The desired end result is to equip teachers who use the text (either as a course text or reference) with the background and skills to address the pronunciation needs of their students. We have selected the North American variety of English for rather obvious reasons: (1) it represents our own variety and that of most of the teachers we train; (2) it is the target variety of the many ESL students living, studying, or working in North America; and (3) it is a variety that has gained a strong foothold in much of the world, where English is taught as a foreign or additional language.

The underlying philosophy of this text is simple: Only through a thorough knowledge of the English sound system and through familiarity with a variety of pedagogical techniques, many of which should be communicatively oriented, can teachers effectively address the pronunciation needs of their students. It is our aim in this text to provide a rich knowledge base, as well as to assist teachers in correctly assessing their learners' pronunciation needs. Given this knowledge base, we believe that teachers can continue to improve their understanding of the English sound system and expand upon the instructional tools that are now – and will become – available to assist learners in this skill area.

EXERCISES

KEY CONCEPTS

Write a brief definition of the following key terms from this chapter. For each, give examples where relevant.

intuitive-imitative approach

analytic-linguistic approach

Grammar Translation/
　reading-based approaches

Direct Method

naturalistic methods

The Reform Movement

International Phonetic Alphabet

Audiolingualism

minimal pair drill

minimal pairs

Cognitive Approach

Silent Way

sound-color chart

Fidel wall charts

Community Language Learning

human computer

Communicative Approach

INTROSPECTING ABOUT YOUR OWN LANGUAGE LEARNING

Think about a foreign language that you have learned in school.

1. What method (or combination of methods) did your teacher use? How did this method address the skill of pronunciation?

2. How successful was this method in improving your pronunciation?

3. Of the methods described in this chapter, which one(s) do you believe would help you most with learning pronunciation in a second language?

DISCUSSION QUESTIONS

1. Match the seven methods below with the statement that best represents their philosophy of pronunciation teaching. Be prepared in the follow-up discussion to explain the techniques employed in each method that relate to the teaching of pronunciation.

   1. Grammar Translation

      a. Pronunciation should be worked on right from the beginning of language instruction. Any words mispronounced by the student should be corrected by the teacher.

   2. Direct Method

      b. Language is not learned by repeating after a model. With visual cues the teacher helps students develop their own inner "criteria" for correctness. They must trust and be responsible for their own production in the target language.

   3. Audiolingual Method

      c. Oral communication is not the primary goal of language instruction. Therefore little attention is given to speaking, and almost none to pronunciation.

   4. Silent Way

      d. Students should work with language at the discourse or suprasentential level. The ultimate goal is communication.

   5. Community Language Learning

      e. Students will begin to speak when they are ready. They are expected to make errors in the initial stage and teachers should be tolerant of them.

   6. Total Physical Response

      f. The pronunciation syllabus is primarily student initiated and designed. Students decide what they want to practice and use the teacher as a resource.

   7. Communicative Approach

      g. Teachers provide students with a model for nativelike speech. By listening and then imitating the modeler, students improve their pronunciation.

      (Adapted from Larsen-Freeman 1986.)

2. Compare your experience learning the pronunciation of another language in a classroom setting with that of a partner. Ask your partner the following questions:

   a. What percentage of instructional time was devoted to pronunciation?

   b. How would you rate the quality of your teacher's pronunciation in the target language (e.g., native/nativelike, good, fair, poor)?

   c. Which of the following standard techniques for teaching pronunciation did your teacher use, and how?

      • articulatory explanation (e.g., "Put your tongue here . . .")

      • phonetic symbols/description

      • imitation and repetition

      • visual aids

   d. What type of feedback (if any) did you receive regarding your pronunciation?

   e. How much use was made of the language laboratory or audiotapes?

   f. What else contributed to your learning the pronunciation of this language?

3. Which method discussed in this chapter seems most suitable for teaching pronunciation in the following situations:

   a. students won't talk

   b. students won't stop talking

   c. monolingual class

   d. multilingual class

   e. large class

   f. small class

   g. children

   h. adults

IN THE CLASSROOM

Assume that you are teaching pronunciation. Here are some common classroom situations that you might encounter. How would you respond?

1. You are teaching a class using Total Physical Response. One of your students asks: "Why aren't we speaking more?"

2. You are using Silent Way with a beginning-level class. One of your students says: "Please correct me every time I make a mistake."

3. You are using the Communicative Approach and doing lots of group work. Your students are unhappy with this. One of them says: "We talk a lot in class but I'm not learning because my partner's accent is worse than mine."

SUGGESTED ACTIVITIES

1. Interview an ESL or EFL teacher. Find out which techniques he or she uses to teach pronunciation.

2. If you are able to locate a teacher who addresses pronunciation systematically, arrange to visit the class. Make a list of the techniques that the teacher employs to teach pronunciation. Can you determine which method(s) is being used and what the teacher's philosophy of teaching pronunciation is?

3. Find out more information about one method of teaching pronunciation. Decide on one technique (e.g., the human computer). Plan a small demonstration lesson and present it in class.

ON THE CASSETTE

Listen to the presentation of the transcription key as represented on page xii. Repeat as needed.

CHAPTER 2

Research on the Teaching and Acquisition of Pronunciation Skills

A s outlined in the preceding chapter, the teaching of pronunciation has experienced the same methodological "swings of the pendulum" (Prator 1991) over the years that have characterized the evolution of ESL teaching. With the wide range of curriculum options now available, and the lack of a clear consensus regarding any one best way to teach pronunciation (Macdonald, Yule, and Powers 1994), informed decisions on the part of the teacher or curriculum designer are of paramount importance. This chapter deals with several factors that underlie the effective teaching of pronunciation. These factors focus on the learner, and involve the effects of age, exposure to the target language, amount and type of prior second language instruction, aptitude, attitude and motivation, and the role of the learner's first language on the phonological acquisition of a second language.[1] Together with the institutional and setting variables (discussed more fully in Chapter 11), insight into these factors helps the reader to identify what is taking place in the complex world of pronunciation research, to judge the current status of research, and to notice the relevance of this research to teaching.

THE LEARNER

The first issue encountered in designing the pronunciation curriculum is perhaps the one most immediately evident – the learners themselves. As Wong (1987b: 17) aptly points out, the teaching of pronunciation "is not exclusively a linguistic matter," and we need to take into consideration such factors as our learners' ages, exposure to the target language, amount and type of prior pronunciation instruction, and perhaps most importantly their attitude toward the target language and their motivation to achieve intelligible speech patterns in the second language.[2]

As teachers in the pronunciation classroom, we clearly have little control over certain of these factors, such as our students' ages and their amount and type of prior language instruction. However, we need to be aware of how these factors figure in determining performance in speaking English (or alternatively in coloring attitudes toward such performance). For those factors that we can influence (i.e., attitude and motivation), we need to be aware to what degree they determine the acquisition of target language phonology.

---

[1]See Leather and James (1991) for an excellent overview of these topics from the researcher's perspective. An alternative teacher-oriented review of relevant research is Pennington (1994).
[2]See Wong (1987b) for a more complete description of the critical role these learner variables play as well as suggestions for helping students become more intelligible within a communicative approach.

Before proceeding to situational variables, let us then briefly examine each of these learner-based factors.

AGE

Given the ability of many adult second language learners to attain targetlike proficiency in morphology and syntax, their apparent inability to attain nativelike proficiency in pronunciation has often intrigued linguists and nonlinguists alike. Scovel (1969, 1988) terms this lack of adult facility in acquiring second language pronunciation the "Joseph Conrad phenomenon" after the famous Polish-born author who, despite the brilliant control of the lexis, syntax, and morphology of English displayed in his literary works, was unable to reach anywhere near the same levels of perfection in his acquisition of English phonology. (Conrad's speech, in fact, remained partly unintelligible to English speakers throughout his life.) Subscribing to the philosophy "You can't teach an old dog new tricks," many would claim along with Scovel that adults are unable to achieve perfect or targetlike pronunciation in a second language. This view goes hand in hand with the generally held notion that prepubescent children with adequate exposure to a second language can achieve perfect or near perfect pronunciation with relative ease.

One line of research that supports these claims was originally formulated by Penfield and Roberts (1959) and Lenneberg (1967). This research posits a period (occurring around puberty) after which brain *lateralization*, or the assigning of certain functions to the different hemispheres of the brain, is completed. The period prior to the completion of lateralization, called the *critical period*, represents the biologically determined period of life during which maximal conditions for language acquisition exist. The implications of this theory as it relates to second language acquisition are quite clear. Scovel (1969) and later Krashen (1973) claimed that along with lateralization (which according to Krashen occurs as early as age 5) comes an increasing loss of brain plasticity, which renders an individual incapable of achieving nativelike pronunciation in a second language after puberty.

Not all second language researchers, however, subscribe to the critical period hypothesis. Flege (1981) cites the lack of empirical evidence to substantiate this claim, contending that "neither physiological maturation nor neurological reorganization renders an adult incapable of speaking a foreign language without an accent" (p. 445). Others (e.g., Brown 1994) would argue that psychomotor considerations figure into the picture as well. In other words, while nativelike command of morphology and syntax in a second language may be the result of plasticity in the central nervous system, the command of second language phonology also involves the neuromuscular realm, which may play an even more crucial role in the overall picture (Bob Jacobs, personal communication). Finally, many would argue that the critical period hypothesis overlooks such differences between child and adult second language acquisition as exposure to the target language, linguistic expectations of interlocutors,[3] ego permeability, attitude toward the second language, and type of motivation.

Overall, then, the importance of the critical period is somewhat downplayed today, and the claim that adults cannot achieve nativelike pronunciation in a second language is not infrequently countered with anecdotes about successful adult second language learners who have "beaten the odds." Scovel (1988), however, argues that the few true successes are balanced out by a comparable number of total failures (i.e., the severely autistic who never even acquire their native language). He also suggests that when native speakers compliment a foreigner on "perfect" pronunciation there is usually some exaggeration involved – for example, when people say, "I'm amazed that you sound just like a

---

[3]For a discussion of the differing expectations that native speakers have of children and adults learning a second language see Hatch, Wagner Gough, and Peck (1985).

native speaker!" they really mean, "You speak my language brilliantly – especially for a foreigner!"

More recently, cognitive scientists have concerned themselves with the issue of aging as it relates to brain plasticity and the creation of perceptual networks. Rather than positing one critical period for language acquisition, these researchers propose that there are a number of *sensitive periods* during which different aspects of language acquisition occur. Research in the field further indicates that children and adults perceive sounds in a very similar manner (Lieberman and Blumstein 1988), and that differences between the two age groups may be related more to the information available (i.e., to external circumstances) than to any innate differences in ability (Massaro 1987). In fact, according to cognitive scientists, the idea of the adult brain "atrophying" or in some way becoming incapable of producing new sounds is an erroneous one, since the brain retains a measure of flexibility or "plasticity" throughout its life (Diamond 1988).

However, it is undoubtedly the case that adults will acquire the phonological system of a second language in a manner different from that of their first language, given that the acquisition of the new sounds in the second language must be integrated into already existing neural networks. As Jacobs puts it (1988: 327), "Biological factors impose limitations much the same as psychological and sociocultural factors . . . , but none of these variables in isolation impose an absolute upper bound on [second language acquisition]." Adults are then capable of rising to the challenge of performing competently in a new sound system.

Of course, factors other than the brain's ability to create new neural networks for the processing and production of the target-language sounds also play a role. Scott (1989), for instance, demonstrates that auditory perception diminishes with age, especially for those over 60 – a factor that would definitely hinder older adults in their attempts to acquire targetlike pronunciation in a second language. A similar caution is sounded by Jacobs (1988), who notes that the environment in which adults typically learn a second language (i.e., the classroom) may not be as rich as that experienced by children acquiring a second language in a more natural, input-rich environment. Thus when we discuss child/adult differences in phonological acquisition we may be comparing the proverbial apples and oranges. Finally, Ausubel (1964), Guiora (1972), Schumann (1975), and others note that the disparity between child and adult performance may be explained through a complex interplay of social and psychological factors (discussed later). In sum, we should be cognizant of such external factors when drawing any conclusions about age.

The implications of the foregoing theories with regard to the teaching of pronunciation deserve reflection. For example, if (as some research indicates) adults are capable of acquiring a high degree of pronunciation accuracy in a second language but are more impeded in their acquisition of target language phonology by nonlinguistic factors than are children, then we need to build into courses for adults more fluency and confidence-building activities;[4] we should also have our adult learners seriously examine their personal goals in the pronunciation class. Likewise, if Scovel's (1988) claims concerning the inability of most adults to achieve targetlike pronunciation are valid, then teachers need to redefine the goal of the pronunciation class as comfortable intelligibility rather than accuracy, and ensure that this goal is reflected in the methods, activities, and materials of the ESL class.

EXPOSURE TO THE TARGET LANGUAGE

According to the language learning theories of Postovsky (1974), Asher (1977), and Krashen (1982), among others, learners acquire language primarily from the input they

---

[4]See also Chapter 10 and the excellent volumes by Wong (1987a) and Bowen and Marks (1992) for a discussion of confidence-building activities.

receive, and they must receive large amounts of comprehensible input before they are required to speak. If true, learners' exposure to the target language will be a critical factor in determining their success. In EFL settings, especially those where students have little opportunity to surround themselves with native input in the target language, the burden will fall more on the teacher to provide an adequate model of the target language, and to ascertain that students have opportunities outside of class (e.g., in language-laboratory or learning-center environments) to experience samples of the authentic oral discourse of native speakers; similarly, it will fall to teachers to encourage out-of-class conversational use of the target language. However, even in ESL settings, where the learners are surrounded by the English-speaking world, many speakers live in linguistic "ghettos" with relatively little exposure to native speakers of the target language in their homes and even in their work sites. Again, in such cases, the teacher should try to maximize students' exposure to the target, and to encourage them to expand their own domains of linguistic competence, stressing the importance of language exposure in the process of acquiring all aspects of language: pronunciation, grammar, and vocabulary.

AMOUNT AND TYPE OF PRIOR PRONUNCIATION INSTRUCTION

Assuming that we are dealing with learners who have had prior exposure to English, we also need to examine the amount and type of prior pronunciation instruction students have had. In EFL settings, instruction may have taken the form of repetition drills led by a teacher whose own pronunciation differed from the target norm. Alternatively, in an ESL multiskills class, pronunciation may not have been explicitly dealt with at all, and students may not have been fully aware of their pronunciation problems. Whatever the scenario, we need to recognize that in any pronunciation class at the intermediate or advanced levels of proficiency, we may be dealing with somewhat fixed or systematic pronunciation errors. Thus the syllabus and techniques that we implement must be tailored to the types of problems we discern among our students.

APTITUDE, ATTITUDE, AND MOTIVATION

Are some learners inherently more capable of acquiring a good pronunciation than others? Skehan's (1989) overview of Carroll's (1965, 1981) research on language aptitude is useful here. According to Carroll, there are four traits that constitute language aptitude:

1. *Phonemic coding ability:* the capacity to discriminate and code foreign sounds such that they can be recalled[5]
2. *Grammatical sensitivity:* the ability to analyze language and figure out rules
3. *Inductive language learning ability:* the capacity to pick up language through exposure
4. *Memory:* the amount of rote learning activity needed to internalize something (a new sound, a lexical item, a grammatical rule, the pronunciation or spelling of a word, etc.)

Our main concern here is the first trait, although the memory trait is also relevant. Some learners are in fact fairly balanced in these four traits, whereas others have very strong patterns of strength and weakness. Learners weak in phonemic coding ability would therefore have much more difficulty achieving a readily intelligible pronunciation than those with high aptitude in this domain. Teachers (and pronunciation syllabuses) need to be sensitive to such learner differences and not expect all learners to achieve the same level of success in the same amount of time.

---

[5]According to Skehan, phonemic coding ability is the language aptitude trait that relates least to one's general intelligence. This suggests that "having an ear for language" may be qualitatively different from other language aptitudes or traits.

Snow and Shapira (1985), on the other hand, discount the importance of aptitude, pointing out that we have all demonstrated language learning ability via acquisition of our native language. One argument against assigning the determining role to aptitude, according to these researchers, is the fact that low-ability learners (as measured by language aptitude tests) are in fact often able to attain fluency in a second language while some high-ability learners are not.[6]

As should be evident by now, the network of factors influencing an individual's acquisition of second language phonology is a tremendously complicated one. Indeed, as Stevick (1976) suggests, we need to go beyond language aptitude and educational or cultural experience to see how individuals and their personalities affect the learning process. Of help in understanding learners' attitudes toward the target language and their motivation (or lack thereof) to acquire this language is research that examines the effect of personality and the acculturation process on language acquisition.

Guiora (1972) notes that personality, or in his words language ego, is at the very core of the language learning process, especially where the skill of pronunciation is concerned. "Speaking a foreign language entails the radical operation of learning and manipulating a new grammar, syntax, and vocabulary and, at the extreme limits of proficiency, modifying one of the basic modes of identification by the self and others, the way we sound" (p. 144). Pointing out the often dramatic discrepancy between certain individuals' attainment in pronunciation versus their attainment in other skill areas, Guiora postulates that accent or pronunciation is a unique feature of language performance – one that can provide "the key to the extent to which the individual is psychologically capable of stepping into a new system of communication" (p. 144).[7]

Following in Guiora's footsteps is Schumann's work on the role that acculturation plays in the process of language acquisition. Schumann (1975) echoes Guiora's hypothesis that *ego permeability* (i.e., the extent to which the ego can be flexible and adapt) and personality factors are at the heart of second language acquisition. Schumann further states that in adults, the development of firm ego boundaries, along with individuals' attitudinal and motivational orientations, can place constraints on the cognitive process of language learning. Given such constraints, adults might well be hindered from attaining their biologically determined capabilities.

Schumann's *acculturation model* (Schumann 1986) clearly delineates the role that social and affective variables may play in language acquisition. This model, based on the premise that certain social and affective variables "cluster" into a single variable of acculturation, states that learners will acquire the target language to the degree that they acculturate. Two types of determining factors are: (1) those concerned with the language learning of a group of people, or sociocultural variables (e.g., social dominance patterns, size of the foreign language population, amount of congruence between the foreign and target language cultures); and (2) factors concerned with individual differences, or affective variables (e.g., ego permeability, personality, type of motivation, degree of culture shock). Schumann notes that sociocultural variables do not prohibit successful second language learning. That is, individuals may learn languages successfully under sociocultural conditions that are not favorable, or vice versa – they may not learn a language under sociocultural conditions that are highly favorable. Thus although the two sets of variables always

---

[6]For a more thorough discussion of the role of aptitude in second language acquisition and a summary of the research on individual differences, see Skehan (1989).

[7]Several studies have attempted to ascertain whether artificially inducing the language ego to become more permeable (i.e., via ingestion of alcohol or valium, or via hypnotism) will result in an increased degree of targetlike pronunciation. The results are somewhat mixed, although the studies provide some evidence of a correlation between ego permeability and accuracy of pronunciation. For details see Guiora (1972), Guiora et al. (1972), and Schumann et al. (1978).

interact, affective variables appear to carry more weight than sociocultural ones in determining any learner's acquisition process.

In applying this model, Schumann differentiates between two types of successful acculturation. In the first type, the learner demonstrates *integrative motivation* – that is, a desire to be socially integrated in the target culture.[8] In the second type of acculturation, the learner demonstrates the same openness to the target culture, but additionally regards target language speakers as his reference group. This second type of motivation appears to be akin to that described by Graham (1985) as *assimilative motivation*, and implies a desire on the part of the learner to become an indistinguishable member of the target speech community. (Assimilative motivation, which is rare among adult second language learners, is what all children have when learning their first language.) Accordingly, one can hypothesize that this second type of learner would willingly embrace the target culture, and would therefore be more apt to acquire targetlike pronunciation in the second language.

Instrumental motivation, in which an individual learns a second language to attain a certain goal, for instance a job promotion, does not contribute to successful acculturation, according to Schumann. However, other researchers such as Lukmani (1972) argue that the intensity of motivation is often as important as the type of motivation at play. In other words, someone with extraordinarily high instrumental motivation (e.g., someone who wants to sound like a native speaker in order to function effectively as an actor or an espionage agent) may well achieve a better pronunciation than someone with integrative motivation that is quite positive yet less intense.

THE ROLE OF THE NATIVE LANGUAGE

Whether our students are from a homogeneous language group (as is most often the case in EFL settings) or from diverse language backgrounds (as is common in ESL classrooms), we need to consider their native language(s) in deciding on pronunciation priorities. For this we can draw on a growing body of research in second language phonology. This field concerns itself with questions such as the following:

1. To what degree is the process of phonological acquisition in one's first language similar to the process of acquiring the sound system of a second language?

2. To what degree do pronunciation patterns acquired in one's first language govern or determine the process of second language phonological acquisition?

3. Are there underlying language universals in the acquisition of phonology? How can these universals help us gain insights into students' pronunciation of the target language?

Six somewhat overlapping theories or hypotheses of second-language phonological acquisition have been proposed: contrastive analysis, error analysis and avoidance, interlanguage analysis, markedness theory, language universals, and information processing theory. Even though these theories are not all mutually exclusive, we will deal with each of them in turn for the purposes of clarity and historical accuracy.

THE CONTRASTIVE ANALYSIS HYPOTHESIS

Certainly the most longstanding theory of phonological acquisition is the *contrastive analysis hypothesis*. Originally proposed to explain all aspects of language acquisition (Lado 1957), this theory holds that second language acquisition is filtered through the learner's first language, with the native language facilitating acquisition in those cases where the target structures are similar, and "interfering" with acquisition in cases where

---

[8]This form of motivation has often been discussed in the literature as a positive force in language acquisition (see Gardner and Lambert 1972).

the target structures are dissimilar or nonexistent. As with many theories, the contrastive analysis hypothesis initially enjoyed widespread acceptance on all fronts – that is, as a valid explanation for the difficulties experienced by learners in the realms of syntax, morphology, and phonology. However, the theory has since been challenged, primarily on the basis of its inability to predict the degree of difficulty learners would experience with a given item and on the basis of conflicting evidence from error analysis and interlanguage research (discussed shortly).

The most enlightened form of the contrastive analysis hypothesis came from Wardhaugh (1970), who rejected the strong version (that contrastive analysis would be able to predict all learning problems) and argued for the validity of a weak version (that contrastive analysis could explain the cause of many, but far from all, systematic language-learning errors). Today most researchers in the field, while minimizing the role that native language interference plays in other areas of language acquisition, would agree that *interference* (now more commonly referred to as *negative transfer*) is valid in second language pronunciation acquisition. Like Lado and Wardhaugh, these researchers hold that negative transfer is a significant factor in accounting for foreign accents, particularly with regard to the acquisition of more general segmental features such as aspiration and of suprasegmental features such as intonation and rhythm (cf. Broselow 1987; Broselow, Hurtig, and Ringen 1987; Sato 1987; Tarone 1987b).

ERROR ANALYSIS AND AVOIDANCE

Banathy and Madarasz (1969) were early critics of contrastive analysis and argued for the need to complement contrastive analysis with *error analysis* (i.e., an analysis of errors that occur in the learners' interlanguage system) – especially if one planned to apply results to language teaching:

> Contrastive linguistics – no matter how refined – can only point toward a potential learning problem or difficulty. On the other hand, error analysis can tell us the intensity of the difficulty or the size of the problem. (p. 92)

Richards (1971), another critic of overreliance on contrastive analysis who was also a proponent of error analysis, proposed a three-way classification of language learning errors that he believed would both shed light on the second language acquisition process and better inform language teaching:

1. *Interlingual errors:* those errors caused by negative transfer from the learner's first language
2. *Intralingual errors:* those errors stemming from marked or complex features in the structure of the target language itself and which thus seem to be committed by all second language learners of the target language regardless of their native language
3. *Developmental errors:* those second language errors that reflect the same problems and strategies that young children encounter and use in acquiring the target language as their first language.

Of course, error analysis has also had its critics, who hold that it tends to focus on learners' problems (i.e., what they do wrong) rather than learners' accomplishments (i.e., what they do right). This line of reasoning helped give rise to interlanguage analysis (see next section). In addition, critics made the argument that error analysis ignores the strategy of avoidance (see Kleinman 1977; Schachter 1974), which occurs when learners take advantage of the paraphrase potential of language to avoid – consciously or unconsciously – the use of words or structures that they find difficult. Thus in English one can avoid using relative clauses by forming a paraphrase with two simple sentences. Likewise, if learners cannot remember whether to say "civility" or "civilness," they can paraphrase with "good behavior" or some such expression.

However, to demonstrate the existence of *avoidance* one has to show that second language learners, given a particular task, are using a particular word or structure they find difficult with a significantly lower frequency than native speakers performing the same task. Thus rather than the presence of a systematic error, one accounts for the systematic absence of a form using theories such as contrastive analysis, performance data, or error analysis.

Schachter (1974) originally argued that avoidance did not occur on the phonological level in the way that it did on the syntactic level or lexical level since one could not, for example, avoid the /ð/ in words like *the, this, that* when speaking English. However, several researchers have reported contexts in which phonological avoidance seems to play a role. Heller (1976) tells of Spanish-speaking adults in evening ESL classes who avoid using similar-sounding English–Spanish cognates (e.g., *quality–qualidad*) in their English because they believe such words are Spanish, not English. Celce-Murcia (1977) describes the speech of Caroline, a 2-year-old child acquiring English and French simultaneously, who selected the word that was easiest for her to articulate or approximate regardless of which language she was using at the time:[9]

Caroline's Speech	French	English
/ku:to/	couteau	*knife
/pu:n/	*cuiller	spoon
/o:m/	*maison	home
/kamyo/	camion	*truck
	(Celce-Murcia 1977: 36)	

Thus it seems as if phonological avoidance is a learning strategy that may occur whenever circumstances permit and that avoidance is not exclusively syntactic and lexical but must be considered a strategy that potentially applies to all areas of second language acquisition.

THE INTERLANGUAGE HYPOTHESIS

At the outset of the 1970s, Selinker (1969, 1972) proposed the notion of *interlanguage*. This term refers to the linguistic codes of second language learners which, according to Selinker, reflect unique systems. At the core of Selinker's construct is the notion that interlanguage grammar can function independently of the speaker's native language or the target language, and that it follows a system all its own based on first language, second language input, language universals, and communication strategies. The term *fossilization*, and its derivatives, also comes from Selinker (1972), who describes it as a plateau in language learning beyond which it is difficult for learners to progress without exceptional effort or motivation.

The notion of interlanguage was further developed by Corder (1974), who visualizes interlanguage as a dynamic continuum along which a second language learner can move toward an increasingly targetlike system. The learner continually processes input from the target language and refines rules or hypotheses in the direction of the target or until there is fossilization.

The research in phonology that was driven by the interlanguage hypothesis centered on the developmental nature of the learner's interlanguage and on investigating the universality of phonological acquisition patterns across age and language groups. Research on

---

[9]See also Ferguson and Farwell's (1975) study on the phonological acquisition of monolingual English-speaking children in which they report that the children persistently avoid particular sounds.

interlanguage phonology in the 1980s (see Ioup and Weinberger 1987) had several focuses, which included: (1) models of phonological development, (2) theories of interlanguage phonology, (3) acquisition of syllable structure, (4) acquisition of suprasegmentals, and (5) the varying phonological production of learners resulting from the formality of the speech situation in which learners are engaged, the anxiety they are experiencing (see Tarone 1988), and so on.

MARKEDNESS THEORY

A fourth theory that has contributed to the field of second language acquisition is *markedness theory*, which proposes that in every linguistic opposition – phonological or semantic – there is one member of any pair of opposites that is psycholinguistically *unmarked* (more basic or neutral, more universal, more frequent, first acquired) and one that is *marked* (more specific, less frequent, more limited, later acquired). This theory is helpful in explaining phonological differences among languages. For example, according to markedness theory, English (which allows both voiceless /p, t, k/ and voiced /b, d, g/ stop consonants in word- or syllable-final position) is more marked with respect to stop consonants in final position than are German and Russian (which permit only voiceless stop consonants /p, t, k/ in this position).

Markedness theory was first proposed and developed by Trubetzkoy (1939) and Jakobson (1941) along with other linguists from the Prague School. In terms of current research on second-language phonological acquisition, markedness theory has been applied by Eckman (1977) in his markedness differential hypothesis. In essence, Eckman's work combines elements of the previously discussed hypotheses, asserting that although it is "necessary to compare descriptions of the native and target languages in order to predict areas of difficulty, . . . this alone is not sufficient" (p. 60).

Eckman's theory is a direct response to criticisms of the contrastive analysis hypothesis – specifically, that it did not (1) accurately predict which areas of target language phonology would be most difficult for learners of a given language group or (2) predict which exact sounds would be substituted by the learner. In the case of German and English, for example, the contrastive analysis hypothesis can establish that these two languages place very different limitations on the positions in which the voiced stops and fricatives /b, d, g, v, z/ occur, with German (with some dialectal variation) allowing them only in syllable-initial position and English allowing a much more varied occurrence (see Moulton 1962). Having established this difference, the contrastive analysis hypothesis can predict that learners from these two language backgrounds would have difficulty pronouncing (i.e., voicing or devoicing) the final stops and fricatives in the other language; contrastive analysis alone, however, is not able to establish a *directionality* of difficulty. In other words, it could not predict whether native English speakers would have more difficulty learning to pronounce the final consonant of the German word *Bad* "bath" as /t/ or whether native German speakers would be more apt to have difficulty voicing the final /d/ of the English word *bad*.

Eckman proposes to remedy this deficiency by constructing a hierarchy of difficulty for phonological acquisition that utilizes insights from markedness theory. His markedness differential hypothesis claims to accurately predict that German speakers (whose language *prohibits* them from voicing stops and fricatives in final position) will, when speaking English, experience difficulty in producing the marked voiced-consonant forms in final position. On the other hand, English speakers (whose native language allows either voiced or voiceless final stops and fricatives) will, when speaking German, experience relatively less difficulty in learning to ignore the marked forms and to use the unmarked forms exclusively in syllable-final position.

This line of linguistic investigation should, according to Eckman, help us augment the insights gained from contrastive analysis and predict not only which sounds learners would have difficulty with, but which problems would be more difficult for a linguistically homogeneous group of learners.

LANGUAGE UNIVERSALS

Rather than assume (as most structural linguists have) that languages can differ from each other unpredictably and without limit (Joos 1958), the linguists who study *language universals* assume that all languages share common properties and that their surface differences might actually be quite unimportant.

The quest for language universals has taken two different paths:

1. Jakobson's (1941) seminal work, which greatly influenced Chomsky's (1986) model of "universal grammar" with its *principles* (given elements) and *parameters* (permitted variations), as well as Chomsky's arguments for positing an innate language acquisition device in all humans

2. Greenberg's (1962) typological or implicational language universals, which examine aspects of language that are common to many, and sometimes all, languages

In terms of sound systems, both versions of the universalist hypothesis start from the observation that given all the sounds the human vocal apparatus could possibly produce, the languages of the world draw on a remarkably finite inventory of sounds and share remarkably similar combinatory and hierarchical principles that explain how natural languages are spoken. For example, all languages have vowel sounds and consonant sounds, and within these categories there are sounds that contrast with each other in predictable ways.

In tandem with these universals about the sound systems of languages, there are related principles of phonological acquisition that predict, for example, that sound A is acquired before sound B. The most influential work regarding language universals in the study of phonological acquisition has been that of Jakobson (1941).[10] Given Jakobson's implicational hierarchy:

$$\text{Stops} \quad \rightarrow \quad \text{Nasals} \quad \rightarrow \quad \text{Fricatives}$$

we can predict that a language with fricatives will also have nasals and stops (but not necessarily vice versa). Likewise, a language with nasals will also have stops (but not necessarily vice versa).

Macken and Ferguson (1987) use Jakobson's hierarchy to state universals of phonological acquisition implied by the hierarchy:

• Stops are acquired before nasals.

• Nasals are acquired before fricatives.

They note that substitutions made in the early stages of acquisition can also be predicted:

• Fricatives will be replaced by stops.

Eckman (1991) combines earlier work on interlanguage analysis, markedness theory, and Greenbergian implicational universals in order to apply the *Interlanguage Structural Conformity Hypothesis* (ISCH) to the acquisition of pronunciation. The ISCH, which holds that implicational universals can be used to explain certain facts about the form of interlanguages without any reference to the learners' first language, was first proposed by

---

[10]Kiparsky and Menn (1987) remind us that Jakobson's hierarchies help us account for, among other things, regularities in the consonant inventories of languages.

Eckman, Moravcsik, and Wirth (1989) in a study that examined syntax (i.e., interrogative structures) rather than phonology. Eckman's 1991 study tested the relevance of the ISCH to phonological acquisition using two implicational universals from Greenberg (1978) as his starting point:

> *Fricative + stop principle:* If a language has at least one final consonant sequence consisting of stop + stop (e.g., *kicked* /kɪkt/), it also has at least one final consonant sequence consisting of fricative + stop (e.g., *risk* /rɪsk/).

> *Resolvability principle:* If a language has a consonant sequence of a given length (e.g., three consonants: *spry* /spray/) in either initial or final position, it also has at least one consonant sequence with one less consonant in the same position (i.e., in this case two consonants: *spy* /spay/).

These principles are hierarchical and do not work in reverse: Languages can have fricative + stop sequences without having stop + stop sequences, and languages can have sequences of two consonants without having sequences of three consonants in the same position.

We expect that further research in language universals will ultimately exploit the links between phonological universals and universals of phonological acquisition (see Leather and James 1991). However, we also agree with Macken and Ferguson (1987), who – based on their learner observation and research – argue that language universals alone will never perfectly predict phonological acquisition. Instead, they put forward two hypotheses that they feel are more accurate:

1. Phonological acquisition, like other forms of linguistic and nonlinguistic learning, involves a process of discovering patterns, via form testing, and revising hypotheses – a process referred to as regularizing.

2. At least some linguistic universals are not due to the operation of an innate language acquisition device; rather, they derive from the interaction of the learner and a patterned input.

With these hypotheses Macken and Ferguson lead us quite logically to a consideration of our last theoretical model for phonological acquisition, information processing theory.

INFORMATION PROCESSING THEORY

Information processing theory, which attempts to account for phonological acquisition without ignoring the effect of the native language on second-language phonological acquisition, derives from work in cognitive science. Within this field, which does not concern itself primarily with language acquisition, the research of Schneider and Schiffrin (1977) and Rumelhart and Norman (1978) provides useful insight into how the brain processes new information. According to Rumelhart and Norman, learners exhibit a distinct tendency to interpret new information in terms of their existing knowledge structures, commonly referred to as *schemata*. Schneider and Schiffrin propose that previously stored information can be processed in one of two manners – either via controlled processing (i.e., processing requiring attention and awareness) or via automatic processing (i.e., processing that is not controlled, modified, or inhibited). Automatic processing differs from controlled processing in that it is not capacity limited, and thus several automatic processes can be carried out in parallel, whereas controlled processes can be carried out only one at a time. These two modes of processing are not mutually exclusive; rather, they are often conducted in tandem as information is accessed.

Information processing theory predicts that in the acquisition of second language phonology, learners will exhibit a distinct tendency to interpret sounds in the second language in terms of the set of sounds that they control as part of their first language system. In addition, they will tend to process phonological information automatically, even in the early stages of second language acquisition, since the higher-level tasks of conceptualizing and formulating in the second language require controlled processing. This automatic processing of phonology, especially prevalent in adults, helps to account for the fossilized nature of much of second language pronunciation (Barbara Baptista, personal communication).

Information processing theory further postulates three modes of learning (Rumelhart and Norman 1978). In the first mode, accretion, the learners add new structures to their existing schemata or knowledge structures. In the second mode, restructuring, learners reorganize already-existing structures and create new schemata based on the preexisting patterns. Finally, in the tuning mode, learners further modify the new and/or old schemata, making them more accurate, general, or specific.

Until this point, the information processing account of second-language phonological acquisition appears to resemble somewhat the contrastive analysis hypothesis discussed earlier. However, second language phonologists who subscribe to an information processing view claim that rather than substitute the native language phoneme for that of the target language, speakers produce a compromise, or "middle ground" between the two – as in Flege's (1981) phonological translation hypothesis. According to Flege, the "seeming compromise between [the native and target language] patterns of phonetic implementation may reflect a restructuring of the phonetic space so that it encompasses the two languages" (p. 451).[11]

To translate this theory into more practical terms, imagine a native speaker of Brazilian Portuguese learning North American English. In this speaker's native-language vowel schema, there are seven oral monophthongal vowels /i, e, ɛ, a, ɔ, o, u/. On confronting the target language, the speaker may notice that the English vowel system contains a similar vowel for each of these native-language vowel sounds.[12] The learner may also recognize that English has the additional unfamiliar vowels /ɪ, æ, ʊ, ʌ/. Following Rumelhart and Norman's theory, acquisition would occur as follows. The speaker would try to add the new vowel sounds to the existing vowel schemata (accretion). Since the existing schemata are inadequate to account for the new input without interfering with the relative position of the vowels, the speaker would be forced to first restructure the existing schemata – ostensibly arriving at the compromise position suggested by Flege. With time and additional input, and assuming no fossilization, the speaker would fine-tune this system, arriving at an increasingly targetlike production of the vowel sounds.[13] As with the other theories discussed here, more empirical evidence is needed to confirm current thought on information processing and validate it as regards a learner's phonological acquisition of a second language. However, this field of research is very promising in terms of providing insight into the role played by first language transfer.

NEW DIRECTIONS IN RESEARCH

Whereas earlier research on the acquisition of English pronunciation by second language speakers tended to focus on the acquisition of individual vowel or consonant phonemes,

---

[11]Note that Flege defends his hypothesis by pointing out that it is in complete accordance with evidence from interlanguage phonology studies indicating that with increased exposure to the target language, the phonological utterances of speakers will become more targetlike.
[12]This assumes that the learner will identify English /ey/ and /ow/ with the Portuguese monophthongs /e/ and /o/ rather than with the Portuguese diphthongs /ei/ and /ou/.
[13]This example is from research by Baptista (1992), who justifies the grouping of English /ey/ and /ow/ with the Portuguese monophthongs /e/ and /o/ by reference to a distinction made by Lehiste and Peterson (1961) between "single-target complex nuclei" like English /ey/ and /ow/ versus true English diphthongs such as /ay/, /aw/, and /ɔy/.

much of the most recent research has dealt with learners' acquisition of English intonation, rhythm, connected speech, and voice quality settings.

INTONATION

One of the pioneering studies in the acquisition of American English intonation (Backmann 1977) used two Spanish-speaking male consultants and one native male speaker of American English as a control. Backmann demonstrated that with increased residence in the United States and better language proficiency, the more advanced Spanish speaker had modified the flatter two-tone intonation contours characteristic of his native Spanish such that his intonation in English better approximated the more highly differentiated three-tone contours typical of the American English speaker. The newly arrived Spanish speaker – with minor modifications – transferred his flatter Spanish intonation to English.

More recently Todaka (1990) compared available instrumental data on the intonation contours typical of similar utterance types in NAE and Japanese and then acoustically measured the English intonation produced by twenty Japanese speakers (ten male, ten female) studying in the United States. Todaka found that the Japanese speakers – like Backmann's Spanish speakers – erred in the direction of transferring their first-language intonation patterns to English. The Japanese speakers did this in two ways: (1) by not utilizing a broad enough pitch range in their English and (2) by not sufficiently stressing and lengthening prominent stressed syllables carrying pitch changes. This difference can be illustrated as follows:

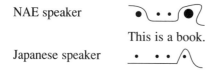

Todaka suggests that by using a "hyper-pronunciation" training method (i.e., one that initially exaggerates pitch contours and the duration of stressed syllables in English), Japanese speakers can be taught to broaden their range of pitch and to give prominent stressed syllables the longer duration that English requires to carry the broader, more dramatic pitch changes characteristic of its intonation.

RHYTHM

As Todaka's (1990) study indicated, accurate intonation is dependent on accurate rhythm. Further interesting research has been done in this area. Anderson-Hsieh and Venkatagiri (1994) acoustically measured the production of intermediate- and high-proficiency Chinese speakers of English and compared syllable duration of stressed syllables as well as pausing with that of native NAE speakers.[14] These researchers found that the intermediate speakers failed to differentiate duration sufficiently in stressed (i.e., prominent) versus unstressed syllables and that they paused frequently and longer, often inappropriately. The high-proficiency Chinese speakers, on the other hand, had acquired near-native proficiency on the variables studied. The researchers conclude that it is indeed possible to learn appropriate syllable duration as well as length and frequency of pauses.

In another study, Chela Flores (1993) claims that rhythm, in particular the appropriate lengthening of stressed syllables and shortening of unstressed syllables in English, is the most widely experienced pronunciation challenge for speakers of other languages. After experimenting with different approaches for teaching English rhythm to Spanish

---

[14]The proficiency level of the subjects in this study was measured by their SPEAK test scores. See Chapter 12 for more information on this test.

speakers, Chela Flores reported that teaching typical English rhythm patterns first in isolation from lexical items or phrases, then by matching patterns to items or phrases, and finally by imposing the patterns on words, phrases, and sentences, her Spanish speakers were able to make great strides toward producing better English rhythm – especially under controlled production conditions. She concluded that extended practice would be needed for the learners to automatize these new rhythmic patterns.

CONNECTED SPEECH

The ability to produce appropriately connected speech is another promising area of research involving suprasegmentals. In a study comparing the connected speech modifications of Japanese ESL learners (five intermediate and five high proficiency) with those of five American English native speakers, Anderson-Hsieh, Riney, and Koehler (1994) examined the effects of language proficiency, native language transfer, and style shifting on speaker performance. The researchers used a sentence-reading task and also elicited more spontaneous speech to investigate speaker performance in four areas: (1) alveolar flapping (in words like *letter*); (2) intersyllabic linking (C-C, C-V, V-V), where C equals any consonant and V equals any vowel; (3) vowel reduction in unstressed syllables; and (4) consonant cluster simplification.[15] For alveolar flapping, overall linking, and consonant cluster simplification there was a significant difference between the intermediate group members (who did not employ these connecting forms appropriately) and the high-proficiency group members (who approximated the performance of native speakers fairly closely). Those areas where the performance of both the intermediate and high-proficiency Japanese speakers differed significantly from that of the native English speakers all involved vowels: C-V linking, V-V linking, and vowel reduction, a tendency due in part to native language transfer. Finally, the researchers in this study found that all three groups produced more linking and deletion on the elicited narrative task than on the sentence reading task; however, both groups of Japanese ESL learners exhibited fewer modifications on this task than the native speakers, who often omitted weak syllables and did rather radical restructuring of underlying phonological forms. The researchers concluded that language proficiency, native language, and style shifting are indeed factors that influence the connected speech of Japanese ESL learners.

VOICE QUALITY

In addition to its vowel and consonant inventory and its characteristic stress and pitch patterns, every language has certain audible characteristics that are present most of the time when native speakers talk (Abercrombie 1967). This phenomenon is referred to as **voice quality**. Laver (1980) describes three types of voice quality settings: supralaryngeal settings (i.e., settings above the larynx that involve phenomena such as tongue position, lip rounding or spreading, presence or absence of nasality, etc.), laryngeal settings or phonation types (i.e., whether the voice can be characterized as whispery, creaky, modal/neutral, or falsetto), and overall muscular tension. He reviews the research before 1980; for example, Hanley, Snidecor, and Ringel (1966) compared pitch and loudness among groups of Spanish, American English, and Japanese speakers and found that the Spanish and Japanese groups spoke with higher pitch and lower volume than did the Americans.[16]

To control for anatomical differences among speakers, which had not been done in earlier studies, Todaka (1993) used a screening test to identify four bilingual speakers (two male, two female) of Japanese and English.[17] Utilizing a variety of physiological and acoustic techniques, he found that both the male and female bilinguals spoke with higher

[15]The topic for the elicited narrative was "the most exciting or dangerous experience that I have ever had."
[16]A good overview of voice quality variation addressed to teachers can be found in Esling (1994).

pitch when speaking Japanese than when speaking English. He also found that the two female bilinguals spoke with a breathier voice in Japanese than in English but that the males did not.[18] Todaka attributed both types of voice quality differences to the interaction of language-specific and sociocultural factors.

More research is needed using either very large subject pools or very well selected bilingual subjects if we are to get accurate information about voice-quality setting contrasts across languages, and if we are to apply these differences to pronunciation instruction (e.g., getting learners to use increased muscle tension when articulating certain sounds, to speak louder or softer, to lower or raise their relative pitch, etc.). For the moment, we know that voice quality differences do contribute to a foreign accent and that they stem from both linguistic and sociocultural factors. Many of the differences reported in the current literature on voice quality are too subjective or too unreliable to merit pedagogical application at the present time. However, we wish to emphasize (as Esling 1994 does) that part of pronunciation acquisition is awareness of and control over voice quality settings appropriate to the second language settings, which may be quite different from those of the first language.

CONCLUSION

We have certainly come a long way from the oversimplified view that a learner's first language background entirely dictates the second language acquisition process. We have also arrived at a much more enlightened view concerning the role of the individual in this process, recognizing that extralinguistic factors also play a very large role in determining the sequence.

Current consensus regarding the acquisition of second language phonology can perhaps best be summed up as follows (see also Macken and Ferguson 1987; Tarone 1987a):

1. Native language transfer plays a role in a learner's acquisition of the sounds of the second language, but it is only one piece of the puzzle.

2. The extent of influence that negative transfer exerts may differ from learner to learner, and may also vary depending on the type of phonetic structure (e.g., segmental or suprasegmental contrast) being acquired.

3. There are some aspects of interlanguage phonology that parallel the first language acquisition of children, indicating the partly developmental and partly universal nature of phonological acquisition.

4. There is variation in performance accuracy among learners, depending on whether they are conversing in more formal (i.e., control-facilitating) or informal (i.e., automaticity-facilitating) registers.

To these observations we believe we can add the following, based on our research survey:

5. Whether discussed in terms of a critical period, a sensitive period, or some other label, the learner's age is a factor in phonological acquisition. Other things being equal, the earlier the learner's exposure to native speakers of the target language, the

---

[17]Subjects were screened by several native speakers of Japanese and several native speakers of English, who independently agreed that the four speakers in the study were native speakers of Japanese and English, respectively.

[18]There are two possible explanations. Perhaps breathiness is gender-based and typically female in Japanese. Alternatively, a post hoc test with monolingual Japanese speakers revealed that the two males were perceived as having a slight accent (i.e., were rated as less fully bilingual than the females). Perhaps the male subjects' lack of breathiness contributed to this assessment of nonnativeness if in fact men tend to have a breathy voice in Japanese.

better the acquisition of phonology; the younger the adult learner, the more his or her pronunciation can be improved.

6. For the overwhelming majority of postpubescent adolescents and adults, a readily intelligible – rather than a nativelike – pronunciation is a more realistic pedagogical goal.

7. Whether we appeal to aptitude (phonemic coding ability), psychomotor skills, or other factors, it appears that acquiring phonology is qualitatively different from acquiring syntax and lexicon. Thus we have young immigrant learners of English who master pronunciation yet have serious gaps in grammar and lexicon. Conversely, there are adults who more or less master English syntax and lexicon yet who have obvious problems with pronunciation.

8. Quite apart from age, aptitude, or first language, the learner's attitude, motivation, language ego, and other sociocultural and sociopsychological factors clearly influence the degree of pronunciation proficiency achieved (or not achieved).

As indicated in Chapter 1, the segmental view of pronunciation has largely given way to a broader, discourse-based view (Pennington and Richards 1986), which includes the interaction between segmental features, voice quality settings, and suprasegmental features. Given this global view, any previously existing perceptions about a division between pronunciation and oral communicative competence is invalidated.

Along with Stevick (1978) and Pennington and Richards (1986), we also point out the vulnerability of learners who, while wishing to attain nativelike pronunciation in the target language in order to avoid the stigma attached to having a foreign accent, may be reluctant to lose their accent for fear of alienating themselves from their native language peers. Thus affective and personality factors (e.g., extroversion, sociability) may either impede or promote acquisition of second language phonology.

In fact, Pennington (1994) suggests that learners perceive three barriers to pronunciation improvement: physiological ("I can't change"), psychological ("I don't need to change"), and sociocultural ("I don't think it's good to change"). She suggests that the goal of instruction is not only to improve learner performance, but also to provide "a basis for change in the psychological and social dimensions of pronunciation" (p. 105).

To be adequately prepared to teach pronunciation, teachers must have at their disposal a working knowledge of articulatory phonetics, theories of second-language phonological acquisition, and an up-to-date command of techniques and procedures to use in the classroom (Parish 1977). But perhaps even more importantly, teachers need to be aware of the affective factors that impede or enhance change so that they can work with students to help them understand how their pronunciation is related not only to their native language but also to their own motivation and personality as well as their view of the target culture (Stevick 1978).

EXERCISES

KEY CONCEPTS

1. Write a brief definition for the following key terms from this chapter. Give examples where relevant.

lateralization

critical period

sensitive period

ego permeability

acculturation model

integrative motivation

assimilative motivation

instrumental motivation

contrastive analysis hypothesis

interference/negative transfer

error analysis

avoidance

interlanguage

fossilization

markedness theory

marked/unmarked

language universals

principles/parameters

Interlanguage Structural Conformity Hypothesis (ISCH)

information processing theory

schemata

voice quality

phonemic coding ability

2. Match each of the following ideas in recent second language acquisition research with its description by writing the corresponding roman numeral in the blanks. Then summarize the controversy surrounding these theories.

__ a.   markedness differential hypothesis

__ b.   critical period hypothesis

__ c.   interlanguage hypothesis

__ d.   information processing theory

__ e.   contrastive analysis hypothesis

__ f.   acculturation model

__ g.   error analysis

__ h.   language universals

   I.   Schumann proposes that learners will acquire a second language to the degree that they desire to integrate with the target culture.

   II.   Eckman predicts sounds that second language learners will find difficult and the order in which learners will acquire these more difficult sounds.

   III.   All languages share common properties, and there is a hierarchy of second language acquisition that is not determined exclusively by the learner's first language.

   IV.   Cognitive science researchers surmise that second language learners initially demonstrate a distinct tendency to interpret sounds in a target language according to the existing stable set of sounds in their first language.

   V.   Selinker proposes that second language learners produce unique utterances that follow a developmental system, partly independent of either the speaker's first language or the target language.

VI. This theory focuses primarily on learner performance rather than on language contrasts.

VII. Lenneberg postulates that the best physiological conditions for acquiring a second language exist before puberty.

VIII. Lado states that the structure of one's first language determines the problems a learner will have in acquiring a second language.

INTROSPECTING ABOUT YOUR OWN LANGUAGE LEARNING

Think about a foreign language that you have learned in school or while living abroad.

1. What pronunciation obstacles have you faced in learning this language? If you have not achieved a targetlike pronunciation, which of the following do you feel help to account for this? Check the boxes that apply.

   ❏ I don't know where my pronunciation problems lie. I don't notice them.

   ❏ I know that I transfer sounds from my native language.

   ❏ I can't hear the difference between some of the target language sounds and my first language sounds.

   ❏ I can't produce the difference between some of the sounds in my native language and similar sounds in the target language.

   ❏ It's not important for me to improve my pronunciation. People understand me without trouble.

   ❏ Even though I can produce some of the target language sounds, it takes too much effort or concentration when I'm speaking.

   ❏ I like my own accent. I don't want to be like a native speaker or sound like one.

   ❏ Native speakers of the language comment that my foreign accent is "cute" or "charming." I don't have any motivation to change.

   ❏ I haven't had enough contact with native speakers. My pronunciation would improve if I had more exposure.

   ❏ There wasn't enough training or practice in pronunciation when I learned the language.

   ❏ I learned the language too late. Only younger people can acquire a foreign language without an accent.

2. In class, discuss these factors with another student. Give specific examples for each item that you checked. To what degree are your experiences the same as your partner's? To what degree are they different?

DISCUSSION QUESTIONS

1. Describe an ideal learning situation as it relates to acquiring targetlike pronunciation in a second language.

2. What is wrong with the following statement? "John is really intelligent. He speaks both Arabic and Chinese with a perfect accent."

3. Do you think that extroverted individuals will learn to pronounce a second language better than introverted individuals?

4. Of what importance to pronunciation teachers is the distinction between instrumental, integrative, and assimilative motivation?

5. For each of the following statements, check the column that best represents your belief. Be prepared to support your choices during subsequent discussion.

Statement	Always True	Sometimes True	Never True	Unsure
1. Imitating a native-speaker model facilitates the acquisition of a targetlike pronunciation.	❑	❑	❑	❑
2. In order to correctly produce the sounds of English, NNS students require a detailed description of the sound system of English.	❑	❑	❑	❑
3. It is possible to change a learner's fossilized pronunciation.	❑	❑	❑	❑
4. A student's first language plays a significant role in his/her phonological acquisition of a second language.	❑	❑	❑	❑
5. Children acquire nativelike pronunciation of a second language more readily than adults.	❑	❑	❑	❑
6. Some students have a better "ear" for language than others, and are thus more gifted in the area of pronunciation.	❑	❑	❑	❑
7. Motivation and personality play a larger role in determining success in the area of pronunciation than aptitude.	❑	❑	❑	❑
8. A learner's desire to socially integrate into a society may determine his/her level of accuracy in second language phonology.	❑	❑	❑	❑

IN THE CLASSROOM

1. How would you respond to a student who says "I don't have the ability to pronounce English properly"?

2. Study the following descriptions of five hypothetical individuals, and rank-order them (i.e., assign a number of 1 to 5, with 1 being the highest) according to their chances of acquiring near-native pronunciation in English. In class, compare your rank ordering with that of your classmates, and attempt to arrive at a consensus.

Ulrike: Ulrike is a 32-year-old immigrant from Germany. She had twelve years of English language training in the German public school system before arriving in the

United States. She is married to an American, and is currently working for a large American corporation as a data processor. She has lived in the United States for two years, and has a 6-month-old daughter.

Alex: Alex arrived in the United States in the company of his parents and two sisters as immigrants from Russia. He was 11 at the time of arrival, and entered a junior high school with a mixed ethnic population. Alex had no English instruction before coming to the United States. He has been in the United States for three years.

Carlos: Carlos was born in Puerto Rico and moved to the United States at the age of 7. He lives in a section of the city where the language spoken is predominantly Spanish, and he uses Spanish at home. He's currently in his junior year of high school, and he wants to be an electrician.

Lan: Lan is a Vietnamese refugee who escaped to Thailand at the age of 16, leaving her entire family behind. After one year in a refugee camp, she managed to enter the United States, completing high school and then enrolling at the university. She completed an undergraduate degree in engineering, and successfully applied for U.S. citizenship. She is currently working for an aviation firm doing design graphics. She's been in the United States seven years, and is engaged to marry a fellow Vietnamese refugee.

Peter: Peter is a Taiwanese immigrant who has been in the United States for eight years. He received a Ph.D. in psychiatry from an American university, and works in the psychiatric ward of a large hospital. His clientele is from mixed ethnic groups. Peter is single.

SUGGESTED ACTIVITIES

1. Interview two or three individuals who have successfully acquired the pronunciation of another language. Find out as much as possible about the strategies they used to acquire the pronunciation of this language. Some questions you may wish to ask include:

    - What motivated you to learn this language?
    - How important was nativelike pronunciation to you?
    - How old were you when you began learning the language?
    - How would you describe the environment in which you learned the language?
    - How would you rate your language aptitude?
    - How similar are the sound systems of your native language and the language that you learned?
    - Were there sounds in this language that you tried to avoid or did not want to pronounce?

2. Select a language with a sound system familiar to you and find a learner of English from this language background. Record the learner describing a family member or friend. Locate five or ten pronunciation errors and analyze these. Do you think the source of error is interlingual, intralingual, or developmental? Bring your recording to class and discuss your findings with other class members.

PART 2

THE SOUND SYSTEM OF NORTH AMERICAN ENGLISH: AN OVERVIEW

One of the characteristic features of the sound system of any language is its inventory of sounds – that is, the particular combination of consonants and vowels that make up the inventory. In fact, all languages are somewhat distinctive in their vowel and consonant inventories, and in the way that these components combine to form words and utterances. Linguists refer to this inventory of vowels and consonants as the *segmental* aspect of language. The first two chapters in this section are devoted to discussing these segmental features and their distinguishing characterists: consonants (Chapter 3) and vowels (Chapter 4).

In addition to having their own inventory of vowels and consonants, languages also have unique features that transcend the segmental level. These *suprasegmental* features involve those phenomena that extend over more than one sound segment. Chapter 5 deals with the more predictable suprasegmental features of word stress, sentence stress, and rhythm along with *adjustments in connected speech* (i.e., the adjustments or modifications that occur within and between words in the stream of speech), such as assimilation and linking. Chapter 6 deals with suprasegmental features that are sensitive to the discourse context and the speaker's intent: prominence and intonation.

The sound system features we describe in Part 2 refer to North American English (NAE) as spoken in the United States and Canada. Throughout the chapters included in this section of the text, we make reference to the principle contrasts between NAE and British English. However, for the reader interested in a more thorough treatment of these differences, we have included a detailed discussion in Appendix 1.

In all four chapters of this section, we include both a detailed description of the features and techniques for teaching them to non-native speakers. Throughout, we intersperse pedagogical tips to the teacher regarding the experiences that can be predicted in teaching these features of English to students, and we suggest techniques that work in the classroom. In this manner, we present the basic knowledge and skills that teachers should possess in order to be able to function effectively in the pronunciation classroom.

The techniques presented in this section have been developed in a variety of class settings and with a variety of populations. In many cases we have included both the instructions and worksheets for an activity in the hope of providing the busy teacher with as many easy-to-adapt ideas as possible. Some techniques are more structured, such as minimal-pair discrimination exercises; others are rather open, such as role plays. We believe there is room for both types of practice in the communicative classroom as students move from structured to free production.

As you read the chapters, you will notice that features are presented within a framework that divides pronunciation teaching into two stages:

1. what teachers themselves need to know about the sound system and which aspects can be conveyed appropriately to learners (planning stage)
2. how these aspects can be presented to learners in a given lesson (teaching stage)

It is clear that there is far more linguistic knowledge that the teacher should possess than can be processed by learners. Thus the teacher must determine in the planning stage how much information to impart to learners and how to sequence and present it effectively. The teaching stage can be divided into several phases, moving from analysis and consciousness raising to listening discrimination and finally production. The following hierarchical framework can be used to plan and present any aspect of pronunciation. In Part 2, we model this framework by applying it to individual teaching points (either segmental, suprasegmental, or connected speech features).

This framework represents our philosophy of how teachers can most effectively teach aspects of the sound system. The specific activities suggested are intended as models only, and should be adapted as necessary when used with specific groups of learners. Ultimately, how teachers apply this framework to teaching pronunciation in their classrooms will depend on a number of variables, which we discuss in Chapter 11 on curriculum design.

A FRAMEWORK FOR TEACHING PRONUNCIATION COMMUNICATIVELY

Planning Stage

1. What the teacher needs to know
   a. information about the features (articulation rules, occurrences in discourse, etc.)
   b. potential problems for students (often based on typical errors by learners from particular language backgrounds)
   c. pedagogical priorities (how important a given feature is for students vis-à-vis their communicative needs)
2. What the student needs to know (of the foregoing information, what should be communicated to the students?)

Teaching Stage

1. Description and analysis (e.g., oral and written illustrations of when and how the feature occurs in order to raise learner consciousness)
2. Listening discrimination (focused listening practice with feedback)
3. Controlled practice and feedback (e.g., oral reading of minimal pair sentences, short dialogues, etc., with special attention paid to the highlighted feature)
4. Guided practice and feedback (e.g., structured communication exercises that enable the learner to monitor for the specified feature, such as information gap activities, cued dialogues)
5. Communicative practice and feedback (e.g., less structured activities that require the learner to attend to both form and content of utterances)

CHAPTER 3

The Consonant System

One way to think of consonant sounds is as the solid blocks with which we construct words, phrases, and sentences. These blocks are connected or held together by a more malleable or fluid material – the vowels of the language. Together, they provide the basic building materials we need to create the architecture of language. Of course, this analogy is a very simple one, and it does not truly capture how consonants and vowels interact to create meaningful sound combinations – about which we will have more to say later. In this chapter, we focus on the consonant system itself, looking first at the minimally distinct sounds and their variants. Next we examine the need for a phonemic alphabet to represent the sounds of the language, and examine in detail the NAE consonant inventory. Finally, we look at how position within a syllable or word can have a strong effect on the articulation of consonant sounds, and we examine the propensity in English for consonants to occur together – as many as four at a time. We now turn to defining some basic concepts needed for our discussion.

Analogy of Vowels and Consonants

PHONEMES AND ALLOPHONES: WHAT THE TEACHER NEEDS TO KNOW

In their description of sound systems, linguists find it useful to focus on those sound differences that distinguish words (i.e., sounds they call *phonemes*) and sounds that are perceptibly different but do not distinguish words (i.e., sounds they call *allophones*). To illustrate the concepts of phoneme and allophone, we can imagine a group of North American tourists visiting a London restaurant and asking for butter. The request will no doubt be understood, and the desired end result obtained. But no sooner will the word *butter* be spoken than the tourists will be recognized as North Americans. Why? The lay explanation is that the tourists have an American accent, but the linguist would explain that the allophone of /t/ that the NAE speakers use in the word *butter* (an alveolar flap [ɾ], discussed later) is quite different from the allophone [t] used by their London counterparts.

Suppose, however, that instead of ordering *butter* the tourists had asked for *batter?* Would they then receive butter? In all likelihood, they would receive a strange stare instead. This substitution of one phoneme for another (the distinctive vowel sound /æ/ for /ʌ/) illustrates the importance of phonemes functioning in *contrastive distribution* – that is, as minimally distinctive units of sound that can alter the meaning of a word.

Another way to think of the concepts of phoneme and allophone is to think of the various allophones of a particular phoneme as all belonging to the same family. Allophones of a given phoneme, like family members, share many of the same characteristics that identify them as belonging to the same kinship group; however, they have their own unique features as well. If we examine the family of the phoneme /p/, for example, we find that it has at least three members in NAE. In other words, the phoneme /p/ itself is an abstraction, or a sum of its allophones; the particular allophone or variety of /p/ that is produced depends on where it occurs in a given word. Linguists refer to this phenomenon as *positional variation* and to the members of any phoneme's family as its *allophones*. Following linguistic convention, phonemes are enclosed between slanted lines / / and allophones are enclosed in square brackets [ ]. The allophones of the English phoneme /p/ are:

[pʰ]   the allophone of /p/ in initial position, which is often heavily
        aspirated or accompanied by a rush of air, as in *pat*

[p]   the allophone of /p/ following an initial /s/, which is not
        aspirated, as in *spin*

[p°]   the allophone of /p/ in final position, in which the lips
        remain closed and the /p/ is unreleased, as in *cup*

Allophones thus represent the specific members of a phoneme that have a fixed or specific distribution; they do not serve to distinguish words in the language in which they occur. In other words, the substitution of one allophone for another (e.g., aspirated [pʰ] for unaspirated [p] in *spin*) does not result in a change of meaning but simply in a nonnative pronunciation. In fact, because allophones are not functionally distinct, native speakers of English may be unaware of the existence of these variations, and may believe that all allophones of a phoneme like /p/ are physically the same sound until the differences are pointed out to them.

Unlike these various allophones of /p/, substitution of the phoneme /b/ for /p/ results in a change of meaning – *pat* vs. *bat, pig* vs. *big, rip* vs. *rib, amble* vs. *ample,* and so forth. However, it is important to note that the distinction between phonemes and allophones is language specific. In other words, although the phonemes /p/ and /b/ are functionally distinct in English, they may not be in some other language, such as Arabic (and speakers of this language may have trouble differentiating and producing the pairs of words listed earlier). Conversely, although aspirated and nonaspirated varieties of /p/ are allophones in English, they may each represent perceptibly distinct sounds (i.e., phonemes) in other languages and thus serve to distinguish words, as in Hindi and Thai. *See*

THE PHONEMIC ALPHABET: WHAT THE TEACHER NEEDS TO KNOW

When attempting to accurately describe the sounds of a language, linguists and teachers often use a set of special symbols commonly referred to as a phonetic alphabet. Since the alphabet we are using in this text is actually phonemic (with some phonetic enhancements), we refer to it as a *phonemic alphabet.* Use of such a system allows us to capture the sounds of the language more accurately since there is a one-to-one correspondence between the symbols used and the sounds they represent. Most of the symbols for consonant sounds will be familiar ones, since they are taken mainly from the Roman alphabet. However, in order to represent each distinct consonant phoneme unambiguously, a few special symbols are introduced. For a comparison of the phonemic alphabet used in this text with some other commonly used phonetic/phonemic alphabets, see Appendix 2.

In the case of English, the use of a phonemic transcription system is especially important because the language has no simple sound–symbol correspondence system – that is, one letter of the alphabet does not represent the same sound all of the time, nor does a specific sound always find its representation in one letter of the alphabet. For example, the

TABLE 3.1 THE ENGLISH CONSONANTS

Sound	Examples	Sound	Examples
1. /b/	boy, cab	14. /ʃ/	shy, dish
2. /p/	pie, lip	15. /h/	his, ahead
3. /d/	dog, bed	16. /tʃ/	cheek, watch
4. /t/	toe, cat	17. /dʒ/	joy, budge
5. /g/	go, beg	18. /m/	me, seem
6. /k/	cat, back	19. /n/	no, sun
7. /v/	view, love	20. /ŋ/	sing, singer
8. /f/	fill, life	21. /l/	long, full
9. /ð/	the, bathe	22. /r/	run, car
10. /θ/	thin, bath	23. /w/	win, away
11. /z/	zoo, goes	24. /hw/	which, what
12. /s/	see, bus	25. /y/	you, soya
13. /ʒ/	leisure, beige		

letter *c* has four different pronunciations in the words *cat, city, ocean,* and *cello;* and the phoneme /s/ has various spelling representations, such as *s, ss, c, ce, sc,* and *ps* (as in *sit, less, city, face, descent,* and *psychology).* In some cases, the same letter within one word can represent two different sounds, as in the pronunciation of the two *c*'s in *success:* First *c* is pronounced /k/ and the second one /s/. Also, combinations of letters are often simply an artifact of the spelling system and do not necessarily indicate that there is more than one actual sound being produced. This is the case with the underlined consonant sounds in words like *stopped, butter,* and *reckon;* it is also the case with the vowel sounds in *feast, bait,* and *road.*

The peculiarities of the English spelling system derive from its highly involved language history, which includes multiple foreign influences and the acquisition of many loan words. We will have more to say in Chapter 9 about the less than perfect (but certainly not unsystematic) sound–spelling correspondences.

A PHONEMIC ALPHABET FOR ENGLISH CONSONANTS

The full inventory of NAE consonant phonemes is shown in Table 3.1.[1] Although the English version of the Roman alphabet is the primary source of symbols for transcribing English consonant phonemes, this alphabet has only twenty-one consonant letters. Since there are twenty-five distinct consonant phonemes in NAE, several additional symbols are needed to represent all the phonemes of the language.

For those who are first encountering a phonemic alphabet, there may be some initial confusion between the phonemic alphabet and English orthography. Note that several letters of the English alphabet – namely *c, x,* and *q* – are typically omitted from phonemic alphabets for English. The letter *c,* as previously pointed out, is used ambiguously in the English spelling system to represent the phonemes /k/, /s/, /ʃ/, and /tʃ/. The letter *x* typically represents /z/ at the beginning of a word (as in *xylophone*), /gz/ in the middle of a word (as in *exact*), or /ks/ at the middle or end of a word (as in *oxen* or *box*). As for *q,* it is followed by the vowel *u* in English orthography, yet it sounds like a sequence of two consonants: a stop followed by an approximant (/kw/ as in *queen*). Thus these letters are

[1]The transcription system used for consonants in this text is a modified International Phonetic Alphabet (IPA) notation system (see Kenworthy 1987 and Ladefoged 1982). We believe that this system is of pedagogical value in helping learners of English approximate these sounds. The one major difference is the use of /y/ instead of the IPA's /j/ to represent the initial sound in *yes, you.*

unsatisfactory choices for symbols. Note also that the orthographic sequence *th* generally represents not a cluster or sequence of consonant sounds but one of two related but different sounds: voiceless /θ/ as in *thick* and *voiced* /ð/ as in *the*. Although initially a bit confusing, these examples of ambiguities in the English spelling system illustrate why a phonemic system is necessary for clarity.

In addition to /θ/ and /ð/, linguists have added other new symbols to the phonemic alphabet. For example, /ʃ/, /tʃ/, and /dʒ/ represent the initial sounds in *sherry*, *cherry*, and *joy* and the final consonant sounds in *wash*, *watch*, and *budge*, respectively. The symbols /ʒ/ and /ŋ/ are needed for the consonant sounds that appear medially in *pleasure* and *singer* and finally in *beige* and *ring*, respectively. The symbol /hw/ is used to represent voiceless *wh* in words like *which* or *what*, as opposed to voiced /w/ in *witch*. In words like *when, whether, which,* and *why*, both the /hw/ and /w/ pronunciations are possible in NAE, with /hw/ representing the older, more conservative pronunciation. In summary, the following eight additional symbols are needed to complete our phonemic alphabet for consonant sounds:

/θ/	thistle
/ð/	those
/tʃ/	chosen
/dʒ/	jury
/ʃ/	sherry
/ʒ/	rouge
/ŋ/	ring
/hw/	whether

THE PHONEMIC ALPHABET: PEDAGOGICAL PRIORITIES

One of the first decisions to make in teaching pronunciation is whether or not to incorporate phonemic transcription in instruction. Naturally, it may depend on the extent of pronunciation instruction anticipated; in the case of occasional lessons in a broad multiskills curriculum, it may seem an unnecessary time investment. However, if weekly lessons are planned over an extended time, phonemic transcription can be indispensable as a means of separating students' perceptions of English sounds from their orthographic representations.

In most language classrooms, it is not essential that the students be able to transcribe words themselves; however, the ability to read phonemic transcriptions will enable the students to comprehend the elements of pronunciation visually as well as aurally. Moreover, students will be better equipped to check pronunciation autonomously in their dictionaries – assuming they use a dictionary that employs a transcription system similar to the one being taught. Even if the system is different, students would be more aware of what sounds were included in this inventory of English phonemes and therefore of what sounds were likely to be represented in the dictionary's inventory of symbols.

PRESENTING THE PHONEMIC ALPHABET TO STUDENTS

How can we make students aware of the need to represent English pronunciation with a phonemic alphabet? English orthography is filled with examples. One focusing technique is to write the word *ghoti* on the blackboard and ask students to pronounce it. They will most certainly not come up with the pronunciation /fɪʃ/ as in the word *fish*. In fact, *ghoti* is a spelling for *fish* invented by George Bernard Shaw, and the corresponding orthography exists in various English words: for example, *gh* = /f/ in *tough* and *rough; o* = /ɪ/ in *women;* and *ti* = /ʃ/ in *nation* and *motion*.

Awareness can also be raised by the following two mock "quiz questions":

How do you pronounce the *a* in *banana?* (Answer: In two different ways. The first and third *a* are pronounced /ə/, whereas the second is pronounced /æ/.)

How do you pronounce *th* in English? (Answer: There are two ways of pronouncing *th:* voiced /ð/ as in *that* and voiceless /θ/ as in *thirty*.)

As a possible follow-up to this activity, teachers can present "Fourteen Ways to Spell /ʃ/," eliciting from students as many examples as possible before presenting them with the following:

FOURTEEN WAYS TO SPELL /ʃ/

<u>sh</u>oe	o<u>ce</u>an
<u>s</u>ugar	nau<u>se</u>ous
i<u>ss</u>ue	con<u>sc</u>ious
man<u>si</u>on	<u>ch</u>aperon
mi<u>ss</u>ion	<u>sch</u>ist
na<u>ti</u>on	fu<u>schi</u>a
suspi<u>ci</u>on	p<u>sh</u>aw

Once students' consciousness of the need for a phonemic alphabet has been raised and the basic consonant symbols have been presented along with sample words, we suggest focusing on listening, beginning with the students transcribing single phonemes. For example, read a list of words and ask students to write the phonemic symbol for the first sound only.

Teacher reads:	Student writes:
phone	/f/
sugar	/ʃ/
thumb	/θ/
chalk	/tʃ/
character	/k/
gun	/g/
George	/dʒ/
very	/v/
than	/ð/
Thomas	/t/
won	/w/
right	/r/

The importance of focusing on sound and not spelling is illustrated particularly in the examples *phone* and *sugar* and the pairs *chalk/character* and *than/Thomas*. Occasionally, students are astounded to discover either that discrepancies between sound and spelling exist or that they have been pronouncing a word incorrectly all along.

The same exercise may be done focusing on the *final* sound in a word.

Teacher reads:	Student writes:
sing	/ŋ/
fish	/ʃ/
was	/z/
judge	/dʒ/
myth	/θ/
match	/tʃ/
mash	/ʃ/
face	/s/

This technique, which focuses on both recognizing consonants and phonemic transcription, provides a convenient bridge to an explanation of the consonant inventory.

THE CONSONANT INVENTORY: WHAT THE TEACHER NEEDS TO KNOW

The twenty-five distinct consonant phonemes of NAE can be distinguished along three main dimensions: *voicing* (whether the vocal cords are vibrating), *place of articulation* (where the sound is made), and *manner of articulation* (how the airflow is affected).[2] Attention to these dimensions helps us to clearly describe the individual consonant phonemes and to distinguish them from each other. We will also rely on some secondary characteristics that enable us to describe these phonemes more accurately. These include whether the sound is aspirated or nonaspirated, released or nonreleased, and whether it is produced with lip rounding. All of these dimensions, which are described in more detail in the following sections, help us to understand what distinguishes NAE consonants from the consonants of other languages and gives NAE its unique quality. They also allow us to differentiate the various allophones of a given phoneme in NAE.

Voicing Before proceeding with a more complete description of the place and manner of articulation of NAE consonants, we need to discuss the phenomenon of **voicing**: whether or not the vocal cords are vibrating. One of the best ways to appreciate the difference between voiced and voiceless consonants is to put the palm of your hand against your Adam's apple (i. e. , larynx) and alternate hissing like a snake /sssssss/ with buzzing like a bee /zzzzz/. When you buzz, you can feel your vocal cords vibrating: /z/ is a voiced sound. When you hiss, however, you feel nothing because the vocal cords are not moving: /s/ is a voiceless sound. Another way to experience the difference is to use your hands to cover your ears firmly while you alternate hissing /sssss/ and buzzing /zzzzzz/. When you hiss, you hear only air escaping; but when you buzz, you can hear the voicing or vibration quite clearly.

Place of articulation In the production of sounds, air passes through one or both of two passageways: the **oral cavity** (mouth) or the **nasal passageway** (nose), depending on whether the nasal passageway is blocked off or not. It is useful to differentiate between the **articulator** (the more movable part of the articulatory system) and the **point** or **place of articulation,** which is where the contact with the articulator occurs.

The main articulators (see Figure 3.1) used to produce sounds are the lower lip and the various parts of the tongue, which for descriptive purposes is further divided into parts: the tip and the blade (which constitute the front of the tongue), the body (which constitutes the mid- and back sections of the tongue), and the root (the back-most section down in the throat, which is not visible). Other articulators include the jaw, the **uvula** (the small moveable flap at the back of the soft palate – it moves when you open your mouth and say "aaah"), the **velum** (the soft palate, which moves to open or close the nasal passageway), and the **vocal cords** (the vibrating bands of tissue within the **larynx**, or voice box).

Important points of articulation in English are the upper lip, the teeth, and the roof of the mouth – beginning with the **alveolar ridge** (the area just behind the front teeth) and continuing back through the hard palate area to the velum. Figure 3.1 shows the sagittal section diagram of these organs of speech.

---

[2]We have relied on many sources to describe the NAE sound system. Some of the sources we can no longer identify for they have become part of our professional knowledge and experience. However, we have relied heavily on Ladefoged (1993) and Patricia Keating (personal communication) to verify our facts and thus would like to single out these two sources for specific acknowledgment.

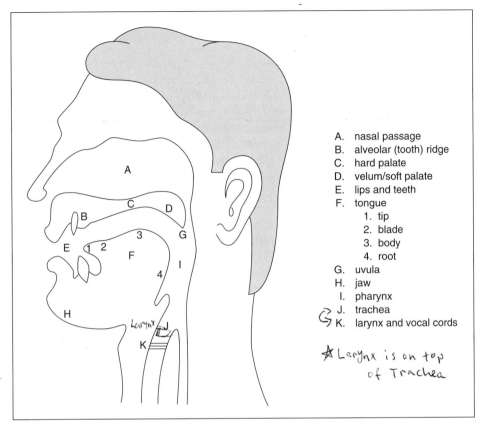

A. nasal passage
B. alveolar (tooth) ridge
C. hard palate
D. velum/soft palate
E. lips and teeth
F. tongue
    1. tip
    2. blade
    3. body
    4. root
G. uvula
H. jaw
I. pharynx
J. trachea
K. larynx and vocal cords

Larynx is on top of Trachea

Figure 3.1 Sagittal section diagram

The places of articulation for NAE consonants can be summarized as the following:

Bilabial: produced with the two lips: /b, p, m, w/ as in <u>buy</u>, <u>pie</u>, <u>my</u>, and <u>wool</u>

Labiodental: produced with the upper teeth and inner lower lip: /f, v/ as in <u>fee</u> and <u>veal</u>

Dental: produced with the tongue tip on or near the inner surface of the upper teeth: /θ, ð/ as in <u>thick</u> and <u>then</u>[3]

Alveolar: produced with the tongue tip on or near the tooth ridge: /t, d, s, z, n, l/ as in <u>to</u>, <u>do</u>, <u>so</u>, <u>zoo</u>, <u>new</u>, and <u>light</u>

Palatal:[4] produced with the tongue blade or body near the hard palate: /ʃ, ʒ, tʃ, dʒ, r, y/ as in <u>show</u>, <u>beige</u>, <u>chow</u>, <u>Jim</u>, <u>rake</u>, and <u>you</u>

Velar: produced with the tongue body on or near the soft palate: /g, k, ŋ/ as in <u>go</u>, <u>kite</u>, and <u>bang</u>

Glottal: produced by air passing from the windpipe through the vocal cords: /h/ as in <u>hi</u>

Manner of articulation In the previous section we discussed the place of articulation – that is, which speech organs are in which position in order for a particular consonant sound to be produced. We still need to describe how those various speech organs interact with each other, providing a further dimension to how consonants are articulated. As mentioned,

---

[3]For some speakers /θ/ and /ð/ are interdental rather than dental; in such cases, the tongue protrudes briefly and slightly between the teeth. This is discussed in more detail later in this chapter.
[4]In some more detailed descriptions, the category "palatal" is further divided into "alveopalatal" and "palatal"; we ignore this distinction in order to simplify our description.

sounds are produced by air moving from the lungs through the articulatory organs and being released through the oral and/or nasal passages. Whereas vowel sounds are articulated with a free airflow, consonant sounds involve some narrowing of the articulatory passageway, or some obstruction of the airflow. In the production of consonant sounds, then, we can think of the air as moving through an obstacle course created by different configurations of the speech organs. As the air encounters these obstacles, different kinds of sounds are produced. The type of obstacle course the air takes, referred to as the **_manner of articulation_**, is another distinguishing feature of how consonants are produced.

For example, when the airstream is blocked or stopped completely before its release, we refer to the resulting explosion of sound as a **_stop_** (or plosive). Thus, the consonants /p/ and /b/ as in _pie_ and _buy_ are formed when the airstream is stopped by the two lips, causing pressure to build slightly before being released through the mouth. Similarly, a barrier resulting in a stop consonant can be created when the tip of the tongue contacts the alveolar ridge in pronouncing /t/ and /d/ as in _tie_ and _die_. Finally, the back of the tongue may rise to meet the velum, temporarily blocking the airflow and resulting in the phonemes /g/ and /k/ as in _great_ and _crate_.

Air passage from the lungs is not always completely stopped. In many cases, the air moves through a narrow passageway created when the articulatory organs approach but do not touch each other. The air being forced through this passage causes friction. We call the resulting sound a **_fricative_**. Fricative sounds can be maintained as long as there is air in the lungs; for this reason they belong to a larger class of consonants known as **continuants**. Consonants classified as fricatives are /f, v, θ, ð, s, z, ʃ, ʒ, h/ as in _feet, vine, think, those, seal, zeal, shield, pleasure_, and _heat_, respectively. In all these instances, the air is restricted by the narrow passage formed by the following articulators: the lower lip and upper teeth for /f, v/; the tongue and the teeth for /θ, ð/; the tongue and the alveolar ridge for /s, z/; the tongue and the hard palate for /ʃ, ʒ/;[5] and the narrow opening of the vocal cords for /h/.

In two instances, sounds are a combination of a stop and a fricative. In the production of these sounds, air pressure is first built up. Rather than being released freely as in the production of a stop, the air is released through a narrow passageway like a fricative. These two sounds, known as **_affricates_**, are /tʃ/ and /dʒ/ as in the initial and final sounds of _church_ and _judge_, respectively. To feel the difference in manner of articulation, try pronouncing the following columns of words, concentrating on the placement of the tongue and the restriction of the airstream.

Stop	Fricative	Affricate
/t/	/ʃ/	/tʃ/
too	shoe	chew
teak	sheik	cheek
tin	shin	chin
tip	ship	chip
/d/	/ʒ/	/dʒ/
bud	—	budge
rude	rouge	—
paid	—	page
bade	beige	—
head	—	hedge

---

[5]The phoneme /ʒ/ occurs most frequently in word-medial and word-final position in English, as in the words _pleasure_ and _mirage_. The few instances of /ʒ/ in word-initial position occur in words of French origin that still retain French pronunciation, such as _genre, Jacques_.

From these examples we can see that /tʃ/ is a combination of a stop somewhat like /t/ and the fricative /ʃ/. Similarly, /dʒ/ is a combination of a stop somewhat like /d/ and the fricative /ʒ/.[6]

In the phonemes we have discussed thus far, the air has passed through the mouth, or oral cavity. However, another set of sounds is produced when air passes through the nasal cavity. As noted earlier, this occurs when the oral passage is closed and the velum moves forward to free the nasal cavity. These **nasal** sounds are /m/ as in _moon,_ /n/ as in _neither,_ and /ŋ/ as in _long._ The three nasal consonants are similar to stops in that there is complete closure of the articulators (i.e., the two lips for /p, b, m/, the tongue and alveolar ridge for /t, d, n/, and the tongue and velum for /k, g, ŋ/. However, the nasals are also similar to the fricatives in that they too are continuants. In other words, they can be held so long as there is air in the lungs to release through the nasal cavity. To see what happens to nasal sounds when the nasal cavity is blocked (for example, when you have a cold), try holding your nose and saying the following sentence, concentrating on your articulation of the consonant sounds indicated:

M̲artha k̲new the re̲mai̲ni̲ng m̲embers would vote agai̲n̲st the m̲easure.

Notice that when the nasal sounds are articulated through the oral cavity, /m/ sounds like /b/, /n/ sounds like /d/, and /ŋ/ sounds like /g/.

Of the nasal consonants, /ŋ/ is the one most likely to pose a challenge to learners; the other two nasals, /m/ and /n/, occur in most languages. The velar nasal /ŋ/ does not occur in initial position in English; it occurs only intervocalically, as in _singing_ or _stinger,_ or in final position – either alone, as in _king_ or _chasing,_ or in final clusters, as in _hangs_ or _longed._ Note also that in words such as _thinker, anchor,_ or _sinks,_ the letter _n_ is actually articulated as /ŋ/ since it occurs together with the velar consonant /k/.

NOTE TO TEACHERS

Medially, the consonant sequences /ŋg/ and /ŋk/ may be difficult for learners to distinguish from /ŋ/. Compare:

/ŋ/	/ŋg/	/ŋk/
singer	finger	thinker
hanger	longer	anchor
banging	bangle	ankle

(There is some dialectal variation among native speakers in the pronunciation of the _ng_ sequence. Although most NAE speakers use [ŋ] when pronouncing words such as singer or Long Island, many New York metropolitan area speakers use [ŋk] instead.)

Similarly, in final position, the contrast between /ŋ/ and /ŋk/ can be difficult. Compare:

/ŋ/	/ŋk/
ring	rink
bang	bank
sung	sunk

Finally, if the airstream moves around the tongue and out the mouth in a relatively unobstructed manner, we call the sound an **approximant.** Within the class of approximants, we further distinguish **liquids** /l/ and /r/ from **glides,** or **semivowels** (/y/ and /w/).

---

[6]Technically, the stops in /tʃ/ and /dʒ/ (which are alveopalatal) are produced farther back in the mouth than the stops /t/ and /d/ (which are alveolar).

Two of the pedagogically most challenging consonants in English, /l/ and /r/, belong to the class of liquids. Since the airstream flows along the sides of the tongue, /l/ is often referred to as a lateral consonant. It has two allophones, *light,* or *clear,* **[l]** and *dark,* or *velarized,* **[ɫ].** The light [l] is formed when the air passes over one or both side(s) of the tongue with the tip of the tongue touching the alveolar ridge, as in <u>l</u>isten and <u>l</u>il<u>y</u>. The dark [ɫ] is formed by air passing over the body of the tongue, which is bunched up in the velar area. In this allophone, the tip of the tongue may or may not remain in contact with the alveolar ridge. Examples are be<u>ll</u> and ca<u>ll</u>. Notice that in Table 3.2, we have included both allophones and thus classified /l/ as both an alveolar and a velar consonant.

The other liquid, /r/, is present in words such as <u>r</u>ing, be<u>rr</u>y, and (in most dialects of NAE) pa<u>r</u>k and ca<u>r</u>.[7] A salient characteristic of /r/ in NAE is that the tongue tip does not touch the roof of the mouth. There are two quite different ways of producing the American /r/. In the method most often described in ESL/EFL pronunciation texts, the tongue tip curls back into the mouth behind the alveolar ridge and the lips are slightly rounded. This is the so-called *retroflex /r/*, which we classify in Table 3.2 as palatal. In the other method of producing /r/, the lips are more rounded, the tongue tip remains low in the mouth, and the body of the tongue bunches up in the alveolar or alveopalatal area. Since this articulation is less common, we have indicated this second articulation in parentheses in the alveolar area. Interestingly, the auditory results of either manner of articulation are similar.

Thus far we have discussed consonant sounds that fall into the following manners of articulation: stops, fricatives, affricates, nasals, and liquids. A final category of consonant sounds involves the glide, or semivowel, sounds, which behave similarly to the liquids in that the airstream moves through the oral chamber in a relatively unobstructed manner. Glides behave like consonants in syllable-initial position yet also represent movements that combine with vowels to form **diphthongs** (a vowel sound followed by a nonadjacent glide within the same syllable, as in b<u>oy</u>). Belonging to this category are the glides /y/ and /w/, as in <u>y</u>ear and <u>w</u>ood. In Table 3.2, /w/ is classified as bilabial due to the extreme lip rounding present in its articulation.[8] The palatal classification of /y/ is explained by the position of the tongue in that region of the mouth.

The following summarizes the information on manner of articulation:

Stop: The airstream is stopped or blocked completely prior to release: /p, b, t, d, k, g/.

Fricative: Air is forced through a narrow passageway in the mouth or throat creating continuous friction: /f, v, θ, ð, s, z, ʃ, ʒ, h/.

Affricate: The sound begins as a stop and is then released as a fricative: /tʃ, dʒ/.

Nasal: Continuous air is released through the nasal cavity while the speech organs assume a stoplike position: /m, n, ŋ/.

Approximant: The airstream moves around the tongue in a relatively unobstructed manner: liquids /l, r/ and glides /w, y/.

Clearly, in the production of any given consonant, both the place and manner of articulation and voicing (along with the other, secondary characteristics) figure prominently in determining what sound is produced. Only by combining all of the relevant articulatory features can we accurately describe English consonant sounds. This information is summarized in Table 3.2, Classification of NAE Consonant Phonemes.

---

[7]Like British English, some NAE dialects in New England, the New York City area, and the South delete postvocalic /r/.

[8]Although we classify /w/ primarily as a bilabial approximant, we would like to acknowledge its simultaneous velar articulation; the velar element in the English /w/ has influenced many phoneticians to classify it as a labiovelar consonant. It also has many of the characteristics of a vowel, leading some phoneticians to characterize it as a nonsyllabic high back vowel.

TABLE 3.2 CLASSIFICATION OF NAE CONSONANT PHONEMES

Manner of Articulation	Place of Articulation						
	Bilabial	Labiodental	Dental	Alveolar	Palatal	Velar	Glottal
Stop voiceless	/p/			/t/		/k/	
voiced	/b/			/d/		/g/	
Fricative voiceless		/f/	/θ/	/s/	/ʃ/		/h/
voiced		/v/	/ð/	/z/	/ʒ/		
Affricate voiceless					/tʃ/		
voiced					/dʒ/		
Nasal voiced	/m/			/n/		/ŋ/	
Liquid voiced				/l/ (/r/)	/r/	[ɬ]	
Glide voiceless	(/hw/)*						
voiced	/w/				/y/		

We have chosen to list /hw/ in parentheses since for many NAE speakers, the initial sounds of *which* and *witch* are not systematically differentiated; rather, the speaker uses /w/ for both words. For other speakers, /hw/ may be simply a variant of /w/ produced in certain words (such as *whether*), or a marker of special emphasis (such as in forceful pronunciations of the question "*What?*").

THE CONSONANT INVENTORY: PEDAGOGICAL PRIORITIES

One decision that must be made when teaching consonants is how detailed an analysis to present to the students. For many ESL/EFL students, a detailed description of the consonant inventory of English is inappropriate. However, for advanced learners focusing on pronunciation or for prospective nonnative teachers of EFL, a comprehensive introduction is essential.

In the following section, we suggest introducing such students to the entire consonant inventory, classifying individual sounds according to their articulatory features. We present consonants in this fashion because we believe that classifying them according to their features can greatly assist students in their discrimination and production efforts. Obviously, when choosing to present consonants in this manner, special attention should be paid to the symbols that differ from regular spelling – /ʃ/, /ʒ/, /tʃ/, /dʒ/, /θ/, /ð/, /ŋ/, and to sound contrasts that do not exist in the students' first language.

There are, however, situations for which such a broad and detailed overview is inappropriate. These include all-skills classes in which there is time to focus only on selected (or problematic) pronunciation contrasts, as well as oral-skills classes that focus on fluency rather than accuracy, and that highlight pronunciation only when it severely impedes communication. The variables of setting, population, and objectives as they relate to curricular choices are discussed more fully in Chapter 11.

PRESENTING THE CONSONANT INVENTORY TO STUDENTS

Begin a discussion of consonants by using a sagittal section of the speech organs (see Figure 3.1). As you present the various speech organs on an overhead transparency or poster board, students can fill in a blank worksheet with the terms. Using a sagittal section diagram and a small hand mirror helps students to see where the sounds are formed, thus familiarizing them with the place of articulation. However, the place of articulation is only one feature that helps distinguish consonants; the manner of articulation and the presence or absence of voicing are also primary characteristics of each consonant.

During the explanation of how consonant sounds are formed, the concept of voicing becomes very important since it is the feature that distinguishes between stops, fricatives, and affricates articulated in the same place. Students can distinguish voiced from voiceless either by feeling their Adam's apple or by putting fingers in their ears and listening to which of the pair of sounds can be heard.

The use of the consonant chart (Table 3.2) offers an organized presentation of these features for students. We suggest giving students a blank worksheet of the table to fill in as you explain the classification of consonants (see Table 3.3).

While students focus on the *place of articulation,* point out how these categories (i.e., *bilabial, labiodental, dental, alveolar, palatal, velar,* and *glottal*) move from the front of the mouth to the back. By looking simultaneously at the sagittal section diagram, students can understand what is meant by each category. This also affords you an opportunity to review word forms and roots and affixes. For example, you can ask:

What does the *bi-* in *bilabial* mean?

What does *labial* mean? (This works if you have any Romance language speakers.)

What does *dental* refer to? What other words do you know with the root *dent-*?

If a sound is described as *labiodental,* which two speech organs are involved?

Each of the categories under *Place of Articulation* ends in either *-al* or *-ar.* What part of speech is each term?

Palatal, velar, and *glottal* refer to which speech organs in the diagram (Figure 3.1)?

TABLE 3.3 STUDENT WORKSHEET: CLASSIFICATION OF NAE CONSONANT PHOEMES

Manner of Articulation	Place of Articulation						
	Bilabial	Labiodental	Dental	Alveolar	Palatal	Velar	Glottal
____ voiceless ____ voiced							
____ voiceless ____ voiced							
____ voiceless ____ voiced							
____ voiced							
____ voiced							
____ voiceless ____ voiced							

Once students know where sounds are formed, they need to know how they are formed – in other words, how the speech organs interact with each other. It is important to start with the basic information that the formation of consonant sounds is a function of air passing from the lungs through either the mouth or nose (again, you may wish to emphasize this using the sagittal section diagram). However, as the air moves, it passes though a type of obstacle course created by various configurations of the speech organs. As the air encounters these obstacles, different sounds are produced.

You should begin the discussion of the various manners of articulation by introducing them one at a time. Students can then record this information and the examples on their blank worksheet. Since the *manner of articulation* of consonants has already been explained in an earlier section of this chapter, we offer the following thumbnail sketch of how you might present stops. Once this category has been explained, you would continue in a like manner to explain fricatives, affricates, nasals, liquids, and glides.

Manner of articulation	The first category is stop/plosive. (Students write this in the left-hand column of their worksheet.)
Teacher explanation	Stops involve a three-step process: the airstream coming from the lungs is completely stopped by the coming together of two speech organs; held and then it is released with a small puff of air. It is like a type of explosion. Once this has happened, the air is free to continue its movement out of the oral cavity. A stop cannot be held or continued.
Ways to elicit examples	Put your lips together. Let the air pressure build up and then release it. What sounds are produced? (Students will likely come up with /p/ and /b/.)
	Put your fingers on your vocal cords and pronounce /p/. Is it voiced or voiceless? What about /b/? (Students are then instructed to write /p/ and /b/ in the respective positions on their consonant charts under the category "bilabial stop.")
	Now, try putting your tongue on the alveolar ridge. Again, let the air build up and then release it. What sounds are produced? (Usually this is enough prompting to elicit /t/ and /d/ and determine voicing; students fill in these sounds on their charts.)
	Finally, start to say *go*. Try to say just the first sound and then stop. Can you feel where your tongue touches? Where do you think the stop /g/ is produced? (Students should feel the back of the tongue meet the velum and be able to place it in this column.)
	Can you produce another stop in the same place? What is it? (Students should come up with /k/ and fill it in on the chart.)

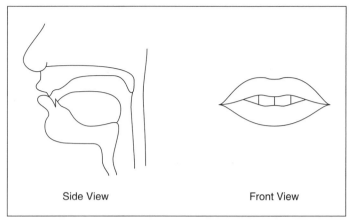

Figure 3.2 Articulation of /v/

PRESENTING CONSONANT CONTRASTS TO STUDENTS

Although consonant sounds can be presented individually, they are often taught in contrast with another consonant. For example, you may choose to teach /ŋ/ in conjunction with /n/ and have students practice minimal pair contrasts, such as "It's a fan/fang." Depending on students' language backgrounds, certain consonants will be harder for them to distinguish than others. Once you have determined which contrasts are most difficult for your students, more focused exercises can be designed.

> **NOTE TO TEACHERS**
>
> It is important to be aware of which individual sounds and which sound contrasts may cause your students difficulty. In classes of students from homogeneous language backgrounds, knowledge of the sound system of the students' first language is especially important, since this can have strong predictive value. Even in heterogeneous classes knowledge of sound systems can be gained through a number of reference sources. We recommend particularly Avery and Ehrlich (1992), Kenworthy (1987), Nilsen and Nilsen (1973), and Swan and Smith (1987).

For less advanced ESL/EFL learners (and especially for beginning learners), the consciousness-raising procedure suggested above is clearly not appropriate. For such learners, problematic consonant sounds can be described using a combination of drawings, visual props, and word and sentence drills. Give articulatory descriptions in informal language; for example, when teaching English /v/ to adult Spanish speakers, you can both demonstrate and show a drawing of how the upper teeth rest inside the lower lip while continuous friction of the vocal cords is produced (Figure 3.2). (Students can be directed to feel the vibration by touching their lower lip or Adam's apple.)

You can then write several example words on the board, such as *van, very, move, drive,* and elicit other words containing /v/ from the students. Students should practice saying all these words aloud first in isolation, then in simple sentences, such as *Vince drives a moving van.*

Finally, students should work in pairs or groups to create their own sentences using the elicited words. These sentences can then be practiced and performed.

USING A COMMUNICATIVE FRAMEWORK TO TEACH PRONUNCIATION

As we suggest in the framework presented in the Part 2 introduction, the presentation of sounds to students should begin with a learner-appropriate description of how the sound is articulated. Teachers should then have students analyze the feature, practice distinguishing it from similar sounds, and then use it in first more controlled and then more guided and communicative contexts. The activities that follow are intended to illustrate the five steps of the communicative framework and are not intended as one single lesson. Depending on the time available for pronunciation practice, we suggest selecting one or two activities in each phase, and if necessary, practicing the different phases in different lessons. We illustrate this progression of classroom activities using the consonant contrast /l/ vs. /r/.

DESCRIPTION AND ANALYSIS: EXAMPLE OF /l/ AND /r/

If your student population includes speakers of Asian languages, especially Japanese, you may find yourself needing to reinforce the distinction between /l/ and /r/. In classroom practice, this would involve beginning with information about these two sound contrasts, perhaps using sagittal section diagrams and the consonant chart to indicate the different points of articulation of these two consonants. For initial /l/, for example, students need to be aware that the tongue makes contact with the roof of the mouth at the alveolar ridge, whereas for /r/, the tongue does not touch anything. For /l/, have students consciously place their tongues on the alveolar ridge, then produce *led* /lɛd/. In order to produce an /r/, have students begin by saying "uh" with a relaxed mouth and jaw. While saying "uh," they should first roll their tongue up and back and then unroll it as they say *red* /rɛd/. Similar exercises would be done to have students experience final /l/ and /r/.

The next step would involve raising students' consciousness as to where these sounds typically occur. In the case of /l/ vs. /r/, a number of rich contexts offer themselves:

Colors: red, yellow, blue, green, brown, purple, maroon, black, gray

Directions: right, left, straight ahead, around the corner, across the street

Professions: bartender, bank teller, waitress, cab driver, doctor, English teacher, lawyer

Places: library, flower shop, grocery store, hairdressing salon, church, temple

Comparatives and superlatives: better, worse, more graceful, less realistic, most terrible

Body parts: elbow, ear, finger, knuckle, ankle, leg, wrist, eyebrow, forehead

Personal names: Ralph, Beverly, Harold, Pearl, Laura, Larry, Marlon, Laverne

Depending on the proficiency level or linguistic sophistication of the students, you may wish to either select one of the categories and (1) present the individual words, or (2) elicit them from students, asking, for example, "How many body parts can you name containing an 'l' or an 'r'?"

LISTENING DISCRIMINATION: /l/ AND /r/

Once the consonant sounds have been classified and contexts have been established, students need practice in distinguishing the sound contrasts. Contextualized discrimination exercises with minimal pairs work well both as a diagnostic tool and as listening practice, for example:

Circle the word you hear:

1. Is that Eileen/Irene?
2. There was a small lake/rake behind the cabin.
3. The teacher collected/corrected the homework.[9]

This discrimination practice can be followed by controlled production exercises in which students produce these types of minimal pair sentences.

CONTROLLED PRACTICE AND FEEDBACK: /l/ AND /r/

Colored rods (see Chapter 1) provide an easy-to-use and effective way of practicing the /l/ vs. /r/ distinction, even with beginning-level students. These small sticks of wood come in different sizes and colors. Thus, color names as well as vocabulary, such as *here/there, left/right,* and *longer/shorter,* can be practiced, first as isolated words if necessary and then in simple sentences.

Question	Answer
Where is the brown rod?	Here.
(pointing) Which rod is there?	The red one.
Which rod is on the left?	The blue one.
Where is the black rod?	On the right.
Which rod is longer?	The yellow one.
Compare the blue rod and red one.	The red rod is longer than the blue one.

Simple vocabulary can also be used to create another controlled practice activity, namely, a dialogue for students to read and perform for the class. They should be told in advance to pay special attention to the pronunciation of /l/ and /r/. Here is an example:

(A police officer stops a car on a busy city street. The driver rolls down his window.)

Ron:	What's the problem, officer?
Police officer:	Didn't you see the traffic light? It was red and you went right through it!
Ron:	Oh no, officer! I'm sure the light was green!
Police officer:	I think you should take off those sunglasses. Your colors are all mixed up! *(He writes out a ticket and hands it to Ron.)*
Ron:	Does this mean I have to go to traffic school?
Police officer:	Well, if you don't want your insurance rates to go up it does. And maybe you should get your eyes checked while you're at it.

Many other contexts exist for practicing the /l/ vs. /r/ distinction. As noted, one of the richest is that of body parts. For younger or lower-level students who are not afraid to stand up and be active, a game of "Simon Says" works well. You can first elicit vocabulary pertaining to parts of the body, and perhaps write these on the board. Then lead the first round, saying either "Simon says touch your elbow" (in which case students should mimic the action) or only "Touch your elbow" (in which case students should *not* mimic the action, and those who do are out of the game). For subsequent rounds, one of the students (perhaps the winner of the previous round) becomes the leader.

---

[9]An excellent resource for such minimal pair sentences is Bowen (1975b).

Another rich context for /l/ vs. /r/ distinctions is directions and place names. Using a map of the immediate vicinity, you can create a map-based activity in which students give each other directions to various locations, for example:

Turn right at the library.

It's across the street from the flower shop.

The park is three blocks straight ahead.

As a variation on this activity, Celce-Murcia and Goodwin (1991) suggest the use of slides of familiar locations (e.g., the college campus) to guide student discussion and to familiarize the class with local points of interest. The teacher would initially narrate the slide show, saying, for example:

(Slide #1) This is Rolfe Hall. It's located across from Royce Hall, where the German and Italian Departments are housed. Rolfe Hall was named after Franklin D. Rolfe, a professor of English and Dean of Humanities at UCLA.

(Slide #2) Here's the Research Library. It has a world-respected collection of resource materials. It's located near the North Campus cafeteria and the Sculpture Garden.

As a follow-up activity, the same slides are shown, but the students provide the oral narrative.

GUIDED PRACTICE WITH FEEDBACK: /l/ AND /r/

An example of slightly less controlled practice in the /l/ vs. /r/ distinction – or indeed in virtually any consonant contrast – is the use of an information gap activity involving two versions of a monthly calendar, each containing different pieces of information about a given individual's plans. This guided practice activity represents a departure from the controlled practice stage in which students simply read aloud sentences or short dialogues focusing on the articulation of a particular sound or sound contrast. Students are especially motivated to participate in this activity when it involves the fictional activities of a popular celebrity such as a politician, movie star, or singer. Figure 3.3 represents Elizabeth Taylor's plans for the month of April. To do the activities you would divide students into pairs, then give each member of the pair a different calendar (version A or B). They fill in

Version A

MONDAY	TUESDAY	WEDNESDAY	THURSDAY	FRIDAY	SATURDAY	SUNDAY
	1 celebrate with friends	2	3	4	5 leave for Berlin	6
7	8	9	10	11	12 horseback riding	13
14 bridge party	15	16	17	18 pick up Harold at airport	19	20
21	22	23	24	25	26	27
28	29	30 conference in Cairo				

Figure 3.3 Calendars for guided practice activity

Version B

MONDAY	TUESDAY	WEDNESDAY	THURSDAY	FRIDAY	SATURDAY	SUNDAY
	1	2	3 *appointment at hairdresser's 3:00*	4	5	6
7	8	9 *return from Berlin*	10	11	12	13 *Hollywood premiere 8:00 p.m.*
14	15	16	17	18	19 *dinner with Barry*	20
21	22	23 *new furniture delivered 4:30 p.m.*	24	25 *fly to London*	26	27
28	29	30				

Figure 3.3 *Continued*

the missing information by asking each other questions about the blank (i.e., unshaded) areas of the calendar. Sample questions are:

What are Elizabeth Taylor's plans on April fourth?

Is she busy on the sixteenth?

What is she doing on April twenty-third?

COMMUNICATIVE PRACTICE AND FEEDBACK: /l/ AND /r/

Once students have had a chance for controlled and guided practice, they should engage in communicative practice using the same consonant contrasts. In this phase of practice, students are provided with a context and key words that contain the targeted sounds. An example of this type of practice involving the /l/ vs. /r/ contrast is to divide students into small groups, give each group a list of words like the following, and have them create a group story selecting their favorite words from the list.

GROUP STORY: /l/ VS. /r/

In your group, choose eight words from the list below. Then create a story using these words in any order.

/r/	/l/
right, write	light
wrong	long
road	load
rate	late
red	led
wrist	list
arrive	alive
pirate	pilot
correct	collect
Irene	Eileen

As each group tells its story, the students in the other groups listen and check off which words on the list were used. They also check whether these words were pronounced correctly and whether they make sense within the context of the story. As a follow-up activity, a different group can try to retell the story, using the words they checked as a guide. An example of a student story might be as follows:

Student 1:   Last summer, my friend <u>Eileen</u> and I went to New York.
Student 2:   Eileen had a <u>long</u> <u>list</u> of things she wanted to see.
Student 3:   Our plane <u>arrived</u> <u>late</u>.
Student 4:   Then our taxi took the <u>wrong</u> <u>road</u> and we had to walk five <u>long</u> blocks carrying a heavy <u>load</u>. What a terrible beginning!

More advanced students can perform role plays – another form of communicative practice – which you can audiotape and play back for self- and peer correction. Although the focus is clearly more on meaning than form in such an activity, students can be asked to concentrate on the particular sound(s) being practiced. Feedback can also be focused on the selected consonant distinction(s). The following role cards set up situations in which /l/ and /r/ occur frequently:

Student A: Role Play #1

Call McDonald's in Ridgemont. You want to find out what hours the restaurant is open, the address, and where to park.

Student B: Role Play #1

You work at Thrifty Drug Store. The phone rings. You answer it. The caller has the wrong number. It's difficult to understand what the caller is saying because it's very noisy. You don't know the phone number or address of the place the caller wishes to reach.

Student A: Role Play #2

Your car broke down on the freeway near the Royal Boulevard exit. Call Lou's Towing Service to have someone come and tow the car to the nearest garage. It's late at night and you are calling from the freeway telephone. Tell them to hurry.

Student B: Role Play #2
You are Lou. You own Lou's Towing Service.
Someone is calling to get a car towed to the
nearest garage. The caller is stranded on the
freeway. Tell the caller that you are located too
far away and to call someone else.

TEACHING OTHER CONSONANT CONTRASTS

The progression from controlled to guided to communicative practice is one we suggest for teaching problematic consonant sounds. We include a few additional activities for teaching other consonant contrasts. These activities demonstrate the range of possible classroom activities for teaching pronunciation contrasts.

The following guiding principles are suggested when developing such activities:

1. Identify your students' problem areas (different groups have different problems).
2. Find lexical/grammatical contexts with many natural occurrences of the problem sounds. Identify contexts for all the positions in which the sounds occur.
3. Draw on these contexts to develop activities for analysis and listening that will assist your students in understanding and recognizing the target sounds.
4. Using the contexts you have chosen, develop a progression of controlled, guided, and communicative tasks that incorporate the sounds for practice.
5. For each stage of practice (i.e., controlled, guided, communicative) develop two or three activities so that you can recycle the problem and keep practicing the target sounds with new contexts.

With this framework in mind, let us survey some sample activities for practicing the consonant sounds that your students may have difficulty distinguishing or producing.

/ʒ/ **in word endings** Within a multiskills class that features work on vocabulary and word building, it can be useful to present students with an analysis activity involving the pronunciation of word endings. The sound /ʒ/, for example, occurs frequently in words ending in -*sure*, such as *pleasure, treasure, measure, leisure,* and *exposure.* Another environment for /ʒ/ is words ending in *rs + -ion* (e.g., *version, excursion*) or vowel + *s + -ion* (e.g., *confusion, decision*).[10] As part of the vocabulary instruction, you can point out that the suffix -*ion* is often used to form a noun from a verb. The following chart illustrates this:

/d/ → /ʒ/		/z/ → /ʒ/		/t/ → /ʒ/	
vowel + -de		**vowel + -se**		**-vert**	
conclude	conclusion	confuse	confusion	convert	conversion
include	inclusion	transfuse	transfusion	invert	inversion
exclude	exclusion	revise	revision	divert	diversion
delude	delusion	supervise	supervision	revert	reversion
divide	division				
decide	decision				
provide	provision				
collide	collision				
explode	explosion				
persuade	persuasion				

[10]Compare, however, *emulsion* and *compulsion,* where the *s* preceding -*ion* is pronounced /ʃ/. See Chapter 9 for further discussion of using spelling patterns as a predictor for pronunciation.

> *Directions:* Choose the word that fits in each blank below and then read the sentence aloud:
>
> exposure   explosion   confusion   diversion
> decision   pleasure   division
>
> 1. Watching television is my favorite _____.
> 2. The river marks the _____ between the two cities.
> 3. Are you here on business or for _____?
> 4. Mary is very wishy-washy and can't seem to make a _____.
> 5. When she lit the gas range there was a loud _____.
> 6. Too much _____ to the sun can cause sunburn.
> 7. There was some _____ because the instructions were unclear.

Figure 3.4 Sentences for controlled practice with /ʒ/

As controlled practice, students could be given the task in Figure 3.4.

/θ/ **and** /ð/ An example of a guided practice activity that provides a rich context for the troublesome sounds /θ/ and /ð/ is "The Family Tree" (Figure 3.5). In the analysis phase, it is important to point out to students that voiced /ð/ occurs commonly in relationship terms, such as *mother, brother,* and *father,* whereas the voiceless /θ/ occurs frequently in personal names. The students should also be alerted to their own substitutions, such as /t/, /s/, and /f/ for voiceless /θ/; and /d/, /z/, and /v/ for voiced /ð/. This activity is also an excellent way to recycle the /s/ and /z/ pronunciations of possessive endings (e.g., *Agatha's* /z/ *mother; Garth's* /s/ *father*), assuming these have been taught previously.

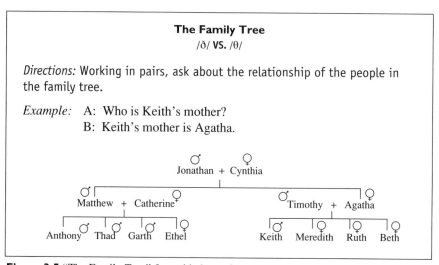

Figure 3.5 "The Family Tree" for guided practice

Once students have moved through the guided practice, they should do a related communicative activity, like the following:

On a sheet of paper, complete your family tree, going back as far as your grandparents. Then tell your partner about your own family.

A more communicative activity involves the same kind of group storytelling activity described for /r/ and /l/, this time designed to practice the distinction between /ð/ and /θ/.

GROUP STORY: /θ/ VS. /ð/

In your group, choose eight words from the list below. Then create a story using these words in any order.

/θ/	/ð/
thief	father
truth	brother
theory	mother
author	this
think	that
through	these
thorough	those
Cynthia	then
Theo	there
Matthew	together

For example:

Student 1: Last Thursday, my sister Cynthia went on a trip to Boston.
Student 2: She wanted to visit my brother Matthew, who lives there.
Student 3: She traveled through many small towns. She didn't know that it was so far.
Student 4: After she arrived, a thief stole her money and she had to return home.

/tʃ/ **and** /dʒ/ Another common difficulty for many students is producing the voiceless affricate /tʃ/ and the voiced /dʒ/.[11] In terms of analysis, it can be useful to explain to students that /tʃ/ is similar to a combination of /t/ and /ʃ/. Have them first produce /t/, then /ʃ/, to get a feel for the position in the mouth. Next try having students put the two sounds together quickly. The same procedure is followed for /dʒ/, which is a combination of /d/ and /ʒ/. Once they are able to produce the sounds in isolation and then in words, adequate opportunity for controlled practice (e.g., having students read short sentences or dialogues containing the target sounds) should be provided. The pair interview exercise in Figure 3.6 is an example of the guided practice that should follow.

/n/ **and** /ŋ/ For learners from certain language backgrounds (e.g., Chinese, Farsi, Portuguese), the distinction between /n/ and /ŋ/ can be difficult both to hear and to produce. The principal difference is in the place of articulation. In the analysis stage, have students use mirrors to see if they are placing the front of their tongue on the alveolar ridge for /n/ and the back of their tongue on the velum for /ŋ/. They may double-check their tongue

[11]For some students, the position in which these sounds occur is a factor. Depending on native language, there may be a tendency for the student to produce only the voiceless affricate /tʃ/ in the final position.

Shopping Interview:
/tʃ/ **VS.** /dʒ/

Directions: Imagine you are going shopping for the things on this list. Working in pairs, decide where you will make your purchases. The list of stores is on the right.

potato chips
a jug of wine
jelly doughnuts
grape juice   Joe's Liquor Store
jumbo shrimp   Churchill's Bakery
cheddar cheese   George's Supermarket
chewing gum
strawberry jam
tangerines
cherry pie
matches
gin
orange marmalade
chicken legs

Now ask and answer the following questions:

A: What will you buy at _____?
B: I'll buy _____.
A: Where will you buy the _____?
B: I'll buy (it/them) at _____.
A: How much/many _____ will you buy?
B: I'll buy _____.

Figure 3.6 Shopping interview for guided practice

placement during a controlled practice exercise involving minimal pair word and sentence contrasts. This would then be followed by a guided practice activity such as that in Figure 3.7 (which is also good for practicing the structure *gone* + VERB-*ing*).

For a communicative extension of the activity in Figure 3.7, the class could play a game of "Twenty Questions." A student volunteer (V) chooses one character from the grid (e.g., Ron) and writes down the name without revealing it to the class. The other students then ask a series of yes/no questions until the name is discovered:[12]

A: Is the person a man?
V: Yes.
B: Has he gone skiing?
V: No.
C: Has he gone swimming?
V: No.
D: Has he gone shopping?
V: Yes.
D: Is it Ron?
V: Yes!

[12]Teachers can reinforce the "Has he/she gone VERB-ing?" pattern by modeling it for students in the instructions for this activity.

Figure 3.7 Guided practice activity for /n/ and /ŋ/

The boxed activity shown in the figure reads:

/n/ **VS.** /ŋ/

Directions: Working in pairs, use the illustrations to ask each other questions.

Example: A: Where's Ron?
             B: He's gone shopping.
             A: Where are Lynn and Owen?
             B: They've gone dancing.

Names in the illustration grid: Virginia, John, Dan, June, Lynn, Owen, Karen, Sean, Brian, Joan, Ken, Ron, Jane, Caroline, Don, Jason

THE EFFECT OF ENVIRONMENT ON CONSONANT QUALITY: WHAT THE TEACHER NEEDS TO KNOW

Thus far we have discussed the characteristics of twenty-five distinct consonant sounds as they are produced in isolation. However, sounds are rarely produced in this manner; rather, they are influenced by the environment in which they occur – by their position within a word and by the sounds that precede or follow them.[13]

POSITIONAL RESTRICTION

Consonants can potentially occur in five different environments: syllable initial, syllable final, intervocalic, initial clusters, and final clusters. Not all consonants occur in all of these environments, and the teacher should keep this in mind when teaching consonants. Consider, for example, the consonants /s/, /tʃ/, and /ŋ/:

---

[13]See the assimilation section in Chapter 5 for a more comprehensive discussion of the influence of environment.

Phoneme	Syllable initial	Syllable final	Intervocalic	Initial clusters	Final clusters
/s/	sing sat Sally	bus loss face	classic passive adjacent	stream scratch slip	burst mask cats
/tʃ/	cheese chin chair	each touch match	teaches butcher watching	(none)	bunch lurch gulch
/ŋ/	(none)	young tongue ring	singer bringing dinghy	(none)	hanged thank wings

Notice in these examples that /s/ can occur in all positions; however, both /tʃ/ and /ŋ/ are somewhat restricted. The following five consonants are also restricted in terms of where they can occur: /hw/, /h/, /ʒ/, /w/, and /y/. For a complete taxonomy of where the twenty-five consonants of NAE can potentially occur, see Appendix 3.

POSITIONAL VARIATION

In addition to the positional restrictions on where consonants can occur, there is also positional variation – that is, the same phoneme is pronounced differently in different positions or environments. Thus teachers need an awareness of the effect that this positional variation has on the production of consonant sounds. This variation is often not obvious to native speakers, who produce the various allophones of a given phoneme unconsciously; yet such variation is often a source of difficulty in pronunciation and listening discrimination for learners in the ESL/EFL classroom.

INITIAL AND FINAL STOP CONSONANTS

One example of how environment can affect the articulation of a sound involves the stop consonants /p, t, k/. Thus far, we have distinguished these sounds from /b, d, g/ in terms of voicing. However, an additional significant feature of voiceless stop consonants in English is **aspiration**, the brief puff of air that accompanies the allophones of /p, t, k/ in words such as *pan, tan,* and *key*. The presence or absence of aspiration is easiest to demonstrate with the bilabial stops /p/ and /b/. If an English speaker says *pie,* the aspiration will often extinguish a lighted match or move a strip of paper placed in front of the speaker's mouth. If the same speaker says *buy,* it will not noticeably affect the flame or the paper. Since /t/ and /k/ are articulated farther back in the mouth than /p/, the aspiration is harder to demonstrate visually than for /p/, but it is nonetheless present and salient.

In general, then, we can say that the voiced stop consonants are not aspirated, whereas the voiceless stop consonants are. However, we need to further qualify this statement, since the occurrence of aspiration with /p, t, k/ depends on the position of the consonant within a word. Try saying the following words, in which /p, t, k/ occur word initially (column 1) and at the beginning of a stressed syllable (column 2):

	1	2
[pʰ]	peal	rePEAL
[tʰ]	test	deTEST
[kʰ]	kin	aKIN

Notice how the stop consonant is aspirated both at the beginning of the words in column 1 and at the beginning of the stressed (i. e. , second) syllable in column 2.

Now compare the unaspirated [p] and [k] that occur at the beginning of unstressed syllables (column 1) with the aspirated [pʰ] and [kʰ] at the beginning of the stressed syllables (column 2) (the consonant /t/ will be discussed separately):

1	2
[p]	**[pʰ]**
Opus	opPOSE
Opal	apPALL

1	2
[k]	**[kʰ]**
REcord (n.)	reCORD (v.)
Ochre	ocCUR

Notice the aspiration when these stop consonants begin a stressed syllable.

We can further see this difference in aspiration when there is a stress shift due to a derivational ending, as in the following case:

[p]	**[pʰ]**
RApid	raPIDity

Again here, there is a noticeable difference between the unaspirated [p] in *rapid* and the aspirated [pʰ] in *rapidity* – clear evidence of the role positional variation plays in determining the aspiration of voiceless stop consonants.

NOTE TO TEACHERS

In many languages, initial voiceless stops are less strongly aspirated than in English, or are even unaspirated. Speakers of these languages may therefore tend to confuse initial /b, d, g/ in English with their own language's unaspirated /p, t, k/ in this position. These learners may be misperceived by English native speakers as producing *back* in place of *pack,* or *die* instead of *tie.* In fact what they may be producing is an unaspirated /p/ or /t/ in place of the English aspirated counterparts. They may, of course, also have difficulty in differentiating such minimal word pairs. For these learners, aspiration can provide a valuable clue to perceiving and producing these words. English speakers, of course, have the reverse problem when learning a foreign language that does not aspirate initial voiceless stops.

In casual speech, the same six stop consonant sounds /p, t, k/ and /b, d, g/ are often not ***released*** in final position. In other words, the process of articulation is not completed. For example, in the word *cat*, the final [t°] is produced with the tip of the tongue remaining in place on the alveolar ridge rather than being released at the end of the word.[14] Similarly, in the word *tub*, the lips remain in place for the articulation of the final [b°]; air is not released subsequently.

---

[14]Alternatively, the final /t/ in words such as *cat, put,* and *but* may become glottalized, with the /t/ accompanied or replaced by a glottal stop [ʔ]. In such cases, the airstream is stopped in the throat by the constriction of the vocal cords.

It can thus be hard for learners to distinguish minimal pairs ending in stop consonants. The real perceptual clue in distinguishing such word pairs tends to be **vowel length;** all things being equal, the vowel sounds in *rip*, *hit*, and *pick* are shorter than the vowel sounds in *rib*, *hid,* and *pig*, respectively. Note that the former words end in a voiceless consonant sound and the latter in a voiced sound. Therefore, learners must be taught that English vowels are systematically shorter before voiceless consonants than before voiced consonants; this will be one of their most reliable clues in distinguishing these consonants in final position.[15] In order to represent lengthened vowels, we use the symbol [:] following the vowel:

Final voiceless consonants (shorter vowel)		Final voiced consonants (longer vowel)	
rip	/rɪp/	rib	/rɪ:b/
hit	/hɪt/	hid	/hɪ:d/
pick	/pɪk/	pig	/pɪ:g/

NOTE TO TEACHERS

Many learners have a tendency to release and aspirate final stops too heavily: for example, *book* [kʰ], *hit* [tʰ], *spot* [tʰ]. Explanation and demonstration of vowel length and unreleased final stops can be helpful in getting them to overcome this tendency. Also, for learners who have experience with British English, it must be explained that the tendency for final stops to be unreleased is stronger in NAE than in British English (see Appendix 1).

NAE FLAP [ɾ]

In the earlier discussion of aspiration with /p, t, k/, we omitted /t/, because /t/ takes on a unique quality for most speakers of NAE when it occurs after a vowel or an /r/ and before an unstressed syllable. This voiced allophone, which we will represent with the symbol [ɾ], occurs in such words as *data, city, putting, dirty, started,* and is called a **flap,** or **tap.**[16] It is produced like /d/, except the tongue touches or flaps against the alveolar ridge only very briefly. Like /d/, the flap is voiced. A flap allophone occurs in the same environments as /d/ as well. In fact, most speakers of NAE make no difference in articulating the words *catty* and *caddy,* or *latter* and *ladder.*[17] The flapping of /t/ and /d/ occurs even across word boundaries, and may even occur when the vowel in a following word is stressed. Consider, for example, the phrases "put it on" and "head it in," in which the underlined sounds are flapped in normal speech.

[handwritten: d sound / but the sound flaps]

[15]In addition to the lengthening effect on vowels of final voiced consonants, we should note the similar lengthening effect of 1) degree of stress and 2) position within a word. With regard to degree of stress, note that the second vowel in comPLAIN is longer than the second vowel in CHAPlain. Second, the vowel /ow/ in GLOBE is longer than its equivalent in GLOBal.

[16]Some linguists differentiate between a flap and a tap, maintaining that a tap is a brief contact of the tongue with the alveolar ridge (as in *data, city*) and a flap consists of the tongue tip brushing against the alveolar ridge (as in *party, dirty*). We will use the term *flap* to refer to both of these processes.

[17]Some speakers may make a distinction in the stressed vowels of such pairs, especially when the vowel is /ay/, as in *writer* vs. *rider.*

In the same environment – that is, before an unstressed syllable – the consonant sound /n/ and the consonant sequence /nt/ can both be realized as a nasalized flap. Thus for many NAE speakers, word pairs like *winner/winter* and *banner/banter* may have virtually the same pronunciation, especially in casual speech. This NAE phenomenon is sometimes referred to as "disappearing *t*," and is particularly common when words with medial /nt/ occur in common phrases (*twen(t)y-one, win(t)er break, the en(t)ertainment business*) and in place names (*San(t)a Ana, Toron(t)o*).

FRICATIVES AND AFFRICATES

English fricatives can be divided into two groups: *sibilants* (those with a high-pitched turbulent sound) and nonsibilants (those produced with much less friction and energy). The sibilant fricatives are /s, z, ʃ, ʒ/, and the nonsibilants are /f, v, θ, ð, h/. Since the two affricates /tʃ, dʒ/ both have a sibilant fricative release, they also qualify as sibilant sounds.

The presence or absence of fricative /h/ is simply a matter of expelling air before the vowel or of having no air before the vowel. Speakers of French, Hebrew, and many other languages have problems producing and distinguishing pairs like these, of which English has many:

No /h/	/h/ present
air	hair
art	heart
ear	hear
and	hand

The sound /h/ generally occurs under the same conditions as aspiration; thus /h/ before unstressed vowels – especially in noninitial position – tends to be deleted:

/h/ articulated	/h/ often deleted
inHIBit	in(h)iBITion
proHIBit	pro(h)iBITion
hiSTORic	pre(h)iSTORic

The English dental fricatives /θ/ and /ð/ vary in place of articulation. Some speakers articulate the sounds with the tongue tip just behind and touching the upper teeth, in which case they are dental, as we describe them; some speakers articulate them with the tongue tip touching the upper teeth but also protruding very briefly and very slightly between the upper and lower teeth, in which case they are interdental. We have not emphasized the interdental articulation because we believe that this does not characterize the speech of most NAE speakers; however, the interdental description of the sounds may be of help pedagogically with the many learners who do not have these sounds in their languages.

A final important observation concerning voiced and voiceless fricatives and affricates is their relation to vowel length. Vowels preceding fricatives and affricates behave similarly to those before stops. In other words, if one considers isolated word pairs, the vowel sounds are clearly longer before the voiced fricatives and affricates than before voiceless:[18]

Final voiceless consonants (shorter vowel)		Final voiced consonants (longer vowel)	
gra<u>ce</u>	/greys/	gra<u>ze</u>	/grey:z/
fi<u>fe</u>	/fayf/	fi<u>ve</u>	/fay:v/
tee<u>th</u>	/tiyθ/	tee<u>the</u>	/tiy:ð/
ba<u>tch</u>	/bætʃ/	ba<u>dge</u>	/bæ:dʒ/

On the other hand, the voiceless fricatives and affricates are perceptibly longer and more strongly released than the voiced ones; as a result, the words in each minimal pair are virtually the same length.

---

[18]The fricative sounds /ʃ/ and /ʒ/ were not included in these lists because there are virtually no minimal pairs for word-final position. The sound /ʒ/ occurs in word-final position in only a few French borrowings, such as *beige* and *rouge*. One can perhaps appreciate the difference in vowel length nonetheless by comparing the words *bei<u>ge</u>* /ʒ/ and *fre<u>sh</u>* /ʃ/.

SYLLABIC CONSONANTS

The nasal consonant /n/ and the liquid /l/ are unusual in that they have the capacity to become *syllabic* or vowel-like; in other words, they have allophones that can function as a weak syllable without the support of a vowel sound.[19] This can happen in words where [n̩] or [l̩] constitute a weakly stressed syllable following a strongly stressed one. Note that the English spelling system often indicates the presence of a vowel where there is in fact a syllabic consonant; however, this is a spelling convention only. Syllabic consonants are transcribed with a small vertical line under the syllabic consonant sound. Syllabic [n̩] and [l̩] occur following stressed syllables ending in alveolar consonants, most frequently /t/, /d/, and /n/:

Syllabic [n̩]		**Syllabic [l̩]**	
kitt<u>en</u>	[kiʔn̩]	kett<u>le</u>	[kɛɾl̩]
butt<u>on</u>	[bʌʔn̩]	litt<u>le</u>	[lɪɾl̩]
did<u>n</u>'t	[dɪdn̩t]	lad<u>le</u>	[leyɾl̩]
should<u>n</u>'t	[ʃʊdn̩t]	tunn<u>el</u>	[tʌnl̩]

A consonant sound often anticipates some following sound. Both /t/ (in words like *butt<u>on</u>* and *kitt<u>en</u>*) and /d/ (in words like *su<u>dd</u>en* and *ha<u>dn</u>'t*) exhibit unusual medial variants before syllabic [n̩]. The /t/ is either glottalized (articulated with a momentary blockage of the airstream in the vocal cords) or it is replaced by a *glottal stop* [ʔ], which is a sound formed by stopping the airstream at the vocal cords. When the consonant /t/ or /d/ is produced before syllabic [n̩], the air used to produce the stop is released through the nose rather than the mouth. Because of these articulatory differences, words with medial /t/ and /d/ before syllabic [n̩] are clearly distinguishable, for example, *su<u>dd</u>en* vs. *Su<u>tt</u>on*, *bi<u>dd</u>en* vs. *bi<u>tt</u>en*.

Before syllabic [l̩] both /t/ and /d/ are usually realized as a laterally released flap [ɾ] (i.e., the flap is released by lowering one or both sides of the tongue for air to escape as the syllabic [l̩] is produced). Words with medial /t/ and /d/ before syllabic [l̩] are therefore not consistently distinguished; there are very few minimal pairs to cause confusion (e.g., *pe<u>t</u>al/pe<u>dd</u>le*, *me<u>t</u>al/me<u>dd</u>le*, or family names such as *Li<u>ttl</u>e/Li<u>ddl</u>e*).

---

[19]In fact, some phoneticians maintain that /m/, /ŋ/, and /r/ also have syllabic allophones. However, since syllabic [n̩] and [l̩] are more frequent and also have a significant effect on the pronunciation of the preceding consonant, we restrict our discussion of syllabic consonants to these two consonant sounds only.

TABLE 3.4 DIFFERENT QUALITIES OF /l/ IN NAE

Lightest /l/ ←———————————————————————→ Darkest [ł]

-ly suffix	Initial position	Initial clusters	Final position	Final clusters[a]
timely	Lee, Lou	clear	fill, fall	fault
dearly	lip, look	glib	pill, pull	bulk
badly	late, loss	blink	well, wool	holes

[a]Darkest [ł] in cluster configuration generally follows back vowels or co-occurs with a velar consonant.

LIGHT VERSUS DARK /l/

In Table 3.2, we listed two variants of /l/, alveolar light (or clear) /l/ and velarized dark [ł].[20] Generally light /l/ occurs syllable-initially or before front vowels and is produced with the tip of the tongue in the alveolar area (e.g., *leap, lip*), whereas dark [ł] occurs syllable-finally or before back vowels and is produced with the body of the tongue approaching the velum (e.g., *full, hole*). In other words, the closer the tongue to the velum, the darker the /l/.

In fact, there is a great deal of variation among native speakers of NAE in where /l/ may be produced. The general tendency in NAE is to use the so-called dark [ł], with varying degrees of "darkness" in different positions. Table 3.4 represents this continuum.

> #### NOTE TO TEACHERS
>
> Many problems can be anticipated in teaching the correct pronunciation of American /l/. Students from certain Asian backgrounds will have problems hearing and producing the /l/ vs. /r/ distinction in all positions, since these sounds may not be distinctive phonemes in their languages. Others (e.g., many speakers of European languages) will have difficulty producing dark [ł] and will use light /l/ in all environments. Some learners will omit final /l/ and /l/ in clusters altogether, and others (e.g., speakers of Brazilian Portuguese) will tend to produce postvocalic /l/ as a vowel resembling /o/ or /u/.

Nineteen of the twenty-five NAE consonant phonemes can occur freely in initial, medial, and final positions. However, they may differ significantly in articulation depending on where they occur in a word or syllable, as we have noted in the preceding discussion of their allophones.

We have also introduced several additional symbols in our discussion of positional variation (note: C = any consonant; V = any vowel):

Symbol	Description
[Cʰ]	aspirated consonant
[C°]	unreleased consonant
[V:]	lengthened vowel
[ɾ]	flap
[Ç]	syllabic consonant
[ʔ]	glottal stop
[ł]	velarized or dark /l/

[20]The best examples of light /l/ can be found in languages other than English. If one compares the light /l/ used in all environments in German (e.g., *Licht* "light," *viel* "much, many") or in French (e.g., *lit* "bed," *île* "island") with the kinds of /l/ that native speakers of NAE produce in virtually any position, one can appreciate the difference between light /l/ and dark [ł]. In fact, the dark quality of /l/ used by NAE speakers when they speak these two languages contributes significantly to their foreign accent.

THE EFFECT OF ENVIRONMENT: PEDAGOGICAL PRIORITIES

Given the preceding discussion, it is obviously important for students to understand how the articulation of a given consonant varies according to where it occurs – in other words, they need to be made aware of the role of positional variation. For example, the difference between /p, t, k/ and /b, d, g/ is initially explained to students as a function of voicing. However, when these sounds come at the beginning of a word, the feature of aspiration becomes very significant. Other effects of positional variation include vowel lengthening, released versus unreleased stop consonants, the flap allophone, and syllabic consonants.

The flap allophone of /t/ and /d/, being a distinct feature of NAE, would be a priority in situations where this variety is being taught. For example, students often complain that when ordering water in a restaurant, they are not understood and have to repeat their request. This is probably a function of their not producing the flap allophone of /t/. Since this distinction is not present in many dictionaries (especially the small bilingual dictionaries), students never discover it. Anecdotes of this nature emphasize the critical need for an awareness of positional variation and a teaching agenda that addresses this need.

PRESENTING INITIAL AND MEDIAL STOP CONSONANTS TO STUDENTS

To convey the concept of aspiration in initial stop consonants to students, hold a match or a light piece of paper in front of your mouth. Demonstrate the noticeable puff of air that accompanies initial /p, t, k/ while saying the following pairs of words:[21]

	/p, b/	/t, d/	/k, g/
Aspiration	pat	tan	cave
No aspiration	bat	Dan	gave

You will notice that the airstream bends down slightly, so that you should hold the paper slightly below the mouth. The flame or piece of paper should flutter during the pronunciation of words in the first row but not in the second. The aspiration may even blow out the match. Students should then try this themselves. This distinction can be important for students who speak languages such as Arabic, French, Italian, and Spanish, in which initial voiceless stops are not aspirated.

You may want to follow up this demonstration with a listening discrimination task, perhaps using pictures instead of sentences (Figure 3.8). This task could also be turned into a controlled speaking/listening activity for groups of three to four students. In each group, the students should secretly mark the pictures they will pronounce when it is their turn. Then, one at a time, each student reads the preselected words while the remaining group members circle the picture of the word they hear. The listeners then tell the speaker what they marked (i.e., heard) as feedback. If the listeners all agree, then any discrepancies are most likely due to a mispronunciation. If the listeners disagree, you may have to intervene to determine whether the speaker or the listener is mistaken.

For more contextualized practice, students can read and perform dialogues, such as:

Pam: Do you have the time, Beth?
Beth: No, I don't, Pam. I don't have any money at all!
Pam: I don't need a *dime*, Beth; I need the *time*.
Beth: Oh, I see. It's about ten after ten.
Pam: Well, I need to go pick up my coat at the cleaners. See you later, Beth.
Beth: Bye, Pam. Take care, and say hi to Ted for me.

---

[21]In the case of /t/ vs. /d/, place the match or paper lower toward the chin since the articulation of these initial consonants will direct the air in a downward direction. For /k/, remember that this is a velar consonant and therefore the puff of air will be less than for /p/.

Directions: Circle the picture of the word you hear.

1.
2.
3.
4.
5.
6.
7.
8.
9.

Figure 3.8 Minimal pair listening discrimination with pictures

With medial stop consonants, students need to be aware of stressed versus unstressed syllables in order to determine which medial voiceless stops are aspirated and which are not. For example, you may write the following words on the board:

apartment   botanical

Students should say these two words aloud and try to see if a strip of paper held in front of their mouths moves as they pronounce the second syllable. Since these voiceless stops come at the beginning of a stressed syllable, they are aspirated in the same way as an initial voiceless consonant.

Not all medial voiceless consonants are aspirated, however. The following examples illustrate this:

bumper   baking

For these examples, the strip of paper held in front of the mouth should not flutter noticeably. The medial voiceless consonant in this case falls at the beginning of an unstressed syllable. Next you can write the words *paper* and *cooking* on the board and ask students, "Are the two /p/'s the same? What about the two /k/'s?" Students can check for aspiration using their strips of paper; they should be able to provide the explanation that only the two initial stop consonants are aspirated, since they come at the beginning of a stressed syllable. This brief awareness-raising activity serves to alert students to the role of position and syllable stress in determining the aspiration of voiceless consonants.

Figure 3.9 shows a listening discrimination exercise that asks students to listen as the words on the list are read aloud. Their task is to decide if the underlined sound is aspirated or not.

		Aspirated	Not aspirated
Example:	photography	X	
1.	mechanical		
2.	upper		
3.	particular		
4.	wrapper		
5.	cooking		
6.	potato		
7.	opinion		
8.	packet		
9.	support		
10.	return		

Figure 3.9 Listening discrimination exercise for aspiration

PRESENTING THE FLAP ALLOPHONE TO STUDENTS

Whereas the British pronounce *water, better,* and *bitter* with an unaspirated voiceless /t/, Americans normally voice and flap any medial *t* that:

1. comes at the beginning of an unstressed syllable and

2. occurs between voiced sounds.

This voicing and quick tongue flap [ɾ] on the alveolar ridge produces a sound more like a quick /d/ than /t/. Thus, common words such as *water, butter, getting, party,* and *pretty* may sound to nonnative speakers as if they are being pronounced with a /d/ instead of a /t/.

One way of presenting this feature is to have students analyze a group of words containing medial -*t*. Begin by having students listen to the following two columns of words. How is /t/ pronounced differently in the following pairs?

	[ɾ]	[t/tʰ]
1.	forty	fourteen
2.	atom	atomic
3.	matter	master

For advanced students, it is useful to have them try to deduce the rules for the flap allophone [ɾ] based on these examples. In the first two sets of words, the distinction appears to be that /ɾ/ comes at the beginning of an unstressed syllable. However, in the third pair, both /t/ allophones (flap [ɾ] and unaspirated medial [t]) fall at the beginning of an unstressed syllable. Thus, a second condition must be met: namely, position between two voiced sounds (not simply between two vowels, as is evident in *forty*).

Examples of flap [ɾ] abound in grammatical contexts. Thus, teaching these grammatical forms can include reference to the many cases of flap [ɾ]:

• In regular past tense verbs and past participles ending in /t/:

-ate	*-ite*	*-ute*	*-ote*	*-ete*	*-eat*
educated	excited	contributed	noted	completed	defeated
related	invited	distributed	voted	secreted	repeated
stated	ignited				
negotiated	united				

- In the comparative and superlative forms of adjectives ending in /t/:

-er	*-est*
greater	shortest
smarter	brightest
neater	sweetest

- In the -*ing* form of verbs ending in /t/:

getting	meeting
putting	eating
sitting	writing

Teachers can also incorporate flap [ɾ] when discussing word forms and endings. The following examples illustrate such occurrences of flap [ɾ]:

- In agent nouns ending in -*er* (derived from verbs):

writer	voter
waiter	babysitter
batter	heater

- In nouns ending in -*ity:*

quality   activity   ability   gravity

It is important to note that flap [ɾ] occurs not only within words but also across word boundaries:

- In questions beginning with *what* followed by an auxiliary verb:

What   +   { is / am / are }   What   +   { (h)ave / (h)as / (h)ad }   (in reduced speech)

- In phrasal verbs ending in /t/:

Get   +   { up / on / in / off }

Hit / Put / Heat / Beat / Shut / Cut / Get / Set   +   it   +   { up / out / away / in / on / over / off }

- In many phrases with prepositions:

a bit of	upset at
a lot of	not at all
the rate of	
the state of	
sort of	

Find the Flap [ɾ]

Directions: In the following passage, circle the instances in which an American speaker would be likely to pronounce a /t/ so that it sounds like a /d/:

Example: He wai(t)ed for me on the corner.

1	What are we going to do today? Well, we're starting
2	with a quiz. You won't have to do any actual writing but
3	you will have to recognize the flaps in this piece of
4	writing. This is an activity to help you analyze a part
5	of pronunciation in English. But if you have trouble
6	finding flaps, then what is the best strategy for
7	completing the quiz? First, it would be a great idea if
8	you located the occurrences of *t* and then decided if the
9	two conditions apply. Of course, you may find a lot of
10	*t*'s that are not at all pronounced like /d/. I hope
11	you won't get upset about all the letter *t*'s. It's not
12	really so complicated. I believe in your capability.
13	Good luck!

Figure 3.10 Analysis activity for locating flap [ɾ]

As an analysis activity, intermediate to advanced students can be asked to locate the flap [ɾ] in a text (Figure 3.10). Once students have predicted where the flap occurs, they can compare answers with a partner. Then the class as a whole can compare answers. Ask questions like "How many flap *t*'s did you find in line 3?" Finally, you can read the passage, so that students can resolve any conflicts and listen for the flaps.

High-beginning to intermediate students can work with the following dialogue for controlled practice:

Betty: Peter, what are you doing tonight?
Peter: Nothing exciting, Betty. What about you?
Betty: Well, Sally and I are meeting some students from our class at a restaurant downtown. Can you come?
Peter: What time?
Betty: Oh, about eight o'clock.
Peter: Sounds great! A lot better than eating at home! Thanks for inviting me.

To use the dialogue activity most effectively, have students:

1. Try to predict the occurrences of flap [ɾ].
2. Listen to the dialogue on tape and check their predictions.
3. Compare answers with a partner.
4. Check answers with the teacher.
5. Perform the dialogue with a partner.

In order to practice the flap in a less controlled manner, you can use the following activity. "What Are They Doing?" is an information gap activity in which students work in pairs. Each student has the same blank grid to begin with (as in Figure 3.11, without the X markings). Along the vertical axis, four people are listed – in this case, people whose names contain a flap [ɾ]. At the top along the horizontal axis, four actions are depicted, all involving verbs which end in /t/ creating a flap [ɾ] environment in the present progressive.

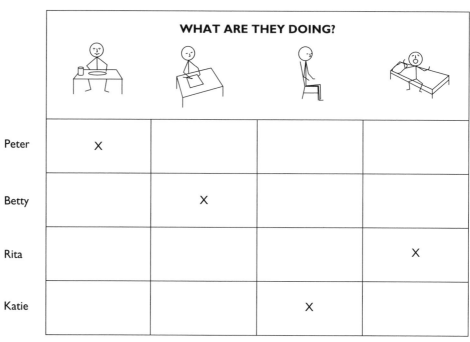

Figure 3.11 Information gap activity for practicing flap [ɾ]

The first step is for both members of the pair to mark four boxes secretly with an X. These can be any of the sixteen boxes – all in one row or column, or randomly spread across the grid, as shown in Figure 3.11. Keeping this information from their partners, students then try to identify which four boxes their partners have marked by asking questions. For example, if Maria and Minh are paired and Maria has marked her box as in Figure 3.11, Minh might ask, "Is Peter eating?" Maria might answer, "Yes, he is," and Minh would then take another turn.[22] If he next asks, "Is Rita sitting?" then Maria answers "No, Rita's not sitting," and Minh forfeits his turn to Maria. The game continues until one partner wins by discovering all four of the other's X's.

PRESENTING FINAL CONSONANTS TO STUDENTS

Like consonants in initial and medial positions, consonants in final position can differ in pronunciation from those same consonants produced in isolation. A good way to introduce the articulation of final consonants to students is to present the example of *bus* vs. *buzz*. If students are asked what the major difference in sound is between these two words, they will most likely focus on the /s/ vs. /z/ distinction, perhaps mentioning the voiced/voiceless difference if they are familiar with this concept. However, it should be pointed out that native speakers discriminate two such words more on the basis of vowel length than on the final consonant difference. The voiceless stops /p, t, k/, the fricatives /f, s, ʃ, θ/, and the affricate /tʃ/ in final position are all preceded by a shorter vowel sound than their voiced counterparts /b, d, g/, /v, z, ʒ, ð/, and /dʒ/. Thus, the learner needs to practice lengthening the vowel preceding these latter voiced consonants when they occur in final position.

---

[22]More advanced students could be encouraged to create more complex sentences, such as "Peter is eating pancakes for breakfast" or "Katie is writing a letter to her aunt."

Voiceless final consonant (shorter vowel)		Voiced final consonant (longer vowel)	
/p/	cap	/b/	cab
/t/	hit	/d/	hid
/k/	back	/g/	bag
/f/	fife	/v/	five
/s/	bus	/z/	buzz
/ʃ/	rush	/ʒ/	rouge[23]
/θ/	teeth	/ð/	teethe
/tʃ/	batch	/dʒ/	badge

Another feature that should be pointed out is force of articulation. The voiceless fricatives and the affricates are articulated with greater length and force in final position than are their voiced counterparts. A visual way of representing the interplay of vowel length, consonant length, and force of articulation on the board is the following:

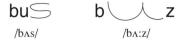

/bʌs/   /bʌːz/

Other pairs of words appropriate for contrasting vowel length, consonant length, and force of articulation include *safe/save, place/plays, teeth/teethe,* and *rich/ridge.*

With stop consonants in final position, the nonrelease of the consonant should be noted. These example sentences illustrate this nonrelease for the voiceless stops:

Wow! The buttons look like they're going to po<u>p</u>! *(lips remain closed)*
Yeah, it's just not going to fi<u>t</u>. *(tongue remains on the alveolar ridge)*
I'm going to take it ba<u>ck</u>. *(back of tongue remains on velum)*

Information about consonants in final position is summarized in Table 3.5.

TABLE 3.5 CONSONANTS IN FINAL POSITION

Type of final consonant	Voiced or voiceless	Example	Tran- scription	Vowel lengthened?	Final consonant unreleased?	Final consonant longer and more forcefully articulated?
Fricative and affricate	Voiced	*eyes, ridge*	/ay:z/ /rɪ:dʒ/	Yes	No	No
	Voiceless	*ice, rich*	/ays/ /rɪtʃ/	No	No	Yes
Stop	Voiced	*cab*	/kæ:b°/	Yes	Yes	No
	Voiceless	*cap*	/kæp°/	No	Yes	No

[23]There are no minimal pairs for /ʃ/ and /ʒ/. The near-minimal pair used here serves to illustrate the difference in vowel length.

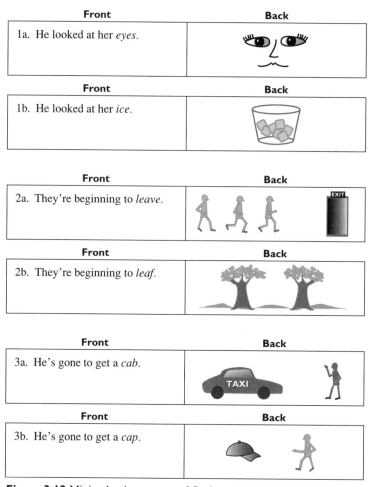

Figure 3.12 Minimal pair contrasts of final consonants
(based on Bowen 1972)

Bowen (1972) devised an enjoyable exercise to practice these final consonant distinctions. For this activity, first make pairs of index cards with drawings representing minimal pair contrasts (Figure 3.12). On the front of the card is the minimal pair sentence; on the back is a visual that cues the minimal pair.

Holding one index card in each hand with the picture facing the students, read one of the two sentences at random while students point to the picture corresponding to the correct sentence. Next, have students agree on a meaningful gesture with which they can associate each of the two sentences. In example 1, the two gestures could be pointing to one's eyes and shaking an imaginary glass with ice cubes in it. Then ask students to perform the gesture corresponding to the sentence uttered rather than to point to the correct picture. Once a majority of students can clearly discriminate between the two sentences, call for a volunteer to come to the front of the class. After making sure that the volunteer knows the two sentences by heart, move to the back of the classroom. All students except the volunteer should be facing the front of the class at this point. Make the gesture or hold up one of the two index cards (which only the volunteer in front can see); the volunteer should utter the correct sentence. The rest of the students signal their comprehension by performing the gesture corresponding to the sentence they have understood. Both you and the volunteer can immediately see which sentence has been understood by observing the class response. Thus, the volunteer receives immediate feedback from peers on his or her pronunciation.

PRESENTING SYLLABIC CONSONANTS TO STUDENTS

Syllabic [n̩] and [l̩] need to be presented to students as a special type of consonant in English. They should know that syllabic consonants occur when syllable-final /t/, /d/, or /n/ is followed by unstressed /l/ or /n/. These latter consonants then take on the quality of an entire syllable – without the articulation of a vowel. The following diagram illustrates this phenomenon for students:

$$
\left.\begin{array}{c} t \\ d \\ n \end{array}\right\} \quad + \quad \text{unstressed} \quad \left\{\begin{array}{c} l \\ n \end{array}\right. \quad = \quad \text{syllabic}
$$

Students should be made aware of the fact that all of these sounds are alveolar: that is, the front of the tongue touches the alveolar ridge to form them.

You can begin showing how syllabic [n̩] is articulated in an example word like *cotton*. Have students first say *cot* with an unreleased final [t°].[24] With the tongue still touching the alveolar ridge (you should open your mouth to show this tongue position), the unreleased [t°] is transformed into an [n̩] by moving the air blocked in the mouth out through the nose to form the nasal sound.

Syllabic [l̩] can be described in a similar way. To have students produce NAE *battle*, tell them to say the first syllable /bæt/ and hold the front of the tongue on the ridge behind the upper front teeth. At this point the airflow will be momentarily blocked by the tongue touching the tooth ridge. Then tell them to release air out over the sides of their tongue to form [l̩], never allowing the tongue to move away from the alveolar ridge.[25]

Productive contexts for practicing syllabic [n̩] and [l̩] include names of families, locations, past participles, and negative contractions:

Family names:	Benton, Barton, Newton, Norton, Little, Kettle, Huddleston
Locations:	Battle Creek, Seattle, Little Rock, Britain, Baton Rouge, Rocky Mountains, Staten Island
Past participles:	bitten, eaten, forgotten, hidden, written, beaten, ridden
Negative contractions:	didn't, couldn't, wouldn't, hadn't, shouldn't

Two stories about a family's travels can be used first as listening comprehension practice, then as a stimulus for production. Begin by drawing an outline of the United States on the blackboard and eliciting an approximate location for each city mentioned in the story (see Figure 3.13). Give students a map outline on a worksheet, or have them copy the map outline on a piece of paper. Then read them the story, which provides practice with syllabic [l̩]. Students listen and write the name of each person next to the appropriate place name. Finally, have students retell the story to the class.

---

[24]Many speakers may use a glottal stop in this position, for example pronouncing *cotton* as [kɑʔn̩].
[25]Note that the flap in *battle* is laterally released and therefore different from the one described earlier in words like *city* and *ladder*.

From Seattle to Brattleboro: The Battle Family

Teacher's script: Jane Battle lives in Seattle, Washington. Her brother, Herb Battle, lives in Little Rock, the capital of Arkansas. Her sister, Marge Battle, lives in Brattleboro, Vermont. The Battles live so far apart, they hardly ever get to see each other.

Task: First, try to place the following cities in the proper location.

Little Rock, Arkansas

Brattleboro, Vermont

Seattle, Washington

As you listen to the story, match the following names to the proper city:

Marge Battle

Jane Battle

Herb Battle

Figure 3.13 Story activity for practicing syllabic [ḷ]

Using the same procedure and the information in Figure 3.14, a similar tale can be told about the Bentons from Britain to practice syllabic [ṇ]. After filling in the map, students should move toward oral practice of syllabic [ṇ] and answer the following questions aloud:

1.   What is the Bentons' route on their trip? *(Show this on the map.)*

2.   Who lives in Canton?

3.   Where does Betty Newton live?

4.   Who lives in Baton Rouge?

5.   Which mountain range will they visit?

6.   Do you know any other mountains in the United States?

The Bentons From Britain

Teacher's script: The Benton family has just arrived from Great Britain to visit
their relatives in the United States. Their first stop is in Scranton, Pennsylvania, to
visit Mrs. Benton's sister, Betty, and Betty's husband, Bill Newton. Next they will
travel to Canton, Ohio, to visit Mr. Benton's brother, Bob, and then go south to Baton
Rouge, Louisiana, to visit their long-forgotten aunt, Sue Hardin. Since they also want
to go out west, they will fly to the Rocky Mountains before returning home.

Task: First, try to place the following cities in the proper location.

Canton, Ohio

Rocky Mountains

Scranton, Pennsylvania

Baton Rouge, Louisiana

As you listen to the story, match the following names to the proper city:

Betty and Bill Newton

Bob Benton

Sue Hardin

Figure 3.14 Story activity for practicing syllabic [n̩]

Another context for syllabic [n̩] can be combined with verb tense instruction. As
Bowen (1972) illustrates, the negative modal perfect offers a natural context for practicing syllabic [n̩]. As part of a grammar lesson, students might be instructed that when we
conclude that something in the past was impossible, we often say, "It *couldn't have*
/kʊdn̩rəv/ happened." Similarly, if we (or others) do something and later regret it, we
often say, "We (or they) *shouldn't have* /ʃʊdn̩rəv/ done it." Have students work in pairs
to complete the worksheet in Figure 3.15 and then read the mini-dialogues aloud. This
exercise is rich in syllabic [n̩] contexts – both the modal forms (e.g., *shouldn't have*,
couldn't have) and other instances (*important, eaten, forgotten*) – thus helping to point out
the frequent contexts for this feature of spoken NAE.

Directions: Respond to the following situations with a sentence using *shouldn't have* or *couldn't have.*

1. A: The phone rang but I was unable to reach it in time. No one called back. Do you think it was important?
    B: No, it _____

    (couldn't have been important)

2. A: Bob ate ten hot dogs at the baseball game and now he's sick.
    B: He _____
    (shouldn't have eaten so many hot dogs)

3: A: My birthday's today, and I haven't received a card from my mother. Do you think she forgot?
    B: No, she _____

    (couldn't have forgotten)

4. A: Our dog Fido bit our kitten and now he's not allowed indoors.
    B: He _____
    (shouldn't have bitten the kitten)

5. A: Betty got home very late last night and now she can't wake up.
    B: She _____
    (shouldn't have gotten home so late)

6. A: My friend Françoise received a letter from Bob in French, but Bob doesn't *know* French. Do you think he wrote it himself?
    B: No, he _____
    (couldn't have written it himself)

Figure 3.15 Mini-dialogues for practicing syllabic [ŋ]

CONSONANT CLUSTERS: WHAT THE TEACHER NEEDS TO KNOW

Because consonants are greatly affected by their position in a word or syllable, we preface the treatment of consonant clusters with a brief discussion of syllable structure. The most general or universal type of syllable structure among the languages of the world is CV, or a syllable composed of a consonant sound followed by a vowel sound.[26] As the following examples show, many English words of one syllable follow this pattern. (Do not be overly concerned about the vowel transcriptions used here. Vowel sounds will be presented and discussed in the next chapter.)

CV PATTERN: ENGLISH WORDS

s<u>ee</u>	/siy/
p<u>ay</u>	/pey/
b<u>uy</u>	/bay/
<u>you</u>	/yuw/

[26]It is even possible to have a one-syllable word that consists of only a single vowel sound: *eye, oh, ow.*

Notice that each of these words consists of two sounds only: the initial consonant sound and the subsequent underlined vowel sound (which, although sometimes represented here by combinations of two letters or two symbols in the phonemic alphabet, such as the *ee* or /iy/ for *see,* is in reality only one vowel sound).

However, many one-syllable English words follow the pattern CVC, or a syllable composed of a consonant followed by a vowel, followed by a consonant. This is the next most common type of syllable structure found among the languages of the world.[27]

CVC PATTERN: ENGLISH WORDS

s<u>ee</u>m	/siym/
p<u>ai</u>d	/peyd/
b<u>i</u>te	/bayt/
d<u>i</u>p	/dɪp/
b<u>e</u>d	/bɛd/
m<u>a</u>t	/mæt/
b<u>oo</u>k	/bʊk/
g<u>oa</u>l	/gowl/
z<u>oo</u>m	/zuwm/

Not all English vowel phonemes can occur in the CV syllable pattern, but all can occur in the CVC pattern. In English syllables, vowels form the core whereas consonants occur at the outer limits, thus forming a package or a container for the vowels.

English has a distinct propensity for **consonant clustering,** in which two or more consonants occur in sequence in syllable-initial or syllable-final position.[28] In word-initial position there are many clusters of two consonants in English and even some with three. With clusters of two, either the first sound is /s/ or the second one is an approximant (/l/, /r/, /w/, or /y/); in some instances both conditions hold:

Two: /sn-/ <u>sn</u>ake; /sp-/ <u>sp</u>eak; /sk-/ <u>sk</u>y; /pl-/ <u>pl</u>ay;

/pr-/ <u>pr</u>ay; /kw-/ <u>qu</u>ite; /hy-/ <u>hu</u>e; /py-/ <u>pu</u>re;

/sl-/ <u>sl</u>ow; /sw-/ <u>sw</u>ift

With initial clusters of three consonants, the first sound is always /s/, the second sound is a voiceless stop (i.e., /p, t, k/), and the third sound is one of the four approximants (i.e., /l, r, w, y/).[29]

Three: /spl-/ <u>spl</u>ash; /str-/ <u>str</u>ong; /skw-/ <u>squ</u>are;

/sky-/ <u>sk</u>ew

---

[27]Again, notice that many single vowel sounds are represented in the spelling or transcription systems by combinations of letters or symbols. Also, notice that although the word *bite* ends with the letter *e,* this letter is silent, and serves only to influence the quality of the preceding vowel sound. Thus the word ends in a consonant rather than a vowel sound.

[28]For a complete listing of possible cluster configurations, see Prator and Robinett (1985).

[29]A voiceless stop that directly follows an initial /s/ is not aspirated. In fact, phonetically it is somewhat voiced in anticipation of the following approximant or vowel. The differences between /p, b/, /t, d/, or /k, g/ in this environment can therefore be described as neutralized. The voiceless stops are used in transcription as a convention since this follows the spelling pattern. Note also that /p, t, k/ generally have no aspiration within a word when they follow /s/ within the same syllable, even if the syllable is stressed: *a<u>sp</u>ire, a<u>st</u>ound, a<u>sk</u>ew.*

In final position there are many more consonant clusters than in initial position. These clusters can consist of two, three, or even four consonants. Many clusters of two or three and virtually all clusters of four are the result of adding a plural /s, z/ or past tense /t, d/ inflection to a stem ending in two or three consonants:

Two: /-lb/ bulb; /-md/ seemed; /-rv/ nerve;
            /-vz/ loves

Three: /-rts/ hearts; /-ldz/ builds; /-sks/ asks;
            /-mpt/ tempt

Four: /-mpts/ tempts; /-ksts/ texts;
            /-ltst/ waltzed

PRODUCING CONSONANT CLUSTERS

When we discussed the effect of environment on consonant quality earlier, we did not say much about what happens to consonants in clusters. But occurrence within a cluster can, not surprisingly, have an effect on the quality of a consonant. We have already seen this in clusters of /s/ + voiceless stop, in which the voiceless stop is not aspirated.

In clusters where the first consonant is voiceless and the second voiced, the voiced consonant (e.g., /n/ in snack, /r/ in through, /w/ in twin) is often partially devoiced. This happens especially in words with /r/ or /l/ in initial clusters:

preach, treat, pray

sly, close, play

What occurs here is a form of assimilation, a process treated in more depth in Chapter 5. Additionally, syllable-initial /tr/ before a stressed vowel (as in tree or true) shows an interaction between the stop action and the aspiration of /t/ and the tongue position and potential lip rounding of /r/. This interaction causes the /tr/ cluster to take on affricatelike qualities that could be transcribed [tʃr].[30]

Another example of assimilation in clusters involves anticipation of the final consonant in an initial cluster. In the cluster /kw/ of quick, for example, a native English speaker will anticipate the /w/ by putting the lips into position for the /w/ before releasing the /k/.

---

[30]For some NAE speakers, this tendency toward affrication also carries over to initial /dr/ clusters. For these speakers, the initial clusters in dream, dry, draw begin to approach [dʒr] in sound.

In final clusters of two consonants, note that when the cluster consists of two stops, the first of the two tends to be unreleased and the second (which is often an inflection) released. For example:

opt [p°t]; act [k°t]; robbed [b°d]; begged [g°d]

However, when the final sequence is a liquid + a stop, it is the final stop that tends to be unreleased – as with final stops after a vowel:

bulb [lb°]; build [ld°]; bird [rd°]; iceberg [rg°]

Even for native speakers, it is not always easy to pronounce two or more consonants together. As a result, they employ certain strategies to make consonant clusters easier to pronounce.

To simplify final clusters, native speakers frequently use the strategy of **cluster reduction.** In other words, they omit one of the consonants in order to make the cluster easier to pronounce. Usually, in final clusters of three or four consonants, it is a middle consonant that is dropped. This strategy is often used by native speakers to simplify clusters created by the addition of grammatical endings, as in the simplification of *asked* /æskt/ to /æst/ or *facts* /fækts/ to /fæks/. It is regularly employed when pronouncing fractions such as *sixths* (reduction of /sɪksθs/ to /sɪks/) or *fifths* (reduction of /fɪfθs/ to /fɪfs/).

Another simplification strategy native speakers use is **resyllabification**. This strategy involves breaking up a final consonant cluster when it is followed by a word beginning with a vowel sound. In this case, the final consonant of the cluster is moved over to the next syllable. For example, in the following phrases, a native speaker will usually pronounce the syllables thus:

She moved it. /ʃi·muwv·dɪt/

He cleaned Art's office. /hi·kliyn·dɑrt·sɔfɪs/

NOTE TO TEACHERS

Learners' pronunciation errors vary in the production of consonant clusters.

Learners whose native language has a simpler syllable structure tend to do one of two things:

1. They may simplify English words by dropping final consonants altogether. They may especially show a tendency to drop important grammatical endings (for example, producing *car* in place of *cars* or *put* in place of *puts*). These students will need instruction on the importance of grammatical endings, and explanation of how native speakers simplify difficult syllable-final consonant configurations without dropping the grammatical markers. Learners from many Asian language backgrounds may delete final consonant clusters entirely; instead of pronouncing *"He has a cold"* /kowld/, a Chinese speaker might simply pronounce /kow/, leaving off the final cluster. Since the articulation of /l/ and /r/ is often challenging for Asian speakers, these two sounds are frequently deleted in clusters (initial or final): *problem* /prɑbləm/ might be articulated as /pɑbəm/, *program* /prowgræm/ as /powgæm/, or *world* /wɜrld/ as /wʊd/.

> 2. A second tendency is to simplify clusters by inserting extra vowels – thereby breaking up the cluster and creating more syllables. This may occur externally (either initially or finally) or internally (between the consonants in initial and final clusters):
>
> | External | sport | → | /ɛspɔrt/ |
> |----------|-------|---|----------|
> | | tempts | → | /tɛmptsu/ |
>
> | Internal | sport | → | /səpɔrt/ |
> |----------|-------|---|----------|
> | | watched | → | /watʃəd/ |
>
> Native Japanese speakers, for example, often produce a stream of CVCVCV syllables, for example, pronouncing *speak* /spiyk/ as /s(u)piku/. Spanish or Farsi speakers might also employ vowel insertion, especially in initial consonant clusters beginning with *s-*. In this case, a Spanish or Farsi learner usually inserts an initial vowel, thus pronouncing *school* /ɛskuwl/ or /əskuwl/, or *street* as /ɛstriyt/ or /əstriyt/.
>
> Some languages have very different consonant cluster configurations from English and require clusters to be either all voiced or all voiceless. For example, Italian speakers, while familiar with consonant clusters in their own language, have different rules governing their pronunciation. In clusters in which /s/ is followed by /l/, /m/, or /n/, English rules allow the voiceless quality of /s/ to predominate. In Italian, on the other hand, the *s-* is voiced by assimilation to the following more dominant consonant. Thus, Italian speakers, if relying on rules of their own language, will pronounce *sleep* as /zliyp/ or *small* as /zmɔl/.

CONSONANT CLUSTERS: PEDAGOGICAL PRIORITIES

Even if learners have gained a certain mastery over English consonants when produced singly, clusters often present a radical departure from the syllable structure rules of their native-language sound system, which (as mentioned previously) may not allow clusters at all, or may have a more limited distribution of clusters either initially or finally. This clustering of consonants makes English difficult to pronounce for speakers whose language follows simple CV or CVC syllable patterns with no consonant clusters. Of course, even in English, not all consonants can occur in all positions in a cluster. It is not necessarily the discrimination or articulation of a particular phoneme that poses the greatest difficulty for the learner; rather it is the perception or articulation of two, three, or even four consonants in a row.

Learners should be made aware that departures from the dictated cluster sequence in English can render their speech very difficult for native speakers to understand. This is especially true in cases where the learners break up cluster sequences in English (by inappropriately inserting a vowel) or omit a consonant in a cluster. If morphological endings are omitted, teachers should call attention to the possible stigmatizing effect that this may have – that is, the native speaker may conclude that the nonnative speaker does not "know" English grammar and thus may arrive at a false conclusion about this speaker's proficiency in English.

On the other hand, students should be encouraged to learn that they are not alone in having difficulty producing clusters: Native English-speaking children often have difficulty with /r/ clusters and compensate by substituting the semivowel /w/. Young children might, for example, pronounce *ice cream* as *ice kweam /ayskwiym/ instead of /ayskriym/. Although this type of substitution is not considered acceptable for older children or adults, learners should be made aware that there are acceptable strategies used by native speakers to simplify consonant clusters in certain systematic ways, as we have discussed. They should be taught these rules explicitly so that they too can employ them.

All of these reasons argue forcefully for including explanation of and practice with NAE consonant cluster sequences in the pronunciation curriculum and for teaching non-native speakers to employ the consonant simplification strategies of native speakers.

PRESENTING CONSONANT CLUSTERS TO STUDENTS

To properly lay the groundwork for teaching consonant clusters to students, teachers must first present some basic information about English syllable structure. English syllables can take the following shapes:

- A syllable can consist of minimally one vowel (as in *I* or *eye*).
- It can consist of a vowel with up to three initial consonants (e.g., *pie* /pay/, *spy* /spay/, *spry* /spray/)
- It can consist of a vowel with up to three final consonants (e.g., *at* /æt/, *ask* /æsk/, *asked* /æskt/)
- It can consist of a vowel with one or more initial consonants and up to four final consonants (e.g., *ten* /tɛn/, *tent* /tɛnt/, *tempt* /tɛmpt/, and *tempts* /tɛmpts/)
- It can consist of a vowel with almost the full range of possible initial and final clusters (e.g., /spl/ *splints* /nts/).

Although English syllable structure can potentially be CCCVCCCC, the only one-syllable example we have found of this is *strengths* when pronounced /strɛŋkθs/ with an epenthetic /k/.[31] The syllable structure of many other languages is much simpler, the simplest and most universal syllable structure being CV. This has important implications for teaching English consonant clusters to speakers of other languages.

It is helpful to summarize this information on the board. You can select common syllable configurations:

V	CV	VC	CVC	VCC	CCV	CVCC	CCVCC (etc.)
oh	see	it	but	arm	fly	silk	slips
eye	buy	us	rag	eats	snow	burn	trust

List several words under each category, enlisting students' help if they are proficient enough.

INITIAL CLUSTERS

We suggest beginning with the presentation of initial clusters because these tend to be easier for students to produce and also represent an environment in which no native-speaker simplification strategies apply. The diagram in Figure 3.16 can assist in raising consciousness about the possibilities for three-consonant initial clusters in English. Have

---

[31]For more information on epenthesis, see Chapter 5.

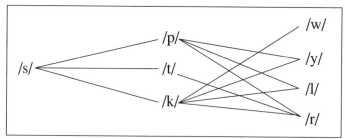

Figure 3.16 Possible combinations for three-consonant initial clusters; combinations with /skl/ (e.g., *sclerosis*) are very infrequent (Adapted from *Manual of American English Pronunciation*. Fourth Edition by Clifford H. Prator and Betty W. Robinett, copyright © 1985 by Holt, Rinehart and Winston, Inc., reproduced by permission of the publisher.)

students work in groups to come up with as many words as possible for each combination of two or three consonants.

Here is an example of what a group might generate:

Clusters of two		Clusters of three
play	spin	splash
crew	swim	stream
tree	skin	scratch

This word-generation activity can be done as a contest with a time limit – the true goal being to have students generate words from their active vocabulary. As groups read off their lists, it will become clear whether certain combinations pose any difficulty for the students.

Appendix 4, which summarizes English syllable structure and initial and final consonant clusters in a concise visual form, can also be used with learners to review and practice consonant clusters.

In remediating problems with initial consonant cluster articulation, it should be pointed out to students that initial clusters cannot be simplified. It is also helpful to discuss the kinds of inappropriate cluster simplification strategies they are using, such as insertion of vowels to break up difficult clusters, insertion of initial /ɛ/ or /ə/, or omission of a given consonant in the sequence.

For the first of these problems, getting students to discriminate lists of minimal pairs like the following can help bring home the point that in English, inserting a vowel in a cluster sequence can potentially change the meaning of the word:

CC-	CVC-
train	terrain
sport	support
scum	succumb
star	sitar

This type of listening discrimination exercise can be done writing the pairs of words on the board. Students can either (1) point to the word they hear or (2) listen to you pronounce two words in sequence (e.g., *scum, scum*) and identify whether these words are the same or different.

For the second type of nonnative simplification strategy in initial consonant sequences (i.e., insertion of /ɛ/ or /ə/ initially), have students focus on the initial /s/ and consciously lengthen it before pronouncing the rest of the cluster:

state	school	Spanish
/ssssteyt/	/sssskuwl/	/sssspænɪʃ/

It should also be pointed out that in English, insertion of an initial vowel may produce a different word, as illustrated in the following pairs:

state	estate
sleep	asleep
steam	esteem
spree	esprit
stride	astride
strange	estrange

Students, notably native Spanish or Farsi speakers, may not be able to hear the distinction between these pairs of words. Therefore, you need to begin with a listening discrimination exercise to attune students' ears to the difference, then get them to practice the first column using an extended /ssss/ sound.

Once students' consciousness has been raised about the environments in which initial clusters occur and their ears have been attuned to listening for these consonant sequences, they can move on to production practice. The initial practice stage should focus on getting students to articulate the two or three consonants in the initial cluster.

Have students begin by building up the initial cluster gradually. Tell them to pronounce the word in the first column and then to anticipate this consonant in the second word. For example, have them pronounce *rain* several times, then anticipate the /r/ with their lips and mouth and rapidly pronounce *train:*

rain	train
lace	place
port	sport
come	scum
tar	star

To help them avoid inserting a schwa between two initial consonants, start with clusters containing consonant + /w/ sequences. Have students position their lips for the /w/ by rounding them and pushing them slightly outward. Then have them try to pronounce *twin, Dwight, question, swim,* and so on.

If students substitute a voiced /z/ sound for an initial /s/, again have them concentrate on lengthening the /s/ without voicing it, then pronounce the following consonant rapidly:

small	snack	slip
/sssmɔl/	/sssnæk/	/ssslɪp/

Students should choose several words that they wish to focus on and then practice them by building up the cluster gradually:

/l/ → /pl/ → /spl/
lash → plash → splash

/r/ → /tr/ → /str/
rap → trap → strap

Students can also use the word list they have created to write dialogues, chain stories, or role plays that incorporate these words.

FINAL CLUSTERS

Teaching final consonant clusters can proceed in much the same way as outlined for initial clusters. For example, having students gradually build up clusters allows them to gain mastery over final clusters of three or four consonants:

Clusters of three:

/ŋ/ → /ŋk/ → /ŋks/
thing → think → thinks

Clusters of four:

/k/ → /ks/ → /ksθ/ → /ksθs/
sick → six → sixth → sixths

The teaching of final consonant clusters deviates from the teaching of initial consonant clusters in the attention that needs to be paid to how native speakers simplify final cluster configurations. Some common examples that could be presented to students include the following:

Reduction			Example
skt	→	st	*asked* /æskt/ becomes /æst/
sks	→	ss	*asks* /æsks/ becomes /æss/
sts	→	ss	*lists* /lɪsts/ becomes /lɪss/
kts	→	ks	*facts* /fækts/ becomes /fæks/
pts	→	ps	*scripts* /skrɪpts/ becomes /skrɪps/

Fractions are also often reduced, losing the voiceless *th* /θ/:

Reduction			Example
fθs	→	fs	*fifths* /fɪfθs/ becomes /fɪfs/
ksθs	→	ks	*sixths* /sɪksθs/ becomes /sɪks/
ntθs	→	n(t)s	*tenths* /tɛntθs/ becomes /tɛn(t)s/

One essential point for students to note is that third person singular present tense and plural endings provide important grammatical signals and are never left off in order to simplify a cluster. Common plurals such as *months* /mʌntθs/ and *clothes* /klowðz/ are therefore never reduced by native speakers to /mʌn(t)θ/ and /klowð/ but rather to /mʌn(t)s/ and /klowz/.

After being presented with native speaker strategies for simplifying clusters, students should be given opportunities to practice these strategies themselves. A brief dialogue to practice one of these examples might be:

Ted: I couldn't finish the sixth problem.

Joe: That's because you forgot to reduce 6/6 (six/sixths) to 1.

The following dialogue also incorporates some examples of consonant clusters NAE speakers might reduce:

A TRIP TO THE VETERINARIAN

Vet: What seems to be the problem with Peppy?

Pet owner: Well, he just isn't very *peppy,* Doc. He <u>acts</u> so tired all the time. He just <u>lifts</u> his head up and sighs.

Vet: And this started two <u>months</u> ago? Can you give me some more <u>facts</u>?

Pet owner: Sure. One of Peppy's big <u>strengths</u> as a guard dog are his <u>bursts</u> of energy. I <u>asked</u> him to fetch the newspaper yesterday and he left three-<u>fourths</u> of it on the doorstep. What does your medical <u>textbook</u> say about that?

Vet: Well, let me look it up under "<u>listless</u> dogs." It says here that "four /<u>fifths</u> of all <u>listlessness</u> in dogs is due to poor diet." Why don't I give you some pep pills? Feed him one every day and we'll see how he <u>acts</u> next week.

More communicative activities for practicing final clusters include using the calendar page for the current month to practice final clusters in ordinals:

What's happening on the
$$\begin{cases} \text{fi}\underline{rst} \\ \text{seco}\underline{nd} \\ \text{thi}\underline{rd} \\ \text{(etc.)} \end{cases}$$
day of the month?

What's taking place on the
$$\begin{cases} \text{four}\underline{th}? \\ \text{thirty-fi}\underline{rst}? \end{cases}$$

Such calendar exercises can, of course, be designed as information gap activities to increase the amount of learner interaction.

Another activity appropriate at the university level or with working adults instructs learners to identify key English words from their field of study or occupation – at least five with initial clusters and five with final clusters. Then each learner presents a personal list to the class and makes a short oral presentation that includes at least eight of the words. Classmates should evaluate the speaker's production of consonant clusters as to how accurate, natural, and easily intelligible they sound.

CONCLUSION

In this discussion on the teaching of consonant sounds, it should be clear that although students may have difficulty with certain individual consonants or consonant contrasts, time should be spent on consonant sounds within words, phrases, and coherent discourse, since how consonants are pronounced in isolation may in fact be quite different from how they are articulated in real speech. In particular, the positional variation of English consonants (e.g., characteristics such as aspiration, released versus unreleased consonants, the flap allophone, syllabic consonants, and consonant cluster configurations and simplification strategies) may be quite unfamiliar to nonnative students.

EXERCISES

KEY CONCEPTS

Write a brief definition for the following key terms from this chapter and the Introduction to Part 2. Give examples where relevant.

segmental	manner of articulation
suprasegmental	stop/plosive
phoneme	fricative
allophone	affricate
contrastive distribution	continuant
positional variation	nasal
phonemic alphabet	approximant
voicing	liquid
oral cavity	glide/semivowel
nasal passageway	retroflex /r/
articulator	diphthong
uvula	aspiration
velum	released/unreleased
vocal cords	vowel length
larynx	flap/tap
alveolar ridge	sibilants
place of articulation	syllabic consonant
bilabial	glottal stop
labiodental	light/clear [l]
dental	dark/velarized [ɫ]
alveolar	consonant clustering
palatal	cluster reduction
velar	resyllabification
glottal	

INTROSPECTING ABOUT YOUR OWN LANGUAGE LEARNING

Think about a foreign language that you have learned in school or while living abroad.

1. What difficulties with consonant sounds did you have?

2. Were these difficulties typical for native speakers of your language? If so, what caused them?

3. What strategies did you use to improve your production of these sounds? Were these successful?

4. If you had language instruction, did the teacher try to help you with pronunciation? If so, how?

DISCUSSION QUESTIONS

1. What are the arguments for and against use of a phonemic alphabet to teach pronunciation?

2. What kinds of ESL/EFL learners would benefit from learning a phonemic alphabet for NAE consonants? What kinds of learners would not?

3. Why is it important to consider positional restrictions and variation when teaching NAE consonants to speakers of other languages? Use a specific consonant sound to illustrate your answer.

4. What differences might there be in the type of articulatory information that you would present to different groups of learners? Consider, for example, children learning English in school in their home country versus international teaching assistants at a North American university.

5. What kinds of consonant articulation problems could be helped by practice with mirrors?

6. Do you think certain consonant difficulties cause a greater breakdown in communication or are more irritating to native speakers than others? If so, which?

IN THE CLASSROOM

Assume that you are teaching pronunciation. Here are some common classroom situations that you might encounter. What technique would you use or what explanation would you give?

1. Your students consistently pronounce *this* as /dɪs/.

2. Your students produce /muwf/ instead of /muw:v/.

3. Your students pronounce *study* /ɛstʌdi/.

4. A student says: "When I learned English in my country, the teacher taught us to pronounce *water* with a /t/ sound. But I hear most Americans pronounce it with a /d/ sound. Which is correct?"

5. You are tutoring a businessman who imports silk flowers. One of his problems is that he pronounces *silk* as /sɪk/. This is causing him to lose business. What would you do to help him?

SUGGESTED ACTIVITIES

1. Locate a description of typical difficulties for the group of learners that you work with or anticipate working with. See for example Avery and Ehrlich (1992), Kenworthy (1987), and Swan and Smith (1987). What insights do you gain into the consonant challenges that this group will experience?

2. Suppose that you were going to tutor one of the two learners in item 6 in the section "On the Cassette" (page 92). What are the top five priorities you would select in terms of helping him or her improve control of the NAE consonant system? Develop an exercise for presenting and practicing the first and second priority.

3. Prepare materials for presenting and practicing one of the following consonant contrasts, each of which is a problem for certain groups of learners:

   /s, z/   /ʃ, tʃ/   /f, v/   /b, v/   /w, v/   /p, b/   /y, dʒ/

4. Develop a communicative activity to practice and reinforce one of the following teaching points:

   • aspiration of initial stop consonants
   • nonrelease of final stop consonants
   • vowel lengthening before final voiced consonants
   • approximating NAE /r/
   • distinguishing light [l] vs. dark [ɫ]

ON THE CASSETTE

1. For words 1–10 on the cassette, transcribe the initial consonant sound you hear.
2. For words 11–20, transcribe the final consonant sound.
3. For words 21–30, transcribe the intervocalic or medial consonant sound.
4. For words 31–40, transcribe the initial consonant cluster.
5. For words 41–50, transcribe the final consonant cluster.
6. Listen to the two spontaneous speech samples from nonnative speakers (several times if necessary), paying particular attention to consonant production. What problems do these speakers have with initial consonants? Final consonants? Intervocalic consonants? Do they have any consonant cluster difficulties?

CHAPTER 4

The Vowel System

Children from their earliest primary school days can name the vowels of the English alphabet: *a, e, i, o,* and *u*. Of course, defining vowel sounds and describing their phonetic properties is not as simple a matter as naming the five orthographic vowels. In fact, when we begin to examine the vowel sounds of North American English more scientifically, we find that there are at least fourteen distinct stressed vowel sounds rather than five, and that what constitutes a vowel is a somewhat contested issue.[1]

THE NAE VOWEL SYSTEM: WHAT THE TEACHER NEEDS TO KNOW

Before turning our attention to the production of NAE vowels, we first need to examine their characteristics and define how vowel sounds differ from their consonant counterparts. What is a **vowel**? An unscientific answer would be that vowels are the tools of poets, since it is vowels that allow poets to create assonance and rhyme, and thus to shape language musically and make it pleasing to the ear. A more scientific answer would be that vowels are the core or "peak" of the syllable. In fact, as we have seen, a syllable can consist minimally of one vowel (V) only, as in the word *eye* (V); alternatively, the vowel in a given syllable can also be surrounded on either or both sides by consonants (C), as in the words *bray* (CCV), *ants* (VCCC), and *pranks* (CCVCCC). Another way of describing vowels is to define them as sounds in which there is continual vibration of the vocal cords and the airstream is allowed to escape from the mouth in an unobstructed manner, without any interruption. These descriptions can help us to differentiate vowels from consonants, since in consonants vocal cord vibration can be interrupted and there is obstruction of the airflow when the various articulators approach each other. Also, a consonant cannot usually constitute the peak of a syllable.

One difficulty in describing vowels has already been alluded to – namely, that in the production of vowel sounds there is no contact of the articulators as there is in the production of consonant sounds. Therefore, the classification of vowels is not as clear-cut as that of consonants. Whereas consonants can be distinguished by place and manner of articulation and by features such as voicing and aspiration, the description of vowels is much

---

[1]The number of vowels and the transcription system chosen to represent these vowels will vary from text to text according to a number of factors: who does the analysis, what dialect of English is being described, what purpose the transcription system is to serve, and so on. In this text, we have chosen to define the number of discrete vowels in NAE that occur in stressed position as fourteen. Notationally, however, we will introduce a fifteenth symbol at a later point to address the issue of *r*-coloring. We will also introduce some additional symbols for reduced vowels.

more elusive. Voicing, for example, is not a distinguishing characteristic since all English vowels are voiced. Moreover, when we discussed consonant articulation, the flow of air was described as moving through a type of obstacle course that modified or blocked it completely. In contrast, vowels involve a relatively unobstructed airflow and take on their peculiar characteristics largely through changes in the shape and size of the oral cavity. Thus, in many respects, vowels can be more clearly delineated in relation to one another than in relation to any external standard of classification.

A CLASSIFICATION OF NAE VOWELS

Let us begin with an overview of the NAE vowel system. Eleven of the fourteen stressed vowels of NAE are either *simple vowels* (vowels without an accompanying glide movement, as in *bed* /ɛ/ or *put* /ʊ/) or vowels with an adjacent *glide* (vowels accompanied by /y/ or /w/, as in *pain* /ey/ or *stone* /ow/). The remaining three vowels are *diphthongs* (i.e., vowels consisting of a vowel sound followed by a nonadjacent glide within the same syllable, as in *boy*).

The eleven simple vowels and vowels with adjacent glides are as follows:

	Sound	Examples		Sound	Examples
1.	/iy/	heat, be	7.	/ʌ/	cut, son
2.	/ɪ/	fit, tin	8.	/ɔ/	thought, law
3.	/ey/	rain, may	9.	/ow/	sew, boat
4.	/ɛ/	get, hen	10.	/ʊ/	look, wool
5.	/æ/	cat, pan	11.	/uw/	blue, room
6.	/ɑ/	ma, hot			

You may have noticed that four of the eleven vowels consist of two symbols each: /iy, ey, ow, uw/. These symbols indicate that the vowel sounds in words like *green* and *rain* begin with /i/ and /e/, respectively, and then glide toward /y/. Similarly, the vowel sounds in words like *bowl* and *blue* begin with /o/ and /u/ and then glide toward /w/. Sometimes we refer to these four vowel sounds as vowel + glide sequences to capture this phonetic fact.

The three phonemic vowel diphthongs, all of which involve even greater movement from a vowel sound produced lower in the mouth to a glide produced higher in the mouth, are:

	Sound	Movement	Examples
12.	/ay/	low central to high front	pie, fine
13.	/aw/	low central to high back	blouse, how
14.	/ɔy/	low back to high front	boy, choice

THE VOWEL QUADRANT

As was stated, the position of the articulatory organs in the production of vowels is not as easily specified as that of consonants; however, as air from the lungs moves past the vibrating vocal cords and out through the oral cavity, the position of the various articulators acts to modify the vowel sound produced. If we think of the oral cavity as a resonance chamber, then the size and shape of this chamber can be modified by the movement of the tongue and the opening or closing of the jaw. Accordingly, vowel sounds can be distinguished from each other by which part of the tongue is involved (front, central, back) and by how high the tongue is when the sound is produced (high, mid, low). When describing /iy/ and /ɪ/, for example, we can speak of them as high front vowels since they are articulated with the front of the tongue high in the mouth near the front of the hard palate and with the jaw in a relatively closed position. The phoneme /ɑ/, on the other hand, is described as a low central vowel since it is articulated in the center of the mouth, with the tongue in its lowest position lying flat on the bottom of the mouth and the jaw in its most open position. These two dimensions are summarized in the stylized NAE *vowel quadrant* (Figure 4.1).

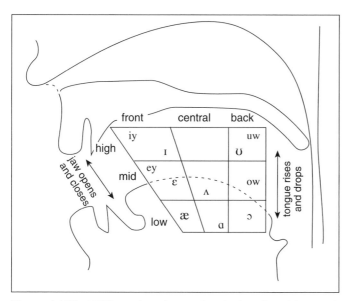

Figure 4.1 The NAE vowel quadrant and sagittal section of the mouth

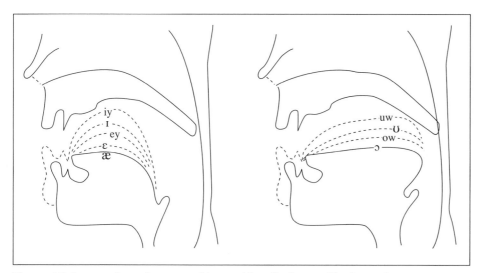

Figure 4.2 A comparison of tongue and jaw positions for front and back vowels

As Figure 4.1 illustrates, the volume of the oral cavity increases as the jaw opens, with the **high, mid,** and **low** sections of the vowel quadrant being differentiated both by the successive opening of the jaw and the lowering of the tongue. The position of the body of the tongue (which influences the shape of the oral cavity) is represented by the **front, central,** and **back** sections. Figure 4.2 shows the tongue and jaw movements (i.e., high to mid to low) of the front and back vowels.

ROUNDED VERSUS SPREAD VOWELS

Another very visible factor that characterizes the production of vowel sounds is lip position. Lip position can be described as **rounded** or **spread** (in varying degrees), or **neutral** (neither rounded nor spread). Although this feature cannot be represented in a side view of the mouth, it is nonetheless an additional determinant of vowel quality. Extreme

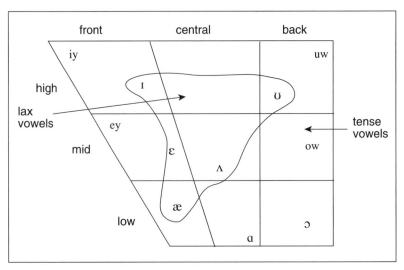

Figure 4.3 Tense versus lax vowels in NAE

rounding of the lips is present in the vowel phonemes /ow/ as in *low* and /uw/ as in *true*, whereas extreme spreading is present in /iy/ as in *she*. (See Table 4.2 on page 103 for a description of lip position and a summary of other NAE vowel characteristics.)

TENSE VERSUS LAX VOWELS

The final distinction we will make for vowels is *tense* versus *lax*. The tense vowels /iy, ey, ɑ, ɔ, ow, uw/ are articulated with more muscle tension than the lax vowels /ɪ, ɛ, æ, ʌ, ʊ/.[2] This added muscle tension serves to stretch the articulation of tense vowel sounds to more extreme peripheral positions in the mouth, making them less centered (see Figure 4.3). Often, tense vowels in English are also accompanied by a glide. This glide quality, or slight *diphthongization,* frequently distinguishes them from similar vowels in other languages that may have a purer quality to them.[3]

Another distinction between tense and lax vowels is that tense vowels can occur in both stressed **open syllables** (syllables without a final consonant sound, as in *tea, may, pa, law, hoe,* and *zoo*) and in stressed **closed syllables** (syllables terminating in a consonant, as in *team, main, pop, lawn, hole,* and *zoom*). The lax vowels /ɪ, ɛ, æ, ʌ, ʊ/, on the other hand, are articulated with more relaxed muscles. They do not usually have the same tendency toward diphthongization as the tense vowels.[4] In monosyllabic words or when stressed, they occur only in closed syllables (*him, met, hand, fun, put*) and never in open syllables. In other words, a consonant is always needed to close a stressed syllable with a lax vowel. Table 4.1 outlines the basic differences between tense and lax vowels.

[2]The classification of tense and lax vowels is somewhat debated by linguists. Where there are counterparts (/iy, ɪ/, /ey, ɛ/, and /uw, ʊ/), the distinction is clear. However, there is some disagreement as to whether /ɑ/, /ɔ/, and /æ/ should be considered tense or lax.
[3]Compare, for example, the "pure" quality of the vowel in the French word *thé* "tea" with the vowel + glide that occurs in the English word *day.*
[4]Some NAE speakers (especially Southerners) diphthongize some of the lax vowels slightly (with a centralizing glide), especially before a final voiced consonant. Many NAE speakers also diphthongize /æ/ in some environments, for example, before nasal and other voiced consonants.

TABLE 4.1 A COMPARISON OF TENSE AND LAX VOWELS IN NAE

Tense vowels /iy, ey, ɑ, ɔ, ow, uw/[a]	Lax vowels /ɪ, ɛ, æ, ʌ, ʊ/
Muscles more tense Certain vowels have a related glide Occur in open or closed syllables	Muscles more relaxed Less tendency to glide Occur only in closed syllables when stressed

[a]The three NAE diphthongs /ay, aw, ɔy/ exhibit the same features as the tense vowels; these are discussed later.

THE TENSE VOWELS OF NAE

How do these multiple features (tongue height and position, jaw opening, lip rounding, tense versus lax quality) work together to produce the fourteen stressed vowels of NAE? Let us begin with the tense vowels. Figure 4.3 shows that the highest front tense vowel is /iy/. To produce this vowel, tongue and jaw position are high, and the body of the tongue is pushed forward. The lips are spread into a wide, smiling position. Although this is a tense vowel, it is difficult to hear the accompanying glide since it is articulated in the same position as the initial vowel. Sample words include _free_ /friy/, _deed_ /diyd/, and _beam_ /biym/. In fact, the potential glide on /iy/ is much more likely to occur or to be perceptible in open syllables: _bee_ /biy/, _me_ /miy/, _tree_ /triy/.

> ### NOTE TO TEACHERS
> Many students will have problems articulating the difference between the adjacent tense/lax vowel phonemes /iy/ and /ɪ/. There are numerous minimal word pairs with this distinction. Students from language backgrounds without glided vowels will have particular difficulty producing /iy/ and may consistently substitute a sound resembling /ɪ/ for /iy/.

The tense mid-front vowel /ey/ occurs in such words as _great_ /greyt/, _trade_ /treyd/, and _ray_ /rey/. In comparison to /iy/, the jaw and tongue are somewhat lower and the lips are not as spread – at least at the beginning. The articulation of /ey/ involves the tongue moving up toward the /y/ glide position and thus is best represented by two symbols, /ey/.

> ### NOTE TO TEACHERS
> A common source of learner error is for students to confuse the adjacent phonemes /ey/ and /ɛ/. Practice with contextualized minimal word pairs and an explanation of the tense/lax distinguishing characteristics of these two vowel sounds can be of help, as can a focus on the less spread position of the lips and the lower jaw position of /ɛ/.

When the jaw is most open and the tongue is lowest, we produce the sound that doctors ask us to make when examining our throat – "aahh" /ɑ/. It occurs in closed syllables in such words as _hot_ /hɑt/ and _clock_ /klɑk/, and in open syllables in words such as _ma_ /mɑ/ and _spa_ /spɑ/; however, it does not have the glide quality of most other tense vowels.[5] The body of the tongue for /ɑ/ is in a central to back position, with the mouth wide open; the tongue lies flat in the mouth and the lips are neither rounded nor spread.

[5]Some phoneticians believe that /ɑ/ has two allophones. The first is a tense allophone that occurs in both open syllables (e.g., _spa, ma, pa_) and in closed syllables ending in a liquid or a nasal (e.g., _car, doll, calm, prom_); the second is a lax allophone that occurs in closed syllables ending in a stop, fricative, or affricate (e.g., _hot, stop, posh, scotch_). This lax allophone was historically a separate phoneme, which still survives in British English as /ɒ/. In /ɔ/-less dialects of NAE, the three historical phonemes /ɒ/, /ɑ/, and /ɔ/ all tend to merge into /ɑ/.

NOTE TO TEACHERS

The production of the low central vowel /ɑ/ does not generally tend to be problematic for speakers learning NAE. However, it is a frequent substitute for the low front vowel /æ/, which does not occur in the first language of many learners. These students should be told to spread their lips slightly more to produce /æ/, and to drop the jaw more with a neutral lip position to produce /ɑ/. Many learners who have previously studied British English will also have difficulty with NAE /æ/ since it occurs in many words where the British produce /ɑ/. Some common examples are *class*, *fast*, *chance*, and *passed*.

As three slight movements are made – the jaw rises, the tongue moves back, and the lips become more rounded – the sound /ɔ/ of *law* /lɔ/ and *caught* /kɔt/ is produced. Although this sound occurs in both open and closed syllables, the vowel /ɔ/ does not have the glide quality of most other tense vowels. It is produced farther back and higher in the mouth than /ɑ/ by NAE speakers who do distinguish the two vowel sounds.

NOTE TO TEACHERS

Many native speakers of NAE both in the United States and Canada do not distinguish /ɔ/ and /ɑ/, but instead use /ɑ/ for both vowels. You should therefore make an informed decision about how much to emphasize the /ɑ/ versus /ɔ/ contrast. This would appear to be more important if students are living in regions where this distinction prevails, and less so in regions (e.g., the western United States) where it does not. In either case, students should be made aware of the dialectal variation, and should be given opportunities to recognize and distinguish the two vowel sounds. Whether or not class time should be devoted to teaching students to produce /ɔ/ would then depend on whether it is determined to be important for the context in which the students will be speaking.

The final two tense vowels, /ow/ and /uw/, are both back vowels. The back vowel /ow/ as in *toe* /tow/ begins in the mid-position but then glides up toward the /w/ glide. The accompanying lip position resembles the closing of a camera shutter as the lips move from a fully rounded open position to a more tightly rounded closed position. The vowel /uw/ as in *boot* /buwt/ is produced with the back of the tongue very high in the mouth. One of the most visible characteristics of /uw/ is its tightly rounded lip position (similar to the lip position for a kiss). The potential /w/ glide of /uw/ is most obvious in open syllables, as in the word *zoo* /zuw/, where two phenomena occur: (1) The lack of a final consonant lengthens the vowel, and (2) this lengthening allows and even encourages production of a glide to complete the syllable.

NOTE TO TEACHERS

The accompanying /w/ glide of these back two vowels may be problematic for speakers of languages in which there are no glided vowels. Frequently, there is learner confusion between /ʊ/ and /uw/, or between /ɔ/ and /ow/. Focusing on the progressive rounding of the lips that accompanies the two vowel + glide combinations can help learners produce these vowel sounds in a more targetlike fashion.

THE LAX VOWELS OF NAE

Several of the lax vowels (see Figure 4.3) appear as counterparts to tense vowels. Beginning with high front vowels, the /ɪ/ sound in p*in* can be viewed as a lax counterpart to /iy/. The muscles relax somewhat when moving from /iy/ to /ɪ/; the jaw also drops slightly, and the lips are not so tightly spread apart. The tongue moves toward a more central position in the mouth. Finally, there is no /y/ glide quality to /ɪ/.

> ### NOTE TO TEACHERS
>
> Some learners may in fact produce a sound midway between /iy/ and /ɪ/, which is perceived as /iy/ when the native speaker expects /ɪ/ and vice versa. One way for these learners to better approximate /ɪ/ is to have them (1) relax the muscles and tongue, and (2) spread the lips less than for /iy/. To approximate /iy/, tell them to spread the lips and raise the tongue forward. This sound contrast is especially difficult for learners to produce. The best strategy is to have them practice dozens of meaningful words in contrast.

The mid-front vowels /ɛ/ and /ey/ can be described as similar counterparts: /ɛ/ is slightly lower and more relaxed and has no glide, has a more central tongue position, and has less spreading of the lips; /ey/ is more tense, longer, higher, and ends in a glide.

The remaining front vowel, the low front vowel /æ/ of h*a*t, is similar to the /ɛ/ of b*e*t. Both are lax vowels, yet there is usually a slight difference in the position of the jaw and often in the amount of lip spreading as well. To produce /ɛ/, the jaw remains relatively stationary in its mid-position and the lips are slightly spread, whereas to produce /æ/, the tongue and jaw are lower or drop slightly during articulation, and there may be more pronounced lip spreading.[6]

> ### NOTE TO TEACHERS
>
> The mid-front vowel /ɛ/ and the low front vowel /æ/ right below it on the vowel quadrant are frequently confused. Try having students place their hand on their jaw and pronounce the word pairs *met* and *mat* or *less* and *lass*, concentrating on the lowering of the tongue and jaw and greater spreading of the lips for the second of the two counterparts.

The low mid-central vowel /ʌ/ is characterized by a relaxed and neutral central position of the jaw, lips, and tongue and occurs in such words as f*un* and c*u*t. It is higher and slightly more forward than NAE /ɑ/; it is also lower and more back than /ɛ/.

> ### NOTE TO TEACHERS
>
> For speakers of first languages with no mid-central vowel (this includes speakers of most languages), the stressed vowel /ʌ/ is very difficult to perceive and produce. For this reason, it tends to be confused with nearby central and back vowels:
>
> | /ʌ/ vs. /ɑ/ | *cut/cot, done/Don, dull/doll* |
> | /ʌ/ vs. /ɔ/ | *cut/caught, gun/gone, dug/dog* |
> | /ʌ/ vs. /ʊ/ | *cud/could, buck/book, putt/put* |
>
> Note that for the many NAE speakers who do not distinguish /ɔ/ and /ɑ/, the second set of contrasts merges with the first. The /ʌ/ versus /ɑ/ contrast is especially important

---

[6]In certain urban dialects of midwestern NAE (e.g., Chicago, Milwaukee, Detroit), /æ/ occurring before nasals and voiced consonants tends to be higher and closer to /ɛ/ than in other NAE dialects. Thus *band* and *bend* or *land* and *lend* sound very much alike, except for a centralizing glide after /æ/.

for learners. One method of helping them to produce this distinction is to have them begin with the jaw in lowered position for /ɑ/, then raise and lower the jaw, producing /ɑ/ and /ʌ/ successively. It may also be useful to demonstrate the almost continuous backward and downward movement of the tongue from mid-front /ɛ/ to low mid-central /ʌ/ to low central /ɑ/:

/ɛ/ peck
↓
/ʌ/ puck
↓
/ɑ/ pock

Alternatively, have them begin by producing *pock* /pɑk/ and then move the tongue up and slightly forward to produce *puck* /pʌk/, or tell them to say *peck* /pɛk/ and then move the tongue back and slightly lower for *puck* /pʌk/.

The high back vowel /ʊ/ as in <u>look</u> is produced without the /w/ glide of its tense counterpart /uw/ as in <u>Luke</u>. In addition, /ʊ/ is slightly lower, more centered, more relaxed, and is produced with less rounded lips than /uw/. The vowels /uw/ vs. /ʊ/ are the back vowel counterparts of /iy/ vs. /ɪ/.

NOTE TO TEACHERS

The tense/lax contrast /ʊ, uw/ presents a learning challenge to many students. Fortunately, this distinction has only a few minimal pair contrasts and thus causes fewer problems in communication than the /iy/ vs. /ɪ/ distinction. To produce /ʊ/, students should practice beginning with the tense rounded position of /uw/, then loosen the muscles and relax the rounded lip position somewhat. This vowel occurs perhaps most frequently in the modals *could*, *would*, and *should* and some common nouns and verbs ending in /k/, such as *book, look, took,* and *cook*. These words can be practiced within a communicative context such as giving advice or making requests.

THE DIPHTHONGS OF NAE

As indicated in Figure 4.4 the three diphthongs /ay/ as in *b<u>i</u>te*, /aw/ as in *b<u>ou</u>t*, and /ɔy/ as in *b<u>oy</u>* are represented by arrows rather than points. This is because they consist of two nonadjacent sounds and involve a broad gliding movement from one point of articulation to the other. Like the vowel + glide sounds /iy, ey, ow, uw/, they are written with two symbols signifying each of the two sounds.[7]

The diphthong /ay/ as in *m<u>y</u>* or *h<u>ei</u>ght* involves a glide from the low central region close to /ɑ/ to the high front region close to /iy/. Instruct students to open their mouths wide for /ɑ/ and then, as they slowly change position to say *eye* /ay/, to notice how the jaw and tongue rise and how their lips change shape to a more spread position. The same exercise can be performed beginning with /ɑ/ and then changing position to produce *ow!* /aw/, although technically, the starting point for both /ay/ and /aw/ is slightly further forward in the mouth than /ɑ/. Again, instruct students to pay attention to the rise of the jaw and tongue and the change to a rounded lip position. Finally, the diphthong /ɔy/ involves a glide from the lowest back vowel /ɔ/ toward the highest front

---

[7]Note that the three diphthongs are tense vowels and share many of the same characteristics with the other tense vowels (e.g., muscle tension during articulation, presence in both open and closed syllables, and lack of a centered position in the mouth).

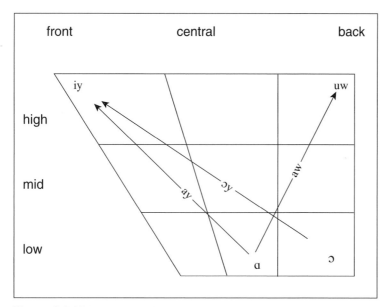

Figure 4.4 Glide movement for the NAE diphthongs

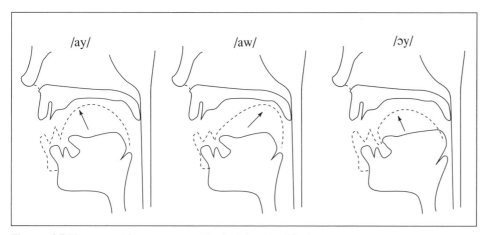

Figure 4.5 Tongue and jaw movements for /ay/, /aw/, and /ɔy/

vowel /iy/. The tongue and jaw movements for these three diphthongs are illustrated in Figure 4.5.

According to O'Grady and Dobrovolsky (1987), the most noticeable feature of some Canadian varieties of NAE is the pronunciation of the diphthongs /ay/ and /aw/ when these sounds occur before a voiceless consonant:

/ay/ → [ʌy]	ice, pipe
/aw/ → [ʌw]	house, shout

As the phonetic notation indicates, before voiceless consonants the onset of both diphthongs is the mid-central vowel sound /ʌ/ rather than the usual English low central /ɑ/.[8]

---

[8]In all other environments /ay/ and /aw/ are virtually similar in the United States and Canada; that is, speakers from both countries pronounce words like *buy* and *lies* with [ay] and *cow* and *crowd* with [aw].

> **NOTE TO TEACHERS**
>
> These three diphthongs are sometimes confused with the tense vowels that are phonetically similar:
>
> | | |
> |---|---|
> | /ay/ versus /ey/ | *might/mate, mine/main, mile/mail* |
> | /aw/ versus /ow/ | *bout/boat, town/tone, towel/toll* |
> | /ɔy/ versus /ɔ/ | *Lloyd/laud, coy/caw, boil/ball* |
>
> For those NAE speakers who do not distinguish /ɑ/ and /ɔ/, this third distinction would be realized as /ɔy/ versus /ɑ/.

SUMMARY OF THE CHARACTERISTICS OF NAE VOWELS AND DIPHTHONGS

We can summarize the primary characteristics of NAE vowels as follows:

- Vowels are classified as high, mid, or low, referring to the level of the tongue within the oral cavity and the accompanying raised or lowered position of the jaw.

- Vowels are also classified as front, central, or back, depending on how far forward or back the tongue is positioned within the oral cavity during articulation and which part of the tongue is involved.

- Vowels can be either tense or lax. These terms refer to the amount of muscle tension used to produce the vowel, the tendency of the vowel to glide, its distribution in closed or open syllables, and its relative place of articulation (i.e., its position in the center or on the periphery of the vowel quadrant).

- Vowels are simple or glided. The latter term refers to vowels with tongue movement occasioned by an accompanying /y/ or /w/ glide. Of these glided vowels, those with an adjacent glide are distinguished from the three phonemic diphthongs, which involve a nonadjacent glide.

- Vowels are characterized by the degree of lip rounding or spreading that occurs during their articulation.

Obviously, no one characteristic is sufficient to describe a given vowel; rather, only the constellation of these factors can adequately characterize a vowel's articulatory features.

Table 4.2 visually depicts the key differences in NAE vowel articulation. Reading from left to right, the sounds move in a U-shape from the high front vowels down to the low central /ɑ/ and back up to the high back /uw/, concluding with the mid-central vowel /ʌ/ and the three diphthongs. Note how the positions of the tongue, jaw, and lips change from the left to the right of this chart. Note also how the tongue and jaw are gradually lowered from the highest front position /iy/ to the lowest central position /ɑ/. Then both the tongue and the jaw begin to rise through the back vowels until the highest back vowel /uw/ is reached. The lips show similar changes, beginning with their most spread position for /iy/, and parting gradually into the wide open position of /ɑ/. Whereas the lips are more spread for the front vowels, they are more rounded for the back vowels. The lip positions for the tense vowels /ey/ and /ow/ involve a rise to an adjacent glide and are therefore marked with an arrow. The lips in the articulation of the three diphthongs also move from one position to another, but the movement is so great that two lip diagrams are used to represent this movement.

THE EFFECT OF ENVIRONMENT ON VOWEL QUALITY: WHAT THE TEACHER NEEDS TO KNOW

Like consonants, vowels are affected by the environment in which they occur. They tend to lengthen before voiced consonants; they are also "colored" or altered significantly in their articulation before certain consonants (especially /r/ and /l/).

TABLE 4.2 CLASSIFICATION OF VOWELS

	/iy/ pea feet	/ɪ/ pin fit	/ey/ paint fate	/ɛ/ pen fed	/æ/ pan fad	/ɑ/ pa fob	/ɔ/ Paul fought	/ow/ pole foe	/ʊ/ put foot	/uw/ pool fool	/ʌ/ pun fun	/ay/ pine fight	/aw/ pound foul	/ɔy/ poise foil
Tense or lax	Tense	Lax	Tense	Lax	Lax	Tense	Tense	Tense	Lax	Tense	Lax	Diphthong	Diphthong	Diphthong
Tongue position	Highest front near top of mouth	High front, but lower and more centered than /iy/	Mid-front, gliding up toward /iy/	Mid-front centered	Lower front than /ɛ/, centered	Lowest, central, lying flat on bottom	Low back	Mid-back, gliding up toward /uw/	High back and more centered than /ow/	Highest, back of tongue pushed up	Relaxed mid-level	Moves low central to high front	Moves low central to high back	Moves low back to high front
Jaw position	High closed	Slightly lower than /iy/	Begins lower than /ɪ/ but rises during glide	Open wider than /ey/	Slightly more open than /ɛ/; may drop a bit lower during articulation	Open widest	Closed slightly	Begins higher than /ɔ/; rises more during glide	Slightly higher	High, closed	Relaxed	Rises with tongue, closes	Rises with tongue, closes	Rises with tongue, closes
Lip position	Widely spread, smiling	Relaxed, slightly parted and spread	Spread more during glide to /iy/	Slightly spread	Spread	Yawn	Oval	Very rounded, closing like a camera shutter	Relaxed, slightly parted, weakly rounded	Closed and rounded, as for whistling	Relaxed, slightly parted	Moves from open to slightly parted and spread	Moves from open to slightly parted and round	Moves from oval to slightly parted and spread

VOWEL LENGTH

In our earlier discussion of consonant sounds, we touched upon the fact that vowels are longer before a final voiced consonant than before a final voiceless consonant. This holds true for all the lax vowels we have discussed. In fact, there is a continuum of vowel lengthening that is related to whether or not the vowel occurs before a **sonorant** (a voiced sound that can function as the peak of a syllable). Sonorants include all vowels, the semivowels /w, y/, the nasals /m, n, ŋ/, and the liquids /r, l/. Lax vowels are longest when they are followed by a sonorant consonant, next longest when followed by a voiced nonsonorant consonant, and shortest when followed by a voiceless consonant (Table 4.3).

Tense vowels are longest when either no consonant or a voiced sonorant consonant follows, next longest when a voiced nonsonorant consonant follows, and shortest when a voiceless consonant follows (Table 4.4).

TABLE 4.3 CONTINUUM OF LAX VOWELS

| | Longer ←——————————————→ Shorter | | |
	Final voiced sonorant consonant	Final voiced nonsonorant consonant	Final voiceless consonant
/ɪ/	hill	hid	hit
/ɛ/	bell	bed	bet
/æ/	bang	bad	bat
/ʊ/	bull	could	cook
/ʌ/	bun	buzz	bus

TABLE 4.4 CONTINUUM OF TENSE VOWELS

| | Longer ←——————————————→ Shorter | | |
	No consonant or final voiced sonorant consonant	Final voiced nonsonorant consonant	Final voiceless consonant
/iy/	bee, beer	bead	beet
/ey/	bay, bale	bayed	bait
/ɑ/[a]	pa, palm	pod	pot
/ɔ/	law, lore	laud	loss
/ow/	go, goal	goad	goat
/uw/	boo, boom	booed	boot
/ay/	buy, pyre	bide	bite
/aw/	plow, our	loud	lout
/ɔy/	boy, boil	void	voice

[a]As previously mentioned, /ɑ/ is believed by some phoneticians to have both a lax and a tense allophone. In the example given, *pa* would be tense, and *pod* and *pot* lax for these phoneticians.

The tendency for vowels to lengthen in certain environments is only part of the picture, and it may be most perceptible when words are spoken in isolation. Within the stream of speech other factors, such as whether the vowel occurs within a stressed or unstressed syllable and whether or not the word receives prominence in the utterance, also influence vowel length. We have more to say about this in later chapters.

/r/-COLORING

Earlier we alluded to the fact that vowels are affected when certain consonants follow them. When the consonant /r/ follows a vowel and occurs in the same syllable (as in *fur*, *pour*, *bird*, *party*), the vowel anticipates and glides toward the central /r/ position and takes on some of the retroflex quality of /r/, often altering its production dramatically. This phenomenon is known as **/r/-coloring**. For example, in the word *beard*, the vowel is colored by /r/ to such an extent that it resembles neither /iy/ nor /ɪ/ strongly. Although conventionally transcribed as /bɪrd/, this transcription may not completely represent or capture the precise articulation of this /r/-colored vowel.

TABLE 4.5 DISTINCTIONS BETWEEN /r/-LESS AND /r/-COLORED VOWELS

Inventory of /r/-less vowels		Inventory of /r/-colored vowels	
/iy/	bead	/ɪr/	beard
/ɪ/	bid	(In some dialects /iyr/ occurs instead.)	
/ey/	bait	/ɛr/	bared[a]
/ɛ/	bed	(In some dialects either /eyr/ or /ær/ occurs instead.)	
/æ/	bad		
/uw/	pool	/ʊr/	poor
/ʊ/	put	(In some dialects /uwr/, /ɜ^{r}/, or even /owr/ occurs instead.)	
/ow/	load	/ɔr/	lord
/ɔ/	laud	(In some dialects /owr/ occurs instead.)	

[a]The NAE neutralization of /ey/, /ɛ/, and /æ/ to /ɛ/ before /r/ is not complete in some East Coast dialects in which speakers continue to distinguish *Mary* /ey/, *merry* /ɛ/, and *marry* /æ/. In more widely spread dialects of NAE where these vowels are neutralized, the vowel in all three of the preceding words would tend to be /ɛ/.

In fact, when the vowel /ʌ/ is followed by /r/, it changes quality so much that many phoneticians use a distinct symbol for this sound. We will represent this sound sequence with the symbol /ɜ^{r}/, and use it to capture the significant difference in quality between the /ʌ/ in *bud* and the /ɜ^{r}/ in *bird*. This adds a fifteenth vowel symbol to our inventory.

The following examples serve to illustrate the degree of /r/-coloring that occurs when /r/ follows the simple vowels /ɪ, ɛ, ʊ, ʌ, a, ɔ/ and the diphthongs /ay, aw/.[9] Compare:

Uncolored vowel		/r/-colored vowel	
/ɪ/	lid	/ɪr/	leered
/ɛ/	fed	/ɛr/	fared
/ʊ/	should	/ʊr/	assured
/ʌ/	hut	/ɜ^{r}/	hurt
/ɑ/	pot	/ɑr/	part
/ɔ/	caught	/ɔr/	court
/ay/	tie	/ayr/	tire
/aw/	ow!	/awr/	our

When vowels are colored by /r/, some of the usual distinctions may merge or disappear, resulting in a smaller vowel inventory for /r/-colored vowels (Table 4.5).

[9]Note that /ɔy/ is not followed by /r/ within the same syllable; words like *lawyer* and *Sawyer* are disyllabic. In fact, if pronounced slowly and carefully, the other two diphthongs /ay/ and /aw/ followed by /r/ also seem to divide into two syllables. In rapid native-speaker speech and in certain dialects, however, this glide may be minimized to /a^{y}r/ and /a^{w}r/, respectively.

> **NOTE TO TEACHERS**
>
> Many learners (especially those from open-syllable languages and those who have difficulty producing NAE /r/) have severe difficulty producing /r/-colored vowels in one-syllable words like *fire* and *our*. For pedagogical purposes it is useful to begin with disyllabic words, such as *skier, lawyer,* or *Sawyer,* and then have learners produce words like *fire* and *our* in a similar manner: that is, pronounced as /fayə^r/ and /awə^r/. This articulation of /ə/ assists learners in their production of syllable-final /r/. In fact, learners should be taught that the production of final /r/ following any diphthong can be facilitated by this insertion of /ə/ between the semivowel /y/ or /w/ and the /r/:
>
> | | **Instead of this:** | **Recommend this:** |
> |---|---|---|
> | our | /awr/ | /awə^r/ |
> | flour | /flawr/ | /flawə^r/ |
> | fire | /fayr/ | /fayə^r/ |
> | hire | /hayr/ | /hayə^r/ |
>
> This can be reinforced by showing learners that words like *flour/flower* and *hire/higher* are pronounced identically.

/l/-COLORING

Postvocalic /l/ also colors a preceding vowel, but not as drastically as /r/ does. It does not, for example, neutralize contrasts. However, the velarized or dark NAE [ɫ] does pull front vowels back in the oral cavity so that they are perceptibly more central than the counterpart front vowel without a following /l/.[10] Compare:

/iy/	see/seal
	seed/sealed
/ɪ/	Mick/milk
/ey/	may/male
	maize/males
/ɛ/	hep/help
/æ/	tack/talc

Central and back vowels, as well as the diphthongs, are also slightly colored (i.e., more raised and more back) by the velar quality of a postvocalic /l/. Compare:

/ɑ/	dot/doll
/ʌ/	duck/dull
/ɔ/	bought/ball
/ow/	coat/coal
/ʊ/	wood/wool
/uw/	tooth/tool
/ay/	my/mile
/aw/	how/howl
/ɔy/	boy/boil

In these contexts, the postvocalic final /l/ sometimes assumes an /ʊ/-like quality for native speakers of some NAE dialects. This is similar to what happens to postvocalic /l/ in Brazilian Portuguese.

---

[10]The /l/ can become syllabic, or nearly syllabic, after tense vowels or diphthongs, as in the words *seal, mail, coal, tool, mile, howl,* and *boil.*

NOTE TO TEACHERS

Many of the same difficulties that learners have producing /r/-colored vowels exist for /l/-colored vowels. Learners should be taught that the production of final /l/ following any vowel + glide or diphthong can be facilitated by the insertion of /ə/ and the production of a more velarized /l/:

	Instead of this:	Recommend this:
seal	/siyl/	/siyəl/
mail	/meyl/	/meyəl/
coal	/kowl/	/kowəl/
tool	/tuwl/	/tuwəl/
mile	/mayl/	/mayəl/
howl	/hawl/	/hawəl/
boil	/bɔyl/	/bɔyəl/

This can be reinforced by showing learners that words like *howl* and *boil* may rhyme with *towel* and *loyal*, respectively.

Finally, the problems inherent in /r/- and /l/-coloring are, of course, exacerbated in those cases where both /r/ and /l/ – in that order only – occur together and color a preceding vowel sound: *girl, world, pearl, curl, Karl*.

NOTE TO TEACHERS

Words in which the /rl/ cluster occurs are particularly difficult for learners to pronounce and should receive special attention with respect to both recognition and production – assuming postvocalic /r/ and /l/ have first been treated independently. It may be easier initially to present this problematic sequence in two-syllable words like *curly, burly,* and then practice the respective cluster configurations, *curl, burl*.

VOWELS COLORED BY NASAL CONSONANTS

The nasal consonants also tend to color the sound of a preceding vowel, resulting in a more **nasalized** quality in NAE (i.e., the velum is partially open during the vowel sound); however, in British English, the velum remains closed longer.[11] Nasals rarely follow /ʊ/ and, as indicated in Appendix 5, /ŋ/ has a very limited distribution with respect to the vowel sounds it can follow. Compare the vowel quality in the following sets of words:

	No final nasal	Final nasal
/iy/	see	seem, seen
/ɪ/	mitt	Tim, lint, ring
/ey/	say	same, sane
/ɛ/	bet	hem, bent
/æ/	cat	tam, can't, rang
/ɑ/	cot	bomb, con
/ɔ/	taught	taunt, tong
/ow/	grow	Rome, groan
/uw/	too	tomb, tune
/ʌ/	but	bum, bunt, rung
/ay/	my	time, fine
/aw/	how	hound
/ɔy/	coy	coin

[11]In many dialects of NAE, the presence of a following nasal also causes the contrast between the lax vowels /ɪ/ and /ɛ/ to be neutralized so that no distinction is made between pairs of words such as *tin/ten, since/sense, him/hem*. This naturalization appears to be spreading.

Actually, NAE has gradations for vowel nasalization. When the nasal consonant precedes the vowel, there is a slight degree of nasalization. When the nasal follows the vowel, a greater degree of nasalization occurs, and when a nasal both precedes and follows a vowel the greatest degree of nasalization occurs (Table 4.6).

TABLE 4.6 DEGREES OF NASALIZATION IN NAE

Least <—————————————————————————————————> Greatest

Initial nasal	Final nasal	Initial and final nasal
maid	aim	main
met	ten	men
gnat	tan	man
note	home	gnome

REDUCED VOWELS

One of the more striking characteristics of English is the frequency with which **reduced vowels** occur in the stream of speech. Also striking is the restricted number of vowels that tend to occur in unstressed position. Before proceeding with a discussion of where stress falls in words, we therefore need to consider carefully the range of reduced vowels occurring in unstressed syllables in NAE.

At the word level, the mid-central reduced vowel /ə/, which is often called *schwa*, is by far the most common of the reduced NAE vowel sounds, especially if one includes with schwa reduced vowels with a postvocalic /r/ as in *father* or *brother*.[12] Schwa, which is closest in position to the stressed vowel /ʌ/, is produced with the muscles relaxed, the tongue in mid-position in the mouth, and the jaw slightly open:

● ·	· ●
/ə/	/ə/
sof<u>a</u>	<u>a</u>bout
aq<u>ua</u>	<u>a</u>round
quot<u>a</u>	s<u>u</u>btract
Sar<u>a</u>	<u>o</u>ffend

The choice of /ə/ over all other reduced vowels is often dialectal or idiosyncratic; however, we believe it is important to recognize that more than one reduced vowel sound exists.

Figure 4.6 presents the inventory of reduced vowels that can occur in unstressed position. Besides /ə/ and /əʳ/, NAE has four other reduced vowel sounds that also occur frequently in unstressed syllables – /ɪ/, /i/, /o/, and /u/.[13] The latter three unstressed vowels are similar to /iy/, /ow/, and /uw/, but without the glide; they are also more central because of the lack of stress:

[12]Because /ə/ is also colored when followed by /r/, it is sometimes transcribed /ɚ/. Given that our alphabet is a pedagogical one, we will not use this convention, and instead use /əʳ/ to transcribe such combinations.

[13]Note that /ɪ/ appears in Figure 4.6 as both a reduced and an unreduced vowel. Since both versions are phonetically very similar, we have opted to use the same symbol to represent both rather than introduce a new symbol. Many phoneticians also consider /ʊ/ to be a common reduced vowel, as in *July*, *judicial* (although often in variation with /ə/).

/ɪ/	/i/	/o/	/o/	/u/
music	city	meadow	hotel	into
reddish	sassy	narrow	motel	venue
sleeping	candy	shadow	rosette	menu

The exact quality of reduced vowel sounds tends to vary. For example, the reduced vowel in the words *behind*, *begin*, and *prefer* may be articulated as /i/, /ɪ/, or /ə/, depending on the speaker, the context, and the dialect.

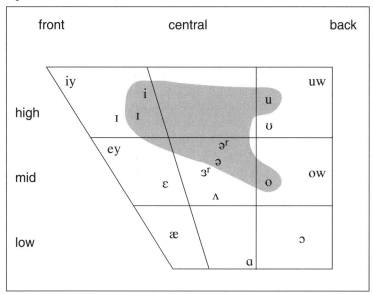

Figure 4.6 Position of the unreduced versus reduced vowels

There are two situations in which a vowel occurs in unstressed position. The first is when a vowel occurs in an unstressed syllable in a multisyllabic word (as in the words *allow, sofa, focus*). The second situation concerns monosyllabic words that have both a stressed **citation form** (a form with a stressed vowel when the word is spoken alone, out of context) and a reduced form (the version of the word that usually occurs in natural speech). The following are some common examples of words that have both stressed citation forms and reduced forms:

Word	Stressed or citation form	Unstressed or reduced form
a	/ey/	/ə/
an	/æn/	/ən/
the	/ðiy/	/ðə/ before consonants /ði/ before vowels
on	/ɑn/, /ɔn/	/ən/
at	/æt/	/ət/
is	/ɪz/	/ɪz/, /əz/
are	/ɑr/	/əʳ/
was	/wʌz/	/wəz/
have	/hæv/	/(h)əv/
has	/hæz/	/(h)əz/
his	/hɪz/	/(h)ɪz, (h)əz/
to	/tuw/	/tə/ before consonants /tu/ before vowels

As is evident from this list (see also Appendix 6), words that often occur in a reduced form in natural speech are function words, such as articles, auxiliary verbs, possessive adjectives, prepositions, and pronouns. Thus we find many reduced vowels occurring in utterances like the following:

| John has washed the car. | /dʒanəzwɔʃtðəkɑr/ |
| He was coming to see us. | /hiwəzkʌmɪŋtəsiyəs/ |

The typically unstressed nature of such words in the stream of speech contributes markedly to English stress and rhythm, which we discuss further in Chapters 5 and 6.

THE NAE VOWEL SYSTEM: PEDAGOGICAL PRIORITIES

The fourteen stressed vowel phonemes of NAE (fifteen if we add /ɜʳ/) make the vowel system incredibly rich and complex. This fact alone deserves attention, since we need to realize that this complexity is a challenge for students learning English as a second language. In fact, many of our students (e.g., speakers of Japanese, Chinese, most Romance languages, Tagalog, Turkish, and many African languages) speak first languages that have only five to eight vowels, and we can therefore expect that these students will have difficulties in mastering the more differentiated vowel system of NAE. However, even those students whose first-language vowel systems are more complex will lack certain English vowels in their first language. For all students, then, we can expect some transfer of the vowel system of their first language to that of English, along with the problems that such transfer entails.

What are the special challenges involved in teaching vowels? First, the place and manner of articulation of vowels is less clear-cut than for consonants, and voicing is not a distinguishing feature since all vowels are voiced. Moreover, the sound-spelling correspondence for vowels exhibits greater variety than for consonants and may thus be misleading, especially since many learners rely much more on what they see written than what they hear. Thus many mispronunciations are clearly induced by English orthography if the learners are not aware of the rules and principles we introduce in Chapter 9.

There are several general learner errors that we can identify. Some ESL/EFL learners clip short all tense vowels such that they may sound like lax vowels. This tendency, which is usually due to native language transfer from a system with vowels that do not glide, not only signals a foreign accent but also makes it difficult for such speakers to distinguish the following pairs of sounds in listening and in speaking: iy/ɪ, ey/ɛ, ow/ɔ, and uw/ʊ. Consider, for example, contrasts such as the following:

Native language	Example	English word
Italian	*si* "yes" /si/	*see* /siy/
Spanish	*de* "of" /de/	*day* /dey/
German	*Foto* "photo" /foto/	*photo* /fowɾo/
French	*rouge* "red" /ruʒ/	*rouge* /ruwʒ/

In these cases, the European vowel sounds contain no accompanying glide whereas their NAE counterparts do.

Learners also tend to confuse vowels that occur in adjacent positions in the vowel quadrant, since these vowels are similar in their articulatory characteristics. Thus the following word pairs may be particularly difficult for students to differentiate, both receptively and productively:

Adjacent vowels	Minimal pair examples
/iy/ vs. /ɪ/	beat/bit, keen/kin, peel/pill
/ey/ vs. /ɛ/	bait/bet, Kane/Ken, tale/tell
/ɛ/ vs. /æ/	bet/bat, men/man, sell/Sal
/ɑ/ vs. /ɔ/[14]	cot/caught, Don/dawn, collar/caller
/ɔ/ vs. /ow/	caught/coat, fawn/phone, ball/bowl
/ʊ/ vs. /uw/	would/wooed, look/Luke, pull/pool

In addition to presenting information on the articulation of individual vowels, learners also need to be made aware of positional variation, since it affects both their listening discrimination ability and their ability to produce targetlike segmental variants. The four areas that we highlighted earlier – vowel length, /r/- and /l/-coloring, nasalization, and vowel reduction – will need to be dealt with systematically in the pronunciation classroom as contexts arise in which these phenomena occur.

Pronunciation courses have often focused on students' correctly differentiating such minimal pair sentences as "My brother beat/bit me" or "Would you test/taste this for me?" Today, many communicatively oriented teachers of pronunciation tend to dismiss such minimal pair practice as contrived and out of context. We agree that minimal pair practice alone will not assist learners in gaining true control over segmental contrasts – especially when learners are called upon to produce language in situations where the focus is on the message rather than the form. Nonetheless, minimal pair sentences do present evidence of how meaning can be misconstrued if a single vowel phoneme is mispronounced or misperceived. If contextualized and followed by more communicative practice, such minimal pair practice can assist learners in gaining control over segmental contrasts. In sum, a comprehensive course in NAE pronunciation needs to include a component that assists learners in mastering the perception and production of vowel sounds in contextualized and communicatively relevant ways and in learning how to predict the pronunciation of vowels from their spelling patterns (see Chapter 9).

PRESENTING THE NAE VOWEL SYSTEM TO STUDENTS

As with consonant sounds, we suggest that you begin the presentation of vowels sounds by providing students with information about their characteristic articulation. You can use the vowel quadrant superimposed on a sagittal section of the mouth as in Figure 4.1 to clarify the importance of the following variables in articulating vowels:

- the height and position of the tongue
- the volume of the oral cavity as determined by jaw movement
- the rounded or spread position of the lips

To facilitate students' understanding, you can demonstrate the principles involved by bringing several partially filled bottles of liquid to class. The bottles should be of different shapes and sizes, and contain varying amounts of liquid. Ask students to blow across the top of each bottle. As they do so, they will discover that bottles with a low level of liquid produce a low-pitched sound, whereas bottles filled closer to the brim produce a high-pitched sound. Bottles of different shapes with the same level of liquid produce slightly different sounds, depending on their total volume. Finally, bottles with a narrow opening produce different sounds from those with a wide opening. Using the bottle as a metaphor

---

[14]As noted, in many dialects of NAE, speakers do not make a distinction between /ɑ/ as in *cot* and /ɔ/ as in *caught*. In these dialects, such word pairs are pronounced the same (i.e., neutralized to /ɑ/). The only exception to this occurs when /ɑ/ or /ɔ/ comes before /r/, as in *card* /kɑrd/ vs. *cord* /kɔrd/. Furthermore, the /ɔ/ vs. /ow/ contrast is usually realized in /ɔ/-less dialects as /ɑ/ vs. /ow/.

for the production of vowel sounds, you can ask students to think of the level of liquid in the bottle as the height of the tongue. The shape of the bottle (i.e., its total volume) can be likened to the shape and volume of the oral cavity, and the size of the bottle opening to the rounded or spread shape of the lips.

The effect of environment on vowels will also require attention. To this end, simple graphics on the board such as the following may assist the teacher in explaining phenomena like vowel lengthening before final voiced consonants:

face   vs.   f⊏⊐z e

peace   vs.   p⊂⊐s

The fact that most English vowel sounds have multiple orthographic representations underscores the need for a system of notation for vowels that does not rely exclusively on regular English spelling. Phonetic symbols can be used if students are sufficiently advanced that the initial investment in learning a phonemic alphabet can be put to good use. This is certainly true if students are using a monolingual dictionary with a pronunciation key. However, it is also possible to use a color-coding system, in which vowels are associated with a specific color. The usefulness of the system we present here lies in the fact that the color words each contain the vowel sound they represent. Thus, the association is not random and memorization is minimal. This system is especially useful if students are preliterate or semiliterate in English and would not be able to use transcription. We suggest the following colors to teach vowel recognition:

/iy/	/ɪ/	/ey/	/ɛ/	/æ/	/ɑ/	/ɔ/	/ow/
green	pink (or silver)	gray	red	black	aqua	mauve	gold

/ʊ/	/uw/	/ʌ/	/ɜʳ/	/ay/	/aw/	/ɔy/
soot	blue	rust	purple	white	brown	oyster

This color-coding system can be taught to students using flashcards. All of the colors should be familiar to intermediate-level students, except perhaps *aqua, mauve, rust, oyster,* and *soot.* (Indeed, in the latter two cases, the definition of color needs to be expanded to *color-texture.*) After one or two quick drills matching color names with a large card of the same color, students should be able to associate the colors and vowel sounds rather easily. At this point, the color cards can be hung around the classroom as an easy reference; you can simply point to the proper color when a vowel is mispronounced. As in the Silent Way, this method of error correction allows you to remain silent while the learner attempts self-correction.

LISTENING DISCRIMINATION

Since vowels are often more easily distinguished in relation to one another than by any external standard of measurement, the perception of contrasts is an essential starting point in the teaching of vowels. Tuning students' ears to the subtle differences between vowels is critical. It is best to begin with a limited number of vowel contrasts, and then build up to asking students to discriminate the full range of vowels. For this purpose, teachers have a variety of listening discrimination activities to choose from.

One option for practicing listening discrimination geared to younger or less literate students is to have the learners circle the picture of the word they hear. As a pre-activity, present the vowel distinction using picture cue cards, making sure each student is familiar with the relevant vocabulary items. Next, distribute a vowel discrimination worksheet such as the following one, which is geared to teaching the vowel contrast /ɛ/ vs. /æ/. For each item on the worksheet, randomly select one of the two words to read aloud, and have learners circle the word they have heard. For example, if learners heard the word *men*, they would circle picture 1b on the worksheet. In the follow-up phase, the students can check their answers with a partner, or you can go over the answers with the class as a whole.

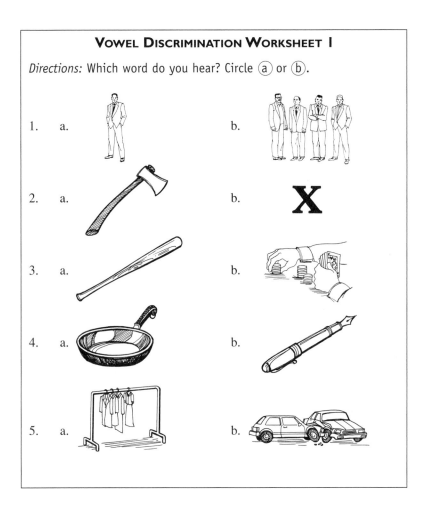

An alternative listening discrimination exercise requires the learner to decide if two words spoken by the teacher are the same or different. This is a relatively easy task to begin with because it contrasts two sounds directly rather than presenting one of the two for students to identify. When working with the /ɪ/ vs. /iy/ distinction, for example, you might read the following list of words to students, who circle the appropriate response on vowel discrimination worksheet 2.

1. sleep   sleep
2. sleep   slip
3. slip   sleep
4. slip   slip
5. sleep   slip

VOWEL DISCRIMINATION WORKSHEET 2

Directions: Listen carefully to each pair of words. Are they the same or different? Circle your answers.

1. same   different
2. same   different
3. same   different
4. same   different
5. same   different

Worksheet 3 presents a similar listening discrimination exercise that incorporates practice with sound-spelling patterns. Each item on the worksheet has four choices, three of which contain the same vowel sound. Students are asked to circle the word with the different vowel sound. Encourage them to make their choices based on what they hear, not on the spelling of the words.

VOWEL DISCRIMINATION WORKSHEET 3

Directions: Listen to each group of four words. Circle the word that has a different vowel sound.

1. foot	good	could	food
2. eat	treat	threat	meat
3. itch	mild	fill	pin
4. close	most	lost	hose
5. sew	threw	blew	grew

If you opt to use a phonemic alphabet with your students, you may wish to have students do simple transcription exercises, limiting the range of possible contrasts in the initial stages. For example, you might write the following on the board:

/ɪ/ vs. /ɛ/

Students would then be responsible only for this contrast, and would transcribe the words you dictate – for example, *tip* /tɪp/, *red* /rɛd/, *gin* /dʒɪn/, *set* /sɛt/, *lid* /lɪd/. For feedback, have students come up to the board and write the words as they have transcribed them. Once this sound contrast is easily distinguished by students, you might add the additional vowel /æ/ to the list on the board and dictate the following words: *pal* /pæl/, *him* /hɪm/, *hid* /hɪd/, *less* /lɛs/, *band* /bænd/, *pet* /pɛt/. This type of transcription exercise is easy to construct, takes very little class time, provides immediate feedback to learners, and lends itself to virtually any vowel contrast.

The foregoing exercises discriminate vowels at the word level. They can, however, easily be adapted to the sentence level. A typical review of vowel contrasts is illustrated by vowel discrimination worksheet 4, in which students listen to minimal pairs embedded in a sentence context and circle the word they hear.

VOWEL DISCRIMINATION WORKSHEET 4

Directions: Which underlined word does the teacher pronounce? Circle the word you hear.

1. There was an ugly <u>bull</u> / <u>bowl</u> in the corner.
2. He wanted to <u>sell</u> / <u>sail</u> the boat.
3. That's the biggest <u>wheel</u> / <u>whale</u> I've ever seen.
4. Susan is going to buy some <u>soap</u> / <u>soup</u>.

CONTROLLED PRACTICE AND FEEDBACK

Listening discrimination exercises like those in the four preceding worksheets serve as a diagnostic to ascertain whether students are perceiving specific vowel contrasts or not. This type of listening discrimination practice should be followed by oral production practice. Finding contexts in which a given vowel or vowel contrast naturally occurs is a key step in teaching pronunciation communicatively. A good way to begin the controlled practice phase of a pronunciation lesson is to choose a subject category and give or elicit sample words containing the targeted vowel sound. Virtually unlimited contexts lend themselves to this activity. The following are a few examples for the vowel contrast /ɪ/ vs. /iy/:

Body parts: wr<u>i</u>st, f<u>i</u>nger, ch<u>i</u>n, h<u>i</u>p, l<u>i</u>p, sh<u>i</u>n, ch<u>ee</u>k, kn<u>ee</u>, t<u>ee</u>th, h<u>ee</u>l, f<u>ee</u>t

Countries: <u>I</u>taly, L<u>i</u>bya, Braz<u>i</u>l, F<u>i</u>nland, <u>I</u>ndia, Gr<u>ee</u>ce, Kor<u>ea</u>, Argent<u>i</u>na, Gu<u>ya</u>na

Food items: m<u>i</u>lk, ch<u>i</u>cken, v<u>i</u>negar, f<u>i</u>sh, p<u>i</u>ckles, t<u>ea</u>, ch<u>ee</u>se, p<u>ea</u>ch, cr<u>ea</u>m, m<u>ea</u>t

Personal names: J<u>i</u>m, R<u>i</u>ck, L<u>i</u>nda, Chr<u>i</u>s, B<u>i</u>ll, M<u>i</u>ck, Ir<u>e</u>ne, P<u>e</u>ter, J<u>ea</u>n, St<u>e</u>ve, T<u>i</u>na

How this preliminary presentation phase is structured depends to a great extent on the proficiency level of the students. If, for example, you are working with beginning-level students, you may opt to set the context and provide the example words. However, with more advanced learners, it may suffice to establish the context (e.g., personal names) and then elicit the individual examples from the students.

An enjoyable follow-up to this elicitation activity is an adaptation of the game "Categories." The worksheet in Table 4.7 can easily be adapted to any minimal pair vowel

TABLE 4.7 WORKSHEET FOR THE GAME "CATEGORIES"

Countries[a] /iy/ /ɪ/	Colors /iy/ /ɪ/	Clothing items /iy/ /ɪ/	Personal names /iy/ /ɪ/
Food items /iy/ /ɪ/	**Hobbies** /iy/ /ɪ/	**Bodies of water** /iy/ /ɪ/	**Cities** /iy/ /ɪ/

[a]Certain of the category headings may change depending on the vowel contrasts selected. For example, to practice the vowel contrast /ʊ/ vs. /uw/, you might want to include the heading "professions" (e.g., *butcher, bookkeeper, cook, movie star, beautician*) in place of one of the other categories, since this category is so rich in words containing the /ʊ/ vs. /uw/ sound contrast.

contrast. The task of this activity is for students to fill the categories by writing a pair (or pairs) of words containing each targeted sound contrast. The first student to finish the task (i.e., the first one to fill all columns with a minimum of one word in each) calls "Stop" and the scores are then tallied in the following manner:

1. The student who called "Stop" receives 5 bonus points.
2. For each correct and unique word (i.e., a word that no other student has), students receive 2 points.
3. For each word that more than one student has written, students receive 1 point.

If this activity is used as a vowel review, the winner (the student receiving the most total points) can suggest the vowel contrast to be selected for the next round of the game.

Another activity that lends itself well to the controlled practice phase involves dialogues containing many words with the contrasting vowel sounds. If students have been taught to associate a given vowel with a color, one possible variation of the standard dialogue reading activity involves using color cards to replace vowels in words. You can put the dialogue on either an overhead transparency or a large sheet of paper or poster board, using colored squares to replace the words being contrasted (e.g., pink and green squares to replace /ɪ/ and /iy/). The students enjoy the first step of figuring out what the color-coded words are. During the second step – the reading of the dialogue in pairs – the use of color highlights the vowel distinctions while reducing the students' need to focus on spelling. The following sample dialogue illustrates this activity:

(Jean and Kim are two sisters who have just visited Disneyland for the first time.)

Jean: Hasn't th[*pink*]s b[*pink*]n a n[*green*]t tr[*pink*]p, K[*pink*]m?

Kim: Yes, just th[*pink*]nk of all the th[*pink*]ngs w[*green*]'ve s[*green*]n at D[*pink*]sneyland.

Jean: I liked the submar[*green*]ne ride best.

Kim: Not m[*green*]. I th[*pink*]nk s[*green*]ing M[*pink*]ckey and M[*pink*]nnie was r[*green*]lly tops!

Dialogues can often help students focus on troublesome vowel contrasts. In the following, students begin by trying to locate all the words containing the /ʊ/ sound. The next step is to find the words pronounced with /uw/, and perhaps mark them with a *blue* pencil or pen to reinforce the vowel and distinguish them from the words with /ʊ/:

Luke: Doobie, you're so stupid! You forgot your book two times this week!

Doobie: Look who's calling me stupid! You're full of baloney, Luke! You should loosen up a little.

Luke: Cool it, Doobie. Last week I took a look at your notes. You'd be a fool to continue in this class.

Doobie: Is this assignment due today? I think I blew it.

Luke: School could be a lot of fun if it weren't so full of fools like you!

Once students have identified the /uw/ vs. /ʊ/ contrasts, they work in pairs to practice and perform the dialogue. This particular dialogue could be combined with the study of idioms. Dialogues can be constructed to practice a variety of vowel contrasts; in fact, more advanced students may enjoy writing their own, individually or in pairs.

Another type of pair practice activity can easily be constructed using worksheets with minimal pair sentences. In the review activity in Figure 4.7, Student A begins by reading

	STUDENT A

STUDENT A

I. Read sentences 1–5 to your partner.

  1. He gave me a hug.

  2. Hand me the pin.

  3. This room is full of cats.

  4. It's very withered.

  5. The men will come soon.

II. Circle the word that your partner reads.

  6. I'd like to see that _____
      (a) chick
      (b) check

  7. That's my _____
      (a) luck
      (b) lock

  8. They _____ around.
      (a) spun
      (b) spin

  9. I fell over the _____
      (a) rock
      (b) rack

  10. They _____ weights at the gym.
      (a) lift
      (b) left

STUDENT B

I. Circle the word that your partner reads.

  1. He gave me a _____
      (a) hug
      (b) hog

  2. Hand me the _____
      (a) pen
      (b) pin

  3. This room is full of _____
      (a) cots
      (b) cats

  4. It's very _____
      (a) withered
      (b) weathered

  5. The _____ will come soon.
      (a) man
      (b) men

II. Read sentences 6–10 to your partner.

  6. I'd like to see that chick.

  7. That's my lock.

  8. They spun around.

  9. I fell over the rock.

  10. They left weights at the gym.

Figure 4.7 Worksheets with minimal pair sentences

his or her sentences aloud while Student B marks the correct word. After five sentences they change roles, so that students practice both as the speaker and the listener.

"Pronunciation Bingo," an activity suggested by Hecht and Ryan (1979), uses the familiar game format of Bingo to practice vowel contrasts. Each student receives a Bingo card containing words instead of numbers. Figure 4.8 illustrates a Bingo card designed to practice the minimal pair contrast /ɛ/ vs. /æ/. The game begins as a listening discrimination exercise with the teacher reading aloud a list of words containing the targeted minimal pair contrast from the Bingo card:

dead	dense	said	letter	mess
end	mass	latter	shell	gas
leather	laughed	**BINGO**	dad	pet
pat	guess	better	dance	left
sad	shall	lather	batter	and

Figure 4.8 "Pronunciation Bingo" card for practicing /ɛ/ vs. /æ/

1. left	5. end	8. dad	11. gas
2. shall	6. better	9. laughed	12. leather
3. pat	7. mass	10. said	13. pet
4. mess			

As you read the words, students mark the appropriate box. Their main challenge is to distinguish the minimal pair contrasts (e.g., *said* or *sad*), since this will determine which box they cross out. Once a row is completely marked (across, down, or diagonally), they call out "Bingo!" The center box is a free space, so that the two diagonal rows and the middle horizontal and vertical rows require only four words each to make Bingo.

In the game illustrated here, Bingo is reached in the middle row across, containing *leather, laughed, dad,* and *pet.* The call sheet is constructed so that everyone should have Bingo as the thirteenth word is read. If a student calls out "Bingo" before the thirteen words are read or does not have Bingo at the end of the list, then the student has misunderstood at least one of the words. As a check, students can compare Bingo cards, or the teacher can verify by rereading the list using a transparency of the Bingo card on an overhead projector.

For more practice with the same Bingo card, you can create four additional call sheets (simply draw up a list of 12–15 words that lead to Bingo as the last word is read). In groups of four, students take turns being the Bingo master and calling out the words on the list. The other three group members are the players for that round. If Bingo is reached by all three at the same time, then the speaker has obviously pronounced the words well and the players have understood correctly. If Bingo is not reached simultaneously, group members can check to see where discrepancies lie.

A technique that we presented earlier in the teaching of consonants can also be adapted for guided practice with vowel contrasts. This technique, originally suggested by Bowen (1972), involves the use of pictures. Each round of the activity stems from a minimal pair contrast in contextualized sentences. For example, to practice the distinction between /ɪ/ and /iy/, two model sentences might be:

Don't sleep on the floor. / Don't slip on the floor.

First, write these two sentences on opposite sides of the blackboard, then say them randomly while students point to the one they hear. This allows you to gain a fair idea of how well students are able to perceive the vowel contrast.

The next step is to erase the sentences and to elicit one gesture to represent each of the two sentences. For example, students may tip their head to the side with two hands clasped underneath to mime a sleeper for: *Don't sleep on the floor*. For the second sentence, students may choose to make a sweeping motion with their hand to represent a slip or fall: *Don't slip on the floor*. Say the two model sentences randomly again, but this time have students make the gesture corresponding to the sentence they comprehend. This is an important step in that students are now associating a meaningful gesture with the input they understand.

Next introduce two pictures (on tagboard or large construction paper) representing the two sentences; in this case, the pictures could be simple diagrams of a stick person sleeping on a floor and a stick person slipping on a floor:

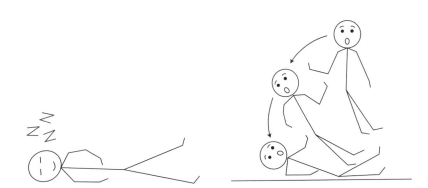

Show the pictures in random order a few times and have the class chorally produce the appropriate sentences.

These pictures are necessary for the next stage of the activity, in which a student volunteer comes to the front of the class. Have this volunteer repeat the sentences a few times for practice, cueing the response with the picture cards. Then move to the back of the room and hold up one of the two pictures randomly as a cue for the volunteer. The student produces the utterance (e.g., *Don't sleep on the floor*), and the class provides immediate feedback by making the gesture corresponding to the sentence they have heard. Assuming that the class response is more or less uniform and correct, the speaker can assume that the distinction was clearly made; if not, the teacher and class members may request a repetition of the utterance.

Other sentence examples for the /ɪ/ vs. /iy/ distinction that are easy to illustrate are the following (see Bowen 1975b and Nilsen and Nilsen 1973 for more examples):

1a.   He bit the man.

1b.   He beat the man.

2a.   Will he leave here?

2b.   Will he live here?

This technique is summarized in the following steps:

1.   Write the two model sentences on opposite sides of the board.
2.   Say them randomly; students point to the one that they hear.
3.   Elicit a gesture to represent each sentence, then erase the sentences from the board.
4.   Again, say the sentences randomly; students make the appropriate gesture.
5.   Produce stick-figure picture cards and show each picture randomly a few times; have the class say the corresponding sentence.
6.   Ask for a volunteer. Make sure the student has memorized the two sentences and can associate them quickly with the pictures.
7.   Move to the back of the classroom. Flash the pictures randomly (only the volunteer can see; the rest of the class should be watching the volunteer *only*). The volunteer should pronounce the appropriate sentence while the rest of the students make the gesture corresponding to the sentence they comprehend.

Generally, students notice quickly whether they are being understood clearly and try to modify their pronunciation accordingly. Thus, 2–3 minutes is usually a long enough period for each volunteer at the front of the class. Of course, the student need not always be a volunteer. The teacher may wish to call on students with particular production problems to see if they are beginning to distinguish a given contrast better.

GUIDED PRACTICE WITH FEEDBACK

In this phase, students are still focused on the relevant contrasts but assume an increasing amount of responsibility for producing language (and the targeted vowel contrasts) creatively, usually within a sentence-length utterance. Information gap activities, which allow students to practice both listening discrimination and spoken production, are an ideal format for providing students with this kind of guided practice. Because attention

STUDENT A

Directions: Eight of the sixteen boxes below are filled in for you. The other eight are empty. Your task is to fill in these empty boxes by asking your partner for the missing information. In turn, your partner will ask you questions about your eight words. You should ask questions like the following:

What is the word in box C2?

What word is in box A4?

	1	2	3	4
A	/ɑ/ bomb		/ʌ/ duck	
B		/ɑ/ not		
C			/ʌ/ cup	/ɑ/ got
D	/ʌ/ cut	/ɑ/ box	/ʌ/ hut	

Follow-up: After you and your partner have finished filling in the missing information, compare your answers to see if you have understood each other correctly. Practice pronouncing any difficult words together.

STUDENT B

Directions: Eight of the sixteen boxes below are filled in for you. The other eight are empty. Your task is to fill in these empty boxes by asking your partner for the missing information. In turn, your partner will ask you questions about your eight words. You should ask questions like the following:

What is the word in box C3?

What word is in box D2?

	1	2	3	4
A		/ʌ/ come		/ʌ/ stuck
B	/ɑ/ sock		/ɑ/ rob	/ɑ/ smog
C	/ʌ/ luck	/ɑ/ cop		
D				/ʌ/ nut

Follow-up: After you and your partner have finished filling in the missing information, compare your answers to see if you have understood each other correctly. Practice pronouncing any difficult words together.

Figure 4.9 Information gap exercise to discriminate between /ɑ/ and /ʌ/

is focused primarily at the sentence level, the potential for the learner to carefully monitor output is great; furthermore, the opportunity for peer feedback is built into the activity. Information gap exercises built around minimal pair contrasts are easily constructed, as in Figure 4.9.

"Simon Says," presented in the previous chapter on consonants, can be adapted for guided practice with vowel contrasts. In this game, the leader "Simon" (in this case, the teacher) gives commands and all participants must either act out the command (it if begins with the words "Simon says") or ignore it (if the leader does not preface the command with the words "Simon says"). For example, if the leader says, "Simon says move your index finger," any participants who fail to act out this command are out of the game and must sit down. However, if the leader says "Touch your cheek," any participants who carry out the command are out of the game and sit down. The last person remaining standing is considered the winner and can then assume the role of "Simon."

This game lends itself especially to practicing the /ɪ/ vs. /iy/ contrast because the names of so many body parts contain these vowel sounds:

/ɪ/	/iy/
wrist	cheek
finger	knee
chin	teeth
hip	heel
lip	feet
shin	

Before beginning the game, you can elicit body parts containing these sounds from the students. For younger students (or adults, for that matter) who enjoy kines-

TABLE 4.8 LIST OF VOWELS WITH COMMUNICATIVE MEANING IN ENGLISH

Written	Pronounced	Used to express	In response to/(situation)
Ahhh!	/ɑː/	Satisfaction, relaxation	(You step into a nice hot tub./ You take a sip of refreshing iced tea on a hot day.)
Aw.	/ɔː/	Sympathy, disappointment	"My dog just died."
Ow!	/aw/	Pain	(A door slams on your finger.)
Oh?	/ow/	Mild surprise, interest	"The new Woody Allen movie is opening tonight."
Oh.	/ow:/	Comprehension	"You have to plug it in before it'll work."
Uh-oh.	/ʔʌʔow/	Trouble	(You're driving over the speed limit and you see a police car in your rear-view mirror.)
Ooh!	/uw:/	Disgust	"Look! There's a fly in your soup!"
Oops!	/uwps/	Recognition of problem	(You spill your coffee while pouring.)
Aha!	/əhɑ/	Discovery	(You finally understand the math problem you've been working on.)
Huh?	/hʌ/ (nasal)	Lack of understanding	(You don't hear what someone says to you, or you think you heard incorrectly.)
Boo!	/buw/	Frightening someone	(You sneak up behind someone and want to scare him or her.)
Uh-uh.	/ʔʌʔə/ (nasal)	No	"Have you ever read this book?"
Uh-huh	/əhʌ/ (nasal)	Yes	"Can I call you?"

A

Read this: **Listen for this:**

What would you say if . . .

1.   . . . you sat down to relax in a big
     comfortable chair after standing all day?   Ahh!

2.   . . . you didn't hear what one of your
     friends just said to you?   Huh?

3.   . . . you saw your teacher coming toward you
     and you had skipped his class twice this week? Oh-oh!

B

Read this: **Listen for this:**

What would you say if . . .

1.   . . . you quietly walked up behind a
     friend to scare her?   Boo!

2.   . . . you dropped your pen on the floor?   Oops! *or* Uh-oh!

3.   . . . your friend told you he had a bad
     cold?   Aw.

Figure 4.10 Worksheets for communicative activity with interjections

thetic reinforcement while learning, this activity provides a welcome opportunity to move about, once the scene has been set by the teacher. Since students can lead the activity, they can practice both listening and production skills.

Single vowels or combinations of vowels and consonants can have an important communicative function or meaning in English. The list in Table 4.8, which can be distributed as a student handout, sets the stage for a pair exercise involving cued responses. Begin by presenting each example with the proper intonation.

Although not commonly taught in the language classroom, these simple interjections are an efficient means of conveying emotions and feelings. Before introducing the pair practice activity, you may want to check how many of these expressions the students already know by eliciting situations or meanings from them and clarifying the pronunciation of each utterance. Once this has been done, each member of the pair receives either Worksheet A or Worksheet B (Figure 4.10) containing situations on the left and appropriate responses on the right. Pairs should take turns reading their situations and checking whether their partner can produce the appropriate cued response.

Chain drills are another appropriate and enjoyable guided activity for both younger children and adult learners. The children's game "I'm Going on a Trip" lends itself well to virtually any individual vowel sound or vowel contrast, for example, the contrast /uw/ vs. /ʊ/. If possible, students should sit in a circle for this activity. First, explain the rules: Each student has to repeat the phrase used by the student before and then add one additional item containing either an /uw/ or /ʊ/ sound. Begin the activity by stating, "I'm going on a trip and I'm going to bring some *shoes.*" The student to your immediate right then says, "I'm going on a trip and I'm going to bring some *shoes* and some *toothpaste.*" Each successive student repeats the previous items, adding one more until someone is not able to supply an appropriate item or has a memory breakdown. At this point, the next student in the circle can begin anew, this time using the /ʊ/ sound (e.g., "I'm going on a trip and I'm going to bring a *book.*") This activity can continue for several rounds, until students have exhausted their repertoire of words containing the targeted sounds. Other possible adaptations of this chain drill activity are, "I'm going shopping and I'm going to buy . . . ," or "I'm cooking a delicious meal and I'm going to make . . ."

COMMUNICATIVE PRACTICE AND FEEDBACK

Most of the preceding activities depend heavily on learners producing targeted contrasts intelligibly enough for their partners to comprehend them. However, although there is an element of negotiated meaning built into the activities, the learners are not yet generating utterances of their own or using language in a truly creative sense. Controlled and guided practice precede the stage of communicative practice, which allows newly acquired pronunciation skills to be practiced in a more genuinely communicative context.

Many of these activities already contain built-in expansion possibilities from more guided to more communicative practice. For example, in the activity on interjections, the next step would be to have pairs or small groups of students write their own "What would you say if . . ." scenarios, and then present them to the class to cue the appropriate response. Similarly, the logical follow-up to a minimal pair dialogue reading activity is to have students write and perform their own dialogues containing the sound contrast being practiced. In this section we mention a few additional communicative practice activities involving vowel sounds. This is by no means an exhaustive list of possible activities, as these are limited only by the teacher's imagination.

Since the letters of the alphabet contain many of the key vowel sounds in English, one relatively communicative activity for vowel practice is an adaptation of the children's game "Hangman." Although most appropriate for low-level students, students engaging in this activity need to have a good command of the alphabet (see Chapter 9) and have a command of certain grammatical structures such as the following:

Is there a/an _____? (e.g., "Is there a *C*?")

Yes, there is.

No, there isn't.

They also need to be able to understand simple phrases, such as "Time is money" or "Help yourself." You need to prepare a selection of such phrases or idioms in advance. To begin the activity, explain the rules of "Hangman": A "man" is being hung and can be saved from his death if the students guess the secret phrase before the hangman is fully drawn.

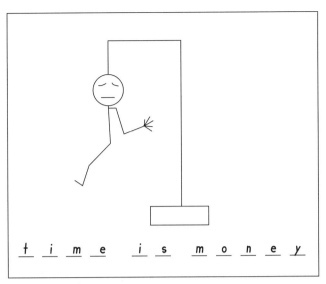

Figure 4.11 Sample "Hangman" drawing

Draw the gallows on the board (see Figure 4.11) and under it indicate the number of letters in each word of the phrase by drawing the appropriate number of blanks. Students take turns guessing; for each wrong guess add a body part of the stick-figure hangman under the gallows, beginning with the head. Younger children especially love this activity, and like to be allowed to go to the board and draw the hangman or fill in the blanks while their classmates participate in the guessing activity.

A more challenging production activity is the strip story. The language base is provided for students in the form of a short narrative passage. Prepare this activity in advance by writing each sentence of the narrative on individual strips of paper, which you give to the students in jumbled order. They must practice their sentence, paying special attention to the vowel contrasts contained, and then memorize it. Students are next arranged in story groups in such a way that every student in a given group has one of the sentences of the narrative. The group task is to unscramble the sentences and rearrange them in their proper narrative order, then present the story orally to the rest of the class. These stories can be written for a variety of vowel contrasts, and present an excellent opportunity for students to negotiate meaning while practicing key sound contrasts. The following sample narrative is written for the vowel contrast /ɛ/ vs. /ey/:

It was a dark and rainy night in November.

It was late, after twelve, and Stella was tired.

As she walked along Main Street, the wind wailed through the trees.

Suddenly, she saw a strange man at the other end of the street.

He had a long red scarf around his neck.

As he approached her, her heart raced faster.

Then, to her relief, she saw that it was her neighbor Ed.

"Oh Ed, I'm so glad that it's you. I was scared."

"Stella, what are you doing out so late? It's dangerous!"

"Let me hail you a taxi. We can share the cab fare and get you home safely."

Once students have sorted out the proper order for the narrative, you can follow-up by having two students (in this case one female and one male) volunteer to be interviewed in the roles of Stella and Ed. Their classmates can be encouraged to pose factual questions, such as, "How did you feel when you saw the strange man at the end of the street?" and even more personal questions, such as, "Do you find Stella attractive?" This follow-up allows the activity to extend into an even more communicative realm, since the questions and answers are no longer directly tied to the language practice material, and students must attend more to meaning than to form.

As we pointed out previously, colors are a rich context for practicing vowel contrasts. Teachers wishing to present a communicative review of the entire range of vowel sounds in NAE can make use of colorful postcard-size museum replicas (or old calendars) to set the context for an activity in which students describe a work of art to a partner. This activity can be more or less structured, depending on student proficiency level and teaching objectives. In the less structured version, students first practice describing their picture to their partner, and give each other feedback on their production while you circulate and give additional feedback as requested or needed. (Selected volunteers may be called upon to describe their picture to the entire class.) A possible follow-up would be to have students tape record their description (either at home on a personal tape recorder or in the language lab) and hand their cassette in to the teacher for evaluation or feedback.

A more structured version of this activity requires that the teacher obtain sets of art postcards that are similar in subject matter and composition – such as Monet's water lilies, Degas' ballerinas, or Kandinsky's abstracts. Each student pair would receive a set of three or four postcards; they could take turns describing one of the works of art to their partner, whose task it would be to decide which work of art was being described. As a follow-up to this version of the activity, students could select their favorite rendition of the subject and tape record their description.

In Chapter 3, we suggested adapting simple role plays for communicatively oriented consonant practice. This works equally well for vowel practice, as illustrated in the sample role cards for practicing the /iy/ vs. /ɪ/ contrast:

Student A

Identity: Jean/Jim Green, student

Situation: Your physics teacher, Mr./Mrs. Bean, has called you into his/her office because he/she suspects you of cheating on the quiz. You explain that you didn't cheat. The heat was making you feel ill and you needed to take a pill.

Student B

Identity: Mr./Mrs. Bean, physics teacher

Situation: You have called your student Jean/Jim into your office because you suspect she/he was cheating on the physics exam. You ask her/him to sit down and explain the situation.

As we have noted, vowels are the tools of poets, and what better way to heighten students' awareness of vowel contrasts than to engage them in a simple poetry-writing activity. Because writing poetry is difficult even for native speakers, the task is simplified for students by providing them with a limerick template, as in Figure 4.12.

Students should be encouraged to use their imagination (i.e., create rhyming nonsense words) and to have fun with this activity. A sample student-generated limerick follows:

/æ/ **VS.** /ʌ/

There once was a student named Pam
Who wanted to dance with a lamb
She tried not to hug it
But she happened to slug it
So the lamb ended up in her Spam.

A final suggestion for creating a context for communicative practice involves setting up a problem-solving situation – in this case a matchmaking scenario involving the vowel contrasts /ɛ/, /ey/, and /æ/. Students are told that they work for an exclusive computer dating service, and that they have been asked by their supervisor to find the perfect match for Jack Beck. They need to justify the potential match, since Mr. Beck is a loyal and steady customer of the firm. A space engineer who works hard and plays hard, Mr. Beck likes gambling, fast cars, and jazz. He hates baseball and women who wear too much makeup. He has a cabin in Colorado, where he loves to spend his vacations. He's frightened of airplanes, since both of his parents died in a plane crash. Information about the three potential "matches" appears in Figure 4.13.

Directions: Using the following guide, work in pairs or small groups to write your own limerick. The words in blanks 1, 2, 5, and 6 should rhyme; the words in blanks 3 and 4 should rhyme. Notice that blanks 2 and 5 contain the same word. See the sample limerick for an example.

Sound Contrasts: / / **vs.** / /

There once was a student named _____
(1) NAME

Who wanted to dance with a/an _____
(2) THING

She tried not to _____ it
(3) VERB

But she happened to _____ it
(4) VERB

So the _____ ended up in her _____.
(5) THING   (6) THING

Sample Limerick: /ɪ/ **vs.** /iy/

There once was a student named Trish
Who wanted to dance with a fish
She tried not to squeeze it
But she happened to freeze it
So the fish ended up in her dish.

Figure 4.12 Worksheet with template for writing limericks

Jane Wayne	Jennifer Black	Pat Kemp
PERSONAL CHARACTERISTICS: jealous, lazy, patient, passive, talented	PERSONAL CHARACTERISTICS: playful, competitive, aggressive	PERSONAL CHARACTERISTICS: chronically late, standoffish, restrained
HOBBIES: classical music, foreign languages, home decorating	HOBBIES: samba dancing, tennis, fencing, home repair	HOBBIES: figure skating, stamp collecting, backpacking
OTHER INFORMATION: likes cats, owns a Jaguar, married three times previously, expensive taste	OTHER INFORMATION: into health food, wears big, floppy hats, loves to travel, athletic	OTHER INFORMATION: lived in Algeria, hates being indoors, has allergies

Figure 4.13 Computer dating: /ey/ vs. /ɛ/ vs. /æ/

CONCLUSION

The challenge of teaching vowels, as with consonants, lies both in how to initially describe the individual phonemes to students and how to find rich, authentic contexts for practice. As we have noted, vowels can be difficult both for the teacher to describe and for the student to master. This is partially because the articulatory characteristics of vowels cannot be pinned down as precisely as those of consonants. A second reason vowels can be so difficult for students is due to the relative complexity of the English vowel system – especially as it compares to the vowel systems of many of our students' first languages.

Vowels are also problematic in that they tend to display much more dialectal variation among native speakers of NAE than consonants do. It is important that native speakers who teach pronunciation become aware of any markedly regional or dialectal features in their own speech so that they can be open and objective with their learners (e.g., "I/people living around here say *pin* and *pen* the same. But many native speakers say them differently."). Teachers should feel free to modify textbook exercises and activities so that when teaching pronunciation they are not forced to produce or spend time teaching distinctions they cannot or simply do not make in their own speech. However, teachers also have the responsibility to expose learners via guest speakers and tape recordings to other widespread dialects of NAE with different target vowel sounds. Teachers who are nonnative speakers should select the target norm that they are most familiar with (and can produce with reasonable accuracy and consistency) and modify classroom activities accordingly.

In this chapter, we have suggested that in presenting vowels, teachers should progress through the various stages of the controlled to communicative hierarchy, in much the same fashion as they would when teaching consonants. We have also suggested possible contexts that can be used to set the scene for teaching vowel contrasts, and have presented numerous activity types that lend themselves to practicing these segmental contrasts.

EXERCISES

KEY CONCEPTS

Write a brief definition for the following key terms from this chapter. Give examples where relevant.

vowel	tense/lax vowel
simple vowel	open/closed syllable
vowel + glide	sonorant
diphthong	/r/- and /l/-coloring
vowel quadrant	nasalization
front/central/back	reduced vowel
high/mid/low	citation vowel
rounded/spread/neutral lip position	

INTROSPECTING ABOUT YOUR OWN LANGUAGE LEARNING

Think about a foreign language that you have learned in school or while living abroad.

1. What difficulties with vowel sounds did you have?

2. Were these difficulties typical for native speakers of your language?

3. What strategies did you use to improve your production of these sounds? Were these successful?

4. If you had language instruction, did the teacher try to help you with pronunciation of vowels? If so, how?

Discussion Questions

1. What do you consider to be the greatest challenges in teaching vowels?

2. In this chapter we suggest several ways of presenting the basic articulatory features of vowels (e.g., use of the vowel quadrant, sagittal diagrams, the analogy of the oral cavity to a resonance chamber). Which of these tools do you find most useful? Would you suggest using different strategies with different populations? Explain.

3. Do you think certain vowel difficulties cause a greater breakdown in communication or are more irritating to native speakers than others? If so, which?

4. Why is it important to consider positional variation when teaching NAE vowels to speakers of other languages? Use a specific vowel sound to illustrate your answer.

In the Classroom

Assume that you are teaching pronunciation. Here are some common classroom situations that you might encounter. What technique would you use or what explanation would you give?

1. Your students consistently pronounce *back* as /bɑk/.

2. A student pronounces *campus* as /kæmpuws/.

3. A student says: "When I learned English in my country, the teacher taught us to pronounce *dance* as /dɑns/. But I hear most Americans pronounce it /dæns/. Which is correct?"

4. A student cannot distinguish *pill* and *peel* and produces /pɪl/ for both.

Suggested Activities

1. Locate a description of typical difficulties for the group of learners that you work with or anticipate working with. See, for example, Avery and Ehrlich (1992), Kenworthy (1987), and Swan and Smith (1987). What insights did you gain into the vowel challenges that this group will experience?

2. Listen again to the recorded segment for the previous chapter, which contains two spontaneous speech samples from nonnative speakers. Listen to the two samples (several times if necessary), paying particular attention to vowel production. What problems do these speakers have with vowels? (Consider not only the articulation of individual vowels but also issues such as /r/- and /l/-coloring, vowel length, nasalization, and reduced vowels.)

3. Suppose that you were going to tutor one of the two learners in (2). What are the top priorities you would select in terms of helping the learner improve control of the NAE vowel system?

4. Prepare an activity for presenting and practicing one of the following vowel contrasts, each of which is a problem for certain groups of learners:

   /ʊ, uw/ /ɪ, iy/ /ey, ɛ/ /ʌ, ɑ/

   You may choose to use any of the activities we have presented in this chapter (e.g., Bowen's minimal pair technique, an information gap, a role play). Specify in which phase of the pronunciation lesson this activity would be used.

On the Cassette

Listen to the cassette and transcribe the vowels in the thirty words read by the speaker.

CHAPTER 5

Stress, Rhythm, and Adjustments in Connected Speech

Many pronunciation teachers would claim that a learner's command of segmental features is less critical to communicative competence than a command of suprasegmental features, since the suprasegmentals carry more of the overall meaning load than do the segmentals. To better understand this point of view, imagine a native speaker of English engaged in conversation with an adult learner. The learner is discussing an incident in which her child had choked on something and could not breathe. "He swallowed a pill," she says. "What kind of peel?" asks the native speaker. "An aspirin," says the learner. "Oh, a *pill!* I thought you said *peel,*" responds the native speaker. Such incidents in native-nonnative speaker conversation involving mispronunciation of a segmental sound usually lead to minor repairable misunderstandings.

With suprasegmentals and connected speech, however, the misunderstanding is apt to be of a more serious nature. Learners who use incorrect rhythm patterns or who do not connect words together are at best frustrating to the native-speaking listener; more seriously, if these learners use improper intonation contours, they can be perceived as abrupt, or even rude; and if the stress and rhythm patterns are too nonnativelike, the speakers who produce them may not be understood at all.

In the sections that follow, we examine and describe the stress and rhythmic patterns of NAE along with its characteristic connected speech features. We also give suggestions on how these areas can be addressed in the ESL/EFL pronunciation curriculum.

WORD STRESS: WHAT THE TEACHER NEEDS TO KNOW

What is *stress*? Stressed syllables are most often defined as those syllables within an utterance that are longer, louder, and higher in pitch. In fact, this definition is not exactly borne out by phonetic facts. Stressed syllables (or rather the vowels of stressed syllables) are often longer, louder, and higher in pitch, but in any given stressed syllable this entire combination of features may not be present. Looking at this phenomenon from the speaker's point of view, stress involves a greater outlay of energy as the speaker expels air from the lungs and articulates syllables. This increase in muscular energy and respiratory activity is undoubtedly what allows the native speaker to tap out the rhythm of syllables within a word or words within an utterance. From the listener's point of view, the most salient features of stress are probably longer vowel duration in the stressed syllable and higher pitch.

The difference between stressed and unstressed syllables is greater in English than in most other languages – with the possible exception of German, its Germanic language cousin. Compare the relatively unstressed pattern of French words with the more differentiated stress pattern of their English cognates:

French				English			
·	·	·	●	●	·	●	·
dé	mo	cra	TIQUE	DE	mo	CRAT	ic
·	·	·	●	·	●	·	·
gé	o	gra	PHIE	ge	OG	raph	y
·	·	·	·	●	●	·	·	●	·
or	ga	ni	sa	TION	OR	gan	i	ZA	tion

To capture this differentiation in stress levels, English language-teaching texts generally speak of three levels of **word stress**, or the pattern of stressed and unstressed syllables within a word. These levels are often referred to as strong, medial, and weak (or, alternatively, primary, secondary, and tertiary). In fact, according to some phoneticians, there are as many as six levels of word stress, not all of which are readily discernible. For pedagogical purposes, we will adhere to the conventional designation of three levels, which we will call **strongly stressed, lightly stressed,** and **unstressed syllables.** We have chosen these designations because we believe that they best represent what occurs on the syllable level. In addition, the designation *unstressed* also parallels our analysis of vowel quality in such syllables, where the more centralized or neutralized unstressed vowels tend to occur. When using normal orthography, we represent these three levels using large capital letters, small capital letters, and lowercase letters, respectively. In multisyllabic words, it is possible for all three levels of word stress to be present, e.g., JAPanESE.

To indicate strongly stressed syllables in phonetic transcription we have chosen the convention of a superscript accent mark (') placed before the syllable; to indicate lightly stressed syllables we use a subscript accent (ˌ); unstressed syllables are not specially marked. Compare:

under	/ˈʌndəʳ/	arrival	/əˈrayvəl/
clockwork	/ˈklɑkˌwɜʳk/	aptitude	/ˈæptəˌtuwd/
preposterous	/prəˈpɑst(ə)rəs/	celebration	/ˌsɛləˈbreyʃən/

Another feature of word stress in English is that it can occur on virtually any syllable, depending in part on the origin of the word. This apparent lack of predictability as to where the stress falls is confusing to learners from language groups in which stress placement is more transparent.

NOTE TO TEACHERS

For speakers of languages with very regular word stress patterns, the more complex rules for assigning word stress in English will undoubtedly cause some difficulty. French almost consistently stresses the last syllable, and this native-language stress pattern frequently carries over to the French speaker's pronunciation of English words – particularly with multisyllabic cognates in the two languages. Czech consistently stresses the first syllable of multisyllabic words, whereas Polish and Swahili have regular word stress on the penultimate syllable.

Far from being random, stress placement in English words derives from the rather colorful history of the language. Today, roughly thirty percent of the vocabulary of English stems from its Old English origins and retains the native Germanic stress patterns.[1] Many of the remaining words have been acquired through historical events, such as the Norman Conquest, which brought much French vocabulary into English, or through the influences of Christian religion and academia, which have done much to secure the position of words of Greek and Latin origin in the English language. In more recent times, English has derived a portion of its vocabulary from the indigenous Native American languages (e.g., *moccasin, moose, hickory*) and from its Spanish-speaking neighbors (e.g., *chocolate, tomato*). It has also acquired vocabulary via trade with more distant neighbors from South America (e.g., *condor, jaguar, tapioca*) and Asia (e.g., *china, jungle, bandana, bungalow, cashmere*). New loan words continue to be assimilated into English and undergo similar changes in spelling and pronunciation as have words that entered the language in earlier eras – until they are no longer perceived as foreign and their origins are all but forgotten to users who do not study etymology.

Overall, then, NAE is very much a "melting pot" language. Although loan words in English may sometimes retain the stress patterns of the language from which they derive, they are more often incorporated into the stress patterns of English, which imposes on them a more indigenous or Germanic stress pattern by moving the stress to an earlier syllable, often the first.[2] We can see this in borrowings such as *GRAMmar* (from French *gramMAIRE*) and *CHOColate* (from Spanish *chocoLAte*). In fact, the longer a borrowed word has been in the English language, the more likely it is that this type of stress shift will occur.

WHERE THE STRESS FALLS IN A WORD

Factors that influence stress placement include the historical origin of a word, affixation, and the word's grammatical function in an utterance.[3] One important difference between words of Germanic origin and those of non-Germanic origin is the way in which stress is assigned. For words of Germanic origin, the first syllable of the base form of a word is typically stressed:

FAther	YELlow	FINger
SISter	OFten	ELbow
FROLic	TWENty	HAMmer
WISdom	FIFty	WAter

Today, even many two-syllable words that have entered English through French and other languages have been assimilated phonologically and follow the Germanic word stress pattern:

PICture	FLOWer	FOReign
MUsic	PURple	REAson
DOCtor	VISit	MANage

[1]Despite the limited number of words in the English language that stem from Germanic origins, these words are used quite frequently. In fact, of the 1,000 most frequently used words in English, approximately 83% are of Germanic origin. Examples of frequently used Germanic root words in English are kinship terms, body parts, numbers, prepositions, and phrasal and irregular verbs.
[2]British English exhibits an even stronger tendency to move stress to an earlier syllable than American English. Compare the British pronunciation of the French loan words *garage* and *ballet* (GARage, BALlet) to the American pronunciation (gaRAGE; balLET). See Appendix 1 for further details.
[3]See Chapter 9 for a discussion of how spelling can help to predict the placement of stress in a word.

Words that have not been assimilated to the Germanic pattern have less predictable word stress in their base forms, but stress is often predictable if certain affixes or spellings are involved.

PREFIXES

As a general rule, words containing prefixes tend to be strongly stressed on the first syllable of the base or root element, with the prefix either unstressed or lightly stressed:

Nouns	Adjectives	Verbs
aWARD	unHEALTHy	deCLARE
surPRISE	beREAVED	exPLAIN
proPOSal	aSLEEP	forGET
comPLAINT	inCREDible	obTAIN

In English, prefixes tend to fall into one of two categories: prefixes of Germanic origin and prefixes of Latinate origin. The Germanic prefixes include: *a-, be-, for-, fore-, mis-, out-, over-, un-, under-, up-,* and *with-* (as in *awake, belief, forgive, forewarn, mistake, outrun, overdo, untie, understand, uphold,* and *withdrawn.*) Some of these prefixes (*a-, be-, for-,* and *with-*) are always unstressed in the words in which they occur. Others usually receive light stress, as in the following highly productive prefix + verb combinations:

un-	*out-*	*over-*	*under-*
• ●	• ●	• · ●	• · ●
UNDO	OUTDO	overLOOK	UNderSTAND
UNLEASH	OUTRUN	overTAKE	UNderRATE
UNTIE	OUTBID	overCOME	UNderCOOK
UNHOOK	OUTCLASS	overDRESS	UNderFUND
UNHITCH	OUTLAST	overDO	UNderPAY

An exception to this general pattern (light or no stress on the prefix and strong stress on the base) occurs when a word with a prefix (such as *fore-, out-, over-, under-,* or *up-*) functions as a noun and has the same pattern as a noun compound (see the following list). In this case, the prefix or its first syllable tends to be strongly stressed, with the noun receiving only light stress:

fore-	*out-*	*over-*	*under-*	*up-*
● •	● •	● · •	● · •	● •
FOREarm	OUTLook	OverALLS	UNderDOG	UPshot
FOREcast	OUTLine	OverCOAT	UNderWEAR	UPkeep
FOREthought	OUTrage	OverDOSE	UNderBRUSH	UProar
FOREsight	OUTput	OverHANG	UNderPASS	UPstart
FOREground	OUTcry	OverPASS	UNderTOW	UPsurge

Notice the difference in word stress in the following examples, where the prefix is attached in one case to a noun and in the other case to a verb.

Prefix + base (functioning as a noun)	Prefix + verb
He has a lot of FOREsight.	Could anyone foreSEE it happening?
He was wounded in the FOREarm.	foreWARNED is foreARMED!
It requires a large financial OUTlay.	The firm needed to outLAY a large amount of capital for the project.
Inflation is an OUTgrowth of excess spending.	My daughter will outGROW these shoes soon.
We couldn't stop the OverFLOW from the tank.	Why did the tank overFLOW?
The truck carried an OverLOAD.	Don't overLOAD the pack animals.

In these examples, the difference in the stress patterns helps to reinforce the differences between parts of speech.[4]

The second category is prefixes of Latinate origin. These include: *a(d)-, com-, de-, dis-, ex-, en-, in-, ob-, per-, pre-, pro-, re-, sub-,* and *sur-* (as in the verbs *complain, discharge, inhale, persuade, subside,* etc.). As with prefixes of Germanic origin, it is usually the base (not the prefix) that receives strong stress. However, unlike Germanic prefixes – many of which receive light stress when added to verbs – the majority of Latinate prefixes are unstressed when part of a verb.[5] Among the most frequent of these Latinate prefixes, which account for hundreds of verbs in English, are the following:

com-	*dis-*	*pro-*	*ex-*
• ●	• ●	• ●	• ●
comMAND	disCUSS	proCLAIM	exIST
comMIT	disPERSE	proDUCE	exPAND
comPARE	disPLAY	proJECT	exPECT
comPEL	disPOSE	proPEL	exPEL
comPLAIN	disTURB	proTEST	exTEND

In all these cases, the unstressed nature of the prefix extends to its variant forms. Thus *com-* would also include its allomorphic variants, *co-, col-, con-,* and *cor-,* just as *in-* also includes *im-, il-,* and *ir-.*

We see similar differences in word stress with the Latinate prefixes. In other words, when these prefixes are part of a word that functions as a noun, the prefix often receives strong stress. Compare the following sentences:[6]

Noun	Verb
He's working on a difficult PROject.	They proJECT that it will take six months to finish.
Fresh PROduce is expensive in the winter.	The new company will proDUCE the goods more cheaply.
The election was so close that they demanded a REcall.	Do you reCALL his name?

[4]The influence of a word's part of speech on its stress pattern is dealt with more thoroughly in Chapter 8.
[5]However, there are also examples of Latinate prefixes that receive light stress because they are still being used to form new words: e.g., *re-* in reDO, reHEAT, reBUILD. In addition, some speakers may use light stress on some of the other Latinate prefixes.
[6]See Chapter 8 for a list of common noun-verb pairs that differ in stress pattern.

SUFFIXES

Suffixes affect word stress in one of three ways:

1. They may have no effect on the stress pattern of the root word.
2. They may receive strong stress themselves.
3. They may cause the stress pattern in the stem to shift from one syllable to another.

For the most part, the neutral suffixes, which do not affect the stress pattern of the root word, are Germanic in origin. These suffixes include, for example, *-hood* (*childhood*), *-less* (*groundless*), *-ship* (*friendship*), and *-ful* (*cheerful*). In fact, if we compare examples of English words that employ such neutral suffixes with their modern-day German equivalents, we can easily see the historical relationship:

Neutral suffix	English	German
-en	THREAT + en	DROH + en
-er	BAK + er	BÄCK + er
-ful	TACT + ful	TAKT + voll
-hood	CHILD + hood	KIND + heit
-ing	OPEN + ing	ÖFFN + ung
-ish	DEVIL + ish	TEUFL + isch
-less	GROUND + less	GRUND + los
-ly	FRIEND + ly	FREUND + lich
-ship	FRIEND + ship	FREUND + schaft

Other neutral suffixes – not all of Germanic origin – that function in the same way include: *-able* (*usable*), *-al* (noun suffix, *arrival*), *-dom* (*kingdom*), *-ess* (*hostess*), *-ling* (*yearling*), *-ness* (*kindness*), *-some* (*handsome*), *-wise* (*clockwise*), and *-y* (*silky*).

Words with Germanic or neutral suffixes (whether the stem is of Germanic origin or not) still tend to maintain the stress pattern of the base form:

WORDS WITH GERMANIC SUFFIXES

BROTHer	HAPpy	EAsy
BROTHers	HAPpier	EAsier
BROTHerly	HAPpiness	unEAsily
unBROTHerly	unHAPpiness	unEAsiness

Unlike the Germanic suffixes, suffixes that have come into the English language via French often cause the final syllable of a word to receive strong stress, with other syllables receiving light or no stress. In most cases, the following categories (from Kreidler, 1989: 307) represent borrowings from modern-day French:[7]

-aire	*-ee*
doctriNAIRE	refuGEE
millionAIRE	tuTEE
questionNAIRE	trusTEE

---

[7] As a general tendency, the longer a word remains as part of the English vocabulary system, the greater the tendency for stress to shift toward the beginning of the word. Note the tendency today, for example, for the pronunciations *cigarETTE* and *millionAIRE* (stress on the final element) to coexist with *CIGarette* and *MILLionaire* (stress on the first element).

-eer	*-ese*
engiNEER	LebaNESE
mountainEER	SudaNESE
volunTEER	VietnaMESE

-esque	*-ique*
groTESQUE	bouTIQUE
araBESQUE	techNIQUE
picturESQUE	anTIQUE

-eur/-euse	*-oon*
masSEUSE	balLOON
chanTEUSE	saLOON
chaufFEUR	basSOON

-ette	*-et /ey/*
basiNETTE	balLET
casSETTE	bouQUET
kitchenETTE	vaLET

Suffixes can also cause a shift of stress in the root word – that is, as certain suffixes are added to a word, they can cause the stress to shift to the syllable immediately preceding the suffix. Note the stress shift caused by the addition of the following suffixes to the root word:[8]

Suffix	Root word	Root with suffix
-eous	adVANtage	ADvanTAgeous
-graphy	PHOto	phoTOGraphy
-ial	PROVerb	proVERBial
-ian	PARis	PaRIsian
-ic	CLImate	cliMATic
-ical	eCOLogy	EcoLOGical
-ious	INjure	inJURious
-ity	TRANquil	tranQUILity
-ion	EDuCATE	EDuCAtion

In these, as in many other words in English, a change of suffix not only brings about a shift in stress but also a change in the accompanying vowel reduction or neutralization in the unstressed syllables. Because of the nature of tense and lax vowels, there is sometimes an accompanying change in syllable structure or syllabification.

aCADemy	ACaDEMic	ACadeMICian
/əˈkædəmi/	/ˌækəˈdɛmɪk/	/ˌækədəˈmɪʃən/

PHOtoGRAPH	phoTOGraphy	PHOtoGRAPHic
/ˈfowɾəˌgræf/	/fəˈtɑgrəfi/	/ˌfowɾəˈgræfɪk/

REaLIZE	reALity	REaLIStic
/ˈriyəˌlayz/	/riˈæləri/	/ˌriyəˈlɪstɪk/

[8]The shift in stress also causes a change of vowel sound, as we discuss more fully in Chapter 9.

In certain cases, suffixation may cause a complete change in vowel quality from tense to lax rather than a shift in stress, as in the words *page* /ey/ vs. *paginate* /æ/, and *mime* /ay/ vs. *mimic* /ɪ/. For more information on this topic, see Chapter 9.

Finally, it is important to note that in cases where the base and the suffix have different historical origins, it is the suffix that determines the English stress pattern. For example, Germanic suffixes such as *-ly* and *-ness,* which can be added to words of Romance origin, cause no shift in stress: *PASsive, PASsively, PASsiveness.* Compare this with the shift from *PASsive* to *passSIVity* that occurs with the addition of the Latinate suffix *-ity.* This stress shift would extend even to a base word of Germanic origin if it were to take a Latinate suffix (e.g., *FOLDable* vs. *foldaBILity*).

NUMBERS

Cardinal and ordinal numbers that represent multiples of ten (20, 30, 40, 50, etc.) have predictable stress on the first syllable.

Cardinal numbers	Ordinal numbers
● (•) •	● (•) • •
TWENty	TWENtieth
THIRty	THIRtieth
FORty	FORtieth
FIFty	FIFtieth
SIXty	SIXtieth
SEVenty	SEVentieth

Two different stress patterns are possible with the *-teen* numbers and their ordinal counterparts:

Pattern 1	Pattern 2
● (•) •	• (•) ●
THIRTEEN(TH)	THIRTEEN(TH)
FOURTEEN(TH)	FOURTEEN(TH)
FIFTEEN(TH)	FIFTEEN(TH)
SIXTEEN(TH)	SIXTEEN(TH)
SEVenTEEN(TH)	SEVenTEEN(TH)
EIGHTEEN(TH)	EIGHTEEN(TH)
NINETEEN(TH)	NINETEEN(TH)

Native speakers tend to use the first of these patterns before a noun in attributive position (e.g., *the THIRteenth man*) and when counting. Overall, the second pattern is more common in phrase-final or utterance-final position, or when speakers are trying to make a deliberate distinction between the ten and teen digits. When pairs of words such as *thirteen* and *thirty* might be confused, native speakers may prefer the second pattern (i.e., strong stress on the second syllable) to differentiate clearly:

● •	• ●
THIRty	THIRTEEN
FORty	FOURTEEN
FIFty	FIFTEEN
SIXty	SIXTEEN

The *-teen* numbers are **compounds** – that is, combinations of two or more base elements.[9] The same is true of all hyphenated numbers: for example, *thirty-seven, eighty-four*. Like the *-teen* numbers, hyphenated numbers have two possible stress patterns depending on the context:

Pattern 1	Pattern 2
● (·) • ● (·)	● (·) • ● (·)
TWENty-THREE	TWENty-THREE
THIRty-SEVen	THIRty-SEVen
SEVenty-SIX	SEVenty-SIX
EIGHty-FOUR	EIGHty-FOUR

If a number is used without another number as a contrast, the first pattern is used – unless the number is utterance final, in which case the second pattern is preferred:

Pattern 1   I have TWENty-THREE dollars.
Pattern 2   John is only TWENty-THREE.

The first pattern is also preferred if the multiple of ten is in contrast or is given special emphasis:

Pattern 1   I said TWENty-THREE, not THIRty-THREE.

If, however, it is the second number in the compound that is contrasted, the second pattern is used:

Pattern 2   I said TWENty-THREE, not TWENty-TWO.

COMPOUNDS

In English noun compounds, the first element of the compound is strongly stressed, whether the compound is simple or complex:

Simple compounds	Complex compounds
● •	● • •
BLACKBIRD	BLACKbird NEST
AIRPLANE	AIRplane WING
COWBOY	COWboy HAT
HOT DOG	HOT dog BUN
TAP DANCE	TAP dance SCHOOL

[9]Some common compound patterns include: noun + noun (*sunglasses, ceiling fan*), noun + verb (*babysit, earmark*), and certain adjective + noun combinations that have assumed special meaning (*blackboard, greenhouse*).

There are two major noun compound patterns: (1) adjective + noun compounds and (2) noun + noun compounds. Since both elements of these two patterns receive stress, they do not exhibit any vowel reduction:[10]

Adjective + noun compounds	Noun + noun compounds
● •	● •
BLACKBOARD	DRUGSTORE
DARKROOM	MAILBOX
EASy STREET	HUBCAP
GREENHOUSE	LIPSTICK

Stress will vary between such "true" noun compounds and words that look like noun compounds but are actually functioning as adjective + noun sequences. Compare:

●   •

Noun compound: The President lives in the WHITE HOUSE.

•   ●

Adjective + noun sequence: John lives in a WHITE HOUSE.

In the first of these sentences, *White House* is functioning as a noun compound – hence the strong stress is placed on the first element of the compound. In the second sentence, *white* is lightly stressed and functions simply as an adjective modifying the noun *house;* thus the strong stress falls on the second (or major) element. Examples of other word sequences that can function as either noun compounds or adjective + noun phrases depending on stress and context are *greenhouse, blackbird, cold cream, yellow jacket, blackboard,* and *hot plate.* (For an excellent and thorough treatment of this area of word stress see Bowen 1975b.) When such word sequences are used as noun compounds, they are often spelled as one word.

The same patterns can occur in more complex contrasts, such as the following:

●   •   •

Billy found a BLACKbird NEST. (= *a nest used by blackbirds*)

•   ●   •

Billy found a BLACK BIRD NEST. (= *a bird nest that happened to be black in color*)

In the first sentence the word sequence *blackbird nest* functions as a complex noun compound, with the first element, *black,* receiving strong stress. In the second sentence, *black* is an adjective modifying the noun compound *bird nest.* It is lightly stressed, with the first element of the noun compound *bird nest* receiving strong stress.

Although noun compounds are the most frequent compounds in English, there are also some adjective compounds and verb compounds, all of which follow the

---

[10]The one exception is compounds with *-man,* which often have the reduced vowel /ə/ in the *-man* syllable: *salesman, fireman, policeman.*

same stress patterns as noun compounds: that is, strong stress falls on the first element of the compound and light stress on the second:

Adjective compounds	Verb compounds[11]
● (·) ● (·)	● (·) ●
WELL TRAINED	HOUSESIT
LIME GREEN	BAbySIT
OFF COLor	LIPREAD
SECondHAND	HANDCUFF
OverWORKED	GHOSTWRITE
GOODLOOKing	TYPEwrite
MIDdle AGED	TIPTOE

Like the compound numbers discussed earlier, the adjective compounds actually take two stress patterns (these are often hyphenated when written):

Pattern 1	Pattern 2
● (·) ● (·)	● (·) ● (·)

The first pattern tends to be used when the adjective compound modifies a noun:

That's a WELL-TRAINED dog.

I don't like OFF-COLor jokes.

The second pattern can occur when the adjective compound occurs in utterance-final position:

The gentleman is MIDdle-AGED.

Mary is frequently overANXious.

REFLEXIVES

One grammatical category that exhibits complete predictability of stress is reflexive pronouns, in which *self/selves* receives strong stress in virtually any environment:

· ●	· ●	· ●	· ●
mySELF	yourSELF	himSELF	themSELVES

PHRASAL VERBS

Phrasal verbs consist of two or three words and are composed of verbs followed by adverbial particles and/or prepositions. They are informal colloquial verbs of

---

[11]Compare these "true" verb compounds, which consist of a noun and a verb, with the prefix + verb combinations discussed earlier. In the case of the verb compound, the noun element receives strong stress and the verb element light stress: *"Did you VIdeoTAPE that program for me?"* In the prefix + verb combinations, it is the verb that receives strong stress and the prefix light stress or no stress: *"Can you reHEAT those leftovers for me?"*

Germanic origin that can often be paraphrased with a more formal single verb of Latinate origin:

Phrasal verb	Latinate verb
look at	regard
look over	peruse
talk about	discuss
talk up	promote
look out for	protect
talk out of	dissuade

The prepositions that are the second element of some two-word phrasal verbs or the third element of three-word phrasal verbs are: *about, at, for, from, of, to,*[12] and *with*. The most common adverbial particles in two-word verbs are: *across, ahead, along, away, back, behind, down, in(to), off, on,*[13] *over, under,* and *up.*

We can distinguish syntactically between the prepositions and the adverbial particles used to form phrasal verbs. In formal registers, prepositions can be fronted with their objects in wh-questions and relative clauses:

Formal   About whom are you talking?

Formal   I know the woman about whom they were talking.

Particles, however, never permit such fronting in any register:

Incorrect   Up what word did you look?

Incorrect   The word up which we looked has four meanings.

As we will explain more fully in our discussion of sentence stress, words that fall into certain grammatical categories, such as nouns, verbs, adjectives, and adverbs, tend to receive stress in a sentence, whereas articles, auxiliary verbs, and prepositions do not. This helps explain why prepositions in phrasal verb units are unstressed and why adverbs receive stress.

In fact, we can classify phrasal verbs into three main patterns. In all three patterns, the verb head has at least one stressed syllable and the following elements are either unstressed (if functioning as prepositions) or stressed (if functioning as adverbial particles):[14]

PATTERN 1	
Verb head	**– Stress particle**
LOOK	at
TALK	about
disPENSE	with
apPROVE	of

PATTERN 2	
Verb head	**+ Stress particle**
FIGure	OUT
DROP	OFF
TAKE	Over
LOOK	BACK

[12]There is one phrasal verb in which *to* functions as a particle rather than a preposition: *come to* meaning "to regain consciousness."

[13]As Dickerson (1994a) points out, the word *on* can function as either an unstressed preposition or a stressed adverbial particle. In phrasal verbs expressing cognitive or communicative activities *on* is an unstressed preposition: *agree on, insist on, settle on, plan on, decide on, count on, call on, lecture on.* If the phrasal verb is not functioning in either of these semantic categories, then *on* is probably a stressed adverbial particle: *put on, turn on, try on, carry on.*

[14]This taxonomy and description draw heavily from Dickerson (1994a); however, we use our own terminology to remain consistent with the analysis of other forms in this chapter and in Chapter 6.

PATTERN 3		
Verb head	**+ Stress particle**	**– Stress particle**
RUN	aWAY	with
WALK	OUT	on
TALK	DOWN	to
GET	aHEAD	of

These stress patterns appear when phrasal verbs are spoken in isolation or when the phrasal verb represents the last piece of new information in the predicate:

Pattern 1   She's LOOKing at it.

Pattern 2   They were STANDing aROUND.

Pattern 3   He RAN aWAY with it.

However, for phrasal verbs in patterns 2 or 3, if some other content (i.e., stressable) word comes after the verb head and carries important new information, then that word is strongly stressed and the verb and particle are only lightly stressed:

He TRIED ON a COAT.

We PUT the DOG OUT.

He RAN aWAY with the MONey.

We PUT UP with the NEW diRECtor.

For phrasal verbs in the first pattern, only the verb head receives light stress if it is followed by some other content word that carries the new information and receives strong stress:

LOOK at the BAby!

They TALKED about the MERger.

We treat related discourse-level matters under the topic of prominence in the following chapter. For a more detailed discussion of stress patterns with phrasal verbs, see Dickerson (1994a).

WORD STRESS: PEDAGOGICAL PRIORITIES

Initially, learners need to understand that a basic characteristic of every English word containing more than one syllable is its stress pattern. They also need to understand that even if all the individual sounds are pronounced correctly, incorrect placement of stress can cause misunderstanding. Thus, our first step as teachers is to clarify:

1.   how native speakers highlight a stressed syllable (length, volume, pitch)

2.   how they produce unstressed syllables (often with vowel reduction)

3.   what the three main levels of stress are (strongly stressed, lightly stressed, unstressed)

Next, we need to examine the primary dilemma faced by our students – namely, hearing and predicting where stress falls in words. As mentioned earlier, word stress in English is not nearly as predictable as it is in languages such as French or Polish; nor does English indicate irregularly placed stress patterns through stress or accent marks in the spelling, which is the case in Spanish.

Nonetheless, stress placement in English words is for the most part a rule-governed phenomenon, and explicit teaching of word stress patterns should be a part of the ESL pronunciation curriculum. When addressing this in the classroom, it is the teacher's task to minimize students' frustration and to clarify the systematicity of stress placement in words.

PRESENTING WORD STRESS TO STUDENTS

There are several systems of notation for marking stress in a written word that can help make the concept visual for students:

CAPitals

boldface

● ·
bubbles

áccents

<u>un</u>derlining

Each method has its advantages and disadvantages. Although capital letters stand out well in print and are easy to create with a typewriter, usually only two levels of stress can be indicated. The addition of boldface type and small capitals, possible in computer-generated materials, opens up the possibilities for indicating additional levels, however. Bubbles also work, especially if the size of the circles can be well differentiated (they may, of course, be written in by hand).

Accents are often used in dictionary pronunciation guides, with an accent *aigu* (´) signaling strong stress and an accent *grave* (`) signaling light stress, and no symbol at all for unstressed syllables: for example, *néwspàper, èducátion*. This type of notation can be accomplished with computer software but not with most typewriters. Also, it may not be as transparent to learners as the systems of capital letters or bubbles.

Many dictionaries mark strong stress with a vertical accent mark before the main stressed syllable: *chapter* /'tʃæptəʳ/. For words containing two or three levels of stress, a subscript accent mark is added to indicate light stress, as in the words *newspaper* /'nuwzˌpeypəʳ/ and *education* /ˌɛdʒə'keyʃən/. This system of vertical subscript and superscript accents is likely to be more intuitive than the notation of *grave* and *aigu* accents, but again is not as visually commanding as capital letters or bubbles. Moreover, the subscript accent mark cannot be found on most typewriters or current software programs (an apostrophe can serve as the superscript accent mark). Whatever system for marking stress teachers ultimately choose, they can add aural reinforcement by humming, clapping, or tapping the stress pattern. This can be done while holding up the fingers of one hand to indicate visually the number of syllables and where the strong stress falls.[15]

We suggest beginning the presentation of word stress with a brief discussion of the nature of stress and its historical origins in English. This can be followed up with an introduction to the fixed stress patterns that occur in certain categories of words such as cardinal and ordinal numbers, compound words, words beginning with prefixes, and other categories such as reflexive pronouns. Because of the complexity of word stress rules in general, we encourage teachers to reinforce classroom explanation of specific word stress rules with both in-class and out-of-class opportunities for students to make predictions about stress placement and apply any new rules they have been exposed to in class.

When treating the issue of compounding in the classroom, it is important to call students' attention to the fact that the stress patterns of these words differ from the same sequence of words when they do not function as a compound. In compounds containing noun elements (e.g., *notebook, drugstore, paper clip*), the first element in the word provides the more specific meaning of the noun compound, whereas the second element has a more generic meaning. This principle provides a useful pedagogical tool: In compounds, distinguishing information tends to be highlighted through stress. Urging students to con-

---

[15]See Chapter 10 for more information regarding the use of paralinguistic cues for visual reinforcement.

sider which element of the compound carries more specific meaning (e.g., answers the question "What kind of a _____?") can thus be of assistance. For example, the question "What kind of a brush is it?" has a variety of possible answers:

a HAIRbrush

a TOOTHbrush

a PAINTbrush

This same pattern applies to many other compounded items, and you can ask students to generate lists of possible noun compounds for common household items, such as:

_____knife

_____book

_____clock

_____plate

By explicitly teaching such patterns of word stress, we introduce learners to productive lexical areas of the English language.

A second pattern of word stress that should be introduced to students involves prefix + verb combinations that function as verbs, such as *understand, overlook,* and *redo.* The stress pattern of these words is the exact opposite of compounds that function as nouns. For example, given a context such as the following, the pattern *re-* + verb can be practiced:

Bob has done a project for his boss. Now the boss tells him the project is unsatisfactory. What advice can you give Bob?

Working in pairs or groups, students will generate as many appropriate *re-* + verb words as possible, using the formula "Bob should _____ the project." Possible words include *redo, rethink, reevaluate, retype, redesign, reorganize.*

For advanced-level professional or university students, it is useful to extend the discussion of word stress to discipline-specific terms. Students can be asked to bring in a list of five to ten multisyllabic words or compounds from their field to share with the class. Volunteers can write examples on the board for the class to analyze. Using the rules of predicting where stress falls, class members first determine stress placement and then try to pronounce the words. For example, a law student might write the following terms on the board:

beneficiary

liability

irrevocability

conservatorship

life insurance trust

pooled income fund

This activity not only allows students to exchange information about their areas of expertise, but it also illustrates how valuable a clue stress can be in determining the correct pronunciation of multisyllabic words.

LISTENING DISCRIMINATION

First, you need to be sure that students can hear the difference between stressed and unstressed syllables. This can be checked at a very basic level using nonsense syllables. In the following exercise, students write whether the two syllables in each pair are the same or different. You read:

Same or different?

1. la LA   la LA
2. LA la   la LA
3. la LA   LA la
4. LA la   LA la
5. la LA   la LA

Awareness of stress placement in specific words can be determined in a variety of ways. In one exercise, you group words together that share a stress pattern, then read each list aloud. The student's task is to circle the syllable containing strong stress:

Directions: Your teacher will read the following groups of words for you.
Circle the number of the syllable that receives the most stress in each group.

1 – ②– 3	1 – 2 – 3	1 – 2 – 3 – 4	1 – 2 – 3 – 4
embarrassed	president	regulation	military
dictation	envelope	satisfaction	ordinary
eraser	holiday	economic	elevator
pajamas	beautiful	artificial	dictionary
banana	bicycle	fascination	cemetery

In this exercise, the number of syllables is given for the students and several examples of a particular stress pattern are provided as reinforcement. In the more challenging exercise that follows, students must decide whether the word they hear has three or four syllables, then determine the pattern by comparing it to a model word (this can obviously be adapted for words with two- and five-syllable stress patterns as well).

Directions: Your teacher will read a list of words. Write each word in the appropriate column according to the number of syllables and the stress pattern:

● · · adjective	· ● · example	· ● · · ability	● · ● · education

Read the following list of words:

potential	photographic	elephant	confusion
community	hospital	professor	philosophy
tomorrow	tradition	bicycle	material
demonstration	excellent	practical	dangerous
political	mysterious	graduation	romantic

For students who already have some knowledge of word stress rules, an additional predictive stage can precede the listening activity. In this stage, students use their own knowledge of word stress rules and spelling patterns to predict the stress pattern before listening to the words.[16]

---

[16]For a more complete discussion of spelling rules, see Chapter 9.

Finally, to practice distinguishing noun compounds from nouns modified by an adjective, you can present students with a listening task in which they circle the item they hear as you randomly read either choice *a* or *b* in each item:

Directions: Listen to your teacher read the following sentences and circle *a* or *b,* depending on which element in the compound receives more stress:

1. I always use
   a. COLD CREAM. (= well-chilled cream)
   b. COLD CREAM. (= face cream)

2. My brother is a successful
   a. HEAD DOCTor. (= chief of staff)
   b. HEAD DOCTor. (= psychiatrist)

3. I've always wanted a
   a. GREEN HOUSE. (= house painted green)
   b. GREENhouse. (= glass house for growing plants)

4. Be careful with that
   a. YELlow JACKet. (= yellow article of clothing)
   b. YELlow JACKet. (= yellow and black insect that stings)

Once you have ascertained that students are able to hear the stressed element, ask them to determine logical responses to the two choices, and provide the appropriate response when they hear a given sentence. For example, if you produce "Be careful with that YELlow JACKet," the students might respond "It's very expensive." If they heard "Be careful with that YELlow JACKet," they would respond "It stings." Obviously, this type of exercise lends itself to pair practice as well as to the suggested teacher-led activity.

CONTROLLED PRACTICE

A first activity that allows students to become comfortable with typical word stress patterns requires students to repeat lists of words (all of which share a rhythmic pattern) in unison after the teacher, often tapping out the rhythmic pattern or clapping as they practice:

TYPICAL TWO-SYLLABLE PATTERNS

● ·	· ●	● ●
table	begin	drugstore
language	arrive	hairdo
window	select	blackboard
teacher	around	toothbrush

TYPICAL THREE-SYLLABLE PATTERNS

● · ·	· ● ·	● · ●
happiness	discover	advertise
usual	behavior	pacify
melody	romantic	organize
bicycle	election	photograph

Obviously, these same kinds of drills can be done with words that are even longer.

In a low-level ESL/EFL classroom, you can present the predominant stress pattern in two-syllable nouns by bringing in a bag of objects and having students go on a shopping spree:

Student A: May I help you?
Student B: Yes, I'd like to buy _____.

The bag might contain such items as a PICture, an APple, some COOKies, some COFfee, a PENcil, some YOghurt, and so on.

GUIDED PRACTICE

Practice in word stress in the multicultural ESL classroom may begin with a guided practice activity using place names. Nonnative speakers are usually aware of place name differences when their home city or country has been translated into English (e.g., *Deutschland/Germany, Nippon/Japan, Guangzhou/Canton*). However, they may be less aware of stress differences when the spelling of these words is the same as or similar to that in their native country but the pronunciation has been Anglicized:

Native pronunciation		Anglicized pronunciation
PaRIS	→	PARis
VeNEZia	→	VENice
BogoTA	→	BOgota
ıTALia	→	ITaly

In many such cases, the stress moves to an earlier syllable and the production of vowel and consonant sounds is assimilated to English.

The following activity allows students to recognize differences in word stress while asking and responding to questions about their home countries and cities:

A: Where are you from?
B: I'm from TOkyo, JaPAN.
      What about you?
A: I'm from VENice, ITaly.

The stress difference in *-ty* and *-teen* cardinal numbers can be practiced in an information gap exercise in which partners try to obtain information about flights from New York to Miami.[17] They might ask questions such as:

When does Flight 790 leave?

Which flight arrives in Miami at 10:30?

What time does Flight 413 arrive in Miami?

A model worksheet for each of the two partners is illustrated in Figure 5.1. After filling the blanks by asking each other questions, the two partners should check their production and comprehension by comparing worksheets. If, for example, Student A has written 2:50 for the arrival time of Flight 413, then they should determine whether the error lies in A's comprehension or B's production of the item.

---

[17]Note that in compound *-teen* numbers like 413 and 8:19, *-teen* tends to receive strong stress. This stress pattern is relatively fixed.

STUDENT A		
Flight #	Leaves New York	Arrives in Miami
790		8:19 p.m.
380	7:13 a.m.	
618		1:50 p.m.
413	11:14 a.m.	

STUDENT B		
Flight #	Leaves New York	Arrives in Miami
790	4:50 p.m.	
380		10:30 a.m.
618	10:40 a.m.	
413		2:15 p.m.

Figure 5.1 Model worksheets for information gap activity with cardinal numbers

Further vocabulary study might involve affixation. As we have pointed out, stress can shift within the various derivatives of the same word stem: *PHOtoGRAPH, phoTOGraphy, PHOtoGRAPHic*. One of the endings that draws strong stress to the syllable preceding it is *-ian*. In order to practice this shift in stress, students can play the game "What Am I?" Distribute index cards on which a simple phrase is written, such as "I do magic." Then model the activity by reading a phrase aloud and adding, "What am I?" The first student to correctly reply "You're a magician!" takes the next turn, giving a similar clue, such as "I fix electrical appliances." The other students respond with, "You're an electrician." Other possible clues are:

I work in a library.   (*librarian*)

I play music.   (*musician*)

I study history.   (*historian*)

I work in politics.   (*politician*)

I do technical work.   (*technician*)

I make people beautiful.   (*beautician*)

I study grammar.   (*grammarian*)

Stress in noun compounds is often misplaced by learners of English, who tend to place strong stress on the second noun of the compound rather than the first, as in *"I'd like to buy a hair BRUSH, please."*[18] Because compounding in English is such a productive area of vocabulary expansion, we present the following two activities for practice.

In the first activity, "Shop Till You Drop" (the idiom will no doubt require explanation), begin by drawing a simple grid on the board as shown in Figure 5.2.

---

[18]Romance language speakers occasionally even reverse the two nouns in the compound – for example, they say *wine table* for *table wine*.

SHOP TILL YOU DROP: NOUN COMPOUNDS				
Furniture store	**Hardware store**	**Drugstore**	**Grocery store**	**Stationery store**

Figure 5.2 Model grid for "Shop Till You Drop" activity

Then distribute one item from the following list of noun compounds to each student in the class. (These items can either be written on index cards or, if you prefer, they can be in the form of small magazine pictures mounted on tagboard or construction paper. In some cases, the actual item, such as a *paper clip, suntan lotion,* or *sunglasses* may be brought in to add authenticity to the activity.)

sunglasses	beach towel	beach ball
ice cream	notebook	bookbag
notepad	pickle relish	pencil sharpener
toothbrush	paper clips	thumbtacks
toilet paper	suntan lotion	coffee beans
picture frame	screwdriver	paintbrush
armchair	foot stool	sleeper sofa
coffee table	floor lamp	end table
bookshelf	cassette rack	file cabinet
pork chops	hairbrush	wastebasket

After you have handed out all the pictures or objects around the class, students (individually or in groups) should decide where the object can be purchased and write the name of the item on the board in the proper column.

Next, students can practice the pronunciation and stress (remembering to place strong stress on the first rather than the second noun of the compound). At this point, students are ready to use the stress pattern in a sentence context. Depending on the level of the student, the utterances might be quite controlled, as in *I'm going to the _____ so I can buy a/some _____*. At a more advanced level, students can actually role-play clerks and customers.

COMMUNICATIVE PRACTICE

A more communicative activity for practicing stress placement in compound words is a variation of the old TV show "Password." This activity benefits from a game show atmosphere – ideally with a talk show "host" or "hostess." Two sets of "contestants" begin by introducing themselves, and then the host explains the rules of the game. They are as follows: One of the two contestants is given the role of clue giver while the other guesses the words (in this case, compound words). The clue giver draws from a pile of words and gives a clue to his or her partner. If the partner guesses correctly, the team gets one point. One restriction on the clue giving is that neither of the words in the compound can be used as clues. If such a violation occurs, the host intervenes to disqualify the clue and the contestants draw another word. A time limit of 3–5 minutes is set for each pair of contestants. For this purpose, a stopwatch or an egg timer is a useful tool.

Here is a sample of how the activity might proceed. The first two contestants, Marie and Ming, are introduced and they begin the game. Marie draws a card with the compound noun *sunglasses* and gives the following clue: "You wear these when it's bright outside." Ming guesses *tanning lotion,* and Marie quickly adds, "No, covering your eyes," whereupon Ming says *sunglasses* and one point is given. For the next word, Marie draws *barbecue sauce.* "It's the sauce you use when you grill steak or chicken," she says. This clue is disqualified since Marie has used one of the two words in the compound. She then draws the next card and she and Ming continue in the same vein until their 3-minute time limit has elapsed. At this point, the second pair of contestants, Ali and Ursula, begin the next round of Password. Once their round has elapsed, the "defending champions" (either Ming and Marie or Ali and Ursula) are pitted against the next pair of contestants. In this way, all members of the class can alternate roles as either contestants or members of the audience.

For this activity to succeed, you need to have prepared in advance a large number of index cards with compounds. Students should not be forced to give a clue for all cards they draw. As in the TV game, the clue giver can choose not to give a clue for a particular word, or the pair of contestants can abandon an aborted communication attempt midstream and select another card. The goal of the classroom activity, as in the actual Password show, is for contestants to get as many points as possible. Once the entire activity is finished, the class can be allowed to vote on which pair should be invited back to compete as the "grand champions."

Another possible communicative activity involves suffixes and draws upon the professions, vocations, or academic fields of the learners. Begin by distributing index cards, each with a name of a different profession or academic field, to pairs or small groups of students. Groups then work to (1) generate all the derivative words (e.g., *electric, electrical, electricity, electrician*) associated with the word assigned and (2) prepare a short description of the profession or field to be delivered orally to the class, focusing on the correct pronunciation and stress of all the derivations. Some possible items for this activity are:

Professions/vocations	Academic fields
secretary/clerk	geology
musician	history
photographer	biology
mechanic	psychology
electrician	economics
architect	chemistry

SENTENCE STRESS AND RHYTHM: WHAT THE TEACHER NEEDS TO KNOW

The previous discussion of word stress provides a useful basis for understanding how stress functions beyond the word level. In fact, the combination of unstressed, lightly stressed, and strongly stressed elements in multisyllabic words also characterizes English utterances. We use the term *sentence stress* to refer to the various stressed elements of each sentence. The following examples illustrate the physical similarities in stress patterns that exist in both multisyllabic words and simple sentences:

● ·	· ●
mother	attend
Do it.	You did?
Pay them.	It hurts.

· **●** ·   ● · **●**

abandon   guarantee
I saw you.   Have some cake.
We found it.   Where's the beef?

● · **●** ·   ● · **●** · ·

education   nationality
Mary saw it.   Come to Canada.
John's a lawyer.   Where's your bicycle?

· ● · **●** ·   · ● · · **●** ·

communication   electrification
I want a soda.   We took a vacation.
I think he's got it.   I went to the station.

Word and sentence stress combine to create the **rhythm** of an English utterance – that is, the regular, patterned beat of stressed and unstressed syllables and pauses. This rhythmic pattern is similar to the rhythm of a musical phrase. Just as in music, English moves in regular, rhythmic beats from stress to stress – no matter how many unstressed syllables fall in between. This **stress-timed** nature of English means that the length of an utterance depends not on the number of syllables (as it would in a **syllable-timed** language like Spanish or Japanese) but rather on the number of stresses. A famous poetic example of this is from the poem "Break, Break, Break" by Tennyson. The first two lines are considered rhythmically equivalent:

(pause) ● / **(pause)** ● / **(pause)** ● /
    Break,   break,   break   *(3 syllables, 3 stresses)*

· · ●/ · ●/ · ●/
On thy cold gray stones, O Sea!   *(7 syllables, 3 stresses)*

This example also exhibits the importance of pauses in English rhythm and how they mark intervals (just as a rest does in a phrase of music). Stress-timed rhythm is the basis for the metrical foot in English poetry and is also strongly present in chants, nursery rhymes, and limericks.

The stressed-timed nature of English can be seen even more clearly if we compare the following sentences:

	●		●	●
	CATS		CHASE	MICE.
The CATS		have	CHASED	MICE.
The CATS		will	CHASE	the MICE.
The CATS		have been	CHASing	the MICE.
The CATS	could have been		CHASing	the MICE.

Even though these sentences differ in the number of actual syllables, they are equivalent in their number of stressed elements; therefore the time needed to say each sentence is roughly equivalent. An obvious consequence of this is that syllable length varies. In the first sentence, which has the fewest syllables, each syllable is longer. In the subsequent sentences, however, there are increasingly more unstressed syllables, which are much shorter than the stressed ones. In addition, the stressed syllables of these sentences are also slightly shorter than the stressed syllables of the first sentence in order to accommodate the extra unstressed syllables.

NOTE TO TEACHERS

Maintaining a regular beat from stressed element to stressed element and reducing the intervening unstressed syllables can be very difficult for students whose native tongue has syllable-timed rhythm patterns. In these syllable-timed languages (such as French, Spanish, Italian, Japanese, and many African languages), rhythm is a function of the number of syllables in a given phrase, not the number of stressed elements. Thus unlike English, phrases with an equal number of syllables take roughly the same time to produce, and the stress received by each syllable is much more even than in English:

Spanish Los lib-ros es-tan en la me-sa.

French Les livres sont sur la ta-ble.

English The books are on the ta-ble.

As a result of these differences in stress level and syllable length, learners from syllable-timed language backgrounds tend to stress syllables in English more equally, without giving sufficient stress to the main words and without sufficiently reducing unstressed syllables.

Table 5.1 categorizes **content words** (i.e., words that carry information) and **function words** (i.e., words that signify grammatical relationships), and illustrates which words in a sentence or utterance tend to receive stress and which do not. Words that carry the most information are usually stressed – generally the nouns, main verbs, and adjectives. We also stress interrogatives (words that begin information questions), such as *who, what, when,* and *where,* and demonstrative pronouns – words that point or emphasize (*this, that, these, those*).[19] Possessive pronouns (*mine, yours,* etc.), adverbs (*always, very, almost,* etc.), adverbial particles following phrasal verbs (*take off, do away with*) and negative contractions (*can't, isn't*), and even the negative particle *not* when uncontracted usually receive stress because of their semantic as well as syntactic salience.

TABLE 5.1 CONTENT WORDS VERSUS FUNCTION WORDS

Content/information words (often stressed)	Function words (usually unstressed, unless in final position or when used emphatically)
nouns	articles
main verbs	auxiliary verbs
adjectives	personal pronouns
possessive pronouns	possessive adjectives
demonstrative pronouns	demonstrative adjectives
interrogatives	prepositions
not/negative contractions	conjunctions
adverbs	
adverbial particles	

[19]Remember that demonstrative pronouns, which generally are stressed, do not modify a head noun. They substitute for an entire noun phrase: *Whose books are <u>these</u>? <u>That's</u> a bad idea.*

On the other hand, words that modify the lexically important nouns and verbs (such as articles and auxiliary verbs) tend not to be stressed. Likewise, words that signal information previously mentioned (e.g., personal pronouns, relative pronouns, possessive and demonstrative adjectives) are usually unstressed. In these unstressed sentence elements, the vowels also tend to be reduced. We discuss this in more detail in Chapter 7, where we treat reduced speech.

SENTENCE STRESS AND RHYTHM: PEDAGOGICAL PRIORITIES

Teachers should build upon students' knowledge of word stress to help them begin to understand sentence stress in English. In addition, students should understand that there is a basic hierarchy in correctly determining stress placement within an utterance. This involves knowing the stress patterns for the individual multisyllabic words in an utterance and deciding which words in an utterance would normally be stressed.

It is a major priority in the pronunciation classroom to explain and illustrate for students the stress-timed nature and rhythm of English. When learners (particularly those whose first language is syllable timed) obscure the distinction between stressed and unstressed syllables in English, native speakers may either fail to comprehend or they may grow impatient at the lack of selective stress on key words. In the beginning, you may find that your ESL/EFL learners believe that they are most clearly understood when they pronounce each word and syllable distinctly. In fact, students are usually quite surprised to find that giving all syllables equal stress actually hinders native speakers' comprehension.

In addition, you need to provide learners with clear guidelines concerning which words (i.e., function or content words) in a sentence tend to receive stress. Table 5.1 provides a useful framework for informing students which types of words in an utterance usually receive stress.

PRESENTING SENTENCE STRESS AND RHYTHM TO STUDENTS

The bridge between word and sentence stress can be illustrated by comparing the stress pattern of some example words with utterances containing equal numbers of syllables and similar stress patterns:

Multisyllabic word	Utterance
● · ●	● · ●
overlook	Tell the cook!
guarantee	Can't you see?
· ● · · ● ·	· ● · · ● ·
electrification	We took a vacation.
identification	We went to the station.

Learners can repeat these examples fairly rapidly in succession while tapping or clapping. This will help them begin to see parallels between word and sentence stress in English.

LISTENING DISCRIMINATION

For many students, especially those from syllable-timed language backgrounds, simply hearing which elements in a sentence receive stress may be difficult initially. Because of their clear rhythmic pattern, nursery rhymes, limericks, and jazz chants (see Graham 1978, 1986, 1991) can provide an effective initial listen-and-repeat practice activity for such students. We recommend providing students with the text and the metrical pattern of the rhyme or limerick and reading it aloud, asking students to concentrate on the rhythmic pattern. To assist them in noting this pattern, you may wish to clap on the major rhythmic beats or tap out the pattern. On subsequent readings, this responsibility can be given to the students, who clap or tap out the rhythmic pattern as you read the poem aloud.[20] The following nursery rhymes work well for this purpose. For this exercise, we have used the poetic conventions (/) to mark stressed elements and (∪) to mark unstressed elements within a rhythmic foot:

MARY, MARY

Mary, Mary	/ ∪ / ∪
Quite contrary	/ ∪ / ∪
How does your garden grow?	/ ∪ ∪ / ∪ /
With silver bells,	∪ / ∪ /
And cockle shells,	∪ / ∪ /
And pretty maids all in a row.	∪ / ∪ ∪ / ∪ ∪ /

LITTLE JACK HORNER

Little Jack Horner	/ ∪ ∪ / ∪
Sat in a corner	/ ∪ ∪ / ∪
Eating his Christmas pie.	/ ∪ ∪ / ∪ /
He stuck in his thumb	∪ / ∪ ∪ /
And pulled out a plum,	∪ / ∪ ∪ /
And said "What a good boy am I."	∪ ∪ / ∪ ∪ / ∪ /

See also Chapter 10 for further suggestions concerning how poetry and other rhythmic exercises can be used.

CONTROLLED PRACTICE

The stress-timed nature of English can be illustrated with either the "Cats chase mice" example cited previously or the following variant:

●		●	●
MICE		EAT	CHEESE.
The MICE		EAT	CHEESE.
The MICE		EAT	the CHEESE.
The MICE	will	EAT	the CHEESE.
The MICE	will have	EATen	the CHEESE.
The MICE	might have been	EATing	the CHEESE.

Initially, students can listen to you read these sentences and try to identify the stressed elements. With minimal assistance, they should notice that stress usually falls on the content words – the words that carry the most meaning. During the second listening, students can

[20]Nursery rhymes, limericks, and the like tend to distort natural stress patterns to achieve their literary end. For this reason we do not recommend making extensive use of them in the classroom, or asking students to read them aloud.

snap their fingers or tap lightly on their desks to experience how the stressed words tend to come at regular intervals – no matter how many unstressed syllables fall in between. Once a clear rhythmic pattern has been established, they can practice, first chorally and then in pairs. In this way, students are provided with a controlled practice activity that reinforces the nature of English as a stress-timed language.

Rhythm drills such as the following provide another means of controlled practice with sentence stress. First model a given pattern by tapping or clapping. Then students repeat the example sentences (all of which share a rhythmic pattern) in unison:

• ● • ● • ● •

She doesn't like to hurry.

Her father cleaned the basement.

I didn't want to leave her.

He hasn't even tried it.

They need some new pajamas.

• ● • • ● • • ●

He wanted to help her forget.

We needed to call them at ten.

It's better to hide it from John.

I wonder who's kissing her now.

I think that he's doing it wrong.

GUIDED PRACTICE

A guided practice activity focusing on sentence stress involves the exchange of personal information about professions. Begin by handing out cards with professions written on them; students then practice the following model dialogue and do a survey of class members (the slash indicates a pause between thought groups):

A: WHAT do you DO?
B: I'm a DOCtor / and I WORK in a HOSpital.
B: WHAT do **YOU** DO? (*addressing C*)
C: I'm a proFESsor / and I LECture at the uniVERsity.

In this manner, you can reinforce the idea that the words carrying the most meaning in English (in many cases, nouns and verbs) are those that receive stress.

COMMUNICATIVE PRACTICE

An effective communicative practice is a role-play activity modeled after the late-night talk show format. For this activity, students are paired, with each receiving a turn both as host and as guest. When it is their turn to be the guest, they receive a role card with an identity on it. Identities created along the lines of Guinness World Record feats work especially well in this activity, for example:

> 1. You are the world record holder for walking on your hands – 36 hours!

> 2. You are winner of the world KISSING marathon. Winning time: 32 hours, 18 minutes.

> 3. You are the first person to cross the Pacific Ocean in a hot air balloon.

The talk show host interviews the guest and takes notes, asking questions such as the following:

What is your name?

What did you do?

What record did you break?

When did you do this?

Where did you do this?

Why did you do this?

You should monitor rhythm and accurate placement of stress, giving appropriate feedback after the practice.

If the identities chosen have a humorous side to them, you may wish to have the pairs perform individually for the class, or audience. This activity, as is true for most of those we present here, can intersect with a lesson on grammar as well as pronunciation – in this case, wh-questions and/or simple past tense.

Several other techniques for teaching sentence stress are discussed in Chapter 10. These include work with poetry, drama, and jazz chants, the use of action cartoon strips and jokes, and reinforcement via kinesthetic techniques.

ADJUSTMENTS IN CONNECTED SPEECH: WHAT THE TEACHER NEEDS TO KNOW

So far in this chapter we have dealt with word stress, sentence stress, and rhythm. We turn now to a discussion of *adjustments in connected speech.* Even in the most rudimentary of English language lessons, we cannot ignore the changes in pronunciation that occur within and between words due to their juxtaposition with neighboring sounds.[21] In teaching the phrases "This is a book" and "This is an apple," we find ourselves discussing the two forms of the indefinite article *a/an,* explaining to our students that *a* precedes words beginning with a consonant sound whereas *an* precedes words beginning with a vowel sound. This simple rule is an example of a far more elaborate language system whereby sounds are influenced by other sounds in their immediate environment, taking on different characteristics as a result. (These processes are common to all languages; however, here they are discussed primarily as they relate to English.) The main function of most of the adjustments we discuss here is to promote the regularity of English rhythm – that is, to squeeze syllables between stressed elements and facilitate their articulation so that regular timing can be maintained.

---

[21]Often, the phenomena to be discussed in this section are referred to as *sandhi* variation – a term that derives from Sanskrit and refers to the "placing together" of sounds within and between words.

In the section that follows, we discuss the processes of linking, assimilation, dissimilation, deletion, and epenthesis as they occur in connected speech.

LINKING

Even to the linguistically naive, a salient characteristic of much of nonnative English speech is its "choppy" quality. The ability to speak English "smoothly," to utter words or syllables that are appropriately connected, entails the use of **linking** (or liaison), which is the connecting of the final sound of one word or syllable to the initial sound of the next. The amount of linking that occurs in native-speaker speech will depend on a number of factors, such as the informality of the situation, the rate of speaking, and of course the individual speech profile (or idiolect) of the speaker. Thus, the amount of linking that occurs is not entirely predictable. However, linking occurs with regularity in the following five environments:

1. Linking with a glide commonly occurs when one word or syllable ends in a tense vowel or diphthong and the next word or syllable begins with a vowel:

/y/ **glides**	/w/ **glides**
/iy/ + V: be‿ʸable, cre‿ʸate	/uw/ + V: blue‿ʷink, Stu‿ʷart
/ey/ + V: say‿ʸit, lay‿ʸette	/ow/ + V: no‿ʷart, no‿ʷel
/ay/ + V: my‿ʸown, na‿ʸive	/aw/ + V: how‿ʷis it, flo‿ʷur
/ɔy/ + V: toy‿ʸairplane, boy‿ʸish	

The two low tense vowels that do not end in a glide typically move smoothly from one vowel to the other, although some speakers of NAE may insert a glottal stop [ʔ] before the second vowel between words:

> /ɑ/ + V: spa owners *or* spa [ʔ] owners
> /ɔ/ + V: saw Ann *or* saw [ʔ] Ann

In this environment or after an /ə/, speakers of some New England and New York City dialects of NAE (and also many speakers of British dialects) tend to add a linking or intrusive /r/ to V + V sequences:[22]

EXAMPLES OF LINKING /r/

> spa /r/ owners
>
> saw /r/ Ann
>
> vanilla /r/ ice cream
>
> media /r/ event

2. When a word or syllable ending in a single consonant is followed by a word or syllable beginning with a vowel, the consonant is often produced intervocalically as if it belonged to both syllables:

> dog‿eat dog
>
> black‿and gray
>
> McLean‿Avenue
>
> Macintosh‿apple

---

[22]Recall that these same dialects have a noticeable absence of postvocalic /r/ in words such as *car, bird, beer*. See Appendix 1 for more differences between NAE and British English.

3. When a word or syllable terminating in a consonant cluster is followed by a word or syllable commencing with a vowel, the final consonant of the cluster is often pronounced as part of the following syllable. This phenomenon is sometimes referred to as *resyllabification:*

lef/t‿arm	/lɛf•tɑrm/
wep/t‿over	/wɛp•towvəʳ/
fin/d‿out	/fayn•dawt/
push/ed‿up	/pʊʃ•tʌp/
las/ting	/læs•tɪŋ/
adap/table	/ə•dæp•tə•bl̩/

Note that resyllabification does not result in any aspiration of voiceless stops. Thus the /t/ in *left arm, wept over,* and *pushed up* is not aspirated.

4. When two identical consonants come together as a result of the juxtaposition of two words, there is one single, elongated articulation of the consonant (i.e., native speakers do not produce the consonant sound twice):

stop pushing	rob Bill
[p:]	[b:]
short time	bad dog
[t:]	[d:]
quick cure	big gap
[k:]	[g:]
classroom management	less serious
[m:]	[s:]

5. When a stop consonant is followed by another stop or by an affricate, the first stop is not released, which facilitates the linking:

pet cat	blackboard	good jury
[t°k]	[k°b]	[d°dʒ]
soap dish	big dipper	big church
[p°d]	[g°d]	[g°tʃ]

ASSIMILATION

A second example of an adjustment in connected speech is the process of **assimilation,** during which a given sound (the assimilating sound) takes on the characteristics of a neighboring sound (the conditioning sound). This is often misunderstood as "lazy" or "sloppy" speech, since the organs of speech involved appear to be taking the path of least resistance. However, such a characterization ignores the fact that assimilation is a universal feature of spoken language. In English it occurs frequently, both within words and between words; it by no means marks a speaker as inarticulate or nonstandard. There are three types of assimilation in English: (1) *progressive* (or perseverative), (2) *regressive* (or anticipatory), and (3) *coalescent.*

In *progressive assimilation* the conditioning sound precedes and affects the following sound. Examples of progressive assimilation in English are the regular plural /s/ vs. /z/ alternation, in which the final sound of the stem conditions the voiced or voiceless form of the suffix. This type of assimilation also occurs in the regular past tense /t/ vs. /d/ alternation:

Conditioning sound	→	Assimilated sound
-s ending		
bags		/bæg → **z**/
backs		/bæk → **s**/
-d ending		
moved		/muwv → **d**/
fished		/fɪʃ → **t**/

For the plural -*s* ending, the voiced /g/ of *bags* conditions the voiced form of the -*s* ending, causing it to be pronounced /z/, whereas the voiceless /k/ of *back* conditions the /s/ pronunciation of the ending. Notice that the same type of conditioning occurs in the -*d* endings.

Progressive assimilation also occurs in some contractions (e.g., *it + is → it's* /ɪt + ɪz → ɪts/), and in some reductions (e.g., *had to → /hædə/*). Most of the progressive assimilation in English occurs at the intersection of phonology and morphology, which is discussed in detail in Chapter 8.

In English, *regressive assimilation* is more pervasive as a purely phonological process than is progressive assimilation. In regressive assimilation, the assimilated sound precedes and is affected by the conditioning sound. Examples of this type of phenomenon are the words *grandpa* (the /p/ causes the /nd/ to be articulated as /m/: /græmpɑ/) and *pancake* (the /k/ causes the /n/ to become /ŋ/: /pæŋkeyk/).

Regressive assimilation occurs commonly in the periphrastic modals *has/have to* (when expressing obligation) and *used to* (when expressing former habitual action):

have	+	to	→	"hafta"[23]
/hæv/	+	/tuw/	→	/hæftə/
has	+	to	→	"hasta"
/hæz/	+	/tuw/	→	/hæstə/
used	+	to	→	"usta"
/yuwzd/	+	/tuw/	→	/yuwstə/

In these examples, the voiceless /t/ of *to* is the conditioning sound that causes the voiced /v/, /z/, and /d/ preceding it to assimilate and become voiceless /f/, /s/, and /t/:

Assimilated sound	←	Conditioning sound
/hæ**f**	←	tə/
/hæ**s**	←	tə/
/yuw**s**	←	tə/

Another clear example of regressive assimilation is reflected in the English spelling system – namely, in the four allomorphic variants of the negative prefix. Note that the unmarked allomorph *in-* occurs in all cases except when the subsequent sound is a bilabial

---

[23]We have opted to use an orthographic representation of assimilation here for purposes of illustration, as found in literary character dialogue, comic strips, and other written examples of spoken English.

or a liquid: *indecent, inept, invalid.*[24] In the case of *im-,* the initial bilabial sound of the root word causes the organs of speech to approach a position closer to that of the conditioning sound, as in *impossible* or *immobile.* Similarly, with the liquids /l/ and /r/, the negative prefix is conditioned or changed to *il-* and *ir-* respectively, as in *illogical* and *irrational:*

in-	*im-*
inoperative	impossible
inflexible	imbalanced
indifferent	immeasurable
inexcusable	immobile
intangible	impartial

il-	*ir-*
illogical	irreplaceable
illegal	irresponsible
illegitimate	irrelevant
illegible	irrational
illiberal	irregular

As exemplified by the negative allomorphs *il-* and *ir-,* assimilated sounds often become identical to the conditioning sound. In rapid native-speaker speech, sequences of sibilants having the form (/s/ or /z/ + /ʃ/) are particularly susceptible to this type of regressive assimilation:

/s/ + /ʃ/	Swi<u>ss ch</u>alet	hor<u>ses</u>hoe
	[ʃ:]	[ʃ:]
/z/ + /ʃ/	hi<u>s sh</u>irt	one'<u>s sh</u>adow
	[ʃ:]	[ʃ:]

With stop consonants, a final /t/ or /d/ may assimilate to a following initial /p, k/ or /b, g/, respectively (i.e., the place of articulation changes but the voiced or voiceless quality of the segment remains constant):

goo<u>d b</u>oy	goo<u>d g</u>irl
[b:]	[g:]
a<u>t p</u>eace	pe<u>t k</u>itten
[p:]	[k:]

Notice that final nasal consonants, especially /n/, may also adjust their place of articulation according to that of a following conditioning consonant:

He's i<u>n p</u>ain.	They're i<u>n K</u>orea.
[m]	[ŋ]
It rains i<u>n M</u>ay.	Be o<u>n g</u>uard!
[m]	[ŋ]

These examples of regressive assimilation all involve a change in place of articulation or in voicing, which are the most common types. There are, however, also some cases of

---

[24]This prefix is spelled *in-* before velar consonants but is pronounced /ɪŋ/: *incoherent, inglorious.*

regressive assimilation with a change in manner of articulation. These tend to occur in informal speech:

Could you g<u>ive me</u> a call?
             /m:/
Let <u>me</u> do that for you.
  /m:/

The third type of assimilation, *coalescent assimilation,* is a type of reciprocal assimilation: The first sound and second sound in a sequence come together and mutually condition the creation of a third sound with features from both original sounds.

$$\text{Sound A} \quad + \quad \text{Sound B}$$
$$\searrow \qquad \swarrow$$
$$\text{Sound C}$$

This process occurs most frequently in English when final alveolar consonants such as /s, z/ and /t, d/ or final alveolar consonant sequences such as /ts, dz/ are followed by initial palatal /y/. They then become palatalized fricatives and affricates, respectively:

Rule			Examples
/s/		/ʃ/	is<u>sue</u> He's coming thi<u>s y</u>ear.
/z/		/ʒ/	plea<u>sure</u> Doe<u>s y</u>our mother know?
/t/	+ /y/ →	/tʃ/	sta<u>ture</u> Is tha<u>t y</u>our dog?
/ts/		/tʃ/	She le<u>ts y</u>our dog in. He ha<u>tes y</u>our hairdo.
/d/		/dʒ/	proce<u>dure</u> Woul<u>d y</u>ou mind moving?
/dz/		/dʒ/	She nee<u>ds y</u>our help. He never hee<u>ds y</u>our advice.

Within words, the /y/ sound (which is generally in an unstressed syllable) may be the initial sound of a suffix or of the subsequent bound part of the word (e.g., *-ure, -ion, -ious*); across words, the /y/ sound comes from a second word beginning in /y/, typically *you* or *your*. This type of assimilation is often referred to as *palatalization.*

As with linking, the amount of assimilation that occurs in native-speaker speech will depend on a number of variables, such as the formality of the situation, the rate of speech, and the style of the speaker.

DISSIMILATION

The process of *dissimilation* occurs when adjacent sounds become more different from each other (rather than more similar, as is the case with assimilation). It is rare in English and not an active process. Some texts cite the pronunciation of the final cluster of *fifths* as [fts] as an example of dissimilation (i.e., of [fθs] to [fts]), which reflects a tendency in some NAE dialects to break up a sequence of three fricatives by replacing the second with a stop. In English, the process of dissimilation can be ignored for pedagogical purposes.

DELETION

An even more radical form of adjustment in connected speech is *deletion* (also known as omission): the process whereby sounds disappear or are not clearly articulated in certain contexts. In some cases, the spelling system of English is sensitive to this phenomenon, representing deletion in the contracted forms of auxiliary verbs plus *not* (e.g., *isn't*). In other cases, however, deletion occurs without any acknowledgment in the spelling system. Even many native speakers may be unaware of where deletion occurs. The process is pervasive.

The following are some of the most typical environments for deletion:

- Loss of /t/ when /nt/ is between two vowels or before a syllabic [l̩]:
  /t/ win~~t~~er, Toron~~t~~o, en~~t~~er, man~~t~~le

- Loss of /t/ or /d/ when they occur second in a sequence or cluster of three consonants:
  /t/ res~~t~~less, lis~~t~~less, exac~~t~~ly

  /d/ win~~d~~mill, kin~~d~~ness, han~~d~~s

- Deletion of word-final /t/ or /d/ in clusters of two at a word boundary when the following word begins with a consonant:[25]

  Deletion
  Eas~~t~~ side
  blin~~d~~ man
  wil~~d~~ boar

However, when the following word begins with a vowel, there is no deletion. Instead, resyllabification occurs.

  **No deletion
  (resyllabification)**
  Eas/t‿end
  blin/d‿eye
  wil/d‿ass

- Loss of an unstressed medial vowel (also referred to as *syncope*), where the unstressed vowel /ə/ or /ɪ/ optionally drops out in some multisyllabic words following the strongly stressed syllable:[26]

  choc~~o~~late, ev~~e~~ry, ev~~e~~ning, cam~~e~~ra, myst~~e~~ry, hist~~o~~ry,

  veg~~e~~table, comp~~a~~rable, lab~~o~~ratory, int~~e~~resting,

  mis~~e~~rable, gen~~e~~rally, asp~~i~~rin, diff~~e~~rent, fav~~o~~rite,

  rest~~au~~rant, bev~~e~~rage, fam~~i~~ly, reas~~o~~nable, em~~e~~rald

In rapid or informal native-speaker speech, deletion occasionally occurs in two-syllable words such as the following, which are reduced to one syllable:

  c~~o~~rrect, p~~a~~rade, p~~o~~lice, s~~u~~ppose, g~~a~~rage

---

[25]There are two exceptions to this rule. First, when the second word begins with /w, h, y, r/, no deletion occurs: *East hill, blind youth, wild ride.* Second, some consonant clusters with final /t/ or /d/ never simplify: /nt, lt, rt, rd/: *plant food, felt pen, shortstop, bird feeder.*
[26]If the last syllable is stressed, syncope does not occur. Compare the verb *separate* /ˈsɛpəˌreyt/ with the adjective *separate* /ˈsɛprət/.

Related to this type of deletion is loss of an unstressed initial vowel or syllable in highly informal speech, a process known as *aphesis:*

'cause, 'bout, 'round

- Loss of the first noninitial /r/ in a word that has another /r/ in a following syllable:[27]

Feb̶ruary, gove̶rnor, su̶rprise, tempe̶rature

- Loss of final /v/ in *of* (i.e., reduction to schwa) before words with initial consonants:

lots <u>of</u> money, waste <u>of</u> time, hearts <u>of</u> palm
  /ə/   /ə/   /ə/

- Loss of initial /h/ and /ð/ in pronominal forms in connected speech:

ask h̶er, help h̶im, tell t̶h̶em

EPENTHESIS

Epenthesis is the insertion of a vowel or consonant segment within an existing string of segments. Although less frequent than deletion in English, epenthesis is by no means uncommon. The most important type of epenthesis in English occurs in certain morphophonological sequences such as the regular plural and past tense endings. Here an epenthetic schwa /ə/ is added to break up clusters of sibilants or alveolar stops. Progressive assimilation alone will not make the morphological endings sufficiently salient. Thus for the plural endings, for which we can posit an underlying {Z} morpheme, we have:

Assimilation	Epenthesis
plate + {Z} = /pleyts/	place + {Z} = /pleysəz/
bag + {Z} = /bægz/	buzz + {Z} = /bʌzəz/

And for regular past tense, for which we can posit an underlying {D} morpheme, we have:

Assimilation	Epenthesis
look + {D} = /lʊkt/	plant + {D} = /plæntəd/
grin + {D} = /grɪnd/	hand + {D} = /hændəd/

Finally, there are also cases of consonant epenthesis in English. Often words like *prince* and *tense,* which end in [ns], are pronounced with an inserted [t] so that they sound just like *prints* and *tents.* In such cases, the insertion of the voiceless stop [t] makes it easier for speakers to produce the voiced nasal plus voiceless fricative sequence. We see the same process at work when some speakers add a [p] between the /m/ and /f/ in *comfort.*[28]

---

[27]We believe that speakers of standard NAE will often omit the first /r/ sound in the listed words; however, in certain words, such as *library,* the loss of the first /r/ is more dialectal.
[28]In some cases an epenthetic consonant is now represented in the spelling of a word or name. Examples are the <u>p</u> in *empty* or *Thom<u>p</u>son* (a variant of *Thomson*).

NOTE TO TEACHERS

As we have already discussed, nonnative speakers often erroneously use the strategy of epenthesis to simplify clusters, both word internally and word externally:

Word-internal epenthesis

film	→	/fɪləm/
please	→	/pəliyz/
judgment	→	/dʒʌdʒəmənt/

Word-external epenthesis

sport → /ɛspɔrt/ (speakers of Spanish and Farsi)

club → /kurabu/ (speakers of Japanese)

All five types of adjustments in connected speech that we have just discussed (i.e., linking, assimilation, dissimilation, deletion, and epenthesis) reflect NAE speakers' attempts to connect words and syllables smoothly in the normal stream of speech. Sometimes underlying sounds are lost or modified – as in the cases of deletion and assimilation. Sometimes other sounds are added, as in epenthesis or some forms of linking. Typically, the motivations for all these modifications seem to be:

1. ease of articulation for the speaker

2. preservation of the preferred English syllable structure

3. preservation of grammatical information

In fact, several of the topics we discuss elsewhere are functionally related to these five phenomena in that they all work to preserve stress-timed rhythm: vowel reduction (Chapter 4), the vowel elision that accompanies syllabic [n̩] and [l̩] (Chapter 3), and contractions and the *h*-elision in noninitial unstressed *he, her, him, his, have, had, has* (Chapter 7).

ADJUSTMENTS IN CONNECTED SPEECH: PEDAGOGICAL PRIORITIES

Learners often attempt to pronounce each individual word so clearly that they fail to blend words within a single thought group smoothly. This can cause their speech to sound choppy. All languages have some rules concerning adjustments in connected speech; however, no other language has exactly the same rules as English, and teaching the conventions specific to English is the pedagogical challenge.

How the teacher opts to present connected speech depends on the teaching context. In a course primarily devoted to pronunciation, the teacher should initially present an overview of connected speech phenomena, and then deal with each feature in more depth using an appropriate context. Initially, we suggest presenting a slightly more simplified picture to students of the rules governing connected speech than was discussed in the previous section. Because they occur frequently in spoken English, the following areas should be highlighted:

- consonant-to-vowel linking

- vowel-to-vowel linking

- consonant assimilation

- palatalization

When pronunciation is integrated into the teaching of other skills, the teacher needs to combine information about connected speech with a particular teaching point, for example, phrasal verbs, imperatives, giving advice. It is probably best to focus on one feature of connected speech at a time, according to the context.

Suppose, for example, that the context being used is proverbs. Begin by introducing several popular proverbs on the board (e.g., "Time is money," "A penny saved is a penny earned"). Then present the consonant-to-vowel and vowel-to-vowel linking, illustrating it by demonstrating where it occurs in the example phrases:

Time‿is money.

A penny save**d‿is‿a** penny‿**ea**rned.

PRESENTING ADJUSTMENTS IN CONNECTED SPEECH TO STUDENTS

When introducing connected speech in the ESL/EFL classroom, you can illustrate the most common patterns using worksheets like those presented in Figure 5.3 (below and continuing to page 169).

STUDENT WORKSHEET 1

Linking consonant to vowel

Rule 1: When a word ends in two consonants and the next begins with a vowel, the final consonant sounds like the initial consonant of the following word:

   Send it sounds like *sen·dit*

   Camp out sounds like *cam·pout*

Rule 2: When a word ends in a single consonant and the next begins with a vowel, the consonant straddles the two syllables:

   Push‿up   Stop‿it
   Come‿in   Take‿off

Practice: Repeat the following phrases, paying attention to linking:

Two consonants + vowel	**Single consonant + vowel**
Hol/d‿on	Is‿it?
Lef/t‿it	Keep‿up
Fin/d‿out	Gone‿in

Your examples:

Think of verbs ending in consonants that would complete the following phrases. Write one verb in each blank. Then practice saying the phrases with your partner.

_____ it in.   _____ at me.

_____ it down.   _____ out.

_____ up.   _____ on it.

Figure 5.3 Student worksheets for presenting patterns in connected speech

STUDENT WORKSHEET 2

Linking vowel to vowel

Rule 1: When a word ending in /iy/, /ey/, /ay/, or /ɔy/ is followed by another word beginning with a vowel, the two words are connected by a /y/ glide:

/iy/
/ey/ } + vowel = /y/ glide
/ay/
/ɔy/

Be‿a sport.
Play‿a game.
Tie‿it up.
Employ‿a professional.

Rule 2: When a word ending in /uw/, /ow/, or /aw/ is followed by another word beginning with a vowel, the two words are connected by a /w/ glide:

/uw/
/ow/ } + vowel = /w/ glide
/aw/

through‿it all
slow‿and steady
How‿are you?

Practice: Repeat the following words and phrases, paying attention to linking within and across words.

	/y/ **glide**	/w/ **glide**
Within words:	re‿action	gradu‿ate
	high‿er	co‿alition
Across words:	We‿aren't coming.	Let's go‿on.
	Try‿it again.	Try to‿understand.
	The boy‿ate an apple.	How‿are you doing?

Your examples:

Match the items in columns 1, 2, and 3 to make complete phrases. Write these phrases in the blanks provided and then practice saying them with your partner.

Column 1	Column 2	Column 3	
do		up	_____
try	it	now	_____
play		again	_____
say			_____
tie			_____
slow		down	_____

Figure 5.3 *Continued*

STUDENT WORKSHEET 3

Linking consonant to consonant

Rule 1: When a stop is followed by another stop or affricate, the first stop is not released or aspirated.

Stop + stop	Stop + affricate
Hot_dog	Bad_judgment
Back_door	Sick_child

Rule 2: If the consonants (whether a stop or not) are identical, the consonant is somewhat lengthened. The two consonants are not articulated separately:

Identical consonants

Keep_practicing!	less_serious
hot_tea	common_names

Practice: Repeat the following phrases, paying attention to connecting the consonants.

Stop + stop	Stop + affricate	Identical consonants
sleep_tight	grape_jam	bad_day
soup_bowl	big_church	June_night
red_tie	red_cherry	pet_turtle

Your examples:

Add a noun to the color terms below. Choose words that follow the patterns described above:

Stop + stop/affricate	Identical consonant
red *tape* _____	purple *lake* _____
black _____	green _____
white _____	pink _____
violet _____	gold _____

Figure 5.3 *Continued*

STUDENT WORKSHEET 4

Palatalization

Rule: When the consonants /s, z, t, d/ are followed by /y/ in an unstressed syllable, the two sounds combine to form a palatalized consonant:

Alveolar consonant	Palatalized form	Example
/s/ + /y/ →	/ʃ/	Pass‿your plate.
/z/ + /y/ →	/ʒ/	Where's‿your fork?
/t/ + /y/ →	/tʃ/	Why didn't‿you eat‿your soup?
/d/ + /y/ →	/dʒ/	Where did‿you hide‿your spoon?

Practice: Read the following phrases, paying attention to the palatalized forms.

We'll miss‿your sweet smile.
You'll freeze‿your toes.
I'd like to meet‿your brother.
Have you read‿your mail yet today?

Practice: It is important to relax and maintain good health. Write *do* and *don't* sentences using the following nouns and verbs.

Verbs: eat, miss, forget, lose, get, count
Nouns: sleep, exercise, temper, rest, vitamins, calories, vegetables

DO	DON'T
<u>Eat</u> your <u>vegetables</u>.	Don't <u>forget</u> your <u>vitamins</u>.
_____ your _____.	Don't _____ your _____.
_____ your _____.	Don't _____ your _____.
_____ your _____.	Don't _____ your _____.

Figure 5.3 *Continued*

CONTROLLED PRACTICE

Once students have been introduced to a particular connected speech pattern, they can be asked to do controlled practice exercises such as the following:

> *Directions:* Underline likely instances of linking in the following dialogue and then read it aloud with a partner.

> *(Two students see their classmate rushing off to catch a bus before school is over.)*

Bob: Hey, where is Ann going in such a hurry?
Marie: I haven't any idea!
Bob: I hope it's not an emergency.
Marie: Me too. Her grandmother is in the hospital. Do
              you think it might be that?
Bob: I'm not sure. She raced out of here so fast I
              didn't get a chance to ask her.

Another good controlled practice activity is to ask students to identify the types of connected speech patterns that occur in geographical expressions:

Cook͜ County	West͜ Indies
South͜ Africa	Cape͜ Cod
New͜ England	Marshall͜ Islands

As with the worksheets in Figure 5.3, students first analyze the patterns and then practice reading the phrases; they would then come up with examples of their own and perhaps exchange information about their native countries.

Excellent sources of controlled practice materials for connected speech are idioms, sayings, and advertising slogans. You can select a context or topic for practice and then allow students to practice the phrases with a partner. The following examples illustrate controlled practice with idioms containing the word *talk,* sayings about poets, and popular advertising slogans:

IDIOMS	SAYINGS
all talk and no action	All poets are mad. (Robert Burton)
talk is cheap	All men are poets at heart. (Ralph Waldo Emerson)
talk a blue streak	A poet is the painter of the soul. (Isaac D'Israel)
talk shop	A good poet's made as well as born. (Ben Jonson)
talk through your hat	Next to being a great poet is the power of
talk someone's head off	understanding one. (Longfellow)

ADVERTISING SLOGANS

Coke is it!

We make money the old-fashioned way: We earn it!

These examples illustrate various instances of linking. However, you can use these same contexts to focus on other connected speech phenomena. To cite one example, you could pick the context of proverbs (e.g., "Don't count your chickens before they're hatched" and "Put your money where your mouth is") to provide practice with palatalization.

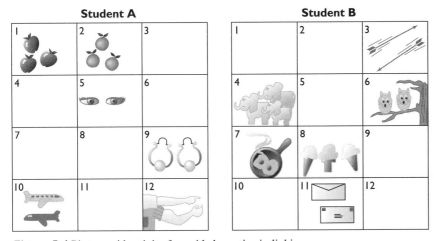

Figure 5.4 Picture grid activity for guided practice in linking

GUIDED PRACTICE

For a low-intermediate to intermediate group, you can use a picture grid activity to have students share information and practice vowel-to-vowel linking using the /y/ glide (after the number *three* /θriy/) and the /w/ glide (after the number *two* /tuw/). In this activity (see Figure 5.4), students share information by asking:

A: What is in square 4?
B: Three elephants.

Student A then draws in the three elephants and Student B takes a turn. Monitor the pair for accuracy of /y/ and /w/ glides.

COMMUNICATIVE PRACTICE

Commands and instructions are useful for communicative practice with linking. Have students work in pairs. Student A has a picture (such as the simple drawing in Figure 5.5) that is not shown to Student B. Instead, Student A instructs Student B to draw the picture using commands such as, "Put a tree in the center of your picture. Add a house in the bottom left corner. Draw a door and two windows on the house."

Figure 5.5 Sample drawing for communicative practice with instructions

Palatalization, which occurs frequently in combinations of verbs with *you* or *your,* lends itself naturally to an advice-giving or suggestion-making activity, which could include sentences cues such as:

Why don't you . . . ?
Would you like to . . . ?
Can't you . . . ?
Could you possibly . . . ?
Did you ever think of . . . ?

For example, you can set a context, such as noisy neighbors, and have students work in groups to create "advice" that they would give to their neighbors using the sentence cues. Students might come up with phrases such as "Could you possibly meet your friends somewhere else?" or "Can't you amuse yourself more quietly?" or "Why don't your fix your stereo so it isn't so noisy?"

As stated earlier, the amount of linking that occurs between words in speech is not entirely predictable. Nonetheless, since the lack of appropriate connections can make a speaker sound markedly nonnative, it is important to address this issue in the language classroom. The amount of time spent on understanding and practicing linking phenomena will depend on the extent of difficulty students have with this natural speech phenomenon; some students and classes will need greater assistance than others.

CONCLUSION

In this chapter we have discussed word stress, sentence stress, rhythm, and adjustments in connected speech. These features allow the speaker to turn the basic building blocks of the sound system (i.e., the vowel and consonant phonemes) into words, meaningful utterances, and extended discourse. Command of these features is therefore as critical as command of the segmental features discussed in Chapters 3 and 4 – if not more so – in achieving successful communication for second language learners.

Stress, rhythm, and adjustments in connected speech can be easily overlooked in the language classroom. Nonetheless, as we will see in Chapter 7, these invisible signals are among the main clues used by listeners to process incoming speech and are thus of primary importance in the speech communication process.

EXERCISES

KEY CONCEPTS

Write a brief definition of the following key terms from this chapter. Give examples where relevant.

stress	regressive assimilation	content word
strongly stressed	palatalization	adjustments in connected speech
unstressed	deletion	resyllabification
phrasal verb	aphesis	progressive assimilation
rhythm	word stress	coalescent assimilation
syllable-timed	lightly stressed	dissimilation
function word	compound	syncope
linking	sentence stress	epenthesis
assimilation	stress-timed	

INTROSPECTING ABOUT YOUR OWN LANGUAGE LEARNING

Think about a foreign language that you have learned in school or while living abroad.

1. How aware are you of the stress and rhythmic patterns of this language? Of linking?

2. What kind of instruction did you receive regarding stress, rhythm, and adjustments in connected speech? Explain. What percentage of instructional time was devoted to these areas?

3. Do you believe that there are significant differences in these features between your first and second languages? Explain.

4. When communicating with native speakers of this language, did you ever feel that you had communication problems that resulted from a lack of awareness of the features discussed in this chapter? Explain.

DISCUSSION QUESTIONS

1. If English is your first language, how do your native-speaker intuitions match up with the description of features in this chapter? If it is your second language, how many of these features were you already aware of? Do any of them seem unnatural to you?

2. In your opinion, what contributes more to a learner's intelligibility – accuracy of consonant and vowel sounds or command of stress, rhythm, and adjustments in connected speech?

3. Regarding stress, rhythm, and adjustments in connected speech, is it more important to stress perception or production? Is your answer the same for all of these features?

4. Think about the learners that you have taught or plan to teach. What challenges do you believe these learners will face in the areas listed in question 3?

5. Comment on the following statement: "Carefully articulated speech is the mark of an educated speaker and should be what our students are striving to achieve."

IN THE CLASSROOM

Assume that you are teaching pronunciation. Here are some common classroom situations that you might encounter. What technique would you use or what explanation would you give?

1. A student says: "Sometimes I hear native speakers say *SUSPECT* and at other times *susPECT*. Which one is correct?"

2. A student asks you for advice, saying: "People can't tell whether I'm saying *thirteen* or *thirty*. What should I do?"

3. Your students have a tendency to insert /ə/ between words in phrases like *cold drink, wet towel,* and *gas station.*

4. One of your students is disturbed about the "bad English" that she hears. For example, she relates that she has heard native speakers saying *takideezy* and *seeyaroun.*

5. A native speaker friend of one of your students has told the student that he pronounces English much too "carefully." The student is perplexed and comes to you for advice.

6. One of your students says that a close friend (who is a native speaker) has told her she sounds very abrupt or aggressive when she speaks. What advice would you give the student?

SUGGESTED ACTIVITIES

1. Survey an ESL/EFL textbook – either an all-skills textbook that explicitly deals with pronunciation or a single-skills text devoted to this skill. How does this textbook sequence the segmentals and suprasegmentals?

2. Select an area of word stress that you might focus on in the classroom (e.g., stress patterns with suffixes, compounds). Construct a brief dialogue that contains multiple examples of this stress pattern. If possible, tape an ESL/EFL learner reading this passage. What difficulties did the learner encounter?

3. Using the list of suffixes on page 137 that cause a shift of stress in the root word (e.g., *-eous, -ical, -ity*), construct a short paragraph-length reading passage to practice these differences in stress. If possible, tape an ESL/EFL learner reading this passage. What difficulties did the learner encounter?

4. Find five common sayings or idioms that illustrate one of the linking patterns described in this chapter. Plan the presentation phase of the lesson using these phrases to illustrate the rule or rules involved.

5. Find a short piece of literature that could be used to practice one or more of the features described in this chapter. Describe how you would use this passage.

ON THE CASSETTE

1. Listen to the following paragraph as it is read on the cassette. Mark the occurrences of linking. Decide which of the linking rules given in this chapter apply. If you need help, ask your instructor.

EARTHQUAKE SAFETY

If indoors, take cover under a desk or table, or brace yourself in a doorway. Stay away from windows. If outdoors, move to an open area away from overhead hazards. If in a car, stop carefully in an open area. Stay in the car. Listen to the car radio for information. Above all, keep calm and don't panic.

2. Listen to the two nonnative speakers on the tape read the same passage. Mark their use of linking. What does their performance on this task indicate about their need for instruction in this area?

CHAPTER 6

Prominence and Intonation in Discourse

In the previous chapter we discussed word stress, sentence stress, rhythm, and adjustments in connected speech. Although there are variations possible in all these areas based on such factors as rate of speech and dialect,[1] these phenomena are largely rule governed and not particularly sensitive to discourse and speaker's intent. This chapter focuses on features of pronunciation that are quite sensitive to the discourse context and the speaker's intent – namely, prominence and intonation. In particular, we focus on the productive use of these features to segment speech and highlight important information.

PROMINENCE: WHAT THE TEACHER NEEDS TO KNOW

Just as individual utterances can be divided into words and these words into syllables, so too the larger stream of speech can be broken into smaller units. The term **thought group** refers to a discrete stretch of speech that forms a semantically and grammatically coherent segment of discourse. When we think about where a speaker can logically pause in the stream of speech, we can separate an utterance into thought groups. Although written discourse provides some markers for these divisions or pauses (i.e., commas, semicolons, periods, dashes), in spoken discourse a speaker may pause at points where such punctuation does not always occur in a written transcription of the utterance.

Similarly, the term **intonation unit** describes this same segment of speech but refers also to the fact that this unit of speech has its own intonation contour or pitch pattern (Gilbert 1983; Schuetze-Coburn 1993) and typically contains one prominent element. A single utterance or sentence may include several intonation units, each with its own prominent element and contour.

To summarize, each typical intonation unit (or thought group):

1. is set off by pauses before and after
2. contains one prominent element
3. has an intonation contour of its own
4. has a grammatically coherent internal structure

There is no foolproof way to divide an utterance into intonation units. In rapid speech, intonation units may be fairly long; in slower speech, they may be shorter, and breaks between

[1]See Appendix 1 for a detailed discussion of differences between NAE and British English.

units will therefore be more frequent. Where the utterance divisions fall will also depend on the individual speaker, with some speakers producing fewer breaks than others. Finally, such divisions are dependent on the performance context. Public speakers, for example, tend to pause frequently to make their message clearer or more emphatic, as in a political statement:

> I promise / to serve / my fellow citizens / to the best / of my ability.

By contrast, if in another context the speaker is communicating urgency, the intonation units may be longer and the speech may contain fewer breaks:

> I promise that I'll get you the back-ordered merchandise / just as soon as it arrives in the warehouse.

There are two additional points to be made regarding intonation units. First, too many pauses (and therefore intonation units) can slow speech down and create too many prominent elements, causing the listener difficulty in processing and comprehending the overall message. Second, blending and linking (see Chapter 5) occur within intonation units, but not across unit boundaries. For example:

Dave: Do you remember (/) when we used to stay
up all night (/) studying for exams?
Howard: Do I ever! / Finals week was such a killer /
that we all drank coffee (/) by the ton.

In this dialogue the slashes indicate possible "(/)" and obligatory "/" intonation unit boundaries. Dave's question could be uttered as one long rapid thought group or as two or three more measured groups; if the latter, there could be as many as three intonation units. Howard has an obligatory intonation unit boundary after the first three words and another after *killer*. The intonation unit boundary between *coffee* and *by the ton* is optional; it depends on how much special prominence is given to *by the ton*.

In fact, the discourse context generally influences which stressed word in a given utterance receives ***prominence*** – that is, which word the speaker wishes to highlight. There are three circumstances governing the placement of prominence. The first, as we have already discussed, is when the speaker places prominence on new information. This has been discussed by Chafe (1980), who points out that within an intonation unit, words expressing old or given information (i.e., semantically predictable information) are unstressed and spoken with lower pitch, whereas words expressing new information are spoken with strong stress and higher pitch. In unmarked utterances, it is the stressed syllable in the last content word that tends to exhibit prominence.

Allen (1971: 77) provides an excellent example of how prominence marks new versus old information; she uses capital letters to signal new information (strong stress and high pitch):

X: I've lost an umBRELla.
Y: A LAdy's umbrella?
X: Yes. A lady's umbrella with STARS on it. GREEN stars.[2]

In this example, *umbrella* functions as new information in X's first utterance. However, in Y's reply, *lady's* receives prominence because it is the new information. In X's second

---

[2]From "Teaching Intonation, From Theory to Practice," by Virginia French Allen, 1971, *TESOL Quarterly, 5* (pp. 76–77). Copyright 1971 by Teachers of English to Speakers of Other Languages, Inc. Used with permission.

utterance, both *umbrella* and *lady's* are old information, whereas *stars* and *green* are new information, thus receiving prominence.

A second, related circumstance governing the placement of prominence is **emphatic stress** – when the speaker wishes to place special emphasis on a particular element. In fact, the element receiving emphatic stress usually communicates new information within the sentence; however, it is differentiated from normal prominence by the greater degree of emphasis placed on it by the speaker. (This greater degree of emphasis is also signaled by pitch level, discussed shortly.) In the phrase "I'm NEVer eating clams again," for example, the speaker might place emphatic stress on *never* to signal a particularly bad reaction she once had when eating clams. Similarly, in the following brief exchange, Speaker B places emphatic stress on *really* to indicate a strong degree of enjoyment:

A: How do you like that new computer you bought?
B: I'm REALly enjoying it!

The third circumstance governing the placement of prominence is **contrastive stress.** In this case, two parallel elements – either explicitly or by implication – can receive prominence within a given utterance. In the question "Is this a LOW or a HIGH impact aerobics class?" for example, the speaker places prominence on both *low* and *high* to signal this important contrast in the sentence. However, note that contrastive stress can occur across speakers without prominence necessarily occurring on both elements (Wayne Dickerson, personal communication):

A: Is this the low impact aeRObics class?
B: No, it's the HIGH impact class.

In this example the contrast becomes apparent only with speaker B's contribution; thus *low* is not stressed by Speaker A, whose focus is on *aerobics*.

We will use the following conventions to indicate word stress, sentence stress, and prominence:

Typeface	Meaning
lowercase letters	unstressed syllable
small capital letters	lightly stressed syllable
large capital letters	strongly stressed (prominent) syllable
boldface capital letters	contrastive or emphatic syllable stress

To better understand the concept of prominence, compare the following two dialogues:

1. A: HOW was the MOvie?
    B: It was TOO LONG.

2. A: Was it a LONG DRIVE?
    B: It was **TOO** LONG.

Although Speaker B says essentially the same thing in both dialogues, *long* is the prominent word in the first dialogue (with *too* also receiving light stress as a content word), since the idea of the movie's being a long one is the main information Speaker B wishes to communicate in answer to *how*. However, in the second dialogue, *too* receives emphatic stress since the speaker, in response to the question about the length of the drive, wishes to highlight its excessiveness. Moreover, in this utterance, *long* is old information and therefore does not receive prominence.

In order to summarize the stress rules of the previous chapter and show how they form an underlying basis for the placement of prominence, the following guidelines are useful:

1. Some degree of sentence stress tends to fall on all content words within an utterance.

2. When any word receiving stress has more than one syllable, it is only the word's most strongly stressed syllable that carries the sentence stress.

3. Within an intonation unit, there may be several words receiving sentence stress but only one main idea or prominent element (or in the case of contrastive stress, two).

4. New information tends to receive prominence and generally occurs toward the end of an utterance.

5. If the speaker wishes to emphasize a given element even more strongly, that element will receive emphatic stress.

6. When contrast between two elements in an intonation unit is signaled, both of these elements tend to receive contrastive stress; in such cases the intonation unit will have two prominent elements.

The following example demonstrates these points:

1. Teacher: We're STUDYing phoNETics in this CLASS.
    (the main idea)

2.   There are WEEKly exAMS.
    (new information)

3.   The exAMS are EVERY THURSday.
    (new information)

4. Student: Did you SAY **TUES**day or **THURS**day?
    (contrast)

5. Teacher: I SAID **THURS**day.
    (clarification and emphasis)

Phonetics is the most meaningful piece of information in line 1, and thus receives prominence. The new, and thus highlighted, information in line 2 is *exams,* just as *Thursday* is the new information in line 3 (not *exams,* which were previously mentioned and are therefore old information). In line 4, the student is not sure of the message and asks for clarification, giving extra emphasis to the contrasting items *Tuesday* and *Thursday.* Finally, in line 5, the teacher clarifies the matter, placing extra emphasis on *Thursday.*

As we have discussed thus far, the main idea or new information receiving prominence tends to come toward the end in unmarked utterances. However, the communicative context can override this general principle. Notice what happens when the speaker intentionally wishes to highlight some other element in the utterance:

1. JOHN'S CAR is WHITE. (unmarked)

2. JOHN'S CAR is **WHITE.** (contrast: not some other color)

3. **JOHN'S** CAR is WHITE. (contrast: not Albert's car)

4. JOHN'S **CAR** is WHITE. (contrast: not his truck)

5. JOHN'S CAR **IS** WHITE. (emphatic assertion: *Why do you say it isn't? I'm absolutely certain it is.*)

In the first statement, the unmarked placement of prominence would occur on the final element, *white.* However, depending on the context, there may be contrast placed on *white* as in statement 2, signaling that the car is white and not some other color. Alternatively, the important contrastive piece of information may be that it is *John's* car that is white and not someone else's, as in statement 3. Or perhaps, as in statement 4, the speaker wishes to make the contrast that it is John's *car* that is white rather than his house or truck. Moreover, should there be a dispute over the color of John's car, the speaker may insist on his or her point of view (i.e., the fact that John's car is indeed white) by emphasizing the verb *be* as in statement 5.

This flexibility allows the speaker to use prominence rather than additional verbiage to get the message across. Here is one more example:

Discourse context	Prominent element
What about John?	He CAN'T GO.
Who can't go?	**HE** CAN'T GO. (*pointing to John*)
Why doesn't John go?	He **CAN'T** GO.

These sentences further demonstrate how the assignment of prominence depends heavily on the discourse and situational context.

In sum, whereas placement of stress within a word is dictated by the word's etymology and other factors, such as affixation, spelling, and grammatical category (which were discussed in Chapter 5 and which will be further elaborated on in Chapters 8 and 9), prominence is sensitive to meaning, discourse, and syntactic boundaries. It reflects the meaning and the context in which a given utterance occurs as well as the speaker's intent.

PROMINENCE: PEDAGOGICAL PRIORITIES

One difficulty learners may encounter entails recognizing and correctly utilizing prominence to highlight the most important information within a thought group. In languages with much more flexible word order, the highlighting of information may often be achieved by moving various sentence elements to the beginning or end of an utterance. It is therefore necessary for teachers to point out the function of prominence as a highlighter in English, with its relatively fixed word order, and to provide students from these language groups with opportunities for practice in this area.

NOTE TO TEACHERS

Although English tends to use prominence and intonation to highlight information that is the focus, many other languages employ quite different means of achieving this same end. For example, in response to the question "Who made the beautiful drawing?" a native English speaker would be likely to reply, "I did," with prominence on *I*, rather than employ the focus construction "It was I who did it." However, a typical reply in Italian would be "L'ho fatto io," with the highlighted element *io* "I" occurring at the end of the utterance. Compare:

English

I DID it.   (unmarked)
I DID it.   (prominence on "I")

Italian

(Io) l'ho fatto.   (unmarked = I did it.)
L'ho fatto io.   (focus on *io*)

Similarly, in German, flexible syntax performs much the same function as prominence in English. Notice how in German the element being highlighted moves to the beginning of the sentence, whereas in English it retains its natural order but receives emphatic stress:

German

Wir fahren nächste Woche los.   (unmarked = We leave next week.)
Nächste Woche fahren wir los.   (focus on *nächste Woche*, "next week")

English

We're LEAVing NEXT WEEK.   (unmarked)
We're LEAVing NEXT **WEEK**.   (not next month)

For learners from languages that tend not to use prominence to highlight or place focus on an element, this function of prominence in English will require explanation and practice.

In sum, teachers should emphasize that prominence in English is used to (1) highlight what is new or important information in an utterance; (2) place special emphasis; and (3) show contrast. Prominence is very sensitive to meaning, discourse, lexical stress, and syntactic boundaries, and thus must be taught in rich contexts that permit learners to see what is new and what is important or contrastive information. This will enable them to understand why prominence occurs where it does. Determining which element of the intonation unit receives prominence, of course, is not the whole story. This is closely related to intonation patterns, which we will discuss shortly.

PRESENTING PROMINENCE TO STUDENTS

Whereas the stress pattern of any multisyllabic English word is more or less established and can be found in the dictionary, prominence can vary a great deal, reflecting changes in the meaning of an utterance. As a consciousness-raising activity to illustrate the discourse influences on prominence, you can write the following three versions of the phrase *I'm listening* on the board:

1. I'm LIStening.
2. **I'M** LIStening.
3. I **AM** LIStening!

Students would first identify which of the three versions you are pronouncing (chosen at random) and then practice producing all three versions, paying attention to placing prominence on the highlighted element. Next ask students three different questions, directing them to answer using one of the three phrases written on the board:

Teacher asks:	Student should respond:
What are you doing?	I'm LIStening.
Who's listening?	**I'M** LIStening.
Why aren't you listening?	I **AM** LIStening![3]

Assuming that students are able to provide the appropriate rejoinder to the questions, you then ask students to provide a rationale for which element receives prominence. Reinforcement

[3]Note that the uncontracted *am* adds extra affirmative emphasis to this statement to contradict the negative question.

for the students' answers can be provided quite simply: First write the three questions next to the appropriate responses and then simply circle the prominent element and relate it back to the question:

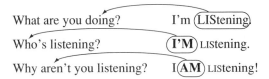

What are you doing?   I'm (LIStening).

Who's listening?   (I'M) LIStening.

Why aren't you listening?   I (AM) LIStening!

To indicate prominence visually, you can employ a variety of notational systems similar to those we suggested for teaching word stress (see Chapter 5):

HOW do you **DO**?

How do you <u>do</u>?

Hòw do you dó?

●   •   •   ●
HOW do you **DO**?

LISTENING DISCRIMINATION

Dialogues are excellent for giving students additional, more real-life practice in distinguishing prominence. Once students understand the basic rule that each thought group contains one prominent element, they can listen to short dialogues such as the following. As they listen, their task is to circle the prominent word in each thought group:

A: I'm (starved.) / Let's go grab a bite to (eat.)

B: Good (idea.) / Where do you want to (go?)

A: (Well,) / there's a nice (Italian) restaurant / about a (block) from here.

B: Do you have your heart set on (Italian?) / What about a (Chinese) place?

A: (Oh,) / do you (know) one?

B: I sure (do.) / The food is (delicious) / and it's right around the (corner.)

A: (Great!) / Let's (go!)

For more advanced learners, the task should be to circle only the strongly stressed syllable of each prominent word rather than the entire word.

CONTROLLED PRACTICE

Controlled practice in assigning prominence can be provided via simple dialogues. Once students have read the dialogue and made predictions about the prominent word or syllable in each thought group, they can compare answers with a partner and then check these predictions against the passage as you read it aloud. Students then perform the dialogues with their partners (in a two-person dialogue, a third student may be assigned the role of "monitor"). Partners should trade roles until everyone has had a chance to practice. During this phase, circulate to give feedback on the students' performance. Although learners may think that they are giving clear prominence to one element over another, unless the listener can hear and identify the prominent element in each thought group, the speaker should be directed to add additional emphasis via volume, length, and/or pitch.

The following dialogues combine practice in placing prominence with options illustrating how native speakers can shift register to express varying degrees of formality/informality:

1. *Relatively formal*

   A: He(llo) / How (are) you?
   B: (Fine,) thank you. / How are (you?) (*or:* And (you?))
   A: (Fine,) thanks.

2. *Neutral*

   A: How have you (been?)
   B: Pretty (good.) / How have (you) been? (*or:* How about (you?))
   A: Just (fine.)

3. *Relatively informal*

   A: (Hey!) / How are you (doing?)
   B: Not (bad.) / How are (you) doing? (*or:* How about your(self?))
   A: O(kay,) thanks.

GUIDED PRACTICE

In the guided practice phase, learners first pattern their production after a model and then exchange limited information. One such activity involves personal information questions and answers. First provide a model dialogue, which students practice in unison:

A: WHERE are you FROM?
B: GERmany. WHAT about **YOU**?
A: I'M from CHIna.

You may also wish to provide some variety in the model dialogue by including alternative rejoinders (e.g., "And **YOU**?" or "How about your**SELF**?"). Once students are comfortable reading the model dialogue, they can be paired off to create new dialogues asking each other about their home countries.

Further guided practice can be provided via dialogues that illustrate the basic rules for prominence, such as the following:

AT THE DELI

Customer:	I'd like some (cheese,) please. (main idea)
Shopkeeper:	What (kind) of cheese? (main idea, new information)
	(Swiss) or (Cheddar?) (contrasting two things)
Customer:	I'll have (Cheddar.) (emphasizing choice)

Once students practice the dialogue with a partner, the activity can take a more communicative bent by having students role-play the customer and the shopkeeper at the deli. Any item that can be bought at a deli counter will work: for example, salad (potato or coleslaw), pickles (sweet or dill), sausage (Polish or Italian), chicken (barbecued or roasted), bread (whole wheat or rye), and so on.

COMMUNICATIVE PRACTICE

One activity that provides communicative practice in placing prominence is a "Spot the Difference" picture activity in which Students A and B each receive similar pictures with

Figure 6.1 Illustrations for Student A (*top*) and Student B (*bottom*) for "Spot the Difference," communicative practice with prominence

several differences (see Figure 6.1). Partners sit facing each other (without showing the picture to each other) and exchange information in order to determine the differences. A sample exchange between two partners might be the following:

A: I have a picture of a lady sitting in a PARK.
B: I have a lady in a park TOO. She's reading a BOOK.
A: Oh, my lady is reading a NEWSpaper.
B: Next to the lady there's a big TREE.
A: There's a big tree in MY picture TOO.
B: My picture has a DOG.
A: My picture has TWO dogs.

COMMON INTONATION PATTERNS: WHAT THE TEACHER NEEDS TO KNOW

As we have seen, one way of highlighting information is through prominence; another is intonation. To understand intonation, it is first necessary to define *pitch,* the relative highness or lowness of the voice. It is important to note that the phonetic notion of pitch is relative, referring to the differentiated pitch levels of a given speaker – not to the lower versus higher pitches of men's and women's voices or the differing pitch variations of different speakers.

In fact, pitch in its phonetic meaning corresponds quite closely to the definition of pitch in music. For example, ascending *do, re,* and *mi* represent progressively higher tones, or musical pitch. We distinguish four levels of phonetic pitch in English:

4 = extra high

3 = high

2 = middle

1 = low

Normal conversation moves between middle and high pitch, with low pitch typically signaling the end of an utterance. The extra high level is generally used to express a strong emotion such as surprise, great enthusiasm, or disbelief, and is the pitch level often used in contrastive or emphatic stress. English makes use of pitch variation over the length of an entire utterance rather than within one word.

NOTE TO TEACHERS

In tonal languages such as Chinese, Navajo, or Yoruba, differences in pitch can signify differences of meaning within a word. The classic example from Mandarin Chinese is the word *ma,* which can mean either "mother," "scold," "hemp," or "horse," depending on its pitch pattern (high level vs. high falling, etc.). Similarly, in Yoruba, a language spoken in Western Nigeria, the sound sequence /ɔkɔ/ can mean "hoe," "vehicle," or "husband," depending on the pitch of the two syllables. Speakers of such languages often have difficulty adjusting to the very different intonational structure of English, and may transfer the tonal structure of their own language to their production of English words.

If we examine the function of pitch within one-word utterances in English, we find that it does not change the fundamental meaning of the word itself. Rather, it reflects the discourse context within which a word occurs. For example, the one-word utterance *now,* produced with a rising pitch contour from middle to high, could signify a question: "Do you want me to do it now?" Produced with a falling pitch contour from high to low, however, this same word could signify a command: "Do it now!"

If pitch represents the individual tones of speech, then *intonation* can be thought of as the entire melodic line. Intonation involves the rising and falling of the voice to various pitch levels during the articulation of an utterance. It performs several unique functions. First, intonation reflects the grammatical function of an utterance. For example:

She's gone.

She's gone?

If the utterance is pronounced with a rising–falling intonation, then it signals speaker certainty, which often corresponds to a declarative statement. However, pronounced with rising intonation, the same sequence of phonemes signals uncertainty and corresponds to a special type of yes/no question with statement word order but rising intonation.[4]

Intonation also performs the function of conveying an attitude or emotion. For example, the simple utterance "Great" can be used to express three different shades of meaning:

1. Great.   (perfunctory)

2. Great.   (enthusiasm)

3. G r e a t.   (sarcasm)

Clearly, the attitude of the speaker will vary in these three instances, with intonation conveying a great deal of the difference. Thus in statement 1, the overall effect of the slightly falling intonation is that the speaker's comment is neutral or perfunctory, whereas in statement 2, the broader movement from high to low signifies that the speaker is genuinely enthusiastic. In contrast, the flatter intonation of the last statement signifies lack of enthusiasm or sarcasm on the part of the speaker.

The movement of pitch within an intonation unit is referred to as the **intonation contour** of that unit. Such contours span the range of extra high pitch to low pitch. These levels are highly dependent on discourse meaning and prominence, with rises in intonation co-occurring with the highlighted or more important words that receive prominence within the sentence. Thus pitch and prominence can be said to have a symbiotic relationship with each other in English, and the interrelationship of these phenomena determines the intonation contour of a given utterance. The next three sections summarize the most common intonation contours in NAE, followed by a discussion of how the discourse context influences the choice of intonation contour.

RISING–FALLING INTONATION

One of the most common patterns is the **rising–falling contour**. In this pattern, the intonation typically begins at a neutral middle level (2) and then rises to a high level (3) on the main stressed element of the utterance. The intonation then falls to either the low level (1) – a terminal fall, signaling certainty and generally corresponding to the end of the utterance – or to the middle level (2) – a nonterminal fall, signaling a weaker degree of certainty and usually corresponding to an unfinished statement, an incomplete thought, or a mood of suspense.

If the prominent syllable is the last syllable in the thought group, the fall is a **glide:**

Computers are fun.
        (glide)

If, on the other hand, the stressed syllable is part of a multisyllabic word with other unstressed syllables after it, then the fall occurs on the unstressed element immediately following the main stressed syllable and is called a **step:**

Computers can also be frustrating.
        (step)

Rising–falling intonation patterns of the 2-3-1 "certainty" type (i.e., the utterance begins at level 2, rises to level 3, and then falls to level 1) typically signal the following

[4]This example illustrates nicely what Ford and Thompson (1996) have shown: that intonation can override syntax in spoken English.

types of utterances: declarative statements, **wh-questions** (questions with the interrogative pronouns *where, when, what, who, why, how much*), and commands or directives.

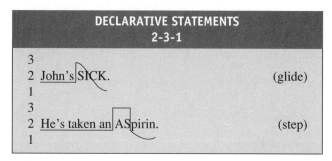

DECLARATIVE STATEMENTS 2-3-1	
3 2 John's SICK. 1	(glide)
3 2 He's taken an ASpirin. 1	(step)

WH-QUESTIONS 2-3-1	
3 2 Who will HELP? 1	(glide)
3 2 What about JONathan? 1	(step)

COMMANDS AND COMMAND-FORM REQUESTS 2-3-1	
3 2 Fix me some SOUP. 1	(glide)
3 2 Please add NOODles. 1	(step)

Two further types of utterances can use rising–falling intonation contours. However, in these cases the pitch levels also vary from the 2-3-1 pattern. The first of these utterances uses a 2-3-2 nonterminal fall with a slight rise at the end, indicating that the utterance is an unfinished statement in which the speaker has left something unsaid or implied:

UNFINISHED STATEMENTS 2-3-2
3 2 John's SICK . . . 1
(. . . *but I think he's going to work anyway.*)
3 2 He's taken an ASpirin . . . 1
(. . . *but I don't know if it helped or not.*)
3 2 She said she was aLONE . . . 1
(. . . *but I'm not sure I believe her.*)

In some unfinished statements, the speaker uses the 2-3-2 pattern with a slight rise at the end to create suspense:[5]

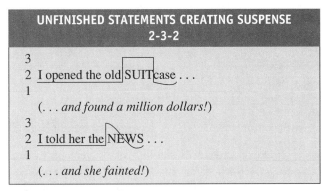

UNFINISHED STATEMENTS CREATING SUSPENSE
2-3-2

3
2 I opened the old SUITcase . . .
1

    (. . . *and found a million dollars!*)

3
2 I told her the NEWS . . .
1

    (. . . *and she fainted!*)

The other utterance using a rising–falling intonation occurs after a 2-3-1 contour and employs a 3-1 contour. This contour occurs in **tag questions eliciting agreement,** in which the speaker is requesting confirmation from the interlocutor. Functioning almost like a statement, they typically signal certainty:

TAG QUESTION ELICITING AGREEMENT
2-3-1   3-1

3
2 We really ought to VIsit him, SHOULDn't we?
1

RISING INTONATION

Another common intonation pattern in English is the **rise.** Rise in intonation usually begins at the syllable with discourse prominence and continues slightly until the end of the phrase:

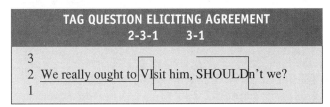

Are you feeling better?

Has he finished it yet?

There are two different rise contours: one that moves from middle to high level (2-3 or 2-4), depending on the amount of emotion being expressed, and another that rises from low to mid level (1-2). The middle-to-high rise (2-3 or 2-4) signals uncertainty. The following utterance types tend to follow this pattern: yes/no questions using question word order, open-choice alternative questions, yes/no questions using statement word order, unfinished statements creating suspense, echo questions, repetition questions, and tag questions signaling uncertainty.

In the first of these, **yes/no questions,** the speaker asks a question, phrased in question word order, to which the expected answer is *yes* or *no.*

YES-NO QUESTIONS WITH QUESTION WORD ORDER
2-3

3
2 Have you GOT a minute?
1

3
2 Can I ask you a QUEStion?
1

[5]Some speakers may drop on the prominent syllable and then rise slightly at the end instead.

In the next pattern, ***open-choice alternative questions,*** the listener has a free choice of the alternatives being offered. It is unclear whether other options are available, but the listener is given the chance to reject all of the alternatives.

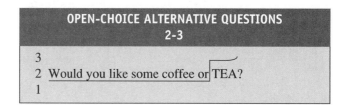

OPEN-CHOICE ALTERNATIVE QUESTIONS
2-3

3
2 Would you like some coffee or TEA?
1

The next category involves utterances that look like statements in terms of their syntax but function as questions. Such statements are unlike normal yes/no questions in that the speaker already has some evidence to confirm the statement. Both 2-3 and 2-4 rise patterns are possible – the latter if surprise or disbelief is being expressed:

YES/NO QUESTIONS WITH STATEMENT WORD ORDER
2-3; 2-4

4
3
2 The plane LEFT already?
1

   (2-3 = neutral confirmation question)
   (2-4 = great surprise or disbelief: *I was supposed to be on it!*)

4
3
2 It left from Gate 47?
1

   (2-3 = neutral question)
   (2-4 = great surprise or disbelief: *They told me Gate 23!*)

Occasionally, as a conversational strategy, a speaker will repeat a question before answering it. In these types of questions, commonly known as ***echo questions,*** there is a 2-3 rise pattern. For example, in answer to Speaker A's question "What are you doing this weekend?" Speaker B might begin with the following echo question:

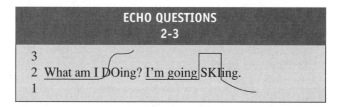

ECHO QUESTIONS
2-3

3
2 What am I DOing? I'm going SKIing.
1

Repetition questions ask for repetition usually because the speaker could not hear what was said or the speaker could not believe what was said. These types of questions can follow statements, yes/no questions, or wh-questions.

In the case of a 2-3 pitch contour, the question means "Could you repeat what you said? I didn't hear you." Suppose that Speaker A asks, "What are you doing this weekend?" to which Speaker B replies, "I'm going skiing." If Speaker A has not understood, a repetition question is asked:

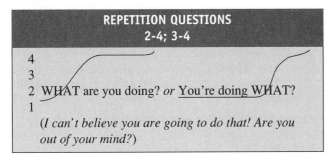

With a more exaggerated pitch rise, on the other hand, the question means "I can't believe what I just heard. Tell me again." Assuming, for example, that Speaker B's answer to the question "What are you doing this weekend?" is "I'm going skydiving," Speaker A might signal disbelief through a rise to level 4:

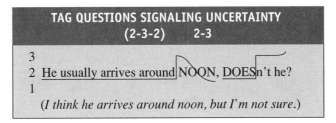

Unlike the category of tag questions eliciting agreement, **tag questions signaling uncertainty** are more like true yes/no questions. The speaker may have some prior assumption but allows for the possibility of either a "yes" or "no" response:

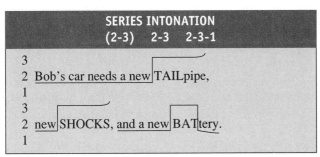

OTHER PATTERNS

As noted previously, there are two basic options for sentence-final intonation in NAE – rising–falling and rising patterns. However, internal to a given sentence, there may also be a series of rises or falls that occur as a result of the syntax.

In the first combination, elements occur in a series, with each item in the series receiving rising intonation (usually 2-3) until the final item, which receives rising-falling intonation (2-3-1).

SERIES INTONATION		
(2-3)	2-3	2-3-1

3
2 Bob's car needs a new TAILpipe,
1
3
2 new SHOCKS, and a new BATtery.
1

The identical pattern is found in ***closed-choice alternative questions.*** Again, each alternative receives rising intonation until the final one – signaling that no other options are available and the speaker is expected to select from the closed set of choices presented.

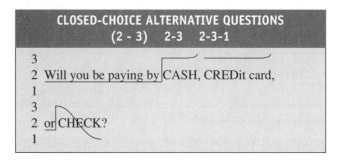

This pattern of closed-choice alternative questions contrasts both in intonation contour and meaning with the open choice alternative questions described earlier. Compare:

Are you going to pay with Master Card or Visa?

(Open choice: *Are you going to pay with a credit card?*)

Are you going to pay with Master Card or Visa?

(Closed choice: *Which credit card are you going to pay with: Master Card or Visa?*)

In ***appositive constructions,*** defined as a phrase or clause that follows and modifies a noun giving added information, the 1-2-1 contour signals that the clarifying appositive information is uttered as an aside.

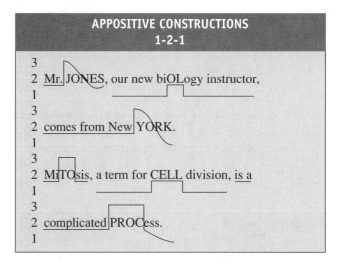

A related construction is the ***parenthetical expression.*** Similar to appositives, these expressions are often uttered as asides, signaled through the intonation contour used by the speaker. Parentheticals include utterances such as direct address (*John, Dr. Martin*), polite expressions (*please, thank you*), adverbials (*unfortunately, once in a while*), expressions of opinion (*I'm afraid, you know*), and epithets or expletives (*that jerk, damn*). These parenthetical elements, when they appear sentence initially, can be signaled either through a rising or a rising–falling pattern:

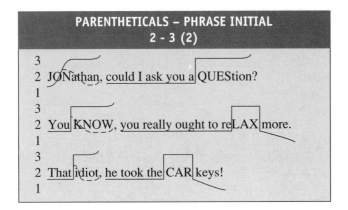

A second pattern used with middle-sentence and sentence-final parentheticals moves from low to middle level (1-2), with the rise in intonation coinciding with the main stressed syllable of the parenthetical:[6]

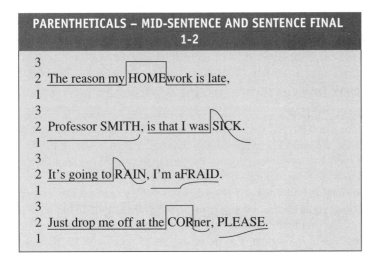

In compound or complex sentences, each clause has its own intonation pattern, which more or less corresponds to the rules given previously. In other words, each clause may terminate in rising intonation or rising–falling intonation, depending on its particular syntax. However, in the case of falling intonation patterns with nonfinal clauses, the fall usually terminates at level 2.

---

[6]In some analyses of sentence-final parentheticals there is no prominence (Dickerson, personal communication). These constructions are marked not only by the absence of a prominent element but also by a low, flat intonation pattern.

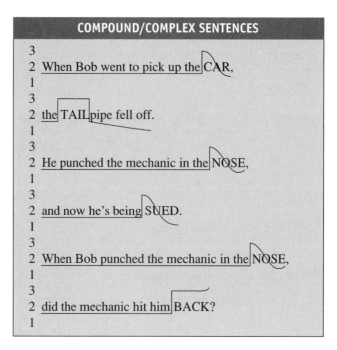

As we mentioned previously, certain basic principles governing English prominence exist; however, the speaker's intentions may override typical patterns in order to assign special prominence to a different element in the utterance. This is also true for intonation. In fact, as we have seen, intonation contours are directly connected to the prominent syllable. Therefore it is logical that if the prominent element shifts according to discourse context, then the intonation pattern will also change.

COMMON INTONATION PATTERNS: PEDAGOGICAL PRIORITIES

It is rare to find a beginning or an intermediate textbook that does not make use of dialogues in both oral and written form. We believe that it is imperative even at the most elementary stage of language instruction that attention be paid not only to the vocabulary, grammar, and functions of these dialogues but also to the prominence and intonation – that is, to the critical role these features play and the meaning they carry.

Certain intonation patterns present difficulties for the learner. For example, learners frequently associate questions exclusively with rising intonation, and as a result may have difficulty correctly producing and/or interpreting many wh-questions, which typically have falling intonation in English. Tag questions are also difficult for nonnative learners, in terms of both grammar and intonation. Most learners use the rising intonation only, thereby signaling uncertainty. Native speakers, on the other hand, use the intonation signaling certainty much more frequently, since they most typically use tags to elicit confirmation, not to express uncertainty. Thus when producing utterances such as "That was a really tough exam, wasn't it?" (with final rising intonation), an ESL/EFL learner might appear to a native-speaker interlocutor to be unusually indecisive or hesitant.

Alternative questions can also be confusing to the nonnative learner, since nonnatives may again have difficulty interpreting or producing the difference between open- or closed-choice alternative questions. A common phenomenon among learners is to interpret closed-choice questions as open-choice. Thus in restaurants, when asked if they would like blue cheese, ranch, or house vinaigrette dressing, learners may answer "yes" instead of selecting from among the three options.

Depending on the language background of the learner, the pitch variation within intonation contours may be either too narrow or too exaggerated. For example, the intonation of languages such as Japanese, Spanish, and Dutch typically has a narrower range – thus making the English intonation of learners from these language groups sound somewhat flat. Speakers of other languages (such as Norwegian or the Swiss dialect of German) use more exaggerated pitch variation within a contour, lending a somewhat sing-song quality to their English.

Whether the teacher opts to present multiple intonation patterns to students at once or to present such patterns one by one as needed based on student difficulties and/or teaching contexts will obviously depend on a number of factors, including the focus of the course, student proficiency level, and curricular goals. We discuss these issues at greater length in Chapter 11.

Since the suprasegmental features of a language are perhaps even less "visible" to the learner than the segmental features, we need to explore concrete ways to make students aware of them. In the following section, we suggest ways in which intonation can be presented and made salient to students.

PRESENTING COMMON INTONATION PATTERNS TO STUDENTS

Once students have understood the concepts of word stress, sentence stress, and rhythm, these can be integrated into the presentation of prominence and intonation in English. In reality, these features cannot be separated naturally. However, we believe that the various intonation patterns and accompanying pitch movements make more sense if word stress, sentence stress, rhythm, and prominence have already been presented.

You can begin a presentation of intonation by explaining that it is similar to the melody or tune of speech, which is made up of individual pitches. To reinforce this analogy, you can illustrate the varying pitch levels using lines similar to a musical staff. This staff and an example sentence can be drawn on the board as follows:[7]

4	EXTRA HIGH			
3	HIGH		red	
2	MID	Joan is wearing		to-
1	LOW			day.

Explain that the typical statement begins at the mid level as shown, and that the prominent element (in this case, *red*) coincides with the main pitch movement. The utterance finishes on a low pitch to show finality. There are usually no extra high-level pitches in a neutral statement such as this one.

An important concept to convey to students is that of the thought group, or intonation unit. Students need to know that a single utterance may include multiple intonation units, each with its own prominent element and contour. Each intonation unit

1. is set off by pauses before and after,

2. contains one prominent element,

3. has an intonation contour of its own, and

4. has a grammatically coherent internal structure.

---

[7]The intonation contours we present in our examples are not the only ones possible because NAE exhibits individual and dialectal variation.

One way to communicate this to students is to take a dialogue from the students' text and write it on the board or project it. For example:

(*On the telephone*)

Mrs. Smith:	Hello?
Joe:	Hello, Mrs. Smith, this is Joe.
Mrs. Smith:	Oh hi, Joe. How are you?
Joe:	Oh, I'm fine. Can I talk to Tom?
Mrs. Smith:	No, he's gone to the library to find a book for his science project. Should I tell him you called?
Joe:	Yeah, could you tell him I won't be able to meet him tonight because my aunt and uncle dropped in from out of town and the whole family is going out for dinner.
Mrs. Smith:	Okay. I'll be sure to tell him that.

Depending on the proficiency level and linguistic sophistication of the students, you can either add slashes (/) to mark the thought groups yourself or elicit from students which segments in each line constitute grammatical thought groups. Then circle or elicit the prominent element in each segment and draw in the intonation contour. Follow this with choral and individual reading of the lines of the dialogue with students, paying special attention to the intonation contours.

Learners should also be made aware that there is no one fixed or rule-governed way to divide an utterance into thought groups. For example, a faster speaker may pause only once in the utterance, whereas a slower speaker might pause as many as four times. You can illustrate this by selecting a longer utterance (such as the following example from the Tennessee Williams play *The Glass Menagerie*) and writing it on the board with the possible thought groups marked, as follows:

Faster speaker   When he sees how lovely and sweet and PRETty she is, /

he'll thank his lucky stars he was asked to DINner.

Slower speaker   When he sees how LOVEly / and SWEET /

and PRETty she is, / he'll thank his lucky STARS /

he was asked to DINner.

In the sentence uttered by the faster speaker, which has two thought groups, the two prominent elements are *pretty* and *dinner*. These prominent elements coincide with the pitch movement of the intonation contour. The sentence uttered by the slower speaker contains five prominent elements (i.e., *lovely, sweet, pretty, stars,* and *dinner*) since it is divided into five thought groups. Again, these prominent elements correspond with the movement in pitch within the intonation unit.

It is helpful to point out that in certain cases, the punctuation found in written English reflects the intonation units of spoken English. For example, a period (or full stop) at the end of a written sentence usually signals a fall to level 1 in the corresponding spoken utterance:

Writing   He's a teacher.

Speech   ˌhiyzəˈtiytʃər

By contrast, a comma at the end of a clause or phrase often signals that the pitch ends at level 2 (or that there is a slight rise), followed by a pause to indicate that the speaker is not yet at the end of the utterance.

In these examples the comma represents a slight rise on the preceding syllable, followed by a pause:

Direct address

JOHN, we're WAITing for YOU.

Listing nonfinal members of a series

(Who came?)   BOB, JOE, and BILL.

However, as Allen (1971) points out, sometimes a written comma does not signal a slight rise and pause in the corresponding spoken utterance, as in the following examples. (Note that in the first two examples the comma separates two equally important pieces of information [specific vs. general]; thus each piece of information receives prominence.)

Place-name divisions

JOE LIVES in SPRINGFIELD, oHIo.

Time divisions

JOE was BORN on AUgust 10, 1981.

Yes/no responses

(Did you see it?)   YES, I DID.

Strong emotion is often signaled by an exclamation point in writing and by more extreme pitch changes in intonation. Compare:

WHAT a BALLGAME!

WHAT a **BALL**GAME!

Similarly, in yes/no questions, the question mark often corresponds to rising intonation:

Is JOHN a TEAcher?

However, the question mark at the end of wh-questions typically corresponds to rising–falling intonation in speech:

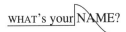

WHAT's your NAME?

As we have seen, English tag questions may either rise or rise and fall, depending on their meaning. However, when they appear in written form, a question mark usually occurs at the end of both types of tags regardless of intonation.

Thus students who are much more comfortable with written English than with spoken English will have to be warned, as Allen (1971) suggests, that punctuation is not a completely reliable guide to intonation. Instead, the structure, meaning, and purpose of the utterance are what must guide the speaker's choice of intonation contour.

LISTENING DISCRIMINATION

To build upon students' knowledge of grammar and punctuation in English and to demonstrate relevance to intonation, you can introduce the following listening activity, based on the one-word exchanges in a dialogue from Allen (1971:76). In this dialogue, the grammatical function (and therefore, the punctuation) of each line is conveyed through intonation alone. Provide students with a version of the dialogue in which the punctuation has been omitted. The students' task is simply to add a period, a question mark, or an exclamation point at the end of each line as you read the dialogue aloud:[8]

Teacher's script		Student worksheet	
He:	Ready? ↗	He:	Ready
She:	No! ↘	She:	No
He:	Why? ↘	He:	Why
She:	Problems. ↘	She:	Problems
He:	Problems? ↗	He:	Problems
She:	Yes. ↘	She:	Yes
He:	What? ↘	He:	What
She:	Babysitter. ↘	She:	Babysitter

To further reinforce students' ability to discriminate between rising and falling intonation, the following kinds of listening exercises are suggested. These activities provide an immediate assessment of the learner's ability to discriminate rising versus rising–falling intonation, and they are easy to construct and administer. However, we recommend that you mark in advance which way you are going to read each item, and even practice or tape-record these before doing the activity in the classroom. Obviously, you would not want to do all of these exercises at once, but rather select the one that corresponds to the feature you are teaching.

QUESTION OR STATEMENT?		
Directions: Listen to the sentences. Check the box that corresponds to the pattern used (rising for yes/no questions; rising–falling for statements).		
Utterance	**Question ↗**	**Statement ↗↘**
1. He left already		
2. Sally's moving		
3. John missed his flight		
4. It's snowing in Tucson		

[8]From "Teaching Intonation, From Theory to Practice," by Virginia French Allen, 1971, *TESOL Quarterly, 5* (pp. 76–77). Copyright 1971 by Teachers of English to Speakers of Other Languages, Inc. Used with permission.

TAG QUESTIONS: SURE OR UNSURE?

Directions: Listen to the sentences. Check the box that corresponds to the intonation pattern used for the tag question (rising–falling if the speaker is sure of the statement; rising if the speaker is unsure).

Utterance	Sure ↗↘	Unsure ↗
1. Your name's George, isn't it?		
2. It's going to rain tomorrow, isn't it?		
3. You wanted to go, didn't you?		
4. We should offer to help, shouldn't we?		

ALTERNATIVE CHOICE QUESTIONS

Directions: Listen to the sentences. Check the box that corresponds to the information pattern used (rising for yes/no questions; rising–falling for forced-choice questions).

Utterance	Yes-No ↗	Choice ↗↘
1. Are you coming Friday or Saturday?		
2. Can you meet us at 8 or 9?		
3. Would you like beer or wine?		
4. Are you going to Spain or Portugal?		

CONTROLLED PRACTICE

Choral reading of dialogues can provide effective practice if the teacher makes a strong effort to guide the speakers in rhythm, stress, and intonation using body and hand movements. If teachers highlight only the more tangible elements, such as vocabulary and grammar (or even the individual pronunciation of sounds and words), they neglect an important aspect of communicating meaning: the stress and intonation patterns of each phrase. In fact, prominence and intonation are key elements used by native speakers to comprehend an utterance or conversation. Look at an example that might occur in a beginning text:

(*Nancy and Bob meet in an evening class.*)
Nancy: Hi! My name's Nancy.
Bob: Hi, Nancy. I'm Bob.
Nancy: Where are you from, Bob?
Bob: I'm from Madison. What about you?
Nancy: I'm from New York.

Although the teacher may pronounce the dialogue very naturally, or may even use prerecorded tapes, it cannot be taken for granted that learners will automatically be able to imitate the intonation accurately. Both prominence and intonation should be visually highlighted for the learner. This can be done by superimposing intonation contours over the written text and also by using hand movements during oral modeling. This might render dialogue as follows:

Nancy: Hi! My name's Nancy.

Bob: Hi, Nancy. I'm Bob.

Nancy: Where are you from, Bob?

Bob: I'm from Madison. What about you?

Nancy: I'm from New York.

The teacher probably will not be able to convey the reasons behind each intonation contour pattern to the beginning-level student but should at least aim for a minimum level of accuracy in this important feature of oral language.

The intonation of tag questions is sometimes puzzling to students because two different possibilities exist. To help clarify this for students, begin by practicing dialogues with tag questions in which ambiguity is removed by the context:

Tag question eliciting agreement

A: It's a beautiful day, isn't it?

B: Yes, it's lovely! Seems like spring is already here!

Tag question signaling uncertainty

A: The library's supposed to be right around the corner here, isn't it?
    I can't seem to find it!

B: Actually, it's on the next corner. You have to go one more block
    and it's on your left.

Focused review of intonation patterns can be achieved using simple teacher-written dialogues. With advanced classes, teachers can ask the students to mark the intonation patterns (alone or in pairs or groups); then, after verifying their predictions, students can read them paying special attention to intonation. The following dialogue is taken from Craig Chaudron (personal communication) and has been marked to assist the teacher:

JACK AND JILL

Jill: Good morning, Jack.

Jack: Hi, Jill. Where are you going?

Jill: Just up the hill. Do you want to come along?

Jack: Sure. What's that you're carrying?

Jill: That's my bucket. I'm going to fetch a pail of water.

Jack: Didn't you hear about the rockslides? After the rains, the
        winds, and the earthquake, they say the path is dangerous.

Jill: Oh, I'm not afraid, and you're not either, are you?

Jack: Oh, I suppose not. Let's go.

An important function of wh-questions is to ask for repetition or clarification. When teaching this function, you can have students practice sequences such as the following while pointing out that the wh-word rises in pitch and the repeated element assumes prominence and is usually accompanied by stronger stress:

Original statement	Clarification question	Repeated information
I'm going to New YORK.	WHERE?	New YORK!
Do you have Mary's PHONE number?	WHOSE?	**MARY's!**
Ted likes the BLUE one best.	WHICH one?	The **BLUE** one!
I can't find the CAR keys.	WHICH keys?	The **CAR** keys!
I'm taking my vacation in NoVEMber.	WHEN?	In NoVEMber.

Another controlled practice technique that works well if a language laboratory is available is that of mirroring or shadowing. To begin, learners read over the written text of a speech sample – be it a conversation or monologue – several times making sure that they understand it well. Then learners listen to the tape several times while reading along silently until their eyes follow the text in coordination with the speaker. Using a two-track tape system, learners record their voice while reading along with the speaker trying to maintain the same speed, rhythm, stress, and intonation. Finally, learners can play back the two simultaneous recordings and compare them.

GUIDED PRACTICE

A guided practice activity focusing on rising versus rising–falling intonation patterns involves the dramatic reading of literature excerpts, such as the following poem by Christina Rosetti (1862), in which the alternating lines contain excellent opportunities for students to practice rising and rising–falling intonation patterns:

UPHILL

Does the road wind uphill all the way?
    Yes, to the very end.
Will the day's journey take the whole long day?
    From morn to night, my friend.

But is there for the night a resting-place?
    A roof for when the slow dark hours begin.
May not the darkness hide it from my face?
    You cannot miss that inn.

Shall I meet other wayfarers at night?
    Those who have gone before.
Then must I knock, or call when just in sight?
    They will not keep you standing at that door.

Shall I find comfort, travel-sore and weak?
    Of labor you shall find the sum.
Will there be beds for me and all who seek?
    Yea, beds for all who come.

COMMUNICATIVE PRACTICE

For more communicative practice in yes/no question intonation, teachers can construct simple games such as the following "Twenty Questions" game. One partner receives a magazine picture of a room interior (e.g., a kitchen, a den, a bathroom) and the second partner must guess the type of room by asking a series of yes/no questions. Next the second partner attempts to identify at least five items in the room. For example:

> Is it a kitchen?
> *No, it isn't.*

> Is it a living room?
> *Yes, it is.*

> Is there a sofa in the living room?
> *Yes, there is.*

> Is there a pillow on the sofa?
> *Yes, there is.*

> Is there a coffee table in front of the sofa?
> *Yes, there is.*

> Are there any bookshelves against the wall?
> *No, there aren't.*

To motivate students, you can set a time limit for the game and award a "prize" to the student who has correctly guessed the most items.

So far we have discussed common intonation patterns and how to present these to students; we now move to a discussion of how discourse considerations influence intonation contours – in other words, how the individual speaker uses intonation to convey meaning in discourse.

INTONATION AND MEANING: WHAT THE TEACHER NEEDS TO KNOW

Individual speakers make very specific use of **prosody** (i.e., intonation, volume, tempo, and rhythm) to convey their meaning in extended spoken discourse. Initially, by marking thought groups or intonation units, a speaker signals "information about thematic cohesion, perspective, message prominence, and distinctions such as those between shared and non-shared, main and subsidiary information" (Gumperz and Kaltman 1980: 62).

The intonation or the pitch contour of a thought group is crucial; Ford and Thompson (1996), for example, demonstrate that in English conversation a complete intonation contour is almost always accompanied by a grammatical completion (a phrase, a clause, etc.). However, the reverse is not true. There are many grammatically complete word strings that are not perceived by the interlocutor as complete. This is because they are not produced with utterance-final intonation, thus indicating that the speaker is not finished. From these findings, we can deduce that intonation is more important than grammar for marking boundaries in conversation (see also Gumperz 1982).

In a similar vein, Chun (1988: 81) notes: "Intonation functions to express whether a speaker is ready and willing to relinquish the floor, to signal that a response is desired, unnecessary, or unwanted, and to differentiate normal information from contrastive or expressive intentions." In other words, intonation performs an important conversation management function, with the speaker being able to subtly signal to the interlocutor to quit talking, to respond in a particular fashion, or to pay particular attention to a piece of highlighted information.

STATEMENTS

Unmarked or neutral versions of most English statements have rising–falling intonation and fairly predictable stress as discussed previously in this chapter. For example:

JOHN COOKED DINner.

However, statements are sometimes marked such that one constituent, for example the subject noun *John,* is singled out for special focus or emphasis. This special marking can be accomplished in a variety of ways. There are grammatical options, such as the cleft construction (*It was John who cooked dinner*), and addition of emphatic markers (*John himself cooked dinner*); yet in everyday spoken English, marking is most commonly accomplished through greater length, extra force, and higher pitch on the prominent syllable. Thus the most typical way to give special prominence to *John* in the statement we are discussing is to say:

JOHN COOKED DINner.

However, it does not make sense to practice the unmarked and marked versions of *John cooked dinner* in isolation and out of context. Learners must understand early on that one version is appropriate in one context, whereas the other is appropriate in another context.

For example, consider the following conversational exchange:

Alice: WHAT HAPpened after you GOT HOME?

Betty: NOTHing unUSual; JOHN COOKED DINner.

In this context the unmarked version of the statement is used. Contrast it with the following:

Alice: Did you COOK DINner after you GOT HOME?

Betty: No, **JOHN** COOKED DINner.

The marked version of the statement is used to counter the false assumption that Betty cooked dinner; the correction is made by emphasizing the name of the person who actually did cook dinner: John.

YES/NO QUESTIONS

When asking yes/no questions, the unmarked syntactic option involves the inversion of the subject and the auxiliary verb (or the addition of *do* as the auxiliary in sentences that have no auxiliary verb). This unmarked option is accompanied by rising intonation. Since the intonation can rise on whichever constituent is in focus, this intonation pattern often has two or three possible contours depending on the syntactic complexity and length of the question, for example:

1a.   Did JOHN COOK DINner?

  b.   Did JOHN COOK DINner?

However, it is also possible with this same syntactic option for the speaker to use a marked rising–falling intonation pattern. This pattern conveys either expectation of an affirmative answer (if normal stress and intonation are used) or impatience, simultaneously implying an additional query (i.e., Are you going to answer my question, or aren't you?) if more exaggerated stress and intonation occur. Again, two contours are possible depending on which constituent is being emphasized:

2a.   Did JOHN COOK DINner?

b.   Did JOHN COOK DINner?

In an even more highly marked version of this yes/no question, there is no inversion: In terms of its syntax, the uninverted question is a statement, yet it still functions as a question because of the rising intonation. This uninverted yes/no question form can take two different prosodic patterns.

The first pattern has the normal stress and intonation of a rising yes/no question but has several possible contours resulting from primary stress and rise on the different constituents in focus:

3a.   JOHN COOKED DINner?   (focus on *dinner*)

b.   JOHN COOKED DINner?   (focus on *John*)

c.   JOHN COOKED DINner?   (focus on *cooked*)

In all of these question contours, the speaker is either asking the interlocutor to repeat or is making an assumption and wants the interlocutor to confirm it (i.e., the speaker has good reason to expect a *yes* answer).

The second prosodic pattern for the uninverted question has emphatic stress, high pitch, and exaggerated intonation on one or two of the constituents that lend themselves to focus. Again, several contours are possible depending on the constituent in focus:

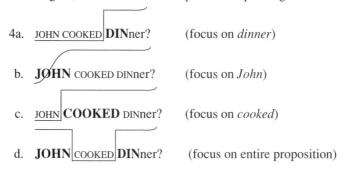

4a.   JOHN COOKED **DIN**ner?   (focus on *dinner*)

b.   **JOHN** COOKED DINner?   (focus on *John*)

c.   JOHN **COOKED** DINner?   (focus on *cooked*)

d.   **JOHN** COOKED **DIN**ner?   (focus on entire proposition)

In these variations the speaker is reacting with surprise or disbelief to certain information just received:

• *dinner:* the fact that it was dinner that John cooked (*a*)

• *John:* the fact that it was John who cooked dinner (*b*)

• *cooking (dinner):* the fact that John cooked it (*c*)

• *the fact that John cooked dinner:* i.e., the whole proposition (*d*)

Each of the foregoing yes/no patterns requires a different discourse context:

1a, b Neutral request for information
2a, b Greater expectation, or impatience
3a–c Request for repetition or confirmation
4a–d Expression of surprise or disbelief

For each of the four contexts below, see if you can find the best match among the three choices provided and explain why it is best.

Context 1

Alice: Bob, Joe, and John kept doing nice things for me because it was Mother's Day. Bob washed the car, and Joe ironed the shirts. Guess what else happened.

Betty: _____?

Alice: Yes.

    (a)   Did JOHN COOK DINner?

    (b)   JOHN COOKED DINner?

    (c)   **JOHN** COOKED **DIN**ner?

Context 2

Alice: The guys kept doing nice things for me because it was Mother's Day. Bob washed the car, Joe ironed the shirts, and John cooked dinner.

Betty: _____?

Alice: Yes, it was quite a surprise to me, too. He's never even boiled an egg before.

    (a)   **JOHN** COOKED **DIN**ner?

    (b)   Did JOHN COOK DINner?

    (c)   JOHN COOKED DINner?

Context 3

Alice: I was really tired when I got home last night, and I just couldn't cook.

Betty: _____?

Alice: Yes, he did.

    (a)   **JOHN** COOKED DINner?

    (b)   Did JOHN COOK DINner?

    (c)   Did JOHN COOK DINner?

Context 4

Alice: I was really tired when I got home last night, and I just couldn't cook dinner.

Betty: Did John?

Alice: I just kicked off my shoes and sat down.

Betty: _____

(a) Did JOHN COOK DINner?

(b) JOHN COOKED DINner?

(c) Did **JOHN** COOK DINner?

Answers:

Context 1 = *b*, because Betty is expressing a fairly confident guess. Choice *a* would indicate that she was impatient and *c* would express her extreme astonishment at the fact that John had cooked dinner.

Context 2 = *a*, because Betty is expressing her surprise and disbelief at the entire proposition. Choice *b* would indicate a normal yes/no question asking for information and *c* would cue confirmation of Betty's presupposition that John had cooked dinner.

Context 3 = *c*, because Betty is asking a focused yes/no question to find out if John cooked dinner. Choice *a* would be inappropriate because it would imply surprise on Betty's part that John had cooked and *b* would be asking a neutral yes/no question without making any assumption.

Context 4 = *c*, because Betty is expressing her impatience at having to repeat the question about John's cooking dinner; the falling intonation with special emphasis on *John* captures this impatience. Both *a* and *b* are true questions and do not express this impatience or annoyance.

WH-QUESTIONS

Wh-questions follow the same rising–falling intonation as statements when they are unmarked, with the rise corresponding to the most prominent element in the utterance:

HOW are you DOing?

WHY is she CRYing?

WHAT can I DO for YOU?

Question words in English generally do not receive prominence; this may differ from the stress pattern in learners' first language.[9] Often with wh-questions, there are two or more

---

[9]However, question words have prominence in certain marked forms of wh-questions, such as uninverted wh-questions ("Ann brought WHAT?" "Two plus two is WHAT?") and questions requesting repetition or clarification (e.g., "WHAT did you say?" "WHICH book is missing?") or expressing surprise or disbelief (e.g., "**WHAT** did he tell you?"); note that many of these are said with rising intonation. The question words may, of course, be given prominence for special emphasis ("But WHY are you going?").

different contours depending on whether the result of the action or the agent of the action is in focus.

1a.   WHAT did ANN BRING?   (focus on *result*)

 b.   WHAT did ANN BRING?   (focus on *agent*)

Such rising–falling intonation often surprises nonnative speakers, who sometimes assume that all questions in English – regardless of type – should be spoken with rising intonation. In fact, even learners who speak languages in which information questions have falling intonation may also hold this assumption.

However, when spoken with rising intonation (which for wh-questions is the marked form), the rise signals "Repeat some of your information. I didn't hear everything you said":

2a.   WHAT did ANN BRING?
 b.   WHAT did ANN BRING?

Here choice *a* means "Tell me again more clearly *what* Ann brought" and *b* means "Tell me again more clearly what *Ann* in particular brought."

Just as with uninverted yes/no questions, there is also a very exaggerated rising intonation pattern that sometimes occurs, as seen in the following two variations of the question:

3a.   **WHAT** did ANN BRING?

 b.   **WHAT** did **ANN** BRING?

Such utterances express the speaker's surprise or disbelief – in question 3*a* concerning whatever was purported to be brought and in *b* about whatever it was that Ann in particular brought. Exaggerated rising intonation may also occur with **uninverted wh-questions** (i.e., questions in which the interrogative pronoun follows the subject and verb). Such questions convey much the same meaning of surprise or disbelief as questions 3*a* and *b*:

4a.   ANN BROUGHT **WHAT**?

Uninverted wh-questions can be used with unmarked rising intonation to request repetition or clarification, or with rising–falling intonation as an *elicitation device* – that is, to obtain a response or information from an interlocutor:

4b.   ANN BROUGHT WHAT?
 c.   ANN BROUGHT WHAT?

In 4b the rising intonation is used to request repetition of the unclear element; in c rising–falling intonation is used to elicit a response. In such a case, the one who asks the question already knows the answer; the interrogator is asking simply to find out if the addressee also knows the answer. Such questions, which are sometimes called **display questions** because they request a display of previously learned or heard information, are frequently asked by teachers, tutors, and adults speaking to children.

Adults to children

Adult: TWO plus TWO is WHAT?

Child: Four.

Adult: Good. What a big girl!

Teacher to students

Teacher: The LAST LETter of the GREEK ALphabet is WHAT?

Student: Omega.

Teacher: That's right.

Now try to decide which version of the wh-questions (from the choices listed after each dialogue) best completes each of the four following contexts:

Context 5

Alice: I brought chips, and Ann brought something to drink.

Betty: _____?

Alice: She brought beer.

    (a) WHAT did ANN BRING?

    (b) WHAT did ANN BRING?

    (c) ANN BROUGHT **WHAT**?

Context 6

Alice: I brought wine, and Mary brought soft drinks.

Betty: _____?

Alice: Beer.

    (a) **WHAT** did ANN BRING?

    (b) WHAT did ANN BRING?

    (c) ANN BROUGHT **WHAT**?

Context 7

Alice: I was amazed, because Ann, who had never even drunk a drop of alcohol in her life, brought a keg of beer to the party.

Betty: _____?

(a) WHAT did ANN BRING?

(b) WHAT did ANN BRING?

(c) ANN BROUGHT WHAT?

Answers:

Context 5 = *a*, because Betty is simply requesting that Alice elaborate more specifically on what Ann brought. Choice *b* would be a marked information question suggesting that Ann had not been mentioned, and *c* would express surprise or disbelief, which is not appropriate here.

Context 6 = *b*, because Betty is asking about Ann and what it was that she brought. Choices *a* and *c* would indicate surprise or disbelief, which are not appropriate in this context.

Context 7 = *c*, because Betty is expressing extreme surprise and disbelief concerning the event of Ann's bringing a keg of beer to the party. Question *a* is a genuine information question, and *b* is a request for repetition of what Ann brought. In *a* Betty knows what other people brought but is inquiring what Ann herself brought; in *b* she is just interested in establishing exactly what it is that Ann brought (mineral water? coffee? etc).

TAG QUESTIONS

Tag questions follow statements, which have rising–falling intonation. When tags are used in their most frequent function – that is, seeking confirmation or making a point – they also have rising–falling intonation:

It's a NICE DAY, ISn't it?

PEOPle are WORried about the eCOnomy, AREN'T they?

Tag questions have rising intonation only when they are used much like yes/no questions normally are: to elicit a *yes* or *no* answer from the addressee or to seek further clarification:

The DODGers WON, DIDn't they?
You DIDn't FINish the CANdy, DID you?

Note that in these latter two examples the statement preceding the tag tends not to fall as low as it does in the former examples because of the general tentativeness the speaker is expressing and anticipation of the upcoming terminal rise in the tag.

The rising–falling pattern is definitely the more frequent contour for tag questions in English. However, in English the same tag question can have different intonation and different meaning depending on the context. See if you can determine which intonation goes with the tag question in the following two contexts:

Context 8

Terry: The score was Dodgers 8, Giants 2 at the bottom of the ninth inning when I had to turn off the TV and go to work.

Jan: Nothing much else happened.

Terry: _____?

Jan: Yeah.

(a)   The DODGers WON, DIDn't they?

(b)   The DODGers WON, DIDn't they?

Context 9

Terry: The score was Dodgers 3, Giants 2 at the bottom of the ninth inning when I had to turn off the TV and go to work.

Jan: Too bad. It was an exciting game.

Terry: _____?

Jan: Yes, they did.

(a)   The DODGers WON, DIDn't they?

(b)   The DODGers WON, DIDn't they?

Answers:

Context 8 = *a*. Terry can assume with a fair degree of confidence that the Dodgers won the baseball game since a game consists of nine innings and they had a strong lead. Thus in her question to Jan, the confirmation-seeking, rising–falling intonation pattern used in choice *a* would be more appropriate than *b*, which signals uncertainty.

Context 9 = *b*. In this situation, the score is so close that confidence cannot be expressed; Terry would probably use the rising intonation in choice *b*, indicating a genuine yes/no question in this context.

ALTERNATIVE QUESTIONS

Closed-choice alternative questions, as we have discussed, contain a rise in the first part, a pause, and then a rise–fall in the second part:

Closed-choice alternative question

Would you LIKE JUICE or SOda?

Closed-choice alternative questions differ semantically, syntactically, and pragmatically from open-choice alternative questions, which have rising intonation and do not force the listener to choose among alternatives:

Open-choice alternative question

Would you LIKE JUICE or SOda?

Either pattern is possible, depending on the speaker's intent. However, in many cases the discourse context itself limits the speaker to one of the two patterns. Consider the following two utterances below and decide which intonation pattern to use (alternative or open choice):

Context 10
Do you want to get something to drink or snack on?

(a)

(b)

Context 11
Do you want to just get a drink or go get some food?

(a)

(b)

> **Answers:**
>
> Context 10 is an open choice; it favors a yes/no question interpretation and thus takes the rising intonation in choice *b*. Context 11 expresses a true alternative or closed choice, thus taking the contrastive rising, rising–falling intonation pattern in choice *a*.

CONTRASTIVE RESPONSES AND NEW INFORMATION

In this chapter we have spent a great deal of time on prosody of questions. The various subtypes of questions nicely illustrate how speakers can use stress and intonation to highlight a particular constituent or even an entire proposition in the process of communicating meaning. For example, consider the following typical greeting sequence:

A: HelLO. HOW ARE you?

B: FINE THANKS. HOW are YOU?

Speaker A first inquires about Speaker B's well-being by emphasizing the verb *be* (i.e., *are*); Speaker B, having responded positively, then focuses contrastively on Speaker A (*you*) and inquires about the interlocutor's well-being.

Noninterrogative utterances also make use of the kinds of options we described earlier with reference to questions. As in the foregoing greeting sequence, it is generally important to note which utterance comes first or initiates the exchange and which utterance comes in response to something said earlier; the response often contrasts with the initial utterance in important ways. This reflects how the focus of information is shifted by first one speaker and then another in an ongoing conversation. Whatever information is new tends to receive special prosodic attention, as indicated in this example (adapted from Allen 1971):

Salesclerk: Can I HELP YOU?

Customer: YES, PLEASE. I'm LOOKing for a BLAzer.

Salesclerk: SOMEthing CASual?

Customer: YES, SOMEthing CASual in LINen or WOOL.

Note the tendency of the new information to come toward the end of the utterance in English and to coincide with prominence and the key change in the intonation contour.

In cases of contradiction or disagreement, the shift in focus from one constituent to another is very clear:

Alice: It's COLD.

Betty: It's NOT COLD.

Alice: It IS COLD.

Betty: COME ON. . . It's REALly NOT THAT COLD.

Here Alice begins by describing the environment and emphasizing the word *cold;* Betty disagrees by restating the same utterance in negative form and stressing the word *not.* Alice responds by reasserting the original proposition, this time by emphasizing the verb *be*, which in its affirmative form contrasts with Betty's prior negation of the proposition. In the final turn, Betty tries to persuade Alice to downgrade the initial assessment; she does this by emphasizing the modifiers *really* and *that*.

INTONATION AND MEANING: PEDAGOGICAL PRIORITIES

From both the receptive and productive points of view, learners need extensive practice in distinguishing the subtle shades of meaning that are conveyed through prosodic clues. Much research (see Gumperz 1982) has shown that nonnative speakers are frequently misinterpreted as rude, abrupt, or disinterested solely because of the prosodics of their speech. This misinterpretation of intent is not limited to individuals who have infrequent contact with nonnative speakers; even those who deal with nonnative speakers on a daily basis (e.g., ESL/EFL teachers and program administrators) may find prosodic features of second language speech – such as choppy, unnatural rhythm; overly flat intonation; or inappropriate application of rise or rise–fall patterns – annoying or difficult to understand.

On the other hand, nonnative speakers often cannot hear important keys to meaning because of their limited command of prosodic clues. This is especially true when humor, sarcasm, anger, irony, and the like are conveyed through prosodic means. Thus, though the verbatim message may be understood, the speaker's intent may be misinterpreted, resulting in the entire meaning being misconstrued. To take a simple example, the phrase "That's a great idea," if spoken sarcastically by a boss to his nonnative employee, is intended by the boss to convey the exact opposite message: "That's a stupid/terrible idea." Without access to these prosodic clues, the nonnative employee might not understand that his or her idea is being negatively evaluated.

When presenting the interplay between intonation and meaning to learners, a top priority should be given to providing them with adequate opportunities to listen for the shades of meaning in authentic conversational exchanges and to check their interpretation against that of a native speaker listening to the same conversational interchange. For this purpose off-air radio excerpts (such as segments from radio talk shows or radio dramas) provide excellent material. Only at the more advanced stages of second language proficiency is it likely that teachers will want to devote time to having their students actually practice expressing these subtle shades of meaning. In the section that follows, we outline a variety of means by which teachers can present this very complex area of the sound system to their students.

PRESENTING INTONATION AND MEANING TO STUDENTS

One way to raise learners' consciousness about intonation and meaning is to present some examples for students to distinguish. Using the same technique we noted earlier, write the word *thanks* on the board and read it in three different ways:

1. Thanks.   (perfunctory)

2. Thanks.   (enthusiastic)

3. T h a n k s.   (sarcastic, drawn out)

Students first listen to see if they hear any differences. If they do, elicit situations in which each example might be appropriate. For example, number 1 could be a checkout clerk at a store who says "Thanks" a hundred times a day; number 2, the recipient of a much longed-for gift; and number 3, a disgruntled employee who has been assigned overtime duty. Although it may be difficult for students to identify exactly what makes each version distinctive, they will usually be able to notice that the three are not pronounced identically and that different meanings are being expressed.

LISTENING DISCRIMINATION

Another discovery technique takes the activity in the preceding section a step further by asking students to finish a mini-dialogue that they hear with an appropriate rejoinder or continuation of thought. Begin by writing the dialogue and three possible interpretations on the board. For example:

Dialogue
A: I've just read a good book.
B: What?

Possible interpretations

1.   I can't believe you actually read a book!

2.   The latest one by Sidney Sheldon.

3.   I've just read a good book.

To allow learners to fine-tune their listening skills so that they can distinguish the shades of meaning communicated by different intonation contours, read the following three versions of the mini-dialogue (adapted from Bowen 1975: 187–8) in which the words are identical but the intonation pattern is different. Ask students to choose the correct completing phrase from the choices provided on the board.

Mini-dialogue 1

A: I've just read a good book.

B: What? (= *What book?*)

Answer: 2. The latest one by Sidney Sheldon.

Mini-dialogue 2

A: I've just read a good book.

B: What? (= *I didn't hear you, could you repeat?*)

Answer: 3. I've just read a good book.

Mini-dialogue 3

A: I've just read a good book.

B: W h a t ? (= *What?! **You** who never reads books? Unbelievable!*)

Answer: 1. I can't believe you actually read a book!

How prominence and intonation affect the meaning of an utterance can further be illustrated for learners by using a matching exercise like the following, which you can either read aloud or record on tape and then play back for the class (adapted from Ravensdale, 1973):

Directions: Each of the following sentences will be read three times in three different ways. Match the meaning of each version to the interpretation on the right. Pay special attention to intonation and stress!

Original sentence	**Intended meaning**
1. What do you think?	
a. WHAT do YOU THINK?	i. *I already know what he thinks.*
b. WHAT do you THINK?	ii. *Should we do it or not?*
c. WHAT do you THINK?	iii. *I'm sorry, I didn't hear what you said.*
2. She didn't take the car.	
a. She DIDn't TAKE the CAR.	i. *Someone else must have.*
b. She DIDn't TAKE the CAR.	ii. *So stop accusing her!*
c. SHE DIDn't TAKE the CAR.	iii. *She must have gone on foot, or by bus . . .*

3. He thought the film was good.

　　a. He THOUGHT the FILM was GOOD.　　　i.　*But the music was awful!*

　　b. He THOUGHT the FILM was GOOD.　　　ii.　*She didn't, though.*

　　c. HE THOUGHT the FILM was GOOD.　　　iii.　*Oh really? The critics hated it!*

In the first round, play the tape or read the three versions of each utterance. Since this exercise may pose some difficulty at first for some learners, there should be free discussion of the meaning of each alternative. In the second round, students can work in pairs, with one partner pronouncing the sentences and the other checking the intended meaning. The answers are: 1 – a(i), b(iii), c(ii); 2 – a(ii), b(iii), c(i); 3 – a(iii), b(i), c(ii).

CONTROLLED PRACTICE

When one speaker corrects another, we have a context very similar to disagreement, from a prosodic point of view:

Sam:　　YOU'RE from DENver, AREN'T you?

Harry:　　NOT DENver. BOULder.

In classes with students from many different countries, this type of exchange can be repeated many times, with individual students taking turns at guessing each classmate's hometown. Learners of English need ample opportunity to practice getting the prominence and intonation right in realistic dialogue sequences.

Many of the earlier examples in this chapter could also be adapted for classroom practice. We particularly suggest simple teacher-constructed dialogues such as the following, which can be used for pair practice and allow students to express a range of meanings and emotions. In the following dialogue, the intonation patterns for Student B's responses are marked. Once Student B has had a chance to practice giving the responses, the students switch roles and Student A has a chance to practice:

NO PANCAKES FOR YOU!

Directions: Read the dialogue with your partner, paying special attention to the intonation patterns and how these help to communicate meaning. Then switch roles.

A:　Get me some pancakes.　　　　　B:　We DON'T SERVE PANcakes.

A:　Three eggs and a short
　　stack of pancakes.　　　　　　B:　We DON'T SERVE PANCAKES.

A:　What do you mean? Every-
　　body serves pancakes.　　　　　B:　WE DON'T SERVE PANCAKES.

A:　For the last time . . . bring
　　me some pancakes and eggs.　　B:　We DON'T SERVE PANcakes.

> *Directions:* Read the information given in Situation 1. Then with a partner, practice the dialogue between the two friends. When you have finished practicing, read the information given for Situations 2 and 3. Read the dialogue again according to the information given. Use prominence and intonation to express the different meanings.
>
> *Situation 1:* Both A and B are male. They are friends and are approximately the same age. A is pleased to hear that his friend is back from his trip.
>
> *Situation 2:* Both A and B are female. A is B's mother. She's a bit upset that her daughter hasn't bothered to call her since returning from her trip.
>
> *Situation 3:* A is male; B is female. He and B have been in a serious relationship for over a year now. He's slightly older than she is, and tends to be the jealous type. He's furious that she didn't call him immediately upon her return from her trip.
>
> **Dialogue**
>
> A: So you're back from your trip?
> B: Yes, I got back two days ago.
> A: Nice of you to call. I hadn't expected to hear from you so soon.
> B: Oh well, I thought I'd just call and see how you were doing.
> A: Fine, just fine.

Figure 6.2 Worksheet for guided practice with intonation contours

GUIDED PRACTICE

An interesting technique that can make a strong impression on learners is to have them (1) listen to and analyze a dialogue read with varying emotions and (2) practice reading the same dialogue themselves. Preface this activity by pointing out that when emotions are strong (either positive or negative), intonation contours tend to be either broader or narrower to convey this. The worksheet in Figure 6.2 above gives situations that can be used to illustrate this.

Short extracts from literary works also lend themselves well to the guided practice of intonation. One example of such a passage is excerpted from *The Glass Menagerie* by Tennessee Williams:[10]

Amanda:	You mean you have asked some nice young man to come over?
Tom:	Yep. I've asked him to dinner.
Amanda:	You really did?
Tom:	I did!
Amanda:	You did, and did he – accept?
Tom:	He did!
Amanda:	Well, well – well! That's – lovely!
Tom:	I thought that you would be pleased.
Amanda:	It's definite, then?
Tom:	Very definite.
Amanda:	Soon?
Tom:	Very soon.
Amanda:	For heaven's sake, stop putting on and tell me some things, will you?
Tom:	What things do you want me to tell you?

[10]Copyright 1945 by Tennessee Williams. Used by permission of New Directions Publishing Corporation.

Amanda:	*Naturally* I would like to know when he's coming!
Tom:	He's coming tomorrow.
Amanda:	*Tomorrow?*
Tom:	Yep. Tomorrow.
Amanda:	But, Tom!
Tom:	Yes, Mother?
Amanda:	Tomorrow gives me no time!
Tom:	Time for what?
Amanda:	Preparations!

Another example is the following extract from Hemingway's short story "Hills Like White Elephants":[11]

"And we could have all this," she said. "And we could have everything and every day
     we make it more impossible."
"What did you say?"
"I said we could have everything."
"We can have everything."
"No, we can't."
"We can have the whole world."
"No, we can't."
"We can go everywhere."
"No, we can't. It isn't ours any more."
"It's ours."
"No, it isn't. And once they take it away, you never get it back."
"But they haven't taken it away."
"We'll wait and see."
"Come on back in the shade," he said. "You mustn't feel that way."
"I don't feel any way," the girl said. "I just know things."
"I don't want you to do anything that you don't want to do —"
"Nor that isn't good for me," she said. "I know. Could we have another beer?"
"All right. But you've got to realize —"
"I realize," the girl said. "Can't we maybe stop talking?"

Begin with controlled oral reading practice, with students carefully monitoring their production of intonation patterns. For the guided phase, students gradually assume more and more responsibility, as the student worksheet in Figure 6.3 outlines.

COMMUNICATIVE PRACTICE

Literary passages offer the further benefit of being easily extended to incorporate communicative practice. To extend the "Hills Like White Elephants" activity, you can ask students to participate in an extemporaneous role-play situation, using the context that has been carefully set as a point of departure for more creative use of language. Once students have had an opportunity to do the rehearsed reading in step 5 of Figure 6.3, they can be videotaped performing an oral dramatic reading of the scene. Pay special attention to the ability of students in this reading to communicate the message via intonation, and give appropriate feedback.

---

[11]From "Hills Like White Elephants." Excerpted with permission of Scribner, a Division of Simon & Schuster, from *The Short Stories of Ernest Hemingway*. Copyright 1927 Charles Scribner's Sons. Copyright renewed 1955 by Ernest Hemingway.
   We thank Patrice Dally for calling our attention to the possibilities that this story provides for practicing the suprasegmental aspects of English.

Background: In the following passage from the Ernest Hemingway story "Hills Like White Elephants," two Americans (a man and a woman) are sitting in the bar of a rural train station in Spain. It's midday and hot; the place is empty except for the barmaid. The two order beer and begin to talk.

1. Read the passage silently to yourself. As you read, decide which character (the man or the woman) is speaking each line of dialogue.

2. Try to imagine yourself as one of the two characters in the train station. Concentrate on the feelings that character has.

3. With the other students in your group, discuss which character you have chosen and why. Together, create a personal history of these two characters. How long have they known each other? What kind of relationship do they have? What incident has led up to the conversation that you are reading?

4. Together with your group members, examine the adjectives below and decide which ones *best* describe the man and woman. Write the adjectives in the appropriate columns below. Note that not all adjectives will apply, and you may want to use some adjectives more than once.

angry	determined	outraged	shallow
arrogant	eager	patient	sincere
conciliatory	frustrated	proud	thoughtful
deep	insincere	secretive	trusting
defiant	mistrustful	sensitive	vain
depressed			

Woman   **Man**

_____   _____

_____   _____

_____   _____

_____   _____

_____   _____

_____   _____

5. Find a partner who has chosen the opposite character from you in step 1. Practice reading the conversation with this partner. Paying attention to prominence, use intonation patterns that represent the emotions and meanings of the two characters.

Figure 6.3 Worksheet for guided practice with "Hills Like White Elephants"

A further communicative extension of the activity is to have the students stay "in character" (i.e., as either the man or the woman in the Hemingway story) and be interviewed about their actions by their peers. Finally, they may be given extemporaneous situations such as the following and be asked to act these out after a brief (e.g., 5-minute) planning period:[12]

Extemporaneous situation #1: You are the man/woman in the scene you just rehearsed, but it is 20 years later. You suddenly encounter the other person (whom you have not seen since that day in Spain when you argued in the train station).

[12]This extension of a rehearsed reading activity is suggested by Stern (1987). The technique is discussed in more detail in Chapter 10.

Extemporaneous situation #2: You are the man/woman in the scene you just rehearsed. Some time has passed, but you are still haunted by the experience. You decide to discuss what happened with your psychoanalyst.

For both of these situations, a videocamera can be used to record the students' performances and assist in giving feedback.

Role plays also lend themselves well to providing students with communicative practice in intonation patterns. In the following activity, Partners A and B are husband and wife (or roommates) who have just set out on a vacation that they had been planning for a long time. Responsibilities for the trip were divided up, with A taking charge of reservations and itinerary for the trip and B taking charge of all the arrangements that needed to be made around the home in order to take off for a long period of time. The partners each receive a role play card such as the following and have several minutes to prepare what they intend to say.

PARTNER A

Context: You're a bit worried that B hasn't taken care of all the responsibilities that were delegated to him/her. You know that B has been busy at work, and also that he/she tends to be forgetful and scattered. You just happen to have a list of the things in your pocket, so you decide to find out if anything really important was forgotten.

Things to do

close the windows
pay the rent
tell the neighbors we'll be away
have the mail held
arrange to have the plants watered
phone Jean to say goodbye
cancel the newspaper
get prescription refilled

PARTNER B

Context: You have been really busy at work over the last week – much busier than you thought you would be just before your vacation. A had given you a list of things to take care of. Just as you got in the car you discovered this list in your pocket. Most of the things have been checked off, but there are several you neglected to do. You hope that A doesn't ask you about them! You know he/she'll be furious.

Things to do

✓close the windows
  pay the rent
  tell the neighbors we'll be away
✓have the mail held
✓arrange to have the plants watered
✓phone Jean to say goodbye
  cancel the newspaper
✓get prescription refilled

We suggest audiotaping or videotaping role plays so that a meaningful feedback phase can be built in following the enactment.

CONCLUSION

In our discussion of prominence, we have indicated that English speakers tend to deemphasize given information (what is already known) and emphasize new or contrastive information. In this chapter, we enlarge upon this basic tendency by presenting general pragmatic strategies used by English speakers in the broader arena of discourse. The main point of this chapter is that although English grammar limits the syntactic possibilities of an utterance, prosodic elements interact with syntax to convey a range of meaning and speaker intent in spoken discourse. In any ESL/EFL class where oral skills are taught, the interaction of discourse, on the one hand, and prosody and grammar, on the other, must be highlighted and taught, since contextually appropriate control of stress and intonation is an essential part of oral communicative competence that is usually not self-evident to nonnative speakers.

Although increased attention has been given to describing the interaction between intonation and discourse in English (e.g., Brazil, Coulthard, and Johns 1980), some of the best pedagogical suggestions to date are in a short article by Allen (1971), who recommends that teachers do the following (p. 73):

- direct students' attention to a few major patterns;
- alert students to differences between the punctuation system and the intonation system;
- distinguish between the intonation of isolated sentences and the intonation of segments in extended discourse;
- teach students to think in terms of the speaker's intention in any given speech situation.

To this list we would add (1) using the notions of given and new information – or contrast, where relevant – to explain shifting focus in ongoing discourse (i.e., the speaker will emphasize contextually salient information and will deemphasize what is given or predictable); and (2) alerting students to similarities and differences in intonation between the native language and the target language – especially in classes where the students share the same native language. For example, Spanish and Japanese are both intonation languages like English; however, they use a much narrower pitch range for their intonation contours than English. Transfer of the narrow L1 intonation range to English often makes these L2 speakers sound disinterested and bored. Also, Japanese has much shorter and less exaggerated intonation peaks than English (Todaka 1990); this can convey the impression of tentativeness or abruptness to English listeners when the L1 intonation patterns are transferred too directly.

In this overview of prosody and discourse we have emphasized the information management functions of intonation. There are also obvious functions related to conversation management whereby a speaker lets the interlocutor know if he or she wishes to continue or is ready to yield the floor. Much more difficult to describe and teach, however, are the social functions of intonation, which may reveal the speaker's degree of interest or involvement, the speaker's reticence or assertiveness, the relationship between speaker and hearer, the speaker's expression of sarcasm, and so on. In this chapter we have touched on only some of the more straightforward emotions, such as surprise, disbelief, impatience, and annoyance, with respect to how they are signaled through intonation. More research is needed before teachers will be able to fully understand and teach the more subtle emotions and social functions signaled by intonation.

EXERCISES

KEY CONCEPTS

Write a brief definition of the following key terms from this chapter. Give examples where relevant.

thought group	rise
intonation unit	yes/no questions
prominence	open-choice alternative question
emphatic stress	echo questions
contrastive stress	repetition question
intonation	tag question signaling uncertainty
pitch	closed-choice alternative question
intonation contour	appositive construction
rising–falling contour	parenthetical expression
glide/step	prosody
wh-question	uninverted wh-question
tag question eliciting agreement	display question

INTROSPECTING ABOUT YOUR OWN LANGUAGE LEARNING

Think about a foreign language that you have learned in school or while living abroad.

1. If English is your first language, when did you first become aware that the language you were learning had prominence or intonation differences with English? What triggered your awareness? If English is your second language, when did you first become aware that it had prominence and intonation differences with your first language?

2. If you have learned an intonation language, can you remember having difficulty with prosody? If you have learned a tonal language, what special challenges did this pose?

3. Did any language teacher ever help you learn the correct prominence and intonation of a language you were studying? If so, what teaching techniques were used?

4. What do you think would help you the most in learning the prosodic features of another language?

DISCUSSION QUESTIONS

1. Why is punctuation an unreliable guide to intonation?

2. Many ESL/EFL teachers think that prosody is a more important part of pronunciation than consonants and vowels. What do you think?

3. What kinds of authentic discourse samples would you suggest to teach prosody? Why?

4. Judy Gilbert regularly demonstrates to teachers at conferences the use of a kazoo to teach intonation. What other tools or techniques do you think might assist learners?

5. Most traditional English language teaching materials emphasize the unmarked forms of intonation patterns. Why is it important to highlight both marked and unmarked forms?

6. Suppose you had to present the type of information contained in this chapter to a class of NAE learners. What level of learner proficiency would you want, and why?

IN THE CLASSROOM

Assume that you are teaching pronunciation. Here are some common classroom situations that you might encounter. What technique would you use or what explanation would you give?

1. Many of your students speak English in a monotone.

2. One of your students has very halting speech (i.e., pauses too frequently and/or inappropriately).

3. One of your students doesn't understand the difference between rising and rising–falling intonation on tag questions.

4. One of your ESL students has many young American peers who regularly use rising intonation with statements. This student asks you about the conflict between this observation and what has been taught in the classroom.

SUGGESTED ACTIVITIES

1. In this chapter we have presented a number exercises in which the situation called for a particular combination of intonation and syntax (e.g., tag questions, alternative questions). Develop a similar exercise that you would use in the ESL/EFL classroom.

2. Read a description of the prosodic features of a language that you are familiar with. What are some of the major contrasts with English? What difficulties with English prosody would you expect a speaker of this language to have in English?

3. Select an intonation pattern and construct a listening discrimination exercise. Administer it to an ESL/EFL learner. What difficulties did the learner encounter?

ON THE CASSETTE

1. Listen to the following dialogue as it is read on the cassette. Use slashes to mark intonation units, underline the most prominent syllables, and draw in the intonation contours.

    (*Maggie, Sara, Jennifer, and Alice are college roommates. Maggie arrives home to find Sara cleaning the bathroom – not one of their favorite duties.*)

Maggie:	Hi, Sara. What's up?
Sara:	I'm cleaning the bathroom.
Maggie:	You're cleaning the bathroom? Wasn't Jennifer supposed to clean it this week?
Sara:	She was, but she can't.
Maggie:	Why not?
Sara:	She has a midterm tomorrow. So she asked Alice, and she couldn't either.
Maggie:	What's her problem?
Sara:	Her parents are here from out of town.

2. Listen to the two nonnative speakers read the above dialogue. What are their major prosodic problems?

3. Set priorities for teaching prosody to one of the two nonnative speakers and develop an exercise to deal with one of the top priorities.

PART 3

INTERSECTIONS OF THE SOUND SYSTEM WITH OTHER AREAS OF LANGUAGE

In the four preceding chapters we provided a comprehensive treatment of the NAE sound system by describing its consonant and vowel inventory along with its characteristic stress, rhythm, and intonation patterns. We also dealt with the adjustments that occur in connected speech and the features of prominence and intonation in discourse. In this section of the book, we explore the various ways in which the English sound system interacts with other systems of the language when native and non-native speakers use English for communication.

Efficient communication involving any skill area (listening, speaking, reading, writing), or any combination of skills, depends on the speaker's ability to integrate knowledge of the English sound system (i.e., phonetics and phonology) with knowledge of grammar (i.e., morphology and syntax) and lexicon. In addition, mastery of listening and speaking presupposes some ability and efficiency in perceiving and producing English sounds, tunes, and rhythms. Mastery of English reading and writing, on the other hand, presupposes knowledge of the writing system (i.e., orthography), which

makes the relationship between the sound system and the writing system another crucial intersection.

To help the reader gain some appreciation of these important connections, we explore the following three topics in this section of the book:

- the sound system and listening
- the sound system and inflectional morphology
- the sound system and orthography

We believe that the intersection of the sound system with these areas is extremely important since the English sound system cannot be learned (and thus should not be taught) in a vacuum. The sound system, a resource for creating meaning and for expressing a variety of functions, relates to every other aspect of the language when the learner listens, speaks, reads, and writes. These natural connections must be understood by teachers if they wish to help learners develop good listening comprehension and intelligible pronunciation as a natural part of their communicative language proficiency.

CHAPTER 7

The Sound System and Listening

W hen listening to spoken English, learners need to perceive and segment the incoming stream of speech in order to make sense of it. How they accomplish this is a topic of great interest to researchers. At the word level, Laufer (1990) has looked at the performance of both native and nonnative English speakers in distinguishing *synforms* – lexical forms that look and sound similar but are in fact different words with different meanings. She found that although nonnative speakers made more errors overall than native speakers, there was a common hierarchy of difficulty for both groups as follows:

1. Identical stems with differences in the suffixes were the most difficult synforms to distinguish (e.g., *discriminating/discriminatory*).

2. Synforms with a vocalic difference were the second most difficult category (e.g., *cost/coast*).

3. Synforms with a prefix difference were the third most difficult type (e.g., *consumption/assumption*).

4. Synforms with a consonantal difference were the fourth most difficult category (e.g., *price/prize*).

Even though Laufer was looking at issues of sequence and order in vocabulary development, all of these lexical confusions are influenced by the sound system of English. Problems 1 and 3 involve syllables that do not receive primary stress and thus are easier to mishear than clearly stressed syllables (see Browman 1980); problems 2 and 4 involve the confusion of vowel and consonant sounds, with the vowels playing a more significant role than the consonants. Interestingly, it is the problems in categories 2 and 4 that have traditionally received emphasis in most pronunciation teaching materials, whereas the problems in categories 1 and 3 have tended to be ignored. These findings suggest that the stress patterns of English words – and the information that unstressed syllables can convey – are an important part of teaching listening discrimination; the ability to process, segment, and decode speech depends not only on the listener's knowledge of lexicon but also on being able to exploit knowledge of the sound system.

Clearly, the incoming stream of speech is not decoded at the word level alone, and thus research is needed into how learners process speech more globally as well. Based on the assumption that one can discover much about how a process works by examining cases of its malfunction, Garnes and Bond (1980) analyzed a corpus of 890 "mishearings" committed by native

English speakers in everyday conversation. Based on their analysis of these data, they propose that listeners process incoming speech by employing the following four strategies (holding the stream of speech in short-term memory would, of course, underlie all four strategies):[1]

1. Listeners attend to stress and intonation and construct a ***metrical template*** – a distinctive pattern of strongly and weakly stressed syllables – to fit the utterance (see Rost 1990).

2. They attend to stressed vowels.[2]

3. They segment the incoming stream of speech and find words that correspond to the stressed vowels and their adjacent consonants.

4. They seek a phrase – with grammar and meaning – compatible with the metrical template identified in the first strategy and the words identified in the third strategy.

It is, of course, highly likely that English listeners are carrying out all four strategies simultaneously while actively attending to context. As they listen to and process speech, they are also calling up their prior knowledge, or ***schemata*** (higher-order mental frameworks that organize and store knowledge), to help them make sense of the bits and pieces of information they perceive and identify using these strategies.

In addition to carrying out these strategies when listening to spoken English, nonnative speakers have to overcome other hurdles, among them lack of background knowledge (including cultural gaps) and lack of knowledge of the sound system, along with a tendency to transfer the rules and features of their first-language sound system to English. These obstacles, as well as incomplete knowledge of English grammar and vocabulary, can distort their perception when they listen to English (see Broselow et al. 1987). All of the factors mentioned may contribute not only to word-level perception errors, such as a nonnative speaker's hearing *thought* for *fraught,* but also to phrase-level mishearings, such as *down the reed* for *Donna Reed* and *more stuff and barrel* for *lock, stock, and barrel.*

These two phrasal nonnative mishearings happen to include a proper name and an idiom, which are prime candidates for mishearing even among native speakers (Celce-Murcia 1980). It is thus likely that the unfamiliarity of the ESL listener with both the name *Donna Reed* and the idiom *lock, stock, and barrel,* in addition to imperfect perception due to L1 distortion, contributed to the mishearings. This may also be true of the word-level error in which *fraught* was misheard as *thought,* since the listener may not have been familiar with the word *fraught.*

The foregoing examples of mishearing are all drawn from written data representing the attempts of advanced nonnative speakers to transcribe authentic native-speaker discourse. Using less proficient nonnative speakers as subjects, research by Voss (1979) and Griffiths (1991) indicates that even the hesitation phenomena produced by native-speakers, such as filled pauses (*uh, hmm,* etc.), can be misconstrued as words.

This information sheds light on an important intersection between pronunciation and listening comprehension, suggesting that the learner's ability to perform the following processes is important in decoding native speaker speech:

• discerning intonation units

• recognizing stressed elements

• interpreting unstressed elements

• determining the full forms underlying reduced speech

[1]Garnes and Bond report that errors in which stress and intonation are misperceived by native speakers are quite rare.
[2]Errors involving the perception of stressed vowels are also rare among native speakers. They occur most often adjacent to consonants that can affect vowel quality – for example, /r/, /l/, /n/ – or among listeners and speakers of divergent dialects that have somewhat different vowel inventories.

A classic method that teachers can use to assess students' command of these processes is dictation. Traditionally, the teacher reads the dictation text, which has been divided into logical thought groups, at a normal rate of speech, pausing at the end of each thought group to allow students to write what has been dictated. The following sample dictation illustrates how this technique can help the teacher assess listening skills:

DICTATION: MEAN DOGS

We all sooner or later encounter mean dogs. There is no set way for handling the situation. Each dog is different. But all dogs tend to conform to certain predictable rules of behavior. When you find yourself face to face with an aggressive animal, knowing these rules can help you avoid trouble. Never stare at a dog. Never run or walk quickly past – or away from – a strange dog. Try to avoid showing your fear. Keep calm.[3]

Student product

We all sooner or later in counter mean dogs. There is no sat way for handeling situation. Each dog is different, but all dogs ten a conform to certen prudectuble rools to behave you. When you will fain youself face to face with an agressive animal no in this rools can halp you avoid a troble. Never stare to the dog, never run or walk quqly past or away from a strange dog. Try to avoid show you fire. Keep call.

Notice that aside from the misspellings, the student's performance reveals difficulties in his ability to hear unstressed elements, segment speech, and process thought groups:

1. Difficulties with unstressed elements
    a. missing or wrong articles and prepositions:
        ORIGINAL TEXT: handling the situation
        STUDENT TEXT: handeling situation
        ORIGINAL TEXT: Never stare at a dog.
        STUDENT TEXT: Never stare to the dog,
    b. missing morphological endings:
        ORIGINAL TEXT: avoid showing your fear
        STUDENT TEXT: avoid show you fire
2. Difficulties in segmenting speech into words or thought groups
        ORIGINAL TEXT: rules of behavior
        STUDENT TEXT: rools to behave you
        ORIGINAL TEXT: knowing these rules
        STUDENT TEXT: no in this rools

What additional clues does this student product provide concerning his knowledge of pronunciation? First, missing prepositions, articles, and morphological endings reveal an inability to hear unstressed syllables and words. There is also evidence that the learner has difficulties with segmentals, such as the vowel contrast /æ/ vs. /ɛ/ (as suggested by the spelling *sat* for *set* and *halp* for *help*), and with hearing final consonants and consonant clusters (as suggested by the substitutions *call* for *calm* and *ten* for *tend*).

---

[3]Used by permission of Michael W. Fox.

A technique related to dictation is to have students transcribe segments of discourse. As illustrated by the following advanced nonnative speaker transcript (in italics) of an authentic native-speaker conversation (nonitalic text), this technique can provide additional evidence as to how learners process the incoming speech stream.

J: I mean, is there any <u>person alive</u> that doesn't want to understand
      I mean, is there any <u>personal life</u> that doesn't want to understand
      the opposite sex a little better than they already do?
      the opposite sex a little better than they already do?

D: Wait, wait, I do think that the current trend, you know,
      Wait, wait, I do think that the current trend, you know,
      is really alarming because very often the man <u>is portrayed</u> as
      is really alarming because very often the man <u>has portray</u> as
      <u>a</u> very negative figure. <u>And so it's</u> very easy for <u>the</u> woman to
      —very negative figure. <u>This is</u> very easy for <u>a</u> woman to
      say "Ah hah, the reason I'm having all these problems in our
      say "Ah hah, the reason I'm having all these problems in our
      relationship really isn't because <u>of</u> me, <u>it's</u> because <u>of all</u> these . . .
      relationship really isn't because <u>for</u> me, because <u>all of</u> these . . .

J: I don't agree with this idea <u>that</u> men <u>are</u> all, you know, bad.
      I don't agree with this idea <u>at</u> men <u>at</u> all. You know, bad.

D: <u>The danger</u> I think of the self-help book is that you read one of
      <u>??</u> I think of the self-help book is that you read one of
      them and you <u>get</u> that one <u>unbalanced</u> opinion in a sense.
      them and you <u>give</u> that one <u>an unbalance</u> opinion in a sense.
      You tend to then just accept that and it does <u>mold</u> your view of
      You tend to then just accept that and it does <u>mode</u> your view of
      the world.
      the world.

Like the student's mean dog dictation cited earlier, this advanced nonnative-speaker transcript reveals difficulties in the areas of segmentation/word boundaries (e.g., *personal life*), morphological endings (e.g., *portray—, unbalance—*), unstressed words (e.g., *has* for *is, at* for *that,* and *a* for *the*), and consonant clusters (*mode* for *mold*).

CHUNKING WORDS INTO INTONATION UNITS

One of the most important realizations that contributes to successful speech processing is that spoken English is divided into chunks of talk, or ***intonation units*** (also referred to as thought groups or prosodic phrases). These intonation units correspond to phrases, clauses, or longer utterances that reflect how speakers organize their thoughts.

    Punctuation often helps the reader mark intonation units in written English. In the following two utterances, which contain the identical sequence of words, the meaning changes completely depending on where the speaker pauses:

    A.   "Alfred," said the boss, "is stupid."   (meaning = Alfred is stupid.)
    B.   Alfred said, "The boss is stupid."   (meaning = The boss is stupid.)[4]

---

[4]These and other Gilbert (1983) examples are taken from "Pronunciation and Learning Comprehension," by Judy Gilbert, in *Cross Currents,* Vol. 10, no. 1, 1983, pp. 53–61. Used with permission.

TABLE 7.1 SIGNALS OF INTONATION BOUNDARIES APPLIED TO GILBERT'S (1983) EXAMPLES

Criteria	Sentence A	Sentence B
	(3 intonation units)	(2 intonation units)
Number of unified pitch contours	3 pitch contours: *Alfred / said the boss / is stupid*	2 pitch contours: *Alfred said / the boss is stupid*
Frequency of lengthening of unit-final stressed syllable	3 lengthened syllables: *ALfred* *BOSS* *STUpid*	2 lengthened syllables: *ALfred* *STUpid*
Number of pauses	3 pauses, after: *Alfred* *boss* *stupid*	2 pauses, after: *said* *stupid*
Frequency of pitch reset	2 pitch resets, at: *said* *is*	1 pitch reset, at: *the boss*

In spoken English there is no punctuation, but there are five signals that can mark the end of one intonation unit and the beginning of another (Gilbert 1983; Schuetze-Coburn 1993):

1. a unified pitch contour
2. a lengthening of the unit-final stressed syllable
3. a pause
4. a reset of pitch
5. an acceleration in producing the unit-initial syllable(s)

Not all of these signals will occur at each intonation unit boundary; however, at least two or three should be perceptible. Let us test these criteria against Gilbert's two examples (Table 7.1).[5] In the two spoken utterances we can notice the following. Sentence A contains three separate intonation units, each having its own pitch contour with two pauses separating these contours. At the beginning of the second and third intonation units, the pitch is reset (i.e., it returns to level 2). In Sentence B, on the other hand, there are only two intonation units and thus two separate pitch contours with one pause separating them. The pitch therefore is reset only once.

These intonation unit signals are not universal. Many non-Indo-European languages (e.g., Korean, Cantonese) use particles to signal the end of main and subordinate clauses and do not rely as heavily on prosodic markers as does English. Even languages that resemble English because they use pause, pitch reset, and syllable lengthening as chunking signals (e.g., Japanese, Spanish, German, French, Turkish) may use these signals quite differently because of syntactic and phonological differences. As a result, we can predict that many learners will need extensive classroom practice in recognizing (and producing) intonation units.

---

[5]These two examples are not really long enough to properly observe criterion 5, unit-initial accelerated speech.

How can we teach the chunking signals of English to those who have special difficulty? One salient feature for students to perceive is the pause between thought groups. To assist them in recognizing intonation units and the pauses that separate them, we suggest providing written texts that have the intonation units already marked. Students should follow along as they listen to the teacher read the text; they are directed to focus on the marked pauses. Any kind of text can be adapted for this purpose, depending on the proficiency level of the student. The following example might be used with intermediate-level students in a listening class:

TODAY'S WEATHER

Today you can expect sunny weather (/) and cloudless skies. / The high for today will reach the mid 80s / with a cool front moving in this evening. / Humidity will remain constant at around 60 percent. / It's a perfect day for the beach!

This ability to process intonation units correctly is a basic listening skill that can be further practiced by adapting simple textbook dialogues. In this activity, students receive an unmarked text and are directed to locate the pauses as the text is read. How students perform on this task will inform the teacher of their ability to hear pauses and intonation contours.

Directions: As your teacher reads the text, mark a slash (/) where you hear the pauses. Hint: There are 6 pauses.

Steve this is my friend Rosemary she's a student at Wilson Middle School
Rosemary this is Steve he's a student too he's in my math class

> **Answers:** Steve / this is my friend Rosemary. / She's a student at Wilson Middle School. / Rosemary / this is Steve. / He's a student too. / He's in my math class.

Another possibility, suggested by Gilbert (1983), is to use a multiple-choice listening format for assessing chunking ability, as the following sample tasks illustrate:

1. Comprehending signals of grammatical difference:
   Do you hear (a) or (b)?
   a. My sister, who lives in Chicago, has two children.
   b. My sister who lives in Chicago has two children.

2. Hearing numbers (for practice taking down addresses, phone numbers, passport numbers, credit card numbers, etc., over the phone):
   Do you hear (a) or (b)?
   a. 047-72-5772
   b. 0477-257-72

3. Comprehending mathematical formulas:
   Do you hear (a) or (b)?
   a. $(A + B) \times C = Y$
   b. $A + (B \times C) = Y$
   Do you hear (c) or (d)?
   c. $(3 + 4) \times 6 = X$
   d. $3 + (4 \times 6) = X$

These and other exercises designed to teach chunking signals as markers of discourse boundaries help forge the link between pronunciation and listening comprehension for the learner. (See Chapter 6 for further information on the links between pronunciation and grammar and discourse.)

To enlarge upon Gilbert's first category, we suggest a listening exercise such as the following. The examples cited illustrate the semantic difference between restrictive and nonrestrictive relative clauses. They also reinforce the role that intonation units play in communicating this grammatical difference aurally (and that punctuation plays in communicating it orthographically).

Directions: Listen to the following statements. Mark the version you hear.

1. _____ a. Children, who are noisy, should be seen but not heard. (= *all children*)

   _____ b. Children who are noisy should be seen but not heard. (= *only those children who are noisy*)

2. _____ a. The climbers, who reached the top, had a magnificent view. (= *all the climbers*)

   _____ b. The climbers who reached the top had a magnificent view. (= *only those who reached the top*)

SENTENCE PROMINENCE

Once the teacher has established that students are able to hear pauses and identify thought groups, the next step is to have them identify the prominent element within a thought group. This step is a critical one in preparing students to identify the metrical templates that will assist them in comprehending spoken English. In the first dialogue that follows, students are simply asked to read along silently and note the prominent elements as the teacher reads the dialogue aloud. In the second dialogue, the students' task is to listen for the prominent element in each thought group and circle it.

WET PAINT

A: Watch (out)! / Don't get near the (wall).

B: (Why)? / What's the (problem)?

A: There's wet (paint).

B: (Where)?

A: On the (door).

B: When did (that) happen?

A: Just about ten (minutes) ago.

AT THE TRAVEL AGENT

A: Where would you like to go?

B: I was thinking about Paris.

A: Terrific. / We have a deal for you.

B: How many days is it?

A: Five days / and four nights.

B: How much does it cost?

A: Only nine hundred dollars.

Similar dialogues can be constructed for the purpose of working with students on identifying the role that discourse plays in determining sentence prominence (see Chapter 6 for a more extended discussion of this phenomenon). Again, the task in the first dialogue that follows is simply to listen while the teacher reads or plays the tape and note the prominent elements. For the second dialogue, students listen and circle the prominent elements themselves.

ARGUING ABOUT A MOVIE

A: It's (great).

B: It's (not) great.

A: It (is) great.

B: (No) it isn't.

A: Yes it (is). It's (truly) great.

B: As far as (I'm) concerned, / it (stinks)!

SOLVING A MATH PROBLEM

A: That's wrong.

B: It's not wrong.

A: It is wrong.

B: No it's not.

A: It's totally wrong.

B: It's not totally wrong.

A: Well maybe partially wrong.

B: It seems okay to me.

A: Well it isn't. / It's wrong!

Yet another source of rich material for working with intonation units and sentence prominence is short anecdotes. Teachers can easily adapt narrative passages from their classroom texts (which often contain selections about famous figures, such as presidents, inventors, writers) for the same purpose:

Walking in the (woods) one day, / the famous (president, / Abraham (Lincoln, / met a young (woman. / He (said,) / "You are a very beautiful (lady." / In turn (she) said / "You are the (ugliest) man / I've ever (seen)" / To which (Lincoln) replied, / "That may be (so) / but you might have (lied) / as (I) did."

The following activity illustrates how our short-term memory retains stressed elements in order to reconstruct and process the spoken stream of speech. The teacher begins by dictating a long sentence or a short passage without the normal pauses used in dictation. Students are allowed to take notes, and in the process they discover that the most salient words also receive the most stress. From these "key" words, they then attempt to reconstruct the text, working individually or in pairs.[6]

It is strictly forbidden to do any of the following things while on board the airplane: no smoking inside the cabin or restrooms, no use of electronic devices during takeoff or landing, and no blocking the aisles during meal services.

In this example, students will probably note down some of the following words: *forbidden, things, airplane, no, smoking, cabin, restrooms, electronic, devices, takeoff, landing, blocking, aisles, meal,* and *services.* Then they work together in pairs to reconstruct the message.

------

[6]This suggestion, along with many other excellent ideas for using dictation in the classroom, is found in Davis and Rinvolucri (1988).

REDUCED SPEECH

There are many *reduced speech forms* that occur in the everyday speech of educated native English speakers. These forms involve unstressed vowels, omitted sounds, and other alternations of the full form, such as assimilation, contraction, and blending. However, many nonnative speakers with long-term exposure to written English lack the necessary exposure to these reduced forms and may mistakenly believe that they represent slang or uneducated speech. When exposed to these forms in classes, learners sometimes insist that they want to learn "proper" or standard English instead.

FUNCTION WORDS

The distinction between stressed content words and unstressed function words (as discussed in Chapter 5) and the corresponding reduction of vowels in function words (as discussed in Chapter 4) underlies the concept of reduced speech. Function words, because they are unstressed in the stream of speech, tend to exhibit various forms of reduction, including the following:

1. Loss of an initial consonant sound (e.g., *his* /hɪz/ → /ɪz/ or *them* /ðɛm/ → /əm/)

2. Loss of a final consonant (e.g., *and* /ænd/ → /ən/ or *of* /ʌv/ → /ə/)

3. The weakening or centralizing of the internal vowel to /ə/ (e.g., *can* /kæn/ → /kən/)

4. In certain phonetic environments (i.e., where syllabic consonants are possible), the reduction of a vowel + consonant sequence to a syllabic consonant (e.g., *and* /ænd/ → [n̩] in the phrases *bread and butter* or *bright and early; will* /wɪl/ → [l̩] in the phrase *What will you do?*)

As can be seen from the foregoing examples, more than one type of reduction can occur within the same word. The following examples show how common function words can be reduced in the stream of speech:

Prepositions:	Early <u>to</u> bed, early <u>to</u> rise . . .	/tuw/ → /tə/
Pronouns:	You can lead a horse to water but you can't make <u>him</u> drink.	/hɪm/ → /ɪm/, /əm/
Auxiliary verbs:	It must <u>have</u> been music to your ears!	/hæv/ → /əv/, /ə/
Conjunctions:	You can't have your cake <u>and</u> eat it, too.	/ænd/ → /ən/
Articles:	John is <u>the</u> life of <u>the</u> party.	/ðiy/ → /ðə/

Seeing transcribed versions of simple utterances like these, in which the vowels of unstressed words are reduced, can heighten learners' awareness. (For a more complete list of commonly reduced function words, see Appendix 6.)

Sometimes, when learners do not attend to (or are unaware of) phonetically subtle differences in English, communication can break down in interesting ways. For example, the modal auxiliary *can* and its negative contraction *can't* are easily confused when they occur in context and are spoken rapidly. We know of one nonnative speaker who was parking her car in Los Angeles when a passerby told her, "You can't park here." Thinking that she had heard "You can park here," she did and thus was very surprised to find a citation on the windshield when she returned to her car.

There are several differences that native speakers can perceive that help them to discriminate these two phrases:

1. YOU can PARK here.   /ˌyukən'pɑrkhɪr/
2. You CAN'T PARK here.   /yəˌkænt'pɑrkhɪr/

The first salient difference is stress. Although the prominent element in both sentences is most likely *park,* the modal *can* in sentence 1 does not normally receive stress, whereas in sentence 2 the negative modal *can't* does. A second difference is the vowel sound, which in unstressed *can* is normally /ə/ or /ɪ/ but in the stressed word *can't* is realized as /æ/.[7] Thus there is a difference in both rhythm and vowel quality to which nonnative speakers must be sensitized. Note that the final /t/ of *can't* is unreleased [t°] and that the /n/ may be realized as a nasalization of the vowel.

An exercise like that in Figure 7.1 would be appropriate to help preliterate or young learners practice hearing the difference between *can* and *can't.* As the teacher reads from a listening script, the learners are instructed to circle the happy face for the *can* and the unhappy face for *can't.*

Teacher reads . . .	Student Worksheet . . .
1. You can park here.	1. ☺ ☹
2. You can speak Spanish.	2. ☺ ☹
3. They can't come.	3. ☺ ☹
4. He can't fix the car.	4. ☺ ☹
5. She can't play the guitar.	5. ☺ ☹
6. They can swim.	6. ☺ ☹

Figure 7.1 Listening discrimination exercise for *can* vs. *can't* for young or preliterate learners

In fact, function words can cause problems for the nonnative listener since in their most highly reduced form, the representations for many common function words are virtually identical:

him them } /əm/[8]   as is } /əz/   or are } /əʳ/

a of have } /ə/   in on an and } /ən/, [n̩]

---

[7]There are, of course, environments in which *can* may be stressed, such as clause- or utterance-final position. An example would be the *can* in "I believe I can," uttered in response to the question "Can you do it?"
[8]Historically, the reduced *'em* did not arise from *them* but from Anglo-Saxon *hem,* which later became *them.*

Thus, for example, there may be little audible difference in a phrase such as the following:

Did you see (him/them)?   /dɪdʒəsiyəm/

If the reduced pronoun refers to one male individual, the full form is *him;* if it refers to more than one individual, it is *them.* Native speakers can generally distinguish reduced *him* from *them* by the quality of the reduced vowel – /ɪ/ vs. /ə/, respectively. The difference is so slight, however, that sometimes even native speakers will not hear a difference or will mishear one for the other.

We suggest that there may be some value in exercises such as the following, which raise learner awareness that these simple function words, when reduced, may all sound identical. Successful completion of the activity would, of course, depend on learners' using their internalized knowledge of English grammar (and in this case, idioms):

> *Directions:* Listen to your teacher read the following sentences. Then, using your knowledge of English, decide which choice is correct.
>
> 1. It's as flat _____ a pancake.
>   a. as
>   b. is
>
> 2. Don't put me _____ a tight spot.
>   a. in
>   b. an
>   c. on
>
> 3. Live _____ learn.
>   a. an
>   b. and
>   c. on
>
> 4. Let's watch _____ step.
>   a. are
>   b. our
>   c. or

Another possibility is to adapt traditional dictation exercises for the purpose of ear training. Instead of dictating the entire text, teachers provide students with a cloze dictation. The teacher may choose to limit these deletions to a specific type of function word, such as articles. In the following example, learners are asked to insert either *a, the,* or nothing (Ø) in the gaps as the teacher dictates the text:

WATER POLLUTION

Everyone agrees that water pollution is ___a___ serious problem today. ___Ø___
$_1$ $_2$

oceans, lakes, and rivers all over ___the___ world are becoming polluted with
$_3$

garbage and dangerous materials. Factories contribute to ___the___ problem because
$_4$

they rely on rivers for disposing of wastes. ___Ø___ oil and other chemicals can
$_5$

kill fish and make water bad for drinking. Polluted water is ___a___ hazard to
$_6$

everyone. Since people are dependent on ___Ø___ water, they should be involved
$_7$

in finding ___a___ solution to this problem.
$_8$

These same kinds of cloze dictations can also be adapted to listening for other function words (e.g., prepositions, conjunctions, auxiliary verbs, pronouns, etc.):

BUY OR RENT?

Is it better ___to___ rent furniture ___or___ to buy your own home furnishings?
1   2

Today, many young people ___are___ renting instead ___of___ buying, ___and___
3   4   5

furniture rental ___is___ one of the fastest-growing businesses ___in___ the
6   7

United States. The reason ___for___ this trend ___is___ quite simple: People prefer
8   9

___to___ wait until they have enough money ___to___ buy furniture ___that___
10   11   12

they really like instead ___of___ buying used ___or___ cheap furniture. Renting
13   14

has another advantage, too. It saves people the cost ___of___ moving their furni-
15

ture ___to___ other parts ___of___ the country when they relocate.
16   17

We also suggest that teachers bring in short taped segments of native-speaker speech (news, weather, conversations, speeches, talk shows, etc.). From these they can create simple fill-in-the-blank exercises such as the following (excerpted from an authentic conversation), which provide students with further assistance in listening to unstressed function words in natural speech:

CALIFORNIA DRIVERS

A: How did you come into work today, then?

B: I drove.

A: What were ___the___ roads like?
1

B: Oh, terrible. You know what California drivers ___are___ like when it's raining. I
2

    saw three accidents ___on___ the way here.
3

A: Three accidents? Was this ___on___ the freeway ___or___ the city streets?
4   5

B: On the freeway.

A: Was anybody hurt, ___do___ you think?
6

B: Oh, I don't think so. The accidents were all sorts ___of___ fender-benders!
7

COMMONLY REDUCED VERBAL PHRASES

Weinstein (1982) has developed listening materials that help ESL/EFL learners recognize and comprehend commonly reduced verbal phrases using orthographic representations of the reductions. These nonstandard orthographic forms are a useful tool for introducing reduced speech in settings where the focus is on listening skills rather than pronunciation; in these settings, the teacher may not wish to introduce a phonetic alphabet. We have added phonemic transcription for use where relevant:[9]

Straightforward reductions

(have) got to	→	gotta	/gɑɾə/
have to	→	hafta	/hæftə/
has to	→	hasta	/hæstə/
want to	→	wanna	/wɔnə/, /wɑnə/
going to	→	gonna	/gʌnə/
don't know	→	donno (dunno)	/dənow/
should have	→	shoulda	/ʃʊdə/
would have	→	woulda	/wʊdə/
could have	→	coulda	/kʊdə/
must have	→	musta	/mʌstə/
may have	→	maya	/meyə/
might have	→	mighta	/mayɾə/

To Weinstein's inventory we add the following:

used to	→	usta	/yuwstə/
supposed to	→	supposta	/səpowstə/
ought to	→	oughta	/ɔɾə,ɑɾə/
shouldn't have		shouldn't've / shouldna	/ʃʊdn̩(t)ə(v)/
couldn't have		couldn't've / couldna	/kʊdn̩(t)ə(v)/
wouldn't have		wouldn't've / wouldna	/wʊdn̩(t)ə(v)/

Ambiguous reductions (also noted by Weinstein)

What do you (mean) / What are you (doing)	Whaddaya	/wʌɾəyə/
What do you (want) / What have you (been doing) / (I don't know) what you (mean)	Whacha (whatcha)	/wʌtʃə/

Notice that several levels of reduction are often possible in common phrases. Take, for example, the utterance "I have got to go now." Depending on the relationship of the speaker, the informality of the setting, and the rapidity of the speech, this can take the following forms:

I have got to go now.	/ay(h)əvgɑ[t°]təgownaw/[10]
I've got to go now.	/ayvgɑ[t°]təgownaw/
I've gotta go now.	/ayvgɑɾəgownaw/
I gotta go now.	/aygɑɾəgownaw/
Gotta go now.	/gɑɾəgownaw/

[9]We are following Weinstein's spelling conventions here and suggest our own alternatives in parentheses. Note that some of these reductions simply take a word one step beyond its usual contracted or blended form in terms of sound reduction. For example, the full form *should have* contracts to *should've*, which then reduces to *shoulda*.

[10]We have chosen to transcribe the verb *have* in this version of the utterance in its reduced form /əv/ since it is unstressed in the stream of speech.

Certainly it is not necessary that nonnative speakers learn to produce all such common reductions automatically. However, it is important that they become aware of them and are able to quickly figure out the underlying forms. To this end, Weinstein (1982) suggests that learners listen to a dialogue containing reduced forms such as those highlighted in the teacher script (or tape script) below:

GOING ON VACATION

Tim: I *dunno* what clothes to take. *Whaddaya* think I should pack?
Jackie: I *dunno*. It depends on *whatcha wanna* do after you get there. I'm *gonna* go
         shopping now. Do you *wanna* come with me?
Tim: I *dunno* if it would help. *Whaddaya* think?
Jackie: It couldn't hurt.

In an accompanying student worksheet, these reduced forms are deleted, with blanks for students to write in the standard spelling of the full text that corresponds to the reductions they hear (Figure 7.2).

To Weinstein's exercise types we would add others that help learners to specifically discriminate ambiguous reductions. For example, in short dialogues like the following, learners should decide whether each instance of *whaddaya* is a reduction of *what do you* or *what are you:*

Bill: Hey, Ann, whaddaya doing this weekend?
Ann: That all depends. Whaddaya have in mind?

The learners should be able to explain how they arrived at their decision.

Directions: In the blanks below, write the standard spelling of the full form for the reduced speech which you hear.

GOING ON VACATION

Tim: I _____ _____ what clothes to take.

         _____ _____ _____ think I should pack?

Jackie: I _____ _____ . It depends on _____

         _____ _____ _____ do after you get there.

         I'm _____ _____ go shopping now.

         Do you _____ _____ come with me?

Tim: I _____ _____ if it would help.

         _____ _____ _____ think?

Jackie: It couldn't hurt.

Figure 7.2 Student worksheet for exercise on reduced forms ("Going on Vacation" scripts adapted from WHADDAYA SAY by Weinstein, © 1983. Reprinted by permission of Prentice-Hall, Inc., Uppersaddle River, NJ.)

For many nonnative speakers it is extremely difficult to distinguish affirmative and negative modal perfects. We recommend exercises such as the following, in which students circle the phrase they hear:

1. You _____ done it.
    a. should have
    b. shouldn't have

2. He _____ arrived on time.
    a. could have
    b. couldn't have

3. Sally _____ been able to fix it.
    a. would have
    b. wouldn't have

Finally, to reinforce the prevalence of reduced speech forms in native-speaker speech, teachers can bring in cartoons and short passages from literature that illustrate reductions in written form. The following dialogue, from the opening scene of Arthur Miller's *Death of a Salesman*,[11] can be analyzed for reduced speech with an intermediate to advanced class:

> [*Willy Loman, a traveling salesman, returns from a business trip prematurely, surprising his wife, Linda. He explains his change of plans.*]
>
> **Willie:** I'm tired to the death. I just couldn't make it. I just couldn't make it, Linda.
> **Linda:** Where were you all day? You look terrible.
> **Willie:** I got as far as a little above Yonkers. I stopped for a cup of coffee. Maybe it was the coffee.
> **Linda:** What?
> **Willie:** I suddenly couldn't drive any more. The car kept going off onto the shoulder, y'know?
> **Linda:** Oh. Maybe it was the steering again . . .
> . . . .
> **Willie:** I was driving along, you understand? And I was fine. I was even observing the scenery. . . I opened the windshield and just let the warm air bathe over me. And then all of a sudden I'm goin' off the road! I'm tellin' ya, I absolutely forgot I was driving. If I'd've gone the other way over the white line I might've killed somebody. So I went on again – and five minutes later I'm dreamin' again, and I nearly . . . I have such thoughts, I have such strange thoughts.

This activity is especially interesting and productive when used in conjunction with an audiotaped or videotaped version of the play.

CONTRACTION AND BLENDING

Related to the larger phenomenon of reduced speech in English are **contractions,** conventionalized written sequences that obscure a word boundary, and **blendings,** spoken two-word sequences that obscure a word boundary.[12] Contractions are a subset of blendings; in other

---

[11]From *Death of a Salesman* by Arthur Miller. Copyright 1949, renewed © 1977 by Arthur Miller. Used by permission of Viking Penguin, a division of Penguin Books USA Inc. (Stage directions have been deleted.)
[12]This analysis follows Hill and Beebe (1980). For other information on contractions, see Dickerson (1989a: 71–77).

words, all written contractions represent a spoken blending, but not all spoken blendings are conventionalized as orthographic contractions:

Contraction = a written convention: *it's, doesn't, you'll*

Blending = related spoken phenomenon: *Bob's (= Bob is / Bob has), this's, there're*

Some research (e.g., Odlin 1978) suggests that among ESL learners, frequency of contracting correlates with English proficiency; however, we have found that even the speech of advanced learners can be marked by the infrequent use of contractions and blending in otherwise fluent speech. Whether or not nonnative speakers choose to use blendings, contractions, and reductions, they must be exposed to the way native speakers use them if they wish to comprehend informal spoken English.

Like the instances of reduced speech discussed earlier, blending in spoken English presents a learning barrier for many students. Orthographic contractions are a logical first step for introducing the concept of blending and reinforcing the pervasiveness of this phenomenon in spoken English.

There are eight English words that occur productively in written contractions (the two most frequently contracted forms are *is* and *not,* according to Hill and Beebe 1980):

is → _____'s   **are → _____'re**
   he's / she's   we're
   it's   they're
   there's   you're
   that's
   where's

has → _____'s   **have → _____'ve**   **had → _____'d**
   he's / she's   I've   I'd
   it's   we've   we'd
   there's   you've   you'd
   that's   they've   he'd / she'd
   where's   they'd

will → _____'ll   **would → _____'d**
   I'll   I'd
   we'll   we'd
   you'll   you'd
   he'll / she'll   he'd / she'd
   they'll   they'd

not → _____n't

isn't   doesn't   can't   don't[13]
aren't   didn't   wouldn't   won't
wasn't   couldn't
weren't   shouldn't
                        mustn't
                        mightn't

---

[13]The two forms *don't* and *won't* are phonologically irregular in that /duw/ changes to /downt/ and /wɪl/ changes to /wownt/.

There are two other special contractions in which two words combine:

I am → I'm

let us → let's

There is the frozen contraction *o'clock,* which derives historically from the phrase "of the clock."

As we have defined it, blending includes all the foregoing contractions and extends them to a number of other environments common in spoken English, such as the following combinations with auxiliary verbs:

Wh-words:	why's, who'll, when'd
Proper names:	Al's, Jane'll, Dr. White'd
Common nouns:	my name's, the play'll, a guy'd
Demonstratives:	this's, that'll, these'd
Existential "there":	there'll, there'd

Despite the pervasiveness of contractions and blendings, there are several constraints on where they occur. These include the formality of speech (i.e., the more formal, the less likely they are to occur) and the position in which they occur. Most contracted and blended forms (with the exception of those with *not*) do not occur in final position within a clause or an utterance. See Appendix 7 for further information on these constraints.

Like the reduced forms of function words mentioned earlier, contractions and blendings with *'s* and *'d* are ambiguous: *'s* can represent *is, has,* or sometimes even *does:*

He_'s_ an athlete.	(He <u>is</u>)
She_'s_ seen that movie.	(She <u>has</u>)
What_'s_ it cost?	(What <u>does</u>)

The contracted or blended form *'d* can represent *had, would,* or sometimes even *did:*

They_'d_ already eaten at 7 p.m.	(They <u>had</u>)
I_'d_ like to see you later.	(I <u>would</u>)
Where_'d_ you go?	(Where <u>did</u>)

One strategy for assisting learners in recognizing the full form of contractions or blendings comes from Bowen (1975a), who recommends that nonnative speakers listen to recordings of sentences read in their naturally reduced form. The learner, who has no access to the written version of the sentence, is instructed to write down the full, uncontracted (or unblended) form of the first two words of each utterance. To do this successfully, learners must make use of their knowledge of grammar as well as phonology. Thus in the sentence "Aren't you sorry you missed it?" the learner should write *are not*. Some sample listening items follow, with the correct answer in parentheses:

Aren't you sorry you missed it?	(Are not)
How's he keep track of the money?	(How does)
It'd be better if he came later.	(It would)
It's been cloudy all day.	(It has)
Don't you know any better?	(Do not)
There're about a dozen.	(There are)
What'll you have for dessert?	(What will)

In addition to the types of exercises Bowen suggests, we recommend that nonnative speakers listen to and transcribe coherent dialogues containing the common contractions and then later reconstruct the full forms of all the contractions they have transcribed in order to become more aware of and sensitive to the use of contractions in spoken English.

Many common contractions have one or more single-word *homophones* – words pronounced the same but spelled differently. Hill and Beebe (1980: 321) present the following useful list:

Contraction/blending	Single-word homophone
I'll	aisle, isle
you're	your
you'll	yule
he'll	heel, hill
he'd	heed
we'll	will, weal
we've	weave
they're	their, there
who's	whose
where's	wears
where're	wearer
why's	wise
why're	wire
why'd	wide
why'll	while
how's	house (v.)
how'll	howl

Homophones can be contextually practiced by learners using dictated passages in which they must use grammatical and contextual information to figure out which form is appropriate (Figure 7.3).

Directions: Your teacher will read the following text. Fill in each blank with the missing word.

When (1) _____ depressed, it often seems as if all (2) _____ friends have abandoned you. (3) _____ depression is a serious condition, (4) _____ is a strong possibility that individuals (5) _____ physicians diagnose them as depressed (6) _____ recover after simple treatment and the passage of time. They may also require more extensive clinical observation. These patients should (7) _____ the advice of (8) _____ physician, and may require drug treatment since (9) _____ potentially dangerous to themselves and others.

Answers: (1) you're; (2) your; (3) While; (4) there; (5) whose; (6) will; (7) heed; (8) their; (9) they're.

Figure 7.3 Student worksheet for a cloze dictation practicing homophones

B.C. By Johnny Hart

By permission of Johnny Hart and Creators Syndicate, Inc.

BIZARRO By Dan Piraro

The "Bizarro" cartoon by Dan Piraro is
reprinted by permission of Chronicle Features,
San Francisco, California. All rights reserved.

Figure 7.4 Examples of false segmentation.

SEGMENTATION

As some of our previous examples suggest, one of the major decoding problems at the phrasal level is the task of segmenting the stream of speech into syllables and words. For example, we may hear an utterance and then wonder if the speaker said *a part* or *apart*. The history of the English language tells us that phrases such as *an apron* and *an adder* were once *a napron* and *a nadder,* indicating that **segmentation,** or the dividing up of utterances into individual words and syllables, has long been a real problem for native as well as nonnative listeners.

In fact, false segmentation is sometimes a source of humor in English, as shown in the comic strips in Figure 7.4. Similarly, recall the nonnative speaker cited at the outset of this chapter who listened to "Is there any person alive that doesn't want to understand this a little better?" and transcribed it as "Is there any personal life that . . . ?" This speaker made a segmentation error and a minor consonant error (mishearing /v/ as /f/), illustrating once again that often several different perception problems – as well as cultural, lexical, and syntactic problems – can conspire to cause mishearing.

Bowen (1975: 153, 259) provides a number of examples of potential segmentation problems:

a tax on city buses	attacks on city buses
Paula praised	Paul appraised

paid A   pay day
Is Ann around?   Is Anna round?
Joan Elson   Joe Nelson

Sometimes more than two segmentations are possible:

same Ann   same man   say man

Some linguists claim that such pairs exhibit differences in **juncture** – that is, perceptible differences in word segmentation; however, we believe that when spoken normally as part of an utterance, such phrases are virtually impossible to distinguish consistently even for English speakers, who use context or their knowledge of the world to help them segment and to choose from competing options. For example:

The violence is getting out of hand. We really
must do something about . . .
a.   attacks on city buses.
b.   a tax on city buses.

The listener will guess that the speaker said "attacks on city buses" and not "a tax on city buses" because the former makes better sense.

Some cases of differences in segmentation do, however, result in differences that native speakers are able to detect:

1	2
nitrate	night rate
why try	white rye
my turn	might earn
a tease	at ease
key punching	keep punching
may Karen	make Karen

Notice that in column 1, the second syllable begins with an aspirated stop [t^h, p^h, k^h]. In column 2, however, the first syllable ends in a stop, causing an allophonic difference that native speakers can easily discern. In the case of *night rate* and *white rye,* the variant used is unreleased [$t°$]; in the case of *might earn* and *at ease,* the /t/ occurs in intervocalic position and is thus articulated as [ɾ]. Finally, in the case of *keep punching* and *make Karen,* the /p/ and the /k/ are not articulated twice, but are rather held or lengthened slightly to [p:] and [k:].

Native speakers can detect differences due to segmentation or juncture in numerous other such cases – for example, *that's cool / that school* and *why choose / white shoes.* As a result, native speakers distinguish fairly consistently between such pairs, and advanced learners might therefore benefit from some practice in discriminating examples of this type. The pedagogical challenge is to contextualize these contrasts at the utterance level so that learners can practice listening discrimination in a reasonably natural way. For example:

Directions: Listen to your teacher read the following sentences. Circle the item you hear.

1. Hal is always . . .
    a.   a tease. (bothersome)
    b.   at ease. (comfortable)

2. We weren't aware of the . . .
    a.   nitrate (chemical compound)
    b.   night rate (fee after 6 p.m.)

Native speakers pick up on other kinds of clues to help them segment speech. For example, the following two-word utterances differ in the addition of an extra unstressed syllable in one of the two word pairs. Compare:

1	**2**
Paula praised	Paula appraised
to the state	to the estate
much steam	much esteem
pineapples	pie and apples

The items in column 2 have an extra unstressed syllable (e.g., *praised* /preyzd/ vs. *appraised* /əpreyzd/) that contrasts with the words in column 1. Examples of this type are relatively common, and advanced nonnative speakers might benefit from choosing between these kinds of options. For example:

Directions: Listen to your teacher read the following sentences. Circle the item you hear.

1. Paula . . . the vase.
    a. praised (said it was gorgeous)
    b. appraised (valued it at $1300)
2. Jonathan . . . it.
    a. proved (showed it to be true)
    b. approved (okayed it)

In this case, the vocabulary involved tends to be fairly advanced, so this type of exercise would be useful only with proficient learners.

Gilbert (1994: 41) offers the following type of exercise to assist learners in listening for additional clues to segmenting speech (such as differences in word stress or phonemes):

1. That's elementary / a lemon tree.
2. We're interested in history / his story.
3. What do you think of this comedy / committee?

SPECIAL LISTENING PROBLEMS WITH NUMBERS

As Bowen (1975b) notes, some numbers in English are also potentially confusing, especially *thirteen* through *nineteen* and the related multiples of ten from *thirty* to *ninety*. Nonnative speakers (and sometimes native speakers) have difficulty in correctly hearing the difference between pairs like these:

1. The book costs (thirteen/thirty) dollars.
2. It cost ten dollars and (sixteen/sixty) cents.
3. There are (seventeen/seventy) of us.
4. Just dial (five-seven-four, twenty-nine, nineteen / five-seven-four, twenty-nine, ninety).
5. Come at (eleven fifteen / eleven fifty).

As pointed out in Chapter 5, the difference comes from the stress level, the initial consonant of the final syllable, and the vowel quality of the second syllable. For *thirteen* (/ˈθɝˌtiyn/ or /ˌθɝˈtiyn/) and the other teen numbers, the second syllable is strongly or lightly stressed, with the vowel /iy/ having a full quality followed by /n/. In *thirty* [ˈθɝɾi] and the other multiples of ten, however, the second syllable is unstressed, the consonant is the flap allophone of /t/ ([ɾ]), and the vowel is reduced to /i/ with no final /n/.

As noted previously, there are two slightly different stress patterns for the teen numbers. When these occur in attributive position (examples 1 and 2), the first syllable tends to be stressed more strongly than the *-teen* syllable:

1. THIRteen DOLlars

2. SIXteen CENTS

In phrase or utterance-final position, however, the *-teen* syllable tends to be strongly stressed:[14]

3. sevenTEEN of us

4. (five-seven-four) (twenty-nine) nineTEEN (a telephone number)

5. (eleven) fifTEEN (the time of day)

Obviously, examples like 1 and 2 are more likely to result in a listening confusion between *tens* and *teens* than the last three, in which the *-teen* syllable is strongly stressed. Listening comprehension exercises that focus on the contrast in attributive position are thus very important for nonnative speakers. The following kind of listening discrimination practice is easy to construct:

Directions: Listen to your teacher read the following sentences. Circle the number you hear.

1. The repairman charged us (sixteen/sixty) dollars.

2. It took us (fifteen/fifty) hours to finish the job.

3. It's (nineteen/ninety) miles to the next gas station.

To provide students with further practice in listening to numbers and to extend this practice into a more communicatively meaningful context, we suggest the following activity:[15]

AMERICAN MEN

Directions: Circle the number you hear.

1. 19/90 percent of American men would like to change their nose.

2. 13/30 percent of American men think everything is changing too fast.

3. 17/70 percent of American men like meat loaf.

4. 14/40 percent of American men are less than 5'6" tall.

5. 15/50 percent of American married men say they do most of the cooking in the household.

6. 18/80 percent of American men live within ten minutes of their work.

7. 16/60 percent of American men weigh two hundred pounds or more.

8. 19/90 percent of American men drive on a regular basis.

9. 13/30 percent of American men have arthritis.

10. 19/90 percent of American men think a happy marriage is possible without children.

Answers: 1. (19 percent); 2. (30 percent); 3. (70 percent); 4. (14 percent); 5. (15 percent); 6. (18 percent); 7. (16 percent); 8. (90 percent); 9. (13 percent); 10. (19 percent).

---

[14]When it is necessary to be very precise, native speakers may use a special type of paraphrase to clarify, for example: "I said three-zero, not one-three," or they may ask for disambiguation: "Did you say three-zero or one-three?"

[15]Adapted from D. Weiss, *100% American* (New York: Poseidon Press, 1988).

In addition to providing focused practice in distinguishing these numbers, this activity also includes a cultural element. Before the teacher reads the sentences, students can be asked to predict the answers. A follow-up discussion could focus on cultural differences.

In other environments, distinguishing numbers is very subtle and can be achieved only by focus on vowel quality, hearing unstressed syllables, and word segmentation. For example:

Bill runs (<u>four to five</u> / <u>forty-five</u>) miles a week.

The plane flew at (<u>sixty-eight thousand</u> / <u>six to eight thousand</u>) feet.

Nonnative speakers need to practice hearing and producing such pairs in context. In this way, they are at least made aware of the problems that might occur and may be able to improve their ability to discriminate and produce such potentially confusing numbers.

CONCLUSION

The very close, careful listening that is required to discriminate functionally distinct sounds and prosodic patterns and to segment the stream of speech into words and phrases is not an easy skill for most adolescents and adults to master in a second or foreign language. It requires time, effort, and practice. In fact, as Yule, Hoffman, and Damico (1987) point out, when intermediate or advanced ESL/EFL learners first receive explicit instruction in listening discrimination, their performance on listening discrimination tests frequently deteriorates briefly. Only later do they become significantly better at perceiving critical differences and significantly more confident about knowing when their identifications are correct. Such self-monitoring skills are very useful to most adults who wish to improve their listening comprehension and their pronunciation.

If students are fully literate, the teacher can also assess listening skills more holistically than with minimal discrimination tests by using dictation (both traditional and gapped) and by having students transcribe spontaneous native-speaker speech. These procedures can reveal the following: whether learners can recognize and process contractions, blendings, and various other phrase-level reductions; whether they can segment continuous speech; whether they ignore (or appropriately transcribe) hesitation phenomena such as filled pauses; and whether they can use prosodic patterns and pauses to identify grammatical boundaries. A range of formal (e.g., news reports) to informal (e.g., talk shows) recordings can be used to expose learners to the pervasiveness and variation of reduced speech among educated native speakers.

Admittedly, the link between perception and production is not entirely clear. There is some evidence that a learner who cannot hear the distinction between, say, *correct* and *collect* may still be taught to produce this distinction; conversely, some learners who can discriminate two sounds may not be able to produce the same difference systematically. However, there is also a body of research that demonstrates a closer correlation between perception and production. Browning (1974), for example, demonstrates that those nonnative speakers who can most accurately evaluate the pronunciation proficiency of other nonnative speakers exhibit better pronunciation themselves than do those who rate others less accurately.

This suggests that lack of internalized knowledge about English stress and intonation, English vowels, and English consonants can all contribute to an inability to perceive, interpret, and evaluate spoken English – not to mention an inability to speak it comprehensibly. In short, listening proficiency plays a critical role in the learner's overall communicative competence, which requires that learners be able to discriminate, as well as produce, functionally significant distinctions in their spoken English.

EXERCISES

KEY CONCEPTS

Write a brief definition of the following key terms from this chapter. Give examples where relevant.

synform	metrical template
schemata	intonation unit
reduced speech form	contraction
blending	homophone
segmentation	juncture

INTROSPECTING ABOUT YOUR OWN LANGUAGE LEARNING

Think about a foreign language that you have learned in school or while living abroad.

1. What are some of the problems you experienced when you were listening to native speakers?

2. How long did it take you to understand a news broadcast on the radio? Were other listening tasks easier?

3. Were some native speakers easier to understand than others? If so, why?

4. In their research, Garnes and Bond (1980) identified four strategies that listeners use in order to process incoming speech. Which ones do you think applied to your own language learning?

5. Remembering the first time you listened to a native speaker of the language you had learned or were learning in the classroom, what surprised you the most about the native speaker's speech?

DISCUSSION QUESTIONS

1. Why can listening comprehension be difficult even for students who have studied English for many years?

2. Why do you think it might help learners improve their listening comprehension skills if they read a transcript and listened to a recording at the same time?

3. Do you believe that learners with good listening comprehension generally have better pronunciation than learners with poor listening skills?

4. In what ways might listening activities be used to help learners understand how English stress, rhythm, and intonation work?

5. Examine the following authentic native-speaker conversation and the learner transcript below it in italics. Locate the errors. What might they reveal about the learner's knowledge of pronunciation?

    I find that the more experienced I become
    I find that the more experience I becoming

    in being a student, the more I'll do ten
    being a student, the more I do ten

    minutes of one thing and then switch and do
    minute of one thing and then switch and do

something else. I may not finish, say, my
something else. I may not finish, say

English homework, I start reading some of my
English homework, I start reading some of

chemistry, and then I get bored with that . . .
chemistry and then I get bore with that . . .

IN THE CLASSROOM

Assume that you are teaching pronunciation. Here are some common classroom situations that you might encounter. What technique would you use or what explanation would you give?

1. Your students keep pleading with you to slow down when you give them a dictation.

2. A student complains that she has trouble understanding when native speakers are saying *can* and when they are saying *can't*.

3. A student brings in a comic from the newspaper with the word *whatcha*. He is confused because he can't find it in his dictionary.

4. A student asks you to explain the two meanings of "My sister who lives in Boston has three children."

5. A student asks you to explain why native speakers say "I should of done it" when she learned that the proper form was "I should have done it."

SUGGESTED ACTIVITIES

1. Tape a sample of spontaneous native-speaker English (e.g., a radio broadcast, an interview) and listen to it. Which of the reduced speech phenomena discussed in this chapter do you notice?

2. Record a conversation between two nonnative speakers. To what extent do they use contractions, blendings, and reductions? Do you think they can easily understand native speakers who use contractions, blendings, and reductions?

3. Design a brief activity to help one of the speakers in (2) with a listening-related pronunciation problem that you were able to diagnose.

4. Find a cartoon or comic strip that illustrates a mishearing and come up with two ways you might use it in the classroom.

5. Choose one of the activities from this chapter (e.g., a multiple-choice listening exercise) and administer it to two or more nonnative speakers. What problems did they have? What might this tell you about their pronunciation skills?

ON THE CASSETTE

1. Administer the recorded dictation "Mean dogs" on page 224 to a group of intermediate-level English learners. Analyze the errors in the learners' dictations. Do they follow the patterns discussed in this chapter?

2. Listen to the short segment of spontaneous native-speaker conversation on the cassette. What contracted and blended speech phenomena can you find? What other connected speech phenomena are used?

3. Have two advanced learners of English listen to and transcribe the conversation in (2). What do their errors suggest about their listening and pronunciation skills in English?

CHAPTER 8

The Sound System and Grammar: Inflectional Morphology and Parts of Speech

Hierarchically, the grammar of English consists of syntax, the study of sentence relationships, and **morphology**, the study of the smallest units of meaning that cannot be subdivided without making the unit meaningless. Morphology further divides into **inflectional morphology** – the grammatical endings that attach to words – and **derivational morphology** – lexical processes like compounding, conversion, and affixation that build words using a stock of roots, stems, and affixes. (Conversion in English refers mainly to nouns that become verbs without the addition of any derivative inflection, such as "He *lunched* with me." "That senator always *stone-walls*.") In the first section of the chapter we focus on how the English sound system interacts with the inflectional morphology of English and with major word classes and parts of speech.

There are **eight regular morphological inflections,** or grammatically marked forms, that English words can take: plural, possessive, third-person singular present tense, past tense, present participle, past participle,[1] comparative degree, and superlative degree. Most have phonologically sensitive realizations. Even some of the irregular forms for these inflections can be described in terms of historically motivated phonological variants, as we discuss in Appendix 8.

Modern English has relatively few morphological inflections in comparison with Old English or with other European languages. The inflections and word-class clues that do remain help the listener process incoming language. For example, certain nouns and/or adjectives exhibit segmental features that distinguish them from etymologically related verbs that are otherwise identical or similar. This is the case with *bath* (noun) and *bathe* (verb), for in addition to the /æ/–/ey/ vowel alternation, the noun ends in a voiceless consonant and the verb in a voiced consonant – a consonant alternation that regularly signals a distinction between noun and verb in related noun–verb pairs. Such differences, which provide redundancy, aid listeners in processing and comprehending spoken English. In multisyllabic words, some part-of-speech differences are also suprasegmental with segmental consequences: Compare the stress and vowel differences between the noun *REcord* /ˈrɛkəʳd/ and the verb *reCORD* /rəˈkɔrd/. If these inflectional and part-of-speech signals are ignored or produced incorrectly by nonnative speakers, confusion or misunderstanding may result.

[1]For regular verbs, the past participle ending is the same as the past tense ending.

REGULAR INFLECTIONAL MORPHOLOGY

Nowhere else in English is the connection between the sound system and inflectional morphology closer than it is in the regular grammatical inflections of the language. Linguists often refer to this area as ***morphophonology.***

THE -*s* INFLECTIONAL ENDING

The regular plural inflection, the third-person singular present-tense inflection, and the possessive inflection all share the same set of pronunciation rules despite the differences in spelling and punctuation for the possessive:

- When the noun or verb ends in a *sibilant* consonant (i.e., /s/, /z/, /ʃ/, /ʒ/, /tʃ/, or /dʒ/), the inflection has an epenthetic vowel and is realized as unstressed /ɪz/ or /əz/.
- When the noun or verb ends in a *voiced nonsibilant* sound, the inflection involves progressive assimilation and is realized as /z/.
- When the noun or verb ends in a *voiceless nonsibilant* consonant, the inflection also involves progressive assimilation and is realized as /s/.

	/z/	/s/	/ɪz/, /əz/
Regular plural	boy<u>s</u>	boat<u>s</u>	bus<u>es</u>
	bag<u>s</u>	lake<u>s</u>	church<u>es</u>
Third-person singular present tense	see<u>s</u>	make<u>s</u>	us<u>es</u>
	run<u>s</u>	hit<u>s</u>	catch<u>es</u>
Possessive	Ray<u>'s</u>	Mike<u>'s</u>	Rose<u>'s</u>
	Marvin<u>'s</u>	Mr. White<u>'s</u>	Dr. Leech<u>'s</u>

When the noun is both plural and possessive, the following rules of pronunciation and punctuation apply:

- When the plural form of the noun ends in -*s* (or -*es*), an apostrophe is placed after the plural inflection to indicate the possessive in writing. Notice that with regular plural nouns, there is no phonetic difference between the singular possessive and the plural possessive modifier:[2] *the girl<u>s'</u> books* (sounds like *the girl<u>'s</u> books*), *the neighbor<u>s'</u> house* (sounds like *the neighbor<u>'s</u> house*).
- When the plural form of the noun is irregular and does not end in /s/ or /z/, the regular possessive inflection rule is applied and the form is spelled with an apostrophe + -*s*: *the childre<u>n's</u> toys, the me<u>n's</u> clothing.*

These rules assume that students are familiar with a phonemic alphabet. Dickerson (1990) shows how the pronunciation of final -*(e)s* or -'*s* can be cued orthographically rather than phonemically when students are low proficiency and have not yet learned a phonemic transcription system.

Students frequently depend on spelling alone when they pronounce plural endings. As a result, many believe that all regular plurals in English should be pronounced /s/ or /ɪs/. Whenever such morphological inflections are introduced or practiced in an ESL/EFL class, sufficient attention and practice should also be given to the pronunciation and spelling rules that complement the morphological rules.

---

[2]The punctuation part of this rule applies to some irregular plurals: *(his) wife's car; (their) wi<u>ves'</u> cars.* However, in these cases there is a phonetic difference between the singular form, which is voiceless, and the plural form, which is voiced.

The inflectional -*s* allomorphs (/s/, /z/, and /ɪz/ or /əz/ for plural nouns, third-person singular present-tense verbs, and possessives) would not normally be presented or practiced at the same time. However, once the three endings for the plural have been taught, the same endings can easily be recycled when presenting or practicing the simple present tense (third-person singular) or when presenting or practicing possessives.

For the following activity on plural nouns, the teacher needs to prepare a stack of index cards by writing one regular plural noun on each card. In the classroom, begin by writing the three endings on the board, listing a few examples of each:

/s/	/z/	/ɪz/, /əz/
book<u>s</u>	bag<u>s</u>	fac<u>es</u>
cat<u>s</u>	eye<u>s</u>	bus<u>es</u>
map<u>s</u>	pencil<u>s</u>	brush<u>es</u>
chief<u>s</u>	moon<u>s</u>	maz<u>es</u>
pack<u>s</u>	bed<u>s</u>	garag<u>es</u>
ant<u>s</u>	key<u>s</u>	judg<u>es</u>

Then elicit or provide the rule governing the pronunciation of these endings. After distributing the index cards to students, ask them to decide which of the categories on the board the noun plural would fall into. After practicing the pronunciation of the singular and plural forms, students come to the front of the class and write their noun in the proper column, citing the appropriate rule. In the final phase of the activity, the cards are reshuffled and students are put in pairs or small groups. They receive the shuffled cards (i.e., a pair would receive two cards and a group of four would receive four cards) and are given the task of constructing a sentence or short dialogue using the plural form of these words.

Sample student-generated sentence: Cats have beautiful green eyes and intelligent faces.

Sample dialogue:
   A: Did you buy any books?
   B: I bought three books and some pencils.

Obviously, similar classroom activities can be done to recognize and practice the three phonetic variations of the -*s* ending for all three morphemes: plural, third-person singular, and possessive as well as contractions and blendings. (Note that the contractions and blendings with *is, has,* and *does* follow the same pronunciation rules as the -*s* endings here: e.g., *it's* /s/, *he's* /z/, and *this's* /ɪz/.)

An enjoyable way to reinforce the different pronunciations of the -*s* ending is to use simple popular songs. The students make predictions by filling out the worksheet and then listen to the song to confirm their predictions. Figure 8.1 illustrates a worksheet to accompany James Taylor's "Sweet Baby James."

A memory chain activity using -*s* endings to practice the possessive and third-person singular present can double as a way for students to get to know each others' names and hobbies. Write the following pattern on the board:

His/Her name'<u>s</u> _____ and he/she like<u>s</u> to _____.

With the students sitting in a large circle, ask the student on your right for his name and favorite activity. Then pointing to the board, say:

His name'<u>s</u> José and he like<u>s</u> to swim.

Directions: With your partner, discuss the pronunciation of the *-(e)s* endings in the words below. Then write the correct pronunciation in the diagonal marks provided: /s/, /z/, or /ɪz/. Listen to the recording or to the teacher and check your predictions. Now practice singing or reading the song, focusing particularly on the correct pronunciation of these endings.

SWEET BABY JAMES

There is a young cowboy, he live<u>s</u> on the range
                              / /

His horse and his cattle are his only companion<u>s</u>
                                        / /

He work<u>s</u> in the saddle and he sleep<u>s</u> in the canyon<u>s</u>
    / /   / /   / /

Waiting for summer, his pasture<u>s</u> to change
                        / /

And as the moon rise<u>s</u> he sit<u>s</u> by his fire
                / /   / /

Thinking about women and glasse<u>s</u> of beer
                      / /

And closing his eye<u>s</u> as the doggie<u>s</u> retire
              / /   / /

He sing<u>s</u> out a song which is soft but it'<u>s</u> clear
    / /   / /

As if maybe someone could hear.

Figure 8.1 Worksheet for predicting pronunciation of *-s* endings in song lyrics (*Sweet Baby James:* Words and music by James Taylor © 1970 EMI Blackwood Music Inc. and Country Road Music Inc. All rights controlled and administered by EMI Blackwood Music Inc. All rights reserved. International copyright secured. Used by permission.)

Then introduce yourself, saying:

> My name'<u>s</u> Joan (or Ms. Smith) and I like to dance.

At this point, the student on your left should repeat José's and your introductions and then add her own using the pattern. The chain continues around the circle to the left. Names may have to be repronounced, but hobbies can be mimed as a memory helper. As a classroom prompt, it can be helpful to have three big signs on the board to point to:

/s/   /z/   /ɪz/, /əz/

These are present to remind students to pronounce these endings clearly and correctly, but they can also be helpful for error correction: You can simply point to one of the signs to cue students that a mispronunciation has occurred.

A guided practice activity that allows students to focus on the production of final /s/, /z/, or /ɪz/ while exchanging information uses a worksheet that compares the cleanliness habits of "Dirty Harry" and "Squeaky Clean Sam" (Figure 8.2). In this activity, students use present-tense verb forms (chosen from the list of verbs provided) and match appropriate items from the worksheet columns to construct meaningful

---

DIRTY HARRY AND SQUEAKY CLEAN SAM

Directions: With your partner, compare the habits of "Dirty Harry" and "Squeaky Clean Sam," paying special attention to the pronunciation of the -s endings. You can select from the verbs listed below to make sentences about Harry and Sam:

brush	fold	rinse
change	hang up	scrub
clean	iron	sweep
dump	mop	wash
dust	polish	wipe

Example: Dirty Harry rarely mops the kitchen floor.
Squeaky Clean Sam dusts his bookshelves twice a week.

	Dirty Harry	Squeaky Clean Sam
teeth		
pants		
sheets		
	once a week	frequently
bookshelves	every Thursday	once in a while
	occasionally	every morning
kitchen floor	never	whenever it's dirty
	only when his mother visits	after each meal
garbage	once a month	twice a week
	rarely	almost daily
clothes	seldom	often
	on Saturdays	usually
shoes	almost never	Tuesdays and Thursdays
	only on holidays	whenever he takes a shower
towels	before a job interview	constantly
shirt		
windows		
hair		

Figure 8.2 "Dirty Harry and Squeaky Clean Sam": guided practice with final -s endings

sentences that allow them to practice the three pronunciations of the present-tense -s morpheme. The results can be humorous when students produce sentences such as "Dirty Harry brushes his teeth only when his mother visits" or "Squeaky Clean Sam brushes his hair constantly."

THE -*ed* INFLECTIONAL ENDING

The regular past tense and the regular past participle inflections (the latter occur in the perfect tenses and the passive voice) also share a common set of pronunciation rules similar to the three allomorphs for the plural, present tense, and possessive inflections:

- When the verb ends in /d/ or /t/, the ending takes an epenthetic vowel and is realized as /ɪd/ or /əd/.
- When the verb ends in a *voiced* sound other than /d/, the ending undergoes progressive assimilation and is pronounced as /d/.
- When the verb ends in a *voiceless* consonant other than /t/, the ending also undergoes progressive assimilation and is pronounced as /t/.

/d/	/t/	/ɪd/, /əd/
cried	walked	chatted
grabbed	passed	waded
moved	kissed	added
viewed	laughed	needed
robbed	stopped	waited

Students should be able to recognize the distinct /d/, /t/, and /ɪd/ sounds from past exposure to these words; if they cannot, the teacher can model them. (For an alternative explanation of how the pronunciation of final past-tense -*ed* can be cued orthographically rather than phonemically, see Dickerson 1990.)

After the teacher's initial explanation, students will be ready for the following activity. Prepare a set of index cards, each containing one regular verb. Write three model words on the board – for example, *cared, picked,* and *wanted.* Then distribute different packs of cards consisting of regular verbs to groups of four to five students. Each group should decide how the -*ed* ending is pronounced for these verbs. One student from each group goes to the board and writes the group's examples under the proper model word. This will create a list of verbs under each model word. In an advanced class, students can try to figure out what all the examples in one column have in common in order to deduce the rule governing the pronunciation. In a beginning or intermediate class, you will most likely have to point the rule out.

As with -*s* endings, students can do a prediction exercise for the pronunciation of -*ed* past tense endings using song lyrics. They can then listen to the recording to verify their predictions. The worksheet in Figure 8.3 accompanies the traditional Australian song "Waltzing Matilda."

Teachers can recycle the past-tense word cards suggested previously to cue production of the past tense. For this activity, students sit in a circle (in a large class, you may wish to form more than one circle). Each student receives a different regular verb card and has to make a sentence beginning: *Yesterday, I _____.* For example, if a student named Yoshi begins and his card reads *play,* he could say, "Yesterday I played baseball." The other class members should decide if Yoshi pronounced the -*ed* correctly. The next student, Silvia, may have a card reading *wash.* She should repeat Yoshi's statement and then add her own: "Yesterday Yoshi played baseball and I washed my car."

This activity constitutes a modified pattern drill. If you desire more open-ended practice, cards can be distributed again to each student in a circle, but each utterance should build on the previous one, creating a unified story:

play   John played the trumpet when he was a boy.
need   He really needed to take lessons.
wash   He washed his trumpet every day.

kiss   One day he kissed his girlfriend Sue.
laugh   She laughed and told him she wasn't a trumpet!

Because the students need to stretch their imagination to create a unified story, the results can be quite humorous.

Directions: With your partner, discuss the pronunciation of the *-ed* endings in the words below. Then write the correct pronunciation in the diagonal marks provided: /t/, /d/, and /ɪd/. Listen to the recording or to the teacher and check your predictions. Now practice singing or reading the song, focusing particularly on the correct pronunciation of these endings.

WALTZING MATILDA

1. Once a jolly *swagman* camp<u>ed</u> by a *billabong*
                                 / /
   Under the shade of a *coolibah* tree,
   And he sang as he watch<u>ed</u> and wait<u>ed</u> till his *billy* boil<u>ed</u>,
                               / /   / /   / /
   You'll come a-waltzing Matilda with me!
   Refrain: *Waltzing Matilda,* Waltzing Matilda,
                   You'll come a-waltzing Matilda with me!
   And he sang as he watch<u>ed</u> and wait<u>ed</u> till his billy boil<u>ed</u>,
                               / /   / /   / /
   "You'll come a-waltzing Matilda with me!"

2. Down came a *jumbuck* to drink at the billabong,
   Up jump<u>ed</u> the swagman and grabb<u>ed</u> him with glee,
            / /   / /
   And he sang as he stow<u>ed</u> the jumbuck in his *tucker* bag,
                     / /
   You'll come a-waltzing Matilda with me! (*refrain*)

3. Up rode the *squatter,* mount<u>ed</u> on his thoroughbred,
                         / /
   Down came the troopers, one, two, three,
   "Where's that jolly jumbuck you've got in your tucker bag?"
   You'll come a-waltzing Matilda with me! (*refrain*)

4. Up jump<u>ed</u> the swagman, sprang into the billabong
            / /
   "You'll never catch me alive," said he
   And his ghost may be heard as you pass by that billabong.
   "You'll come a-waltzing Matilda with me!" (*refrain*)

Glossary

swagman: a tramp	*Waltzing Matilda:* to go on a tramp
billabong: a water hole	*jumbuck:* a sheep
collibah: eucalyptus tree	*tucker:* food
billy: tin can used to boil tea	*squatter:* sheep farmer
swag: a bundle (carried by the tramp)	

Figure 8.3 Worksheet for predicting pronunciation of past-tense *-ed* endings in song lyrics ["Waltzing Matilda" by A. B. (Banjo) Paterson. Copyright ©1936, 1941 by Carl Fischer, Inc. All rights reserved. Reprinted by permission. Glossary is from Dick and Beth Best, eds., *The New Song Fest,* New York: Crown, 1959 pp. 5–6.]

For guided practice with the past-tense *-ed* ending, students can compare the past habits of "Sloppy Sarah" and "Neat Nelly," two college roommates. This activity is modeled on the "Dirty Harry and Squeaky Clean Sam" exercise (Figure 8.2). In this activity, students again select appropriate verbs and items from the worksheet columns to create meaningful sentences about the past habitual actions of the two characters, focusing attention on the various pronunciations of the *-ed* endings (Figure 8.4).

SLOPPY SARAH AND NEAT NELLY

Directions: With your partner, compare the past habits of "Sloppy Sarah" and "Neat Nelly," two roommates who lived together during their last year of college. Pay special attention to the pronunciation of the past tense endings. You can select from the verbs listed below to make sentences about Sarah and Nelly:

change	iron	scour
clean	mop	scrub
dump	pick up	vacuum
dust	polish	wash
fold	rinse	wipe

Example: Sloppy Sarah chang*ed* the bed sheets every other month.
Neat Nelly scour*ed* the toilet almost daily.

	Sloppy Sarah	Neat Nelly
dishes		
kitchen sink		
bed sheets		
bookshelves	every other month	after every meal
	never	routinely
kitchen floor	only when her mother visited	whenever it was dirty
	once a month	once in a while
garbage	rarely	twice a week
	seldom	frequently
the laundry	on Saturdays	often
	almost never	every week
the hallway	only on major holidays	usually
	never	Tuesdays and Thursdays
clothes	once a week	almost daily
	occasionally	once a month
the toilet		
windows		
the blinds		

Figure 8.4 "Sloppy Sarah and Neat Nelly": guided practice with past-tense *-ed* endings

If one introduces and practices the predictable phonetic variants for the simple past tense of regular verbs along with the past tense inflection, this information can be reviewed and applied again when perfect verb tenses or the passive voice are presented and practiced with regular verbs. For example, using a list of regular verbs such as the following, students can work in pairs or groups:

visit	stay	date
travel	touch	love
taste	walk	want

Students ask each other questions about their past experiences, making use of the present perfect with attention to the pronunciation of -ed. For example:

A: Have you ever traveled to China?
B: No. Have you ever dated someone from another country?
A: Yes, I once dated someone from France.

In a similar exercise with a different set of regular verbs, students can practice the present perfect passive, again with attention to the pronunciation of -ed. For example:

annoy	amuse	frighten	depress
surprise	startle	please	irritate

A: Have you ever been annoyed by a neighbor?
B: Yes, I was annoyed by my neighbors upstairs. They had a very noisy party
last Saturday.

Students who lack knowledge of these phonological rules (in particular students from language backgrounds in which final consonant clustering is more restricted than in English) often pronounce every -ed ending as a fully syllabic /ɪd/ or /ɛd/. This is a distracting pronunciation error since relatively few verb stems end in /d/ or /t/ – the only final sounds that justify the addition of unstressed /ɪd/. When such students are at the intermediate or advanced stage of acquiring English, it is very difficult to get them to suppress their syllabic /ɪd/ and merely add consonantal /d/ or /t/ to the end of verbs as appropriate.

We have now discussed five of the eight regular morphological inflections of English in relation to regular nouns and verbs (i.e., regular plural, third-person singular present, possessive, regular past tense, and regular past participle). However, not all English nouns and verbs are regular; later we will mention some of the pronunciation patterns that can be used to describe and teach irregular nouns and verbs.

THE PARTICIPIAL INFLECTION *-ing*

Of the three remaining regular inflections, the progressive (or present) participle has a relatively invariant pronunciation. It always consists of -ing (pronounced /ɪŋ/) added to the base form of the verb. In informal conversation, this ending can be pronounced /ɪn/, which is often represented orthographically as -in'. This substitution, however, is conditioned by degree of informality and rate of speech and thus is not like the morphophonologically conditioned variants for -s and -ed. The pronunciation of this inflection can be reviewed whenever a progressive verb form is presented or practiced.

THE COMPARATIVE AND SUPERLATIVE INFLECTIONAL ENDINGS

The two remaining regular inflections are the comparative *-er* /ə^r/ and the superlative *-est* /əst/. There is a metrical principle based on syllable structure that in many cases helps native speakers decide when to apply these inflections and when to use the **periphrastic** comparative and superlative forms – those with *more* and *most*. (There is some degree of choice in the use of the periphrastic form rather than the inflection, since only the periphrastic form can carry utterance prominence when this is called for – for example, in the phrase "When I saw Yves again last night, his eyes were even MORE blue than I had remembered.")

First, adjectives and adverbs of one syllable take the inflectional ending as do two-syllable adjectives with a final *-y* suffix (pronounced as unstressed /i/).[3]

Base form	/ə^r/	/əst/
big	bigger	biggest
tall	taller	tallest
soon	sooner	sooner
hard	harder	hardest
happy	happier	happiest
noisy	noisier	noisiest

Second, many other two-syllable adjectives that have a stressed first syllable and an unstressed second syllable ending in *-ly* /li/, *-ow* /o/, or *-le* (syllabic [l̩])[4] also take the inflection, although it is certainly possible to use the periphrastic form in certain contexts, such as when extra emphasis is being placed on the comparative or superlative element ("She is the MOST friendly person I know").

Base form	/ə^r/	/əst/
friendly	friendlier	friendliest
	(more friendly)	(most friendly)
narrow	narrower	narrowest
	(more narrow)	(most narrow)
gentle	gentler	gentlest
	(more gentle)	(most gentle)

Note also that these two-syllable adjectives can add derivational prefixes and still take the same inflections as the base form (e.g., *unhappier, unfriendliest,* etc).

Third, all two-syllable adverbs ending in *-ly* that do not have an adjective homonym take the periphrastic form.

Adverbs taking the periphrastic form

slowly	more/most slowly	(*not* slowlier/iest)
brusquely	more/most brusquely	(*not* brusquelier/iest)
sharply	more/most sharply	(*not* sharplier/iest)

Fourth, there are adjectives that seem more suited to the periphrastic comparative and superlative forms but that also occur with inflectional endings, especially in informal use. These include two-syllable adjectives that: (a) end in *-er* or *-ure,* such as *tender, mature;*

---

[3]There are a few one-syllable adjectives that are exceptional in that they take only periphrastic *more* or *most: real, right, wrong,* and *like* (= similar to).
[4]Syllabic [l̩] in this context generally becomes consonantal when the inflection is added.

(b) end in a weakly stressed vowel followed by nothing more than a final /d/ or /t/, such as *stupid, quiet;* and (c) end in a weakly stressed *-some,* such as *handsome, awesome.*

Base form	"More"	"Most"
tender	more tender (tenderer)	most tender (tenderest)
stupid	more stupid (stupider)	most stupid (stupidest)
handsome	more handsome (handsomer)	most handsome (handsomest)

Fifth, adjectives and adverbs with two syllables having any ending other than those described previously, and all adjectives and adverbs of three or more syllables, take only the periphrastic forms:

	Base form	"More"	"Most"
Adjective	curious	more curious[5]	most curious
	pleasant	more pleasant	most pleasant
	beautiful	more beautiful	most beautiful
Adverb	skillfully	more skillfully	most skillfully
	cautiously	more cautiously	most cautiously
	independently	more independently	most independently

The rules for the comparative and superlative inflections are not as rigid as those for the plural or past tense inflections. We regularly hear English speakers use a periphrastic form for emphasis (e.g., "Before this happened, I didn't believe I could be more sad") when the "rule" would predict the inflection. There is also some individual variation, and thus some speakers may prefer *quieter* and *stupider* over *more quiet* and *more stupid.* In fact, we should speak of a tendency rather than a rule when discussing this phenomenon: The variation that occurs among NAE speakers can be partially explained by the fact that the second and fourth groups of adjectives and adverbs listed above can take both the periphrastic and the inflectional forms.

For teaching purposes, once again a set of index cards with adjectives that illustrate each tendency could be used to practice the comparative and superlative inflections. The cards are divided among groups of three. After discussion and consensus, the students in each group generate sentences about themselves using the comparative and superlative forms of the adjectives they have been given. For example:

tall	José is taller than Ana, but Lev is (the) tallest (one in the group).
cautious	Chen is more cautious than Ali, but Susana is the most cautious person in the group.

If the students have any problems with the endings, you can first do a card-sort activity (as described previously) to focus on the rules before proceeding. The three choices could be set up as follows on the board:

-er/-est	"More"/"Most"	*-er/-est* [or] "More"/"Most"
short	cautious	clever
big	intelligent	quiet
tall	abrasive	subtle

[5]The use of the inflection is sometimes deliberately extended as in *Alice in Wonderland,* where author Lewis Carroll had Alice say "curiouser and curiouser" to achieve a special effect.

IRREGULAR NOUN PLURALS

There are more foreign-borrowed irregular plurals in English than native-English irregular plurals. We will not give phonological rules for Latin and Greek plurals; these are for the most part highly learned vocabulary items for which plurals must be memorized, since they have no phonological basis in English (e.g., *focus/foci; criterion/criteria; datum/data*). We will also omit treatment of those native English nouns that generally have identical singular and plural forms, since there is no phonologically based rule governing these either (e.g., *deer, elk, sheep, moose, fish*).

There are, however, some irregular English plurals that retain vestiges of the Germanic **umlaut** system. In this system, the vowel in the plural noun form becomes more fronted and/or higher because of assimilation to a vowel in the following syllable. Thus in modern German the singular *T̲a̲nz* /ɑ/ "dance" becomes *Tänze* /ɛ/ "dances" in the plural. In modern-day English, the "following syllable" is no longer in evidence, having been lost through historical change. Nonetheless, what we see today in nouns such as *foot/feet, tooth/teeth, goose/geese, man/men, mouse/mice,* and *louse/lice* are the remains of an earlier, more productive umlauting rule. This can be most clearly seen if we compare modern English to modern German, where the umlaut in spelling (¨) signals a phonetically higher or more fronted and sometimes also more rounded vowel:

Modern English	Modern German
goose/geese	Gans/Gänse
foot/feet	Fuss/Füsse
tooth/teeth	Zahn/Zähne
man/men	Mann/Männer
mouse/mice	Maus/Mäuse
louse/lice	Laus/Läuse

There are, of course, other ways of forming irregular plurals in English, such as the *-en* plural ending, which when added to singular *ox* results in the plural *oxen*. This *-en* plural also combines with vowel shortening and umlauting, respectively, when singular *child* and *brother* become plural *children* and *brethren* (although the form *brethren* is now specialized or archaic; the regular plural *brothers* is used in most contexts). Sometimes the historical umlauting process even affects two syllables, as is the case when singular *woman* /wʊmən/ becomes plural *women* /wɪmɪn/.

Another historically motivated phonological pattern occurring with irregular plurals involves those nouns that end in voiceless /f/ yet form their plural with voiced /vz/:

$$/f/ \rightarrow /vz/$$

leaf/leaves	wife/wives	shelf/shelves
half/halves	knife/knives	self/selves
wolf/wolves	scarf/scarves	thief/thieves
sheaf/sheaves	elf/elves	life/lives

This Germanic rule in English has weakened. Originally /f/ became /v/ intervocalically (which occurred when the plural inflection was added). This condition, of course, no longer applies. The weakening of the rule was probably assisted by the fact that several non-Germanic words that end in /f/ have an *-s* plural (e.g., *chief/chiefs; chef/chefs*). In fact, even some words of Germanic origin have a simple *-s* plural (e.g., *belief/beliefs, cliff/cliffs, roof/roofs*). The plural forms of certain other words appear to be in flux (*hooves vs. hoofs,* *dwarves vs. dwarfs).* Note that more recently coined countable nouns ending in /f/ take /s/ as their plural and do not end in /vz/ (e.g., *spoof/spoofs*).

Less pervasive than the singular /f/ to plural /vz/ pattern but part of the same historical voiceless to voiced alternation are singular forms ending in voiceless /θ/ and the plural in voiced /ðz/ without any corresponding change in spelling, as in *path/paths, bath/baths, moth/moths, truth/truths.* However, for many speakers of NAE, voicing of the final consonant in the plural in these word pairs does not occur.[6] There is also at least one pair in which final voiceless /s/ in the singular becomes voiced /zɪz/ in the plural *(house/houses).*

IRREGULAR VERBS

Irregular verbs are more common in English than irregular nouns. Except for a few of the most frequent examples, such as *be* and *go,* English irregular verbs tend to have phonologically definable inflectional patterns that are historically motivated (e.g., the /ɪ-æ-ʌ/ alternation of verbs like *sing/sang/sung* and *begin/began/begun).*[7] These recognizable patterns make it easier to learn irregular verbs than if the forms were totally arbitrary. (See Appendix 8 for a detailed discussion of irregular verbs.)

The following six sound-based groups of irregular verbs are derived from the Old English *weak verb* system, which indicated a change in tense through the addition of a dental ending:

1. Verbs with /d/ in the base form and /t/ in the past tense and the participle:

/d/	/t/	/t/
build	built	built
lend	lent	lent
send	sent	sent

2. Verbs ending in /d/ or /t/ undergoing no change in the past tense and participle forms:

let	let	let
put	put	put
rid	rid	rid

3. Verbs with /iy/ in the base form and /ɛ/ + /t/ in the past tense and past participle forms:

/iy/	/ɛ/	/ɛ/
creep	crept	crept
leave	left	left
mean	meant	meant

4. Verbs with historically shortened vowels in the past tense and past participle forms:

/iy/	/ɛ/	/ɛ/
feed	fed	fed
read	read	read

/ay/	/ɪ/	/ɪ/
light	lit	lit
slide	slid	slid

---

[6]Such variation may occur because the spelling does not reflect the sound change as it does in cases like *life/lives.*

[7]For comprehensive accounts of the irregular verb system in English, see R. E. Diamond (1970) and Brinton (1989).

/uw/	/ɑ, ɔ/	/ɑ, ɔ/
lose	lost	lost
shoot	shot	shot

5. Verbs with past tense and past participle forms ending in /ɔt/, spelled *-aught* or *-ought:*

buy	bought	bought
catch	caught	caught
think	thought	thought

6. Verbs with /ɛ/ + /l/ in the base form and /ow/ + /ld/ in the past tense and past participle forms:

/ɛ/	/ow/	/ow/
sell	sold	sold
tell	told	told

In addition, there are seven groups of verbs deriving from the Old English **strong verb** system, which indicated a change in tense through a change in the root vowel:

1. Verbs exhibiting a three-part vowel change from base form to past tense to past participle forms:

/ɪ/	/æ/	/ʌ/
begin	began	begun
ring	rang	rung
swim	swam	swum

2. Verbs with identical past tense and past participle forms:

dig	dug	dug
hold	held	held
win	won	won

3. Verbs with the same vowel sound in the past tense and past participle + an *-n* /n/ or *-en* /ən/ ending in the participle:

freeze	froze	frozen
steal	stole	stolen
weave	wove	woven

4. Verbs with long *i* /ay/ in the base form, /ow/ in the past tense, and short *i* /ɪ/ with *-en* in the participle:

/ay/	/ow/	/ɪ/
drive	drove	driven
rise	rose	risen
write	wrote	written

5. Verbs with identical base forms and past participle forms with a vowel change in the past tense only:

run	ran	run
come	came	come

6. Verbs with a vowel change in the past tense form but with base and past participle forms that are identical except for the addition of a final -*n* /n/ or -*en* /ən/ to the participle:

blow	blew	blown
eat	ate	eaten
fall	fell	fallen

7. Verbs that are completely irregular (i.e., are a composite of forms from originally different verbs and thus follow no discernible pattern):

go	went	gone
am/is/are	was/were	been

The teacher who is aware of these patterns can use the sounds as an effective aid to presenting English irregular verbs. One controlled practice suggestion drawn from Olson and Shalek (1981) directs teachers to prepare two large poster-board pocket charts (one for each of the historical classes deriving from the Old English verb system). The charts would contain a representation of a tree with the pockets representing its branches – six for the weak verb system and seven for the strong verb system. Each pocket would be illustrated with one example of the three principal parts of a verb belonging to that class. The teacher should prepare in advance a stack of index cards, each indicating the base form of a verb belonging to the weak or strong verbs system, respectively (see Appendix 8 for a more comprehensive list). The cards should be distributed among class members, who are asked to produce the principal parts of the verb and place the card in the correct pocket. More advanced learners can be asked to create simple sentences illustrating the verb tenses before placing the card in the pocket chart.

The two charts should not be presented simultaneously to students due to the amount of information being transmitted. Instead, we suggest that teachers focusing on irregular verbs familiarize their students first with one historical class of verbs and then the other. Each pocket chart can be used for brief review and practice sessions over the course of several lessons and can later be used to recycle the topic as the need arises.

PART-OF-SPEECH ALTERNATIONS

The part of speech of English words is often signaled phonologically. For example, there are etymologically related nouns and verbs where the noun ends in a voiceless fricative and the verb in a voiced fricative (e.g., *excuse* /ɪk'skyuws/ and *excuse* /ɪk'skyuwz/). Examples of these etymologically related word pairs (which may include other minor vowel-sound differences between the alternating forms) include:

Noun (voiceless final consonant)	Verb (voiced final consonant)
/s/	/z/
use	use
house	house
abuse	abuse
excuse	excuse
spouse	espouse
loss	lose
advice	advise
choice	choose

/θ/	/ð/
bath	bathe
teeth	teethe
mouth	mouthe
cloth	clothe

/f/	/v/
shelf	shelve
life	live
grief	grieve
half	halve
safe	save
belief	believe
relief	relieve
proof	prove

Note that these noun–verb pairs involve the same voicing changes and the same sounds that we observed earlier for the singular and plural forms of certain irregular nouns.

Whether they function as verbs or adjectives, most English words ending in the *-ed* suffix follow the same phonological rules as the past tense inflectional ending (e.g., *striped* /t/, *forked* /t/, *cultured* /d/, *used* /d/, *moneyed* /d/, *furrowed* /d/, *good-natured* /d/, *gray-haired* /d/, *blue-eyed* /d/). There are, however, historically based differences in pronunciation between certain forms ending in *-ed,* depending on whether they function as adjectives or verbs. The *-ed* adjectives in this category have an extra syllable and take the /ɪd/ pronunciation,[8] whereas the verbs simply take /t/ or /d/, following the rules for the regular past tense and regular past participle outlined earlier:

Verb	**Adjective**
blessed /t/	blessed /ɪd/
(He blessed us.)	*(the blessed virgin)*
beloved /d/	beloved /ɪd/
(She is beloved by him.)	*(a beloved elder)*
learned /d/	learned /ɪd/
(We learned a lot.)	*(a learned gentleman)*
dogged /d/	dogged /ɪd/
(They dogged my steps.)	*(dogged determination)*
legged /d/	legged /ɪd/
(We legged it out of there.)	*(a three-legged stool)*

Sometimes, even when there is an adjective with no corresponding verb, the adjective is still pronounced /ɪd/ *(naked, wretched, rugged, wicked).*[9] Also, in some cases the pronunciation of an *-ed* adjective may vary from speaker to speaker or according to (1) the meaning the word has (e.g., *a learned gentleman* /ɪd/ vs. *learned behavior* /d/) or (2) the register (e.g., poetic language vs. ordinary conversation).

Teachers wishing to review the three possible pronunciations of the *-ed* suffix with students may wish to have them practice reading simple dialogues that focus attention on this particular aspect of the English sound system. For example, Figure 8.5 shows a

[8]Occasionally there can also be a noun form derived from an /ɪd/ adjective (e.g., "This is my *beloved*").
[9]Adverbs ending in *-edly* and nouns ending in *-edness* generally pronounce the *-ed* as /ɪd/ (*supposedly, advisedly, (un)reservedly, markedly;* also *markedness, (un)reservedness*). This is true even if there is a related adjective form that is pronounced as /t/ or /d/ (e.g., marked /t/, reserved /d/).

Directions: With your partner, discuss the pronunciation of the *-ed* endings in the words below. Then write the correct pronunciation in the diagonal marks provided: /t/, /d/, and /ɪd/. Listen to the dialogue and check your predictions. Practice reading the dialogue, focusing particularly on the correct pronunciation of the endings.

Sam: So, you visit<u>ed</u> the marital counselor I recommend<u>ed</u>?
        / /   / /

Laura: Yes, we visit<u>ed</u> him, and wast<u>ed</u> fifteen minutes of our
        / /   / /

        valuable time!

Larry: Not to mention the fact that he char<u>ged</u> us an arm and a leg!
                                              / /

Laura: For once, I agree with you. We were definitely ripp<u>ed</u> off!
                                                            / /

Larry: Well, I warn<u>ed</u> you it would be a waste of time, but
                  / /

        you insist<u>ed</u> we go.
              / /

Laura: I insist<u>ed</u>? You drag<u>ged</u> me there!
              / /   / /

Sam: Laura, Larry, control yourselves! You should
        be asham<u>ed</u>, fighting like a pack of four-leg<u>ged</u> animals.
              / /   / /

Larry: She start<u>ed</u> it.
              / /

Laura: No, he did. He claim<u>ed</u> it was my fault.
                          / /

Sam: Let's stick to the nak<u>ed</u> facts. Tell me exactly what
                            / /

        Dr. Otter talk<u>ed</u> to you about.
                   / /

Laura: Not a bless<u>ed</u> thing! We wait<u>ed</u> over an hour in the reception
              / /   / /

        room, and then his secretary usher<u>ed</u> us into the office.
                                          / /

Larry: Then after five minutes, he glan<u>ced</u> at his watch and
                                        / /

        stat<u>ed</u> that he had another appointment.
        / /

Laura: What wretch<u>ed</u> treatment! I've never been so offend<u>ed</u>!
                  / /   / /

Larry: I warn<u>ed</u> you it would be a waste of time, didn't I?
              / /

Laura: You warn<u>ed</u> me? Who call<u>ed</u> and made the appointment?
              / /   / /

Figure 8.5 Worksheet for predicting pronunciation of past-tense and adjective *-ed* endings in a dialogue

teacher-written dialogue in which Laura and Larry discuss a visit they made to a marital counselor with their neighbor Sam.

Another type of verb and noun/adjective alternation is words ending in *-ate;* the verbs always end in a lightly stressed syllable with a full vowel sound /eyt/, whereas the adjectives or nouns generally end in an unstressed syllable with a reduced vowel sound /ət/:

Verb form:	DUplicATE	/eyt/
Adjective or noun form:	DUplicATE	/ət/

Words exhibiting this duality in their part of speech for most speakers of NAE include: *advocate, alternate, animate, appropriate, approximate, articulate, associate, delegate, deliberate, duplicate, elaborate, estimate, graduate, intimate, legitimate, moderate, precipitate,* and *separate.* There are also many *-ate* words that function only as verbs and thus occur only with the /eyt/ ending, for example: *celebrate, collate, demonstrate, appreciate, depreciate, dominate, educate, elevate, evaluate, fascinate, inundate, relegate, rotate,* and *simulate.* A smaller number of words function only as adjectives (and/or nouns) and thus end only in /ət/, for example:[10] *accurate, consulate, (in)adequate, desperate, (un)fortunate, delicate,* and *passionate.*

There are also part-of-speech differences signaled by word stress patterns in two-syllable prefix + stem nouns and verbs of Latinate origin, which we noted in Chapter 5:

Noun		**Verb**[11]	
CONduct	/ˈkɑnˌdʌkt/	conDUCT	/kənˈdʌkt/
CONflict	/ˈkɑnˌflɪkt/	conFLICT	/kənˈflɪkt/
CONtest	/ˈkɑnˌtɛst/	conTEST	/kənˈtɛst/
CONtract	/ˈkɑnˌtrækt/	conTRACT	/kənˈtrækt/
CONtrast	/ˈkɑnˌtræst/	conTRAST	/kənˈtræst/
CONvert	/ˈkɑnˌvɜʳt/	conVERT	/kənˈvɜʳt/
DESert	/ˈdɛzəʳt/	deSERT	/dəˈzɜʳt/
INcline	/ˈɪnˌklayn/	inCLINE	/ɪnˈklayn/
INcrease	/ˈɪnˌkriys/	inCREASE	/ɪnˈkriys/
INsert	/ˈɪnˌsɜʳt/	inSERT	/ɪnˈsɜʳt/
INsult	/ˈɪnˌsʌlt/	inSULT	/ɪnˈsʌlt/
OBject	/ˈɑbˌdʒɪkt/	obJECT	/əbˈdʒɛkt/
PERmit	/ˈpɜʳˌmɪt/	perMIT	/pəʳˈmɪt/
PROgress	/ˈprɑˌgrɛs/	proGRESS	/prəˈgrɛs/
PROject	/ˈprɑˌdʒɛkt/	proJECT	/prəˈdʒɛkt/
PROtest	/ˈprowˌtɛst/	proTEST	/prəˈtɛst/
REBel	/ˈrɛbəl/	reBEL	/rəˈbɛl/
RECord	/ˈrɛkəʳd/	reCORD	/rəˈkɔrd/
SURvey	/ˈsɜʳˌvey/	surVEY	/səʳˈvey/
SUSpect	/ˈsʌsˌpɛkt/	suSPECT	/səˈspɛkt/

[10]There are some exceptions for *-ate* nouns and adjectives. Those that regularly are pronounced /eyt/ instead of /ət/ include: *mandate, acetate, magistrate,* and *concentrate.*

[11]There is some variation among NAE speakers showing a tendency to stress the first syllable of the verb as well as the noun. For example, some speakers say *to PROtest,* or *to SURvey.* (List adapted from *Manual of English Pronunciation.* Fourth Edition by Clifford H. Prator and Betty W. Robinett, copyright © by Holt, Rinehart and Winston, Inc., reproduced by permission.)

This tendency toward stress differences does not constitute a rule, however, since in a number of such pairs both the noun and verb members have the same stress pattern:

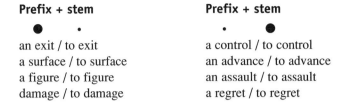

Prefix + stem	Prefix + stem
● ·	· ●
an exit / to exit	a control / to control
a surface / to surface	an advance / to advance
a figure / to figure	an assault / to assault
damage / to damage	a regret / to regret

Part-of-speech differences are also signaled through word stress differences in certain Germanic noun and verb pairs that consist of a prefix + stem combination. In such cases, the nouns behave like noun compounds and have strong stress on the prefix element and light stress on the stem; verbs have light stress on the prefix element and strong stress on the stem:[12]

Noun (prefix + stem)	Verb (prefix + stem)
● (·) ·	· (·) ●
an OverFLOW	to overFLOW
an OverLOAD	to overLOAD
an OverCHARGE	to overCHARGE
an OverLAP	to overLAP
an OverRUN	to overRUN
an OUTGROWTH	to OUTGROW
an OFFSET	to OFFSET

Many such prefix + stem words exist only as nouns, and they reflect that fact in their stress pattern:

● ·

OFFSPRING
OUTPUT
OUTLET
OUTLOOK

However, even more such prefix + stem words exist only as verbs; again, the part of speech is reflected in the stress pattern:

· ●	· · ●
OUTDO	overHEAT
OUTCLASS	overCOME
OUTBID	overEAT
OUTPLAY	overDO
OUTLIVE	overSLEEP

---

[12]Occasionally the noun will end with some other derivational signal *(-th, -er)* that helps to identify the part-of-speech difference reflected in the stress pattern.

THE GENERATION GAP

Directions: Read the following passage to yourself and try to determine the stress pattern and pronunciation of each underlined word. Then read it aloud before discussing the topic at the end.

    Sometimes there is a <u>conflict</u> of interest between parents and teenagers. Young people feel the need to <u>rebel</u>, to become <u>separate</u> individuals in their own right. Parents often feel such <u>conduct</u> is not <u>appropriate</u>, especially when their sons or daughters <u>isolate</u> themselves from the family or when they <u>insult</u> their elders. Young people <u>advocate</u> that they be <u>permitted</u> to set their own limits and not be <u>obligated</u> to follow their parents' "rigid" ideas. However, most parents still prefer to exercise some control over their children until they <u>graduate</u> from high school. Perhaps children should feel <u>fortunate</u> to have parents who are willing to guide their <u>offspring</u> at the risk of losing their affection.

Discussion topic: Describe the relationship between parents and teenagers in your country.

Figure 8.6 Worksheet for controlled and communicative practice with stress differences

When teaching how differences in stress can signal the part of speech, the teacher can highlight noun/adjective and verb pairs such as:

Noun/adjective	Verb
RECord	reCORD
CONflict	conFLICT
GRADuate	GRADuATE
OFFset	offSET

One technique for raising students' awareness of these stress differences is to write the grammatical category on the board, provide a few examples, and elicit further examples from students.

    The passage in Figure 8.6 above contains several examples of these types of words. Note that the first step (reading the passage aloud) is quite controlled, allowing the student to rehearse vocabulary relevant to the topic. The second step then moves into more communicative practice. Students can also record this passage as homework and bring it in for the teacher to evaluate.

    Students who are engaged in using English for academic or professional purposes should be encouraged to look for instances of words like these in the texts they read. Using the explanations that have been presented in class, they can then begin to determine the accurate pronunciation of the words.

CONCLUSION

Although second language learners often receive extensive grammar instruction (including past tense, plurals, possessive, parts of speech) at an early stage, the pronunciation aspect of such grammar lessons is not always well addressed. This lack of integration between grammar and pronunciation can affect other areas of language proficiency, such as listening, speaking, and writing. For example, if learners are unaware of the three phonological realizations for the regular past tense ending, they are likely to confuse present and past tense utterances. In addition, these markers may be missing from their speech and writing. Thus, this is clearly an area where teachers and textbook writers, especially at the beginning level, need to give greater attention to pronunciation.

In this chapter we have examined many of the segmental and suprasegmental sound alternations that reflect the regular morphological inflections and part-of-speech alterations in English – that is, the major relationships between phonology and morphology. We have also provided teachers with specific pedagogical suggestions for highlighting these connections. The next chapter deals with the relationship between the English sound system and the English writing system.

EXERCISES

KEY CONCEPTS

Write a brief definition of the following key terms from this chapter. Give examples where relevant.

morphology	periphrastic comparative
inflectional morphology	umlaut
derivational morphology	weak verb
8 regular inflections	strong verb
morphophonology	

INTROSPECTING ABOUT YOUR OWN LANGUAGE LEARNING

If you are a native speaker of English, think about a foreign language that you have learned in school or while living abroad. If you are a nonnative speaker of English, think about your learning of English.

1. Can you recall any grammatical aspect of the language that was related to pronunciation? If so, did your instructor explicitly show you these relationships? How?

2. Do you recall learning any phonological differences in the parts of speech?

DISCUSSION QUESTIONS

1. Why is it important to integrate work with morphophonology into a general skills language course?

2. When and how should dictation be used to reinforce and practice work in inflectional morphology?

3. If a student pronounces *cats* as /kæt/ and *dogs* as /dɔg/, how can a teacher determine whether the student has a grammatical problem or a pronunciation problem?

4. Which information about the history of English in this chapter or in Appendix 8 do you think would be most essential to teach to ESL/EFL learners?

IN THE CLASSROOM

Assume that you are teaching pronunciation. Here are some common classroom situations that you might encounter. What technique would you use or what explanation would you give?

1. You have a student who pronounces the past tense of all regular verbs with an /ɛd/ ending when he speaks.

2. Several of your students pronounce all words ending in -ate as /eyt/ regardless of the part of speech.

3. The inability of two of your students to distinguish /s/ and /z/ extends to their pronunciation of plural nouns and other parts of speech.

4. A student asks you why the plural of *wife* is *wives* but the plural of *chief* is *chiefs*.

5. You have students who do not know the major parts of speech (noun, verb, adjective). Choose one of the rules described in this chapter (e.g., plural of regular nouns, past tense of regular verbs, comparative forms of adjectives) and discuss how you would present it.

SUGGESTED ACTIVITIES

1. Interview and record a nonnative speaker about a past event in his or her life. Does the student have pronunciation problems with past tense endings? Do you notice any other problems with inflectional morphology or part-of-speech distinctions?

2. Look at the passage entitled "The Generation Gap" (Figure 8.6), which has been created to practice part-of-speech differences in stress. Write an original passage that would provide learners with contextualized practice in applying stress patterns in part-of-speech alternations.

3. Select one of the functions of the -s morphological ending (plurals, possessive, third-person singular) and write a short dialogue to provide students with practice in pronouncing this ending.

4. Develop an activity for teaching the -s ending for third-person singular present tense to an ESL/EFL class that includes a pronunciation focus.

5. Read an article about a second language acquisition study that focuses on the acquisition of morphemes in ESL. What did you learn from the paper? Did the author(s) mention phonological factors or pronunciation? If so, explain.

ON THE CASSETTE

1. Listen to the cassette and transcribe the -s endings used for words 1–20.
2. For words 21–40, transcribe the -ed endings.

CHAPTER 9

The Sound System and Orthography

It is important for ESL/EFL teachers to understand the correspondences between English phonology and English orthography so that they can teach their learners (1) how to predict the pronunciation of a word given its spelling and (2) how to come up with a plausible spelling for a word given its pronunciation. English learners who are already literate in their first language may experience learning problems due to the writing system of their first language. The system may be completely different from English (i.e., nonalphabetic) or it may involve a different alphabet (e.g., Cyrillic). It may even be a Roman alphabet with different sound–letter correspondences (e.g., Spanish vs. English). Each situation brings special challenges in teaching spelling, reading, and pronunciation.

It is also important for teachers to be aware that the English writing system often has an influence on how literate users of English perceive the English sound system, whether or not they are native speakers. For example, we occasionally hear from our teachers-to-be and advanced ESL/EFL students misconceptions such as "English has five vowel sounds" or "the choice between *a* and *an* depends on how the following word is spelled." We will return to these misconceptions in the conclusion of this chapter.

When they are fluent speakers but not highly literate, both native and nonnative speakers of English tend to allow their knowledge of the spoken language to influence their spelling. Such native speakers may write *photagraph* instead of *photograph, grammer* instead of *grammar;* such nonnative speakers may write *grin* instead of *green, writting* instead of *writing, light* instead of *right*. The nonnative spellings may reflect the learners' imperfect control of the English sound system, transfer from the sound system of their native language, or inadequate understanding and control of English orthographic conventions – especially sound–spelling correspondences. Thus both native and nonnative misspellings can be better analyzed if we understand from the outset that English spelling is based on morphological and lexical as well as phonological regularities.

It has long been established that English spelling has an indirect and somewhat complex relationship with pronunciation (see Chomsky and Halle 1968). As Carol Chomsky (1970) points out, English spelling frequently correlates with lexical representation, a level of linguistic processing that is beneath the surface and that is related to pronunciation by regular morphophonological processes – some of which are sometimes fairly complex, as we shall illustrate.

In the case of students who are fully literate, we disagree with language teaching professionals who believe that English pronunciation should be taught using only the writing system, without imposing the burden of a phonemic alphabet or additional symbols. English orthography, although fairly systematic in its own right, is simply too abstract to be phonetically (or phonemically) optimal, for it lacks the principle of one-to-one symbol–sound correspondence. It is our experience that a separate phonemic alphabet is a useful tool not only for teaching pronunciation but for creating some psychological distance between the sound system and the writing system. Such a separation helps both in teaching pronunciation and in presenting the correspondences between the English writing system and the English sound system. It is also useful for presenting some of the conventions of English spelling, which has many rules that are based in part on sounds.

Of course, when ESL learners are preliterate or semiliterate, the situation is different and the introduction of a phonemic alphabet is unnecessarily burdensome. See Chapters 3–5 (and also our discussion of Silent Way in Chapter 1) for suggestions on teaching pronunciation and spelling to this type of learner population.

THE ALPHABET

One of the most basic connections between the English sound system and the writing system is the pronunciation of the letters of the English alphabet.[1] Over the years we have had many ESL/EFL students who could not accurately comprehend and pronounce the letters of the English alphabet, often to the detriment of their ability to communicate. Even some of our intermediate and advanced learners could not orally spell their names and other basic information in a comprehensible manner.

There are five groupings of letters according to the vowel sound used to pronounce them:

The /iy/ group:	B, C, D, E, G, P, T, V, Z
The /ɛ/ group:	F, L, M, N, S, X
The /ey/ group:	A, H, J, K
The /yuw/ group:	Q, U, W
The /ay/ group:	I, Y

The two remaining letters, (*o* /ow/ and *r* /ɑr/, have unique sounds. There is one notable difference between British English and NAE in the way the alphabet is pronounced: In NAE *z* is in the /iy/ group and is pronounced /ziy/, but in British English it is in the /ɛ/ group and pronounced /zɛd/.

It is important for learners of English to be able to pronounce the English alphabet clearly and accurately, for they are often asked in the course of everyday communication to spell their names or other words for accuracy or clarification. Conversely, native speakers will orally spell personal names and place names for learners on the assumption that the learners can process and comprehend the letters of the English alphabet.

With reference to the alphabet, it is also important for teachers and learners to know which letters can represent vowel sounds and which can represent consonant sounds. The following six vowel letters each represent two or more vowel sounds (long and short vowel sounds will be discussed shortly): *a, e, i, o, u,* and *y* (although *i* and *y* represent more or less the same set of sounds).

Vowel digraphs are sequences of two vowel letters that may be the same or different: *seem, lead*. They may also be sequences of V + *y* (*day, boy*), V + *w* (*row, pew*) or *y* + *e* (*dye, rye*).[2]

---

[1]The children's game "Hangman," as explained in Chapter 4, provides an enjoyable way to practice in the pronunciation of the English alphabet letters.
[2]There are even a few vowel trigraphs with *y* and *w* as the second letter: *aye, ewe.*

The following letters represent consonant sounds: *b, c, d, f, g, h, j, k, l, m, n, p, q, r, s, t, v, w, x, y,* and *z.* In addition, the letter *u* represents a consonant pronounced as /w/ in the following environments:

- between *q* and a vowel letter that is not final *e: qᴜestion, seqᴜence, liqᴜid*
- between *ng* and a vowel letter that is not final *e: langᴜage, distingᴜish, pengᴜin*

On the other hand, the letter *u* is silent in the following environments:

- between *q* and final *e: critiqᴜe, mosqᴜe, physiqᴜe*
- between *g* and the vowel letters *e* and *i: gᴜest, disgᴜise, tongᴜe*

Elsewhere in NAE *u* represents a consonant + vowel (CV) sequence when it is pronounced /yuw/ – that is, syllable initially and after *b, c, f, h,* and *p* in long-vowel patterns: *ᴜse, ᴜranium, bᴜtte, cᴜte, fᴜse, hᴜge, pᴜre.*[3]

Thus we have three letters (*y, w,* and *u*) that can be listed among both the letters representing vowel sounds and the letters representing consonant sounds. The *u* is a vowel except in those limited environments where it serves the two consonant functions. The *w* represents a vowel only as the second letter in vowel digraphs (*boᴡ, peᴡ, broᴡn*); in all other contexts (i.e., syllable initially), *w* represents a consonant sound (*ᴡe, aᴡay*). The *y* represents a vowel after a consonant letter (C*y*), as in *style, gym, my,* and after a vowel letter (V*y*), as in *guy, gray, enjoy.*

The vowel letter *y* (like *i*) represents two stressed vowel sounds:

	/ɪ/	/ay/
y	cyst	my, type
i	fist	hi, ripe

Although all combinations of letter and syllable type are possible for *i* and *y,* in closed syllables, *i* is the most common spelling for these two sounds. In open syllables, *y* occurs frequently as a word-final letter representing both stressed and unstressed vowels: stressed *my, sky, why;* unstressed *lucky, gladly, glory.*

SPELLING-TO-SOUND CORRESPONDENCES FOR VOWELS

The English language uses the five vowel letters of the Roman alphabet *(a, e, i, o, u)* and the letters *y* and *w* (C*y*, V*y*, V*w*) to represent more than a dozen distinct vowel sounds. These vowel letters and vowel digraphs can represent ten different stressed sounds that are traditionally contrasted as "short" and "long" vowels:

Letter	Short sound		Long sound	
a	/æ/	fat	/ey/	fate, Fay
e	/ɛ/	met	/iy/	meat, me
i, y	/ɪ/	bit, tryst	/ay/	bite, hi, type, by
o	/ɑ/	mop	/ow/	mope, mow
u	/ʌ/	mutt	/(y)uw/	mute, moo

These short and long vowel sounds include all stressed English vowel sounds other than /ʊ/, /ɔ/, /ɔy/, /aw/, and /ɝ/, which do not have long and short vowel counterparts but are nevertheless spelled in distinctive ways with some of the same vowel letters. Although

---

[3]Note that *u* is also /yuw/ after *t, d,* and *n* in British English in long-vowel patterns: *tune, due, news.* See Appendix 1 for other British vs. NAE differences in pronunciation.

the "short" sound for each letter in the foregoing list tends to reflect the phonemic transcription of the vowel, the "long" sound represents the pronunciation of the vowel letter.

As we explained previously, phonologists often use the terms *lax* (or lenis) and *tense* (or fortis) rather than *short* and *long*. Although historically there was a difference in length, this no longer applies. Rather, today the differences between the two kinds of vowel sounds are due to differences in muscular tension rather than to differences in length. Thus we will henceforth refer to this distinction as tense and lax rather than long and short (see also Chapter 4). Also, the tense–lax distinction is phonologically important since lax vowels cannot occur in open syllables and must be followed by a consonant – that is, the syllable must be closed ((C)VC). Tense vowels, on the other hand, can occur either in syllable–final open syllables ((C)V) or in closed syllables ((C)VC).

These tense–lax vowel distinctions are signaled through at least four orthographic means (see also Dickerson 1994b):

1. Lax sounds are often spelled with a vowel letter followed by at least one consonant letter (VC). Tense vowels are often spelled with a vowel letter followed by a consonant plus a word-final silent *e* (VC*e*).

Letter	Lax vowel		Tense vowel	
a	rat	/æ/	rate	/ey/
e	met	/ɛ/	mete	/iy/
i	bit	/ɪ/	bite	/ay/
o	rot	/ɑ/	rote	/ow/
u	cut	/ʌ/	cute	/(y)uw/

Some syllables with lax vowels end in two consonant letters (which may be identical or different): *add, tell, off, pend, felt, loft.*

2. Another means of signaling lax vowels is through medial consonant letters doubling, which does not occur with tense vowels. Compare:

Letter	Lax vowel		Tense vowel	
a	latter	/æ/	later	/ey/
e	Eddie	/ɛ/	Edie	/iy/
i	pinning	/ɪ/	pining	/ay/
o	mopping	/ɑ/	moping	/ow/
u	rubble	/ʌ/	ruble	/uw/

3. In closed syllables, tense vowels can be signaled by the use of a vowel digraph before the final consonant: e.g., *eat, meet, boot, boat, bail, boil, bawl, bowl.*[4]

4. In open syllables, tense vowels are signaled through the use of a vowel digraph ending in *w* or *y: low, how, may, buy.* In closed syllables, tense vowels can be signaled with a vowel digraph ending in *w: howl, dawn, sewn.*

THE GREAT ENGLISH VOWEL SHIFT

Historically, the so-called pairs of tense and lax vowel sounds were indeed closer to being long and short variants of a similar sound; however, during an earlier period in most dialects of English, all of the long vowels shifted upward very gradually and developed glides. For example, the two highest long vowels, /i:/ and /u:/, moved down toward /a/ but

---

[4]This combination does not always signal a tense vowel. There are numerous exceptions in words spelled with the digraphs *ea, oo,* and *ou: bread, look, could.*

revealed their historical source as glides in the diphthongs /ay/ and /aw/. That is, the approximant /y/ is phonologically related to the vowel /iy/, and the approximant /w/ is related to the vowel /uw/:

Before shift (Middle English)		After shift (Modern English)	
/æ:/	*næme* "name"	/ey/	name
/e:/	*hete* "heat"	/iy/	heat
/i:/	*i* "I"	/ay/	I
/o:/	*mone* "moon"	/uw/	moon
/u:/	*hus* "house"	/aw/	house

Historical linguists refer to this sound change as the **Great English Vowel Shift;** it was a long and gradual process that took place approximately between 1450 and 1700 and that was fully generalized by about 1750.

English spelling is abstract and generally reflects the lexicon and morphology of the language (i.e., etymological and grammatical relations). This can be seen very clearly if we examine derivational suffixes such as *-ity, -ic(al),* and *-tion.* When such suffixes do not change the stress pattern of the word in question, the stressed vowel will systematically change from tense in the base to lax in the corresponding derivative for the five vowels we have been discussing. This reinforces the lexical-etymological relationship between these tense and lax sounds:

Letter	Vowel shift	Base form (stressed tense vowel)	Derivative form (stressed lax vowel)
a	/ey/ → /æ/	sane, state	sanity, static
e	/iy/ → /ɛ/	serene, discreet	serenity, discretion
i	/ay/ → /ɪ/	cycle, divine	cyclic, divinity
o	/ow/ → /ɑ/	tone, verbose	tonic, verbosity
u	/uw/ → /ʌ/	assume, reduce	assumption, reduction

See Appendix 9 for a more complete listing of these five tense–lax vowel shift patterns in such base forms and derivatives.

STRESSED AND UNSTRESSED VOWELS AND THEIR SPELLING PATTERNS

The spelling patterns in closed syllables that traditionally reflect lax vowel sounds ((C)VC or (C)VCC) and in patterns that typically suggest tense vowel sounds ((C)VC*e*, (C)VVC, and (C)V*y* or (C)V*w*), although useful, have their limitations; they work only for words of one syllable or in words where the syllable with the vowel in question is stressed. Often the problem for the learner is knowing whether the vowel is stressed or not. In multisyllabic words, in fact, we are dealing with several vowel qualities: tense and lax, stressed and unstressed. (See Chapters 5 and 7 for additional stress rules.)

KEY STRONG STRESS RULE

To predict the stress pattern of multisyllabic words from their spelling, we turn to the work of Dickerson (1981, 1987b, 1989a,b, 1994b), which gives us a number of very useful rules. One such rule applies to 10,000 or so English words ending in suffixes with an *i*V sequence, where *i* is followed by *a, o,* or *u* in the suffixes *-ion, -ian, -ial, -ious, -ia, -io, -ium,* and *-ius.* According to this **key strong stress rule,** the syllable to the left of the *i*V sequence, called the **key syllable,** is strongly stressed, leaving the *i*V sequence itself (and any second syllable to the left of the stressed syllable) unstressed (the following examples reflect Dickerson's lexical syllable divisions rather than conventional dictionary entries):

AS•ia	LES•ion	NOX•ious
aph•AS•ia	co•HES·ion	ob•NOX•ious

If there is an additional (i.e., third) syllable on the left of the iV sequence, this syllable receives light stress:

PO•ly•NES•ia   OP•er•AT•ion   SU•per•CIL•ious

If the stressed syllable is spelled (C)VC, it has a tense vowel unless it is spelled iC (*initial*). If it is spelled VCC or CVCC, it has a lax vowel sound.[5]

STRESS IN POLYSYLLABIC WORDS WITH WEAK ENDINGS

Dickerson (1987b, 1989a) provides two more rules for predicting stress from the spelling of those polysyllabic words that have weak endings. These endings include *-al, -an, -ance, -ancy, -ant, -en* (noun), *-ence, -ency, -ent, -ide, -is, -ite, -oid, -on, -um,* and *-us*.[6] In short, this set includes many of the word endings not in the iV set discussed earlier. Several conditions govern these weak endings in multisyllabic words:

• If only one syllable precedes the weak ending, that preceding syllable is stressed. If the preceding syllable has a (C)VC spelling pattern, which standing alone would signal a lax vowel, the vowel of this preceding syllable is tense when followed by a weak ending, which functions much like a silent *e* to lengthen the preceding vowel sound:

CVC (lax vowel)	CVC + weak ending (tense vowel)
sin	sin + us
pot	pot + ent
cub	cub + oid
leg	leg + al
fat	fat + al

• When there are two or more syllables to the left of the weak ending, the key syllable always begins with a vowel letter. If this key syllable is spelled V or VC, the stress falls on the **left syllable** – that is, the syllable to the left of the key syllable. Left syllables contain lax vowels. The only exception to this would be left syllables containing the spelling *u*, in which case the left syllable has a tense vowel:

V key syllable	VC key syllable	VC key syllable with "u" in left syllable
GRAD•(u)•al	a•NAL•(ys)•is	NUM•(er)•ous
STREN•(u)•ous	MED•(ic)•al	a•LUM•(in)•um
con•TIN•(u)•um	MIL•(it)•ant	PUN•(it)•ive

---

[5]Recall that the letter *x* stands for two consonant sounds: /ks/.
[6]The weak endings noted are clues to use the V/VC Weak Stress Rule, discussed shortly. Other weak endings, namely, *-able, -age, -ar, -ary, -ative, -atory, -ature, -ed, -en, -er, -ery, -est, -ile, -ish* (adj.), *-ive, -or, -ory, -ure,* and *-y* (adj.) are clues to use the second weak stress rule, the Prefix Weak Stress Rule.

- If the key syllable is spelled VV(C) or VCC – or any way other than V or VC – then the key syllable retains strong stress, with VV(C) signaling a tense vowel and VCC a lax vowel quality:

VV(C) key **(tense vowel)**	**VCC key** **(lax vowel)**
flamb•(OY)•ant	ab•(YSM)•al
am•(OEB)•oid	pat•(ERN)•al
thes•(AUR)•us	syn•(OPS)•is

To further simplify these rules, Dickerson (1989a) reduces the three conditions to one, and calls the rule the V/VC Weak Stress Rule:

RULE: From a V or VC key, stress left; if you cannot stress left, stress key.

With such formulations, Dickerson shows that stress patterns and vowel quality can be predicted from spelling. From his articles and practical materials, we learn that it is both possible and desirable to teach nonnative speakers to make these kinds of predictions about word stress and vowel quality.

STRESS IN WORDS WITH TERMINAL -Y

One further very useful rule from Dickerson (1984, 1989a) applies to most words with a terminal -y.[7] To predict the stress, Dickerson suggests that students find the key syllable to the left of the -y and underline it. Next, they need to find the left syllable and stress it.[8] The key syllable is unstressed as is any other syllable immediately preceding the left syllable. The stressed left syllable has a lax vowel if it is (C)VC:

Word	Unstressed other syllable	Stressed left syllable (C)VC	Unstressed key syllable	-y
vanity		**VAN**	it	y
profanity	pro	**FAN**	it	y
melody		**MEL**	od	y
energy		**EN**	erg	y
anomaly	a	**NOM**	al	y

When the left syllable is (C)V, the stressed vowel is tense:

Word	Stressed left syllable (C)V	Unstressed key syllable	-y
deity	**DE**	it	y
laity	**LA**	it	y
poetry	**PO**	etr	y

---

[7]This rule accounts for the stress-final -y nouns of three or more syllables and final -fy verbs but excludes words with final -ary, -ery, -ory, -ancy, -ency, -iary, -iancy, and -iency, which represent either weak endings or the -iV sequence rule.

[8]For those -y terminal words with only two syllables, the key syllable is stressed: DIRTy, TREATy, PITy, BOOTy.

This rule can be extended by noting that the terminal *-y* becomes *-i* before a weak ending (e.g., *modifier, melodies*). In such cases the key is to the left of the whole weak ending including the *-i* terminal, and the same rules apply:

Word	Unstressed other syllable	Stressed left syllable	Unstressed key syllable	Terminal + weak ending
melodies		**MEL**	od	ies
modifier		**MOD**	if	ier
indemnities	in	**DEMN**	it	ies

English spelling often reflects an underlying morphological or lexical relationship more closely than it does phonetic form. This explains why the vowel letters in the same syllable of related words (Can*a*da, Can*a*dian) are the same whether the vowel is stressed or unstressed. The tense or lax vowel quality of the stressed vowel is predicted by Dickerson's rules:

Letter	Unstressed vowel	Stressed vowel	
		Tense	Lax
a	Can*a*da	Can*a*dian	
	gramm*a*r		gramm*a*tical
e	eth*e*r	eth*e*real	
	numb*e*r		num*e*rical
i	var*i*ous	var*i*ety	
	prod*i*gal		prod*i*gious
o	profess*o*r	profess*o*rial	
	phot*o*graph		phot*o*graphy
u	sulph*u*r	sulph*u*ric	
	prod*u*ct		prod*u*ction

Students who understand this concept will be less likely to produce common misspellings, such as *grammer* and *photagraph*.

CONSONANT LETTER–SOUND CORRESPONDENCES: SPELLING VARIATIONS AND PHONOLOGICAL ALTERNATIONS

Many English consonant letters and **consonant digraphs** (two-letter consonant sequences) represent stable letter–sound correspondences – especially in initial but sometimes also final position (e.g., *dog, dish, do; pad, hid, bud*). In medial position, consonant letters are doubled after lax vowels (e.g., *saddle*), *addict, pudding*) but single after tense vowels (e.g., *lady, poodle, idler*). Besides the doubling of syllable-final consonants after lax vowels and before certain derivational endings,[9] some consonants and digraphs have additional variants in medial or final position. For example, *dd* can also occur in word-final position after lax vowels (*odd, add*). See Appendix 10 for further information on the spelling patterns and pronunciation of the consonant letters and digraphs.

Four of the consonant letters – namely, *c, g, q,* and *x* – require fuller discussion. As noted in Chapter 3, the letters *c* and *g* both correspond to more than one sound. The letter *c* is generally pronounced as /k/ when it occurs (1) before *a, o,* and *u*, as in *cat, coat, cut;*

---

[9]The spelling rules for many derivational endings are discussed in the previous section as well as later in the section on spelling rules.

(2) before a consonant, as in <u>c</u>lean, <u>c</u>rime; and (3) word finally, as in ti<u>c</u>, chi<u>c</u>, and zin<u>c</u>. It is generally pronounced /s/ when it occurs before i, y, and e, as in <u>c</u>ity, <u>c</u>yst, <u>c</u>ede, i<u>c</u>e, pie<u>c</u>e. This rule holds not only in short words like these but also in more complex etymologically related words in which the /k/ and /s/ variants of c surface:

c + e, i, y = /s/	Elsewhere: c = /k/
electri<u>c</u>ity	electri<u>c</u>
romanti<u>c</u>ism	romanti<u>c</u>
eccentri<u>c</u>ity	eccentri<u>c</u>
criti<u>c</u>ize	criti<u>c</u>al
plasti<u>c</u>ity	plasti<u>c</u>
medi<u>c</u>ine	medi<u>c</u>ate
produ<u>c</u>e	produ<u>c</u>tion
dedu<u>c</u>e	dedu<u>c</u>tion
inno<u>c</u>ent	inno<u>c</u>uous
commer<u>c</u>e	mer<u>c</u>antile
<u>c</u>ylinder	cy<u>c</u>le

There is, of course, an important difference in the /k/–/s/ alternation in *king* and *sing* as opposed to *electric* and *electricity*. In the former pair the contrast distinguishes two different lexical items, and there is both a phonemic and a lexical difference; in the latter pair, the contrast can be captured by a morphophonological rule, with the spelling and the underlying lexical representation of the base form remaining the same (C. Chomsky 1970).

Likewise, the letter g is generally pronounced /g/ (1) before consonants, as in *glee, grass, grumpy;* (2) before the vowels a, o, and u, as in *gas, go, gun;* and (3) word finally, as in *log, bag, dig.* It is also pronounced /g/ before e and i in words of Germanic origin: *get, give.* However, in many cases, especially before i, y, and e, the letter g is pronounced /dʒ/: *gentle, giant, gyro, gesture, gem, gist.* Most of these /dʒ/ words are of Romance origin but are words that have become **anglicized** – incorporated into the English lexicon and phonology. Again the same rule holds true for more complex etymologically related words, featuring /g/ and /dʒ/ variants of *g:*

g + e, i, y = /dʒ/	Elsewhere g = /g/
analo<u>g</u>y	analo<u>g</u>(ue)
sa<u>g</u>e	sa<u>g</u>acity
dialo<u>g</u>ist	dialo<u>g</u>(ue)
prodi<u>g</u>ious	prodi<u>g</u>al
ideolo<u>g</u>y	ideolo<u>g</u>(ue)

A two-part rule that captures such alternations as we have described for c and g is the following (Schane 1970):

• c and g → /s/ and /dʒ/, respectively, before e, i, and y;

• elsewhere, they are pronounced /k/ and /g/, respectively.

There are, of course, some English words with final *ge* that still sound French. These words are often pronounced with a final /ʒ/: *beige, rouge, loge, luge.* In NAE *garage* fits this pattern, with stress on the second syllable and a preference for final /ʒ/ (although final /dʒ/ is also heard), whereas in British English the word has been fully anglicized with stress on the first syllable and a final /dʒ/ sound as standard.

As mentioned earlier, the letter q regularly combines with u to represent the consonant cluster /kw/ before any vowel that is not final e: *quite, queen, acquaint.* The letter sequence *-qu(e)* also can represent a /k/ sound in words of French or Romance origin: *clique, pique, mosquito, conquer, liquor, bouquet.*

Medially and finally the letter *x* represents the sound sequence /ks/ – *e<u>x</u>tra, la<u>x</u>ity, bo<u>x</u>, fi<u>x</u>* – although intervocalically before a stressed syllable *x* often is voiced and becomes /gz/ – *e<u>x</u>act, e<u>x</u>ample.* Rare occurrences of *x* in initial position are usually pronounced /z/: *<u>x</u>ylophone, <u>x</u>erox, <u>x</u>enophobia.*

WORD-INTERNAL PALATALIZATION

In Chapter 5 we discussed coalescent assimilation as a linking process whereby two words spoken in sequence without any pause could produce a palatal consonant at the word boundary. This process is also called palatalization:

$$
\begin{array}{ccc}
\text{coul\underline{d}} & + & \text{\underline{y}ou} \\
\text{/d/} & & \text{/y/} \\
& \searrow \quad \swarrow & \\
& \text{/dʒ/} &
\end{array}
$$

No spelling changes accompany this word-linking palatalization.

As the following discussion will attest, such palatalization may also occur word internally without any change in spelling. However, as a preliminary to a full understanding of word-internal palatalization, we need to understand the rules for Dickerson's (1985) **invisible /y/.**

Because of the regularity with which learners of English pronounce a word like *music* as /muwzɪk/, it is important for teachers and learners of English to understand that there is an *invisible* (or unspelled) /y/ sound added before the vowels in words like *huge* and *puny*, but not before words like *hug* and *pun*. Furthermore, it is important to understand that the addition of invisible /y/ is highly rule-based, as follows:[10]

- Invisible /y/ occurs before the vowel sound /uw/ if it is spelled *eu* or *ew* and is not preceded by the letters *j, r,* or *ch:*

eu = /yuw/	*ew* = /yuw/	*eu, ew* ≠ /yuw/
feud	few	jewelry
eulogy	ewe, yew	threw
eucharist	hewn	Reuben
eucalyptus	mews	crew
heuristic	pewter	chew

Exceptions: Invisible /y/ does not occur in the NAE pronunciation of words with *eu* or *ew* if they are preceded by the letters *t, d, s, z, n, l: Teutonic, dew, sewage, Zeus, neuter, lewd.* [11]

- Unless preceded by *j, r,* or *ch*, invisible /y/ is inserted before the vowel letter *u:*[12]

Invisible /y/	No invisible /y/
menu	jury
confuse	junior
revue	rude
fuel	rule
music	rumor
humid	chute
acute	Manchuria
unity	brochure

[10]In addition to the words that follow the given rules, there are also other spellings that signal words with invisible /y/, notably *view, beauty, butte.*

[11]For many of these words, British English speakers still insert an invisible /y/ between the consonant and *eu* or *ew.*

[12]This does not apply if *u* is not a vowel letter (e.g., after *g* and *q*): *guess, penguin, quest, antiqued.*

Suffixes such as *-ual* and *-ular* also fit the rule pattern. Thus the following words add the invisible /y/ before *u: manual, annual, muscular, uvular*.

Exceptions: Invisible /y/ does not occur in the NAE pronunciation of words with the letter *u* preceded by the letters *t, d, s, z, n, l, x: tune, duty, assume, Zulu, nude, illusive, exude*.[13] It also does not occur in *au, ou, uC,* or *uCC* sequences:

au	*ou*	*uC*	*uCC*
sauce	mouse	pub	rust
caution	couch	jug	punch
applaud	touching	cub	fully

It is interesting to examine the phenomenon of palatalization as it relates to invisible /y/. For example, speakers of British English have a tendency to pronounce an invisible /y/ in certain words with *u* spellings (e.g., words with *u* after alveolar consonants). When the /y/ is fully articulated, palatalization does not occur. NAE speakers, on the other hand, combine the invisible /y/ with the preceding consonant and palatalize it:

British English		NAE	
issue	/sy/	issue	/s + y/ → /ʃ/
virtue	/ty/	virtue	/t + y/ → /tʃ/
arduous	/dy/	arduous	/d + y/ → /dʒ/
sexual	/ksy/	sexual	/ks + y/ → /kʃ/

This is, in fact, entirely consistent with Dickerson's (1989a) claim that word-internal palatalization is typically triggered in NAE when an alveolar stop /t, d/ or fricative /s, z/ is followed by certain word endings beginning with *i, e,* or invisible /y/:

i/e		Invisible /y/	
-ion	-ious	-uate	-ure
-ial	-eous	-ual	-uous
-ian		-ular	-ue

Palatalization pattern	Alveolar consonant + *i/e* ending	Alveolar consonant + invisible /y/ + *u* ending
/t/ → /ʃ/	vacation, redemption, expeditious, residential, attention[14]	N/A
/t/ → /tʃ/	question, digestion, righteous	actual, creature, fatuous, virtue, perpetual
/d/ → /dʒ/	N/A	graduate, modular, individual
/s/ → /ʃ/	expansion, gaseous, expression, mission, mansion, racial, electrician	tissue, issue, erasure
/z/ → /ʒ/	revision, incision	usual, measure
/ks/ → /kʃ/	anxious, complexion	sexual, flexure

[13]Again, for many of these words, British English speakers still insert an invisible /y/ between the consonant and *u*.
[14]For words in this pattern spelled *-ntion*, many NAE speakers palatalize using /tʃ/ instead of /ʃ/.

In these pairs of words illustrating word-internal palatalization, there is no change in orthography between any underlying stem and derived word as a result of the palatalization. We should add, however, that occasionally English spelling is less abstract, with the result that phonological and morphological changes are reflected more directly in the spelling of consonant sounds. This is the case for those irregular nouns discussed in Chapter 7 in which final *-f* /f/ in the singular becomes final *-ves* /vz/ in the plural (e.g., *leaf/leaves; wife/wives*). This is also the case for some pairs of words in which *t* /t/ in one word corresponds to *c* /s/ in an etymologically related word (see C. Chomsky 1970) or in which *d* /d/ in one word corresponds to *s* /ʒ/ in an etymologically related word:

t /t/	*c* /s/
coinciden<u>t</u>al	coinciden<u>c</u>e
pira<u>t</u>e	pira<u>c</u>y
presiden<u>t</u>	presiden<u>c</u>y
presen<u>t</u>	presen<u>c</u>e
luna<u>t</u>ic	luna<u>c</u>y

d /d/	*s* /ʒ/
explo<u>d</u>e	explo<u>s</u>ion
conclu<u>d</u>e	conclu<u>s</u>ion
deri<u>d</u>e	deri<u>s</u>ion
delu<u>d</u>e	delu<u>s</u>ion

English spelling is thus not fully consistent in its level of abstraction: It directly reflects the three morphophonological changes $f \rightarrow v$, $t \rightarrow c$, and $d \rightarrow s$, yet ignores most of the other phonological processes illustrated earlier in this section concerning the alternation of consonant sounds. Nevertheless, the appropriate consonant sounds can be predicted reliably by the symbol-to-sound rules introduced here.

SILENT CONSONANT LETTERS

Apart from the consonant digraphs discussed in Appendix 10, there are many initial consonant letters occurring in two-letter sequences that are not pronounced as two sounds. We refer to these as silent consonant letters. There are two possible reasons for these silent consonants: (1) The sounds that they represent have been lost through historical sound changes, or (2) the letters represent foreign borrowings with initial clusters that are not part of the consonant cluster inventory for English and have therefore been modified to reflect English pronunciation:

- initial *k* preceding *n:* /n/ as in <u>kn</u>ock, <u>kn</u>ee, <u>kn</u>ack
- initial *g* preceding *n:* /n/ as in <u>gn</u>at, <u>gn</u>aw, <u>gn</u>ash, <u>gn</u>ome
- initial *p* preceding *n:* /n/ as in <u>pn</u>eumatic, <u>pn</u>eumonia
- initial *m* preceding *n:* /n/ as in <u>mn</u>emonic, <u>mn</u>emonomy

All four cases can be explained by one pedagogical rule: When an initial consonant immediately precedes *n,* ignore the initial consonant when you pronounce the word and simply produce /n/ (Kreidler 1972).

There are at least two other consonant digraphs representing silent initial consonant letters in English:

- initial *p* preceding *s:* /s/ as in <u>ps</u>ychic, <u>ps</u>ychology, <u>ps</u>alm, <u>ps</u>eudonym
- initial *w* preceding *r:* /r/ as in <u>wr</u>ite, <u>wr</u>ong, <u>wr</u>ist

Even more silent consonant letters occur in syllable-final and word-medial position than in initial position:

- *l* after *a* and preceding *f/v:* /f/ as in *ca<u>l</u>f, ha<u>l</u>f;* /vz/ as in *ca<u>lv</u>es, ha<u>lv</u>es.* Compare *elf* and *so<u>lv</u>e* (both *l* and *f/v* are pronounced).

- *l* after *a* and preceding *k:* /k/ as in *wa<u>l</u>k, ta<u>l</u>k, ba<u>l</u>k, cha<u>l</u>k.* Compare *si<u>l</u>k, e<u>l</u>k, bu<u>l</u>k* (/l/ is clearly pronounced).

- *l* after *a* and preceding *m:* /m/ as in *ca<u>l</u>m, ba<u>l</u>m, pa<u>l</u>m, a<u>l</u>mond.* Compare *fi<u>l</u>m* and *he<u>l</u>m* (both /l/ and /m/ are clearly pronounced).[15]

- postvocalic *l* preceding *d* (in modal verbs): /d/ as in *cou<u>l</u>d, wou<u>l</u>d, shou<u>l</u>d.* Compare *co<u>l</u>d, he<u>l</u>d* (both /l/ and /d/ are pronounced).

- postvocalic *g* before final nasals: /n/ or /m/ as in *si<u>g</u>n, ali<u>g</u>n, paradi<u>g</u>m.*

- word-final *b* after *m:* /m/ as in *com<u>b</u>, thum<u>b</u>, lam<u>b</u>, lim<u>b</u>, bom<u>b</u>.*

- word-final *n* after *m:* /m/ as in *dam<u>n</u>, autum<u>n</u>, colum<u>n</u>.*

- *t* after *f/s* and before *-en:* /f/ or /s/ as in *of<u>t</u>en,*[16] *sof<u>t</u>en, lis<u>t</u>en, glis<u>t</u>en.*

Under certain conditions, some of these "silent" consonant letters are pronounced in word-medial position, thus changing the syllable structure of the word. This resyllabication typically occurs when derivational affixes are added. In such cases, the first letter of the digraph represents the sound that ends the first syllable, and the second letter of the digraph represents the sound that begins the next syllable. Retaining such consonants in the spelling – even when they are not pronounced – serves to link words morphologically and etymologically:

/m/	bomb	crumb	thumb
/m-b/	bombard	crumble	thimble
/m/	autumn	damn	condemn	solemn
/m-n/	autumnal	damnation	condemnation	solemnity
/n/	sign	malign	design	gnostic
/g-n/	signify	malignant	designation	agnostic
/m/	paradigm	phlegm	diaphragm
/g-m/	paradigmatic	phlegmatic	diaphragmatic

For a few of these consonant pairs, there seems to be only one obvious pair of etymologically related words:

/n/	know		**/s/**	muscle
/k-n/	acknowledge		**/s-k/**	muscular

AMERICAN SPELLING: EMERGENCE AND REFORMS[17]

English orthography exhibited considerable variation until the middle of the 1700s, at which time the effects of the Great English Vowel Shift had been largely achieved. In Britain, Thomas Dilworth's *Aby-sel-pha,* a spelling book published in 1740, and Samuel Johnson's two-volume dictionary of the English language, first published in 1755, finally

---

[15]Due to dialectal variation or spelling pronunciations, some native speakers pronounce the *l* in *calm, balm, palm, almond.*

[16]Many people pronounce the *t* in *often* as a spelling pronunciation and say the word as it is spelled rather than preserving the historical sound change.

[17]This section is based primarily on information in Mencken (1963), with input from Baugh (1957).

provided standardization and authoritative guidance. These two sources had a great influence in Britain and, initially, also in the United States.[18]

After the American Revolution, Benjamin Franklin championed the notion of American *spelling reform* and was able to convert to this cause Noah Webster, a lawyer by education who had turned to teaching. Webster applied his ardently patriotic zeal to the task of making American spelling simpler, more consistent, and in some ways closer to the spoken language. He also deliberately set out to make American spelling different from the British model. (For historical and political reasons, Canadian Anglophones have always favored the British rather than the U.S. standard for orthography.) From the first publication of his *Spelling-Book* in 1783 (which in reissue sold more than 80 million copies in 100 years) to the publication of the first of his many American dictionaries in 1806, Webster worked to undermine the authority of Dilworth and Johnson in the United States. Some of Webster's successful proposals were:

- drop *u* from *-our* words: *color, honor, labor, harbor* (cf. British *colour, honour*)
- drop redundant consonants: *traveler, wagon* (cf. British *traveller, waggon*)
- drop final *k* from *frolic, physic, traffic, almanac* (cf. Johnson's *frolick, physick*)
- transpose *r* and *e* in *center, theater, fiber* (cf. British *centre, theatre, fibre*)
- change *c* to *s* in *defense, pretense, recompense* (cf. British *defence*)

Not all of Webster's proposals were successful. The following, for example, were not taken up by literate Americans:

- drop silent vowels in words like *bre<u>a</u>d, giv<u>e</u>, b<u>ui</u>lt, tong<u>ue</u>* (i.e., *bred, giv, bilt, tung*) and silent consonants in *i<u>s</u>land, thum<u>b</u>* (i.e., *iland, thum*)
- replace certain vowel and consonant sequences with phonetically more straightforward counterparts (e.g., *ruf* and *tuf* for *rough* and *tough*, respectively)
- replace *ch* with *k* in words like *chorus, choir, character* (i.e., *korus, koir*)
- replace *Negro* and *zebra* with *neger* and *zeber*[19]

Webster's proposals regarding generally more economical English spellings have encouraged a host of other spelling reformers. Their work has resulted in British-American differences such as the following:

British	American
gaol(er)	jail(er)
practise (v.)	practice (v.)
tyre	tire
plough	plow
grey	gray
blonde	blond
pedlar	peddler
kerb	curb
axe	ax
draught	draft
tsar	czar
pyjamas	pajamas
storey (of a house)	story (of a house)
whisky	whiskey

[18]Even today, British spelling has undeniable snob appeal and overtones of sophistication for many Americans. We can see evidence of this in proper nouns that disregard the American spelling convention, such as *The Theatre, Bar Harbour,* and the like.

[19]This proposal makes one wonder what Webster's pronunciation of these words was.

See Appendix 11 for a listing of the more systematic American and British spelling differences.

Inspired in part by Noah Webster, a committee of the American Philological Association recommended eleven additional simplified spellings in 1897. Three of these recommendations have been partially successful: *catalog, tho, thru.* The other eight (several of which echoed Webster's earlier proposals) were not: *definit, infinit, ar, gard, giv, hav, liv,* and *wisht.* Some more recent developments that many Americans have accepted, at least in informal writing, include: *sox, thanx, hiway, nite, lite,* and *donut.*

Some of the American spelling reforms and changes described here have served to bring English orthography more closely in line with NAE pronunciation; others have served to simplify the system of sound–spelling correspondences. In fact, some of these reforms are even beginning to appear in the writing of those who ostensibly follow the British standard.[20] Undoubtedly, additional spelling reforms and changes will be proposed in the future. Those proposals that follow established sound–spelling correspondences will tend to be more successful than those that do not.

SOME COMMON ENGLISH SPELLING RULES

How does the English spelling system relate to the morphological inflections we discussed in the preceding chapter? When we add certain inflectional endings to words, systematic rules of spelling apply. The major rules for such cases follow.

Omission of final silent or "mute" e When we add the regular past tense *(-ed)* or the progressive aspect *(-ing)* to verbs ending in a tense vowel + consonant + silent *e,* these verbs drop the silent *e:*

    face   + *ed* → faced
    please + *ed* → pleased
    name   + *ing* → naming
    tease + *ing* → teasing

Doubling of final consonants A word with a single final consonant after a lax vowel typically doubles the consonant when weak inflectional endings beginning with a vowel sound are added:

    step + *ed* → stepped
    fit + *ing* → fitting
    big + *er* → bigger
    sad + *est* → saddest

However, words with a single final consonant following a tense vowel – often spelled with a vowel digraph – do not exhibit consonant doubling when such inflections are added:

    beam + *ed* → beamed
    group + *ing* → grouping
    soon + *er* → sooner
    mean + *est* → meanest

---

[20]As Baugh (1957) notes, even today the differences between British and American spelling often pass unnoticed because some British spellings are still current in the United States, because some American spellings are now common in England, and because both countries tolerate certain variations in orthography.

When weak endings are added to multisyllabic words with a final unstressed syllable consisting of a vowel and one consonant, there is no doubling.[21]

TRAVel + *ed* → traveled
EDit   + *ing* → editing

However, if the final syllable is stressed, then the final consonant letter is doubled if the vowel is lax:

occUR + *ed* → occu<u>rr</u>ed
adMIT + *ing* → admi<u>tt</u>ing

Words ending with -y   Another set of systematic spelling rules concerns nouns, verbs, and adjectives ending in a *y* that is preceded by one or more consonant letters. These rules can be represented as follows:

• No change occurs with the addition of *-ing: rel<u>y</u> + -ing = rel<u>y</u>ing; den<u>y</u> + -ing = den<u>y</u>ing.*
• *y* changes to *i* if the inflectional ending begins with the vowel *e* (e.g., *-ed, -er, -est*): *happ<u>y</u> + -er = happier; read<u>y</u> + -ed = readied; laz<u>y</u> + -est = laziest.*
• If *y* is preceded by a consonant and the inflectional ending begins with a consonant (e.g., *-s*), *y* changes to *ie: lad<u>y</u> + -s = ladies; fl<u>y</u> + -s = flies.*
• If *y* is preceded by a vowel, no change occurs whether the inflectional ending begins with a consonant or vowel: *bo<u>y</u> + -s = bo<u>y</u>s; sta<u>y</u> + -ed = sta<u>y</u>ed.*

Mnemonic devices   There are other so-called spelling rules that are *mnemonic devices* rather than systematic rules like the preceding ones:

• *i* before *e*, except after *c* or when sounded like /ey/, as in *neighbor* and *weigh*

Such a rule accounts for the two possible orders of the vowel letters *i* and *e* yielding patterns such as these:

"*i* before *e*": *chief, thief, believe, grief, friend*
"EXCEPT after *c*": *receive, perceive, deceive, receipt*
"or when sounded like /ey/ as in *neighbor* and *weigh*": *deign, reign, weight, vein*

However, as useful as such mnemonic devices are, they typically have some exceptions: for example, *seize, either, neither.*

There are other less frequently mentioned morphophonologically based spelling rules that can be useful for intermediate and advanced English learners. For example, the rule distinguishing use of *-al* and *-ally* as suffixal allomorphs that change adjectives into adverbs specifies that *-ally* occurs if the adjective is multisyllabic and ends in *-ic*. Elsewhere, *-ly* is used:[22]

-ly	*-ally*
bad<u>ly</u>	bas<u>ically</u>
adequate<u>ly</u>	enthusiast<u>ically</u>
express<u>ly</u>	scientif<u>ically</u>
perfect<u>ly</u>	microscop<u>ically</u>

[21]In British spelling not all words follow this rule, and spellings such as *travelled* and *travelling* are standard. For American spelling, however, the rule is consistent.
[22]The one exception to this rule is the adjective *public*, which becomes *publicly* rather than *publically*.

As another example, let us consider using *-able* or *-ible* to make a word root into an adjective. The following rules concerning the pronunciation of *c* and *g* and the spelling of *-able/-ible* may be of use to some students:

- *-able:* If *c* and *g* are pronounced as /k/ and /g/, respectively, the ending is always *-able: applic<u>able</u>, eradic<u>able</u>, navig<u>able</u>.*

- *-ible:* When *c* and *g* are pronounced as /s/ and /dʒ/, respectively, there is at least a 3:1 chance that the spelling will be *-ible: elig<u>ible</u>, leg<u>ible</u>, invinc<u>ible</u>, reduc<u>ible</u>.*[23]

Of course, these rules depend on the learner's ability to pronounce the word in the first place, and therefore may have limited value for second language learners. To extend this rule, students should learn that if they can add *-ation* to a word root to form the noun, they should use *-able* to form the adjective:

Word root	*-ation*	*-able*
consider	consideration	considerable
irritate	irritation	irritable
repute	reputation	reputable
apply	application	applicable

However, if the other related forms of the word family are spelled with *-ion, -ition,* or *-ive,* then the spelling *-ible* is the appropriate one:

Word root	*-ion*	*-ition*	*-ive*	*-ible*
defense			defensive	defensible
depress	depression			depressible
add		addition	additive	addible
digest	digestion		digestive	digestible
permit	permission		permissive	permissible

Unfortunately, there are a few cases for which this rule predicts *-ible* but when actually *-able* is used: *supportive/supportable, adoption/adoptable.* (The exceptions to the rule for using *-able/-ible* always select *-able* where *-ible* is predicted; the reverse does not occur.) Moreover, in some cases where application of the rule would predict *-ible,* the dictionary lists both spellings: *detectable/detectible; evadable/evadible.* In general, we can surmise that *-able* is the more salient and productive form of the two allomorphs and that *-ible* may slowly be losing ground to *-able.* Until this change is complete, however, the general tendencies outlined here provide useful guidelines for teachers and learners alike.

Many other English spelling rules are based on morphophonological principles. The spelling rules given here are but a brief sketch covering some of the most common ones in English. We have included them since they are often problematic for learners; teachers thus need to be fully aware of them. Readers who wish more detailed information on English spelling rules should consult references such as Venezky (1970) or textbooks such as Smith (1966) and Dickerson (1989a). Unlike traditional spelling texts, Dickerson also shows the learners how to predict a word's pronunciation from its spelling.

---

[23]If, however, such a word takes the *-able* suffix, then the base word retains the silent *e* to preserve the pronunciation of *c* and *g* as /s/ and /dʒ/; for example, *serviceable, changeable.*

CONCLUSION

Our own teaching experience suggests that literate ESL/EFL students with a first language such as French, with an orthography that has a morphemic-lexical basis like English, may well master English spelling more easily than students whose first language exhibits much more transparent sound–spelling correspondences than English (e.g., Spanish, German, Italian). The latter group as well as learners whose first language has a completely different writing system (e.g., Japanese, Korean, Chinese, Hebrew, Farsi, Arabic) can benefit from receiving (in small increments) a systematic presentation of how English sounds and spellings relate to each other and how the pronunciation of a word can be predicted to a large degree from its spelling. Such a presentation would involve, among other things, pronunciation of the alphabet, the tense versus lax vowel system and associated spelling patterns, tense/lax vowel shifts, rules for predicting word stress, rules for predicting vowel quality in reduced and stressed vowels, common consonant alternations, and the most frequent and useful spelling rules. Even native English speakers who have problems with spelling can benefit from such instruction.

In the opening paragraph of this chapter we mentioned two misconceptions. The first concerns "the number of vowels" in English. The information in this chapter and in Chapter 4 should help learners and teachers understand that although NAE may have five vowel letters (six if we also count *y*), it has many more vowel sounds (i.e., fourteen or fifteen stressed vowel sounds and several unstressed vowel sounds). The second misconception concerns the choice between the two forms of the indefinite article. This must be presented as a choice based on sound, not spelling; in other words, *an* precedes a noun beginning with a vowel sound, whereas *a* precedes a noun beginning with a consonant sound. The teacher who presents this rule based on spelling instead of sound induces errors such as *an European* and *a hour* in unsuspecting learners. This is why teachers and learners alike must be able to distinguish what is orthographic, what is phonetic, and what is morphophonological. In other words, they should be aware of the most important differences as well as the significant correspondences between the English sound system and English orthography.

Finally, it is false to state that English orthography is defective because it violates the one sound–one symbol principle. English spelling is an abstract lexical and morphophonemic system that has continued to be useful over time (despite the many sound changes in the English language) and over space (despite phonetic differences among dialects of English). By giving priority to morphemic and lexical information, English orthography favors readers rather than spellers; this in turn is what makes the accurate spelling of English words difficult for many learners, both native and nonnative.

EXERCISES

KEY CONCEPTS

Write a brief definition of the following key terms from this chapter. Give examples where relevant.

vowel digraph	consonant digraph
the Great English Vowel Shift	anglicized pronounciation
key strong stress rule	invisible /y/
key syllable	silent consonant letters
left syllable	spelling reform

INTROSPECTING ABOUT YOUR OWN LANGUAGE LEARNING

Think about a foreign language that you have learned in school or while living abroad.

1. Describe the problems you have had using the spelling/writing system of English and of another language you have studied.

2. Did you receive explicit instruction regarding the spelling/writing system of either of these languages? If so, was it useful?

3. Does the writing system of any language you have studied have a near one-to-one correlation with the sound system? How did this affect your spelling? Your pronunciation?

4. Was it easier for you to learn to pronounce or to spell this language? Why?

DISCUSSION QUESTIONS

1. Do you believe there is any relation between a learner's ability to spell English and the ability to pronounce it? Why or why not?

2. What advantages does a phonetic alphabet offer for teaching orthography? Are there cases when this is not appropriate?

3. Do you feel that the concept of "long" and "short" vowels is useful for understanding the relationship between English spelling and pronunciation? Why or why not?

4. Do you agree or disagree with the commonly heard statement that English spelling is unsystematic? Explain.

5. Why are history, morphology, and etymology so important when we talk about English spelling?

6. Do you think that spelling reform is a good idea? If so, what are one or two areas of American English spelling that you think are most in need of reform?

IN THE CLASSROOM

Assume that you are teaching the relationship between English spelling and pronunciation. Here are some common situations that you might encounter. What technique would you use and what explanation would you give?

1. One of your students consistently misspells verb forms such as the following: *stoped, prefered, runing,* and *begining.*

2. A Spanish-speaking student pronounces all of the following words with the same vowel, which resembles the Spanish /o/: *comes, other, go, from, both.*

3. In the writing of a native English-speaking student you are tutoring, you find the following misspellings: *absance, independance, consistance, permanance.*

4. Your students ask you to explain what long and short vowels are.

5. Your advanced-level students ask you to explain why *s/ss* are sometimes pronounced /s/ as in *re_s_earch, a_ss_ume, nece_ss_ary,* and sometimes /ʃ/ as in *preten_s_ion, pre_ss_ure, nau_s_eous.*

SUGGESTED ACTIVITIES

1. Write a dialogue for students to practice the various pronunciations of *s/ss:* /s/, /z/, /ʃ/, and /ʒ/.

2. Choose three pairs/sets of words from the following list and create mnemonic devices that you could use to help students remember the spelling differences between them:

accept (take) vs. *except* (excluding)
capital (city) vs. *capitol* (state house)
coarse (rough) vs. *course* (direction)
foreword (preface) vs. *forward* (ahead)
hangar (for airplanes) vs. *hanger* (for clothes)
loose (not tight) vs. *lose* (misplace)
passed (went by) vs. *past* (previous)
peace (not war) vs. *piece* (part)
pray (implore) vs. *prey* (victim)
principle (guiding rule) vs. *principal* (school director)
stationary (not moving) vs. *stationery* (paper)
two (number) vs. *too* (also) vs. *to* (direction)
there (direction) vs. *their* (possession) vs. *they're* (they are)

3. Using the principle of word stress, formulate a rule to help account for the spelling *-ery* vs. *-ary*. The following words can be used as examples. (Note: The rule works most of the time, not all of the time.)

-ery	*-ary*
imagery	secretary
battery	ordinary
mockery	corollary
finery	necessary

4. Look at the following definitions written by a university-level ESL student. What spelling errors can you find? How would you assist the student?

- An axon is a long fiber extention from the neuron. It carrys information and passes it to the dendrite.
- Counterconditioning is a process by which a conditioned stimulus is associated with an incompatable stimulus.
- Developemental psychologists focus on the developement of children and their relationships.

5. Administer a dictation to a small group of nonnative speakers, then identify which of their errors are due to misconceptions about English spelling. Bring these to class to discuss with your peers.

6. Find a joke or cartoon that depends on sound–spelling differences for its humor. Bring it to class and discuss how it might be used in the ESL/EFL classroom.

ON THE CASSETTE

The ten items on the cassette are nonsense words that could but do not exist in English. First, transcribe the words. Then propose one or more plausible spellings. In class, discuss any rules that apply to your spelling.

PART 4

ISSUES IN IMPLEMENTATION

At this point in the text you have a historical overview of pronunciation instruction and of research on the acquisition of pronunciation. You have a description of the English sound system and a framework for teaching pronunciation with many example exercises and activities. You also have a sense of how the English sound system intersects in important ways with other areas of the language.

What remains, and what we treat in this final part, are three areas that help you integrate all your previous knowledge so that you can better meet your students' needs. The innovative techniques that we discuss in Chapter 10 provide alternative ways to better respond to students' learning styles and preferences. The issues in curriculum design that we discuss in Chapter 11 provide you with decision-making tools for selecting, arranging, and presenting a pronunciation course or a pronunciation component. Chapter 12, the final chapter, deals with testing and evaluation and thus spans the entire teaching process, from pre-course diagnostic testing and placement through ongoing assessment and feedback to course-final evaluation of learner achievement.

CHAPTER 10

New Directions in the Teaching of Pronunciation

In Chapter 1, we presented an overview of the time-tested (or "traditional") classroom techniques that have been used to teach pronunciation. These techniques include the use of a phonetic alphabet, transcription practice, and diagnostic passages; detailed description of the articulatory system; recognition/discrimination tasks; approximation drills; focused production tasks (e.g., minimal pair drills, contextualized sentence practice, reading of short passages or dialogues); and other techniques such as tongue twisters, games (e.g., "Pronunciation Bingo"), and the like. Throughout this text, we have illustrated how these "tools of the trade" can be used in teaching the segmental and suprasegmental features of NAE to students. This chapter expands the teacher's repertoire by providing an overview of newer techniques and resources available to teachers of second language pronunciation.

Gilbert (1994) provides three guiding principles that can assist teachers in moving beyond traditional teaching practices. These include (1) using methods other than mechanical drills or rules, (2) emphasizing the musical aspects of pronunciation more than sounds, and (3) teaching real speech patterns and giving students practice in efficient guessing of what discourse signals imply.

Often the means suggested in this chapter come from other fields, such as drama, psychology, and speech pathology, and are adapted for use in the second language classroom. Whatever their origin, these techniques may not initially appeal to all teachers, as they occasionally depart from established teaching practices and challenge such long-standing pedagogical beliefs as the following: that nativelike speech should be the target model, that the teacher should decide on the instructional agenda and lead instructional activities, that the sole focus of pronunciation lessons should be accuracy, and finally that instruction occurs exclusively inside the classroom. The techniques that we highlight in this chapter fall into several areas: the use of fluency-building activities as well as accuracy-oriented exercises, appeals to multisensory modes of learning, adaptation of authentic materials, and use of instructional technology in the teaching of pronunciation.

FLUENCY-BUILDING ACTIVITIES

Although the focus of ESL/EFL pronunciation lessons is generally on accuracy (i.e., on getting students to produce targetlike sounds, rhythms, and intonation patterns), fluency and accuracy are interconnected to the extent that students' fluency levels will almost certainly affect their accuracy, and vice versa. This interaction has caused many classroom practitioners to question the scope of pronunciation instruction, which has traditionally been defined as the accurate production of the sounds, rhythms, and intonation patterns of a language. By so defining itself, pronunciation has stood apart from the communicative language teaching movement because it has often ignored the interaction of the sound system with function and meaning.

Wong (1987a) notes that the halting speech of "tongue-tied" students often interferes with the accuracy of their speech patterns. This is of course especially true of suprasegmentals, since in tongue-tied speech, sentence stress and intonation patterns tend to be distorted by frequent pauses that affect the overall intelligibility of the utterance. Students who exhibit such halting speech can often benefit from focused work in fluency building. Wong (1987a: 15–20) discusses the following two techniques to boost students' confidence level while promoting fluency:

- *Effective listening exercise:* The instructor first models supportive listening behavior by having a student volunteer come to the front of the class and converse with the instructor on a topic of the student's choice for 3 minutes. During this period, the other students act as observers, taking notes on the instructor's behavior. Following the 3-minute conversation, the class members discuss the strategies used by the teacher and how these served to encourage the speaker. Students are then divided into groups of three, with one student taking the role of the listener, one the role of the observer, and the third taking the role of the speaker. The speakers can choose from topics suggested by the teacher (e.g., a student's job or living accommodations) or select their own topics. The listeners practice implementing supportive listening techniques while the observers take notes on how these techniques influence the speaker. Five minutes are allowed for this phase of the activity, including 2 minutes set aside for the observers to report their observations to the other two participants. Following this, roles are switched, until each member of the triad has had a chance to assume all three roles.

- *Fluency workshop:* Students are instructed to stand in a large circle. They are paired off and alternately designated "A" (speaker) and "B" (listener). The teacher assigns a discussion topic for the speakers and reminds the listeners to use supportive listening techniques. For the first round, students are given 4 minutes for discussion. Speakers are then told to move clockwise and begin their discussion anew with their next discussion partner. This time, they are given only 2 minutes. In the final round, they again move clockwise and are given 1 minute for discussion. At this point, the teacher asks selected B students to report on what they have heard, and then assigns them a new topic. This time, the B students are the speakers, and the A students serve as the listeners. The B students again engage in three rounds of conversation. As a culminating activity, the teacher can ask students to discuss how their fluency level differed in the three rounds of conversation. An alternate form of this exercise is for students to form two concentric circles. In this version, the students standing in the outside circle move in a clockwise fashion each time they are told to change partners, while the students in the inside circle remain fixed in place.

Klippel (1984) is another invaluable source of fluency activities. The following two activities are particularly geared to the type of oral fluency building that Wong (1987a) suggests students do to improve their pronunciation:

- *Discussion Wheel:* The Discussion Wheel reproduced in Figure 10.1 is used for groups of up to six students; there should be a copy for each group in the class.

Discussion

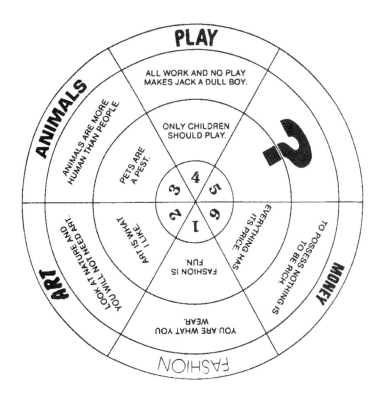

Wheel

Figure 10.1 "Discussion Wheel" for fluency practice (From F. Klippel, *Keep Talking,* Cambridge: Cambridge University Press, 1984, p. 170. Reprinted with permission of Cambridge University Press.)

Students count off one to six. Each group has three dice, which are tossed before each turn. The first two dice indicate which students take part in the discussion for that turn; the third indicates which topic will be discussed. (Note that topic 5 is a free discussion topic – i.e., the students decide the topic.) Pairs of students, each taking one of the two opposing points of view, talk for a given period of time; then the other student observers can join in the discussion. Once the topic is exhausted, the dice are tossed again, and a new turn begins.

• *Values Topics:* This board game (Figure 10.2), which is designed for groups of up to five students, is similar to the discussion wheel activity. Again, the boards should be available in multiple sets for a large-class activity. The rules are simple: One by one, the players toss the dice and move their counters forward the indicated number of spaces. If they land on a topic square, they must discuss that topic for a specified amount of time (e.g., 1 minute). If they land on a "free question" square, the other players can pose a question, which the player can either refuse to answer or choose to elaborate on. The game continues to be played until all players reach the end. If desired, they can start again.

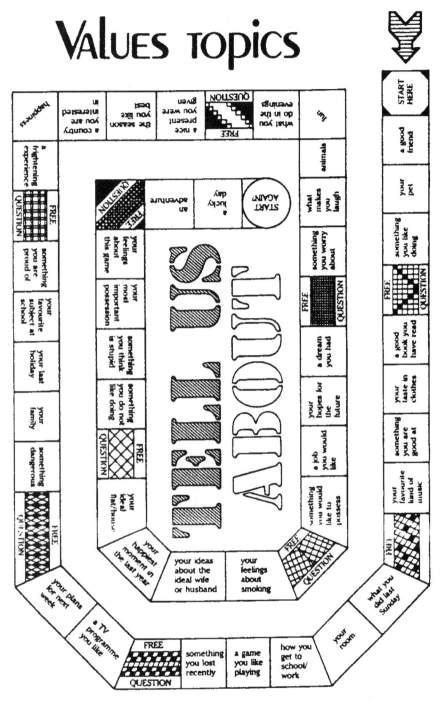

Figure 10.2 "Values Topics" board game for fluency practice (From F. Klippel, *Keep Talking,* Cambridge: Cambridge University Press, 1984, p. 175. Reprinted with permission of Cambridge University Press.)

Our own suggestion for fluency practice in the pronunciation classroom is the Personal Introduction Collage, which lends itself especially to the first day or two of instruction:

• *Personal Introduction Collage:* This activity combines fluency practice with student-created visual support materials. In the first phase of the activity, the teacher models a

Figure 10.3 Sample poster for "Personal Introduction Collage"

personal introduction by introducing herself to students via a sample posterboard collage such as that in Figure 10.3. The teacher should hold up the collage and point to the relevant visuals as she introduces herself:

I'm a native Californian. In fact, my father was born in Los Angeles, too, and both he and I graduated from UCLA, which is where I currently work teaching English as a Second Language. Here I am at the age of one. You can see that I was a messy eater. Even today I'm not the neatest person. You should see my desk! It's always covered with piles of papers. I like reading and writing, and I've even written several textbooks about teaching English. In my free time, you won't find me at home doing the laundry. I'm usually outside, lying in the sun at the beach, hiking in the mountains, or skiing (that's me at age three on the ski slopes). Being active is my stress management technique!

Next, the teacher explains to students that they should prepare their own personal introduction collage and rehearse it until they can speak freely and fluently. Depending on the amount of class time available and the nature of the students, this can be an in-class or a homework activity. If done in class, the teacher should bring in magazines, scissors, glue, and large sheets of construction paper to distribute to the students. In the presentation phase, students should be reminded to refer to their collage, which serves as a skeletal outline to cue and prompt the content of their oral self-introduction.

To better address the accuracy/fluency interaction, pronunciation teaching can certainly benefit by shifting away from an isolated interest in form. Fluency-building activities of the sorts described here are perhaps best incorporated into the initial stages of the pronunciation class – into first-week introductory activities, or as warmups (to loosen up students and prepare them for further practice) at the outset of each class. However, the decision concerning when and how to incorporate fluency building into the syllabus is obviously left to the individual teacher and will depend on other factors, such as the types of learners and the goals of the class.

USING MULTISENSORY MODES IN TEACHING PRONUNCIATION

Perhaps more than any other skill, pronunciation is intertwined with learners' egos (i.e., with their degree of self-confidence, their perception of self-value, and their awareness of how others view them). Many might argue that learners with strong egos retain a marked foreign flavor in their speech because they are reluctant to alter or abandon their self-image and that, conversely, those with more permeable egos are more likely to acquire a more targetlike accent. Although this view is somewhat oversimplified, there is some evidence to support it (see Chapter 2).

Much of the literature today suggests that employing multisensory modes in the pronunciation class can help to break down the ego boundaries of learners, hence making them more receptive to undergoing change in their fossilized pronunciation systems. (Pat Grogan 1990 gives an excellent summary of this literature.)

VISUAL AND AUDITORY REINFORCEMENT

The teaching of pronunciation has always been closely allied with the use of visual support, both in the traditional pronunciation classroom and (as we have seen with the Silent Way) in nontraditional methods. The foregoing chapters have presented numerous ways in which *visual reinforcement* can be built into the teaching of pronunciation – via charts, diagrams, and sketches on the board or the overhead projector, through the use of flashcards and wall charts, and so on. It is therefore clear that visuals are very much at home in the pronunciation classroom.

Another mode of reinforcement that has claimed a strong foothold in the traditional pronunciation classroom is the aural mode, or *auditory reinforcement*. Although we have long since emerged from the "listen and imitate" era of pronunciation teaching (see Chapter 1), and no longer believe that endless repetition of phrases following a native-speaker model will lead to students' forming correct habits in the target language, we nonetheless continue to use "listen and repeat" as a primary teaching tool.

Today's pronunciation classroom tends to view the role of auditory reinforcement somewhat differently. Firth (1992a), for example, discusses its use as a mnemonic device, or *memory peg*. One example of such a memory device is thinking of the sound of a moving train ("choo, choo, choo, choo") as a peg to help produce /tʃ/, or imagining the sound of a buzzing bee to assist in producing /z/. Students can also peg a given sound by associating it with a set phrase. For example, to help prompt correct production of certain phonemes, they can associate /iy/ with the phrase "the bees' knees," /ey/ with "The rain in Spain stays mainly in the plain," and /aw/ with "How now, brown cow?"

TACTILE REINFORCEMENT

A less frequently discussed mode is *tactile reinforcement,* or reinforcement through the sense of touch. This type of reinforcement is frequently used in pronunciation teaching today and may take a variety of forms – including simple tactile descriptions given to students (e.g., "when you pronounce /r/, your tongue feels liquid and your jaw is tight"). Another example is to have students place their fingers on their throat or cup their hands over their ears to experience the vibration of their vocal cords, or have them place their fingers in front of their mouth to ascertain when aspiration is occurring.

Woven throughout this text are suggestions for visual and tactile reinforcement, such as bringing in props or household items to demonstrate and reinforce features of the English sound system. Items that are useful to teachers are matches (for demonstrating the puff of air that accompanies the production of aspirated consonants); rubber bands (for demonstrating differences in vowel length); mirrors (for making students aware of the positions and movement of their speech organs and for allowing them, for example, to more closely monitor lip position when producing English vowels); Q-tips, drinking straws, popsicle sticks, or tongue depressors (to monitor tongue position for contrasts such as /l/ vs. /r/ or to practice lip rounding in /uw/, /ow/, etc.); kazoos (for illustrating intonation patterns); partially filled bottles (as described in Chapter 4) for demonstrating tongue position and related pitch factors in English vowel production; and dental molds (see Gilbert 1991) to provide a tactile experience of where vowel and consonant sounds are articulated.

The following use of tactile reinforcement is reminiscent of the scene in *My Fair Lady* in which Professor Higgins has his Cockney-speaking tutee, Eliza, articulate phrases with pebbles in her mouth. Instead of pebbles, students are provided with jelly beans and chewing gum, which they chew while practicing reductions, linking, and intonation. The following excerpt from the William Saroyan play *The Time of Your Life*[1] lends itself well to this activity:

Joe:	Get it all?
Tom:	Yeah. I had a little trouble finding the jelly beans.
Joe:	Let's take a look at them.
Tom:	These are the jelly beans.
	(*Joe puts his hand into the cellophane bag and takes out a handful of the jelly beans, looks at them, smiles, and tosses a couple into his mouth.*)
Joe:	Same as ever. Have some. (He offers the bag to *Kit*.)
Kit Carson:	Thanks! I remember the first time I ever ate jelly beans. I was six, or at the most seven. Must have been in (*slowly*) eighteen-seventy-seven. Seven or eight. Baltimore.
Joe:	Have some, Tom.
	(*Tom takes some.*)
Tom:	Thanks, Joe.
Joe:	Let's have some of that chewing gum. (*He dumps all the packages of gum out of the bag onto the table.*)
Kit Carson:	Me and a boy named Clark. Quinton Clark. Became a Senator.
Joe:	Yeah. Tutti-frutti, all right. (*He opens a package and folds all five pieces into his mouth.*) Always wanted to see how many I could chew at one time. Tell you what, Tom. I'll bet I can chew more at one time than you can.

[1]Excerpt printed with permission of the William Saroyan Foundation.

Tom:	(*delighted*). All right. (*They both begin to fold gum into their mouths.*)
Kit Carson:	I'll referee. Now, one at a time. How many you got?
Joe:	Six.
Kit Carson:	All right. Let Tom catch up with you.
Joe:	(*while Tom's catching up*). Did you give a dollar to a news-kid?
Tom:	Yeah, sure.
Joe:	What'd he say?
Tom:	Thanks.
Joe:	What sort of a kid was he?
Tom:	Little, dark kid. I guess he's Italian.
Joe:	Did he seem pleased?
Tom:	Yeah.
Joe:	That's good. Did you give a dollar to an old man?
Tom:	Yeah.
Joe:	Was he pleased?
Tom:	Yeah.
Joe:	Good. How many you got in your mouth?
Tom:	Six.
Joe:	All right. I got six too. (*Folds one more in his mouth. Tom folds one too.*)
Kit Carson:	Seven. Seven each. (*They each fold one more into their mouths, very solemnly, chewing them into the main hunk of gum.*) Eight. Nine. Ten.
Joe:	(*delighted*) Always wanted to do this. (*He picks up one of the magazines.*) Let's see what's going on in the world. (*He turns the pages and keeps folding gum into his mouth and chewing.*)

Using this extract, teachers can first model the reading task for students, all the while following stage directions (i.e., popping jelly beans and chewing gum into their mouths and chewing them as directed). Next, students follow suit, directing their attention to specific suprasegmental aspects, such as linking ("Same as ever," "Me and a boy named Clark"), reduction ("at them" becoming /ærəm/, "sort of" becoming /sɔrrə/, "was he" becoming /wəzi/), palatalization ("Did you" becoming /dɪdʒə/), and the like. This exercise works well with students in groups of three (or four, if one serves as listener or "drama coach") doing three separate readings so that each can practice the different roles.

KINESTHETIC REINFORCEMENT

Another form of reinforcement often neglected in traditional pronunciation classes is *kinesthetic reinforcement,* in which hand signals and body movements augment other instructional practices. Chan (1988), for example, suggests the following practices, which involve teacher and student use of hand signals and kinesthetic techniques:

- having students trace intonational contours with arms and fingers extended in front of them as they pronounce a given utterance
- having listeners identify the number of syllables by holding up the corresponding numbers of fingers as they pronounce multisyllabic words or phrases
- placing a finger on one's nose to more fully experience nasal sounds
- using two hands to "construct" a model of the mouth (with the fingers of the top hand as teeth, the lower hand as tongue, and parts of the upper palm as the gum ridge, the roof of the mouth, and the velar region) when demonstrating and practicing segmental positions
- indicating vowel length by holding up the thumb and index fingers outstretched and leaving smaller or larger spaces between them, respectively
- moving the hand in a circular flowing motion to illustrate the drawn-out quality of continuants (e.g., fricatives, nasals, and liquids)

An even more radical use of gesture and body movement is suggested by Acton (1984, 1986, 1991), who advocates that students systematically practice extended reading aloud or recitation in conjunction with some form of body movement – a technique he calls "poetry in motion." Acton's techniques involve the use of breathing exercises and head movements when practicing intonational contours. He further suggests that while reading aloud, students should wave a pencil and/or move their bodies according to the thought groups.

An extension of kinesthetic reinforcement is exercises that focus on the pronounced rhythmic beat or stress timing of English. While the teacher reads the passage aloud, students can clap, snap their fingers, or tap out the rhythm of the passage. Subsequently, they themselves can practice reading as their peers tap out the rhythm. One alternative to tapping out the rhythm is for the teacher to bring in a metronome and set it at a particular speed. This technique works well, as the speed can be increased gradually and students can thus be pushed to overcome their tendency to read word for word. The following passage (Prator 1951: 23), in which the rhythmic beats are designated by the symbol (*), is designed to demonstrate for students the regular "beat" of the English language:

*Stresses in *English *tend to oc*cur at
*regular *intervals of *time. (*) It is
*perfectly *possible to *tap on the *stresses
in *time with a *metronome. (*) The *rhythm
can *even be *said to de*termine the *length of
the *pause between *phrases. (*) An *extra
*tap can be *put in the *silence, (*) as
*shown by the *marks with*in the pa*rentheses.

This type of focused rhythm practice can be supplemented by the use of *jazz chants,* a rhythmic reinforcement technique that is particularly suited to practicing the suprasegmental features of English. Carolyn Graham's books on jazz chants (1978, 1986) are excellent sources. Alternatively, teachers can write their own chants, such as we have:

HARD SELL

Buy now. Pay later.
Get it now. Don't delay.
    Just a minute.
    Let me think.
    I need time.
    More time.
Get it now. Don't delay.
It's a steal! Such a deal!
    Just a minute.
    Let me think.
    I can't decide.
    Not now.
Why wait? Get it now.
Don't delay. Take a chance!
    Why the rush?
    Give me time.
    Let me think.
    Go away!
All right. But do come back.
Don't forget! It's a deal!

SORRY I WASN'T IN CLASS

Sorry I wasn't in class.
I said, I'm sorry I wasn't in class.
> I had the flu.
> My cat got sick.
> My car broke down.
> I lost my keys.

Sorry I wasn't in class.
I said, so sorry I missed your class.
> I overslept.
> I missed the bus.
> I met a friend.
> I had a date.

So sorry I missed class.
I know I should have come.
It's the only way to learn.

Jazz chants are most effective in class when teachers first model the rhythm and beat by either reading the chant aloud or playing a taped version. They should then ask students to repeat chorally, snapping their fingers or clapping to emphasize the beat. Once students can repeat the chant confidently, they can be divided into two groups and allowed to perform the alternating parts chorally. Encouraging a spirit of competition between the groups helps to enliven this activity.

An updated version of jazz chanting involves having students tap out the rhythm as they listen to rap music, and then write and record their own rap passage. Students may feel inhibited doing this in class, so teachers may want to assign this as an out-of-class activity. It also works well in a language laboratory setting, where students have the privacy to record their own passage; once finished, students can trade tapes and listen to their peers' rap creations.

USE OF AUTHENTIC MATERIALS IN TEACHING PRONUNCIATION

Although commercially produced materials for teaching pronunciation provide excellent sources for the presentation and practice of segmental and suprasegmental features, teachers should not overlook the rich resources available to them through the use of authentic materials, such as anecdotes, jokes, advertising copy, comic strips, passages from literature, and the like. These materials can easily be adapted to the teacher's specific teaching purpose.

As the following example attests, limericks are an excellent source of material for illustrating the segmental and suprasegmental features of English:

> There was an old man of Peru
> Who dreamed he was eating his shoe
> > He awoke in the night
> > In a terrible fright
> And found it was perfectly true!

Similarly, cheers, children's rhymes, advertising slogans, and marching chants provide a rich source of practice material:

CHEER

2 – 4 – 6 – 8
Who do we appreciate?
Tommy, Tommy, hurrah!

CHILDREN'S RHYMES

Eeny, meeny, miny, moe
Catch a tiger by the toe.
If he hollers, let him go
Eenie, meenie, minie, moe.

Cinderella dressed in yellow
Went uptown to meet a fellow.
She walked so slow
She met her beau
He took her to the picture show.
How many kisses did he give her?
One, two, three, four (etc).

NURSERY RHYME

Little Jack Horner
Sat in a corner
Eating a Christmas pie.
He stuck in his thumb
And pulled out a plum
And said, "What a good boy am I!"

ADVERTISING SLOGAN

You'll wonder where the yellow went
When you brush your teeth with Pepsodent.

MARCHING CHANT

Left, left, left-right-left.
I left my wife and twenty-one kids
Alone in the kitchen
In starving condition
Without any gingerbread
[*repeat line one and continue*]

Advertising copy often depends on linguistic devices such as alliteration and contrastive stress. We suggest practicing these features with the activity "Shopping for Sounds." For this activity, teachers prepare a collage of products taken from newspaper or magazine ads. The ads should highlight a particular teaching point, such as the /s/ vs. /z/ minimal pair contrast. Students then "shop" for the sounds by examining the collage and locating /z/ and /s/ sounds in the pictures of products depicted (see Figure 10.4). For example, they can locate /s/ in "Spice Rack Cinnamon Sticks" and in "Oscar Mayer Beef

Figure 10.4 Collage for "Shopping for Sounds" activity

Franks"; /z/ in Renuzit Carpet Deodorizer" and in "Luvs diapers"; /s/ and /z/ in "Smucker's Strawberry preserves" and "Crispy Wheaties 'n Raisins cereal."

Single- or multiple-frame comic strips can serve as a humorous introduction to minimal pair contrasts or to suprasegmental features such as blending, intonation, and sentence prominence (see Figure 10.5). In *The Far Side* strip, the /ay/ vs. /ʌ/ contrast is highlighted as the slug in a tenement apartment sights the slug landlord (i.e., the *slum*lord) approaching and exclaims to her slug companion, "Uh-oh, Lenny . . . It's the *slime*lord." Aside from the obvious opportunity of pointing out the minimal pair contrast, this cartoon also provides an opportunity for cultural asides on the topic of slums, landlords, and renters' rights.

Similarly, *The Wizard of Id* (Figure 10.5) provides a challenging opportunity for students to investigate the change of meaning that occurs when the verb + preposition combination is stressed either as a true two-word verb (*turn ON* "to excite") or as a verb-particle combination (*TURN on* "to attack"). Moreover, it allows the teacher to present this point inductively rather than deductively, thus varying the learning task.

THE FAR SIDE By GARY LARSON

"Uh-oh, Lenny. . .It's the slimelord."

THE WIZARD OF ID   by Brant parker and Johnny hart

By permission of Johnny Hart and Creators Syndicate, Inc.

THE AMAZING SPIDER-MAN By Stan Lee

CROCK By Bill Rechin and Don Wilder

Figure 10.5 Examples of comics that provide focus points for teaching pronounciation

The syndicated comic strip columns of the daily newspaper are full of such linguistic word plays, and teachers are well advised to collect these as they find them and keep them in a file for easy retrieval. In addition to these examples, strips such as *Blondie, Garfield, Cathy,* and *Calvin and Hobbes* can also provide excellent focus points for teaching pronunciation. Action comics such as *The Amazing Spider-Man* or humorous strips such as *Crock* (Figure 10.5) often provide clues in the boldface type that can assist students in their understanding of intonation and sentence prominence, and aid students in practicing these phenomena.

Jokes are another resource for presenting and practicing word stress, sentence prominence, and other suprasegmental features. Students can be assigned jokes to practice and recite for their classmates. Wong (1987a) includes a number of jokes that lend themselves to pronunciation practice and suggests that once students have practiced jokes in class, they can be assigned to collect their own from native speakers or sources such as *Reader's Digest*. The students should then share these jokes with class members. One example of the type of joke that works well in the classroom is the following:

Question: What happens when you play a country music song backward?

Answer: You get your wife back, your job back, your money back, your house back, your truck back . . .

Note that telling this joke involves not only insight into the common themes of American country music (i.e., losing one's wife, one's job, one's money) but also helps learners practice correct placement of sentence prominence (". . . your WIFE back, your JOB back," etc.) and the corresponding slight rise in intonation on each of these content words as they are stressed.

Of course, literature of all types (humorous or serious, classic or contemporary) lends itself quite naturally to the teaching of pronunciation, as we have already mentioned in Chapter 5. Poetry and verse can be especially effective for demonstrating the stress-timed nature of English and in providing students with authentic practice in its rhythmic features. Depending on the focus of the lesson and/or the proficiency level of the students, the following activities may be chosen:

- Students listen to the poem or verse as it is read aloud by the teacher (or as an audiotaped recording is played); as they listen, the students mark the elements that receive stress.

- Without benefit of hearing the poem or verse, students work in pairs or in groups to mark its rhythmic pattern and stressed elements; subsequently, they hear it read aloud and revise their markings of the passage.

- Students mark and revise their efforts as in the previous suggestion; they are subsequently given time to read and perform the passage for their classmates.

- Students practice the poem or verse from a marked passage; they then record it (at home or in the language lab) and listen to their recording. The tapes can be turned in to the teacher for evaluation or played for their classmates. The latter suggestion is particularly interesting if students are allowed to choose their own English poem or verse to record.

To illustrate the power of rhythm in English, poems or verse with traditional rhythmic feet (e.g., iamb, trochee, dactyl) and meters (e.g., pentameter, hexameter) work best. Thus ballads such as "Barbara Allen" or "Stagolee," with their alternations of four and three feet per line, are ideal vehicles for students to practice rhythm, and serve the double purpose of introducing them to classics of American folklore. Humorous poems[2] such

[2]Excellent sources of light verse are anthologies by Shel Silverstein, Ogden Nash, and Theodore Geisel's Dr. Seuss books.

as "The Irish Pig" contain similarly predictable rhythmic patterns and can lend an element of levity to the pronunciation classroom:

THE IRISH PIG

'Twas an evening in November
As I very well remember
I was strolling down the street in drunken pride.
But my knees were all aflutter
So I landed in the gutter,
And a pig came up and lay down by my side.

Yes, I lay there in the gutter,
Thinking thoughts I could not utter,
When a lady passing by did softly say:
'You can tell a man who boozes
By the company he chooses' –
And the pig got up and slowly walked away!

If carefully selected, poetry and verse can be used even at beginning proficiency levels. One example of such a poem is Dudley Randall's "After the Killing" (used with permission of Broadside Press):

AFTER THE KILLING

"We will kill,"
said the blood-thirster,
"and after the killing
there will be peace."

But after the killing
their sons
killed his sons,
and his sons
killed their sons, and their sons killed his sons

until

at last

a blood-thirster said,
"We will kill.
And after the killing
there will be   peace."

More advanced classes can easily be enticed by the serious themes of poems such as E. A. Robinson's "The Dark Hills":[3]

THE DARK HILLS

Dark hills at evening in the west,
Where sunset hovers like a sound
Of golden horns that sang to rest
Old bones of warriors under ground,
Far now from all the bannered ways
Where flash the legions of the sun
You fade – as if the last of days
Were fading, and all wars were done.

[3]Reprinted with permission of Simon & Schuster from *Collected Poems* by Edwin Arlington Robinson. Copyright © 1920 by Macmillan Publishing Company, Renewed 1948 by Ruth Nivison.

To supplement poems by such time-honored, classic poets as Robinson, Auden, Emily Dickinson, and Robert Frost, it can be interesting to select poems that "break" the traditional rules so that students can examine the effect of nonstandard language and rhythm on meaning. The blueslike poetry of Langston Hughes exemplified in "Down and Out"[4] is appealing due to the simplicity of language, the raw strength of the content, and the driving force of the rhythm:

DOWN AND OUT

Baby, if you love me
Help me when I'm down and out.
If you love me, baby,
Help me when I'm down and out,
I'm a po' gal
Nobody gives a damn about.

The credit man's done took ma clothes
And rent time's nearly here.
I'd like to buy a straightenin' comb,
An' I need a dime fo' beer.
I need a dime fo' beer.

Gwendolyn Brooks's "We Real Cool" (used with permission of Third World Press) is ideal for the same purposes, and with appropriate vocabulary glossing it can appeal to even beginning levels of proficiency:

WE REAL COOL

The Pool Players.
Seven at the Golden Shovel.

We real cool. We
Left school. We

Lurk late. We
Strike straight. We

Sing sin. We
Thin gin. We

Jazz June. We
Die soon.

TECHNIQUES FROM PSYCHOLOGY, THEATER ARTS, AND OTHER DISCIPLINES

Anecdotal evidence from second language learners suggests that the accurate pronunciation of a second language fluctuates sharply with the degree of confidence a speaker feels (for example, in a given setting, or with a given conversational partner) and with the degree to which the speaker feels relaxed. The research supporting this claim is far from exhaustive, but those findings that do exist appear to support the anecdotal evidence. As noted in Chapter 2, ingestion of a moderate amount of alcohol (Guiora et al. 1972) and hypnotism (Schumann et al. 1978) both were found to effect limited improvement in pronunciation, indicating that experimental subjects in an induced, relaxed frame of mind were better able to produce targetlike sounds in the second language.

Just how far we can extend these research findings to the classroom is, of course, questionable. Clearly, many institutions would object to the use of hypnotism or alcoholic beverages in the classroom. However, other techniques adapted from psychology, theater arts, and related disciplines are rapidly gaining respect in the pronunciation classroom.

TECHNIQUES FROM PSYCHOLOGY

Borrowing from the field of psychology, many teachers find relaxation techniques to be particularly useful in the warmup phase of the lesson. These include breathing exercises in which students stand and place their hands on their diaphragms, breathing deeply in and out as instructed. Often, such exercises are accompanied by **guided imagery activities** – visualization activities in which the teacher gets the students to call up images. When doing guided imagery, it helps to turn down lights or close window shades. Relaxing jazz or light classical music in the background can help to further enhance the activity. Here is one example:

> Sit back in your chair, close your eyes, and relax. Take a deep breath and hold it for a count of 3 (1, 2, 3), then slowly exhale. Your body is in a comfortable position and your eyes are closed. Take another deep breath, even deeper than before, and hold the air for a count of 5 (1, 2, 3, 4, 5). Again, slowly let your breath out. Notice how relaxed and loose your body feels. Now inhale again, from the center of your body, and hold your breath for the count of 8 (1, 2, 3, 4, 5, 6, 7, 8). Picture yourself at home. It's Saturday morning and you have slept in until you felt ready to rise and face the day. You have no particular responsibilities to attend to, and you are enjoying the feeling of peace and quiet that surrounds you. You wander into the kitchen and make yourself a nice strong cup of coffee. Looking out the window, you notice that it's a sunny winter's day. There's a slight breeze and you can see the branches of the trees swaying in the wind. You open the front door and stoop down to pick up the newspaper. The cold outside contrasts with the cozy warmth of your home. You decide to put on some music, and select one of your favorite recordings that you haven't listened to for a long time. You light a fire in the fireplace, and settle into your easy chair. The front page headlines catch your interest and you start to read. From time to time, you sip your coffee. The sound of the crackling fire is pleasant and adds to the sense of peace that surrounds you. You are in a stage of pleasant relaxation, and at this particular moment in time, you don't have a care in the world.

Warm-up activities such as this guided imagery exercise often help students feel relaxed during the rest of the lesson, which can be very important for teaching pronunciation.

Also borrowed from psychology is **neurolinguistic programming** (NLP) – a set of pedagogical beliefs rooted in Counseling-Learning theory and Gestalt therapy (see Bandler and Grinder 1975, 1979, 1982 or Jensen 1988 for more complete information on NLP). NLP concerns itself with the connection between the body, thoughts, and emotions, and is based on the premise that only through changes in one of these elements can changes in the other two occur.

Central to NLP are the concepts of *states* or neurological processes occurring within us at any given moment in time. These states, which generally occur without any conscious effort on our part, are critical components of the learning process. Achieving an understanding of such states and finding methods of altering one's state thus become key elements for attaining change – which in the case of accent improvement translates into altering fossilized phonological patterns. According to NLP, teachers can effect state changes in their students through a variety of methods, such as changing instructional routines, using music, employing breathing exercises, and having students use physical movement. Once the desired state (e.g., relaxation, attentiveness) is effected, teachers may wish to "anchor" such states for future recall by having students mark the state in some manner. For example, they may ask the students to associate the state with a particular location within the classroom, or they may have them mark the state by squeezing their wrists. Once anchored, states can be recalled at will by activating the trigger mechanism.

Although it is not our purpose here to treat NLP in an exhaustive manner, a brief look at some NLP practices as they relate to changing fossilized pronunciation is in order. For this purpose, we have chosen to cite from the diary study of an ESL teacher who reports on the use of NLP to change the fossilized pronunciation of her student, Adolfo, a native speaker of Spanish.[5] The author describes her general accent reduction strategy as follows:

> My technique when dealing with an isolated sound is pretty standard. First we discuss what we want to work on. Then I have Adolfo turn his back and repeat an isolated word for a few repetitions, then in common phrases (whatever I can think of). When the production is consistently good, I have him turn around (luckily we have swivel chairs) and use the same words in phrases he thinks of. Some of them overlap with mine of course, but the important aspect, from my point of view, is that they come from his own consciousness. They are phrases he knows and uses, not ones from a text.

Several "tools" of NLP emerge in this diary study, the first of which is visualizing, or imaging – a technique believed to help the subject build new neurological pathways and thus more readily achieve change. Two examples of this follow:

> (1) On Thursday, we worked on the /ɪ/ sound in depth. When we began, I had Adolfo do some imaging in terms of relaxing and feeling the bubble of air in one's mouth one works with when one talks. He found it to be behind his teeth, without any prompting from me. I then indicated he should move it back so that it was inside the dome of his palate. Proof of the effectiveness of this as an awareness technique came when I had him speak Spanish with the air within the palate dome. He immediately said the Spanish had an American accent. I thought so too. When he subsequently spoke English it had a more slurred, casual, sloppy American quality than does his usual English. He maintained this through most of our session, with a little help, of course.

> (2) The second part of the lesson was devoted to the /z/ sound. Adolfo had indicated that he didn't say it. He even thought he didn't hear it, but a quick minimal pair test indicated he did hear it, at least in isolation. The lesson took the form of sounds with the /z/ sound. We played with sounds such as "zoom," "zap," "zot," and "buzz." I explained how we used these sounds and then we played with making them and changing them in various ways. For example, we imagined a highway with a few cars going by and then one with heavy traffic. We imagined an ant eater finding a few ants and then having a feast. We played "Flight of the Bumble Bee" with our mouths. It was fun and Adolfo's /z/ went from "thin and watery" to robust, at least momentarily.

A second tool of NLP discussed in this study is that of *reframing,* or changing the context that surrounds a given event. In this case, the tutor attempted to have the learner reframe himself as an American – with somewhat less success than she had experienced with a previous subject:

> I also explained the neuro-linguistic programming reframing technique and asked if Adolfo would like to try it. We visualized him as a person with a completely American accent a couple of times and he agreed to continue with the technique

[5]Our most sincere thanks to Ann Aguirre for allowing us to cite from her unpublished pronunciation tutoring journal (1988), submitted as a course project for TESL and Applied Linquistics 103 at UCLA.

for a few days. I was not as encouraged by Adolfo's response as I was by that of Leo, one of my [other] tutees . . . [who had] immediately changed his posture from a very Chinese one . . . to a much more expansive American one . . . Upon thinking about this, I realized that I had been more careful to discuss with Leo any objections he might have to being perceived as an American if he lost his accent . . . Another factor which might be critical is that with Leo we had only visualized him speaking native-like English at work. I had been very careful in my visualizing instructions to indicate that at home, he would be Chinese.

TECHNIQUES FROM THEATER ARTS

Like the techniques drawn from pschology and psychotherapy, techniques used in the field of theater arts can be adapted equally well to the teaching of pronunciation (see Archibald 1987; Dougill 1987; Maley and Duff 1982; Stern 1983; Via 1976). The rationale underlying the use of drama in the general language classroom extends to its use in teaching pronunciation – namely, that the context provided by the dramatic situation and the emotional involvement occasioned by drama foster communicative competence, which is the ultimate goal of the language classroom. More specifically as it relates to teaching pronunciation, however, there is evidence that psychological factors are at work (e.g., increased empathy and self-esteem along with a decreased sensitivity to rejection) that enable students to transcend the normal limits of their fluency and accuracy, leading to more fluid and comprehensible speech, especially in the realms of intonation and inflection (see Stern 1983).

One means by which drama techniques can enter the pronunciation classroom is for teachers to employ the voice modulation techniques typically used by drama coaches. Archibald (1987) discusses several of these, which are intended to give students better control over their articulation – specifically, their pitch, volume, and rate of speech. Performance of these simple exercises can be likened to playing scales on the piano: Students practice various phoneme sequences, concentrating on the position of the various articulators until the phonemes in question take on a familiar character and their production becomes semiautomatized. For example, students might practice simple vowel–consonant articulation sequences as indicated:

1. la – lee – lay – low – lu   (*practice in differentiating /l/ and /r/*)
   ra – ree – ray – row – ru

2. pit – tip – pit – tip – pit – tip   (*practice in differentiating between initial*
   pin – nip – pin – nip – pin – nip   *aspirated $[p^h]$ and final unreleased $[p°]$*)
   pill – lip – pill – lip – pill – lip

Similarly, they might practice volume control by producing words or sound sequences that get progessively louder or softer:

noоOO

heIIоOOO

whoooaaaa

Or they might practice rate of delivery by reading the following passages as indicated:

Slow, relaxed mode of delivery

I am not in a hurry. I can take it easy and relax. Everything around me is calm and time seems to be standing still.

Quick, rushed mode of delivery

I can't stand it. Life is so hectic. Everywhere, people are rushing around.
Traffic is terrible. There isn't time enough in the day to do all the things that
have to get done.

As Archibald (1987) suggests, students can be encouraged to write their own passages
similar to these, to practice them at home, and then to perform them for their classmates.
Finally, students who do not vary their pitch enough in English can be given exercises in
which they are asked to consciously raise and lower the pitch of either isolated sounds or
short sentences such as the following:

They asked me to come.   (*relatively low pitch, uninterested*)
They asked me to come.   (*slightly higher pitch, interested*)
They asked me to come.   (*even higher pitch, excited*)
They asked me to come.   (*very high pitch, ecstatic*)

Obviously, the more students can be asked to put all of these building blocks of articulated speech together, the better, and thus teachers are encouraged to have students practice
more extensive, contextualized stretches of text in which they vary both the pitch and the
volume, or the volume and rate of delivery. In line with this practice, White (1977: 49)
suggests the following exercise, in which students must use a combination of pitch, volume, and rate modulation to express differing emotions when reading this dialogue:

GROUCHY MARY (MARY IN A HURRY, ETC.)

John: Hi, Mary.

Mary: Hi.

John: Did you have a nice weekend?

Mary: What?

John: I asked if you'd had a nice weekend.

Mary: Why?

John: What do you mean, why?

Mary: I mean, why do you want to know?

John: Want to know what?

Mary: Look, first you asked me if I'd had a nice weekend. Then, I asked you why you
        wanted to know. What's the problem? Don't you speak English?

John: Let's just forget the whole thing.

Mary: Forget what?

John: What I asked you.

Mary: What did you ask me?

John: I've forgotten . . . See you Mary. (*John walks away.*)

The beauty of White's dialogue is that it is ripe with potentially different interpretations.
Thus when practicing this dialogue, students can be given several alternate "stage directions" – for example, to read the dialogue as if Mary were grouchy, in a rush, bored, hard
of hearing, exasperated, and so on – each necessitating a change in the intonation contours,
volume, pitch, and rate of delivery with which the dialogue is presented.

 The dramatic technique of mimicry, or imitation, is employed by Davis and Rinvolucri
(1990), who suggest a technique they call "mouthing." This technique is intended to build
beginning-level students' confidence in producing the new sounds of the second language.

Students are asked to remember a dialogue they have practiced, then come to the front of the class and "mime" the dialogue, without words. Next, they mouth the words silently as they mime the dialogue. As a rationale for the activity, the authors note that for many students, the "jump from listening to a language to actually articulating things in it is a breathtaking one" (p. 10).

Mouthing shares characteristics with several other imitation techniques typically used in accent reduction classes – *mirroring, tracking,* and *shadowing.* In essence, all these techniques involve imitation of a native-speaker model, although with minor variations in how the learners go about this process. The terms are used rather loosely (and sometimes interchangeably) in the literature. However, for our purposes, we will define them as follows:

Mirroring: A technique that involves repeating simultaneously with a speaker (in person or on television) while imitating all the speakers' gestures, eye movements, and body posturing.

Tracking: A technique in which students repeat simultaneously with a speaker (either in person or on television, radio, or audiotape) but do not mirror the speakers' movements.

Shadowing (echoing): A technique in which learners repeat as in tracking, although slightly *after* rather than *along with* the speakers.

There is no consensus in the literature about which of these techniques is most effective; we advise teachers to experiment with them and get feedback from their students, as the learners themselves are the ultimate judges of what they find most useful.

Teachers who wish to implement drama more comprehensively in the pronunciation classroom will undoubtedly want to have students practice selected scenes from plays or perhaps even to perform entire short one-act plays. Some teachers may decide to assign roles and have students perform the passage without actually memorizing the text; other teachers may prefer to have students memorize their roles. Needless to say, in either case adequate class time should be allowed for students to practice, so that the teacher can circulate and act as drama coach, supervising the pronunciation of unknown words, suggesting intonation contours, directing the volume and pace of delivery, monitoring paralinguistic support, and so on. When the play is performed, attention to props and stage directions all contribute to the professionalism of the performance and the amount of investment students bring to this activity. Ultimately, the more students are able to feel that they are truly performing and are able to enter into another dramatic persona, the better the results will be. Stern (1987) suggests the following sequence for drama in the classroom:

1. *Enactment:* Students in their various roles enact the scene from the play with appropriate props, stage directions, and so on.

2. *Interview:* Following the performance, students remain in their roles and answer probing questions from the instructor and the audience (i.e., their fellow students) concerning their actions and feelings.

3. *Improvisation:* The characters involved in the enactment stage are next given an improvisational "prompt" from the teacher with a limited time period to prepare for the improvisation; then they perform this for their classmates. Often these prompts involve imaginary sequels to the scene just performed, or performance of off-stage actions referred to in the text. They may also involve a significant twist or change to the plot – for example, a role reversal or a lapse of time between the scene performed and the characters' subsequent meeting.

4. *Feedback:* In this final stage, the teacher and/or classmates give feedback on selected linguistic aspects of the performance. This may be restricted to an aspect

of pronunciation that was the focus of a recent lesson (e.g., wh-question intonation patterns) or may be individualized for each student (e.g., focus on the clear articulation of -ed endings with a student from a Spanish-speaking background). The feedback phase is facilitated greatly by the use of instructional technology, since teachers can play back portions of audio- or videotaped student performances to point out progress in a particular area, or to discuss the need for further improvement with a given area of the language.

Other drama-based activities that also lend themselves to promoting fluency in the pronunciation classroom are **sociodramas** and **simulations**. These activities are similar to Stern's stages 2 and 3 for drama in that the students do not have a written text on which they are basing their performance. However, in both sociodrama and simulation students adopt a dramatic persona and use their available linguistic repertoire to react to a given dramatic situation. In sociodramas, for example (Scarcella 1983), the skeleton of a situation involving significant conflict is sketched for the students, who are then assigned roles and encouraged to improvise from the open-ended scenario presented. Similarly, in simulations, there exists a more formalized version of extended role play with distinctly outlined stages (scene setting, role assignment, debriefing, appraisal, etc.). In both techniques, students are presented with a real-life scenario. Once roles are distributed, this scenario takes on a life of its own, allowing students to transcend the barriers of their own egos. As with other drama activities, there are reports of increased fluidity and phonological accuracy in the speech of students. See the excellent volumes on simulation by Jones (1982) and Crookall and Oxford (1990) for many possible simulations to use in the ESL/EFL classroom.

THE ROLE OF INSTRUCTIONAL TECHNOLOGY IN THE TEACHING OF PRONUNCIATION

As we noted at the outset of this volume, behavioral psychology reigned supreme in the 1950s and early 60s, informing most of our language teaching practices. During this era, teachers based their teaching practices on the assumption that habit formation was the basis of language learning. Much like the beginning piano student who practiced scales in order to later perform pieces by Chopin or Debussy, repetition and drill were the primary means whereby language was practiced by learners.

Nowhere during this era was instructional technology more heralded as an avenue for improving the skills of language learners than in the domain of pronunciation instruction, since it was felt that learners with enough exposure to and imitation of native models of pronunciation would be able to "mimic" or correctly produce the targeted item. The audiotape recorder and its favored environment – the language laboratory – were the medium and setting of choice for such learning to occur. With the demise of behavioral psychology and the resulting disenchantment in the field of linguistics with the Audiolingual Method, however, the language lab environment and instructional technology in general fell into disfavor. In fact, this occurred not so much because technology itself was at fault, but because the methods and materials (audio software) were felt to be passé, to have limited applications, and to be tedious or unstimulating.

Today the language lab is still around, often masquerading as a multimedia environment with video viewing or computer work stations, laser disc players, satellite receivers, and a host of other high-tech hardware items stationed alongside the tried but true audio console and student listening booths. In a sense, this rebirth of the language lab represents a triumph of technology over method and provides a testimonial to the role instructional technology can play in language teaching. In the following section, we examine this role vis-à-vis the teaching of pronunciation.

AUDIO FEEDBACK

In traditional methods of teaching pronunciation, the audio medium has served a dual purpose: It has provided students access to appropriate samples of native-speaker discourse while at the same time allowing them to record and replay their own speech in order to judge the accuracy of their pronunciation. Today, audio recordings and the language lab setting continue to be valued in pronunciation instruction – particularly as more and more high quality commercial pronunciation courses with ancillary tape materials appear on the market.

In its updated version, the language lab is again serving a serious pedagogical purpose, particularly as it relates to the teaching of pronunciation. Given the availability of authentic audio material, the lab can provide almost unlimited access to native-speaker discourse in all its permutations (dialect, register, sex, etc.). In addition, the lab can provide students with other desirable conditions: a large amount of practice not possible in the typical classroom environment; an uninhibiting environment for mimicry; a focused opportunity to compare their own production with a model; and (in library-style learning, in which students select and work on their own assignments) learner control of materials, sequence, and pace.

Today's lab, with its updated technological capabilities and large variety of software materials, offers learners a range of appropriate target models. Furthermore, it presents pronunciation teachers with more opportunities than ever before for configuring lab activities. They can exercise total control over the program they send out to students; they can allow students control of their own audio stations so that they can work at their own pace on preselected materials; they can individualize the programs to suit the individual needs of the students; and, finally, they can set up conference groups so that peers can interact and give feedback to each other.

One innovative technique employing the audiotape medium and/or the language lab setting is the **oral dialogue journal** (Allan 1991; Duke-Lay 1987; Goodwin 1988). This technique, which aims at promoting oral fluency and providing feedback on selected aspects of accuracy, requires students to tape weekly entries, to which the teacher responds.[6] Although responding is somewhat time-consuming for the teacher (especially if class size is large), many teachers believe that the individualized feedback on students' oral production achieved through this means is well worth the time spent, as is the opportunity the journals provide for students to communicate about matters of personal importance. The following procedures are recommended:

1. Students provide the teacher with a blank cassette tape.

2. The teacher initiates the dialogue exchange by taping an introductory message to the student (either individualized or a general introductory remark to all students). If the latter method is chosen, the message can be dubbed at high speed onto the tape.

3. The tapes are returned to the individual students with the following written instructions from the teacher:
    a. *Listen to my message and then stop the recorder. Do not rewind or erase my message.*
    b. *Record your answer AFTER mine (5–7 minutes maximum).*
    c. *After you finish, rewind your tape to the beginning of your message (I will do the same after my entries for your convenience.)*

[6]Alternatively, another native-speaker dialogue journal correspondent may be chosen. In the university setting, we have experimented with using an anonymous conversation correspondent (a graduate student who volunteered for the task and subsequently used the data for research purposes) with great success. Since the students did not know their correspondent, they took extra care to prepare their dialogue journal entries and commented very favorably on the use of this technique in their pronunciation class.

4. As outlined, students tape their comments, either on their personal tape recorders or in the language lab.

5. The tapes are collected on a regular basis, commented on in terms of content and pronunciation (also occasionally on grammar and vocabulary), and then returned to the students. They listen to the teacher's or tutor's response and tape a new entry.

6. This cycle continues throughout the course, with students being asked to introspect on their progress for their last entry. Ideally, teachers should assign a portion of the final course grade to the completion of the oral dialogue journal, as students then take the task more seriously.

In our experience, teachers tend to use the dialogue journal entries as opportunities to comment generally on the content of the entry, to encourage or compliment their students in their oral production, to contrast certain nontargetlike features of the students' pronunciation with their own pronunciation, to explain certain features (e.g., of the articulatory system, or of intonational contours), and to ask students to focus on certain aspects of their pronunciation, such as missing *-ed* endings, misplaced word or sentence stress, or inappropriate consonant cluster reduction. In response to students' requests, teachers may also listen to written passages recorded by the students and give feedback;[7] or teachers may (at the student's request) read and tape passages, such as a paragraph of prose from the student's academic field of interest, a poem, or the like.

USING MULTIMEDIA IN THE TEACHING OF PRONUNCIATION

Much of what we have written concerning the audio medium holds true for the use of multimedia learning aids, such as videorecorders, computers, and other sophisticated computerized displays of speech patterns (see Edney 1990 for a more thorough discussion). These electronic aids present a number of advantages, including:

1. access to a wide variety of native-speaker speech samplings

2. sheltered practice sessions in which the learner can take risks without stress and fear of error

3. opportunity for self-pacing and self-monitoring of progress

4. one-on-one contact without a teachers' constant supervision

5. an entertaining, gamelike atmosphere for learning

Of course, with the addition of visual support (e.g., the on-screen images that accompany the audio soundtrack of a video or computer-assisted instructional program), a dimension that was missing from the audiotape medium is added. Not only do learners receive audio feedback by comparing their rendition of an utterance with that of a native speaker, but they also have access to a new range of feedback modes – all with an added visual element. These include viewing a closeup of native-speaker lip positions used in the production of vowel sounds, comparing students' own computer-displayed pitch contour with that of a native speaker, or testing phoneme discrimination skills by playing a computerized version of "Pronunciation Bingo." Clearly, the sophisticated level of practice and the gamelike atmosphere of such advanced technologies (e.g., digital audio recorders, computer software programs, and other electronic devices for speech analysis) offer advantages that the simpler technologies, including the language laboratory, do not.

---

[7]In such cases, students may submit a photocopy of the written text along with the audiotape so that the teacher can mark the text as well as offer oral comments.

VIDEO

Undoubtedly, the most commonly used of all these advanced technologies is the video camera/recorder, which has made its way into the language classroom just as it found its way into the average household.[8] Like the audiotape medium, video can function both as a feedback tool and, in the case of prerecorded programs (both commmercial and non-commercial), as the source of learning material.

As a feedback tool, video is a powerful medium – more so than its audio counterpart due to the visual element. Students who have been videotaped attest that the ability to not only hear themselves but to see themselves as others see them has a certain shock value. In the pronunciation classroom, this shock value can translate positively. It appears to provide students with incentive to attend to features of their pronunciation that they might not otherwise monitor; it also captures paralinguistic elements of the communicative process. Since so much of the communicative message (and by extension the reception and intelligibility of the speaker) can hinge on paralinguistic elements of communication, it is undoubtedly worth the investment of time and effort for teachers to experiment with this valuable tool in the pronunciation classroom, and to determine its applicability to their own teaching situation.

Several activities suggest themselves with regard to using the videocamera for pronunciation teaching. The most common activity is to tape student speeches, skits, discussions, debates, simulations, role plays, and the like, and then subsequently play the tape back for analysis and evaluation (see Chapter 12 for ideas on possible evaluation instruments to use in conjunction with such activities). The playback and feedback sessions can occur in class immediately following the taping, or they may be designed as outside-of-class activities. In the latter case, the tapes are usually placed in a video viewing lab, where students can view and evaluate their own or a peer's performance. This can be done either in conjunction with an evaluation instrument, such as a speech checklist, or with a specific task. For example, in an accent reduction class aimed at working professionals, participants can be asked to view their simulated job interview and identify job-related terms that were mispronounced or in which word stress was misplaced. Once students have viewed the tape, they meet individually with the teacher for a feedback session.

Another option is to focus on the vocal apparatus (i.e., the visible aspects) by taping closeup video frames of students' faces or mouths as they speak. When viewing these closeup frames, students should be asked to examine the visible elements of articulation and determine whether the sound was produced in a targetlike manner – for example, whether /b/ was produced bilabially, whether the lips were rounded in the articulation of /w/, and so on. If the focus is voice quality setting, students might be asked to check off items on a voice quality checklist.

As a source of prerecorded learning materials, video use appears considerably more restricted because of the scarcity of video software programs that focus on pronunciation. Chan (1991) discusses several video programs for teaching pronunciation, perhaps the most interesting of which is a 20-minute "workout tape" in which students are guided to relax their vocal apparatus, practicing the tensing and flexing of various speech organs. However, because such programs are not readily available, pronunciation teachers use video primarily as a feedback tool.

COMPUTER-ASSISTED INSTRUCTION

Unlike the video camera/recorder, the computer remains a somewhat foreign presence in the language classroom. At first glance, this might appear curious, since computers (like

---

[8]For the purpose of this discussion, we do not discuss the various video formats (videotape, videodisc) separately, although obviously there are differences and advantages inherent in each variation of the medium.

video) are commonly found in households, and thus most teachers and students have overcome any initial anxiety in approaching this medium. However, whereas teachers typically transport the video machine into their classroom, computers are most frequently relegated to their own separate domain in school and institutional settings – the computer lab. Computer labs are dedicated to a multitude of competing uses, only one of which is the teaching of pronunciation. Compounding this situation is the fact that computer labs are costly to install and service, so that in many school settings these facilities may not be well enough maintained or large enough to meet user needs. Finally, as with video, there is to date an insufficient number of software programs for language teaching in general (and for the teaching of pronunciation specifically).

This is not to imply that computers do not hold tremendous promise for the teaching of pronunciation or that they are not fulfilling an already vital role. In fact, the medium appears ideally suited to teaching pronunciation, as an overview of the currently available software for the teaching of pronunciation demonstrates. In addition to traditional minimal-pair listening discrimination exercises and digitized sound representations of the basic vowels and consonants, these programs can also function more interactively. Among programs currently on the market are several that allow students to record their utterances and compare a visual display of their own intonation contours with prerecorded native-speaker models, others that present the vocal apparatus via computer animation, and even one in which students can move a figure around a maze by producing sounds of different pitches (Edney 1990). In short, the major advantages for learners using this medium are (depending, of course, on the quality of the program) the added visual feedback; the entertaining, gamelike quality of the programs; and the opportunity to objectively (via the visual speech displays) ascertain the degree to which students' utterances match a native-speaker model with regard to the targeted feature.

The limitations of computers in the teaching of pronunciation, then, do not reside in the medium itself. Rather, they are an artifact of current hardware and software availability. Luckily, these limitations promise to be short-lived, as there are growing numbers of software and hardware/software packages specifically designed for teaching pronunciation or doing speech analysis, as well as sophisticated authoring systems that allow teachers (with some amount of training) to create their own programs.

SPEECH SPECTOGRAPHIC DEVICES

One outgrowth of electronic technology worthy of special mention here is the work being done with *speech spectographic devices* or computers with built-in speech/voice analyzers, such as Visipitch or CECIL (see Anderson-Hsieh 1990, 1992; Chun 1989; Edney 1990; de Bot and Mailfert 1982; and Molholt 1988 for a detailed discussion). These devices are similar to those developed for linguists studying phonetic features of a language and can be found in most phonetics labs today. Adapted for the teaching of pronunciation to nonnative speakers, they visually display the pitch, length, and loudness of an utterance on a screen, thereby allowing teachers and students to focus on intonation, rhythm, word and sentence stress, linking and juncture, degree of aspiration, and a number of other suprasegmental features. The split-screen feature of Visipitch allows students to compare the visual display of their spoken output with that of a native speaker, receiving immediate objective feedback on their production. Although still somewhat unaffordable for many school districts and in their infancy as far as pedagogical applications go, speech spectographic devices hold much promise for the teaching of pronunciation. When combined with traditional classroom instruction, they may provide the key for working with learners whose pronunciation is severely fossilized and who thus need special instruction in how to adjust their speech habits and fine-tune their vocal apparatus to make their speech more intelligible to other English speakers.

CONCLUSION

The activities and techniques suggested in this chapter cover a wide territory and present teachers of pronunciation with exciting classroom options. Some of the ideas represent relatively well-established practices in the teaching of pronunciation, whereas others provide only glimpses into the classroom experimentations of individual teachers. Whether they belong to the first or second category, these activities and techniques for teaching pronunciation represent a move away from the structurally influenced era of the 1940s, 1950s, and early 1960s and solidify the position of those who argue that teaching pronunciation should be a communication-based enterprise. Taken as a whole, the techniques and activities in this chapter suggest the following:

1. that pronunciation teaching must focus on issues of oral fluency at the same time that it addresses students' accuracy

2. that such teaching should extend beyond the isolated word or sentence level to encompass the discourse level as well

3. that it should be firmly grounded in communicative language teaching practice

4. that it must take into account variation in learning style by appealing to multiple learner modes (e.g., visual, auditory, kinesthetic)

5. that it should include areas of sociopsychological concern previously not thought to belong to the realm of pronunciation teaching, such as ego boundaries and identity issues

6. that it should be open to influences from other disciplines, such as drama, speech pathology, and neurolinguistics

7. that the quality of pronunciation feedback and practice can benefit from the contributions of instructional technology

8. that pronunciation teaching should recognize the autonomy and authority of students, allowing for student-centered classrooms and self-paced or directed learning.

Today, as we look forward to the as yet unpredictable advances that will be made in pedagogy/educational technology during the next ten or twenty years, it is all the more important that we take a minute to consider the foregoing points. For communicatively trained teachers, many of these conclusions will be self-evident; and yet three or four decades ago, many of these statements would have engendered resistance if not heated debate among language teaching professionals. Today they are generally (if not wholeheartedly) embraced. Whether empirical evidence can show that they contribute to more effective pronunciation teaching or not remains to be seen. However, we do know that these conclusions represent the current best efforts of pronunciation teaching practice to inform itself via pedagogically oriented research. As such, they codify important new directions in pronunciation teaching.

EXERCISES

KEY CONCEPTS

Write a brief definition of the following key terms from this chapter. Give examples where relevant.

visual reinforcement	mirroring
auditory reinforcement	tracking
memory peg	shadowing
tactile reinforcement	sociodrama

kinesthetic reinforcement	simulation
jazz chant	oral dialogue journal
guided imagery activity	speech spectographic devices
neurolinguistic programming	

INTROSPECTING ABOUT YOUR OWN LANGUAGE LEARNING

Think about a foreign language that you have learned in school or while living abroad.

1. How did the teacher address the fluency/accuracy issue in teaching speaking skills? Which was emphasized more?

2. What kind of accuracy-oriented practice was used?

3. What about fluency-oriented practice?

4. Did you experience the language laboratory or other forms of instructional media? What were your reactions to them?

5. Were any of the materials used to teach pronunciation authentic? If so, describe them.

6. Were any drama techniques or excerpts from literature used to focus on oral production skills? Describe them.

DISCUSSION QUESTIONS

1. Do you believe that learners with strong egos have more difficulty learning to pronounce a second language than learners with more flexible ego boundaries? What evidence for and/or against this view can you cite?

2. Does neurolinguistic programming share any features with Counseling-Learning and Silent Way (as described in Chapter 1)? If so, what?

3. What advantages do authentic materials offer in terms of teaching pronunciation? What challenges exist in using such material for the teacher? The learner?

4. In what ways does fluency building seem like a valid undertaking for teachers of pronunciation? What reservations might teachers and students of pronunciation have about fluency exercises? How might these reservations be overcome?

5. Instructional technology has made tremendous strides forward in the past few decades. What currently available means do you find most exciting for the teaching of pronunciation? What kinds of advances can you envision in the future?

6. Do you believe that students are more readily able to pronounce English in a targetlike manner when they assume another role (e.g., in a role play, a sociodrama, or a dramatic enactment)? If so, what factors cause this to happen? How might the teacher of pronunciation achieve this same effect via other means?

IN THE CLASSROOM

Assume that you are teaching pronunciation. Here are some common classroom situations that you might encounter. What technique would you use or what explanation would you give?

1. During a fluency-building activity, a student remarks that he cannot see how this is helping his pronunciation.

2. One of your students has difficulty hearing or producing the difference in the quality of /p/ in the words *pit* and *nip*.

3. A student can't hear the difference in vowel length in words such as /bæt/ vs. /bæd/ or /pɪk/ vs. /pɪg/.

4. Many of your students seem to feel uncomfortable clapping or tapping out the rhythms of the exercises you've asked them to practice. Several of them told you they think this is a pointless activity.

5. You've done a guided imagery exercise with your students in which you asked them to think of themselves as native speakers of English. Several of them have objected to this activity, saying that they want to retain their own cultural identities.

SUGGESTED ACTIVITIES

1. Create a magazine collage that provides learners with authentic, contextualized practice in a certain feature (segmental or suprasegmental) of English.

2. Locate a poem or piece of literature that you believe is particularly appropriate for practicing a given feature (or features) of NAE pronunciation. Be prepared to discuss why you chose this particular item and how you would use it in the classroom.

3. With your classmates, try out the guided imagery activity (one student should volunteer as the leader). What are your reactions to this technique? Do you believe that this kind of activity can have an effect on learners' production? You may also wish to try writing your own guided imagery activity.

4. Try writing your own limerick or jazz chant. Then try it out using your peers as students. What features of the language does it help students practice? What are your peers' reactions?

5. With a partner, try reading the dialogue on page 313 in three different ways (e.g., annoyed, in a hurry, bored). What differences in the suprasegmental features are you able to pinpoint? How can learners be taught to recognize and produce these differences?

ON THE CASSETTE

1. Listen to the three different recordings of the following three sentences. For each, decide whether the speaker is uninterested, interested, or excited. Circle the appropriate answer. What clues help you to differentiate the speaker's frame of mind?
   a. *How's your wife?*
      Version 1:   uninterested   interested   excited
      Version 2:   uninterested   interested   excited
      Version 3:   uninterested   interested   excited
   b. *It's good to see you.*
      Version 1:   uninterested   interested   excited
      Version 2:   uninterested   interested   excited
      Version 3:   uninterested   interested   excited
   c. *Harold's on the phone.*
      Version 1:   uninterested   interested   excited
      Version 2:   uninterested   interested   excited
      Version 3:   uninterested   interested   excited

2. Listen to the student self-introduction activity. What clues are you able to gain about this student's fluency and accuracy?

3. Listen to the segment of two students performing a role play. Do you think that these students are more focused on fluency or accuracy? Is this, in your opinion, an appropriate activity for the pronunciation classroom?

4. Listen to the dialogue journal exchange between a teacher and student. Try to pinpoint the areas in which the teacher gives the student assistance with pronunciation. Describe your reactions to this technique. Do you think you will try to use it?

CHAPTER 11

Pronunciation in the Language Curriculum

The focus of the preceding chapters has been on the knowledge and tools that ESL/EFL teachers require to address pronunciation issues. This includes the complex network of linguistic considerations that they must consider when teaching pronunciation, the linguistic knowledge they need to impart to their students, and the range of techniques that they must be able to draw on to function effectively. In covering this territory, we have thus far sidestepped the issue of how to integrate pronunciation into the language syllabus. This would be a serious omission indeed, since it would leave teachers without guidance in formulating pronunciation goals and objectives and in realizing these objectives in the classroom. In this chapter, we attempt to more clearly delineate the decision-making process that teachers and others involved with syllabus construction go through in determining which aspects of pronunciation to highlight for which populations and settings. Furthermore, we discuss the relative weighting of pronunciation in the curriculum depending on the institutional setting and the student population.

As Stern (1992) notes, the fundamental questions instructors face when they undertake to teach a language class are the basic "interrogatives": what to teach, when to teach it, in what sequence, and how. The language *syllabus,* or organized teaching plan, is the road map the teacher depends on to answer these questions. This road map, even though subject to last-minute changes and ongoing revisions, provides teachers with the guidance needed to reach the end goal of effective instruction with a minimum of detours and roadblocks. To provide guidance, the syllabus must go beyond simply defining the objectives to be taught; it must determine the course content and indicate the sequence or progression in which this content is to be delivered. Furthermore, it must lay all of this out within the more global teaching plan, or course *curriculum.*

VARIABLES TO CONSIDER IN SYLLABUS CONSTRUCTION

The syllabus design process varies along numerous dimensions – not the least of which is the specific skill being highlighted and the context within which this skill is being addressed. Stern (1992) also notes a further methodological dimension, stating that over time (from the late nineteenth century to today), the relative emphasis on pronunciation and the attitude toward explicitly teaching this skill have varied greatly. We can therefore conclude that designing the syllabus is a task that must take into account a number of variables: those associated with the learners themselves, or *learner variables;* those connected with constraints placed on the syllabus by the locale in which the language syllabus is being implemented, or *setting variables;* those dealing with the educational situation in which the learners find themselves, or *institutional variables;* those having to do with the first language(s) of the learners, or *linguistic variables;* and finally, *methodological variables,* which are related to the specific teaching approach adopted by the teacher or institution. We discuss each of these in more depth in the following sections.

LEARNER VARIABLES

When constructing the pronunciation syllabus, it is necessary to consider a host of factors related to the learner. These include the learner's age, proficiency level, linguistic and cultural background, prior exposure to the target language, amount and type of prior pronunciation instruction, language aptitude, learning style, and previous exposure to a second language. Also of importance are attitude toward the target language and motivation to achieve intelligible (or perhaps even targetlike) speech patterns. (See Chapter 2 for a related discussion of learner variables; also see Wong 1987b and Strevens 1991.)

Because learner variables play such an important role in the effective design of a pronunciation course (or component of a course), we recommend that teachers carry out a formal or informal analysis of these variables at the outset of the course. Such a needs analysis certainly is most essential when a course is being first implemented in the curriculum. However, even for courses that have a longer institutional history, the results of the needs analysis can allow the classroom teacher to fine-tune course objectives and tailor them to the enrolled student population. Appendix 12 presents a sample student profile questionnaire used to determine learner variables in a university-level ESL pronunciation course.

As we noted in Chapter 2, the teacher has little or no control over many of these variables: age, sex, target-language proficiency, language and sociocultural background, previous educational experience, personality and cognitive style, social and emotional needs, educational or occupational needs. Nonetheless, certain of these factors play an important role in the syllabus design process. For example, the pronunciation component of a course designed for young children learning general English as a required school subject will assume a quite different shape and focus from an accent improvement course for adult nurse's aides who want to improve their oral communicative skills for vocational purposes. Similarly, a pronunciation course for preliterate adult immigrant learners will have unique objectives and will depend on radically different teaching materials and activities than a practical phonetics course for matriculated university students.

Which learner variables, then, play the greatest role in determining the pronunciation teaching agenda in a given course? We feel that apart from linguistic background (which we discuss in more detail shortly), the learner's literacy level and prior exposure to pronunciation instruction will be most critical, since this combination of factors will determine whether the use of a phonemic alphabet and inclusion of descriptive information about the sound system are feasible and/or justifiable. Also of prime importance is the learner's need or perceived need for intelligible or targetlike speech. In the case of a multiskills curriculum, learner need (or interest) will certainly assist in determining the relative weighting of pronunciation in the syllabus; it may also suggest the desirability of devoting an entire course within the curriculum to this skill. Finally, age and level of proficiency will also be key factors, since with young or beginning-level learners, some early emphasis on correctly producing the segmental and suprasegmental features of the language may be very fruitful in ensuring good pronunciation and in preventing fossilization.

SETTING VARIABLES

During the course of their careers, many teachers will have occasion to teach in a variety of settings. Setting, another important variable in the syllabus design process, is used here to refer to the general context (educational, corporate, etc.) rather than the specific institution in which a teacher works. Typically, we differentiate two primary settings in which language teachers function – the foreign language and the second language setting.

In the *foreign language setting,* the target language is not an official, a semiofficial, or a native language of the country.[1] Most often, the language teaching occurs within a school or institutional setting to homogeneous groups of first-language learners. Examples might be Thai secondary school students learning English as a school subject or Mexican tourist industry personnel taking a "brush up" English language course to improve their oral fluency.

In the *second language setting,* on the other hand, the target language is a native or an official language of the country and is being taught to speakers of other languages. Often the learners in the second language classroom are culturally and linguistically heterogeneous. Examples of this setting would be English summer vacation language courses taught to mixed-nationality groups of young adults in Britain, ESL classes taught in Australia to newly arrived adult immigrants from various Pacific Rim countries, and elementary school ESL pull-out classes for limited English proficient students in the United States.

In fact, as Dubin and Olshtain (1986) point out, characterizing English language teaching settings as having a bipolar nature does not do justice to the actual range of settings, which is far more complex. We should also take into consideration the purpose for deciding whether a language be taught in a given society and the role that the target language plays within the host language community. To achieve this, Dubin and Olshtain define four societally governed settings in which the teaching of English to nonnative speakers occurs:

1. monolingual English-speaking communities
2. multilingual communities in which English functions either as an officially recognized language, a lingua franca, or an auxiliary language
3. communities that recognize English as an international language of wider communication
4. communities for which English is truly a foreign language or school subject

The first two settings have typically been characterized as ESL and the latter two as EFL.

What are some of the implications of these settings as they relate to the teaching of pronunciation? First, in foreign language settings, there may not be easy access to the target language outside of the classroom. Teachers in these settings tend not to be native speakers of the target language and may speak an accented variety of English – sometimes causing them to be reluctant to focus on pronunciation in the classroom. As a result, learners' exposure to nativelike pronunciation is often limited. A similar reluctance to deal with pronunciation may also be found in overseas ESL settings where English is a lingua franca (such as in India or in anglophone African countries). Here, local varieties of English may exist and vie for acceptance with standard British or American varieties, and the teachers themselves may be speakers of the local variety. Thus there may be disagreement about what the target norm is, with a resulting lack of focus on pronunciation in the school curriculum.[2]

---

[1]In countries such as Israel or Holland, for example, English is not an official or native language. Yet English is so important for educational, international, and business purposes that virtually everyone who has completed secondary school in those countries has some facility in English.
[2]Von Schon (1987) suggests that, at the risk of being called ethnocentric, teachers not allow their tolerance for variation to be unlimited, but rather decide on the dialect or variety of English to be taught based on the following compound criteria: the variety of English that is locally "admired," the eventual uses to which students will put the language, the attitude of the institution in which the language is being taught toward the various available dialects, and the availability of materials to teach a given variety of English.

All of these factors would seem to argue against the teaching of pronunciation in overseas settings. However, the task of the EFL pronunciation teacher is somewhat simplified by the relatively homogeneous first-language background of the learners in such settings, since knowledge of the students' first language(s) can generally be brought to bear in constructing the pronunciation syllabus.

In domestic second language settings, learners have easier access to the target language, since it surrounds them. In addition, the target norm is usually clearly identified as the variety of English spoken in the host culture, and the teacher in the classroom is most often a native speaker of that variety. However, the task of analyzing the pronunciation needs of the students is often complicated by the multilingual first language makeup of the classroom, and teachers may be further hampered by their lack of knowledge about many of their students' linguistic backgrounds.

National language policy also plays a critical role in the teaching of the target language. Language policy not only determines how soon learners are exposed to the language, how many hours a week they study, what kind of training teachers must have, and what kinds of materials and methods are employed in the language classroom. It also (and more importantly perhaps for the teaching of pronunciation) influences the support within society for the learning of the target language, the political importance ascribed to it vis-à-vis trade and economy, and group and individual attitudes toward speakers of the target language and culture. Learners and teachers alike are impacted by language policy. Thus adult businessmen in Japan learning English may view the learning of English and attainment of a relatively high degree of accuracy in their pronunciation as critical for their economic welfare. Adolescent learners of English in Italy may exhibit a similar enthusiastic embrace of the language based on support within their society for learning this language plus their own avid interest in British or American popular culture. However, they may be less motivated to study English pronunciation, since it does not directly affect their well-being. Thus, the experience of the teachers in these two settings is colored by language policy issues quite outside of their immediate control.

INSTITUTIONAL VARIABLES

Each teaching situation brings with it certain restrictions on what is possible or even feasible. Included in the institutional variables to be weighed when making decisions about pronunciation teaching are the following issues:

- *Teacher issues:* Do the teachers have a basic knowledge of the sound system of the English language? Are they versed in methods of teaching practical phonetics?[3] If they are nonnative speakers of English, does their own pronunciation in English provide an adequate model for students?

- *Curriculum and materials issues:* Is the curriculum school-mandated or client based? Is it single or multiskills oriented? What importance is given to oral skills in general (and to pronunciation in particular)? Are appropriate teaching materials available for the students' level of proficiency and needs? If not, are the teachers proficient in materials development?

- *Other institutional issues:* What type of audiovisual facilities and equipment are available (e.g., overhead projectors, audio/video recording and playback, language laboratory, computer laboratory)? Do students have access to tutors to supplement their classroom instruction? Is class size conducive to paying adequate attention to each student's pronunciation?

Obviously, in the best of all possible situations, teachers would have adequate training both in practical phonetics and in curriculum and materials development. Their own

---

[3]Yalden (1987) rightfully notes that the limitations of teachers can often constrain course design. This is certainly true in the case of teachers who do not have the necessary training to teach pronunciation.

target language pronunciation (native or nonnative) would provide a good model for students to emulate. The curriculum would provide a course or courses devoted to oral skills development, or else there would be room within a multiskills curriculum for dealing overtly with pronunciation in the classroom. In other words, pronunciation would not suffer from the "Cinderella syndrome" – kept behind doors and out of sight – and there would be attractive, engaging materials (commercially available or teacher-developed) to promote the acquisition of this skill. Finally, in this ideal world there would also be limits on class size and appropriate facilities available for students to practice both inside and outside of class, either with a tutor or in the institution's audiovisual facilities.

Lest we give the misleading impression that this ideal world must be in place for effective pronunciation teaching to occur, we should note that even though such conditions seldom exist, teachers around the world somehow manage to teach their students to pronounce English quite intelligibly. (However, in some contexts, such as certain English for specific purposes curricula aimed at teaching students to read technological materials, pronunciation may not be a necessary skill to include in the curriculum.) Institutional variables are thus only one part of the total picture that informs the decision-making process.

LINGUISTIC VARIABLES

As we noted in Chapter 2, students' first languages color their perception and production of English in many ways, and pronunciation is the one area of language in which, most specialists would agree, first-language transfer can play a major role. In other words, differences in the phonological systems and phonetic inventories of languages can cause students to substitute rather predictably known sounds from their first language for new, or unknown, sounds in the target language.

Traditional thinking on syllabus design suggests that on the segmental level, we should focus on the production of those phonemes in the second language that do not exist in the first language, or that we should focus on areas in which allophonic or distributional differences may cause particular production difficulties.[4] This course of action would suggest, for example, that in terms of teaching the NAE consonants to first-language speakers of German, we would need to focus on the consonant phonemes /θ, ð, dʒ, w/, since they do not exist in German. However, we would also need to pay special attention to the issue of voicing, since in standard German the voiceless fricative /s/ does not occur initially and certain voiced consonants (/b, v, d, z, ʒ/) do not occur in final position.

More current research, however, indicates that the suprasegmental and prosodic aspects of language contribute more to intelligibility (and lack thereof) than do the segmental aspects (see McNerney and Mendelsohn 1992; Pennington and Richards 1986), suggesting that an emphasis on suprasegmentals and prosody must precede and/or be integrated with any initial treatment of segmental contrasts. Crawford (1987) defends the following "pioneering" pedagogical sequence suggested by Prator (1971), adding only that in light of current research more emphasis should be placed on processes such as vowel reduction, assimilation, syllable restructuring, and palatalization:[5]

1. suprasegmental intonation and stress

2. segmental phonemes (distinctive vowel and consonant sounds)

3. relationships between spelling and sounds

---

[4]Standwell (1991) notes that whereas most literature on the teaching of pronunciation suggests concentrating first on the phoneme and only later on allophonic differences, the phoneme is in fact only an abstract concept. He therefore suggests that it is pedagogically more appropriate to concentrate on those allophonic differences that are most challenging.
[5]Note that the fourth and most recent edition of Prator and Robinett's *Manual of American English Pronunciation* (1985) reflects this additional emphasis.

4. allophones in complementary distribution

5. allophones in free alternation (i.e., idiosyncratic or dialectal variations)

Prator's hierarchy provides a useful schema for selecting and sequencing pronunciation items. However, we caution against dogmatically applying this schema across all settings, since other factors may provide an equal if not a better basis for determining the scope and sequence of the pronunciation component of a course. Some issues we find very useful to consider are the following:

1. Is the student's first language stress timed or syllable timed? Students from a syllable-timed language background will no doubt have difficulty in assigning greater length to the stressed syllables of content words within a sentence; they will also be challenged to appropriately reduce the length of function words and all unstressed syllables to maintain the characteristic stress-timed rhythm of English. The pedagogical implications for such learners are that rhythm exercises (e.g., jazz chants, limericks, or poetry) may have equal or greater priority over exercises that focus on "difficult" segmental contrasts.

2. Is the universal syllable structure in the student's first language closed or open? Students who come from language backgrounds with a predominantly open syllable structure will tend to have difficulty with syllable-final consonants and will need special guidance in producing final single consonants and consonant cluster configurations.

3. Is the student's first language tonal or intonational? Students from tonal language backgrounds may experience difficulty sustaining intonation contours over large stretches of discourse, and thus will require more attention to the various intonation contours of NAE. Furthermore, they will need focused instruction in how intonation affects the meaning of an utterance, and how to express their intended meanings using appropriate intonation contours. Even those students speaking an intonational first language will need to distinguish patterns in their first language from those in the target language, especially if their language is syllable timed (e.g., Spanish or Japanese).

4. Are there subtle differences in the voice onset time of consonants such that what sounds like a /p/ to native Spanish speakers sounds like a /b/ to native English speakers? If so, this problem needs to be addressed along with aspiration, vowel length, and other general underlying differences.

5. Are there culturally based voice quality characteristics and speech patterns (e.g., the very soft and high-pitched voice quality of Japanese females) that could impede intelligibility in English?

Exactly how to determine syllabus priorities given linguistic and sociolinguistic variables is still somewhat a matter of conjecture. It goes without saying that the contrastive analysis approach is useful only insofar as the students in a class share a first language background. If students are from mixed first language backgrounds, other methods of determining priorities, such as the frequency of an item in speech, the functional load of an item (Brown 1991; Catford 1987), and distinctive feature analysis (Leahy 1991), have been suggested. Concerning functional load, the suggestion is that phonemic contrasts that serve to distinguish a large number of words (e.g., /iy/ and /ɪ/) should receive priority over a contrast that distinguishes relatively few words (e.g., /ʊ/ and /uw/). In terms of distinctive feature analysis, the salient features of English (e.g., aspiration and onset of voicing) that serve to differentiate its sounds from those of the language groups found in the second language pronunciation classroom are first isolated and then systematically taught.

Ultimately, linguistic variables play a large role in determining what to teach and when to teach it. As Brown (1991: 211) notes, the teacher must "decide which features of language, on the one hand, are important and therefore merit precious class time and which, on the other hand, are relatively unimportant and may be overlooked until a more advanced stage."

METHODOLOGICAL VARIABLES

We have now come full circle from Chapter 1, in which we provided a historical perspective on the various techniques employed in and attitudes held toward the teaching of pronunciation in foreign and second language instruction, and from Chapter 2, in which we surveyed research on the acquisition of pronunciation. As Richards (1990) points out, the conception of a syllabus is inextricably linked to the syllabus designer's view of language and second language learning, and hence to method. Over time, as we have seen, there have been marked differences in the relative emphasis given to pronunciation depending on the language teaching method in vogue at that particular time. For example, methods that give little explicit attention to pronunciation (albeit for different reasons) are Grammar-Translation and the Communicative Approach; methods that place a high emphasis on this skill are Audiolingualism and the Silent Way. Table 11.1 summarizes these methodological differences for a variety of teaching methods.

The design of the pronunciation syllabus is inevitably constrained by the methodological persuasion of the teaching institute (at the institutional level) and by language policy (at the global level). Teachers may find themselves in situations in which correction is emphasized and much time is devoted to pronunciation. By contrast, they may find themselves giving pronunciation short shrift – despite learner need – because of a teaching philosophy which holds that exposure to native-speaker speech over time is as effective as linguistic description and practice.

APPLYING THE VARIABLES IN PRONUNCIATION SYLLABUS DESIGN

At the outset of the language learning process, pronunciation instruction tends to be incorporated into the general skills language course. The approach used generally involves encouraging the learner to mimic a native-speaker or near native-speaker model and providing the learner with a nontechnical description of the new pronunciation features. Later in the learning process, pronunciation may receive more emphasis, either as one component of a special oral skills course or as a separate practical phonetics course designed for advanced learners. In either of these cases, more specific detail about the sound system of English is included. Just how much information to include for a given group of learners and how to sequence this information in a pedagogically meaningful fashion is the major task of the syllabus designer. Thus beyond the methodologically influenced decision of whether to teach pronunciation overtly, there are also the issues of selection, arrangement, and presentation.

Regarding *selection of objectives,* or what is taught, Catford (1987) points out that in many English language courses, there is often either an attempt to teach every aspect of pronunciation or to avoid teaching this skill altogether (with the course designers often admitting that they ignore it because pronunciation is too vast an area to deal with adequately in the time available). Selecting appropriate items to focus on with a specific group of learners can indeed be a challenge for curriculum designers, and in many traditional pronunciation courses "peripheral frills," such as the suprasegmental features of rhythm, sentence prominence, and intonation, were given short shrift compared to the segmental features, which were deemed more worthy of attention. (See McNerney and

TABLE 11.1 TEACHING PRONUNCIATION: METHODOLOGICAL VARIATION

Method	Focus	Tolerance of pronunciation errors	Method used	Summary
Grammar-Translation	N/A	Relatively tolerant	Teacher correction via lecture/ explanation	Little or no attention is paid to pronunciation.
Direct Method	Accuracy	Relatively intolerant	Teacher correction and repetition	Students learn to pronounce by listening to and repeating the teacher's model of a word or phrase.
Audiolingual	Accuracy	Relatively intolerant	Teacher correction Repetition drill and practice in the language lab Minimal pair drill	Pronunciation is emphasized and taught from the beginning.
Silent Way	Accuracy first, then fluency	Not tolerant	Teacher correction cued by sound/color charts and Fidel charts; use of gesture and facial expression	There is a strong emphasis on accuracy of production; words and phrases are repeated until they are near nativelike.
Community Language Learning	Fluency, then accuracy	Somewhat tolerant	Teacher correction via repetition	Learner decides what degree of accuracy in pronunciation to aim for.
Total Physical Response and Natural Approach	N/A	Very tolerant	Native-speaker input	Production is delayed until learners are ready to speak, which gives them time to internalize the sounds of the new language; thus good pronunciation is assumed to come naturally.

TABLE 11.1 (Continued)

Method	Focus	Tolerance of pronunciation errors	Method used	Summary
Communicative Approach	Fluency obligatory; accuracy optional	Relatively tolerant	Learner engagement in authentic listening and speaking tasks	Communicatively adequate pronunciation is generally assumed to be a by-product of appropriate practice over a sufficient period of time.
Suggesto-pedia	Fluency	Relatively tolerant	Peripheral learning; dialogue dramatization	Music, visualization, a comfortable setting, low lights, and new names/identities are used to reduce learner inhibitions. Lengthy dialogues are read aloud by the teacher, who matches his or her voice to the rhythm and pitch of the music; these are subsequently performed by the learners.

Mendelsohn 1992 for a convincing argument concerning the selection and early sequencing of suprasegmentals in the pronunciation curriculum.) Obviously, all the variables come into play when determining the agenda of language items to be taught. No pronunciation course can teach everything. Even in a single-skills course devoted to pronunciation, time is limited and certain items must be prioritized over others deemed less necessary or vital to the learner (see Firth 1992b for further discussion). In certain cases (e.g., courses designed for advanced-level learners from heterogeneous language groups for whom intelligibility is a primary concern) the syllabus may be more heavily weighted on suprasegmental features; in others (e.g., courses designed for beginning learners from a homogeneous language background for whom groundwork in the pronunciation of English language sounds is being laid) it may be more heavily weighted on segmental features.

A second syllabus design consideration concerns *arrangement of objectives,* or the sequence in which items are taught. We outline this decision-making process in the following section on case studies. However, as a rule of thumb we can safely state that whatever is deemed as having the greatest impact on the learner's comprehensibility and fluency should receive the highest priority and weighting in the curriculum, with other high-priority items ranked accordingly. Assessing the needs of learners (including a general assessment of the learner variables and a collection and diagnosis of speech samples) is therefore crucial to making sequencing decisions. Ultimately, "teachability" enters into this decision-making process, since some items (even though they are determined to be high-priority needs) may be determined as less teachable at the outset of a course. A concrete example of the teachability factor may be seen in the case of *-ed* and *-s* endings taught in an EFL course designed for Spanish speakers. Because of the nature of the pronunciation rules governing these morphological endings in English, learners must first be taught to distinguish voiced and voiceless consonants before the pronunciation of either of these morphemes can be taught.

A final consideration in the syllabus design process is **presentation of objectives,** which refers to the manner in which learners are exposed to new material – for example, whether they are taught the phonemic alphabet or whether audiovisual aids, such as sagittal section diagrams and tapes, are used. Catford (1987) notes that whatever the selection and arrangement of items in the syllabus, sounds should be described precisely, with concentration on the underlying features of a sound. Thus when discussing the phonemes /θ/ and /ð/, teachers might wish to stress the flatness of the tongue, which is their primary feature, rather than their dentality, a secondary feature. In addition, room in the syllabus should be set aside for silent introspection and practice by the learners and for opportunities to compare and contrast the new target language sounds with known items in the students' first language.

CASE STUDIES

The preceding remarks about the place of pronunciation within the language syllabus are useful insofar as they provide general guidelines. However, when faced with the task of applying these guidelines to a specific setting, teachers may still find themselves puzzled about the decision-making process. The case studies that follow portray this decision-making process as it is carried out in a variety of prototypical EFL and ESL settings:

1. *Context:* One-on-one instruction of a Japanese businessman
   Setting: EFL (company site in Japan)

2. *Context:* Italian middle school students
   Setting: EFL (Italian middle school)

3. *Context:* Low-level adult immigrant students with emerging literacy skills
   Setting: ESL (adult school in a U.S. urban area)

4. *Context:* International teaching assistants
   Setting: ESL (U.S. university)

5. *Context:* An inservice course in teaching pronunciation for Egyptian teachers of English
   Setting: ESL for EFL teachers (Canadian university)

Each case study is organized as follows. First, we briefly describe the context in terms of the different variables (learner, language, setting, institution, and methodology). Next, we list a set of pronunciation objectives (not comprehensive course objectives), since in most cases pronunciation is not the sole focus of the course. These are followed by a discussion of how specific pronunciation teaching points in the syllabus are selected, arranged, and presented in the course. Finally, we discuss the application of the case study to other contexts and settings.

CASE STUDY 1: ONE-ON-ONE INSTRUCTION OF A JAPANESE BUSINESSMAN

The client, a 42-year-old businessman working for an international electronics company, is receiving private tutoring on-site at his company in Japan in order to improve his oral skills in English. He is university educated and is instrumentally motivated to improve, since his work involves frequent use of English as a medium of communication (both with native English speakers and English-speaking businesspeople from other parts of the world). Prior English language exposure includes English as a school subject, a short post-university refresher course, and several business and pleasure trips to the United States and Australia. His language proficiency level is high intermediate, and his English is fluent, although heavily accented.

The tutor is a native speaker of NAE teaching in Japan. She has a Certificate in TESL, during which course of study she took an introductory linguistics course that included a phonetics component. Tutor and tutee meet once a week for two hours. Audio- and videotaping facilities are available. The syllabus for this course is flexible and constantly undergoing revision based on a needs analysis of the learner; text materials (culled from a variety of sources) are provided by the tutor as determined appropriate. Course emphasis is placed on both oral presentation skills and pronunciation. Attention to pronunciation is integrated into the oral language practice and is often manifested as feedback and correction exercises.

Pronunciation objectives The pronunciation objectives are:

1. to comprehend and effectively use English sentence prominence and intonation patterns both in face-to-face interactions and over the telephone
2. to gain control over common word stress patterns and apply these to business and marketing terms, especially those describing electronic products
3. to gain a command of the stress-timed rhythm of English
4. to apply rules of connected speech (e.g., linking, vowel reduction) to spontaneous oral output
5. to recognize and gain conscious control over specific vowel and consonant substitution patterns

Selection The pronunciation objectives were selected after a preliminary audiotaped interview with the client. This interview served the dual purpose of providing a diagnostic speech sample and assisting in needs analysis. A reference text comparing the sound systems of Japanese and English was also consulted, and the information obtained from this was compared with the client's output. Routine discourse functions that the client needs to perform for his job (and that he noted during the interview) were prioritized for presentation and practice. Additional information is obtained via observations or recordings of the client at his job site interacting with English speakers.

Arrangement Since this is a one-on-one instructional situation dependent upon the learner's needs, there is no prescribed sequence of instruction. Although the tutor formulated a general plan of action to follow with the client based on the initial needs analysis, much of the specific practice occurs as a result of what transpires in the individual tutoring sessions. Because the learner comes from a syllable-timed language, a high priority is given to work on rhythm and stress. Time is also spent on reduced syllables (i.e., /ə/ and other reduced vowels), on the more highly differentiated vowel system of English (as opposed to the five-vowel system of Japanese), and to consonant clusters and other consonant sounds that the client has difficulty articulating (e.g., /l, r, f, v, b, θ, ð/ and initial /h/). The following sample of language functions addressed in the oral skills program shows how pronunciation is integrated into the overall course of study:

Social language

Intonation patterns of common greetings and closings, politeness formulas, yes/no
and wh-questions used as conversational openers
Sentence prominence
/θ/ and /ð/; initial /h/

Business terminology

Stress patterns in compound nouns
Stress patterns in multisyllabic words
Stress shift in word families (e.g., *electric, electricity, electronic, electronically*)
/l/, /r/, /b/, /v/, /f/

Describing and presenting a product

Vowel and consonant substitutions in high-frequency vocabulary items, as determined by error analysis
Stress shifting (recycled)
Linking and reduction
Series intonation
Consonant clusters

Persuasion and negotiation

Sentence prominence (recycled)
Contrastive stress
Palatalization
Thought groups and pausing
Intonation of tag questions, echo questions, and unfinished statements

Presentation As stated earlier, pronunciation is integrated into the oral language functions covered in each session. A brief explanation of the pronunciation feature (often accompanied by drill and practice using ancillary text materials) is followed by an application activity, such as a role play in which the client is asked to meet a potential business partner for the first time, describe a product to this potential "buyer," negotiate a deal, and so forth (with the opposite role assumed by the tutor). These simulations are either audio- or videotaped, and focused feedback sessions follow. Frequent recycling of previously practiced items and on-the-spot correction (followed by additional drill) occur.

Application Every one-on-one instructional situation is unique in the sense that it depends on the client's needs and interests. It is the responsibility of the tutor to raise the client's consciousness about his or her language patterns and provide a forum for practice that relates to the client's personal (social, occupational/professional) experiences. The needs analysis procedure is critical in assisting the tutor to determine the tutoring agenda. Once needs have been determined, the material covered and the tasks assigned must be carefully tailored to reflect these real-life needs.

CASE STUDY 2: ITALIAN MIDDLE SCHOOL STUDENTS

This is a beginning-level class of thirty-five 12-year-olds in an Italian middle school *(scuola media)*. They come from a variety of socioeconomic backgrounds and although some will eventually go on to university, they have not yet been streamed into one of the many types of secondary schools common in the European system. In most cases, the only exposure these children have had to English is through hearing popular songs on the radio, some contact with tourists, and the bits and pieces of English present in advertising or on articles of clothing. A few of the students, however, have visited England on family vacations. Since many of them speak a regional dialect of Italian at home but standard Italian at school, they are somewhat familiar with language differences. Their need for English and intelligible pronunciation is relatively low at this point. Motivation varies widely – for some, English is simply a required school subject; for others, high marks are essential in all subjects to gain admission to the desired secondary school and university; for yet others English is a useful tool for future travel or study abroad.

This English class meets four hours a week; approximately half an hour per week is devoted to integrated pronunciation teaching. The class is taught by an Italian teacher whose university study of English focused primarily on literature, not on language and linguistics. However, the teacher has spent several summers in Great Britain and has attended inservice training programs offered by the Italian Ministry of Public Instruction. Although the instructor feels somewhat uncomfortable teaching pronunciation, she has integrated it into the standardized curriculum, which favors a communicative approach. The school is equipped with cassette recorders.

Pronunciation objectives The pronunciation objectives are:

1. to increase comprehension of spoken English by understanding the basic rules of stress, intonation, and reduced speech

2. to develop appropriate intonation and stress patterns in everyday communication in English

3. to understand the main differences in consonant and vowel production between Italian and English

4. to improve the ability to monitor one's own speech when focusing on form

Selection The selection of teaching points is determined primarily by two factors: (1) the prescribed curriculum and textbook for these students and (2) a contrastive analysis of Italian and English sound systems. Areas of anticipated difficulty include vowel reduction, vowel length, final consonants, consonant clusters, linking, word stress, rhythm, sentence prominence, and basic intonation patterns. The class uses a beginning-level multiskills textbook that focuses on communicative fluency. Each unit contains a list of useful phrases and several dialogues.

Arrangement Since the textbook is organized according to communicative functions, pronunciation lessons are adapted to these materials and sequenced accordingly. Following is a sample of the communicative functions covered in the textbook and the corresponding pronunciation teaching points.

Communicative function	Pronunciation point	Example
Greetings and introductions	Intonation in short statements; linking	Hello. Good morning. My name is _____.
Requesting personal information	Intonation in wh-questions and echo questions; linking; sentence prominence; /θ/	How are you? I'm fine, thanks. And you?
Identifying classroom objects	Word stress with special focus on compound nouns; linking (in particular, avoiding the insertion of /ə/); /ð/	What's this? What's that? It's a notebook. It's a blackboard.

Describing people and relationships	-*s* endings; /iy/ vs. /ɪ/	He's my brother. His name's Mario. He wears glasses. He's 5 feet tall and very thin. He has three sisters.

Presentation Teaching points are derived from the content of each lesson. Students first listen to the dialogues and phrases for meaning before focusing on pronunciation. The teacher either highlights the point (e.g., stressed words, higher pitch, rising or falling intonation patterns) or elicits it from the students. Once a point has been presented, the teacher uses strong aural or visual reinforcement (e.g., tapping on the desk for stress and rhythm, sweeping hand gestures for intonation, rubber band stretched apart for vowel length). In addition, students add pronunciation markings to the dialogues and phrases in their text by circling stressed syllables, drawing intonation contours, connecting linked words, drawing a line through reduced vowels, and so forth. Fluency is balanced with accuracy in pronunciation, and feedback is given not only on grammatical errors but on pronunciation errors as well.

Application European public schools share a similar approach to foreign language education. Very often, since the textbooks are selected at a regional or national level, the teacher may have to adapt the required textbook to include a pronunciation component. The communicative approach is widespread and there has been a strong emphasis on fluency rather than accuracy; however, as this case study illustrates, speaking activities can easily include a focus on pronunciation in order to achieve both fluency and intelligibility.

CASE STUDY 3: LOW-LEVEL ADULT IMMIGRANT STUDENTS WITH EMERGING LITERACY SKILLS

This study concerns an ESL literacy class offered to a group of low-level proficiency learners in a large urban center in the United States. Linguistically and culturally the class is mixed; most students are Spanish-speaking (although at home some may speak an American Indian dialect) and are from Mexico or Central America. Some of the students are not currently employed. A smaller percentage of the students are first-language Hmong speakers from Southeast Asia. Both groups of students are recent arrivals in the United States. None has first-language literacy skills; literacy in English is just emerging, with some students already familiar with the alphabet and able to read familiar words and others still learning the alphabet. A few have no literacy in English at all. The Hmong speakers have had some prior instruction in English in a refugee camp setting during their transition to the United States. Pronunciation instruction in this setting was limited to "listen and repeat." Language aptitude in this group is mixed; their learning style (because of lack of prior literacy training) is heavily dependent on the aural/oral mode. Although surrounded by English in this ESL setting, many of the learners live and/or work in neighborhoods where English is not the primary language and may have little exposure to English outside of the classroom. Nonetheless, their desire to learn English is strong and instrumentally motivated: They want to find jobs that enable them to live decently, and they view improved English language skills as an avenue to achieving this goal.

  The setting for this class is a government-funded adult education program. The class, varying in size from twenty-five to forty on any given evening, takes place on a high school campus four days a week for 2½ hours. Because of the funding, the program is open entry, open exit; as a result, the student population is somewhat unstable, with some students attending class much longer than others. The focus of the curriculum is on providing students with a combination of life skills (e.g., housing, transportation) and basic (linguistic) skills. The methodology is whole-language oriented, with most of the activities revolving around the students' lives and their needs. The teacher is certified to teach adult education and has a Certificate in TESL. The reading materials are primarily student-produced, in keeping with the whole-language approach. The teacher supplements this with authentic materials.

Pronunciation objectives The pronunciation objectives are:

1. to pronounce numbers and letters of the alphabet, and give and spell personal information (e.g., address, telephone number, first and last name) intelligibly

2. to distinguish and produce selected vowel and consonant distinctions when reading at the word level (especially if this ability is impeded by the student's first language background)

3. to produce both initial and final consonant clusters intelligibly when reading at the word level (especially clusters with /l/ and /r/ and final clusters with /s/ or /z/)

4. to apply linking and blending when reading at the phrase or sentence level

5. to apply appropriate rising or rising/falling intonation when reading aloud stretches of connected discourse

Selection Because of the whole-language emphasis in the curriculum, no predetermined pronunciation agenda can be set. Reading materials consist of texts that evolve from the learners' life experiences and are initially dictated to the teacher and copied by the students. These materials comprise the course "reader."

Although there is relatively little overt emphasis on pronunciation in the teaching materials themselves, pronunciation skills are nonetheless deemed important in this early language-learning experience. Items to be taught are selected based on an error analysis of the learners' output; correction is usually on the spot, with the focus on intelligibility rather than accuracy. Because of the literacy focus, pronunciation of segmental contrasts is highlighted for word-reading skills; suprasegmental features such as intonation and blending also play a large role when students read their literacy materials aloud.

Arrangement The arrangement of items to be taught is primarily decided via the teacher's analysis of students' reading miscues. Thus no specific arrangement of pronunciation items is spelled out in the curriculum. In general, however, since word-reading practice precedes sentence-reading practice, it is clear that work on segmental contrasts and consonant clusters precedes work on blending and intonation.

Presentation For each reading passage, the teacher and students collaboratively create a "word bank" of the new key words in the text. Using this word bank, the teacher focuses on the segmental contrasts that students are having difficulty producing. This is achieved by the teacher pointing to the articulators (e.g., the lips and teeth when demonstrating the difference between /b/ and /v/), by using simple drawings on the board (e.g., the lip positions for /iy/ and /ɪ/), or by using rubber bands to indicate vowel length. This descriptive stage is followed by choral then individual "listen and repeat" practice. Students often write the key words on index cards and practice reading them in pairs as the teacher circulates and provides feedback (including more individualized pronunciation work).

The reading texts themselves are initially written by the teacher on large pieces of butcher paper. After reading this text aloud as a model and highlighting the pronunciation of more difficult words, the teacher has the students read the text chorally, phrase by phrase. It is at this point that work on blending and intonation occurs. The teacher uses a pointer to indicate linking between words, and sometimes hums the melody or employs a kazoo to illustrate the intonation patterns of selected phrases. Sentence rhythm and prominence are emphasized by clapping or tapping out the rhythm on the desk.

Application This teaching agenda is equally applicable to other, less general kinds of literacy courses, such as migrant farmworker projects, or workplace literacy or parent literacy programs. In such cases, however, the learner populations share a more defined need. Thus the materials chosen should relate more specifically to either the learners' immediate environment (in the agricultural domain or factory workplace) or to the children's course of study at school and the parents' need to communicate with teachers (in parent literacy programs).

CASE STUDY 4: INTERNATIONAL TEACHING ASSISTANTS

A group of twelve Chinese and Korean graduate students in their twenties and thirties are international teaching assistants (ITAs) at a U.S. university.[6] They are from the Department of Mathematics and have a low-intermediate to high-intermediate level of English proficiency. In their native countries, they generally learned English at school and had little or no contact with American speakers before coming to the United States. None has had a course in pronunciation but several students were taught the International Phonetic Alphabet. Language aptitude and learning style vary, and only a few have had any instruction in a second language besides English. Their literacy level is quite high and, as teaching assistants of American undergraduates, their need for intelligible pronunciation is great. However, since this oral skills class is required, their initial motivation is somewhat lacking.

Pronunciation is one component of this four-week summer course conducted on campus by a lecturer in TESL trained in teaching pronunciation. The other components include public speaking skills and the culture of the American classroom. Students meet ten hours per week (two hours each weekday). Facilities include a video camera and a language laboratory with both audio and video playback.

Pronunciation objectives The pronunciation objectives are:

1. to learn the phonemic alphabet in order to make effective use of the pronunciation key in a standard English-English learners' dictionary

2. to improve the ability to monitor one's own speech when focusing on form

3. to analyze and develop appropriate intonation and stress patterns for typical classroom discourse in mathematics (problem solving)

4. to increase comprehension of undergraduate discourse in problem-solving discussion sections led by ITAs

5. to understand common word stress patterns and apply these to mathematical terms

6. to gain a basic knowledge of consonant and vowel production targeting individual areas of difficulty

7. to develop a personal plan for improvement beyond this course using available lab and tutoring facilities on the campus

Selection The selection of teaching points is based on the initial diagnostic speech samples of these twelve students and videotaped examples of spoken discourse in mathematics problem-solving sessions. Points to be covered include clear and dark /l/, final consonants,

---

[6]Excellent sources to consult for the design of ITA courses are Bauer (1991) and Madden and Myers (1994).

consonant clusters (particularly those involving /r/ or /l/), vowel quality and length, word stress, vowel reduction, sentence prominence and rhythm, thought groups, linking, and common intonation patterns used in pedagogical discourse.

Arrangement The sequence of teaching points is as follows:

Background

Initial assessment of each student's pronunciation in terms of both segmental and
   suprasegmental features
Introduction to the phonemic alphabet
Basic overview of the sound system
Practice using the pronunciation key in the required student dictionary

Mathematical terminology

Quality of stressed vowels
Word stress patterns
Vowel length
Vowel reduction
Clear and dark /l/
Consonant clusters

Defining a concept

Thought groups and pausing
Linking between words
Final consonants

Problem solving at the board

Sentence prominence and rhythm
Contrastive stress
Intonation in statements, wh-questions, yes/no questions, unfinished statements,
   and tag questions

Presentation Pronunciation teaching materials are derived from videotaped examples of native-speaking mathematics teaching assistants (TAs) leading problem-solving sessions. First, the videotaped excerpts are presented as listening comprehension practice. Next, written transcripts of the excerpts are examined to analyze the TAs' classroom discourse, to observe their interaction with undergraduates, and to focus on specific pronunciation points. Students practice these points in class in paired dialogues and small-group role plays. Outside of class, students use the transcripts as reading-aloud practice by recording them in audiotaped dialogue journal entries, which are responded to by the instructor. Finally, teaching points are practiced in videotaped minipresentations and are followed up by individual consultations with the instructor.

Application This case study is applicable to the most common ITA teaching situations – pre-sessional orientation courses and semester-long concurrent (in-sessional) courses. If a course is required, motivation may be lacking, in which case the use of actual TAs and undergraduates on tape has proved to be quite stimulating. In a course with ITAs who teach a variety of disciplines, it is necessary to use more generalized and varied examples, but these can be supplemented by having ITAs interview and observe native-speaking TAs in their own departments.

CASE STUDY 5: AN INSERVICE COURSE IN TEACHING PRONUNCIATION FOR EGYPTIAN TEACHERS OF ENGLISH

A group of twenty-five Egyptian secondary school teachers of English are participants in a government-sponsored summer inservice training course at a Canadian university. They are all highly educated native Arabic speakers whose overall English language proficiency is quite advanced. Although their university study concentrated on literature rather than linguistics, all are quite familiar with the International Phonetic Alphabet. Their command of English pronunciation varies – mostly in relation to the opportunities each has had to visit and study in English-speaking countries or to work with native English-speaking colleagues. Most have been taught to speak British English, and they are thus less familiar with NAE pronunciation. Language aptitude is high and many speak a second foreign language (French). These teachers are extremely motivated both by a desire to be a good model for their students and to learn more about English.

This 6-week summer institute includes a number of courses in methodology, of which teaching pronunciation is one. The instructor is a professor of TESL/Applied Linguistics with a strong interest in pronunciation pedagogy. The aim of the course is neither theoretical phonetics nor remedial pronunciation but rather an overview of current methods of teaching pronunciation communicatively, geared to the background level of the participants as well as their goal to be good models of spoken English for their students.

Pronunciation objectives   The pronunciation objectives are:

1. to examine the major contrasts between the Arabic and English sound systems
2. to expand the participants' knowledge of methods of teaching pronunciation communicatively
3. to gain the ability to analyze diagnostic speech samples, in particular of Arabic speakers of English
4. to gain the ability to recognize and highlight selected patterns of stress, intonation, and connected speech in taped samples of authentic spoken English
5. to prioritize pronunciation teaching points for students learning English in the Egyptian secondary school system

The following objectives are optional:

6. to analyze a personal diagnostic speech sample in consultation with the instructor
7. to develop a personal plan for improvement targeting specific areas of difficulty

Selection   The pronunciation features to be presented in this course are selected from three sources:

1. individual diagnostic speech samples
2. the major contrasts between the Arabic and English sound systems
3. typical classroom discourse and the basic communicative patterns of English routinely taught to Egyptian secondary school students

Potential teaching points include vowel contrasts, linking, the voiced/voiceless distinction, consonant clusters, /p/ vs. /b/, /r/, word stress, vowel reduction, sentence prominence, reduced speech, contrastive stress, and sound-spelling correspondences.

Arrangement   Because this is such a highly motivated group of experienced teachers with strong personal goals, the syllabus is generated by distributing a questionnaire on the first day to allow the trainees themselves to select and sequence the pronunciation features they wish to have covered in the course. The resulting consensus is based on a balance among the following factors:

1. an in-depth treatment of the sound system, targeting areas of personal interest and/or difficulty
2. exposure to a variety of communicative techniques for teaching pronunciation
3. the practical application of the first two factors to the participants' own teaching situation

Presentation Initially, the trainees are introduced to several pronunciation diagnostic instruments and are given the opportunity to analyze their own pronunciation in consultation with the instructor. Once the scope and sequence of the course has been defined, sessions are organized as follows:

Awareness stage: Multiple examples of spoken discourse containing the pronunciation feature are presented either on audio- or videotape for trainees to analyze (e.g., *Describe the intonation pattern of the tag questions in this conversation. Which ones rise? Which ones fall? What is the communicative function of the rises and the falls?*).

Analysis stage: The rule or pattern is presented and illustrated using a written transcript of the taped example along with several other contexts. If appropriate, visual representations of the feature or pattern are discussed and used to mark the transcript.

Experiential stage: A variety of contextualized and communicative activities (listening; controlled, guided, and free practice) are presented with trainees acting as the learners. Afterward, trainees discuss each activity in terms of difficulty, enjoyment, and the appropriateness and practicality of the activity for the Egyptian public school context.

Materials development stage: In groups, trainees adapt these activities for their own students or work on creating new ones of a similar type. Outside of class, trainees are encouraged to collect authentic samples of spoken discourse to use as a basis for further materials development.

Application Because it is designed for experienced teachers of English, this case study can best be applied to inservice teacher training programs. However, the pronunciation improvement component can easily be expanded for less proficient speakers (e.g., teachers in training) by including a more comprehensive overview of the sound system before targeting specific features.

CONCLUSION

Obviously, one possible case study that we do not treat here is a preservice practical phonetics course for graduate students pursuing a certificate or master's degree in teaching English as a second or foreign language. Such a syllabus description would be redundant in that this very volume contains what we would hope to convey to such students in a comprehensive university course. Both the descriptive content and the chapter-final questions and exercises are relevant to the objectives selected and their arrangement and presentation.

Another possible case study that we could have treated is the advanced heterogeneous ESL class for students learning English for academic purposes. This, however, is the situation for which most of the currently available commercial ESL/EFL pronunciation textbooks have been designed. Thus there is no problem in finding guidance in developing such a course. In our estimation, the greater challenge lies in integrating pronunciation into other types of courses or contexts.

Although the immediate classroom goal of any pronunciation lesson may be to enable students under closely monitored conditions to reproduce accurately a given sound or sound contrast, in most teaching settings accuracy of learner output is not a realistic goal for the pronunciation course. Thus the pronunciation syllabus should aim at the long-term goal of intelligibility rather than accuracy – that is, it should aim to reduce but not necessarily eradicate foreign accent. A result of implementing this goal of intelligibility is that the phonemic-based view of pronunciation has largely given way to a broader, discourse-based view, which includes the interaction between segmental features, voice quality settings, and prosodic features. With this discourse-based view, the argument that communicative practice should assume its place in the teaching of pronunciation is strongly underscored.

In this chapter we have presented factors that must be considered when designing the pronunciation syllabus (or the pronunciation component of a multiskills course). The relative weighting of pronunciation within the overall syllabus varies greatly, depending on general language policy issues, the proficiency level of the learners, the curriculum at the institution where study is being conducted, the method being practiced, and of course the communicative needs of the learners. Expectations of accuracy vary accordingly. Other differences are whether learners are presented with detailed information on the English sound system and whether they are expected to learn and use a phonemic alphabet.

What is common to the ideal pronunciation syllabus (quite divorced from the learner population for which it is intended) is that there should be a focus on both discrimination and production of selected features; furthermore, once instructed, learners should be able to reproduce these features intelligibly, both in isolation and within a larger discourse context. Where possible, they should be exposed to authentic speech samples that allow them to analyze and focus on a feature before any attempt at articulation. Finally, since no pronunciation syllabus can hope to address all aspects of the sound system, it should instead prioritize objectives according to the learner's communicative needs, highlighting those aspects of oral communication that have the greatest impact on the learner's comprehensibility.

In the last chapter of this book we discuss the very critical questions of how to assess learners' pronunciation skills at the outset of a course, how to provide ongoing feedback, and how to evaluate progress at the end of a course. The diagnostic function of pronunciation assessment will prove a critical piece of the puzzle for syllabus design, since it is a key to accurately assessing learners' needs.

EXERCISES

KEY CONCEPTS

Write a brief definition of the following key terms from this chapter. Give examples where relevant.

syllabus	methodological variables
curriculum	foreign language setting
learner variables	second language setting
setting variables	selection of objectives
institutional variables	arrangement of objectives
linguistic variables	presentation of objectives

INTROSPECTING ABOUT YOUR OWN LANGUAGE LEARNING

Think about a foreign language that you have learned in school or while living abroad.

1. Was pronunciation a part of the syllabus? If so, try to reconstruct what features were explicitly covered (e.g., segmentals, suprasegmentals, voice quality). Can you determine an underlying rationale for highlighting the feature(s)?

2. Have your second/foreign language teachers been native or nonnative speakers of the target language? What effect, if any, do you think this had on their teaching of pronunciation?

3. If English is not your native language, how confident do you feel about teaching English pronunciation? If English is your native language, think of the foreign language you know best. How confident would you be about teaching the pronunciation of this language?

DISCUSSION QUESTIONS

1. In terms of teaching pronunciation, how would the foreign versus second language setting influence your syllabus design?

2. Which do you think would be easier – teaching pronunciation to a homogeneous class in a foreign language setting or a heterogeneous class in a second language setting? Why?

3. Describe the ideal conditions (e.g., setting, class size) for teaching pronunciation.

4. As a teacher, to what extent and in what ways do learner variables affect the design of your pronunciation syllabus?

5. If you are teaching or have taught a language class that included a pronunciation component, which of the following variables have affected your teaching of pronunciation the most: linguistic, learner, setting, institutional, or methodological?

IN THE CLASSROOM

Assume that you are designing a pronunciation course or component. Here are some possible groups of learners that you might be called upon to teach.

1. You are tutoring a small group (two to three people). What adjustments to the syllabus for the individual tutoring format would you make (see case study 1)?

2. You are teaching pronunciation to ten people in an industrial setting in a foreign country. The group consists of learners ranging from executives to clerical workers, all with varying levels of pronunciation ability. How would you structure pronunciation practice to deal sensitively with the status issue?

3. You are teaching a multiskills EFL course. The textbook is communicatively oriented but provides no activities or exercises for pronunciation practice. You believe that the students need to work on their pronunciation. What would you do?

4. You have been asked to teach an oral skills course to English majors in their first year of study at a foreign university. To what extent and in what ways would you incorporate pronunciation into this course?

SUGGESTED ACTIVITIES

1. Examine a current ESL text that explicitly treats the skill of pronunciation (either an all-skills text, or a text devoted exclusively to pronunciation). Answer the following questions:

   a. What is the author's philosophy of teaching pronunciation? Does it reflect a segmental view or a more global, communicative approach?

   b. Does the text teach pronunciation in isolation, or does it integrate the teaching of pronunciation with that of other skills?

   c. To what degree does the organization of the text correlate with the sequence suggested by Prator (summarized in this chapter)? Are you comfortable with the sequencing as it exists?

   d. Do you consider the coverage of pronunciation issues adequate given the intended population? Why or why not?

2. Choose and define a population that you have taught or expect to teach. Describe the population in terms of the variables discussed. Then, using the case study framework presented in this chapter, design a course of study for pronunciation.

3. Interview an experienced teacher of pronunciation. Ask this teacher for a copy of a pronunciation course syllabus and find out about the procedure used to design the course. What variables influenced his or her determination of objectives?

CHAPTER 12

Testing and Evaluation

In the existing literature on teaching pronunciation, little attention is paid to issues of testing and evaluation. In part, this absence can be explained by the fact that the large body of literature on language assessment applies to pronunciation just as it does to any skill – reading, listening, speaking. But unlike these other areas, there are features unique to pronunciation that affect how evaluation is carried out, how feedback is provided, and at which stages of instruction feedback is most appropriately given. Primary among these unique aspects is the fact that pronunciation involves not only the application of relevant rules (e.g., when -s endings are pronounced /s/, /z/, or /ɪz/; or when word-internal palatalization of stops and fricatives occurs) but also perception and production. In this chapter, we discuss diagnostic procedures (including those formal oral proficiency tests that include pronunciation as one component) and treat ongoing feedback and evaluation, and classroom testing. (See also Goodwin, Brinton, and Celce-Murcia 1994 for additional discussion of pronunciation assessment issues.)

Many of the evaluation techniques discussed in this chapter will resemble the teaching techniques presented in Part 2 of this text. This is completely intentional. It is our belief that the most productive evaluation techniques are those that offer learners the greatest opportunity for feedback on their performance. Hence this is also one of our primary criteria for choosing effective classroom activities. Moreover, the more familiar the learners are with the format of a test, the greater the chance that their performance will reflect their true competence in that area. The second important point to remember when reading this chapter is that listening discrimination skills are considered to be an important part of developing intelligible oral production and thus are also a major part of evaluating overall pronunciation.

DIAGNOSTIC EVALUATION

Diagnostic evaluation of pronunciation, as of any skill, is a means of determining a learner's level of proficiency, usually for the purposes of *screening* (determining whether the learner can perform a certain task or function) or *placement* (deciding on a suitable class level given the learner's level of language proficiency). Within a particular course, diagnostic evaluation is also the teacher's initial method of setting or adjusting curricular objectives for a specific population of students and of determining individual needs. In short, it is a global assessment of the class's – and each learner's – perception and production.

DIAGNOSING PERCEPTION

Diagnostic tests of listening discrimination, which can be given either in class or in a language laboratory, should test the learner's ability to distinguish both segmental and suprasegmental features. This can be done in a number of ways.

Consonant–vowel discrimination In order to determine the learner's ability to distinguish vowel and consonant sounds, the teacher can use minimal-pair discrimination exercises. In the following examples, the teacher reads a sentence with one of the two choices in the minimal pair or uses a tape recording.

Directions: Mark the word you hear.

a. Don't (slip / sleep) on the floor.

b. He's gone to (back up / pack up) the car.

or:

Directions: Mark which one of the two illustrations represents the sentence you hear.

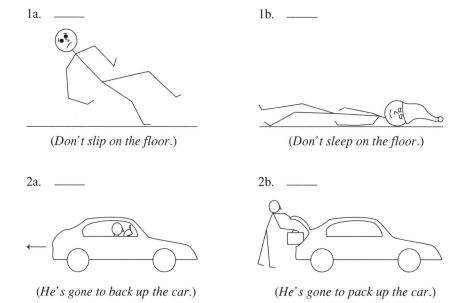

1a. _____

(Don't slip on the floor.)

1b. _____

(Don't sleep on the floor.)

2a. _____

(He's gone to back up the car.)

2b. _____

(He's gone to pack up the car.)

Word stress Recognition of English word stress patterns can be tested by asking learners to choose the correct stress pattern for words or sentences in a text or dialogue that is recorded or read aloud by the teacher:

Directions: Mark the choice that shows the syllable receiving the main stress (capitals = main stress).

(*on cassette*) 1. <u>Photography</u> is one of my favorite <u>activities</u>.

        a. PHOtography   d. ACtivities

        b. phoTOGraphy   e. acTIVities

        c. photoGRAPHy   f. actiVITies

2. I really enjoy taking pictures of <u>ordinary</u> scenes that most people might not even notice.

    a. ORdinary

    b. orDINary

    c. ordiNARy

Prominence Testing formats that diagnose learners' abilities to perceive the most prominent element can resemble those used for word stress.

Directions: Listen to the following utterances and mark the choice that best represents the proper stress pattern (capitals = stress).

1. Joe: Hi, I'm Joe Miller. What's your name?
   a. HI, I'm JOE Miller. WHAT'S your name?
   b. HI, I'M Joe MILLer. What's YOUR name?
   c. Hi, I'M Joe Miller. What's your NAME?

2. Pat: Patricia Langley, but you can call me Pat.
   a. PaTRIcia LANGley, BUT you can call ME Pat.
   b. PATricia LangLEY, but you CAN call me PAT.
   c. PaTRIcia LANGley, but YOU can call me PAT.

Intonation For testing the learner's discrimination of intonation patterns, two types of tests may be used. First, the learner is asked to determine whether the utterance has rising or rising-falling intonation.

Directions: Listen to the following utterances. Check the box that corresponds to the intonation pattern used (rising for questions or rising-falling for statements).

Utterance	Question ↗	Statement ↗ ↘
1. Mary's gone home	☐	☐
2. The VCR doesn't work	☐	☐
3. Jim and Jessica had triplets	☐	☐

This format can easily be adapted to other grammatical forms that are differentiated by means of rising or falling intonation:

Directions: Check the box that corresponds to the intonation pattern used (rising-falling for tag questions in which the speaker is sure of the answer; rising for those in which the speaker is unsure).

Utterance	Sure ↗ ↘	Unsure ↗
1. He hasn't finished fixing the car, has he?	☐	☐
2. The situation's getting worse, isn't it?	☐	☐
3. The stores will be really crowded this time of year, won't they?	☐	☐

More advanced learners could be asked to identify – in a multiple choice format – the intonation contours of utterances.

Directions: Listen to the following utterances and mark the contour that best represents the intonation pattern of the speaker.

1. *Would you like some coffee or tea?*

    a.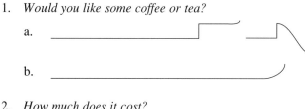

    b.

2. *How much does it cost?*

    a.

    b.

Second, a multiple choice format can also be used to test the learner's ability to distinguish the shades of meaning expressed by different stress and intonation patterns for the same utterance. For this type of assessment, the learner hears the initial utterance and then must determine which interpretation or response is the correct one.

Directions: Listen to the following statements and choose the one that best represents the meaning of the speaker.

1. *Can you come to dinner on* 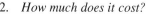 *FRIday?*

    a. I know he can't, but can you?
    b. OK, if you can't make it on Saturday, how about Friday?
    c. If lunch is inconvenient, what about dinner?

2. *What do* YOU *think?*

    a. I already know what he thinks.
    b. Is it a good idea or not?
    c. I'm sorry, I didn't hear you.

Reduced speech   For testing the learner's comprehension of reduced speech, the following format utilizes a cloze passage in which commonly reduced and unstressed words have been deleted. Students then provide the missing words as they listen to the taped passage or dialogue.

Directions: Listen to the following recorded weather report and fill in the missing word(s) in each blank.

This is the WPRO weather update. The weather on Friday is expected _____
                                                                   1. *(to)*

be cool _____ cloudy. There will be a fifty percent chance _____
          2. *(and)*   **3.** *(of)*

showers in the morning, but it _____ clear up by late afternoon. Temperatures
                                4. *(should)*

will range _____ a low of forty-five degrees to a high of sixty-two.
            5. *(from)*

In the following dialogue, there may be more than one word missing in each blank. This format is designed to be slightly more challenging.

Directions: One or more words are missing in each blank. Listen to the two speakers and write in missing words.

A: Where _____ go?
            1. *(did he)*

B: I _____ . I haven't seen _____ .
      2. *(don't know)*   **3.** *(him)*

A: Well, where _____ think _____ went?
           4. *(do you)*   **5.** *(he)*

B: If I _____ tell you I would, but I can't!
         6. *(could)*

The foregoing are only a sample of test item formats that a teacher might use to diagnose a learner's perception and its potential impact on pronunciation. The advantage of these diagnostic techniques is that they can be performed with large populations in a laboratory setting. Individual interviews would certainly provide additional valuable information regarding the learner's ability to perceive and process natural spoken English, if such an option is available.

DIAGNOSING PRODUCTION IN THE CLASSROOM

It is best to obtain two types of spoken production samples at the outset of instruction:

1. a standardized sample of the learner reading aloud
2. a sample of the learner's free speech

These two samples complement each other and assist the teacher in confirming the extent to which learners require instruction in a particular area of spoken production.

In eliciting the first of these two samples, teachers often use a written text known as a *diagnostic passage* to assess a student's command of pronunciation features that might not necessarily occur in a natural speech context. These include the learner's ability to produce certain consonant cluster configurations or the ability to use appropriate intonation in alternative (i.e., closed-choice) questions. In fact, diagnostic passages are typically constructed to contain all or most of the segmental and suprasegmental features of English so that the learner's command of these features can be accurately diagnosed and the teacher can determine where to place the focus of instruction. See Appendix 13 for a sample diagnostic passage and feedback guide.[1]

When administering the diagnostic passage, teachers should first allow the learners to hear a native-speaker rendition of it (either the teacher reading aloud or a taped version); they should then be allowed time to practice before recording the passage. Although this idea of rehearsal may seem counterintuitive to many (after all, this is a "test"), the goal of diagnostic assessment of pronunciation is for the teacher to obtain as true a representation of the learner's typical speech patterns as possible. Even for articulate native speakers, the reading aloud of an unfamiliar passage can result in an unnatural flow, awkward pauses or stumbling over words, restarts, and the like. Practicing a diagnostic passage in advance allows learners to avoid some of the unnatural reading features that might otherwise occur. Obviously, the passage will never truly represent the learners' spontaneous speech. However, allowing learners to rehearse until they feel comfortable reading the passage aloud will allow the teacher to obtain the truest sampling of individual errors.

Both the practice and recording phases are facilitated by the availability of a language laboratory, since an entire class can easily complete the recording in one sitting. However,

[1]Perhaps the best-known example of a diagnostic passage is Prator and Robinett's "Diagnostic Passage and Accent Inventory" accompanying *A Manual of American English Pronunciation* (1985). Today many commercially available pronunciation texts include similar diagnostic reading passages as part of establishing an initial pronunciation profile.

barring this, students can be allowed to tape the passage at home and return it to the teacher for subsequent analysis and written feedback.[2] We suggest using the same diagnostic passage at both the beginning of instruction (to analyze student needs) and at the end (to chart student progress). It is our experience that under carefully monitored conditions (in which students can focus primarily on form rather than meaning) student production can improve substantially, thus motivating students to continue working on their pronunciation.

Since reading aloud does not provide the most natural evidence of a speaker's pronunciation (and may, as stated earlier, induce certain kinds of errors), it is also essential to obtain a more spontaneous sample of spoken English from all students. In this *free speech sample,* students focus primarily on meaning rather than form. This allows confirmation or reassessment of the impressions gained from the analysis of the diagnostic passage.

In order to obtain a free speech sample, the teacher can ask learners to speak for one or two minutes about a familiar topic, such as their family, their hometown, a favorite childhood memory, their major field of interest, or their current occupation and why they chose it. Of primary importance in selecting the topic is that the learner should feel at ease in talking about it. Many teachers prefer to give learners several topics to choose from. An obvious advantage of this is that learners are more apt to provide a fluent speech sample on a topic selected from a range of choices; a possible disadvantage of offering choice is the resulting lack of uniformity in the speech samples obtained from different students.

If the teacher prefers a certain amount of uniformity in these free speech samples, this can be accomplished by using a visual stimulus (such as an illustrated story sequence or cartoon strip without text). Figure 12.1 shows an example from Graham (1991: 30) of the type of prompt we have used. These free speech samples may be recorded on either audiotape or videotape. Since the focus is pronunciation and not presentation skills, an audio recording is quite adequate. Nevertheless, videotapes can be used effectively if closeups of the speakers' faces have been recorded. Closeups may provide certain articulatory information about the learners' pronunciation, such as a tendency to keep the jaw in a somewhat fixed position or a systematic lack of lip closure in final bilabial consonants (e.g., *from* pronounced as /frɑ/).

FORMAL ORAL PROFICIENCY TESTING INSTRUMENTS

Several *formal oral proficiency tests* exist on the market today. Most provide a global oral proficiency score without evaluating any of the subcomponents separately, and focus on production rather than perception. Tests such as the English Language Testing Services (ELTS) examination and the Royal Society of Arts CUEFL (Communicative Use of English as a Foreign Language) examinations evaluate general oral proficiency against a scale consisting of levels described by characteristic linguistic or target performance features. Other oral proficiency tests measure grammatical accuracy and/or functional appropriacy without any reference to pronunciation (e.g., the Ilyin Oral Interview). In oral proficiency tests in which pronunciation is evaluated, it is usually rated globally, as is the case with the Basic English Skills Test (BEST). A summary and review of these and other proficiency tests, oral and written, can be found in the TESOL publication *Reviews of English Language Proficiency Tests* (Alderson, Krahnke, and Stansfield 1987).

Among the most widely used tests of oral proficiency is the *Test of Spoken English* (TSE), designed by the Educational Testing Service (ETS) and administered overseas in the same manner as the Test of English as a Foreign Language (TOEFL). It is a semidirect

[2]This written feedback may take various forms. For example, in the Prator and Robinett (1985) version, teachers use the "Accent Inventory," a comprehensive checklist of problems. Teachers may also simply wish to write the substituted features on the diagnostic passage itself, or to give the learner feedback using a more open-ended summary table, such as the Accent Checklist included in Appendix 13.

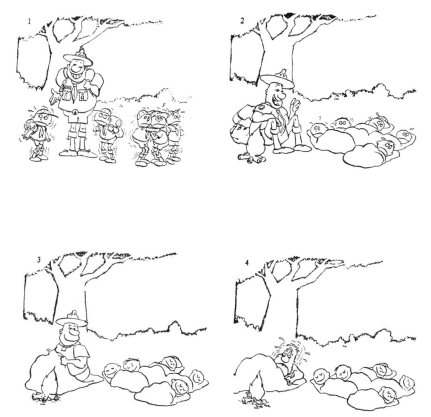

Figure 12.1 Illustrated story sequence to prompt free speech (From *Rhythm and Role Play*, C. Graham and S. Aragones, JAG Publications, 1991.)

measure in which examinees provide verbal responses to tape-recorded and written prompts in a language laboratory setting. Tasks include reading aloud, describing a picture, telling a story from a series of pictures, sentence completion, presenting a schedule or syllabus, and either expressing one's opinion about a controversial topic or describing a familiar object. The total score, reported on a 0 to 300 scale, reflects the examinee's overall comprehensibility; subscores for pronunciation, grammar, and fluency are also given. Pronunciation is rated on a scale from 0 to 3 according to the following descriptors (Educational Testing Service 1992: 13):

0.0–0.4 Frequent phonemic errors and foreign stress and intonation patterns that cause the speaker to be unintelligible

0.5–1.4 Frequent phonemic errors and foreign stress and intonation patterns that cause the speaker to be occasionally unintelligible

1.5–2.4 Some consistent phonemic errors and foreign stress and intonation patterns, but speaker is intelligible

2.5–3.0 Occasional nonnative pronunciation errors, but speaker is always intelligible

A retired version of the Test of Spoken English – the Spoken English Assessment Kit, or **SPEAK Test** – has been released by the Educational Testing Service for institutional use in the United States and is frequently used to screen nonnative graduate teaching assistants at universities.

Another test of oral proficiency that measures pronunciation is the Interagency Language Roundtable Oral Proficiency Interview (ILR), formerly referred to as the Foreign Service Oral Interview (FSI). This 30-minute test is conducted by two trained interviewers, one of whom conducts the interview while the other observes and takes notes on the examinee's performance. It consists of four parts: the warmup (to put the examinee at ease), the level check (to find the examinee's level of performance), the probe (to discover the upper limits of performance and where it begins to break down), and the winddown (to return the examinee to a comfortable level of performance before closing). Pronunciation and fluency are two of the components for which the two interviewers give holistic ratings on a scale of 0 to 5 points.

The ILR Oral Interview was originally designed for government use but has been adapted by the American Council on the Teaching of Foreign Languages (ACTFL) and ETS for use in academic settings. The scale has been expanded at the lower levels of proficiency (0–2+) to reflect finer distinctions. (We provide the ACTFL Proficiency Guidelines for speaking in Appendix 14.)

An alternative scale that incorporates not only a description of the learner's speech but also the impact of the learner's speech on communication is Morley's (1994b) Speech Intelligibility/Communicability Index (see Appendix 15). In the index, Morley identifies three basic levels of speech intelligibility: a pre-threshold level (essentially uncommunicative) followed by two threshold levels (partially communicative and fully communicative).

The recent interest in and necessity of screening nonnative graduate teaching assistants at universities has created new formats for evaluating pronunciation, which is certainly one of the principal factors in a graduate instructor's oral communicative competence. One popular method is the simulated teaching demonstration, which provides a 15- to 20-minute videotaped sample of a discipline-specific presentation in a teaching context. Discrete tasks may include a short presentation of first-day announcements, a mini-lesson, and a simulated office hour. These screening/diagnostic tests are usually administered by trained ESL professionals with actual university students listening to the presentation and asking questions. Scoring may vary from an overall impression of a speaker's pronunciation to measurement of the actual production against a scale in which each level of pronunciation and speech flow has its own description and additional open comments about specific errors. Appendix 16 is an example of this type of scale.

ONGOING EVALUATION WITH FEEDBACK

Once a diagnostic evaluation of the learner's perception and production has been made, the teacher is able to address the most pressing pronunciation needs of the students within the time frame and curricular objectives of a particular course.

The purpose of such *ongoing evaluation and feedback* during the lesson is twofold. On the one hand, the teacher needs to determine the progress students are making in order to provide as much individualization as possible and to revise the curriculum, if necessary. Furthermore, in order for each learner to improve during the period of instruction, the teacher should provide continuous informal feedback on individual progress. This may take the form of opportunities for self-monitoring and correction, peer feedback, or teacher correction.

SELF-MONITORING AND CORRECTION

Theoretically, there is still much disagreement on the degree to which learners can *self-monitor* – notice their own inaccuracies in production – and *self-correct* – produce more targetlike language upon recognition of a production error. Nonetheless, self-monitoring has always played a central role in pronunciation teaching, and most language teachers believe that their students must first be able to recognize that they are making mistakes before they can correct them. In fact, there is some limited evidence to suggest that, with guidance, learners *can* improve in their ability to monitor their pronunciation errors.[3]

Coupled with today's focus on self-directed learning and the development of learner autonomy, monitoring is assuming a larger role than it has previously played in language teaching. As part of learners' taking responsibility for their own learning, self-monitoring is vital to learners' sense of control over their progress. This appears to be particularly true in the realm of pronunciation, for many teachers recognize that the responsibility for monitoring and correcting should rest primarily with the learner, and that the key to forging a closer connection between these two skills depends on learners' accepting responsibility for their own production.

In keeping with these beliefs, one technique revolutionizing the teaching of pronunciation today is self-directed learning. Practitioners such as Acton (1984), Browne and Huckin (1987), Firth (1992a), and Ricard (1986) articulate the following principles:

1. Students should define their own learning objectives.
2. They should have control of their learning activities.
3. They need to be able to select techniques and methodologies that suit their individual learning styles.
4. They should control such aspects of learning as the physical setting, the time of learning, their degree of autonomy, and the rate at which they learn.
5. They should have a voice in evaluating their progress.

These practitioners differ slightly in their methods for implementing self-directed learning. Acton places a strong emphasis on **contract learning,** stressing that the most important changes in pronunciation will occur outside of the classroom. In his pronunciation workshops, the instructor and student individually negotiate the learning objectives. Total responsibility is therefore placed upon the students themselves, who generate and sign "contracts" committing themselves to the changes they wish to make in their pronunciation, the methods they intend to pursue, and the time and place that they will carry out corrective practice. Ricard places a similar emphasis on student-generated strategies; as a part of the course requirements, students collaboratively produce a type of self-help manual detailing ways in which to improve pronunciation.

Dickerson (1984, 1987a) refers to **covert rehearsal,** in which learners practice privately – preparing for interactions, creating conversations, thinking about the accuracy of their utterances, comparing them with their memory of native-speaker models and with the rules of pronunciation they know. Some of the techniques he suggests include:

1. raising learners' awareness about the importance of talking to themselves out loud in the target language as a strategy used by good language learners, noting that actors and public speakers often rehearse before speaking
2. having learners make predictions of word stress, vowel quality, sentence prominence, and so on in the exercises they do at home followed by reading these same exercises aloud
3. having learners make tape recordings of the material presented in class to encourage covert rehearsal at home
4. providing a checklist that identifies the pronunciation features for which the teacher will be listening

---

[3]For an empirical study of this claim, see Yule et al. (1987). They comment on the complex interaction between learners' accuracy levels and their self-assessments of accuracy, noting that "accuracy seemed to have a more solid basis in terms of the learners' self-monitoring skills" (p. 768).

Dickerson points out that with such a checklist, learners consciously monitor themselves on specific points and adjust their production accordingly.

Despite slight differences in focus, pronunciation programs emphasizing self-directed learning share a number of philosophical underpinnings. Primary among these, of course, is the emphasis on the individual's assuming responsibility for change. For this reason, self-directed learning programs make creative use of tutors and learning centers to help students accomplish their goals. These programs also stress the relationship between learners' internal states and their pronunciation,[4] paying much attention to how changes in such external aspects of behavior as breathing, posture, and body tension can affect production. Finally, they emphasize the achievement of realistic goals, stating unequivocally that the aim of pronunciation instruction is to improve learners' intelligibility, not to achieve total accuracy.

In addition to encouraging learners to more systematically self-monitor outside of class, teachers need to generate an atmosphere in class that encourages self-correction. This can be done in any of the following ways:

1. By writing the utterance on the board and underlining the mispronounced feature:
    In conclu<u>sion</u>,...
    (The student had pronounced /dʒ/ instead of /ʒ/.)

2. By writing the type of error on the board:
    r/l
    (The student had said: "My f<u>r</u>ight is at 2 p.m.")

3. By pointing to wall charts posted around the classroom that signify the type of error:

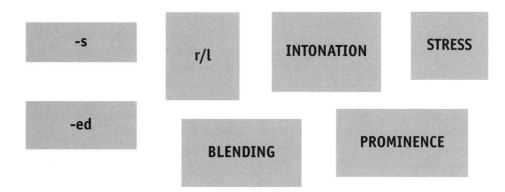

This technique borrows rather liberally from methods such as the Silent Way and Suggestopedia, which use wall charts and posters as a standard part of the language class-room. (See Larsen-Freeman 1986 and Chapter 1 of this text for a more comprehensive overview of these methods.) Obviously, it can be employed only if the students understand the rules underlying the features on the charts. In this example these involve:

*   how *-ed* and *-s* endings are pronounced
*   how the articulation of /r/ differs from that of /l/
*   basic word and sentence stress rules
*   basic intonation patterns
*   typical occasions for blending words in English

---

[4]Acton (1984) discusses at length the issues of *inside out change* (internal changes in emotion and/or affect that relate to changes in ego permeability) and *outside in change* (external, behavioral changes in body posture, etc., which affect production).

4. By having the learner transcribe one portion (or all) of a recorded performance and then try to locate errors before meeting with the teacher.

5. By having the learner evaluate a recorded performance using a guide. Appendix 17 contains an example of a worksheet that has been used by advanced learners to evaluate their own pronunciation following a paired interview role play in which the participants alternately performed the roles of a famous personality and a talk show host. (Interview formats work particularly well for self-feedback purposes.)

PEER FEEDBACK

In order for all students to benefit from interaction in the classroom, it is useful to have peers serve as both monitors and givers of feedback. This helps to sharpen their own listening skills and to put their knowledge of pronunciation rules to immediate use. If a learner is unable to self-correct, then the teacher should try to elicit the correction from a classmate.

One way of structuring peer feedback is to have students work in groups. Groups of three or four often work better than pairs because at any given moment, there are two or three listeners (i.e., evaluators) to determine if the speaker has pronounced an utterance correctly. (In pair work there can be disagreement about whether the speaker *pronounced* the utterance incorrectly or the listener *heard* it incorrectly – so the consensus of several listeners helps resolve the question.)

A simple example of this is a minimal pair worksheet such as the following, which tests learners' abilities to perceive and produce voiced versus voiceless consonants in word-final position:

Directions: Listen and mark the words you hear.

1. Only two <u>seats</u> / <u>seeds</u> are left.
2. They're going to <u>lunch</u> / <u>lunge</u>.
3. I found ten <u>bucks</u> / <u>bugs</u>.
4. She wasn't able to <u>face</u> / <u>faze</u> him.

Suppose that an exercise contains twenty such minimal pair sentences. Each student in a group of four can be responsible for five of the twenty sentences. Students should privately mark in advance which five words they intend to pronounce, and then read these aloud while the other three group members silently check the word that they hear. If, for example, all three listeners marked *seats* in sentence 1, but the speaker's intent was to say *seeds,* it is likely that the word was pronounced incorrectly. If the listeners disagree on which word was pronounced, the teacher may have to intervene and mediate the confusion by asking the speaker to repeat. Using group members as listeners is valuable for two reasons: More students are involved in speaking at one time (the teacher is free to move around monitoring different groups) and students practice both pronunciation and listening discrimination skills.

Peers can also provide focused feedback during more unfocused practice, such as unscripted oral presentations and role plays. In these cases, students can be instructed to listen for whether a particular feature is pronounced correctly, such as -*s* endings, word stress, yes/no question intonation, or blending between words.

An additional activity, which can be done if the class performs paired interviews or role plays, is to have the two speakers transcribe both their own and their partner's utterances and then go over the errors together before meeting with the instructor. This allows for maximum self- and peer correction before teacher intervention.

TEACHER FEEDBACK AND CORRECTION

During classroom activities, the teacher will not want to interrupt each speaker every time an error is made, so it is useful to keep an informal written tally of errors for later correction. In general, the teacher's principal role is to call attention to errors – on the spot or later – as unobtrusively as possible, giving learners every opportunity to begin applying the rules of pronunciation they are learning in order to monitor their own (and others') speech more effectively. Unfortunately, students usually lack a concrete way to hold on to the feedback and models used in class. For this reason, teachers should ideally make use of an audiocassette recorder.

One advantage of in-class recordings (as opposed to language lab recordings) is the opportunity for peer and teacher feedback. This allows the speaker(s) to receive immediate feedback and the peers a chance to increase their listening skills. It is best to have classmates listen for a particular feature agreed upon in advance. A taped recording permits all parties to review the performance afterward and to fill out an evaluation form. Another useful activity is to have students transcribe (in normal orthography) one portion or all of their audiotaped performance and then try to locate pronunciation errors before consulting with the instructor. Often the most useful feedback comes when the teacher and student listen to the recording and go over the errors together. It is particularly helpful for teachers to have a second tape recorder handy in their offices in order to tape the conference. The student can then take home the cassette recording of the conference and review it.

A highly successful form of individual feedback can be provided outside of class through audiotaped dialogue journals, as described in Chapter 10. These oral exchanges can be recorded as homework and can follow a variety of formats: e.g., redoing a lesson from class, rehearsing an oral report, reading a passage aloud, asking questions. To maximize the usefulness of the journal as a way of making students more aware of their own speech patterns, students should listen to their entry and then follow it up by tape recording their own evaluation of it, including any errors that they are able to notice. This exercise encourages both active listening discrimination and the ability to self-monitor. In this way, the teacher can first respond to the self-evaluation and then add feedback. It is best to take notes while listening to the student entry, keeping track of errors on a separate piece of paper. In this way, the speaker can be alerted to any noticeable patterns of error, rather than simply be given a laundry list of unconnected errors. The learner should then be encouraged to make use of this feedback by incorporating the troublesome pronunciation features into the following entry in some way. This technique has proved to be effective in helping students to locate systematic errors, review corrective input, direct their own learning, and note progress over time.

CLASSROOM TESTING

Whereas the diagnostic tests discussed at the beginning of this chapter screen or place learners based on their overall command of English perception and production, classroom tests focus on the material that has been taught and are therefore used to indicate the student's progress and achievement within the context of a specific course and curriculum. Since both diagnostic and classroom tests may be similar in design, the example items presented in the section on diagnostic procedures could, in many cases, serve as classroom test items as well.

It is important to note, however, that the scope of a classroom test is generally much narrower than that of a diagnostic test, since the areas to be tested are determined by what has been emphasized in class. In addition, unlike a diagnostic test, which is administered at the outset of instruction, classroom tests occur at various points in time over the duration of the course, often measuring achievement in a limited area, such as command of consonant contrasts or mastery of stress and intonation patterns. In general, pronunciation tests are most easily administered in the language laboratory, where students can complete the listening section and respond to the speaking tasks in their individual booths.

In the section that follows, we have again divided the discussion into assessment of perception and assessment of production. An additional format, tests of phonetic knowledge, is also discussed as it relates to assessment in a practical phonetics course for advanced learners or prospective teachers.

TESTS OF PERCEPTION

The following are test prototypes. They can be tape recorded or read aloud by the teacher.

Consonant and vowel discrimination

1. In each line of four words, circle the word that has a different initial sound.
   a. sugar   sun   city   sock
   b. cure   kite   car   church
   c. thigh   then   this   there

2. In each line of four words, circle the word that has a different vowel sound.
   a. does   son   what   on
   b. look   fool   wood   book
   c. sake   paid   aid   salve

For the following test formats, a basic knowledge of phonetics is necessary.

1. Circle all the words that have an /iy/ sound.
   neat   kit   deep   great
   elite   dream   fit   complete
   sleep   time   bite   reach

2. Put the following words into the proper column according to their vowel sound:
   dull   pull   wool   book
   fool   mud   room   should
   good   luck   took   pool

/ʊ/	/uw/	/ʌ/

3. Write the phonetic symbol for the initial sound you hear.
   a. (photograph)
   b. (sugar)
   c. (thimble)
   d. (children)

4. Write the phonetic symbol for the final sound you hear.
   a. (enough)
   b. (which)
   c. (says)
   d. (taped)

5. Write the phonetic symbol of the vowel sound you hear.
   a. (foot)
   b. (said)
   c. (light)
   d. (toast)

6. Write the word you hear in phonetic symbols.
    a. (just)
    b. (threw)
    c. (reach)
    d. (lice)

Word stress

Directions: Listen to the following words as they are read aloud and circle the syllable that receives primary stress.

Example: po•(ten)•tial

pho•to•graph•ic   dem•on•stra•tion   suc•cess•ful
in•no•cent   tel•e•vi•sion   ir•rel•e•vant

Prominence

1. Circle the answer that best corresponds to the meaning of the speaker.
   [*on tape*] She enjoys THIS class . . .
   a. but I don't.
   b. but not history.
   c. She really thinks it's great!

   [*on tape*] Sam DIDn't take the car.
   a. Quit accusing him!
   b. Celia did!
   c. He took the bus.

2. Circle the stressed words/syllables in the following dialogue as you listen.
   Example: (What) do you (want) to (do) to(night)?
   Bob: Why did you turn the television on?
   Judy: I want to see the news on Channel Two.
   Bob: Doesn't it come on at six?
   Judy: Normally, yes. But today there's a special report on rain forests.

Intonation

Directions: Listen to the following conversation and mark the intonation contours of each sentence. The first line is marked for you as an example.

A: How are you doing?

B: Fine, thanks. And you?

A: Pretty good. Are you ready to go?

B: Sure. Just let me get my car keys.

Reduced speech

Directions: Read the conversation as you listen to it on the tape. In each blank, fill
in the missing words. More than one word may be missing from a blank.

Larry: I wondered if I _____ borrow your car _____ while.
                        1. *(could)*   **2.** *(for a)*

Mike: What _____ mean by "a while"?
              3. *(do you)*

Larry: Well, _____ pick up my sister _____ airport
                    4. *(I have to)*   **5.** *(at the)*

          _____ plane's _____ a little late.
                6. *(but her)*   **7.** *(going to be)*

Mike: I _____ if I _____ lend it to
                  8. *(don't know)*   **9.** *(can)*

          _____ entire afternoon or anything but . . .
                10. *(you for an)*

TESTS OF PRODUCTION

As with tests of perception, tests of production should focus on features that have been taught in class. The speaking portion of a classroom test can consist of various short passages that the student reads aloud onto the tape. Scoring of such production exercises should be straightforward, with points counted only for the individual items being evaluated. Since one of the skills we are teaching is how to monitor one's own speech, students should have adequate opportunities to rehearse before recording. As with diagnostic assessment, this rehearsal phase is essential. Its purpose is twofold: First, it allows learners to familiarize themselves with the passage; second, it provides them with time to think consciously about the pronunciation features we are teaching them and about which rules to apply. In fact, we encourage students to record themselves, listen to the recording, and then to rerecord the passage if they perceive an error they wish to correct. Since these production tests are intended to measure the learner's command of features presented in class when focusing consciously on pronunciation, we suggest choosing a specific focus for each passage and making sure students pay attention to applying the rules for this feature. For example:

Directions: Read the following aloud, paying special attention to linking between words.

June‿and Bill‿are classmates‿in‿an‿Italian conversation course. This‿afternoon they‿are having‿a drink together‿at an‿outdoor cafe near the school. They‿are talking‿about how much they would like to go‿on‿a trip to‿Italy next‿year.

Similar exercises can be designed to focus on such features as *-ed* and *-s* endings, vowel or consonant contrasts, word stress, sentence stress, reduced speech, and intonation. For example:

Directions: Record the following passage, paying special attention to the underlined vowel sounds.

EARTHQUAKE PRECAUTIONS

Living in California, we f<u>a</u>ce the constant thr<u>ea</u>t of earthquakes. M<u>a</u>ny people today are <u>a</u>sking what we can d<u>o</u> to prepare <u>ou</u>rselves better. In fact, there are n<u>u</u>merous simple prec<u>au</u>tions that we can take. For example, we can st<u>o</u>ck up on earthquake s<u>u</u>pplies, such as w<u>a</u>ter, canned goods, n<u>u</u>ts, and dried fr<u>ui</u>t, and keep these on hand. We can also prepare an earthquake k<u>i</u>t with essential <u>i</u>tems, such as warm cl<u>o</u>thing and blankets, a flashlight, a pocket r<u>a</u>dio, simple tools, and first <u>ai</u>d supplies. <u>A</u>nchor your b<u>oo</u>kcases and other h<u>ea</u>vy items to the wall, and don't hang pictures ab<u>o</u>ve your bed. P<u>e</u>rhaps most importantly, get to know your n<u>ei</u>ghbors.

As an alternative to monologue reading, teachers may wish to have students read one part of a cued dialogue, as in the following example:[5]

Directions: On tape, you will hear the sentences read by Speaker A in the left-hand column below. Read Speaker B's responses, paying special attention to sentence prominence.

Speaker A	**Speaker B**
A: Come into my shop. I've got the best rugs in the market.	
	B: No, thank you. I've got enough rugs as it is. I surely don't need any more.
A: But wait. I can see you like this rug. Come into my shop and have a cup of tea and I'll show you some beautiful carpets.	
	B: Sorry, I'd like to, but I'm broke and I've got to get going. I'm going to be late.
A: But for you, I'll make a special price. Why don't you come on in and take a look at what we've got. You don't have to stay long.	
	B: Well, no harm in just looking, I suppose. But only as long as I don't have to buy anything.
A: It's from the north. How do you like it?	
	B: Yeah, it is pretty!
A: And it's got a nice design. Look at the borders.	
	B: Well, I'm afraid to ask, but how much does this one run, anyway?
A: For you, I'll let it go for 388 dollars.	
	B: What did you say? You must have said 318 'cause 388's just out of the question! Who could ever pay so much?
A: I'll tell you what! For you, I'll give it to you for 380.	
	B: Sorry, but I knew I shouldn't have come in here. I couldn't even afford 360 or 340. I told you I'm broke!
A: But 380's a great deal. This carpet's unique. Believe me! It's one of a kind. How much can you afford to spend?	
	B: No, I think I'd better be leaving now. I'm really not supposed to be buying any more carpets. Thanks, anyway.

[5]This example is from Purpura (1991) and is used with his permission.

As part of the classroom test, instructors may also wish to evaluate the learner's control of pronunciation when not focusing exclusively on form. In this case, it is necessary to elicit and record a sample of free speech. Several formats are possible. It is easy to add a brief discussion topic at the end of the reading-aloud portion of a test. The topic might depend on the feature(s) being tested. For example, if testing spontaneous mastery of the various *-ed* endings, then teachers could ask students about last summer's vacation or yesterday's experiences. If facilities for videotaping exist, students can be asked to give an oral presentation, interview a classmate, or perform a role play with one or two other students. Although oral presentations are sometimes preferred because of their focus on individual performance, interviews and role plays are useful because there is more opportunity for varied intonation patterns. In addition, the interactional aspect lends authenticity to the task and helps to relax the students. Whatever the task, if students' free speech is being evaluated as part of a classroom test, it is necessary that the teacher evaluate all student samples using the same criteria. For this purpose, an evaluation and feedback instrument such as that in Table 12.1 is useful.

TABLE 12.1 ORAL PRESENTATION EVALUATION FORM

	Excellent	Good	Fair
I. Message content *Was the topic appropriate? Interesting? Did the speaker demonstrate knowledge of the topic? Was the speaker enthusiastic and convincing?*	3	2	1
II. Organization *Was there a clear introduction to the topic? Was evidence or support presented in a logical fashion? Did the speaker give a conclusion?*	3	2	1
III. Physical delivery *Were gestures used appropriately? Did the speaker have good posture and make appropriate eye contact? Was the speaker relaxed? Was his or her facial expression pleasant and animated? Were audiovisual aids used to clarify or illustrate?*	3	2	1
IV. Clarity *Was the speaker's voice loud enough? Did the speaker enunciate clearly? Was the speed okay? Was the message intelligible?*	3	2	1
V. Pronunciation *Did the speaker use appropriate stress and intonation? Were vowels and consonants pronounced correctly? Were words linked, blended, and reduced appropriately?*	3	2	1

TOTAL = _____/15 points

TESTS OF PHONETIC KNOWLEDGE

In the case of a practical phonetics course offered to advanced learners or prospective teachers, a third format that tests phonetic knowledge or awareness may also be desirable. In this format, which is appropriate only if rules of the sound system have been clearly presented and explained, learners are asked (as a paper and pen test) to apply rules they have learned.[6] By applying rules, learners can demonstrate their understanding of how a particular feature operates, even though their ability to perceive and/or produce this feature may still be developing. Tests of phonetic knowledge may be used alone, or together with tests of perception and production. Certainly, testing the application of rules does not replace either tests of perception or tests of production; nonetheless, it reveals one aspect of a learner's proficiency that might not be evident in listening or speaking tests.

Allophonic variation

Directions: In the following sentence, circle the /t/ sounds that are normally articulated as a flap [ɾ].

She was the brightest, most beautiful of his three daughters, and no matter who set out to ask for her hand in marriage, her father refused the offer.

Word stress

Directions: Put each word into the proper column according to its stress pattern. One model word is provided for each pattern.

horrible	decision	beautiful
matinee	bicycle	understand
according	instrument	determine
presented	overturn	furniture

● ∙ ∙	∙ ● ∙	∙ ∙ ●
TALented	proDUCtion	guaranTEE

Prominence

Directions: Read the following dialogue. Then circle the letter of the word that receives prominence in Sam's response.[7]

Joe: Hi. I'm thinking of putting a swimming pool in my back yard, but I want something different.

Sam: We can build any kind of pool your heart desires.
           (a)   (b)   (c) (d)

Joe: How about a heart-shaped pool?

---

[6]Many of the formats used in tests of phonetic knowledge closely resemble those used in tests of perception, with the exception that a taped version of the utterance(s) is not available, and learners must instead apply their knowledge of the rule to the instance given.

[7]This example is from Purpura (1991) and is used with his permission.

Reduced speech

Directions: In the following dialogue, strike through the consonants that would be omitted in consonant cluster configurations in rapid native-speaker speech.[8]

Romeo: I'm worried about Juliet. Lately, she acts strangely whenever I see her.

Mercutio: Didn't I tell you to avoid women? They'll go to great lengths to break your heart. He who trusts his fate to the "fairer sex" asks for trouble.

Romeo: What are you telling me?

Mercutio: Nine tenths of all women are poisonous. A relationship with one of these creatures lasts only as long as the first glow of love. Then the unsuspecting male victim plunges into the depths of depression.

Romeo: But I've been consumed with passion for months!

Mercutio: Then I can't help you, my friend. Best of luck!

CONCLUSION

In conclusion, the issue of feedback and evaluation is a crucial one in the teaching of pronunciation. It is essential to diagnose both listening discrimination and spoken production in order to determine the most effective course of instruction. Similarly, classroom testing of both perception and production is necessary, whether pronunciation is the focus of the course or simply an integrated component of a multiskills curriculum. Furthermore, classroom exercises should promote learners' cognitive ability to correct both themselves and their peers. The best tool we can provide our students is teaching them how to elicit feedback on their pronunciation from their environment and then how to make constructive use of this feedback.

Most importantly, teachers should take special care not to set unrealistic goals or judge progress unrealistically. Complete reversal of speech habits is unlikely to occur. However, progress may be noted in students' abilities to repair a mispronounced utterance when it occurs, or to monitor their speech carefully for commonly occurring substitutions or omissions. Creating autonomous learners who are able to perform such tasks is a primary goal of all language instruction, pronunciation included.

EXERCISES

KEY CONCEPTS

Write a brief definition of the following key terms from this chapter. Give examples where relevant.

diagnostic evaluation	Test of Spoken English
screening	SPEAK Test
placement	ongoing evaluation and feedback
diagnostic passage	self-monitoring/self-correction
free speech sample	contract learning
formal oral proficiency tests	covert rehearsal

[8]This example is from Purpura (1991) and is used with his permission.

INTROSPECTING ABOUT YOUR OWN LANGUAGE LEARNING

Think about a foreign language that you have learned in school or while living abroad.

1. Examine the ACTFL Proficiency Guidelines for speaking in Appendix 14. Where would you place your own proficiency in a foreign language that you speak?

2. If you have learned a language at school, how was your production evaluated? Your perception?

3. Were any self- or peer evaluation techniques used by the instructor? If so, describe them.

4. What kind of ongoing feedback did you receive on your pronunciation?

5. How were pronunciation errors treated by your instructor? Was this effective, in your opinion?

6. Were most classroom tests written tests only or did you have oral performances evaluated as well?

DISCUSSION QUESTIONS

1. Review the techniques for diagnostic and placement testing in this chapter. Which ones are better for:
   a. a university ESL course focusing on pronunciation?
   b. a beginning ESL adult school class?
   c. an advanced EFL high school conversation class?

2. What value is there in using formal oral proficiency testing instruments in the classroom?

3. What advantages and disadvantages do you see in using audiotaped dialogue journals?

4. Of the self-correction techniques presented in this chapter, which appeals to you most as a learner?

5. Compare audiotaping versus videotaping as a means of giving feedback and evaluating production.

IN THE CLASSROOM

Assume that you are teaching pronunciation. Here are some common classroom situations that you might encounter. What technique would you use or what explanation would you give?

1. In an activity using peer feedback, a student complains that she wants only teacher feedback because her classmate's pronunciation is worse than hers.

2. One of your students cannot see any value in evaluating her own production and thinks it is a useless activity.

3. Although diagnostic evaluation has revealed that your students have difficulty with blending and reduced speech, they want to focus on consonant and vowel production.

4. One of your students is very nervous about being videotaped. What rationale for the activity would you give and how would you calm the student's fears?

SUGGESTED ACTIVITIES

1. Administer the diagnostic reading passage in Appendix 13 to a nonnative speaker and evaluate the speaker's performance.

2. Use the wordless cartoon strip in Figure 12.1 to elicit a free speech sample from a nonnative speaker.

3. Compare the results obtained in activity 1 to those obtained in activity 2.

4. Think about a population of students you are or will be teaching. Research the typical pronunciation errors of speakers from that language background when learning English and write up a short profile. Some useful sources are Avery and Ehrlich (1992), Kenworthy (1987), and Swan and Smith (1987).

ON THE CASSETTE

1. Listen to the three samples of nonnative speakers telling a story based on the wordless cartoon in Figure 12.1. For each sample, pinpoint two or three difficulties and devise a response that gives constructive feedback.

2. Listen to the two free speech samples. Then answer the following questions for each speaker:

   a. What language background do you think this speaker has?
   b. What features does this speaker systematically omit?
   c. How can you make the speaker aware of this?
   d. What exercises/activities can you recommend or create to help the student overcome this difficulty?

3. Listen to the native speaker rendition of the diagnostic passage in Appendix 13.

4. Listen to the two nonnative speakers reading the same passage. Using the accent checklist in Appendix 13, diagnose each learner's production.

Appendices

APPENDIX 1
Differences Between NAE and British English

There are a number of noticeable differences between standard Southern British and standard NAE pronunciation. These differences are summarized here in terms of the (1) phonemic inventories; (2) allophonic variation; (3) pronunciation of common words; (4) word stress; (5) sentence stress; (6) intonation; and (7) overall sound and voice quality. Useful sources of information on this topic are Ladefoged (1993), Shakhbagova (1982, 1993), Cruttenden (1986), Catford (1988), and Giegerich (1992).

Despite the minor differences mentioned throughout this text concerning Canadian and U.S. English, we concur with the British applied linguist Peter Strevens (1977: 148) that "differences between English in the U.S. and Canada are such as to be indistinguishable to most speakers of English from other parts of the world." Therefore, for the purposes of this appendix, the general comments about NAE can be understood to include both the U.S. and Canadian varieties. However, it should be noted that Canadian varieties often follow the British model in the pronunciation of many lexical items (see section III of this appendix).

A comparison of British and American spelling can be found in Appendix 11.

I. DIFFERENCES IN PHONEMIC INVENTORIES

DIFFERENCES IN THE CONSONANT INVENTORIES

One minor difference in the consonant inventories of NAE and British English is that some dialects of NAE still have the voiceless /hw/ sound distinct from the voiced approximant /w/ (e.g., in words such as _what, which,_ and _whether_). (This /hw/ sound is also still common in Scottish standard.) Such speakers have the contrast _witch/which_. Speakers of Southern British English, however, and many NAE speakers as well no longer have the /hw/ sound in their phonemic inventories.

DIFFERENCES IN THE VOWEL INVENTORIES

The phonemic differences between NAE and British English vowel inventories are considerably greater than the differences in their consonant inventories, particularly in the area of the low back vowels. For example, both dialects use unrounded /ɑ/ in words like _spa_ and _car;_ however, British English has a low-back lax vowel /ɒ/, which is slightly rounded and occurs in words such as _spot, nod, rock,_ whereas NAE has unrounded /ɑ/ in these words. Also, whereas virtually all British speakers have rounded /ɔ/ as a distinct low back vowel (slightly higher and tenser than /ɒ/ in words such as _law, taught, walk, awe,_ many speakers of NAE no longer have a distinct /ɔ/ phoneme and have merged this sound with /ɑ/. Thus British English has three low back vowels, whereas NAE has two or (in many dialects) only one:

Word	British English	Midwestern NAE	Western NAE
spa	/ɑ/	/ɑ/	/ɑ/
stop	/ɒ/	/ɑ/	/ɑ/
straw	/ɔ/	/ɔ/	/ɑ/

This results in some very noticeable differences in the pronunciation of words with low back vowel sounds. For example, the word *long* is pronounced /lɒŋ/ in British English and either /lɔŋ/ or /lɑŋ/ in NAE.

II. DIFFERENCES IN ALLOPHONIC VARIATION

DIFFERENCES IN VOWEL PRODUCTION

The differences in allophonic variation between British English and NAE are much more extensive than the differences in their phonemic inventories. Because most British vowels tend to be less glided than NAE vowels, a different notation (Jones 1991) is used for the tense vowels and diphthongs:

Word	NAE	British English
beat	/iy/	/i:/
boot	/uw/	/u:/
bait	/ey/	/eɪ/
boat	/ow/	/əʊ/
bite	/ay/	/aɪ/
bout	/aw/	/aʊ/
boil	/ɔy/	/ɔɪ/

In these vowels, the most obvious phonetic difference occurs in words like *boat* and *note*, where NAE has /ow/ and British English has the more centralized /əʊ/.

There are also some minor differences in the quality of lax vowel sounds. NAE /ʊ/ is less rounded than British /ʊ/ in words such as *b__oo__k, p__u__t, p__u__ll*. Also NAE /ʌ/ is often slightly higher than British /ʌ/ in words such as *h__u__t, s__o__n, r__u__st*.

DIFFERENCES IN CONSONANT PRODUCTION

One of the most noticeable differences between NAE and British English is the pronunciation of /r/. In prevocalic position (e.g., *__r__ed, __r__ice, __r__ow*) the British /r/ is produced farther forward in the mouth than the NAE /r/, which tends to be produced as an approximant with the body of the tongue in a /ə/-like position but with the tip slightly curled up. In intervocalic position British English may have a flap [ɾ] in certain words such as *very*, but it is much more usual to hear a very weak articulation with almost no /r/ at all. Speakers of NAE dialects, on the other hand, produce a slightly more velarized version of the prevocalic initial allophone that they use in *__r__ed*. In postvocalic position NAE speakers simply produce a darker and often slightly pharyngealized version of initial or medial /r/. Southern British English speakers omit the /r/ completely in this position and produce instead a lengthened or centralized vowel sound; in unstressed syllables, they also omit postvocalic /r/.

Word	NAE	British English
beard	/biyrd/	/bɪəd/
scarce	/skɛrs/	/skɛəs/
car	/kɑr/	/kɑː/
sport	/spɔrt/	/spɔːt/
pure	/pyʊr/	/pyʊə/
bird	/bɜʳd/	/bɜːd/
sister	/sɪstəʳ/	/sɪstə/

Regarding the pronunciation of /l/, NAE speakers tend to produce a darker, more velarized allophone in all positions, whereas British speakers produce a very distinct clear or light allophone in prevocalic position. This British [l] is especially clear before front vowels–as opposed to the dark [ɫ] that occurs in postvocalic position – especially after back vowels.

Clear [l]	Dark [ɫ]
lily	bull
leap	pull
less	bowl
peeling	peel

Note that *peeling* has a clear [l] because of the following /ɪ/ vowel, whereas *peel* has a dark [ɫ] because there is no following high front vowel.

There are also some major allophonic variations in the pronunciation of /t/ in NAE and British English. Intervocalically before a weakly stressed vowel or after a vowel + /r/ and before a weakly stressed vowel, NAE speakers tend to produce a voiced flap /ɾ/: *city, better, latest, forty, party*. This means that pairs such as the following, which are distinct in British English, tend to share the same pronunciation in NAE: *writer/rider, latter/ladder*. Also, NAE speakers tend to drop /t/ altogether after /n/ and before a weakly stressed vowel: *twen(t)y, San(t)a Ana, Toron(t)o, win(t)er*. In British English, on the other hand, none of these changes occur. Intervocalically, British speakers tend to produce a voiceless alveolar stop (less aspirated than initial /t/) except before syllabic [n̩], where they tend to produce a glottal stop /ʔ/ in place of /t/, as in *button* /bʌʔn̩/. In fact, Giegerich (1992) claims that despite being frowned upon by conservative speakers of British Received Pronunciation (RP), postvocalic /t/ is often glottalized [ʔt] or even replaced by a glottal stop [ʔ] in the extremely casual speech of even standard dialect speakers. Such glottalization occurs most often word finally or before nasal syllabics as in *pit, belt, sat, bottom*. In fact, for many British speakers all word-final voiceless stops after stressed vowels tend to be somewhat glottalized:

hip [hɪʔp]	bet [bɛʔt]	buck [bʌʔk]

In NAE these final stops tend to be unreleased when they are in a stressed syllable in word-final position. Some speakers also insert a glottal stop before unreleased stops.

hip [hɪp°]	bet [bɛt°]	buck [bʌk°]
hip [hɪʔp°]	bet [bɛʔt°]	buck [bʌʔk°]

III. DIFFERENT PRONUNCIATIONS OF COMMON WORDS

WORDS SPELLED WITH *a*

Many words spelled with *a* are pronounced with the vowel /ɑ/ in British English but with the vowel /æ/ in NAE: *ask, answer, can't, dance, branch, half, path, plant, grass, cast, laugh*. Such words tend to have an alveolar nasal /n/ or a voiceless fricative /s, f, θ/ after the vowel.

WORDS WITH SYLLABLE-INITIAL ALVEOLAR CONSONANTS

Many words with a syllable-initial alveolar consonant (i.e., /t, d, n/ and now less frequently /l, s, z/) before an /uw/ sound spelled *u, ew,* or *eu* have a more distinct /y/ glide between the consonant and the vowel in British and Canadian English (see Pringle 1985) than in other varieties of NAE, which have lost the /u/ vs. /yu/ distinction even after /t/, /d/, and /n/:

Word	NAE	British English
tune	/tuwn/	/tyu:n/
duke	/duwk/	/dyu:k/
new	/nuw/	/nyu:/
lewd	/luwd/	/lyu:d, lu:d/
suit	/suwt/	/syu:t, su:t/
Zeus	/zuws/	/zyu:s, zu:s/

Note that British English does not have a /y/ glide in words like *two* or *moon,* which have different spelling patterns.

WORDS WITH *u* SPELLINGS FOLLOWING ALVEOLAR CONSONANTS

As we discussed in Chapter 9, some speakers of British English have a tendency to pronounce /y/ in certain words with *u* spellings (i.e., those following alveolar consonants) whereas NAE speakers generally palatalize the consonant following this *u* spelling instead:

Word	NAE	British English
issue	/ʃ/	/sy/
virtue	/tʃ/	/ty/
arduous	/dʒ/	/dy/
sexual	/kʃ/	/ksy/
Parisian	/ʒ/	/zy/

WORDS SPELLED WITH *er*

Some words and names spelled *er* are pronounced /ɑr/ in British English but /ɝ/ in NAE: *clerk, derby, Kerr*.

WORDS ENDING IN *-ile*

Words that end in *-ile* tend to be pronounced /aɪl/ in British English and /əl/ or [l] in NAE: *hostile, futile, tactile, fertile, docile, sterile, agile, fragile, missile*.

OTHER WORDS

There are many individual English words in common use in both dialects with the same spelling that are routinely pronounced differently:

Word	NAE	British English
been	/bɪn/	/biːn/
herb	/ɝb/	/hɜːb/
ate	/eyt/	/ɛt/
vase	/veys/	/vɑːz/
either	/iyðər/	/aɪðə/
neither	/niyðər/	/naɪðə/
figure	/fɪg(y)ər/	/fɪgə/
schedule	/'skɛˌdʒəl/	/'ʃɛˌdyuːl/
tomato	/tə'meyˌto/	/tə'mɑˌto/
leisure	/'liyʒər/	/'lɛʒə/
process	/'prɑˌsɛs/	/'prəʊˌsɛs/

Note that Canadians would pronounce many of these words with the British rather than the American pronunciation.

IV. DIFFERENCES IN WORD STRESS

There are also numerous words in British English and NAE in which the primary difference in pronunciation can be traced to differences in word stress.

VERBS ENDING IN -*ate*

In many two-syllable verbs ending in -*ate*, NAE tends to stress the root syllable and British English the suffix:

NAE	British English
DICtate	dicTATE
FIXate	fixATE
ROtate	roTATE
VIbrate	viBRATE

These words ending in -*ate* seem to represent an exception in that NAE speakers generally put primary stress later in a multisyllabic word than British speakers.

WORDS OF FRENCH ORIGIN

In words of French origin, NAE tends to mirror the French syllable-final stress pattern, whereas British English anglicizes these words with stress on the first syllable:

NAE	British English
garAGE	GARage
balLET	BALlet
fronTIER	FRONtier
bourGEOIS	BOURgeois
cabaRET	CABaret
debuTANTE	DEButante

STRESS IN THREE- OR FOUR-SYLLABLE WORDS

There are also several types of three- or four-syllable words in which stress falls on the second syllable in NAE but on the first syllable in British English.

NAE	British English
comPOSite	COMposite
subALtern	SUBaltern
arISTocrat	ARistocrat
priMARily	PRImarily

SECONDARY STRESS DIFFERENCES IN WORDS ENDING IN *-ily*

There are many five-syllable words ending in *-ily* for which British English gives primary stress to the first syllable whereas NAE gives primary stress to the third syllable. In these same words, British English speakers also tend to reduce or drop the third syllable, thus pronouncing them with four rather than five syllables:

Word	NAE	British English
customarily	/ˌkʌstə'mɛrəli/	/'kʌstəm(ə)rlɪ/
momentarily	/ˌmowmən'tɛrəli/	/'məʊmənt(ə)rəlɪ/
necessarily	/ˌnɛsə'sɛrəli/	/'nɛsəs(ə)rəlɪ/
ordinarily	/ˌɔːdɪ'nɛrəli/	/'ɔːdɪn(ə)rəlɪ/
voluntarily	/ˌvɑlən'tɛrəli/	/'vɒlənt(ə)rəlɪ/

WORDS ENDING IN *-ary, -ery, -ory,* AND *-mony*

There is also a tendency for NAE to give some stress to penultimate syllables that tend to drop out in British English; this gives many words ending in *-ary, -ery, -ory,* and *-mony* rather different rhythmic patterns in the two dialects:

Word	NAE	British English
necessary	/'nɛsəˌsɛri/	/'nɛsəsrɪ/
territory	/'tɛrəˌtɔri/	/'tɛrətrɪ/
customary	/'kʌstəˌmɛri/	/'kʌstəmrɪ/
dictionary	/'dɪkʃəˌnɛri/	/'dɪkʃənrɪ/
ordinary	/'ɔrdɪˌnɛri/	/'ɔːdɪnrɪ/
category	/'kætəˌgɔri/	/'kætəgrɪ/
monastery	/'mɑnəsˌtɛri/	/'mɒnəstrɪ/
cemetery	/'sɛməˌtɛri/	/'sɛmətrɪ/
testimony	/'tɛstəˌmowni/	/'tɛstəmənɪ/
matrimony	/'mætrəˌmowni/	/'mætrəmənɪ/

WORDS ENDING IN *-day*

In days of the week, the *-day* syllable is unstressed and has a reduced vowel in the British variety; however, it has a full vowel and is stressed, albeit weakly, in NAE:

Word	NAE	British English
Sunday	/'sʌndey/	/'sʌndɪ/
Monday	/'mʌndey/	/'mʌndɪ/
Tuesday	/'tuwzdey/	/'tyuːzdɪ/
Wednesday	/'wɛnzdey/	/'wɛnzdɪ/
Thursday	/'θɜʳzdey/	/'θɜːzdɪ/
Friday	/'fraydey/	/'fraɪdɪ/
Saturday	/'sætəʳdey/	/'sætərdɪ/

PLACE NAMES ENDING IN *-aster/-ester*

Place names ending in *-aster/-ester* have a different stress pattern in NAE and British English, since the latter variety gives less stress to the penultimate syllable:

Word	NAE	British English
Lancaster	/ˈlæŋˌkæstər/	/ˈlæŋkəstə/
Rochester	/ˈrɑˌtʃɛstər/	/ˈrɒtʃəstə/

An extreme example of the British tendency can be seen in a name such as *Worcester*, which becomes /wʊstə/: The posvocalic /r/ and the entire middle syllable (except for the /s/) drop out. This tendency also extends to place names ending in *-ham* or *-wood*, which receive some stress on the final syllable in NAE but are stressed only on the initial syllable in British English, with resulting loss of the /h/ in *-ham*:

Word	NAE	British English
Birmingham	/ˈbɜ^{r}mɪŋˌhæm/	/ˈbɛːmɪŋəm/
Buckingham	/ˈbʌkɪŋhæm/	/ˈbʌkɪŋəm/
Hollywood	/ˈhɒlɪˌwʊd/	/ˈhɒlɪwəd/

OTHER WORD STRESS DIFFERENCES

In some cases, words in NAE and British English have the same number of syllables but simply take different stress patterns, with concomitant differences in pronunciation:

Word	NAE	British English
laboratory	/ˈlæbrəˌtɔri/	/ləˈbɒrətri/
advertisement	/ˌædvə^{r}ˈtayzmənt/	/ədˈvɜːtɪsmənt/
corollary	/ˈkɔrəˌlɛri/	/kəˈrɒlərɪ/

In sum, many words and place names have different rhythmic patterns in NAE and British English. As a general trend, there is more syllable reduction in multisyllabic words in British English and greater use of light stress in NAE along with a tendency to retain syllables.

V. DIFFERENCES IN SENTENCE STRESS

There is very little empirical research available on differences in sentence stress between NAE and British English. One area in which differences have been noticed (Shakhbagova 1993) is yes/no questions; British English sometimes gives light stress to the fronted auxiliary verb whereas NAE usually does not:

● · ●
British: ɪs it NICE?

· · ●
NAE: Is it NICE?

We suspect that there are a number of other such differences in sentence stress. More research is needed.

VI. DIFFERENCES IN INTONATION

Differences in neutral and unemotional British and NAE intonation are marked enough such that speakers of both varieties seem to develop stereotyped perceptions of the other group. NAE speakers tend to perceive British speakers as pretentious and mannered, and British speakers tend to perceive Americans as monotonous and negative. Consider this example from Cruttenden (1986: 52):

British: It's not quite the right shade of blue.

NAE: It's not quite the right shade of blue.

The British intonation begins with a marked rise, then a gradual fall with a final glide down on the last syllable. The NAE intonation begins with a much smaller rise-fall, maintaining a mid-level pitch with a marked rise-and-fall glide on the final syllable. In other words, British English has a greater pitch range and a more steplike movement from high to low whereas NAE maintains a flat or slightly wavy mid-level until the final contour of the utterance.

Cruttenden (1986) points out that in yes/no questions that are not responses, the British low rise is polite whereas a high rise signals incredulity. In NAE, however, the high rise is polite and not incredulous; the extra high rise signals incredulity. Cruttenden also explains that the British low rise sounds patronizing or ingratiating to North Americans whereas the NAE high rise appears casual and almost flippant to British ears. Contributing further to this sense of casualness is the NAE tendency to use a high fall-rise more commonly than British speakers would:

Did he pass the exam?

He certainly did!

According to Cruttenden (1986), the use of the high rise in NAE is increasing even on declarative utterances as a marker of casualness, particularly among adolescents and teenagers, and particularly in narrative monologues. This is clearly another area where further empirical research would be extremely enlightening.

VI. DIFFERENCES IN OVERALL SOUND AND VOICE QUALITY

With the exception of certain regional varieties of British English (such as Norfolk and the Home Counties, from which many of the New Englanders and other settlers emigrated during the seventeenth century), NAE has a more nasal quality than British English. This occurs because the nasal passage is more frequently open or partly open in NAE speakers; also, the liquids /r/ and /l/ tend to be articulated more toward the back of the mouth in NAE pronunciation than in British pronunciation, thereby giving NAE liquids a more velarized quality. The more frequent use of the glottal stop as well as glottalized stop consonants in final position gives British English its more clipped and precise quality, whereas the more glided and lengthened vowels of NAE as well as the occurrence of unreleased stop consonants in final position give it a more drawn out or "drawled" quality. According to Esling and Wong (1983) and Esling (1994), spread lips are common to both NAE and British English whereas a somewhat open jaw position during speech is more common to NAE than to British English. A lowered larynx, which gives the voice a deeper, hollowed – and presumably prestigious – sound, is characteristic of radio and television announcers and politicians in NAE. This would be an unusual feature for British English speakers, who tend to speak with a creaky voice, something which also occurs in NAE (especially if the voice is low pitched) but often only on the final stressed syllable of an utterance.

APPENDIX 2
Comparison of Phonetic and Phonemic Alphabets

The transcription system used to represent NAE consonants and vowels in this text deviates in some respects from other commonly used transcription systems, especially with regard to the vowel symbols used. We have made these modifications to (1) allow the transcription system to more accurately reflect the sound system of NAE and (2) be of pedagogical value in helping learners of English approximate the segmental features of the language. The following table presents a comparison of our alphabet with several other commonly used systems. The IPA symbols given are from Jones (1991) and represent British Received Pronunciation (RP).

COMPARISON CHART: A PHONETIC ALPHABET FOR NAE

KEY WORD	Celce-Murcia, Brinton, & Goodwin	International Phonetic Alphabet (Jones 1991)	Oxford Student's Dictionary of American English (1986)	Longman Dictionary of American English (1983)	Prator & Robinett (1985)	Bowen (1975b)	Avery & Ehrlich (1992)
The NAE Consonants							
1. pen	/p/	/p/	/p/	/p/	/p/	/p/	/p/
2. back	/b/	/b/	/b/	/b/	/b/	/b/	/b/
3. ten	/t/	/t/	/t/	/t/	/t/	/t/	/t/
4. dive	/d/	/d/	/d/	/d/	/d/	/d/	/d/
5. cart	/k/	/k/	/k/	/k/	/k/	/k/	/k/
6. go	/g/	/g/	/g/	/g/	/g/	/g/	/g/
7. chin	/tʃ/	/tʃ/	/tʃ/	/tʃ/	/tš/	/ch/	/tʃ/
8. jam	/dʒ/	/dʒ/	/dʒ/	/dʒ/	/dž/	/j/	/dʒ/
9. fit	/f/	/f/	/f/	/f/	/f/	/f/	/f/
10. vat	/v/	/v/	/v/	/v/	/v/	/v/	/v/
11. thin	/θ/	/θ/	/θ/	/θ/	/θ/	/th/	/θ/
12. then	/ð/	/ð/	/ð/	/ð/	/ð/	/dh/	/ð/
13. set	/s/	/s/	/s/	/s/	/s/	/s/	/s/
14. zoo	/z/	/z/	/z/	/z/	/z/	/z/	/z/
15. shoe	/ʃ/	/ʃ/	/ʃ/	/ʃ/	/š/	/sh/	/ʃ/
16. beige	/ʒ/	/ʒ/	/ʒ/	/ʒ/	/ž/	/zh/	/ʒ/
17. how	/h/	/h/	/h/	/h/	/h/	/h/	/h/
18. mat	/m/	/m/	/m/	/m/	/m/	/m/	/m/
19. net	/n/	/n/	/n/	/n/	/n/	/n/	/n/
20. ring	/ŋ/	/ŋ/	/ŋ/	/ŋ/	/ŋ/	/ng/	/ŋ/
21. win	/w/	/w/	/w/	/w/	/w/	/w/	/w/
22. when	/(h)w/	/(h)w/	/(h)w/	/hw/	/hw/	/hw/	/w/
23. late	/l/	/l/	/l/	/l/	/l/	/l/	/l/
24. red	/r/	/r/	/r/	/r/	/r/	/r/	/r/
25. yes	/y/	/j/	/y/	/y/	/y/	/y/	/y/

COMPARISON CHART (Continued)

KEY WORD		Celce-Murcia, Brinton, & Goodwin	International Phonetic Alphabet (Jones 1991)	Oxford Student's Dictionary of American English (1986)	Longman Dictionary of American English (1983)	Prator & Robinett (1985)	Bowen (1975b)	Avery & Ehrlich (1992)
The NAE Stressed Vowels								
1.	b<u>ea</u>t	/iy/	/i:/	/i/	/i^y/	/iy/	/iy/	/iy/
2.	p<u>i</u>t	/ɪ/	/ɪ/	/ɪ/	/ɪ/	/ɪ/	/ɪ	/ɪ/
3.	d<u>a</u>te	/ey/	/eɪ/	/ei/	/e^y/	/ey/	/ey/	/ey/
4.	s<u>e</u>t	/ɛ/	/e/	/e/	/ɛ/	/ɛ/	/ɛ/	/ɛ/
5.	m<u>a</u>t	/æ/	/æ/	/æ/	/æ/	/æ/	/æ/	/æ/
6.	p<u>o</u>t	/ɑ/	/ɒ/	/a/	/ɑ/	/a/	/ɑ/	/a/
7.	b<u>ou</u>ght	/ɔ/	/ɔ:/	/ɔ/	/ɔ/	/ɔ/	/ɔ/	/ɔ/
8.	s<u>o</u>	/ow/	/əʊ/	/ou/	/o^w/	/ow/	/ow/	/ow/
9.	g<u>oo</u>d	/ʊ/	/ʊ/	/ʊ/	/ʊ/	/ʊ/	/ʊ/	/ʊ/
10.	b<u>oo</u>t	/uw/	/u:/	/u/	/u^w/	/uw/	/uw/	/uw/
11.	t<u>i</u>me	/ay/	/aɪ/	/ai/	/aɪ/	/ay/	/ay/	/ay/
12.	h<u>ow</u>	/aw/	/aʊ/	/au/	/aʊ/	/aw/	/aw/	/aw/
13.	b<u>oy</u>	/ɔy/	/ɔɪ/	/ɔi/	/ɔɪ/	/ɔy/	/oy/	/oy/
14.	s<u>o</u>me	/ʌ/	/ʌ/	/ə/	/ʌ/	/ə/	/ə/	/ʌ/
15.	b<u>ir</u>d	/ɜ^r/	/ɜ:/	/ər/	/ɜr/	/ər/	/ər/	/ər/
The NAE Unstressed Vowels								
16.	<u>a</u>bout	/ə/	/ə/	/ə/	/ə/	/ə/	/ə/	/ə/
17.	butt<u>er</u>	/ə^r/	/ə/	/ər/	/ər/	/ər/	/ər/	/ər/
18.	cit<u>y</u>	/i/	/ɪ/	/i/	/i^y/	/ɪ/	/iy/	/iy/
19.	mus<u>i</u>c	/ɪ/	/ɪ/	/ɪ/	/ɪ/	/ɪ/	/ɪ/	/ɪ/
20.	h<u>o</u>tel	/o/	/əʊ/	/ou/	/o^w/	/ow/	/ow/	/ow/
21.	int<u>o</u>	/u/	/ʊ, u:, ə/	/ə, u/	/ə, ʊ, u^w/	/ə,uw/	/ə,uw/	/ə,uw/

APPENDIX 3
Positional Occurrence of NAE Consonants

Listed below are the five positions in which consonants can potentially occur. For each consonant, we provide example words for each position in which it can occur. Note that if consonants occur only rarely in a given position, we have indicated this by placing the example word in parentheses. Usually, these are either personal or brand names (e.g., *Mr. de Vries, Vlasic pickles*), words of place (*Vladivostok*), or other words (e.g., the ono-matopoeic use of the word *vroom* to describe the sound a car makes). We have also placed the initial occurrences of /hw/ in parentheses to indicate that not all NAE speakers use this phoneme in the words listed; instead they use /w/.

Phoneme	Syllable initial	Syllable final	Intervocalic	Initial clusters	Final clusters
1. /b/	bed	tub	habit	bread	bulb
	bird	crab	hobby	blast	sobbed
	bald	robe	robbing	bright	curbs
2. /p/	peach	tap	kipper	pretty	camp
	party	cape	happy	plaster	kept
	pill	leap	seeping	spot	clasped
3. /d/	deep	bid	ladder	dream	hard
	dark	glade	bidding	dragon	bold
	do	wood	loudest	dwell	finds
4. /t/	toe	bat	bitter	tree	quilt
	terrible	mitt	catty	twin	built
	tension	great	beating	star	rafts
5. /g/	girl	tag	bigger	grape	bags
	go	log	sagging	glance	tagged
	gas	rig	snuggest	(Gwen)	icebergs
6. /k/	king	lick	thicker	creep	dark
	calf	ache	picking	quip	tacks
	cook	rake	rocket	clap	text
7. /v/	vine	give	clover	(Vlasik)	fives
	vow	move	having	(vroom)	curved
	voice	live	given	(Vries)	elves
8. /f/	five	knife	heifer	fly	left
	phone	loaf	laughing	frost	laughs
	fair	rough	office	few	surfed
9. /ð/	the	bathe	mother		bathed
	this	teethe	teething	(none)	teethes
	then	writhe	worthy		loathes
10. /θ/	thank	bath	ether	thread	myths
	thick	teeth	mythic	thwart	width
	thought	cloth	breathy	thrash	months
11. /z/	zoo	buzz	cousin		caused
	zinc	choose	busy	(none)	pans
	zap	lose	fazes		elves

Phoneme	Syllable initial	Syllable final	Intervocalic	Initial clusters	Final clusters
12. /s/	sang cinder sorry	bus loss face	classic passive adjacent	stream scratch slip	burst mask carts
13. /ʒ/	(genre) (Jacques)	rouge beige garage	azure pleasure lesion	(none)	rouged (rare)
14. /ʃ/	shoe sugar chaperon	clash bush lush	issue nation glacier	shrink shrapnel (Schwartz)	harsh hushed rushed
15. /h/	hat hi hoot	(none)	ahead rehabilitate behold	hue humor huge	(none)
16. /tʃ/	cheese chair cello	each touch match	teaches butcher watching	(none)	church gulch bunched
17. /dʒ/	joy juice jazz	badge wage ridge	lodging wager pages	(none)	barge budged lunged
18. /m/	meat moose mice	rum clam some	simmer coming tumor	smell smack smile	comes bump realm
19. /n/	noose neat nor	tune clan sun	sinner cunning tuner	snow snake sneeze	banned barn turns
20. /ŋ/	(none)	young tongue wrong	singer bringing dinghy	(none)	hanged thank wings
21. /l/	leap late lose	tall sail gale	falling sailor gallant	fly sleep clear	filled girl helps
22. /r/	read rice wrong	fire car poor	daring forest errant	freeze creep street	curb works bursts
23. /w/	we walk wood	(occurs as vowel glide only)	away beware await	dwell sweet quick	(occurs as vowel glide only)
24. /hw/	(which) (what) (when)	(none)	awhile (rare)	(none)	(none)
25. /y/	you yes yarn	(occurs as vowel glide only)	voyeur lawyer royal	butte hue cure	(occurs as vowel glide only)

APPENDIX 4
English Syllable Structure

The following chart of consonant cluster configurations can be provided for student reference and practice:

ENGLISH SYLLABLE STRUCTURE

The English syllable can consist minimally of one vowel (e.g., *I, Oh!, Ow!*), and maximally of three initial consonants and a vowel followed by four consonants. The latter cluster configuration is extremely rare:

Minimal Syllable Structure	Maximal Syllable Structure
V	CCCVCCCC

Other common cluster configurations (excluding CCVCCCC, which is also extremely rare as in *twelfths*) are as follows:

VC	CV	CCV	CCCV
up	my	pry	screw
an	hoe	grow	spray
in	so	free	stray

VCC	VCCC	CVCCC	CVCCCC
old	Olds	tests	thirsts
and	ants	tenths	texts
ink	amps	lunged	worlds

CVC	CCVC	CVCC	CCVCC
bed	bred	bald	brand
set	dread	sand	trains
cap	stone	hunt	swings

CCCVC	CCCVCC	CCVCCC	CCCVCCC
strut	struts	slurps	scrimps
squat	squats	prints	sprints
sprain	sprained	flirts	squelched

APPENDIX 5
Distribution of Vowels Before Nasal Consonants

As shown in the chart below, all the NAE vowels can occur before a nonnasal consonant. However, the vowel distribution before nasal consonants is more restricted. For example, nasals do not generally occur after /ʊ/. The bilabial nasal /m/ also cannot follow /ɔ/ and /ɔy/, and the velar nasal /ŋ/ can only follow six vowels. Note that for NAE speakers with no /ɔ/ in their dialect, *pond, taunt, Congress,* and *song* would all be pronounced with /ɑ/.

Vowel phonemes	Vowels preceding nonnasal consonants	Vowels preceding nasal -/m/	Vowels preceding nasal -/n/	Vowels preceding nasal -/ŋ/
/iy/	seat	seem	seen	
/ɪ/	sit	him	sin	sing
/ey/	sake	same	sane	
/ɛ/	heck	hem	hen	length
/æ/	sat	Sam	fan	sang
/ɑ/	pot	palm	pond	Congress
/ɔ/	taught		taunt	song
/ʌ/	rut	rum	run	rung
/ow/	grope	gnome	groan	
/ʊ/	put			
/uw/	toot	tomb	tune	
/ay/	might	mime	mine	
/aw/	shout	(Baum)	hound	
/ɔy/	annoyed		annoint	

APPENDIX 6
Commonly Reduced Function Words

Listed by grammatical category are the common function words that exhibit reduction, with some examples to illustrate them.

I. Conjunctions

and	Long live rock *and* roll!	/ən/
	She's footloose *and* fancy free.	/ən/
	Eat your bread *and* butter.	[n̩]
	We got up bright *and* early.	[n̩]
or	There are five *or* six people coming.	/ər/
	You can either stay *or* leave.	/ər/
	It's a life *or* death matter.	/ər/
	Did you help him for love *or* money?	/ər/
as	It's *as* cold *as* ice.	/əz/
	The apartment is *as* clean *as* a whistle.	/əz/
	Sue is *as* happy *as* a clam.	/əz/
	He did it *as* quick *as* a wink.	/əz/
than	Are you taller *than* me?	/ðən/
	Alaska is bigger *than* Texas.	/ðən/
	Max is slower *than* molasses.	/ðən/
	She's nuttier *than* a fruitcake.	/ðən/

II. Prepositions

to	Please talk *to* me.	/tə/
	Let's get back *to* basics.	/tə/
	The score is ten *to* two.	/tə/
	He cut me *to* the quick.	/tə/
for	Let's have one *for* the road.	/fəʳ/
	You don't get more *for* less.	/fəʳ/
	They're having a two *for* one sale.	/fəʳ/
	You're looking *for* trouble.	/fəʳ/
of	That's the best *of* all.	/əv/
	It's one *of* the best movies I've seen!	/əv/, /ə/
	Tom was born on the fifth *of* June.	/əv/, /ə/
	It's the event *of* the century.	/əv/, /ə/
on	Put it *on* the table.	/ɑn/, /ən/
	Take it *on* faith.	/ɑn/, /ən/
	He lives *on* Maple Street.	/ɑn/, /ən/
	You get *on* my nerves!	/ɑn/, /ən/
from	How soon will he fall *from* grace?	/frəm/
	Ida sells cosmetics *from* door to door.	/frəm/
	I mean it *from* the bottom of my heart.	/frəm/
	The plane disappeared *from* sight.	/frəm/

at	She made eyes *at* him.	/ət/
	He's down *at* the heel.	/ət/
	The star player is up *at* bat.	/ət/
	Who's *at* the helm?	/ət/

in	She's one *in* a million.	/ɪn/, /ən/
	It's *in* the bag.	/ɪn/, /ən/
	I'll do it *in* a jiffy.	/ɪn/, /ən/
	He disappeared *in* a flash.	/ɪn/, /ən/

III. Copula *be*

are	How *are* you feeling?	/əʳ/
	Why *are* your shoes unlaced?	/əʳ/
	What *are* your earliest memories?	/əʳ/
	Pat and Sam *are* coming.	/əʳ/

am	Why *am* I so blue?	/əm/
	Who *am* I to tell you that?	/əm/
	How *am* I doing?	/əm/
	What *am* I missing?	/əm/

IV. Auxiliary verbs

have	The books *have* arrived.	/əv/
	He was supposed to *have* finished it.	/əv/
	The children *have* gone to bed.	/əv/
	He must *have* done it!	/əv/, /ə/

has	Max *has* gone to New York.	/əz/
	Chris *has* bought a computer.	/əz/
	The tennis match *has* been cancelled.	/əz/
	Where *has* my pen disappeared?	/əz/

can	I *can* do it for you.	/kən/
	What *can* you offer me?	/kən/
	How *can* I help you?	/kən/
	Now *can* you see it?	/kən/

do	How *do* you do?	/də/
	Where *do* you live?	/də/
	Who *do* you work with?	/də/
	Why *do* you think that?	/də/

will	Things *will* get better.	/əl/
	Time *will* heal all wounds.	/əl/
	Where *will* you go?	[l̩]
	What *will* you do?	[l̩]

V. Pronouns

he	What did *he* see?	/i/
	Where should *he* go?	/i/
	Why does *he* want to?	/i/
	How can *he* pay for it?	/i/

you	Do *you* mind?	/yə/
	Are *you* going?	/yə/
	He doesn't think *you* can do it.	/yə/
	You should ask him for permission.	/yə/
his	What is *his* problem?	/ɪz/
	Do you have *his* address?	/ɪz/
	How much did *his* new car cost?	/ɪz/
	He packed *his* bags already.	/ɪz/
her	Did Jane give *her* the money?	/əʳ/
	The book is in *her* room.	/əʳ/
	We gave *her* free rein.	/əʳ/
	Where did she put *her* car keys?	/əʳ/
him	Did the police book *him?*	/əm/, /ɪm/
	She looked at *him* suspiciously.	/əm/, /ɪm/
	Stella swept *him* off his feet.	/əm/, /ɪm/
	Harold gave *him* a hand.	/əm/, /ɪm/
them	We invited *them* to the party.	/ðəm/, /əm/
	I saw *them* yesterday.	/ðəm/, /əm/
	Didn't she take *them* to lunch?	/ðəm/, /əm/
	The accident frightened *them* to death.	/ðəm/, /əm/
our	It's *our* prerogative.	/ɑr/
	He's *our* man.	/ɑr/
	Did you see *our* new paintings?	/ɑr/
	We can't seem to get *our* energy up.	/ɑr/
your	Everything is at *your* fingertips.	/yəʳ/
	I saw *your* wife yesterday.	/yəʳ/
	It isn't any of *your* business.	/yəʳ/
	What's *your* hidden agenda?	/yəʳ/
that	Alex said *that* he was leaving soon.	/ðət/
	It's a shame *that* she can't make it.	/ðət/
	It's so small *that* you can't see it.	/ðət/
	I made up my mind *that* I'm going.	/ðət/

VI. Articles

the	It's off *the* record.	/ðə/
	That's begging *the* question.	/ðə/
	You should turn *the* other cheek.	/ði/
	We faced *the* eye of the storm.	/ði/
a, an	It's *a* small world.	/ə/
	I feel as weak as *a* kitten.	/ə/
	He's *an* absolute idiot.	/ən/
	Marvin is strong as *an* ox.	/ən/

APPENDIX 7
Constraints on Contraction and Blending

Although contractions and blendings are widely used in spoken (and in the case of contractions, in written) English, there are several constraints on where they can occur. Below, we summarize from Hill and Beebe (1980) the most common constraints on these reduced speech forms.

I. REGISTER

One general constraint is register: The more informal the context and the more rapid the speech, the greater the frequency of contractions and blendings. Conversely, the more formal the context and deliberate the speech, the lower the frequency. This is of course even more so if the language is written.

II. ADJACENCY

Another general constraint on contractions and blendings is that these processes are generally restricted to two adjacent words:

He isn't.	*or*	He's not.	*but not*	*He'sn't.
She wouldn't.	*or*	She'd not.	*but not*	*She'dn't.

However, on rare occasions spoken contractions involving three words seem to occur:

She *couldn't've* come.	(could not have)
They *mustn't've* known.	(must not have)
I*'d've* gone if you asked.	(I would have)

All such phonetically possible triple contractions that we are aware of consist of a modal + *not* + *have* sequence or a pronoun + modal + *have* sequence.

III. PHONOLOGICAL CONTEXT

As Hill and Beebe (1980) point out, certain dissimilatory phonological contexts also seem to dramatically lower the possibility of contractions and blendings:

• *Is* or *has* are not contracted and are less frequently blended after nouns or pro-forms ending in a sibilant (especially *-s*):
   Mavis's coming over tonight.
   Liz's picking me up.
   This's been going on for a while now.

• *Are* is not contracted and is less frequently blended after *there:*
   There're many problems to solve.

• *Will* is not contracted and is less frequently blended after a noun ending in /l/:
   Jill'll come late.

• *Would* and *had* are not contracted and are less frequently blended after *it, what, that,* or nouns ending in an alveolar consonant:
   It'd be nice.
   That'd broken earlier.
   Albert'd be a good choice.

IV. ENVIRONMENT

Finally, other than contractions with *not,* contraction and blending cannot occur in clause- or utterance-final position; only full forms occur in this environment:

(Will you go?) Yes, *I'll.
She hasn't gone, but *they've.
Bill's more tired than *Joan's.
(Who will do it?) I wish *he'd.
I don't know what time *it's.
That's just the way that *I'm.

APPENDIX 8
Irregular Verbs in English

All English verbs are identified according to their three principal parts: the infinitive (or base form), the past tense, and the past participle. In Modern English, regular verbs are characterized by the addition of the inflectional ending *-ed* (pronounced /d/, /t/, or /ɪd/, /əd/) to the past tense and past participle forms; these verbs tend to derive from the Old English weak verb system. Irregular verbs, on the other hand, are characterized by stem-internal vowel changes; they derive from both the Old English weak and strong verb systems.

I. IRREGULAR VERBS FROM THE OLD ENGLISH WEAK VERB SYSTEM

Old English had three classes of weak verbs, all of which formed their past tense by adding the dental consonant /d/ or /t/ to the stem. However, the three weak verb classes of Old English did not merge completely in the Modern English regular verb system. Furthermore, there were already some irregularities in the Old English weak verb system and more arose due to sound changes in Middle English. One result of all these historical developments is that some of the irregular verbs in Modern English derive from the Old English weak verb system: Six main groups of these verbs exist.

1. One such group of irregular verbs simply changes a final /d/ following an /n/ or /l/ in the base form to a final /t/ in the past tense and the participle:

Base form	Past tense	Past participle
-/d/	-/t/	-/t/
build	built	built
bend	bent	bent
spend	spent	spent
send	sent	sent
lend	lent	lent

In British English, this pattern also applies to the verbs *burn, learn, smell, spell, spill,* and *spoil.*

2. A second group of irregular verbs appears to undergo no change at all. The base form of these verbs, which typically ends in a /t/ (or occasionally a /d/), originally added a dental suffix (*-te* or *-de*). The resulting double consonant (*tt* or *dd*) was subsequently shortened.

Base form	Past tense	Past participle
hit	hit	hit
quit	quit	quit
split	split	split
rid	rid	rid
bid	bid	bid
bet	bet	bet
let	let	let
set	set	set
shed	shed	shed
spread	spread	spread
put	put	put
hurt	hurt	hurt

Base form	Past tense	Past participle
burst	burst	burst
cost	cost	cost
cast	cast	cast

3. In the third group, the base form adds /t/ in the past tense and past participle, and the vowel changes from long /iy/ to historically related short /ɛ/:

Base form	Past tense	Past participle
/iy/	/ɛ/	/ɛ/
creep	crept	crept
weep	wept	wept
sleep	slept	slept
keep	kept	kept
sweep	swept	swept
mean	meant	meant
feel	felt	felt
leave	left	left
kneel	knelt	knelt

4. Verbs in this group originally added a dental suffix that resulted in a consonant cluster (-*tt*/-*dd*). The cluster led to the shortening of the vowel sound, after which the consonant cluster simplified:

Base form	Past tense	Past participle
/iy/	/ɛ/	/ɛ/
meet	met	met
feed	fed	fed
lead	led	led
bleed	bled	bled
read	read	read
speed	sped	sped
breed	bred	bred
/ay/	/ɪ/	/ɪ/
light	lit	lit
slide	slid	slid
/uw/	/ɑ, ɔ/	/ɑ, ɔ/
shoot	shot	shot
lose	lost	lost

5. There are many historically irregular weak verbs that have been preserved in Modern English. These verbs have a variety of vowel sounds in the base form, but all have a past tense and past participle ending in /ɔt/–spelled -*aught* or -*ought*:

Base form	Past tense	Past participle
buy	bought	bought
bring	brought	brought
fight	fought	fought
seek	sought	sought
think	thought	thought
teach	taught	taught
catch	caught	caught

6. A final group of historically irregular weak verbs has the vowel /ɛ/ and ends in /l/ in the base form. In the past tense and past participle, the vowel changes to /ow/ and adds a dental /d/.

Base form	Past tense	Past participle
/ɛ/	/ow/	/ow/
tell	told	told
sell	sold	sold

II. IRREGULAR VERBS FROM THE OLD ENGLISH STRONG VERB SYSTEM

The other irregular verbs in Modern English derive from the Old English strong verb system. This system consisted of seven traditional classes that formed their past tense and participle by varying the vowel sound of the stem, a process referred to as ablauting. Modern reflexes of the Old English strong verb system, however, have little direct historical relationship with the seven Old English classes.

1. A number of such irregular verbs undergo a three-part vowel change from base form to past tense to past participle:

Base form	Past tense	Past participle
/ɪ/	/æ/	/ʌ/
sing	sang	sung
ring	rang	rung
drink	drank	drunk
sink	sank	sunk
swim	swam	swum
begin	began	begun

2. In the second pattern, there is only one vowel change, resulting in identical past tense and past participle forms:

Base form	Past tense	Past participle
win	won	won
dig	dug	dug
stick	stuck	stuck
strike	struck	struck
find	found	found
bind	bound	bound
wind	wound	wound
stand	stood	stood
hang	hung	hung
hold	held	held

3. In this pattern, verbs have the same vowel sound in the past tense and participle, but the participle has an additional -n /n/ or -en /ən/ ending:

Base form	Past tense	Past participle
(for)get	(for)got	(for)gotten
freeze	froze	frozen
bite	bit	bitten
hide	hid	hidden
lie	lay	lain

Base form	Past tense	Past participle
speak	spoke	spoken
steal	stole	stolen
weave	wove	woven
swear	swore	sworn
wear	wore	worn
tear	tore	torn

4.   A fourth pattern for irregular verbs deriving from the Old English strong verb system has a long *i* /ay/ in the base form, /ow/ in the past tense, and short *i* /ɪ/ with *-en* in the participle:

Base form /ay/	Past tense /ow/	Past participle /ɪ/
(a)rise	(a)rose	(a)risen
drive	drove	driven
strive	strove	striven
write	wrote	written

5.   A few irregular verbs deriving from the Old English strong verb system have identical base forms and past participles with a vowel change in the past tense only:

Base form	Past tense	Past participle
run	ran	run
come	came	come

6.   Many more such irregular verbs have similar base forms and past participles: Once again, a vowel change occurs in the past tense only – the difference here being that the participle now has a final *-n* /n/ or *-en* /ən/ that distinguishes it from the infinitive:

Base form	Past tense	Past participle
blow	blew	blown
know	knew	known
grow	grew	grown
throw	threw	thrown
eat	ate	eaten
see	saw	seen
give	gave	given
shake	shook	shaken
take	took	taken
draw	drew	drawn
fall	fell	fallen

7.   A few of the most common irregular verbs are suppletive forms (i.e., are a composite of forms from originally different verbs) and thus follow no discernible pattern:

Base form	Past tense	Past participle
go	went	gone
am/is/are	was/were	been

The foregoing are a fairly comprehensive but not an exhaustive listing of English irregular verbs. The majority of irregular verbs, however, do belong to one of the phonological patterns described here.

The precise etymology of each verb cited is not necessarily historically consistent in that a verb could start in one class and move to another: Typically there is simplification whereby irregular verbs either simplify (e.g., lose an /n/ or /ən/) or become regular verbs, a process that still continues today and accounts for variation among speakers and dialects. Compare irregular British *dream-dreamt-dreamt* or *leap-lept-lept* with regular NAE *dream-dreamed-dreamed* or *leap-leaped-leaped;* also compare the more conservative NAE *(for)get-(for)got-(for)gotten* to simplified British *(for)get-(for)got-(for)got.*

APPENDIX 9
Tense–Lax Vowel Alternations in Stressed Syllables of Base Forms and Derived Words

Today, we can still see the tense–lax vowel relationships reflected in many etymologically related pairs of words where the base form has the tense (or long) vowel sound and the derived form has the lax (or short) vowel sound.

a   **tense** /ey/ – **lax** /æ/

cave – cavity	nation – national
chaste – chastity	nature – natural
exclaim – exclamatory	navy – navigate
defame – defamatory	opaque – opacity
deprave – depravity	page – paginate
grade – graduation	profane – profanity
grain – granular	sacred – sacrament
grateful – gratitude	sane – sanity
grave – gravity	state – static
humane – humanity	table – tabular

e   **tense** /iy/ – **lax** /ɛ/

athlete – athletic	meter – metric
austere – austerity	obscene – obscenity
brief – brevity	proceed – procession
clean – cleanliness	receive – reception
concede – concession	repeat – repetitive
convene – convention	serene – serenity
deceive – deception	severe – severity
discreet – discretion	sincere – sincerity
extreme – extremity	supreme – supremacy

i   **tense** /ay/ – **lax** /ɪ/

Bible – Biblical	line – linear
collide – collision	mime – mimic
crime – criminal	mine – mineral
cycle – cyclical	sign – signal
decide – decision	title – titular
derive – derivative	type – typical
divine – divinity	wide – width
expedite – expedition	wild – wilderness

o   **tense /ow/ – lax /ɑ/**

code – codify	locate – locative
compose – composite	microscope – microscopic
cone – conic	mode – modular
episode – episodic	omen – ominous
evoke – evocative	phone – phonics
expose – expository	solo – solitude
globe – globular	tone – tonic
holy – holiday	verbose – verbosity
joke – jocular	vocal – vocative
know – knowledge	

u   **tense /(y)uw/ – lax /ʌ/**

adjudicate – adjudge	produce – production
assume – assumption	punitive – punish
consume – consumption	reduce – reduction
crucify – crux	repugn – repugnant
duke – duchy	resume – resumption
numeral – number	seduce – seduction
presume – presumption	

APPENDIX 10
Consonant Letter–Sound Correspondences and Variations
(including digraphs)

I. GRAPHEME–PHONEME CORRESPONDENCE

Unlike some other languages, the English spelling system does not demonstrate a direct one-to-one correspondence between grapheme and phoneme. Instead, it represents a more abstract morphophonemic system, which is related to pronunciation in a somewhat complex way. Nonetheless, especially in initial position, many of the English consonant letters represent a relatively stable sound–letter correspondence. The following list shows the consonant letters of the English alphabet and their common pronunciations and positional variants.

Letter	Phoneme(s)	Examples and discussion
b	/b/	*boy, bog, break, bleary, lab, curb* Word initially and finally, *b* is pronounced /b/. *Positional variants:* Medially, /b/ is often represented by *bb* after lax vowels, as in *abbot, rabbit, lobby, sabbath*. After tense vowels, *be* is common: *babe, robe*.
c	/k/	*cat, cart, cry, cling* In initial position before central and back vowels and before consonants, /k/ is represented by *c*. *Positional variants:* Although it may appear as *c* (e.g., *relic, picnic, chic*), final and medial /k/ are generally represented by *ck* (*back, rock, docker, stacking, thickset*). Medially, /k/ may also be spelled *cc: succumb, succulent, baccalaureate, accurate*.
	/s/	*celery, cyst, citation, celsius* In initial position before *i, y,* or *e, c* can be pronounced as /s/. *Positional variant:* In medial and final position, /s/ is often realized as *ce: pace, twice, peaceful, traceable*.
	/ʃ/	*musician, capricious, vicious* In medial position before an *i*V sequence, *c* is pronounced as /ʃ/.
d	/d/	*dog, dish, do, dream, pad, hard* Word initially and finally, *d* is pronounced /d/. *Positional variants:* In medial position, /d/ is often represented by *dd* after lax vowels, as in *saddle, addict, paddy*. It also sometimes appears as *dd* in final position, as in *odd, add*. After tense vowels, *-de* is common: *code, shade*.
	/dʒ/	*modular, graduate, individual* Word medially before an unstressed *u* vowel spelling, *d* is pronounced as /dʒ/.

Letter	Phoneme(s)	Examples and discussion
f	/f/	*fat, fun, fill, flat, freedom* Initial *f* is pronounced /f/. *Positional variants:* /f/ is sometimes spelled *ph: phonics, phobia, physics, aphasia.* Medial and final /f/ are often spelled *gh*, as in *laughter, tough;* final *f* can also appear as *fe* after tense vowels, as in *life, chafe.* Medial and final *f* are often doubled after a lax vowel, as in *off, puff, stiff, muffin, raffle.*
g	/g/	*go, gun, glee, target, log, bag, dig* Before the vowels *a, o,* and *u,* and before consonants, syllable-initial *g* is pronounced /g/. In syllable-final position, /g/ also occurs as *g* and is often doubled to *gg* medially after lax vowels: *giggle, bugged.*
	/dʒ/	*gentle, giant, gesture, gem, gypsy* Word initially, the letter *g* before *i, y,* and *e* is often pronounced /dʒ/. *Positional variant:* Medial and final /dʒ/ are also spelled *-dg(e)* or *-g(e)*, as in *lodge, badger, page, raging, wager.*
	/ʒ/	*beige, rouge, loge, luge* In words of French origin, /ʒ/ is often spelled with *ge* finally. In at least one word, *genre*, it is spelled with *g* initially.
h	/h/	*how, heel, huge, hug, horror* Initial *h* is pronounced /h/. *Exceptions:* In some words of Romance origin, an initial *h* goes unpronounced, as in *hour, honor.* In final position *h* generally serves merely to signal a long preceding vowel, as in *oh, rah, ah.* The role of *h* in digraphs is discussed later.
j	/dʒ/	*joy, just, jeep, ajar, pajamas* Word and syllable initially, *j* represents /dʒ/. *Exceptions:* In some words borrowed from Spanish, *j* represents /h/: *junta, frijoles.*
k	/k/	*kin, kiss, look, work, broker, okay* The letter *k* can represent /k/ in initial, medial, or final position. *Positional variants:* Medial and final /k/ are often spelled *ck* after lax vowels, as in *kick, chicken.* Also, *ke* represents /k/ after tense vowels: *cake, woke.*
l	/l/	*list, lame, lose, pal, pool* Initial and final *l* are pronounced /l/. *Positional variants:* In medial and final position, *l* is often doubled after lax vowels, as in *dollar, mill, bell.* Double *ll* also occurs initially in some words borrowed from Spanish (e.g., *llama*). After tense vowels, *le* is common: *role, tile.*

Letter	Phoneme(s)	Examples and discussion
m	/m/	*may, mile, mouse, room, dim* Initial and final *m* represent /m/. *Positional variants:* In medial position, *m* is frequently doubled after lax vowels as in *common, hammer, commute, drummer.* Also, *me* can represent /m/ after tense vowels: *time, name.*
n	/n/	*new, name, nice, man, own* Initial and final *n* represent /n/. *Positional variants:* In medial position, *n* is frequently doubled after lax vowels, as in *manner, uncanny, inning, connect.* Also, *ne* can represent /n/ after tense vowels: *tone, liner.*
p	/p/	*pie, pack, pull, leap, hop* Initial and final *p* represent /p/. *Positional variants:* In medial position, *p* is frequently doubled after lax vowels, as in *supper, apply, opportunity, yuppie.* After tense vowels, *pe* is common for /p/: *hope, ripe.*
r	/r/	*ring, roast, run, four, car* In initial and final position, the letter *r* represents /r/. *Positional variant:* In medial position, *r* is frequently doubled after lax vowels, as in *sherry, marry, barrel, ferry.* Also, *re* is common especially after tense vowels: *wire, core, lure.*
s	/s/	*see, so, say, bus, task* In initial and final position, the letter *s* usually represents /s/. *Positional variants:* In medial and final position, /s/ is often represented by *ss*, as in *tassle, assort, bass.* Also, *se* occurs after tense vowels: *base, use, dose.*
	/z/	*peas, plays, logs, please, raise* The letter *s* often represents the sound /z/ finally after a voiced sound or in a final sequence before final silent *e*. It can also be pronounced as /z/ intervocalically: *pleasant, reason.*
	/ʒ/	*measure, leisure, vision, aphasia* Word-medial *s* after a vowel letter and before an unstressed *u* vowel or an *i*V sequence is pronounced as /ʒ/.
	/ʃ/	*pressure, mission, insure, tension* Medially, *s* after a consonant letter (which may be another *s*) and before an unstressed *u* vowel letter or an *i*V sequence represents the sound /ʃ/. *Exception:* The letter *s* is also pronounced /ʃ/ before a stressed *u* vowel spelling in the words *sugar* and *(as)sure.*

Letter	Phoneme(s)	Examples and discussion
t	/t/	*tea, tune, taste, cat, sit* In initial and final position, the letter *t* represents /t/. *Positional variants:* Intervocalic *t* is often realized as a flap /ɾ/, as in *letter, batter;* it sometimes drops out following medial *n*, as in *twenty, quantity.* Medial /t/ is often represented by *tt* before lax vowels, as in *cattle, attend, mutter;* this is also sometimes the case with final /t/, as in *mitt.* Also, *te* occurs after tense vowels: *quote, mate.*
	/ʃ/	*ration, nation, expedition* In medial position, especially before *i*V sequences such as *-ion*, the letter *t* is pronounced as /ʃ/.
	/tʃ/	*question, natural, pasture* In medial position, *t* after *s* and before an *i*V sequence is pronounced as /tʃ/. It is also pronounced as /tʃ/ before an unstressed *u* vowel spelling.
v	/v/	*vote, vice, veto, avid, beaver* In initial and medial position, the letter *v* is realized as /v/. *Positional variant:* In final position, /v/ is virtually always spelled *ve* whether the preceding vowel is tense or lax: *live, have, move.* The exceptions to this are proper names and colloquialisms: *Bev, rev.*
w	/w/	*we, way, wore, between, toward* In initial and medial position, the consonant *w* is pronounced /w/. *Positional variant:* In syllable-final position, *w* is always part of a vowel sound, as in *saw, low.*
x	/ks/	*extra, laxity, box, fix, taxes* The most common pronununciation for *x* is as the consonant cluster /ks/. *Positional variant:* In intervocalic position before a stressed syllable, *x* represents /gz/, as in *exact, example, exaggerate.*
	/z/	*xylophone, xerox, xenophobia, Xavier* The letter *x* in initial position is pronounced /z/.
y	/y/	*yes, you, yam, beyond, unyielding* The consonant *y* in syllable-initial position is pronounced /y/. *Positional variant:* After a vowel letter, *y* or *y(e)* is always part of a vowel sound, as in *boy, eye;* after a consonant letter, *y* always represents a vowel sound, as in *try, style, gym.*

Letter	Phoneme(s)	Examples and discussion
z	/z/	*zone, zip, kazoo, bazooka* In syllable-initial position, *z* represents /z/. *Positional variant:* In medial and final position, /z/ is often represented as *zz: buzz, fuzzy, dazzle, fizzle.* The sound /z/ is probably more frequently represented by *s(e)* than by *z* (*please, raise, days, wins*), although *ze* sometimes occurs after tense vowels (*gaze, size*).

II. DIGRAPH–PHONEME CORRESPONDENCE

Like the consonant letters of English, the consonant digraphs, or two-letter sequences, demonstrate a relatively consistent letter–sound correspondence. The following is a list of the English consonant digraphs and their common pronunciations and positional variants.

Letter	Phoneme(s)	Examples and discussion
sh	/ʃ/	*show, shirt, push, washer* The consonant digraph *sh* represents /ʃ/ initially, medially, and finally.
ph	/f/	*telephone, phase, phantom, Ralph* The consonant digraph *ph* represents /f/ initially, medially, and finally.
wh	/w/ /hw/	*which, where, what, when, whether, awhile* The digraph *wh* occurs in syllable-initial position only. Note that the selection of /w/ or /hw/ depends on the dialect and/or the individual speaker.
gh	/g/	*ghost, ghetto, ghoul, spaghetti* In syllable-initial position, *gh* is realized as /g/.
	/f/	*tough, laugh, enough* Syllable finally, *gh* is realized as /f/. *Note:* The final digraph *gh* can also be silent; in such cases, it signals a preceding tense vowel: *through, though, caught.*
ch	/tʃ/	*child, chew, chalk, recharge* The consonant digraph *ch* often represents /tʃ/ in syllable-initial position. *Positional variant:* The spelling *tch* also occurs medially and finally, as in *pitcher, catch.*
	/k/	*chlorine, charisma, chemistry, stomach, mechanic(al)* Another possible pronunciation for the digraph *ch* is as /k/, which can occur in initial, medial, or final position.
	/ʃ/	*chic, machine, Chicago, Michigan* In words and place names of French origin, *ch* is pronounced /ʃ/. *Positional variant:* In final position, this pronunciation is often spelled *che: cache, creche.*

Letter	Phoneme(s)	Examples and discussion
th	/θ/	*think, thing, bath, mathematics* The digraph *th* represents /θ/ initially in lexical verbs such as *to think, to threaten, to thank;* initially and finally it occurs in common nouns, adjectives, adverbs, and prepositions: *bath, path, throat, threat, thunder, thin, thrice, through.* It also occurs in proper nouns: *Theodore, Thelma, Garth, Thorpe.*
	/ð/	*this, then, those, bathe, bother* The digraph *th* followed by a vowel letter represents /ð/ in function words such as *the, this, although, that, then, thus.* It occurs medially in nouns such as *mother, brother, lather, bother, heathen,* and finally in some plural nouns such as *baths, paths.* It also occurs in verbs before a final silent *e: bathe, teethe, loathe.*
	/t/	*Thomas, Thames, Thompson, thyme* In rarer cases (mainly proper nouns), *th* is pronounced /t/.
ng	/ŋ/	*singer, ringing, bring, long, hang* Medially and finally, *ng* is pronounced /ŋ/.
	/ŋg/	*longer, finger* In some cases when it occurs medially, *ng* is pronounced /ŋg/. *Note:* In some dialects (e.g., New York), medial and final *ng* may also be pronounced /ŋg/: *singer, long, song.*
	/ndʒ/	*range, stranger, ranging, grungy* Before final silent *e, ng* is pronounced /ndʒ/ rather than /ŋ/. This is also the case before some morphological endings beginning in *-e, -i,* or *-y.*
qu	/kw/	*quick, queen, quest, jonquil, aqua* The letter *q* combines with *u* to represent the consonant cluster /kw/ in syllable-initial and medial positions. *Positional variant:* In final position, *-qu(e)* may represent /k/: *clique, plaque, pique.*

APPENDIX 11
Systematic Differences in British and American Spelling

The following list, based largely on Clark, Moran, and Burrows (1981) and Bolton and Snowball (1993), represents the more systematic differences in the British and American spelling systems. Not included are spelling differences that mirror differences in pronunciation and morphology, such as American *burned* and British *burnt*. For a comparison of pronunciation differences in British and American English, see Appendix 1.

	British and Canadian spelling	**American spelling**
ae/e	anaesthesia	anesthesia
	encyclopaedia	encyclopedia
oe/e	oesophagus	esophogus
	foetus	fetus
-exion/-ection	connexion	connection
	reflexion	reflection
-ence/-ense	defence	defense
	licence	license
-re/-er	theatre	theater
	fibre	fiber
-ise/-ize	realise	realize
	organise	organize
-isation/-ization	civilisation	civilization
	naturalisation	naturalization
-il/-ill	fulfil	fulfill
	skilful	skillful
ll/l	traveller	traveler
	jeweller	jeweler
-mme/-m	programme, program	program
	kilogramme, kilogram	kilogram
-ement/-ment	judgement	judgment
	arguement	argument
-our/-or	favour	favor
	honour	honor
-que/-(c)k	cheque	check
	masque	mask
-gue/-g	catalogue	catalog, catalogue
	dialogue	dialog, dialogue
en-/in-	enquire	inquire
	ensure	insure, ensure
em-/im-	empale	impale
	empanel	impanel

APPENDIX 12
Profile Questionnaire Used at UCLA

This questionnaire is a way for me to get to know each of you better right from the start. This will help me to teach the most useful course for you. I want to ask you some questions about your motivation, background, and situation. Please answer as completely as you can.

General Background

1. What is your name? _____

2. What is your native language? _____

3. What is your major? _____

4. Are you an undergraduate or a graduate student? _____

5. How long have you been at UCLA? _____

6. How long have you lived in the U.S.? _____

7. Approximately what percentage of time do you speak English each day (as opposed to your native language)?
   Circle one: 0–20%   20%–40%   40%–60%   60%–80%   80%–100%

English Study Background

8. Please describe your experience in learning English (*e.g., how long, where, what kind of courses, what kind of teachers, exposure to native speakers of English in your country, your travel/study experiences, whether you consider your experience learning English pleasant or successful so far, etc.*).

9. Have you had more experience with British or with American English (*or some other variety, such as Australian, Indian, South African, etc.*)? Please explain.

Knowledge of English Pronunciation

10. Do you ever use the pronunciation key or guide in your dictionary to get an idea of how a word is pronounced?

11. Are you familiar with a phonemic alphabet or any phonetic/phonemic symbols? (*If yes, and you know the name of the alphabet – e.g., IPA – please add this information.*)

12. Have any of your previous English teachers taught you about pronunciation? If yes, can you give some details?

Motivation for Taking This Course

13. Why do you want to take a pronunciation course?

14. For graduate students: Are you a Teaching Assistant or do you think you will become one in the future?

15. If yes, what kind of courses do you teach or would you teach in your department?

16. Do you ever have to give presentations in classes or at conferences? (*Please explain.*)

Self-Awareness

17. Please describe any situations in which you feel that Americans have misunderstood you because of your pronunciation.

18. Have you ever asked an American for help with pronunciation? If yes, please explain if or how this has helped you.

19. Is there a particular situation that makes you anxious about your pronunciation (*e.g., on the phone, at the bank, in office hours with a professor, etc.*)?

20. In what situation do you feel the most comfortable speaking English?

21. What are your biggest pronunciation difficulties in English?

22. What area of pronunciation would you like to work on most and what are your goals for this course?

APPENDIX 13
Diagnostic Passage and Accent Checklist

If English is not your native language, people may have noticed that you come from another country because of your "foreign accent." Why do people usually have an accent when they speak a second language? Several theories address this issue. Many people believe that only young children can learn a second language without an accent, but applied linguists have reported cases of older individuals who have mastered a second language without an accent. Another common belief is that your first language influences your pronunciation in a second language. Most native speakers of English can, for example, recognize people from France by their French accents. They may also be able to identify Spanish or Arabic speakers over the telephone, just by listening carefully to their pronunciation. Does this mean that accents can't be changed? Not at all! But old habits won't change without a lot of hard work, will they? In the end, the path to learning to speak a second language without an accent appears to be a combination of hard work, a good ear, and a strong desire to sound like a native speaker. You also need accurate information about the English sound system and lots of exposure to the spoken language. Will you manage to make progress, or will you just give up? Only time will tell, I'm afraid. Good luck, and don't forget to work hard!

ACCENT CHECKLIST

Note major problems in these areas:

I.   Vowels

     Stressed

     Unstressed

II.   Consonants

     Initial

     Medial

     Final

     Clusters (initial/final)

III.   Intonation

     Statements

     Questions

     Other

IV.   Stress and prominence

     Word-level

     Phrase-level

V.   Adjustments in connected speech

Additional comments:

APPENDIX 14
ACTFL Proficiency Guidelines for Speaking

GENERIC DESCRIPTIONS – SPEAKING

Novice

The Novice level is characterized by the ability to communicate minimally with learned material.

Novice-Low

Oral production consists of isolated words and perhaps a few high-frequency phrases. Essentially no functional communicative ability.

Novice-Mid

Oral production continues to consist of isolated words and learned phrases within very predictable areas of need, although quantity is increased. Vocabulary is sufficient only for handling simple, elementary needs and expressing basic courtesies. Utterances rarely consist of more than two or three words and show frequent long pauses and repetition of interlocutor's words. Speaker may have some difficulty producing even the simplest utterances. Some Novice-Mid speakers will be understood only with great difficulty.

Novice-High

Able to satisfy partially the requirements of basic communicative exchanges by relying heavily on learned utterances but occasionally expanding these through simple recombinations of their elements. Can ask questions or make statements involving learned material. Shows signs of spontaneity although this falls short of real autonomy of expression. Speech continues to consist of learned utterances rather than of personalized, situationally adapted ones. Vocabulary centers on areas such as basic objects, places, and most common kinship terms. Pronunciation may still be strongly influenced by first language. Errors are frequent and, in spite of repetition, some Novice-High speakers will have difficulty being understood even by sympathetic interlocutors.

Intermediate

The Intermediate level is characterized by the speaker's ability to:
– create with the language by combining and recombining learned elements, though primarily in a reactive mode;
– initiate, minimally sustain, and close in a simple way basic communicative tasks;
– and ask and answer questions.

Intermediate-Low

Able to handle successfully a limited number of interactive, task-oriented and social situations. Can ask and answer questions, initiate and respond to simple statements, and maintain face-to-face conversation, although in a highly restricted manner and with much linguistic inaccuracy. Within these limitations, can perform such tasks as introducing self, ordering a meal, asking directions, and making purchases. Vocabulary is adequate to express only the most elementary needs. Strong interference from native language may occur. Misunderstandings frequently arise, but with repetition, the Intermediate-Low speaker can generally be understood by sympathetic interlocutors.

Intermediate-Mid   Able to handle successfully a variety of uncomplicated, basic and communicative tasks and social situations. Can talk simply about self and family members. Can ask and answer questions and participate in simple conversations on topics beyond the most immediate needs; e.g., personal history and leisure time activities. Utterance length increases slightly, but speech may continue to be characterized by frequent long pauses, since the smooth incorporation of even basic conversational strategies is often hindered as the speaker struggles to create appropriate language forms. Pronunciation may continue to be strongly influenced by first language and fluency may still be strained. Although misunderstandings still arise, the Intermediate-Mid speaker can generally be understood by sympathetic interlocutors.

Intermediate-High   Able to handle successfully most uncomplicated communicative tasks and social situations. Can initiate, sustain, and close a general conversation with a number of strategies appropriate to a range of circumstances and topics, but errors are evident. Limited vocabulary still necessitates hesitation and may bring about slightly unexpected circumlocution. There is emerging evidence of connected discourse, particularly for simple narration and/or description. The Intermediate-High speaker can generally be understood even by interlocutors not accustomed to dealing with speakers at this level, but repetition may still be required.

Advanced   The Advanced level is characterized by the speaker's ability to:
– converse in a clearly participatory fashion;
– initiate, sustain, and bring to closure a wide variety of communicative tasks, including those that require an increased ability to convey meaning with diverse language strategies due to a complication or an unforeseen turn of events;
– satisfy the requirements of school and work situations; and
– narrate and describe with paragraph-length connected discourse.

Advanced   Able to satisfy the requirements of everyday situations and routine school and work requirements. Can handle with confidence but not with facility complicated tasks and social situations, such as elaborating, complaining, and apologizing. Can narrate and describe with some details, linking sentences together smoothly. Can communicate facts and talk casually about topics of current public and personal interest, using general vocabulary. Shortcomings can often be smoothed over by communicative strategies, such as pause fillers, stalling devices, and different rates of speech. Circumlocution which arises from vocabulary or syntactic limita-

	tions very often is quite successful, though some groping for words may still be evident. The Advanced-level speaker can be understood without difficulty by native interlocutors.
Advanced-Plus	Able to satisfy the requirements of a broad variety of everyday, school, and work situations. Can discuss concrete topics relating to particular interests and special fields of competence. There is emerging evidence of ability to support opinions, explain in detail, and hypothesize. The Advanced-Plus speaker often shows a well developed ability to compensate for an imperfect grasp of some forms with confident use of communicative strategies, such as paraphrasing and circumlocution. Differentiated vocabulary and intonation are effectively used to communicated fine shades of meaning. The Advanced-Plus speaker often shows remarkable fluency and ease of speech but under the demands of Superior-level, complex tasks, language may break down or prove inadequate.
Superior	The Superior level is characterized by the speaker's ability to:
	– participate effectively in most formal and informal conversations on practical, social, professional, and abstract topics; and
	– support opinions and hypothesize using native-like discourse.
Superior	Able to speak the language with sufficient accuracy to participate effectively in most formal and informal conversations on practical, social, professional, and abstract topics. Can discuss special fields of competence and interest with ease. Can support opinions and hypothesize, but may not be able to tailor language to audience or discuss in depth highly abstract or unfamiliar topics. Usually the Superior level speaker is only partially familiar with regional or other dialectical variants. The Superior level speaker commands a wide variety of interactive strategies and shows good awareness of discourse strategies. The latter involves the ability to distinguish main ideas from supporting information through syntactic, lexical, and suprasegmental features (pitch, stress, intonation). Sporadic errors may occur, particularly in low-frequency structures and some complex high-frequency structures more common to formal writing, but no patterns of error are evident. Errors do not disturb the native speaker or interfere with communication.

APPENDIX 15
Speech Intelligibility/Communicability Index for Describing Speech and Evaluating Its Impact on Communication

Level	Description	Impact on communication
1	Speech is basically unintelligible; only an occasional word or phrase can be recognized.	Accent precludes functional oral communication.
2	Speech is largely unintelligible; great listener effort is required; constant repetition and verifications are required.	Accent causes severe interference with oral communication.

Communicative Threshold A

Level	Description	Impact on communication
3	Speech is reasonably intelligible, but significant listener effort is required because of the speaker's pronunciation or grammatical errors, which impede communication and distract the listener; there is an ongoing need for repetition and verification.	Accent causes frequent interference with communication through the combined effect of the individual features of mispronunciation and the global impact of the variant speech pattern.
4	Speech is largely intelligible; although sound and prosodic variances from the NS norm are obvious, listeners can understand if they concentrate on the message.	Accent causes interference primarily via distraction; the listener's attention is often diverted away from the content to focus instead on the novelty of the speech pattern.

Communicative Threshold B

Level	Description	Impact on communication
5	Speech is fully intelligible; occasional sound and prosodic variances from the NS norm are present but not seriously distracting to the listener.	Accent causes little interference; speech is fully functional for effective communication.
6	Speech is near-native; only minimal features of divergence from NS speech can be detected; near-native sound and prosodic patterning.	Accent is virtually nonexistent.

From "A Multidemensional Curriculum Design," by Joan Morley, 1994, in Joan Morley (Ed.), *Pronunciation Pedagogy and Theory: New Views, New Directions* (pp. 76–77). Copyright 1994 by Teachers of English to Speakers of Other Languages, Inc. Used with permission.

APPENDIX 16

Speaking Performance Scale for UCLA Oral Proficiency Test for Nonnative TAs

Rating	Pronunciation	Speech flow	Grammar	Vocabulary	Organization	Listening comprehension	Question-handling
4	Rarely mispronounces	High degree of fluency; effortless; smooth	Only occasional errors; no pattern; uses high-level discourse structures	Extensive, appropriate; precise to specific task; includes vocabulary explanations to avoid talking over the heads of students	Complete, clear, well-developed, logical explanations & discourse clearly marked; sufficient redundancy	Appears to understand administrator and undergraduate completely	Clear, not usually confused by questions; can clarify misunderstandings; no long delay in responding
3	Accent may be foreign; never interferes; rarely disturbs NS[a]	Speaks with facility; rarely has to grope; uses paraphrase & circumlocution easily	Full range of basic structures; uses complex structures; some error patterns but meaning conveyed accurately	Adequate to cover specific task; occasional error with noncritical vocabulary	Clear explanation with sufficient detail; some digressions but not overly redundant	Adequate to follow most speech; occasional need for clarification or repetition	Responds clearly; may hesitate while responding; may be confused by unclearly stated questions
2	Often faulty but intelligible with effort	Speaks with confidence but not facility; hesitant; some paraphrasing; choppy	Meaning expressed accurately in simple sentences; complex grammar avoided or misused	Sufficient to speak simply with some circumlocution about the specific task	Simple, clear explanation; transitions may be awkward; some lack of supporting examples; may lack necessary redundancy	OK in face-to-face communication of well-known subject matter; frequent need for clarification & explanation	Has difficulty responding; unable to clarify unclearly stated questions
1	Errors frequent; only intelligible to NS used to dealing with NNS[b]	Slow, strained except for routine expressions	Errors frequent; intelligible only to NS used to dealing with NNS	Lacking in vocabulary necessary to perform the specific task	Overall structure of explanation unclear; difficult to follow sequence & development of ideas	Some misunderstanding despite clarification & repetition	Often confused by questions; may answer illogically
0	Unintelligible	So halting that conversation is impossible	Nonexistent	Inadequate even for simple speech	Impossible to follow explanation	Inadequate even for simple face-to-face situations	May ignore questions; no strategies to clarify misunderstandings

[a]NS = native speaker.
[b]NNS = nonnative speaker.

Scale adapted from *Interagency Language Roundtable Proficiency Test*.

APPENDIX 17
Self-Evaluation Form: Interview Role Plays

NAME: _____ DATE: _____

Directions: Watch your videotaped role play and fill out the following evaluation form.

INTONATION

Listen for any yes/no questions you asked. Write down two examples and mark your intonation. Was it appropriate? Why/why not?

a. _____

b. _____

Do the same for wh-questions.

a. _____

b. _____

Listen to your statements. Does your voice pitch fall (↘) at the end of thoughts and statements to show completion? Give two examples.

a. _____

b. _____

PROMINENCE/STRESS

Prominence: Did you highlight the words that are important or that show new information? Give two examples and mark the words you stressed.

a. _____

b. _____

Word stress: In multisyllabic words, did you stress the proper syllable(s)? Give five examples and mark the syllable(s) you stressed.

a. _____   c. _____   e. _____

b. _____   d. _____

REDUCED SPEECH/REDUCTION OF VOWELS IN UNSTRESSED SYLLABLES

Were you able to reduce unstressed function words within sentences (words like *the, did, have, or, for, and,* etc.)? Give two examples, circling the words that you reduced:

a. _____

b. _____

Were you able to reduce the vowels in unstressed syllables? Give five examples, indicating the reduced vowels with a slash mark (e.g., *bønanø*).

a. _____   c. _____   e. _____

b. _____   d. _____

BLENDING

Were you able to blend words together appropriately? Give two examples, marking the linked words (e.g., *"Are‿you‿an‿active person?"*).

a. _____

b. _____

VOWELS

Are there any vowel distinctions you had difficulty making? Give examples, circling the difficult vowels.

a. _____   c. _____   e. _____

b. _____   d. _____

CONSONANTS

Are there any consonant distinctions you had difficulty making? Give examples, circling the difficult consonants.

a. _____   c. _____   e. _____

b. _____   d. _____

Bibliography

Abercrombie, D. (1967). *Elements of general phonetics.* Edinburgh: Edinburgh University Press.

Acton, W. (1984). Changing fossilized pronunciation. *TESOL Quarterly, 18*(1), 71–85.

———. (1986). Current perspectives on pronunciation: Suprasegmentals. Colloquium presented at the 20th Annual TESOL Convention, Anaheim, CA.

———. (1991). Integrating pronunciation into the second language curriculum: Where the rubber band meets the road. Colloquium presented at the 25th Annual TESOL Convention, New York.

Agnello, V. L., & Garcia, C. (1990). *Vocal rehabilitation: A practice book for voice improvement.* Austin: Pro-Ed.

Aguirre, A. (1988). Dialogue journal: TESL 103 – Instructor Donna Brinton. Unpublished manuscript, University of California, Department of TESL and Applied Linguistics, Los Angeles.

Alderson, J. C.; Krahnke, K.; & Stansfield, C. W. (Eds.). (1987). *Reviews of English language proficiency tests.* Alexandria, VA: TESOL.

Allan, D. (1991). Tape journals: Bridging the gap between communication and correction. *ELT Journal, 45*(1), 61–66.

Allen, V. F. (1971). Teaching intonation: From theory to practice. *TESOL Quarterly, 5*(1), 73–81.

Anderson-Hsieh, J. (1990). Teaching stress, rhythm, and intonation through visual feedback. Paper presented at the 24th Annual TESOL Convention, San Francisco.

———. (1992). Using electronic feedback to teach suprasegmentals. *System, 20*(1), 51–62.

Anderson-Hsieh, J.; Riney, T.; & Koehler, K. (1994). Connected speech modifications in the English of Japanese ESL learners. *IDEAL, 7,* 31–52.

Anderson-Hsieh, J., & Venkatagiri, H. (1994). Syllable duration and pausing in the speech of Chinese ESL speakers. *TESOL Quarterly, 28*(4), 807–812.

Archibald, J. (1987). Developing natural and confident speech: Drama techniques in the pronunciation classroom. In P. Avery & S. Ehrlich (Eds.), *The teaching of pronunciation: An introduction for teachers of English as a second language* (pp. 153–159). Theme issue of *TESL Talk, 17*(1). Toronto: Ontario Ministry of Citizenship & Culture.

Asher, J. J. (1977). *Learning another language through actions: The complete teachers' guidebook.* Los Gatos, CA: Sky Oaks Productions.

Ausubel, D. P. (1964). Adults versus children in second-language learning: Psychological considerations. *Modern Language Journal, 48,* 420–424.

Avery, P., & Ehrlich, S. (1992). *Teaching American English pronunciation.* Oxford: Oxford University Press.

Backmann, N. (1977). Learner intonation: A pilot study. In C. A. Henning (Ed.), *Proceedings of the First Second Language Research Forum* (pp. 30–37). Los Angeles: Department of English, ESL Section, University of California.

Banathy, B. H., & Madarasz, P. H. (1969). Contrastive analysis and error analysis. *Journal of English as a Second Language, 4*(3), 77–92.

Bandler, R., & Grinder, J. (1975). *The structure of magic: A book about language and therapy.* Palo Alto, CA: Science & Behavior Books.

———. (1979). *Frogs into princes: Neuro-linguistic programming.* Moab, UT: Real People Press.

———. (1982). *Reframing: Neuro-linguistic programming.* Moab, UT: Real People Press.

Baptista, B. O. (1992). The acquisition of English vowels by eleven Brazilian Portuguese speakers: An acoustic analysis. Unpublished doctoral dissertation, University of California, Los Angeles.

Bauer, G. (1991). Instructional communication concerns of international (non-native English speaking) teaching assistants: A qualitative analysis. In J. D. Nyquist, R. D. Abbott, D. H. Wulff, & J. Sprague (Eds.), *Preparing the professoriate of tomorrow to teach: Selected readings in TA training* (pp. 420–426). Dubuque, IA: Kendall/Hunt.

Baugh, A. C. (1957). *A history of the English language,* 2nd ed. Englewood Cliffs, NJ: Prentice-Hall.

Blair, R. W. (1991). Innovative approaches. In M. Celce-Murcia (Ed.), *Teaching English as a second or foreign language,* 2nd ed. (pp. 23–45). New York: Newbury House.

———. (Ed.). (1982). *Innovative approaches to language teaching.* Cambridge, MA: Newbury House.

Bloomfield, L. (1933). *Language.* New York: Holt.

Bolinger, D. (1986). *Intonation and its parts.* Palo Alto, CA: Stanford University Press.

Bolton, F., & Snowball, D. (1993). *Teaching spelling: A practical resource.* Portsmouth, NH: Heinemann.

Bowen, J. D. (1972). Contextualizing pronunciation practice in the ESOL classroom. *TESOL Quarterly, 6*(1), 83–94.

———. (1975a). An experimental integrative test of English grammar. *UCLA Workpapers in Teaching English as a Second Language, 9,* 3–15.

———. (1975b). *Patterns of English pronunciation.* Rowley, MA: Newbury House.

Bowen, T., & Marks, J. (1992). *The pronunciation book: Student-centred activities for pronunciation work.* Burnt Mill, Harlow: Longman.

Brazil, D.; Coulthard, M.; & Johns, C. (1980). *Discourse intonation and language teaching.* London: Longman.

Brinton, L. J. (1989). *Independent study guide to accompany English 320 – History of the English Language.* Vancouver: University of British Columbia.

Broselow, E. (1987). An investigation of transfer in second language phonology. In G. Ioup & S. H. Weinberger (Eds.), *Interlanguage phonology: The acquisition of a second language sound system* (pp. 261–278). New York: Newbury House.

Broselow, E.; Hurtig, R.; & Ringen, C. (1987). The perception of second language prosody. In G. Ioup & S. H. Weinberger (Eds.), *Interlanguage phonology: The acquisition of a second language sound system* (pp. 350–362). New York: Newbury House.

Browman, C. P. (1980). Perceptual processing: Evidence from slips of the ear. In V. A. Fromkin (Ed.), *Errors in linguistic performance: Slips of the tongue, ear, pen, and hand* (pp. 213–230). New York: Academic Press.

Brown, A. (1991). Functional load and the teaching of pronunciation. In A. Brown (Ed.), *Teaching English pronunciation: A book of readings* (pp. 211–224). London: Routledge.

Brown, H. D. (1994). *Principles of language learning and teaching,* 3rd ed. Englewood Cliffs, NJ: Prentice-Hall.

Browne, S. C., & Huckin, T. N. (1987). Pronunciation tutorials for nonnative technical professionals: A program description. In J. Morley (Ed.), *Current perspectives on pronunciation: Practices anchored in theory* (pp. 41–58). Alexandria, VA: TESOL.

Browning, G. (1974). Testing pronunciation indirectly: An experiment. Unpublished master's thesis, University of California, Los Angeles.

Brumfit, C. J., & Johnson, K. (Eds.). (1979). *The communicative approach to language teaching.* Oxford: Oxford University Press.

Carroll, J. B. (1962). The prediction of success in intensive foreign language training. In R. Glaser (Ed.), *Training, research, and education* (pp. 87–136). Pittsburgh: University of Pittsburgh Press.

———. (1981). Twenty-five years of research on foreign language aptitude. In K. C. Diller (Ed.), *Individual differences and universals in language learning aptitude* (pp. 83–118). Rowley, MA: Newbury House.

Catford, J. C. (1987). Phonetics and the teaching of pronunciation. In J. Morley (Ed.), *Current perspectives on pronunciation: Practices anchored in theory* (pp. 83–100). Alexandria, VA: TESOL.

———. (1988). *A practical introduction to phonetics.* Oxford: Oxford University Press.

Celce-Murcia, M. (1977). Phonological factors in vocabulary acquisition: A case study of a two-year-old, English-French bilingual. *Working Papers in Bilingualism, 13,* 27–41.

———. (1980). On Meringer's corpus of "slips of the ear." In V. A. Fromkin (Ed.), *Errors in linguistic performance: Slips of the tongue, ear, pen, and hand* (pp. 199–211). New York: Academic Press.

———. (1983). Teaching pronunciation communicatively. *MEXTESOL Journal, 7*(1), 10–25.

———. (1987). Teaching pronunciation as communication. In J. Morley (Ed.), *Current perspectives on pronunciation: Practices anchored in theory* (pp. 5–12). Alexandria, VA: TESOL.

Celce-Murcia, M., & Goodwin, J. (1991). Teaching pronunciation. In M. Celce-Murcia (Ed.), *Teaching English as a second or foreign language,* 2nd ed. (pp. 136-153). NewYork: Newbury House.

Chafe, W. (1980). *The pear stories III: Advances in discourse processes.* Norwood, NJ: Ablex.

Chan, M. (1988). Using your hands to teach pronunciation. Paper presented at the 22nd Annual TESOL Convention, Chicago.

———. (1991). Why is their speech hard to understand? Paper presented at the 22nd Annual CATESOL Convention, Santa Clara, CA.

Chela Flores, B. (1993). On the acquisition of English rhythm: Theoretical and practical issues. *Lenguas Modernes, 20,* 151–164.

Chomsky, C. (1970). Reading, writing, and phonology. *Harvard Educational Review, 40*(2), 287–309.

Chomsky, N. (1957). *Syntactic structures.* The Hague: Mouton.

———. (1965). *Aspects of the theory of syntax.* Cambridge, MA: MIT Press.

———. (1986). *Knowledge of language: Its nature, origin, and use.* New York: Praeger.

Chomsky, N., & Halle, M. (1968). *The sound pattern of English.* New York: Harper & Row.

Chun, D. M. (1988). Teaching intonation as part of communicative competence: Suggestions for the classroom. *Die Unterrichtspraxis, 21,* 81–88.

———. (1989). Teaching tone and intonation with microcomputers. *CALICO Journal,* 21–46.

Clark, R. C.; Moran, P. R.; & Burrows, A. A. (1981). *The ESL miscellany.* Brattleboro, VT: Pro Lingua.

Corder, S. P. (1974). Idiosyncratic dialects and error analysis. In J. Schumann & N. Stenson (Eds.), *New frontiers in second language learning* (pp. 100–113). Rowley, MA: Newbury House.

Crawford, W. W. (1987). The pronunciation monitor: L2 acquisition considerations and pedagogical priorities. In J. Morley (Ed.), *Current perspectives on pronunciation* (pp. 101–121). Alexandria, VA: TESOL.

Crookall, D., & Oxford, R. L. (1990). *Simulation, gaming, and language learning.* New York: Newbury House.

Cruttenden, A. (1986). *Intonation.* Cambridge: Cambridge University Press.

Curran, C. A. (1976). *Counseling-Learning in second language learning.* East Dubuque, IL: Counseling-Learning Publications.

Davis, P., & Rinvolucri, M. (1988). *Dictation: New methods, new possibilities.* Cambridge: Cambridge University Press.

———. (1990). *The confidence book: Building trust in the language classroom.* Essex, England: Longman.

de Bot, K., & Mailfert, K. (1982). The teaching of intonation: Fundamental research and classroom applications. *TESOL Quarterly, 16*(1), 71–77.

Diamond, M. C. (1988). *Enriching heredity: The impact of the environment on the anatomy of the brain.* New York: Free Press.

Diamond, R. E. (1970). *Old English grammar and reader.* Detroit: Wayne State University Press.

Dickerson, W. B. (1981). A pedagogical interpretation of generative phonology II: The main word stress rules of English. *TESL Studies, 4,* 57–93.

———. (1984). The role of formal rules in pronunciation. In J. Handscombe, R. A. Orem, & B. P. Taylor (Eds.), *On TESOL '83: The question of control* (pp. 135–148). Alexandria, VA: TESOL.

———. (1985). The invisible *y:* A case for spelling in pronunciation learning. *TESOL Quarterly, 19*(2), 303–316.

———. (1987a). Explicit rules and the developing interlanguage phonology. In A. James & L. Leather (Eds.), *Sound patterns in second language acquisition* (pp. 121–140). Amsterdam: Foris.

———. (1987b). Orthography as pronunciation resource. *World Englishes, 6*(1), 11–20.

———. (1989a). *Stress in the speech stream: The rhythm of spoken English,* Student Text. Urbana: University of Illinois Press.

———. (1989b). *Stress in the speech stream: The rhythm of spoken English,* Teacher's Manual. Urbana: University of Illinois Press.

———. (1990). Morphology via orthography: A visual approach to oral decisions. *Applied Linguistics, 11*(3), 238–252.

———. (1994a). Discourse stress and phrasal verbs. *IDEAL, 7,* 53–66.

———. (1994b). Empowering students with predictive skills. In J. Morley (Ed.), *Pronunciation pedagogy and theory: New directions, new views* (pp. 17–35). Alexandria, VA: TESOL.

Dougill, J. (1987). *Drama activities for language learning.* London: Macmillan.

Dubin, F., & Olshtain, E. (1986). *Course design: Developing programs and materials for language learning.* Cambridge: Cambridge University Press.

Duke-Lay, N. (1987). Communicative strategy in the classroom: The oral journal. *ESL in Higher Education Newsletter, 6*(2), 7.

Eckman, F. (1987). Markedness and the contrastive analysis hypothesis. In G. Ioup & S. H. Weinberger (Eds.), *Interlanguage phonology: The acquisition of a second language sound system* (pp. 55–69). New York: Newbury House.

———. (1991). The structural conformity hypothesis and the acquisition of consonant clusters. *Studies in Second Language Acquisition, 13,* 23–41.

Eckman, F.; Moravcsik, E.; & Wirth, J. (1989). Implicational universals and interrogative structures in the interlanguage of ESL learners. *Language Learning, 39,* 173–205.

Edney, B. L. (1990). New technological aids for pronunciation instruction and evaluation. *TESOL Newsletter, 24*(6), 9, 20, 26.

Educational Testing Service. (1992). *Test of Spoken English manual for score users,* 4th ed. Princeton, NJ: Author.

Esling, J. H. (1994). Some perspectives on accent: Range of voice quality variation, the periphery, and focusing. In J. Morley (Ed.), *Pronunciation pedagogy and theory: New views, new dimensions* (pp. 49–63). Alexandria, VA: TESOL.

Esling, J. H., & Wong, R. F. (1983). Voice quality settings and the teaching of pronunciation. *TESOL Quarterly, 17*(1), 89–96.

Ferguson, C. A., & Farwell, C. B. (1975). Words and sounds in early language acquisition. *Language, 51,* 419–439.

Firth, S. (1992a). Developing self-correcting and self-monitoring strategies. In P. Avery & S. Ehrlich (Eds.), *Teaching American English pronunciation* (pp. 215–219). Oxford: Oxford University Press.

———. (1992b). Pronunciation syllabus design: A question of focus. In P. Avery & S. Ehrlich (Eds.), *Teaching American English pronunciation* (pp. 173–183). Oxford: Oxford University Press.

Flege, J. E. (1981). The phonological basis of foreign accent: A hypothesis. *TESOL Quarterly, 15*(4), 443–455.

Ford, C. E., & Thompson, S. A. (1996). Interactional units in conversation: Syntactic, intonational, and pragmatic resources for the management of turns. In E. Ochs, E. A. Schegloff, & S. A. Thompson (Eds.), *Interaction and grammar (pp. 134–184).* New York: Cambridge University Press.

Gardner, R. C., & Lambert, W. E. (1972). *Attitudes and motivation in second language learning.* Rowley, MA: Newbury House.

Garnes, S., and Bond, Z. S. (l980). A slip of the ear: A snip of the ear? A slip of the year? In V. A. Fromkin (Ed.), *Errors in linguistic performance: Slips of the tongue, ear, pen, and hand* (pp. 231–240). New York: Academic Press.

Gattegno, C. (1972). *Teaching foreign languages in schools: The Silent Way.* New York: Educational Solutions.

———. (1976). *The common sense of teaching foreign languages.* New York: Educational Solutions.

———. (1985a). *The learning and teaching of foreign languages.* New York: Educational Solutions.

———. (1985b). *The science of education.* New York: Educational Solutions.

Giegerich, H. J. (1992). *English phonology: An introduction.* Cambridge: Cambridge University Press.

Gilbert, J. B. (l983). Pronunciation and listening comprehension. *Cross Currents, 10*(1), 53–61.

———. (1991). Gadgets: Non-verbal tools for teaching pronunciation. In A. Brown (Ed.), *Teaching English pronunciation: A book of readings* (pp. 308–322). London: Routledge.

———. (l993). *Clear speech: Pronunciation and listening comprehension in North American English,* Student's Book, 2nd ed. New York: Cambridge University Press.

———. (1994). Intonation: A navigation guide for the listener. In J. Morley (Ed.), *Pronunciation pedagogy and theory: New views, new dimensions* (pp. 36–48). Alexandria, VA: TESOL.

Goodwin, J. (1988). Using audiotaped dialogue journals to individualize pronunciation instruction. Paper presented at the 19th Annual CATESOL Conference, San Francisco.

Goodwin, J.; Brinton, D.; & Celce-Murcia, M. (1994). Pronunciation assessment in the ESL/EFL curriculum. In J. Morley (Ed.), *Pronunciation pedagogy and theory: New views, new dimensions* (pp. 3–16). Alexandria, VA: TESOL.

Graham, C. (1978). *Jazz chants.* New York: Oxford University Press.

———. (1986). *Small talk.* New York: Oxford University Press.

———. (1991). *Rhythm and role play.* Studio City, CA: JAG Publications.

Graham, R. C. (1985). Beyond integrative motivation: The development and influence of assimilative motivation. In P. Larson, E. L. Judd, & D. S. Messerschmidt (Eds.), *On TESOL '84* (pp. 75–87). Alexandria, VA: TESOL.

Greenberg, J. (1962). *Universals of language.* Cambridge, MA: MIT Press.

———. (1978). Some generalizations concerning initial and final consonant clusters. In J. Greenberg, C. A. Ferguson, & E. Moravcsik (Eds.), *Universals of human language,* vol. 2 (pp. 243–279). Stanford, CA: Stanford University Press.

Griffiths, R. (1991). The paradox of comprehensible input: Hesitation phenomena in L2 teacher talk. *JALT Journal, 13*(1), 23–41.

Grogan, P. (1990). Teaching pronunciation: Multisensory methods make sense. Paper presented at the 24th Annual TESOL Convention, San Francisco.

Guiora, A. Z. (1972). Construct validity and transpositional research: Toward an empirical study of psychoanalytic concepts. *Comprehensive Psychiatry, 13*(2), 139–150.

Guiora, A. Z.; Beit-Hallami, B.; Brannon, R. C. L.; Dull, C. Y.; & Scovel, T. (1972). The effects of experimentally induced changes in ego states on pronunciation ability in a second language: An exploratory study. *Comprehensive Psychiatry 13,* 421–428.

Gumperz, J. (1982). *Discourse strategies.* Cambridge: Cambridge University Press.

Gumperz, J., & Kaltman, H. (1980). Prosody, linguistic diffusion and conversational inference. *Berkeley Linguistic Society, 6,* 44–65.

Hanley, T. D.; Snidecor, J. C.; & Ringel, R. L. (1966). Some acoustic differences among languages. *Phonetics, 14,* 97–107.

Hatch, E.; Wagner Gough, J.; & Peck, S. (1985). What case studies reveal about system, sequence, and variation in second language acquisition. In M. Celce-Murcia (Ed.), *Beyond basics: Issues and research in TESOL* (pp. 37–59). Rowley, MA: Newbury House.

Hecht, E., & Ryan, G. (1979). *Survival pronunciation: Vowel contrasts.* Hayward, CA: Alemany Press.

Heller, L. (1976). TESL 250K Term Paper – Professor Evelyn Hatch. Unpublished manuscript, University of California, English as a Second Language Section, Los Angeles.

Higgs, T., & Clifford, R. (1982). The push toward communication. In T. V. Higgs (Ed.), *Curriculum, competence, and the foreign language teacher.* ACTFL Foreign Language Education Series, vol. 13. Lincolnwood, IL: National Textbook.

Hill, C., & Beebe, L. M. (1980). Contraction and blending: The use of orthographic clues in teaching pronunciation. *TESOL Quarterly, 14*(3), 299–323.

Hinofotis, F., & Bailey, K. M. (l980). American undergraduates' reactions to the communication skills of foreign teaching assistants. In J. C. Fisher, M. A. Clarke, & J. Schachter (Eds.), *On TESOL '80* (pp. 120–135). Alexandria, VA: TESOL.

Howatt, A. P. R. (l984). *A history of English language teaching.* Oxford: Oxford University Press.

Ioup, G., & Weinberger, S. H. (Eds.). (1987). *Interlanguage phonology: The acquisition of a second language sound system.* New York: Newbury House.

Jacobs, B. (1988). Neurobiological differentiation of primary and secondary language acquisition. *Studies in Second Language Acquisition, 10,* 303–337.

Jakobson, R. (1941). *Kindersprache, Aphasie, und allgemeine Lautgesetze.* Uppsala: Almqvist & Wiksell. (For translation, see Jakobson 1968.)

———. (1968). *Child language, aphasia, and phonological universals.* A. R. Keiler, trans. The Hague: Mouton.

Jensen, E. P. (1988). *Super-teaching: Master strategies for building student success.* Del Mar, CA: Turning Point for Teachers.

Jones, D. (1991). *English pronouncing dictionary,* 14th ed. Cambridge: Cambridge University Press.

Jones, K. (1982). *Simulations in language teaching.* Cambridge: Cambridge University Press.

Joos, M. (1958). *Readings in linguistics,* 2nd ed. New York: American Council of Learned Societies.

Kelly, L. G. (1969). *25 centuries of language teaching.* Rowley, MA: Newbury House.

Kenworthy, J. (1987). *Teaching English pronunciation.* London: Longman.

Kenyon, J. S., & Knott, T. A. (1953). *A pronouncing dictionary of American English.* Springfield, MA: G & C Merriam.

Kiparsky, P., & Menn, L. (1987). On the acquisition of phonology. In G. Ioup & S. H. Weinberger (Eds.), *Interlanguage phonology: The acquisition of a second language sound system* (pp. 23–52). New York: Newbury House.

Kleinmann, H. (1977). Avoidance behavior in adult second language acquisition. *Language Learning, 27*(1), 93–107.

Klippel, F. (1984). *Keep talking: Communicative fluency activities.* Cambridge: Cambridge University Press.

Krashen, S. D. (1973). Lateralization, language learning, and the critical period: Some new evidence. *Language Learning, 23,* 63–74.

———. (1982). *Principles and practice in second language acquisition.* Oxford: Pergamon Institute.

Krashen, S. D., & Terrell, T. D. (1983). *The Natural Approach.* Hayward, CA: Alemany Press.

Kreidler, C. (1972). Teaching English spelling and pronunciation. *TESOL Quarterly, 6*(1), 3–12.

Kreidler, C. W. (1989). *The pronunciation of English: A course book in phonology.* Oxford: Basil Blackwell.

Ladefoged, P. (1993). *A course in phonetics,* 3rd ed. Fort Worth: Harcourt, Brace, Jovanovich.

Lado, R. (1957). *Linguistics across cultures.* Ann Arbor: University of Michigan Press.

Larsen-Freeman, D. (1986). *Techniques and principles in language teaching.* New York: Oxford University Press.

Laufer, B. (1990). "Sequence" and "order" in the development of L2 lexis: Some evidence from lexical confusions. *Applied Linguistics, 11*(3), 281–290.

Laver, J. (1980). *The phonetic description of voice quality.* Cambridge: Cambridge University Press.

Leahy, R. M. (1991). A practical approach for teaching ESL pronunciation based on distinctive feature analysis. In A. Brown (Ed.), *Teaching English pronunciation: A book of readings* (pp. 146–158). London: Routledge.

Leather, J., & James, A. (1991). The acquisition of second language speech. *Studies in Second Language Acquisition, 13,* 305–341.

Lehiste, I., & Peterson, G. E. (1961). Transitions, glides, and diphthongs. *Journal of the Acoustical Society of America, 33*(3), 268–272.

Lenneberg, E. (1967). *Biological foundations of language.* New York: Wiley.

Lieberman, P., & Blumstein, S. E. (1988). *Speech physiology, speech perception, and acoustic phonetics.* Cambridge: Cambridge University Press.

Llado-Torres, N. (1991). Pronunciation practice doesn't have to be boring. Paper presented at the 22nd Annual CATESOL Conference, Santa Clara, CA.

Longman dictionary of American English: A dictionary for learners of English. (1983). White Plains, NY: Longman.

Lukmani, Y. (1972). Motivation to learn and learning proficiency. *Language Learning, 22,* 261–273.

Macdonald, D.; Yule, G.; & Powers, M. (1994). Attempts to improve English L2 pronunciation: The variable effects of different types of instruction. *Language Learning, 44*(1), 75–100.

Macken, M. A., & Ferguson, C. (1987). Phonological universals in language acquisition. In G. Ioup & S. H. Weinberger (Eds.), *Interlanguage phonology: The acquisition of a second language sound system* (pp. 3–22). New York: Newbury House.

Madden, C. G., & Myers, C. L. (Eds.). (1994). *Discourse and performance of international teaching assistants.* Alexandria, VA: TESOL.

Maley, A., & Duff, A. (1982). *Drama techniques in language learning.* Cambridge: Cambridge University Press.

Massaro, D. M. (1987). *Speech perception by eye and ear: A paradigm for psychological inquiry.* Hillsdale, NJ: Lawrence Erlbaum.

McNerney, M., & Mendelsohn, D. (1992). Suprasegmentals in the pronunciation class: Setting priorities. In P. Avery & S. Ehrlich (Eds.), *Teaching American English pronunciation* (pp. 185–196). Oxford: Oxford University Press.

Mencken, H. L. (1963). *The American language: An inquiry into the development of English in the United States,* 4th ed. New York: Knopf.

Molholt, G. (1988). Computer-assisted instruction in pronunciation for Chinese speakers of American English. *TESOL Quarterly, 22*(1), 91–113.

Morley, J. (Ed.). (1987). *Current perspectives on pronunciation.* Alexandria, VA: TESOL.

————. (Ed.). (1994a). *Pronunciation pedagogy and theory: New views, new dimensions.* Alexandria, VA: TESOL.

————. (1994b). A multidimensional curriculum design for speech-pronunciation instruction. In J. Morley (Ed.), *Pronunciation pedagogy and theory: New views, new dimensions* (pp. 64–91). Alexandria, VA: TESOL.

Moulton, W. G. (1962). *The sounds of English and German.* Chicago: The University of Chicago Press.

Neisser, U. (1967). *Cognitive psychology.* New York: Appleton-Century-Crofts.

Nilsen, D. L. F., & Nilsen, A. P. (1973). *Pronunciation contrasts in English.* New York: Regents.

O'Grady, W., & Dobrovolsky, M. (1987). *Contemporary linguistic analysis: An introduction.* Toronto: Copp Clark Pitman.

O'Hanlon, W. H. (1987). *Taproots.* New York: Norton.

Odlin, T. (1978). Variable rules in the acquisition of English contractions. *TESOL Quarterly, 12*(4), 451–458.

Oller, D. K. (1974). Simplification as the goal of phonological processes in child speech. *Language Learning, 25,* 299–304.

Olson, C., & Shalek, S. (1981). Games and activities based on grammatical areas which are problems for the intermediate ESL student. Unpublished manuscript. School for International Training, Brattleboro, VT.

Omaggio, A. (1983). *Proficiency-oriented classroom testing.* Washington, DC: Center for Applied Linguistics.

Oxford student's dictionary of American English, 2nd ed. 1986. New York: Oxford University Press.

Parish, C. (1977). A practical philosophy of pronunciation. *TESOL Quarterly, 11*(3), 311–317.

Penfield, W., & Roberts, L. (1959). *Speech and brain mechanisms.* Princeton, NJ: Princeton University Press.

Pennington, M. C. (1994). Recent research in L2 phonology: Implications for practice. In J. Morley (Ed.), *Pronunciation pedagogy and theory: New views, new dimensions* (pp. 92–108). Alexandria, VA: TESOL.

Pennington, M. C., & Richards, J. C. (1986). Pronunciation revisited. *TESOL Quarterly, 20*(2), 207–225.

Pica, T. (1984). Pronunciation activities with an accent on communication. *English Teaching Forum, 22*(3), 2–6.

Postovsky, V. (1974). Effects of delay in oral practice at the beginning of second language learning. *Modern Language Journal, 58*(3), 229–239.

Prator, C. H. (1951). *Manual of American English pronunciation for adult foreign students.* New York: Holt, Rinehart, & Winston.

———. (1971). Phonetics vs. phonemics in the ESL classroom: When is allophonic accuracy important? *TESOL Quarterly, 5*(1), 61–72.

———. (1991). The cornerstones of method. In M. Celce-Murcia (Ed.), *Teaching English as a second or foreign language,* 2nd ed. (pp. 11–22). Boston: Heinle & Heinle.

Prator, C. H., & Robinett, B. J. (l985). *A manual of American English pronunciation,* 4th ed. New York: Holt, Rinehart, & Winston.

Pringle, I. (1985). Attitudes to Canadian English. In S. Greenbaum (Ed.), *The English language today* (pp. 183–205). Oxford: Pergamon Press.

Purpura, J. (1991). Testing pronunciation: Prediction, perception, and production. Unpublished manuscript, University of California, Department of TESL and Applied Linguistics, Los Angeles.

Ravensdale, A. (1973). *Listening comprehension practice in English.* London: St. George's Press.

Ricard, E. (1986). Beyond fossilization: A course on strategies and techniques in pronunciation for advanced adult learners. *TESL Canada Journal,* Special Issue 1, 243–253.

Richards, J. C. (1971). A non-contrastive approach to error analysis. *English Language Teaching Journal, 25*(3), 204–219.

———. (1990). *The language teaching matrix.* Cambridge: Cambridge University Press.

Robbins, A. (1986). *Unlimited power: The new sciences of personal achievement.* New York: Simon & Schuster.

Rogers, C. R. (1951). *Client-centered therapy: Its current practice, implications, and theory.* Boston: Houghton Mifflin.

Rost, M. (1990). *Listening in language learning.* London: Longman.

Rumelhart, D. E., & Norman, D. A. (1978). Accretion, tuning, and restructuring: Three modes of learning. In J. Cotton & R. Klatzky (Eds.), *Semantic factors in cognition* (pp. 37–53). Hillsdale, NJ: Laurence Erlbaum.

Sato, C. J. (1987). Phonological processes in second language acquisition: Another look at interlanguage syllable structure. In G. Ioup & S. H. Weinberger (Eds.), *Interlanguage phonology: The acquisition of a second language sound system* (pp. 248–260). New York: Newbury House.

Scarcella, R. (1983). Sociodrama for social interaction. In J. W. Oller, Jr., & P. A. Richard-Amato (Eds.), *Methods that work: A smorgasbord of ideas for language teachers* (pp. 239–245). Rowley, MA: Newbury House.

Schachter, J. (1974). An error in error analysis. *Language Learning, 24*(2), 205–214.

Schane, S. (1970). Linguistics, spelling, and pronunciation. *TESOL Quarterly, 4*(2), 137–141.

Schneider, W., & Schiffrin, R. M. (1977). Controlled and automatic processing I: Detection, search, and attention. *Psychological Review, 84,* 1–64.

Schuetze-Coburn, S. (1993). The segmentation of discourse. Unpublished doctoral dissertation, University of California, Los Angeles.

Schumann, J. H. (1975). Affective factors and the problem of age in second language acquisition. *Language Learning*, 25(2), 209–235.

———. (1986). Research on the acculturation model for second language acquisition. *Journal of Multilingual and Multicultural Development, 7*(5), 379–392.

Schumann, J. H.; Holroyd, J.; Campbell, R. N.; & Ward, F. A. (1978). Improvement of foreign language pronunciation under hypnosis: A preliminary study. *Language Learning, 28*(1), 143–148.

Scott, M. L. (1989). Younger and older adult second language learners: A comparison of auditory memory and perception. Unpublished doctoral dissertation, University of California, Los Angeles.

Scovel, T. (1969). Foreign accent: Language acquisition and cerebral dominance. *Language Learning, 19,* 245–254.

———. (1988). *A time to speak: A psycholinguistic inquiry into the critical period for human speech.* New York: Newbury House.

Selinker, L. (1969). Language transfer. *General Linguistics, 9,* 67–92.

———. (1972). Interlanguage. *International Review of Applied Linguistics, 10,* 209–231.

Shakhbagova, J. (1982). *Varieties of English pronunciation.* Moscow: Vishaya Shkola.

———. (1993). *British-American-Russian Russian-American-British glossary.* Moscow: Prostreks.

Skehan, P. (1989). *Individual differences in second-language learning.* London: Edward Arnold.

Smith, G. L. (1966). *Spelling by principles: A programmed text.* New York: Appleton-Century-Crofts.

Snow, M. A., & Shapira, R. (1985). The role of social-psychological factors in second language learning. In M. Celce-Murcia (Ed.), *Beyond basics: Issues and research in TESOL* (pp. 3–15). Rowley, MA: Newbury House.

Standwell, G. J. B. (1991). The phoneme, a red herring for language teaching? In A. Brown (Ed.), *Teaching English pronunciation: A book of readings* (pp. 139–145). London: Routledge.

Stern, H. H. (1992). *Issues and options in language teaching.* Oxford: Oxford University Press.

Stern, S. (1983). Why drama works: A psycholinguistic perspective. In J. W. Oller, Jr., & P. A. Richard-Amato (Eds.), *Methods that work: A smorgasbord of ideas for language teachers* (pp. 207–225). Rowley, MA: Newbury House.

———. (1987). Expanded dimensions to literature in ESL/EFL: An integrated approach. *Forum, 25*(4), 47–55.

Stevick, E. (1976). *Memory, meaning and method: Some psychological perspectives on language learning.* Rowley, MA: Newbury House.

———. (1978). Toward a practical philosophy of pronunciation: Another view. *TESOL Quarterly, 12*(2), 145–150.

———. (1980). *Teaching languages: A way and ways.* Rowley, MA: Newbury House.

Strevens, P. (1977). *New orientations in the teaching of English.* Oxford: Oxford University Press.

———. (1991). A rationale for teaching pronunciation: The rival virtues of innocence and sophistication. In A. Brown (Ed.), *Teaching English pronunciation: A book of readings* (pp. 96–103). London: Routledge.

Swan, M., & Smith, B. (1987). *Learner English.* Cambridge: Cambridge University Press.

Tarone, E. E. (1987a). The phonology of interlanguage. In G. Ioup & S. H. Weinberger (Eds.), *Interlanguage phonology: The acquisition of a second language sound system* (pp. 70–85). New York: Newbury House.

———. (1987b). Some influences on the syllable structure of interlanguage phonology. In G. Ioup & S. H. Weinberger (Eds.), *Interlanguage phonology: The acquisition of a second language sound system* (pp. 232–247). New York: Newbury House.

———. (1988). *Variation in interlanguage.* London: Edward Arnold.

Temperley, M. S. (1987). Linking and deletion in final consonant clusters. In J. Morley (Ed.), *Current perspectives on pronunciation: Practices anchored in theory* (pp. 59–82). Alexandria, VA: TESOL.

Todaka, Y. (1990). An error analysis of Japanese students' intonation and its pedagogical applications. Unpublished master's thesis, University of California, Los Angeles.

———. (1993). A cross-language study of voice quality: Bilingual Japanese and American speakers. Unpublished doctoral dissertation, University of California, Los Angeles.

Trager, G., & Smith, H. L. (1951). *An outline of English structure.* Norman, OK: Battenberg Press.

Trubetzkoy, N. S. (1939). *Grundzüge der Phonologie.* Prague: Cercle Linguistique de Prague.

Venezky, R. L. (1970). *The structure of English orthography.* The Hague: Mouton.

Via, R. (1976). *English in three acts.* Honolulu: East West Center, University of Hawaii.

von Schon, C. V. (1987). The question of pronunciation. *English Teaching Forum, 25*(4), 22–27.

Voss, B. (1979). Hesitation phenomena as sources of perceptual errors for non-native speakers. *Language and Speech, 22,* 129–144.

Wardhaugh, R. (1970). The contrastive analysis hypothesis. *TESOL Quarterly, 4*(2), 123–130.

Weinstein, N. (1979). *Whaddaya say?* Culver City, CA: English Language Services.

White, M. (1977). Is anybody listening? Adventures in techniques of teaching aural comprehension. *TESL Talk, 8*(4), 47–56.

Widdowson, H. (1978). *Teaching language as communication.* Oxford: Oxford University Press.

Wong, R. (1987a). *Teaching pronunciation: Focus on English rhythm and intonation.* Englewood Cliffs, NJ: Prentice Hall Regents.

———. (1987b). Learner variables and prepronunciation considerations in teaching pronunciation. In J. Morley (Ed.), *Current perspectives on pronunciation* (pp. 13–28). Alexandria, VA: TESOL.

Yalden, J. (1987). *Principles of course design for language teaching.* Cambridge: Cambridge University Press.

Young-Scholten, M. (1993). *The acquisition of prosodic structure in a second language.* Tübingen: Max Niemeyer Verlag.

Yule, G.; Hoffman, P.; & Damico, J. (1987). Paying attention to pronunciation: The role of self-monitoring in perception. *TESOL Quarterly, 21*(4), 765–768.

Answer Key for "On the Cassette" Exercises

CHAPTER 1   No exercises
CHAPTER 2   No exercises
CHAPTER 3

Questions 1–5

1.	/tʃ/	–	chip	18.	/tʃ/	–	church	35.	/kw/	–	quiet
2.	/k/	–	character	19.	/p/	–	top	36.	/fr/	–	French
3.	/ʃ/	–	sugar	20.	/n/	–	scene	37.	/skw/	–	square
4.	/s/	–	send	21.	/k/	–	lucky	38.	/sw/	–	sweet
5.	/f/	–	photo	22.	/p/	–	paper	39.	/bl/	–	blue
6.	/p/	–	paint	23.	/n/	–	sinner	40.	/gl/	–	glass
7.	/w/	–	wish	24.	/ŋ/	–	singer	41.	/zd/	–	closed
8.	/y/	–	yes	25.	/l/	–	yellow	42.	/st/	–	rust
9.	/dʒ/	–	jam	26.	/r/	–	correct	43.	/nts/	–	prince
10.	/ð/	–	then	27.	/s/	–	messy	44.	/ntʃ/	–	bunch
11.	/s/	–	dance	28.	/z/	–	hazard	45.	/rnz/	–	learns
12.	/θ/	–	bath	29.	/θ/	–	author	46.	/ŋθ/	–	length
13.	/f/	–	graph	30.	/ð/	–	brother	47.	/pt/	–	clapped
14.	/s/	–	box	31.	/tr/	–	train	48.	/fs/	–	laughs
15.	/dʒ/	–	judge	32.	/θr/	–	three	49.	/rθ/	–	birth
16.	/z/	–	buzz	33.	/pr/	–	pretty	50.	/rdz/	–	words
17.	/f/	–	safe	34.	/kl/	–	cloud				

Question 6

NNS 1: This speaker confuses unitial /b,v/ as in *very;* inserts a vowel similar to /ɛ/ before initial /s/ and in *satisfied* or *stay;* she also simplifies the final clusters in *think* /ŋk/, *things* /ŋgz/, and *experience* /n(t)s/ to /n/ and simplifies the final cluster in *first* /rst/ to /rs/.

NNS 2: This speaker articulates consonant sounds fairly well; the quality of initial /r/ is off – that is, slightly trilled; she substitutes initial /d/ for /ð/ in words like *that* and leaves off final sounds in consonant clusters, many of which are inflections; for example, *Korean*s̸, *sometime*s̸, *mentione*d̸.

CHAPTER 4

1.	/ɔ/	–	walk	11.	/ɪ/	–	lid	21.	/ɔy/	–	boys
2.	/ey/	–	plate	12.	/aw/	–	brown	22.	/ey/	–	rain
3.	/ay/	–	fine	13.	/ʌ/	–	but	23.	/ɪ/	–	milk
4.	/ɔy/	–	boil	14.	/æ/	–	hand	24.	/aw/	–	shout
5.	/iy/	–	see	15.	/uw/	–	lose	25.	/ɜʳ/	–	shirt
6.	/ɜʳ/	–	heard	16.	/ʌ/	–	fun	26.	/ɛ/	–	tell
7.	/ɑ/	–	hot	17.	/ow/	–	cold	27.	/æ/	–	cat
8.	/ow/	–	show	18.	/iy/	–	creep	28.	/ɑ/	–	stop
9.	/ɛ/	–	bed	19.	/ɔ/	–	taught	29.	/ʊ/	–	look
10.	/ʊ/	–	could	20.	/ay/	–	flight	30.	/uw/	–	mood

CHAPTER 5

Question 1

NS 1: As indicated in the marked text below, the native speaker employs linking in the following ways:

- lots of C + V linking: *if indoors, if outdoors, if in a car, in an open area*, etc.
- C lengthening: /k/ *take cover*, /r/ *car radio*
- V + V linking: *stay away, to an, stay in*
  y   w   y

- non-release of the first consonant when two different stop consonants occur in sequence: *outdoors, stop carefully, keep calm, don't panic*

If indoors, take cover under a desk or table, or brace yourself in a doorway. Stay away from win-
                k: y
dows. If outdoors, move to an open area away from overhead hazards. If in a car, stop carefully
         [tᵒ]   w   [pᵒ]
in an open area. Stay in the car. Listen to the car radio for information. Above all, keep calm and
                  y   r: [pᵒ]
don't panic.
[tᵒ]

Question 2

NNS 1: This speaker has an obvious problem with C + V linking. She can't carry over the consonants in segments like the following, and needs good instruction and practice in this area:

    if indoors   desk or   from overhead

    cove under   yourself in   above all

Linking problems were not as obvious in the other areas, so instruction can focus on the above.

NNS 2: This speaker also has some problems with C + V linking:

    if indoors   if outdoors   if in a car   above all

He also has minor difficulty with V + V linking (for example, *stay away*) and C + C linking (for example, *overhead hazards*), which suggests that a general overview of linking phenomena in English would be useful for this speaker.

CHAPTER 6

Question 1

The following passage is marked for stress and intonation to represent the reading be the two NSs. Note that underlined syllables represent stressed elements in the sentence, and underlined and bold elements represent prominent elements.

Maggie: Hi, **Sara**, What's **up**?

Sara: I'm cleaning the **bath**room.

Maggie: **You're** cleaning the bathroom? Wasn't **Jen**nifer supposed to clean it this week?

Sara: She **was**, but she **can't**.

Maggie: Why **not**?

Sara: She has a **midterm** tomorrow. So she asked **Al**ice, and **she** couldn't either.

Maggie: What's **her** problem?

Sara: Her **pa**rents are here from out of **town**.

Question 2

NNS 1 (reading Maggie's part): This speaker has a steplike intonation that seems somewhat random, and she uses few glides (one should be used, for example, on *her* in *"What's HER problem?"*). She doesn't stress the prominent contrastive pronouns in cases like *"YOU'RE cleaning the bathroom?"* and stresses pronouns that are not prominent, for example, in *". . . supposed to clean <u>it</u> this week?"* Also, her pitch fell when she said this phrase instead of rising as the native speaker did. She needs major work on her stress and intonation to sound more natural.

NNS 2 (reading Sara's part): This speaker has reasonably accurate but flat intonation that makes her sound bored or disinterested when compared with the native speaker. She made a stress error in *". . . she asked Alice, and she couldn't either,"* where she gave greater prominence to *couldn't* than to *she*. She made a minor intonation error at the very end on "out of town," where she rose and fell on *out* instead of *town*.

Question 3

Answers will vary depending on the speaker chosen. See the preceding analysis and ask your instructor to check your list of priorities.

CHAPTER 7

Question 1

Responses will vary.

Question 2

In this conversation, there are several standard, unambiguous contractions: *hasn't, doesn't, haven't, I'm.* There are also some ambiguous contractions or blends: *it's* (= it has) in the opening line and *it's* (= it is) in two other places; *who's* (= who is) and *we'd* (= we would) also occur. There are two reduced verb forms where the following *to* gets assimilated to the verb: *wanna* (= want to) and *gonna* (= going to). The speaker Janet frequently informally reduces final /ŋ/ to /n/ in *-ing* forms such as *having, doing, keeping, helping*. The transcript of the conversation follows.

Donna: It's been beautiful weather lately, hasn't it?

Janet: Yeah, really gorgeous. Makes you wanna go out and hike every weekend, doesn't it?

Donna: Mmhmm.

Janet: Have you been hiking lately?

Donna: No . . . I haven't been exercising AT ALL? I mean, I'm just getting fatter and fatter.

Janet: Well, I actually took the bull by the horns and started an exercise class, and, um, I must say sometimes I'm really, I'm really having a hard time keeping up with the instructor who's one of these sort of fitness experts, you know, and aerobic people. But I think it's doing a lot of good. I feel like I'm a little more relaxed in my neck and my back and . . .

Donna: Yeah, I was gonna say you haven't had any back problems lately, have you?

Janet: No. No. Actually it's been pretty good, so . . . knock on wood, and um I think the class is helping a lot.

Donna: I should probably take a class too.

Janet: Yeah, we'd love to have you come join us!

Donna: [laughs] Maybe . . . next . . . month . . . [laughs]

Janet: Okay.

Question 3

Responses will vary. Use the transcript provided above for your analysis.

CHAPTER 8

Question 1

1.	/z/	– toys	6.	/əz, ɪz/ – matches	11.	/s/	– moths	16.	/z/ – teams
2.	/z/	– ribs	7.	/z/ – hangs	12.	/s/	– ships	17.	/s/ – trucks
3.	/əz, ɪz/	– kisses	8.	/z/ – saves	13.	/əz, ɪz/	– washes	18.	/s/ – hats
4.	/z/	– sheds	9.	/əz, ɪz/ – ridges	14.	/z/	– legs	19.	/z/ – stars
5.	/z/	– hills	10.	/z/ – bathes	15.	/s/	– bluffs	20.	/z/ – bees

Question 2

1.	/d/	– played	8.	/t/	– crunched	15.	/t/	– baked
2.	/əd, ɪd/	– added	9.	/t/	– cashed	16.	/d/	– mugged
3.	/d/	– filled	10.	/t/	– missed	17.	/əd, ɪd/	– waited
4.	/d/	– banged	11.	/d/	– amused	18.	/d/	– bored
5.	/d/	– pinned	12.	/d/	– teethed	19.	/t/	– shaped
6.	/əd, ɪd/	– scolded	13.	/t/	– coughed	20.	/d/	– robbed
7.	/d/	– budged	14.	/əd, ɪd/	– planted			

CHAPTER 9

1. /pæf/ – paf, paff
2. /kʌtʃ/ – cutch, cuch, kutch, kuch
3. /dɪnts/ – dints, dince, dinse
4. /kweyt/ – quate, quait
5. /fɔk/ – falk, faulk
6. /kiym/ – keem, keam, keme, cheme, cheam, cheem
7. /dʒɛpl̩/ – jepple, gepple
8. /sɛri/ – sarry, serry, sary, sery
9. /kayp/ – kipe, kype, chype
10. /wown/ – wone, wown, woan

Note: A few of the preceding nonsense words (e.g., *Falk*) may in fact be proper names in English, but they do not serve as common nouns.

CHAPTER 10

Question 1

a. How's your wife?
    Version 1: interested (*clue:* slightly exaggerated intonation)
    Version 2: excited (*clue:* highly exaggerated intonation)
    Version 3: uninterested (*clue:* flat and relatively undifferentiated intonation)

b. It's good to see you.
    Version 1: uninterested (*clue:* flat and relatively undifferentiated intonation)
    Version 2: interested (*clue:* slightly exaggerated intonation)
    Version 3: excited (*clue:* highly exaggerated intonation)

c. Harold's on the phone.
    Version 1: excited (*clue:* highly exaggerated intonation)
    Version 2: interested (*clue:* slightly exaggerated intonation)
    Version 3: uninterested (*clue:* flat and relatively undifferentiated intonation)

Question 2

The speaker has generally good fluency and good command of suprasegmentals in her speech. When fluency breaks down, it is generally related to a problem with accuracy. For example, she inserts a vowel like /ɛ/ before initial /s/ in *Spanish* and *student*. She deletes many final consonants, both as morphological endings (*months*, *American*) and as clusters (*department*). She reduces *and* to /an/ instead of /ən/, which is distracting – potentially causing the listener to wonder if the intended word is *and, an, on, Anne,* etc.

Question 3

   In this role play, the two speakers are focusing on communication or fluency rather than accuracy. Speaker A (the voice for Lou's towing service) has comprehensible but accented speech. Speaker B (the one who needs a towing service) is initially very difficult to understand (e.g., *Royal Boulevard Exit*), but gets somewhat better as the role play progresses.

   Such activities are especially useful for teaching pronunciation if they can be recorded and then played back and analyzed to identity (and get learners to self-identify) problems with fluency and accuracy. Such samples usually provide more natural data on a learner's speech than do more controlled sampling techniques such as reading prepared dialogues or passages.

Question 4

   In this taped dialogue journal, Pierre, the student, asks his teacher about when to pronounce *h* and when to leave it out. He also wants some advice on how to pronounce *th* in different environments.

   In her response, the teacher gives Pierre feedback on the pronunciation of initial *h*, saying that it is normally pronounced except for a few words borrowed from Romance languages such as *hour, heir,* and *honor.* She adds that most borrowed words have been Anglicized and that we now pronounce the *h: hazard, hotel,* etc.

   For Pierre's question about *th,* the teacher reviews the voiced /ð/ and voiceless /θ/ phonemes. For plural or possessive nouns ending in *ths* or *th's,* she points out that they are usually /θs/ but for verbs ending in *th(e)s,* the ending is usually /ðz/. She adds a comment on the simplification of /θ/ when it occurs in a cluster between two other consonants; that is, it usually drops out such that words like *months* and *ninths* are pronounced /ns/, not /nθs/.

   We feel this is an effective way for teachers to deal individually with students' questions and problems. In this case, Pierre was the only French student in the class, so the dialogue journal provided the teacher with a systematic way to individually address pronunciation problems which are typical for French speakers.

CHAPTER II No exercises

CHAPTER 12

Question 1

NNS 1: This speaker has problems with initial clusters with /r/, for example, *troop,* and leaves off final /l/ as in *while.* She also tends to leave off final inflectional endings in clusters: *tells, scared, boys.*

NNS 2: This speaker seems to make errors occasionally rather than regularly. She has some problems with /l/. in initial clusters (e.g., *sleeping*) and some problems with /ɪ/, which is too close to /iy/, for example, in *with* and *kids.* She sometimes leaves off endings: *kids.*

NNS 3: This speaker regularly produces /æ/ as /a/: *m<u>a</u>n, <u>a</u>nimal, c<u>a</u>mping.* She substitutes /iy/ for /ɪ/ as in *k<u>i</u>ds* and sometimes adds a vowel like /ɛ/ before initial /s/: *sleep, sleeping.*

   Your corrective feedback should reflect the difficulties you have identified. For example, the first speaker could be made aware of her tendency to delete final /l/, to delete final inflections, and to mispronounce initial /tr/ clusters. She should be given an opportunity to listen to her own recording to see if she can hear these errors. For the other two speakers, compare your prepared feedback strategy with that of several classmates and ask your instructor to check it if you have any questions.

Question 2
NNS 1:

  a. This speaker's native language is hard to identify from her pronunciation. The errors suggest an Asian language, but the accent is so light that her first language, which happens to be Japanese, is not obvious.
  b. She omits some final consonants in clusters, for example, *find,* and produces /l/ in *friendly* more like an /r/.
  c. Make her aware of each problem and then let her listen and compare her pronunciation on the tape with that of a native speaker.
  d. For practicing the *-ly* ending, we would ask her to produce manner adverbs:
    The ballerina dances _____.
    The sprinter runs _____.

For the final consonants, she could be asked to write a story incorporating words supplied by the teacher and could then practice reciting the story with special attention to the final clusters:

| hand(s) | last | girl(s) |
| sand | left | skirts(s) |

NNS 2:

  a. His native language is obviously French.
  b. His problems are not ommissions but rather substitutions. For example, he substitutes /z/ for /ð/ in *the* and *there;* /iy/ for /ɪ/ in *is* and *this.* There is also misplaced stress (*TexAS*) and lack of vowel reduction (the speaker overarticulates *and* even devoices the final /d/ to /t/ instead of reducing this unstressed function word to /ən/).
  c. The problems can be pointed out and the speaker can be asked to listen to his production and to compare it with that of a native speaker. He needs to make /ð/ less sibilant and /ɪ/ more lax.
  d. The two phoneme substitutions could be treated in a series of dialogues like the following. The speaker should be directed to clearly distinguish /ð/ from /z/ and to work on /ɪ/ in words like *in, is, city:*
    A: Where is the zoo?
    B: It's in the city.
The stress problems and vowel reduction could be practiced using the names of two conjoined U.S. states in questions that the student would read and then answer:
    1: Have you visited Texas and Kansas?
    2: What do you know about Washington and Oregon?

Question 4
NNS 1:
General comments: This speaker had some problems reading, though his pronunciation is generally good and his accent is not heavy.

Notes on the "Accent Checklist" :
I.   Stessed vowels: substitution of /ɛ/ for /ɪ/ in *theory;* /æ/ for /ʌ/ in *young,* /ɪ/ for /ay/ in *identify;* /iy/ for /ɪ/ in *system;* something close to /ɛ/ for /ʌ/ in *luck.* Unstressed vowels: substitution of /ey/ for /ə/ in *accurate.*
II. Accurate production of initial consonants; missing medial invisible /y/ in *individ_uals;* occasional dropped final consonant, for example, *changed;* trouble with medial consonant sequence in *accent,* which is produced as /s/ instead of /k.s/.
III. Intonation on the confirmation tag *will they?* went up when it should have come down.
IV. Two incorrect word-level stresses: *influENces* and *arABic.* Lack of linking at the phrasal level in *"Only time will tell, I'm afraid,"* which is produced as two separate phrases with a long pause between (this changes the meaning of the phrase).

V. Need to reduce unstressed syllables in connected speech more – for example, /ə/ instead of /a/ in sec<u>o</u>nd and /ə/ instead of /ey/ in the indefinite article *a*.

Additional comments: If the speaker had correctly pronounced the word *accent*, he would have sounded very good. Perhaps he also has problems pronouncing words like *accident* and *accelerate*, where *cc* (before *i* or *e*) gets pronounced as /k.s/. This should be checked.

NNS 2:

General comments: She has a heavier accent than speaker 1.

Notes on the "Accent Checklist":
I.   Stessed vowels: substitution of /iy/ for /ɪ/ in *if* and g<u>i</u>ve and /ɛr/ for /ɜʳ/ in *l<u>ear</u>n*. Unstressed vowels: substitution of full vowel /ow/ for schwa /ə/ in *rec<u>o</u>gnize* and of the full vowel /ɛ/ for schwa /ə/ in *man<u>a</u>ge*.

II. Initial position: substitution .0of /d/ and sometimes /z/ for /ð/ in <u>*the*</u>, <u>*their*</u>, <u>*that*</u>, and <u>*the*</u>. Substitution of /s/ for /θ/ in <u>*theories*</u>, which sounds like *series*; substitution of something like /h/ for /f/ in <u>*forget*</u>. Medial position: substitution of /z/ for /ð/ in *wi<u>th</u>out*; palatalization of /s/ to /ʃ/ in *pronun<u>ci</u>ation*. Medial clusters: simplification of the /gw/ in *lang<u>ua</u>ge* to /g/. Final clusters: regular deletion of the final sound (often an inflection): *accent~~s~~, speaker~~s~~, master~~ed~~, change~~d~~*, etc.

III. Intonation is not a major problem other than the fact that it is too flat overall. Intonation rose much too high on "*. . . without an accent, but . . . ,*" where a 1-2 rise-fall is required. Inappropriate intonation contour (i.e., rise on both *progress* and *give up* instead of a rise and fall on *give up*) in the sentence. "*Will you manage to make progress, or will you just give up?*"; this was not recognized as a closed choice alternative question.

IV. Stress and prominence are good except for the lack of adequate differentiation between stressed and unstressed syllables and inadequate reduction of unstressed vowels.

V.   Speech in much too choppy overall, indicating the need for work on all aspects of adjustments in connected speech; strong tendency to pronounce each word separately and in isolation from surrounding words. This is the major problem area for this speaker.

Additional comments: The speaker read the word *exposure* as *explosure*, stumbling over the word which she apparently did not know. This should be checked.

Author Index

Subject Index